FROM POPULAR SOVEREIGNTY
TO THE SOVEREIGNTY OF LAW

FROM
Popular Sovereignty
TO THE
Sovereignty of Law

Law, Society, and Politics in Fifth-Century Athens

MARTIN OSTWALD

University of California Press
Berkeley, Los Angeles, London

University of California Press
Berkeley and Los Angeles, California

University of California Press, Ltd.
London, England

Library of Congress Cataloging in Publication Data

Ostwald, Martin, 1922-
  From popular sovereignty to the sovereignty of law.

  Bibliography: p.
  Includes index.
  1. Law—Greece—Athens—History and criticism.
2. Athens (Greece)—Constitutional history. 3. Rule of law—Greece—
Athens. 4. Democracy. 5. Athens (Greece)—Politics and government.
I. Title.
LAW   342.495'12   85-690
ISBN 0-520-05426-1   344.951202
ISBN 0-520-06798-3 (ppbk)

Printed in the United States of America

2   3   4   5   6   7   8   9

To Lore, Mark, and David

CONTENTS

PREFACE

THIS book began as an attempt to pursue into the fifth century the study of the relation between *nomos* and democracy on which I had embarked in *Nomos and the Beginnings of the Athenian Democracy* (Oxford, 1969). More specifically, I wanted to trace the steps by which Cleisthenic *isonomia* developed into *dēmokratia*, the system of government in which sovereign power is vested in the people. That a system in which considerations of social class continued to play a large part in eligibility to the high executive offices should be called a democracy appeared paradoxical; it soon became apparent that the philological method employed to explain the seeming contradiction had to be complemented by a historical approach. Taking a cue from Aristotle's insistence that the jury courts constituted the heart and soul of the Athenian democracy, I devoted my attention to the development of the Athenian judiciary and its role in the political life of the city.

Occupation with the Athenian judiciary made me aware that a full explanation of my paradox demanded a close examination also of the opposition encountered by democracy and the *nomos* that embodied it, an opposition whose most visible manifestation, the *nomos-physis* controversy, left its mark on the thought and the politics of the last quarter of the fifth century. The delicate interrelations between intellectual trends, social currents, and political events posed new substantive problems: to define the nature of the opposition and its aims, and to show how the Athenian democracy responded to its challenge by becoming a new kind of democracy, which subordinated the will of the people to the regulating hand of the law.

Thus, the task I set myself in this book is one of interpretation rather than of discovering facts previously unknown. If this has compelled me to traverse, often in laborious detail, features that have long been recognized as integral to Athenian democracy, I feel no need to apologize. For a new, coherent, and comprehensive picture of the Athenian democracy cannot be given without seeing old facts in a new perspective and without bringing to bear on the question of popular sovereignty cultural phenomena that have in the past been discussed in isolation from politics.

Though this book is primarily addressed to students of the classics and of ancient history, I have tried to make it accessible to Greekless readers by either translating or explaining Greek words and phrases in the text or by translating them in footnotes. To pursue my aim consistently proved especially difficult in Chapter 2, where most of my argument depends on a careful examination of linguistic usage. I have adopted the principle of transliterating Greek expressions wherever possible and of printing in Greek only where the use of a given word by a specific author in a specific passage seemed to me vital to my argument. Still, even in these instances I have transliterated in parentheses the first occurrence of every important word. Those readers who find this procedure inadequate will, I hope, find the substance of that chapter sufficiently distilled in its last section (pp. 129-36).

The widening scope of this book has delayed its completion longer than I had anticipated despite the leisure afforded by a generous leave policy, for which I gratefully acknowledge a debt to my two home institutions, Swarthmore College and the University of Pennsylvania. Other debts were incurred that allowed me to take full advantage of the time the leaves afforded me. A Senior Fellowship granted by the National Endowment for the Humanities enabled me to start the project in 1970–1971 in the most stimulating personal and intellectual atmosphere of Balliol College, Oxford, whose Master and Fellows had done me the signal honor of appointing me to a Visiting Fellowship. In 1974–1975 and again in 1981–1982, I had the privilege of pursuing my work at the Institute for Advanced Study in Princeton under conditions so ideal that they can be fully appreciated only by those who have themselves experienced them. Much in this book is indebted to daily contact with such scholars as Homer A. Thompson, Harold Cherniss, and Christian Habicht. During my most recent tenure at the Institute I was also the beneficiary of an institutional grant awarded to the Institute by the National Endowment for the Humanities. An additional fruitful year in Oxford was made possible through a generous fellowship awarded by the John Simon Guggenheim Memorial Foundation for 1977–1978. The Foundation has put me still further into its debt by a magnanimous subvention toward the publication of this book.

I owe a debt of a different kind to a number of friends whose critical readings of various sections of the manuscript improved it and saved it from errors. Professors J. K. Davies and W. G. Forrest and Drs. Russell Meiggs and Paul Cartledge read earlier versions of Part One; Dr. N. J. Richardson subjected Chapter 3 to a critical perusal, and Professor Richard P. Saller read the complete manuscript. The comments of Professors Malcolm F. McGregor and Philip A. Stadter, as readers for the University of California Press, were invaluable aids for improving and streamlining both style and content, and further suggestions came from Professors Harold Drake and Ronald S. Stroud, who read the manuscript as members of the editorial committee of the press. While credit for much that is good in this book belongs to them, they in no way share blame for its shortcomings and errors of fact or of judgment.

Special thanks go to Sarah S. Fought for producing with speed and accuracy an almost perfect typescript, containing much Greek, from my often undecipherable *manu*script. For Part One her task was made easier by the excellent typescript of an earlier version produced by Barbara Rosenblum-Wolfe. Kerry Christensen and Leslie Mechem compiled with painstaking care and devotion the Index Locorum. For checking and updating the bibliography, also compiled by Kerry Christensen, I am indebted to Laurie Williams and for help with the proofreading to Margaret Somerville. To Doris Kretschmer and her staff at the University of California Press, especially Mary Lamprech and Paul Psoinos, I owe thanks for unfailing and courteous help in the editing and physical preparation of this book.

A more fundamental debt is inadequately acknowledged in the dedication.

Swarthmore and Philadelphia
September 1984

ABBREVIATIONS

FOR references to ancient authors and their works and for standard reference books the abbreviations recommended in the *Oxford Classical Dictionary*, 2d ed. (Oxford, 1970), ix–xxii, in H. G. Liddell, R. Scott, and H. S. Jones, *A Greek-English Lexicon*, 9th ed. (Oxford, 1940), xvi–xlviii, and in the annual issues of *L'Année Philologique* have been used, with exceptions included in the list below.

Bengtson, *SVA* 2²	H. Bengtson, ed., *Die Staatsverträge des Altertums* 2, 2d ed. (Munich and Berlin, 1975)
Blass, *AB*²	F. Blass, *Die attische Beredsamkeit*, 2d ed., 3 vols. (Leipzig, 1887–98)
Bonner-Smith	R. J. Bonner and G. Smith, *The Administration of Justice from Homer to Aristotle*, 2 vols. (Chicago, 1930–38)
Busolt, *GG*	G. Busolt, *Griechische Geschichte*, 3 vols. in 4 (Gotha, 1893–1904)
Busolt-Swoboda	G. Busolt and H. Swoboda, *Griechische Staatskunde*, 2 vols. (Munich, 1920–26)
Davies, *APF*	J. K. Davies, *Athenian Propertied Families 600–300 B.C.* (Oxford, 1971)
DK⁶	H. Diels and W. Kranz, eds. *Die Fragmente der Vorsokratiker*, 6th ed., 3 vols. (Berlin, 1951–52)
Dover, *Clouds*	K. J. Dover, ed., *Aristophanes: Clouds* (Oxford, 1968)

FGH   F. Jacoby, ed., *Die Fragmente der griechischen Historiker* (Berlin and Leiden, 1923–58)

Fornara, *ABG*   C. W. Fornara, *The Athenian Board of Generals from 501 to 404*, Historia Einzelschrift 16 (Wiesbaden, 1971)

Fornara, *ATEP*   C. W. Fornara, ed. and tr., *Translated Documents of Greece and Rome*, vol. 1: *Archaic Times to the End of the Peloponnesian War* (Baltimore and London, 1977)

Gernet-Bizos, *Lysias*   L. Gernet and M. Bizos, *Lysias: Discours* 1, 4th ed. (Paris, 1959)

Guthrie, *HGP*   W. K. C. Guthrie, *A History of Greek Philosophy*, 6 vols. (Cambridge, 1962–81)

HCT   A. W. Gomme, A. Andrewes, and K. J. Dover, *A Historical Commentary on Thucydides*, 5 vols. (Oxford, 1948–81)

Hansen, *PAUP*   M. H. Hansen, *The Sovereignty of the People's Court in Athens in the Fourth Century B.C. and the Public Action against Unconstitutional Proposals* (Odense, 1974)

Harrison, *LA*   A. R. W. Harrison, *The Law of Athens*, 2 vols. (Oxford, 1968–1971)

Hatzfeld   J. Hatzfeld, *Alcibiade* (Paris, 1951)

Heinimann, *NP*   F. Heinimann, *Nomos und Physis*, Schweizerische Beiträge zur Altertumswissenschaft 1 (Basel, 1945)

Hignett, *HAC*   C. Hignett, *A History of the Athenian Constitution to the End of the Fifth Century B.C.* (Oxford, 1952)

Jones, *AD*   A. H. M. Jones, *Athenian Democracy* (Oxford, 1957)

Kerferd, *SM*   G. B. Kerferd, *The Sophistic Movement* (Cambridge, 1981)

Kirchner, *PA*   J. Kirchner, *Prosopographia Attica*, 2 vols. (Berlin, 1901–3)

Krentz, *TA*   P. Krentz, *The Thirty at Athens* (Ithaca, N.Y., 1982)

Lipsius, *ARRV*	J. H. Lipsius, *Das attische Recht und Rechtsverfahren* (Leipzig, 1905–15)
MacDowell, *Andokides*	D. [M.] MacDowell, ed., *Andokides: On the Mysteries* (Oxford, 1962)
MacDowell, *LCA*	D. M. MacDowell, *The Law in Classical Athens* (London, 1978)
MacDowell, *Wasps*	D. M. MacDowell, ed., *Aristophanes: Wasps* (Oxford, 1971)
Meiggs, *AE*	R. Meiggs, *The Athenian Empire* (Oxford, 1972)
Meritt, *AFD*	B. D. Meritt, *Athenian Financial Documents of the Fifth Century* (Ann Arbor, Mich., 1932)
ML	R. Meiggs and D. [M.] Lewis, *A Selection of Greek Historical Inscriptions to the End of the Fifth Century B.C.* (Oxford, 1969)
Page, *PMG*	D. [L.] Page, *Poetae Melici Graeci* (Oxford, 1962)
Rhodes, *AB*	P. J. Rhodes, *The Athenian Boule* (Oxford, 1972)
Rhodes, *CAAP*	P. J. Rhodes, *A Commentary on the Aristotelian Athenaion Politeia* (Oxford, 1981)
de Ste. Croix, *OPW*	G. E. M. de Ste. Croix, *The Origins of the Peloponnesian War* (London, 1972)
TGrF	B. Snell, ed., *Tragicorum Graecorum Fragmenta* 1 (Göttingen, 1971)
Tod, *GHI*	M. N. Tod, *A Selection of Greek Historical Inscriptions*, 2 vols. (Oxford, 1946²–48)

PROLEGOMENA:
SCOPE AND PURPOSE

THE purpose of this book is to trace the growth of popular power in ancient Athens to the point at which it became popular sovereignty, to investigate the challenges popular sovereignty had to face, and to show how a principle of the sovereignty of law emerged from these challenges. This book is thus on democracy, specifically the Athenian democracy of the fifth century B.C., but it differs from other works that have traced the same development in its attempt to come closer to the realities of fifth-century Athens by treating the growth of popular power not as an exclusively political phenomenon but as a movement that came to encompass all major aspects of public life. The absence in ancient Greek of a distinction between "state" and "society" justifies this approach, since it indicates that the social and political facets of community life were not as sharply differentiated one from the other as they are for us. The same is true of the economy and, to a lesser extent, of religion. As a result, changes in one sphere of life were bound to have repercussions on the others: the increasing power of the people in politics affected religious beliefs, practices, and attitudes of the Athenians and engendered changes in the social norms that make up the ethos of a people. Social and religious developments had, in their turn, a decisive impact on the political challenges to which popular power came to be exposed. Accordingly, we do not pretend here to make a contribution to the theory of sovereignty, which has vexed political scientists, but rather use the term in a hierarchical sense similar to that in which Aristotle speaks of τὸ κύριον to express the element in a society or in an institution that is decisive in authenticating its character. In the context of the Athenian democracy, it is, therefore, inevitable to give the concept of popular sovereignty not merely political but also religious and social dimensions.

The period with which we are concerned has the restoration of democracy at the end of the fifth-century B.C. as its logical terminus; for at that time the principle of the sovereignty of law was given official primacy over the principle of popular sovereignty. The selection of a starting point for our inquiry, however, is a less straightforward matter. Popular sovereignty reached its peak in the wake of the reforms of Ephialtes of 462/1 B.C. But Ephialtes' work is unthinkable without the work of Cleisthenes, who had reformed the Athenian state some forty-five years earlier; Cleisthenes' achievement, in its turn, was made possible only by the consequences of Solon's activity at the beginning of the sixth century; and Solon's reforms were based on developments, inscrutable to us, that had followed the unification of Attica attributed by legend to Theseus. None of these reforms, as far as we can tell, tried to implement a preconceived ideological pattern that made the rule of the people by the people a desirable political end for its own sake. All were responses to historical situations that, as a by-product, led to the increase of popular power to the point at which the sovereignty of the people in all public affairs came to be a recognized principle, which could then become an ideology.

This means that ideally the beginning of Athenian history, at least from the time of the unification of Attica—the so-called *synoikismos*—ought to be our starting point. But the dearth of surviving evidence makes that impossible. Of the three kinds of evidence on which we depend for the reconstruction of the past, literary, epigraphical, and archaeological, only the last two are contemporary with events, and only the last is available, and that to a very limited extent, for the period before Solon. Yet without some literary evidence, archaeology and epigraphy provide no answers to the questions that we are raising here. Only with Solon, whose poems afford us a glimpse into contemporary thinking, do the outlines of a picture emerge, even though that picture would remain unintelligible if we could not supplement the poems with later accounts, especially Aristotle's *Constitution of Athens*,[1] which was written more than a

---

[1]   The authorship of the *Athēnaiōn Politeia* has been a matter of controversy ever since its rediscovery in 1891. Though its origin in Aristotle's school is beyond doubt, it is fashionable these days to deny Aristotle himself the authorship, largely for

century and a half after the Solonian reforms, and Plutarch's *Solon*, which is separated from them by some seven centuries. Contemporary evidence for the development of popular power in Athens is rarely so explicit as it is in another *Constitution of Athens*, which has come down to us among the works of Xenophon. For the first two-thirds of the fifth century, we get some information from Herodotus and Thucydides, but usually only incidentally, so that it needs to be sifted by laborious interpretation. We are a little better off for the last third of the fifth century, when Aristophanes and the early Attic orators can be drawn upon, but the pitfalls are considerable. In Aristophanes it is often hard to distinguish the serious from the frivolous, and dispassionate statements cannot easily be culled from the orators. Tragedy, which spans the whole of the fifth century, rarely yields good historical information, because its imaginative nature tends to obscure references to historical reality. Inscriptions, the most contemporary of all ancient evidence, offer occasional valuable insights. Their availability depends, however, on chance discovery and survival; to find a context for them we depend almost exclusively on literary sources, the most coherent of which are late. Yet even late sources have value in that they preserve traditions to which we have no other access, although that value is tempered by the constant possibility that a late author no longer understood distant events or that he interpreted them in the light of late events or of the conditions of his own time. Only a cautious juggling of all surviving evidence, aided by an informed and controlled imagination, gives any hope of piecing together an intelligible account of the development of popular sovereignty.

One final observation is in order. There appears to be something paradoxical about the use of expressions "democracy," "popular sovereignty," "power of the people," and so forth, in discussions of fifth-century Athens. "Democracy" was for all Greeks more restricted than it is for us; it did not imply the potential participation of all adult citizens in every aspect of political life. To exclude women from active participation in politics is not as puzzling in this respect

---

reasons of composition and style; see most recently Rhodes, *CAAP* 1–63, esp. 58–63. Since, however, none of the other 157 "constitutions" with which Aristotle's school is credited is available for stylistic comparison, I regard these arguments as inconclusive and prefer to ascribe the work to the author to whom tradition assigns it. Further, since its authenticity is not in question, it is immaterial for historical purposes whether or not Aristotle was himself its author.

as is the fact that even in the heyday of democracy noble birth and wealth remained important criteria for eligibility to some high offices. The political rights of women are of too recent a vintage for us to expect the Athenians to have countenanced them. What is much harder to understand is that they could speak of δημοκρατία (rule by the people) when there were offices to which the lower classes were denied access. To show that it is nevertheless correct to use terms such as "democracy" and "popular sovereignty" in describing the government of Athens in the fifth century and to trace the growth of the phenomenon inherent in these terms is the purpose of the first part of this book. On the basis of its results, we shall proceed in Parts Two and Three to show how reaction against popular sovereignty set in and how this resulted in a democracy in which law was to be sovereign.

Part I

THE GROWTH OF POPULAR SOVEREIGNTY

CHAPTER ONE

Popular Sovereignty and the Control of Government

SOCIAL ORDER AND POPULAR POWER FROM SOLON TO CLEISTHENES

Since time immemorial the political leadership of Attica had been in the hands of men whose claim to social prominence rested on a combination of landed wealth with membership in old and distinguished families and clans. That membership was primarily conferred by birth; to what extent it was acquired by marriage we do not know. For that reason it is tempting to speak of the governing class as "nobility" or "aristocracy," and if in the following we adhere to this practice of modern scholars, we do so for convenience only and in the knowledge that no titles or other appellations differentiated the members of this class from commoners and that we have no way of telling to what extent wealth or social status depended on inheritance. Though the reforms of Solon achieved their purpose of ameliorating the desperate economic straits of the lower classes,[1] popular participation in government may have been confined to the right to elect the magistrates.[2] The same remains true of the period between Solon and Cleisthenes. The family of the tyrant Peisistratus traced its descent back to the Neleids of Pylos;[3] his opponents, Megacles and Lycurgus, belonged to the distinguished *genē* (clans) of the

---

1 Arist. *Ath.Pol.* 6.1–2; Plut. *Sol.* 15.2–6, with A. Andrewes, "The Growth of the Athenian State," *CAH²* 3.3. (1982) 377–84.
2 Arist. *Pol.* 2.12, 1274ᵃ16–17, with Andrewes, "Growth" 384–89.
3 Hdt. 5.65.3 with Davies, *APF* 445.

Alcmaeonids and the Eteobutads, respectively.[4] The fragmentary archon list covering the years 528/7–522/1 B.C. seems to contain the names only of members of noble *genē*, and the only known opposition to the tyranny of Hippias came from the upper class.[5] Regardless of whether we interpret the political conflict within Attica in the sixth century B.C. as regional, social, economic, personal, or gentilician,[6] what political power the commons had manifested itself exclusively in the support they gave to prominent citizens: the only Assembly vote of which we know in this period gave Peisistratus his bodyguard, with whose help he established himself as a tyrant.[7]

After the expulsion of the Peisistratids, dynastic rivalries among noble families characterized Athenian politics again, in the shape of a struggle for supremacy between the Alcmaeonid Cleisthenes and Isagoras, scion of an equally old and distinguished family.[8] The reforms of Cleisthenes, which resulted from this struggle, took the

---

4   Hdt. 1.59.3; Arist. *Ath.Pol.* 13.4; Plut. *Sol.* 29.1. That Lycurgus was an Eteobutad is assumed by J. Toepffer, *Attische Genealogie* (Berlin, 1889) 122; cf. Davies, *APF* 349.

5   To the first publication of the archon list by B. D. Meritt, "Greek Inscriptions (14–27)," *Hesp.* 8 (1939) 59–65 (= *SEG* 10. 352), D. W. Bradeen has added some further fragments, "The Fifth-Century Archon List," *Hesp.* 32 (1963) 187–208. The "tyrannicides" Harmodius and Aristogeiton belonged to the old *genos* of the Gephyraioi (Hdt. 5.55); the Alcmaeonids were exiled (Hdt. 5.62.2; Thuc. 6.59.4; Arist. *Ath.Pol.* 19.3); the Cimonid Miltiades was dispatched to the Thracian Chersonese (Hdt. 6.34–35); Leogoras, the great-grandfather of Andocides, who came from an old and prominent family, went into voluntary exile (Andoc. 2.26); and Kedon as well as the dead of Leipsydrion are described as aristocratic opponents of the tyranny (Arist. *Ath.Pol.* 19.3, 20.5). For a detailed discussion of aristocratic political families in the sixth century B.C., see D. M. Lewis, "Cleisthenes and Attica," *Hist.* 12 (1963) 22–40, esp. 22–26.

6   There is no need here to enter this part of the debate, to which the more important recent contributions are: R. Sealey, "Regionalism in Archaic Athens," *Hist.* 9 (1960) 155–80; C. Mossé, "Classes sociales et régionalisme à Athènes au début du VIᵉ siècle," *Ant.Class.* 33 (1964) 401–13; D. Kienast, "Die innenpolitische Entwicklung Athens im 6. Jh. und die Reformen von 508," *HZ* 200 (1965) 265–83; E. Kluwe, "Bemerkungen zu den Diskussionen über die drei 'Parteien' in Attika zur Zeit der Machtergreifung des Peisistratos," *Klio* 54 (1972) 101–24; F. Ghinatti, *I Gruppi politici ateniesi fino alle guerre persiane*, Università degli studi di Padova: Pubblicazioni dell'Istituto di Storia Antica 8 (Rome, 1970) 43–73; A. Mele, "La Lotta politica nell'Atene arcaica," *Riv.Filol.* 3d ser., 101 (1973) 385–95; C. Ampolo, "Politica istituzionale e politica edilizia di Pisistrato," *Parola del Passato* 28 (1973) 271–74; G. D. Rocchi, "Aristocrazia genetica ed organizzazione politica arcaica," ibid. 92–116.

7   Arist. *Ath.Pol.* 14.1; cf. Hdt. 1.59.5.

8   Hdt. 5.66.1; Arist. *Ath.Pol.* 20.1.

first step toward increasing the power of the people. But the way was paved for them by the judicial reforms of Solon.

Solon and the Administration of Justice

Some people believe that Solon was a good lawgiver: he abolished an oligarchy that was too unmixed; he put an end to the slavery of the people; and he established the ancestral democracy by introducing a good constitutional blend, in which the Council of the Areopagus is said to constitute an oligarchical element, the fact that the magistrates are elected an aristocratic element, and the law courts an institution favoring the people. However, it seems that in fact the Council and the election of magistrates existed before Solon and were not abolished by him, but that he established popular power by opening membership in the law courts to all. For that very reason some people censure him, alleging that he abolished the other two by making the law court, whose members are chosen by lot, sovereign in all matters.[9]

That Aristotle saw the mainstay of popular sovereignty in Athens in the judicial power of the *dēmos* as vested in the jury courts (*dikastēria*) is evident not only from this passage from the *Politics* but from its presence like a thread through the entire historical part of his *Constitution of Athens*, from the account of Solon's reforms (9.1) to the characterization of the democracy in Aristotle's own day (41.2).[10] Since Aristotle does not elaborate on his reasons for regarding popular participation in the administration of justice as tantamount to the establishment of popular power, modern scholars have tried to come to terms with this baffling statement in different ways. The most influential explanation of the powers of the Athenian judiciary advanced in recent times attributes the authority of the popular law courts (*dikastēria*) to the fact that their judgments had to fill gaps in the Athenian legal system (*Rechtslücken*) as well as gaps left in the

9 Arist. *Pol*. 2.12, 1273^b35–74^a5: Σόλωνα δ' ἔνιοι μὲν οἴονται νομοθέτην γενέσθαι σπουδαῖον· ὀλιγαρχίαν τε γὰρ καταλῦσαι λίαν ἄκρατον οὖσαν, καὶ δουλεύοντα τὸν δῆμον παῦσαι, καὶ δημοκρατίαν καταστῆσαι τὴν πάτριον, μείξαντα καλῶς τὴν πολιτείαν· εἶναι γὰρ τὴν μὲν ἐν 'Αρείῳ πάγῳ βουλὴν ὀλιγαρχικόν, τὸ δὲ τὰς ἀρχὰς αἱρετὰς ἀριστοκρατικόν, τὰ δὲ δικαστήρια δημοτικόν. ἔοικε δὲ Σόλων ἐκεῖνα μὲν ὑπάρχοντα πρότερον οὐ καταλῦσαι, τήν τε βουλὴν καὶ τὴν τῶν ἀρχῶν αἵρεσιν, τὸν δὲ δῆμον καταστῆσαι, τὰ δικαστήρια ποιήσας ἐκ πάντων. διὸ καὶ μέμφονταί τινες αὐτῷ· λῦσαι γὰρ θάτερα, κύριον ποιήσαντα τὸ δικαστήριον πάντων, κληρωτὸν ὄν.

10 The relevant passages are conveniently assembled by E. Ruschenbusch, "Δικαστήριον πάντων κύριον," *Hist*. 6 (1957) 257–74, esp. 257–58.

laws (*Gesetzeslücken*) deliberately or inadvertently by the lawgiver.[11] *Rechtslücken* are, in this view, gaps left by lack of legislation: since Athenian law did not deal with crimes such as parricide, with a father's murder of his son, or with purchase on credit, it was, on this argument, up to the jurors sitting in such cases to supply the deficiency in arriving at their verdicts. Similarly, *Gesetzeslücken*, such as the absence of a clear definition of what constituted treason, arson, theft, and the like, had to be remedied at the discretion of the jurors by their improvising as they went along. However, it is difficult to envisage how the jurors' discretion in such cases can have given the *dikastēria* the authority and control that Aristotle claims for them. What we regard as gaps in the legal system were not gaps for the Athenians but matters that they handled differently from us. There are two reasons why the Solonian laws contained no special provisions for handling murder within the family. First, the relationship between murderer and victim, relevant though it might be in religion, was immaterial in Athenian law;[12] second, inasmuch as trials for murder could be initiated only by the victim's family, such cases were left to the family to handle. If there was no legislation regulating purchase on credit, it was because the Athenians had not developed a concept of credit but treated creditlike transactions as they treated loans. The same is true of ill-defined crimes. Prosecution and defense played a larger part in defining the crime committed in a given case than did the judgment of the jurors: Antiphon's speech *On the Murder of Herodes* shows clearly that the question whether a particular homicide was to be defined as murder (*phonos*) or malicious mischief (*kakourgia*) was an issue between prosecution and defense. But even at that, cases of this sort cannot have been so common or so vital to the larger community as to mark the *dikastēria* as the backbone of the democracy or their verdicts as giving them control over the democracy.

To account for that control we must not look to the function of the jury courts in the settlement of disputes between private individuals but to the role they played in cases affecting the state and the officials entrusted with its administration. From pre-Solonian times on, there were in Athens two kinds of law court. Most private litigation fell within the jurisdiction of one of the nine archons, each

---

11 Ruschenbusch, "Δικαστήριον."
12 Pl. *Euthyphr*. 4b–e.

in charge of his own tribunal and each within a well-defined sphere of competence, "authorized to judge lawsuits in their own right, and not, as they do nowadays, merely to conduct the preliminary inquiry" (Arist. *Ath.Pol.* 3.5). Other cases regarded as private were tried before the Areopagus, which had, at all times in Athenian history, jurisdiction in all cases of homicide, of wounding or poisoning with intent to kill, of arson, and such religious matters as the care of the sacred olive trees.[13] Of greater interest for our present purposes, however, is the jurisdiction of the Areopagus in public cases, at least under the Solonian constitution, if indeed the formal term "jurisdiction" is appropriate to describe its political functions in the archaic state. Since its membership consisted of ex-archons, all of whom belonged to the upper classes, and since it was believed to be the oldest and most venerable political body in Athens even before Solon, it had considerable and presumably undefined powers, which are usually described in the ancient sources as "guardianship of the laws" (*nomophylakein*) or in similar terms.[14] With the benefit of the hindsight that later developments provide, it is possible to distinguish three areas of public law in which we ascribe jurisdiction to the Areopagus: it tried crimes against the state, it held magistrates accountable for their official acts (*euthyna*), and it scrutinized elected officials before they embarked upon their term of office to ensure that they possessed the formal qualifications for the office to which they had been elected (*dokimasia*). We cannot claim that this is an exhaustive list of the political functions of the Areopagus in the archaic state. Its mandate will have been wider and vaguer than our scant evidence permits us to reconstruct. But we know that in these three areas it exercised powers that, when they later went into the hands of the people, constituted the political popular sovereignty we call democracy.

The majority of modern scholars concede that the guardianship of the laws included jurisdiction in crimes against the state.[15] But this is

13 Lipsius, *ARRV* 123–33; Hignett, *HAC* 89–98.
14 See Arist. *Ath.Pol.* 3.6 (διατηρεῖν τοὺς νόμους), 4.4 (φύλαξ τῶν νόμων), 8.4 (νομοφυλακεῖν), 25.2 (ἡ τῆς πολιτείας φυλακή); Plut. *Sol.* 19.2 (ἐπίσκοπον πάντων καὶ φύλακα τῶν νόμων).
15 Reluctantly by M. H. Hansen, *Eisangelia: The Sovereignty of the People's Court in Athens in the Fourth Century B.C. and the Impeachment of Generals and Politicians* (Odense, 1975) 18–19 and "Eisangelia in Athens: A Reply," *JHS* 100 (1980) 91; but see P. J. Rhodes, "Εἰσαγγελία in Athens," *JHS* 99 (1979) 104–5.

also attested by Aristotle's statement that the Areopagus τοὺς ἐπὶ καταλύσει τοῦ δήμου συνισταμένους ἔκρινεν, Σόλωνος θέντος νόμον εἰσαγγελίας περὶ αὐτῶν.[16] Unfortunately, there are a number of difficulties of interpretation. The first is that the expression κατάλυσις τοῦ δήμου, which in all its other occurrences refers to the overthrow of the Athenian democracy,[17] is clearly anachronistic. If it has any historical substance, its minimal meaning will be that the law was devised to protect Solon's constitution against tyranny;[18] but since later legislation differentiated κατάλυσις τοῦ δήμου at least verbally from attempts at establishing tyranny, and since the law under discussion was not invoked against the Peisistratids after their overthrow,[19] it makes more sense to see in Aristotle's description a reflection of a broader measure, designed to protect the public institutions of Athens against any kind of subversion, that is, against any crime against the state.

It is more difficult to understand on what basis Aristotle credits Solon with the introduction of a procedure of *eisangelia* in such cases. Obviously, his statement is anachronistic if we understand by *eisangelia* the complex procedure that in the fifth and fourth centuries involved the Council and the Assembly or the jury courts.[20] But this is not what Aristotle claims: the absence of an article before νόμον indicates that Solon enacted *a* law, not *the* law of *eisangelia* — in other words, legislation like, but not identical with, that which later

16   Arist. *Ath.Pol*. 8.4: "And it tried those who banded together for the overthrow of the people, as Solon had enacted a law of impeachment concerning them."

17   The earliest occurrence of the concept, in the verbal form καταλύειν τὴν δημοκρατίαν, with δημοκρατίαν substituted for the concrete δῆμον, is in the decree of Demophantus of 410 B.C. as cited by Andoc. 1.96–98. Both verbal and nominal forms appear in the fourth-century νόμος εἰσαγγελτικός cited by Hyp. 4.7–8, and in Lycurg. 1.125–26; and the verbal form appears with both δῆμον and δημοκρατίαν in Eucrates' decree of 336 B.C., in *SEG* 12.87. The anachronism is recognized in the most recent discussions of *Ath.Pol*. 8.4 by Hansen, *Eisangelia* 17–19 and 56–57; by P. J. Rhodes, "Εἰσαγγελία" 103–14, esp. 104; and by M. H. Hansen, "Eisangelia: A Reply" 89–95, esp. 90–91.

18   So Rhodes, *CAAP* 156.

19   The oaths of Demophantus's decree at Andoc. 1.97 and of Eucrates' decree (*SEG* 12.87.7–10) include clauses both against κατάλυσις τοῦ δήμου and/or τῆς δημοκρατίας and against the establishment of tyranny. Moreover, if the old law against tyranny cited at *Ath.Pol*. 16.10 is Solonian, as argued by M. Gagarin, "The Thesmothetai and the Earliest Athenian Tyranny Law," *TAPA* 111 (1981) 71–77, even Solon's legislation differentiated between the two offenses.

20   So, rightly, Hansen, "Eisangelia: A Reply" 90–91.

came to regulate proceedings of *eisangelia*. Still, the question remains why Aristotle chose this term to describe the Solonian innovation. To answer it, we have to take a look at the procedural innovations attributed to Solon.

A characteristic feature of *eisangelia* in classical times was that it could be initiated by any citizen, usually before the Council but on occasion also in the Assembly (Arist. *Ath.Pol.* 43.4). While we may assume on the basis of the promise made to the followers of Cylon that a judicial procedure existed for crimes against the state before Solon, probably a trial before the Areopagus,[21] we cannot assume that such action could be initiated by any citizen before Solon introduced "the right for any person [τῷ βουλομένῳ] to take legal action in behalf of the injured party."[22] We are poorly informed about the cases to which this right applied, and as a result scholarly opinion is divided.[23] However, there are reasons to believe that it was confined to those public lawsuits later called *graphai* and that its purpose was to obtain legal redress "in those cases of private injury where the injured party was unable, either in law or for obvious personal reasons, to prosecute on his own account";[24] it also applied to crimes against the state, in which the injured party was not an individual but the community as a whole.[25] This, then, seems to be the reason why Aristotle credits Solon with the enactment of a law of *eisangelia* in cases of crimes against the state.

A second contribution of Solon's to the judicial system of Athens consists in the introduction of the procedure called by Aristotle ἡ εἰς τὸ δικαστήριον ἔφεσις, usually translated "appeal to the law court."[26] This means that Solon added to the jurisdictions of the nine archons and of the Areopagus a new tribunal, whose function was limited to hearing cases that came to it by *ephesis*. That Solon's name for the new tribunal was *hēliaia* and that any citizen regardless of wealth or

---

21   Plut. *Sol*. 12.1; schol. Ar. *Eq*. 445 with M. Ostwald, "The Athenian Legislation against Tyranny and Subversion," *TAPA* 86 (1955) 103–28, esp. 105 with n. 10.

22   Arist. *Ath.Pol*. 9.1: τὸ ἐξεῖναι τῷ βουλομένῳ τιμωρεῖν ὑπὲρ τῶν ἀδικουμένων. Cf. also Plut. *Sol*. 18.6. The spurious Draconian constitution, *Ath.Pol*. 4.4, gives access to the Areopagus only to the injured party (τῷ ἀδικουμένῳ).

23   For a good summary, see E. Ruschenbusch, *Untersuchungen zur Geschichte des athenischen Strafrechts*, Graezistische Abhandlungen 4, (Cologne and Graz, 1968) 48, whose own views (pp.47–53) are adopted here.

24   Rhodes, *CAAP* 160.

25   Ruschenbusch, *Untersuchungen* 53; Harrison, *LA* 2.76–78.

26   Arist. *Ath.Pol*. 9.1; cf. Plut. *Sol*. 18.3.

social status was eligible to serve on it are generally agreed.²⁷ Less firmly established is how it was constituted. Still, the prevalent view, based largely on the etymology of ἡλιαία, that it was a meeting of all citizens sitting as a jury court and differentiated by its name from the Assembly meeting as a political body (ἐκκλησία),²⁸ has not been invalidated by recent attacks.²⁹ Accordingly, it seems that originally

27 Solon's use of ἡλιαία is guaranteed by quotations in Lys. 10.16 and Dem. 24.105, and its identity with τὸ δικαστήριον is established by Dem. 24.114; cf. Rhodes, *CAAP* 160, and M. H. Hansen, "The Athenian *Heliaia* from Solon to Aristotle," *C&M* 33 (1981–82) 9–47, esp. 27–28 with n. 82. That its correct spelling has a smooth breathing was established by H. T. Wade-Gery, *Essays in Greek History* (Oxford, 1958) 173–74 with n. 4 and 195 with n. 4. To the evidence he cites add now αλιαια on two late seventh-century inscriptions from Tiryns: see N. Verdelis, M. Jameson, and Io. Papachristodoulou, "'Αρχαϊκαί ἐπιγραφαί ἐκ Τίρυνθος," *AE*, 1975, 150–205, esp. 168 and 172 with comment on 192–93. Nevertheless, the conventional spelling will be retained here in transliterations.

28 See MacDowell, *LCA* 30–32 with n. 20, where Rhodes, "Εἰσαγγελία" 104 and *CAAP* 160 are to be added to the bibliography.

29 The attacks have come primarily from M. H. Hansen (a) in *Eisangelia* 51–52, (b) in "*Demos, Ecclesia* and *Dicasterion* in Classical Athens," *GRBS* 19 (1978) 127–46, and (c) in "Athenian *Heliaia*." Since (a) has been answered by Rhodes, "Εἰσαγγελία" 104, and since (b) has been restated and strengthened in (c), I shall confine myself here to a few remarks critical of (c).

Hansen challenges the prevalent opinion on three scores: (1) that it is based on a debatable etymology and interpretation of ἡλιαία, (2) that it rests on a misinterpretation of Arist. *Ath.Pol.* 9.1–2, and (3) that it depends on a questionable set of *a priori* assumptions about the development of Athenian institutions. He sets out to prove that the ἡλιαία was in fact a new body of government instituted by Solon and divided by him into panels of δικαστήρια chosen by lot, in which form we know it from the fourth century. My response to each point follows.

1. I agree with Hansen's contention ("Athenian *Heliaia*" 29) that, since ἡλιαία "may apply equally well to the entire people or to a major section, . . . the argument from etymology carries no weight." However, the fact that the noun is never found in the plural, even when referring to a tribunal rather than to a building, gives pause, since we should have expected to find some instances of the plural if the division into panels went back to Solon. Hansen correctly states that the new name suggests a new institution (pp. 29–30), but the new institution can have been constituted from the same body that constituted the ἐκκλησία, that is, from the people as a whole. This does not mean, however, that every meeting of the people as a whole in a judicial capacity should have been referred to as a meeting of the ἡλιαία: according to the prevalent view, when the ἡλιαία as constituted by the people as a whole ceased to function after the reforms of Ephialtes, some of its functions went over to the ἐκκλησία. In view of this, Hansen's argument that a judicial session of the Assembly in the late fifth century is called ἐκκλησία and not ἡλιαία (p. 30) proves nothing, especially since the case referred to is the "trial" of the generals of Arginusae (n. 91), which is acknowledged to have been procedurally illegal. Similarly, Hansen's appeal to Solon's law on

theft at Dem. 24.105 is irrelevant to the question whether Solon gave the people as a whole participation in the ἡλιαία (pp. 30–31): even if ὁ βουλόμενος in that law does refer to the prosecutor, the presence of the clause ὅταν περὶ τοῦ τιμήματος ᾖ (omitted by Hansen) shows that the proposal of a penalty by prosecution and defense in an ἀγὼν τιμητός is at issue; since there is no reason to credit Solon with this institution, this clause will have been inserted after Solon and is, therefore, not germane to the question of how his ἡλιαία was recruited. Again, the law on bribery of judges at [Dem.] 46.26 (pp. 31–32) is irrelevant to the issue: a distinction is made there between the ἡλιαία and δικαστηρίων τι, indicating that the former refers to the people's court, whereas the latter makes sense only if δικαστήριον is taken in a nontechnical meaning, as referring to any tribunal (other than the people's court), including, for example, the Areopagus. The use of ἡλιαία can best be explained by the stylistic impossibility of saying τὸ δικαστήριον ἢ τῶν δικαστηρίων τι.

2.   Hansen (pp. 32–34) cites the use of singular and plural of δικαστήριον in Arist. *Pol.* 2.12, 1273ᵇ35–74ᵃ5, and at *Ath.Pol.* 7.3 and 9.1 to show that Aristotle believed Solon to have instituted dikastic panels and the phrases τὰ δικαστήρια ποιήσας ἐκ πάντων (*Pol.* 1274ᵃ3) and κληρωτὸν ὄν (ibid. 5) for Aristotle's belief that the lot was used to determine the composition of each popular tribunal under Solon as it was in the fourth century. Apart from the facts that τὰ δικαστήρια ποιήσας ἐκ πάντων does not necessarily imply "selection" from the entire people (so Hansen, p. 33) but may equally well mean "composed of the entire people" (and is, therefore, compatible with the view that the ἡλιαία consisted of the people as a whole) and that κληρωτὸν ὄν is clearly part of the fourth-century censure of Solon and not part of Aristotle's own views of the Solonian constitution, Rhodes ("Εἰσαγγελία" 104) has already pointed out that in the context of *Pol.* 2.12 Aristotle is addressing a fourth-century controversy whether Solon's judicial reforms were responsible for the fourth-century democracy; his own point (1274ᵃ5–21) is that this development was not part of Solon's intention. His discussion of the δικαστήρια and of the use of the lot in assigning jurors to a particular court on a particular day envisages the situation in the fourth century and is not an antiquarian endeavor to find out what Solon actually did, beyond stating that Solon gave the people judicial power. His switch from δικαστήρια (1274ᵃ3) to δικαστήριον (1274ᵃ5) is therefore compatible both with the view that the Solonian ἡλιαία was composed of the people as a whole and with the view that it consisted of dikastic panels. The switch from plural to singular in *Ath.Pol.* 7.3 vs. 9.1 is similarly inconclusive, since the plural at 7.3 may envisage the situation in the fourth century or may describe the judicial powers of the people as such. After all, the Areopagus also functioned as a δικαστήριον, but, unlike the ἡλιαία, it was not constituted ἐκ πάντων.

3.   The ancient evidence on the Solonian reforms is too sparse and imprecise to enable us to explain it without *a priori* assumptions about the development of Athenian institutions. Though Hansen (p. 35) is right in his argument that sortition existed under Solon, it is highly unlikely that so sophisticated an institution as dikastic panels should have sprung fully developed from Solon's head, especially at a period that will have been less litigious than the fifth and fourth centuries. Moreover, *ephesis* is not likely to have been so common in the sixth century that several panels had to be created in order to cope with all cases.

the same persons who constituted the *ekklēsia* also constituted the *hēliaia*, that *dēmos* could describe either institution, and that the difference between the two terms signified merely the purpose for which the people had been convoked and the fact that the *hēliaia* had taken the heliastic oath.[30]

Since no record of any case of *ephesis* has come down to us from the sixth century, the nature of this procedure, the cases to which it was applicable, and the purpose for which Solon instituted it must remain largely matters for conjecture. In Solon's time, *ephesis* presumably had the effect of a modern appeals procedure in that it enabled a litigant dissatisfied with an archon's verdict to appeal to the *hēliaia* for a new trial.[31] Did the Solonian system also allow for *ephesis* in cases in which the Areopagus had passed the initial verdict? The answer is negative for homicide and for all those other cases for which the Areopagus never lost its judicial competence and in which its verdict was final in all known periods of Athenian history.[32] As far as its verdicts in political cases are concerned, we shall have to consider the evidence for crimes against the state, cases of accountability, and cases of scrutiny each on its own merit. For the moment it is sufficient to state that from the time of Solon we have no indication whatever to affirm or deny that the verdict of the Areopagus was final in crimes against the state.

The right to hold magistrates accountable for their conduct in office was, according to Aristotle, another constituent element of the guardianship of the laws with which the Areopagus was entrusted under Solon: "It disciplined [ηὔθυνεν] offenders, being competent to impose fines and penalties, and it took the payments due onto the Acropolis without recording the reason why they had been exacted." Only the use of the verb ηὔθυνεν suggests that disciplinary proceedings against public officials are envisaged here and not punitive measures against other kinds of offenders.[33] The language used

---

30   This is suggested by the circumstance that the oath taken by the dikasts in the fourth century was still called "heliastic." The version preserved in Dem. 24.148–51 is no doubt a development of an original version, which may go back to the time of Solon.

31   Plut. *Sol*. 18.3 with Bonner-Smith 1.159 and 2.232–35; Wade-Gery, *Essays* 173–74; Harrison, *LA* 2.72–74; MacDowell, *LCA* 30–32.

32   Dem. 23.22 and Arist. *Ath.Pol*. 60.2 with Lysias 7; cf. Busolt-Swoboda 851.

33   Arist. *Ath.Pol*. 8.4: καὶ τοὺς ἁμαρτάνοντας ηὔθυνεν κυρία οὖσα καὶ [ζη]μιοῦν καὶ κολάζειν, καὶ τὰς ἐκτίσεις ἀνέφερεν εἰς πόλιν, οὐκ ἐπιγράφουσα τὴν πρόφασιν δι' ὃ [τὸ ἐ]κτ[ίν]εσθαι. For similar functions of the Areopagus in the pre-Solonian period,

does not permit the inference that the Areopagus before or under Solon regularly conducted *euthynai* of the kind with which we are familiar from the fifth century on, when they were mandatory for all magistrates upon the expiration of their term of office. It merely indicates that the Areopagus was empowered to exercise disciplinary control over any magistrate at any time when an offense had been imputed to him, and may well have included the power to remove him from office before he had completed his term.

Were decisions of the Areopagus in these cases subject to appeal (*ephesis*) to the *hēliaia*? Though the tenor of the present Aristotelian passage creates the impression that the verdict of the Areopagus was final, two passages in the *Politics* mention the conduct of *euthynai* as one of the powers given by the Solon to the *dēmos*.[34] Unless we are to assume either that these passages are as anachronistic about the *euthyna* as the *Constitution of Athens* (8.4) is about κατάλυσις τοῦ δήμου and εἰσαγγελία,[35] or that εὐθύνειν has a different meaning here from the one it has in the *Constitution of Athens*,[36] the conflict between the two treatises can be resolved by assuming that the principle of ὁ βουλόμενος[37] was applicable to these cases also: complaints from private citizens against magistrates could be lodged before the Areopagus at their *euthynai*, and/or, the statement in the *Constitution of Athens* notwithstanding, there were circumstances in which an adverse decision by the Areopagus in a *euthyna* proceeding—perhaps one in which the complaint of a private citizen against a magistrate had been ignored—could be appealed to the *dēmos* sitting in its judicial capacity as the *hēliaia*.[38] In other words, though our only source, Aristotle, leaves room for the interpretation that *ephesis* from

---

see *Ath.Pol.* 3.6 and also the spurious Draconian constitution at 4.4. The alleged involvement of the *dēmos* in *euthynai* under Solon at Arist. *Pol.* 2.12, 1274ᵃ15–17, and 3.11, 1281ᵇ32–34, will be discussed below. Rhodes, *CAAP* 155, takes the phrase to refer to offenders in general but fails to consider that it appears here in the context of the administration of public affairs and that from the fifth century on the verb and its cognates are used almost exclusively for proceedings against public officials; cf. M. Piérart, "Les εὔθυνοι athéniens," *Ant.Class.* 40 (1971) 526–73, esp. 543–49.

34 Arist. *Pol.* 2.12, 1274ᵃ15–17, and 3.11, 1281ᵇ32–34.
35 See above, p. 8 with nn. 17 and 20.
36 Hignett, *HAC* 204; Rhodes, *CAAP* 155.
37 See above, p. 9 with nn. 22–25.
38 Arist. *Ath.Pol.* 9.1 may in this sense have been a Solonian corrective of the situation described ibid. 4.4, where an injured party could report to the Areopagus παρ' ὃν ἀδικεῖται νόμον, if that situation is indeed historical. A similar point about *ephesis* in *euthyna* proceedings under Solon is made by Bonner-Smith 1.164–65.

the decisions of the Areopagus in *euthynai* may have been possible, it is not likely that in fact recourse was often had to it; in short, it seems that the conduct of *euthynai* was firmly in the hands of the Areopagus.

Scrutiny (*dokimasia*) of elected officials between their election and the inception of their term of office was a further way in which control over magistrates was exercised at Athens. The antiquity of the *dokimasia* is attested by Aristotle's statement that "in ancient times [sc. before Solon] the Council of the Areopagus by itself summoned and judged the person suitable for each office and commissioned him to its tenure for one year."[39] The passage is often taken to mean that the election of magistrates in pre-Solonian times rested entirely with the Areopagus and is therefore believed to contradict Aristotle's statement elsewhere that Solon introduced no change in the election of the magistrates.[40] But in its context in the *Constitution of Athens* the role of the Areopagus need not preclude a prior popular election of the archons; the procedure described may have consisted simply in summoning those elected, submitting them to some kind of scrutiny, and assigning to each that office for which the Areopagites regarded him as best fitted, without regard to his property class and without the procedure of mixed election and lot (κλήρωσις ἐκ προκρίτων), the institution of which Aristotle attributes to Solon.[41] If this interpretation is plausible, it remains the only description of a *dokimasia*-like procedure that we possess before the end of the fifth century. Regardless of any changes the institution may have undergone before then, there can be no doubt that the Areopagus was in control of it under the Solonian constitution.

Three Solonian measures are credited by Aristotle (*Ath.Pol.* 9.1) with having furthered the cause of the common people (δημοτικώτατα). The first, the prohibition against giving loans on the security of the person of the debtor, created the minimal social and economic prerequisite for the common man's exercise of citizenship.

---

39   Arist. *Ath.Pol.* 8.2: τὸ γὰρ ἀρχαῖον ἡ ἐν Ἀ[ρεί]ῳ [πάγῳ βουλ]ὴ ἀνακαλεσαμένη καὶ κρίνασα καθ' αὑτὴν, τὸν ἐπιτήδειον ἐφ' ἑκάστῃ τῶν ἀρχῶν ἐπ' [ἐν]ια[υτ]ὸν [δια-τάξα]σα ἀπέστελλεν.

40   Arist. *Pol.* 2.12, 1273ᵇ41–1274ᵃ3; 1274ᵃ15–17, with Hignett, *HAC* 78–79, 321–22.

41   The assignment of a particular archonship by the Areopagites in the pre-Solonian state may thus have been a predecessor of the kind of allotment envisaged for the polemarch by E. Badian, "Archons and *Strategoi*," *Antichthon* 5 (1971) 1–34, esp. 25.

The second populist measure, the extension to any person of the right to take legal action in behalf of an injured party, constituted a major step toward the advancement of popular power: it enabled any citizen, regardless of social status, to contribute to the enforcement of Solon's laws by initiating legal action, especially in cases in which the state as a whole was the injured party. It showed that the new economic rights of the common man had not only judicial but also political implications. To determine what specific actions violated the laws and were detrimental to the state was no longer the monopoly of the upper classes; any interested citizen had henceforth the right to bring public offenders to justice. In most cases the legal proceedings themselves will have remained in the hands of the upper class, but the final and most important populist measure, the institution of an appeals procedure, *ephesis*, and of a new court, the *hēliaia*, to hear appeals, provided—at least theoretically—a check against the arbitrary administration of justice on the part of the aristocratic establishment. It made the people the court of last resort. From this seed, as we shall see later, popular sovereignty was to develop in Athens.

Cleisthenes and Legislative Procedure

Solon's reforms of the administration of justice were left untouched by Cleisthenes, whose contribution to the growth of popular power was a by-product of the solution to a different set of fundamental problems. Herodotus equates Cleisthenes' tribal reforms with the establishment of the Athenian democracy.[42] This identification can, however, be justified only as a retrospective inference drawn from effects to origins. The origins themselves, as described by Herodotus and Aristotle, show that Cleisthenes' aim was not to place the decisive power of governing the state (*kratos*) into the hands of the *dēmos*,[43] but rather to ameliorate conditions that

42 Hdt. 6.131.1: ὁ τὰς φυλὰς καὶ τὴν δημοκρατίην Ἀθηναίοισι καταστήσας.

43 Whatever the origin of the term δημοκρατία may have been, its meaning even from its earliest occurrences, in Hdt. 6.43.3 and 131.1, denotes the power of the people as a whole. I am convinced neither by the attempt of R. Sealey, "The Origins of *Demokratia*," *CSCA* 6 (1973) 253–95, to show that δημοκρατία was not an "empirically descriptive" term in the fifth century but implied approval or disapproval, nor by the ingenious argument of K. H. Kinzl, "Δημοκρατία. Studie zur Frühgeschichte des Begriffes," *Gymnasium* 85 (1978) 117–27 and 312–26, that the term originated in Cleisthenes' circle to describe at once the principle of majority rule and an administration based on δῆμοι (demes). For earlier attempts to trace the history of the term, see Kinzl, "Δημοκρατία" 117 n. 2.

had first brought about tyranny in Athens and had resulted in political strife as soon as the Peisistratids had been expelled in 511/10 B.C. Cleisthenes was, in other words, no ideological democrat but a practical statesman and politician concerned with eliminating the roots of internal conflict from the society in which he lived.[44] In his struggle with Isagoras, he had himself become involved in the fight for power among aristocratic clans, which had torn Attica apart earlier in the sixth century. That Cleisthenes lost the first battle[45] probably means no more than that Isagoras was elected archon for 508/7 B.C.,[46] but the significant point is that Aristotle ascribes his defeat ταῖς ἑταιρείαις. This indicates that in their struggle for dynastic supremacy both Isagoras and Cleisthenes had relied on the support of their ἑταῖροι, their upper-class friends and retainers, and that the following Isagoras could muster proved stronger and more effective than that of Cleisthenes.[47]

At this point Herodotus credits Cleisthenes with the discovery of the common people as a source of political power: upon his defeat by Isagoras, Cleisthenes "completely attracted to his faction the Athenian commons, which had previously been rejected."[48] The description of this attraction by the words τὸν δῆμον προσεταιρίζεται (5.66.2) implies that Cleisthenes used the commons for purposes for which ἑταῖροι had been used before, or, concretely, that Cleisthenes, acting as a private citizen in opposition to the ruling archon, used the *dēmos*—presumably meaning Council and Assembly—as the forum for passing his reforms.[49] That this was a revolutionary step to take is

44 For this point, see J. Martin, "Von Kleisthenes zu Ephialtes," *Chiron* 4 (1974) 5–42, esp. 40–42.

45 Hdt. 5.66.2; Arist. *Ath.Pol.* 20.1.

46 Dion. Hal. *Ant.Rom.* 1.74.6, 5.1.1.

47 Ghinatti, *Gruppi* 90–110. That ἑταιρεῖαι in the late fifth-century sense of the term (for which see below, pp. 356–57) are not likely to have existed in Athens in the sixth century was shown by Wade-Gery, *Essays* 138.

48 Hdt. 5.69.2: τὸν 'Αθηναίων δῆμον πρότερον ἀπωσμένον τότε πάντως πρὸς τὴν ἑωυτοῦ μοῖραν προσεθήκατο. For a different interpretation, see C. W. Fornara, "The *Diapsephismos* of *Ath.Pol.* 13.5," *CP* 65 (1970) 243–46, esp. 246, whose belief (that Cleisthenes restored to the people powers that they had possessed before Isagoras's oligarchy of the Three Hundred was installed) is untenable, because there is no evidence that such an oligarchy was ever actually installed or that the proposal to install it preceded Cleomenes' intervention on the side of Isagoras against Cleisthenes' proposed reforms.

49 Wade-Gery *Essays* 136, 142–43; T. J. Cadoux, "The Athenian Archons from Kreon to Hypsichides," *JHS* 68 (1948) 70–123, esp. 114–16 n. 249; R. A. De Laix, *Probouleusis at Athens: A Study of Political Decision-Making,* University of California

evident, but it does not follow that the political aims to be achieved by this procedure were equally radical. There is no indication that Cleisthenes designed to overthrow the privilege of birth and wealth in order to put the effective control of the state entirely into the hands of the commons. If that had been his goal from the beginning, he would not initially have joined the upper classes in rejecting the common people,[50] and he would not have been successful in implementing it, because until at least the death of Pericles, in 429 B.C., high birth remained in fact a precondition for political leadership in Athens.[51] If, on the other hand, Cleisthenes' partnership with the people was motivated by sheer opportunism, subservient to the goal of acquiring power for himself or his *genos* when he saw himself

---

Publications in History 83 (Berkeley and Los Angeles, 1973) 19–20. With most modern scholars I believe that Solon established a Council of Four Hundred, whose functions were merely probouleutic. The case for this has been convincingly restated by Rhodes, *AB* 208–9 with relevant bibliography at 208 n. 2 (cf. also his *CAAP* 153–54) and by De Laix, *Probouleusis* 13–17, whose arguments prevail over those of Hignett, *HAC* 92–96, and of E. Will in "Bulletins historiques: Histoire grecque," *Rev.Hist.* 233 (1965) 414 with n. 1; in "Bulletin historique: Histoire grecque," ibid. 238 (1967) 394–95 n. 1., and in his review of M. Ostwald, *Nomos and the Beginnings of the Athenian Democracy* (Oxford, 1969), *Rev.Phil.* 45 (1971) 112 n. 1. The procedure followed by Cleisthenes must remain a matter of conjecture: since Herodotus describes Cleisthenes' approach to the *dēmos* as an unusual step, a direct appeal to the *ekklēsia* without requesting a prior *probouleuma* from the Council cannot be ruled out. On the other hand, the fact that the *boulē*, which must still have been the old Solonian Council of Four Hundred (so Rhodes, *AB* 208–9 and *CAAP* 153–54, and C. Meier, "Clisthène et le problème politique de la polis grecque," *RIDA*, 3d ser., 20 [1973] 115–59, esp. 134 n. 61), gave leadership to the commons in resisting the designs of Cleomenes and Isagoras (Hdt. 5.72.2; Arist. *Ath.Pol.* 20.3) would support the view that Cleisthenes had obtained a *probouleuma* from the Council before submitting his proposals to the Assembly. If we may assume with Hignett, *HAC* 150–51, and Rhodes, *AB* 21 with n. 4 and 209, that the archon—or, less probably, the college of nine archons—presided over the meetings of the *ekklēsia* as well as of the *boulē* before the introduction of prytanies, either of these procedures would have resulted in a direct confrontation between Cleisthenes and Isagoras and would help explain why Isagoras summoned Cleomenes' help as promptly as he did. The problem of the Council is not faced by D. W. Knight, *Some Studies in Athenian Politics in the Fifth Century B.C,* Historia Einzelschrift 13 (Wiesbaden, 1970) 13–24, who dates the reform proposals to the time between Isagoras's election to the archonship and his assumption of office. It is hard to see, however, on what authority Isagoras could have summoned Cleomenes at that moment.

50   Hdt. 5.69.2, where it is grammatically even possible to interpret the rejection as referring to Cleisthenes alone; see De Laix, *Probouleusis* 19 with n. 45.

51   The aristocratic character of the leadership of the developing democracy is well brought out by Martin, "Kleisthenes." Cf. also W. R. Connor, *The New Politicians of Fifth-Century Athens* (Princeton, 1971) chaps. 1 and 2.

unable to muster a dynastic faction strong enough to assert himself against other dynasts,[52] he could and probably would have gratified his desire for power in ways that would have put it more durably into his hands or the hands of the Alcmaeonids. For example, the strong popular support with which his proposals were received and the popularity evinced by the resistance Council and people offered to Isagoras and Cleomenes when Cleisthenes was himself in exile[53] could have been turned by him upon his return to an advantage greater than having his kinsman Alcmaeon elected archon for the following year, 507/6 B.C.[54] For this, as far as we know, was the only personal benefit Cleisthenes derived from his reforms for himself or for his *genos*.[55]

The nature of Cleisthenes' goals can only be inferred from his acts and from the immediate consequences of his measures on the internal life of Athens. Since his reforms put an end to the dynastic factionalism that had beset Athens through much of the sixth century, yet without diminishing the hold that birth and wealth kept on the government of Athens, and since they increased the participation of the common people in public affairs, there has been a tendency in recent scholarship to emphasize one of these aspects at the expense of the other.[56] Neither of these views manages to capture what seems to be the essential point. The view that Cleisthenes took his case to the common people because he failed to attract sufficient dynastic aristocratic support is not irreconcilable with attributing to

52   Martin, "Kleisthenes" 12–18.
53   Hdt. 5.70–72.2; Arist. *Ath.Pol*. 20.2–3.
54   Poll. 8.110 with Cadoux, "Archons" 114 with n. 248. For a cautionary note, see C. W. J. Eliot, *Coastal Demes of Attika. A Study of the Policy of Kleisthenes*, Phoenix Supplement 5, (Toronto, 1962) 146–47 n. 18.
55   P. J. Bicknell, *Studies in Athenian Politics and Genealogy*, Historia Einzelschrift 19, (Wiesbaden, 1972) 1–45, ingeniously argues that Cleisthenes deliberately arranged the deme quotas in the Council in such a way that pro-Peisistratids would be underrepresented while Alcmaeonids and other anti-Peisistratids would be overrepresented. Apart from the general uncertainty of his data, acknowledged on his p. 45, and apart from the fact that a plausible case can be made only for the tribe Aiantis (pp. 32–37), Bicknell's hypothesis is based on assumptions about the importance of the Council in the reforms themselves and in the period immediately following them that have now been invalidated by the work of Rhodes, *AB* 209–11, 223, *et passim*. Cf. also the remarks of Martin, "Kleisthenes" 16–17.
56   Martin, "Kleisthenes," stresses the aristocratic element that persisted in the Athenian constitution after Cleisthenes, whereas Meier, "Clisthène" 115–59, overemphazises and idealizes the democratic aspect.

him a more general perception that the dynastic rivalries rampant in the early and again in the late sixth century had created a disunity harmful to Athens's political development. Accordingly, he devised a system that would neutralize the political influence wielded by dynastic factions by making the power of the people an instrument to counterbalance the upper classes in the making of political decisions. This goal, I believe, lies behind the "mixing" policy (in a geographical as well as social sense) that Aristotle attributes to Cleisthenes. The philosopher sees this goal implemented in the substitution of ten new tribes for the Solonian four,[57] in the new trittyes upon which the new tribes were based,[58] and in the use of the deme as the smallest political unit by which a citizen might be identified, explained as designed to avoid the use of patronymics, which would have created undesirable distinctions between new citizens and those of older stock.[59]

The mixing process that Aristotle saw at the center of Cleisthenes' reforms applies in an even wider sense than he recognized to the blend of aristocratic with democratic elements in the constitution those reforms produced. To accomplish his ends, Cleisthenes, on the negative side, had to break the monopoly of political power that birth and wealth held through its control of the electorate, which had been responsible for the dynastic rivalries that had characterized the politics of sixth-century Athens before, during, and after the tyranny, without at the same time eliminating from the political scene the upper classes, whose economic power, social prestige, and military expertise made them indispensable for the management of public affairs. On the positive side, he had to create in Council and Assembly an effective counterweight to aristocratic power. The reforms accomplished both these ends at almost every level.

---

57 Arist. *Ath.Pol.* 21.2: ἀναμεῖξαι βουλόμενος, ὅπως μετάσχωσι πλείους τῆς πολιτείας. Cf. also *Pol.* 6.4, 1319ᵇ19–27, where the increase in the number of tribes and the consolidation of many private into fewer public cults is motivated ὅπως ἂν ὅτι μάλιστα ἀναμειχθῶσι πάντες ἀλλήλοις.

58 Arist. *Ath.Pol.* 21.3 and 4: ὥστ' οὐ συνέπιπτεν <ἂν> ἀναμίσγεσθαι τὸ πλῆθος, sc. if the old trittyes had been kept; and ὅπως ἑκάστη <sc. φυλὴ> μετέχῃ πάντων τῶν τόπων. For an entirely different explanation of the trittyes, see P. Siewert, *Die Trittyen Attikas und die Heeresreform des Kleisthenes*, Vestigia 33 (Munich, 1982), esp. 131–38 and 156–63, with the review by D. M. Lewis in *Gnomon* 55 (1983) 431–36.

59 Arist. *Ath.Pol.* 21.4: ἵνα μὴ πατρόθεν προσαγορεύοντες ἐξελέγχωσιν τοὺς νεοπολίτας. I have offered an explanation of the probable identity of these νεοπολῖται in *Nomos* 151–52.

Although Aristotle may be attributing too much importance to the role played by the new citizens in his explanation of the introduction of the deme as the smallest political unit,[60] he is probably right in interpreting the new importance assigned to the demes as a measure aimed at old established families. In any event, it is now generally recognized that the demes undermined the dependencies on which the upper class had relied for its political support.[61] The use of patronymics for naming some of his newly created demes proves the point: "Boutad" was henceforth not only the name of a descendant of noble Boutes but also of any person, however humble, who resided in the deme of that name.[62] Apart from enjoying a certain amount of local self-government, each deme contributed an assigned quota to the tribal contingent that represented it in the Council and to some other boards of minor officials.[63] But though the thetes, the lowest property class, could no doubt vote in the deme assemblies that elected prospective members of the Council, they do not yet seem to have been eligible for membership in this most democratic of all elected bodies in Athens.[64]

Similarly the trittyes seem to have been organized to ensure the participation of all citizens in public life without eliminating at the same time the role of birth and wealth altogether. Although we know little about the precise nature of the twelve Solonian trittyes, there is every reason to believe that they were dominated by old established families and clans and were, therefore, not suitable as a

---

60　Arist. *Ath.Pol.* 21.4.

61　Cf. D. W. Bradeen, "The Trittyes in Cleisthenes' Reforms," *TAPA* 86 (1955) 22–30, esp. 24; Martin, "Kleisthenes" 13–15 and 17.

62　D. Lewis, "Cleisthenes" 26–27.

63　For self-government, see R. J. Hopper, *The Basis of the Athenian Democracy* (Inaug. Lect., Sheffield, 1957) and Ostwald, *Nomos* 152–53; for deme assemblies, see B. Haussoulier, *La Vie municipale en Attique* (Paris, 1883) 4–93; for deme representation in the Council, see Arist. *Ath.Pol.* 62.1, with Hignett, *HAC* 150, and Rhodes, *AB* 12; and for a recent attempt to ascertain the deme quotas, see J. S. Traill, *The Political Organization of Attica*, Hesperia Supplement 14, (Princeton, 1975) 56–72. After 487/6 B.C. the demes are said by Arist. *Ath.Pol.* 22.5 to have played a part in the πρόκρισις of the archons, but see Badian, "Archons" 19. Minor officials are mentioned in Arist. *Ath.Pol.* 62.1.

64　Arist. *Ath.Pol.* 7.3, with Hignett, *HAC* 142–43, Jones, *AD* 105, and Rhodes, *AB* 2 and *CAAP* 140–41, 145–46. Cf. also De Laix, *Probouleusis* 21–23, who argues on more general grounds that Cleisthenes did not intend "to set up a radically democratic constitution that would subvert the influence of the καλοὶ κἀγαθοί in public life."

basis for the new tribes. The ingenuity with which Cleisthenes created his thirty trittyes so as to break up important cult organizations dominated by the *genē* by distributing the clans over different trittyes has been admirably demonstrated by D. M. Lewis.[65] The trittyes were designed to prevent the use of religious cults for purposes of dynastic politics; they were not designed to eliminate the upper class from the political life of Athens. A given *genos* could no longer exploit its domination of certain cults or priesthoods as a base for political power; but the fact that each tribe contained one trittys from the city, in and near which the old families were concentrated, ensured that aristocratic influence would remain strong in the tribes. At the same time, that influence would be balanced by the presence in the same tribe of members of other *genē* as well as of inhabitants— rich and poor—of the other two regions of Attica, each with its own local interests.[66]

The elimination from political life of the four kinship tribes, dominated by the *genē*, which Solon had made the electoral units for his constitution, and the substitution of ten new tribes, each composed of a trittys from each of the three regions of Attica, was regarded as a democratic measure already in antiquity.[67] For although tribes had played a part in the election of the most important magistrates ever since the reforms of Solon,[68] it will have made a difference that the Cleisthenic tribes were based on local demes and trittyes, whose allegiances would differ from those that had been owed to the *genē* by their retainers; henceforth candidates for office could no longer take the existence of a constituency for granted but had to convince of their political attractiveness their neighbors in deme and trittys as well as fellow tribesmen from the two regions other than that in which their own trittys was situated. Still, Cleisthenes did not abolish the Solonian property requirements for eligibility to high office, so that the major magistracies will have remained in the hands of the high-born and wealthy.[69] The archon-

---

65 D. Lewis, "Cleisthenes" 27–36, whose main point is not invalidated by Siewert, *Trittyen* 118–20.

66 Cf. Bradeen "Trittyes" 28–30, who applies this influence to the Council and *stratēgia*.

67 Hdt. 6.131.1 (cf. 5.69.2); Arist. *Pol.* 6.4, 1319[b]19–27.

68 Arist. *Ath.Pol.* 8.1–2; *Pol.* 2.12, 1274[a]2 and 16–17.

69 Arist. *Ath.Pol.* 7.3, where I read, with M. Chambers, "Notes on the Text of the *Ath.Pol.*," *TAPA* 96 (1965) 31–39, esp. 34–35, καὶ τὰς μεγάλας ἀρχὰς ἀπένειμεν. See also 8.1.

ship was open only to the highest—possibly the highest two—property classes,[70] and it remained closed to the zeugitai until 457/6 B.C. (Arist. *Ath.Pol.* 26.2). In short, the tribes could appoint candidates for high office and elect them in the Assembly, but only members of the upper classes could be elected.

The structure of the citizen body and its classes was, in the classical period, reflected in the organization of Greek armies, nonprofessional as they were.[71] The question whether or not the appointment of generals as such was a constitutional innovation need not concern us here,[72] but doubtless their appointment brought the organization of the army in line with the tribal reforms of Cleisthenes. Ten generals, one elected from each of the new tribes,[73] henceforth each commanded one of the ten tribal contingents (τάξεις) that made up the army[74] and acted as a counterweight yet subordinate to the polemarch, who, as one of the archons, was elected without regard to tribal distinction and from among the highest property class.[75] We do not know of any property requirement for eligibility to the

---

70 Badian, "Archons" 9–10 with n. 23.

71 Cf. P. Vidal-Naquet, "La Tradition de l'hoplite athénien," in J.-P. Vernant, ed., *Problèmes de la guerre en Grèce ancienne* (Paris and The Hague, 1968) 161–81, esp. 161–62.

72 N. G. L. Hammond, "Strategia and Hegemonia in Fifth-Century Athens," *CQ*, n.s., 19 (1969) 111–44, esp. 111–14, defends the view that στρατηγοί were elected (113 n. 1) even before 501/0 B.C., whereas Fornara, *ABG* 1–10, believes the institution as such to be an innovation. I am inclined to accept Fornara's view, since all references to pre-Cleisthenean στρατηγοί in the *Ath.Pol.* and elsewhere, listed by Hammond (p. 113), are to individual commanders of specific expeditions and do not suggest that the office was a regular—to say nothing of collegial—institution before 501/0 B.C.; cf. also Martin, "Kleisthenes" 23–24. The mention of στρατηγοί in the so-called Draconian constitution at *Ath.Pol.* 4.2 is of doubtful historical value, and in the statement attributed to Androtion (*FGH* 324 F6) on Peisistratus's tyranny στρατηγός can be no more technical in meaning than δημαγωγός. Cf. also Fornara, *ABG* 7 n. 22. Siewert's contention (*Trittyen* 139–59) that the purpose of Cleisthenes' reforms was military in that the trittyes were arranged along the main roads so as to facilitate mobilization rests on weak foundations: not only are trittys-based *lochoi* (see n. 74 below) conjectural, but we know nothing about the antiquity of the roads on which he bases his argument, and internal considerations are likely to have outweighed considerations of external threats in the structure of the trittyes.

73 Arist. *Ath.Pol.* 22.2–3, who dates the institution to the twelfth year before Marathon, with Fornara, *ABG* 1–10.

74 Bicknell, *Studies* 20–21 plausibly suggests that the three λόχοι that made up each τάξις were composed of the units each trittys contributed to the tribal contingent.

75 Arist. *Ath.Pol.* 7.3 with Plut. *Arist.* 1.2. Cf. Badian, "Archons" 25–27, 28–30.

generalship, but the military capacity required of the office will have confined it in fact if not in law to the higher property classes.[76] Still, it is safe to say that the people as a whole, presumably in the Assembly, elected these commanders of each tribal contingent[77] and that the ten generals, who enjoyed absolute equality with one another, constituted a democratic element in the Cleisthenic constitution in that the leadership of the armed forces was determined by popular election. Moreover, if Herodotus's description (6.109–10) of the situation before Marathon is any guide, the position of the polemarch as supreme commander of the army ensured a unified command even when there was dissension among the generals.

But even the army was not so democratic as one might suppose. Not every citizen capable of bearing arms was enrolled in the *taxis* of his tribe, for from the time of Cleisthenes until at least the battle of Marathon only hoplites, that is, members of the top three property classes, were admitted to military service;[78] this meant that the thetes, who at the time constituted about two-thirds of the citizen body,[79] were not permitted to fight. Since the privilege of fighting must have reflected political status, we can conclude that the Cleisthenic democracy was more of a "schéma idéal d'une république des hoplites"[80] than a democracy in the later sense of the term: it extended major political rights only to those of hoplite status and above, thereby excluding approximately two-thirds of the Athenian citizenry from full participation in the affairs of state.

The effect this restructuring of the Athenian state had on the working of the constitution is summed up by Aristotle in the words ἀποδιδοὺς τῷ πλήθει τὴν πολιτείαν, which signify that Cleisthenes gave the common people, whose support had enabled him to enact his reforms, a voice in the management of public affairs; this had previously been the exclusive province of the upper classes.[81] That the common people had participated in the election of magistrates at

---

76 Hignett, *HAC* 191–92 with 191 n. 7.

77 Hdt. 6.104.2 says of Miltiades at Marathon: στρατηγὸς . . .'Αθηναίων ἀπεδέχθη, αἱρεθεὶς ὑπὸ τοῦ δήμου.

78 Vidal-Naquet, "Tradition" 165–70.

79 Jones, *AD* 8, and Vidal-Naquet, "Tradition" 170.

80 I borrow this felicitous expression from Vidal-Naquet, "Tradition" 166.

81 Arist. *Ath.Pol.* 20.1 with Rhodes, *CAAP* 244–45, who cogently argues against Wade-Gery's interpretation (*Essays* 147–48) of τῷ πλήθει = *universo populo*; cf. also Martin, "Kleisthenes" 19 with n. 76, and Fornara, *"Diapsephismos"* 245–46, with the reservation expressed in n. 48 above.

least as early as Solon has already been stated.[82] Moreover, the Assembly will have had a hand in the approval of some other measures, although the only one of which we know before the reforms of Cleisthenes is the authorization of a bodyguard for Peisistratus on the motion of Aristion.[83] Still, Cleisthenes will have enlarged the legislative authority of the common people by relying on their support for getting his reforms passed, and passage by the Assembly remained henceforth a prerequisite for the validation of new legislation. Two decrees passed soon after Cleisthenes' reforms may reflect a consciousness of this newly acquired right; they mention authorization by the *dēmos* alone without the addition of the Council. The earlier of them determined the conditions under which Athenian cleruchs were to be settled on Salamis, and it assigned certain tasks arising from this settlement to a magistrate.[84] The second, the so-called Hecatompedon decree of 485/4 B.C., regulated among other things the conduct of worshipers and gave instructions to the treasurers, making them liable to a fine to be exacted by the prytaneis if they failed to keep the rooms of the Hecatompedon open at specified times.[85] The people as a whole, nobles and commoners, now gave directions to magistrates.

The composition of the Council of Five Hundred, which controlled the agenda of Assembly meetings and thus practically all legislation, will also have acted as a counterweight to the power exercised by the nobility through its tenure of the major magistracies. Although the thetes may have been initially excluded, the Council was, in a sense, as representative of the people as a whole as was the Assembly.[86] Each tribe contributed fifty member chosen in such a way that the smallest political units, the demes, were repre-

---

82   See n. 68 above.

83   Arist. *Ath.Pol.* 14.1; cf. Hdt. 1.59.4–5. The role assigned to the people in the Cylonian revolt by Thucydides 1.126.7–8 is spontaneous rather than organized.

84   ML, no. 14, esp. 1, 7–8, and 11, dated on p. 27 "before the cleruchy sent to Chalkis after the Athenian victory of 506 (Hdt. v.77.2)," but after the reforms of Cleisthenes. What part, if any, the Council played in passing this decree remains uncertain; line 12 suggests that it played some part.

85   *IG* I³ 4, esp. A14–15, 16, B3–8, 8–13, 17–25, and 26. It is doubtful that the πρύτανις is at this time a tribal official of the Council; see Rhodes, *AB* 17. Cf. also πρυτάνειον on the Xanthippus ostrakon in ML, p. 42. For an interesting discussion of the moral aspects of this decree, see G. Màddoli, "Responsabilità e sanzione nei 'decreta de Hecatompedo,'" *MH* 24 (1967) 1–11.

86   See V. Ehrenberg, *The Greek State*² (London, 1969) 63.

sented in each tribal contingent in proportion to their numerical strength in the tribe as a whole.[87] The injunction against a tenure of more than two nonconsecutive years of office will have ensured that every adult male of hoplite status might reasonably expect to serve as councilor at least once in his life,[88] but it will have proved unworkable in the long run without extending eligibility to the thetes. Of the political powers the Council enjoyed before the reforms of Ephialtes in 462/1 B.C. we know so little that it remains doubtful whether Cleisthenes added any to the probouleutic functions that it must have been given already by Solon;[89] that is, it deliberated on policies and legislation before these were submitted as motions to the Assembly and had, therefore, from the beginning the control over the agenda of Assembly meetings that we know it possessed in the fourth century (Arist. *Ath.Pol.* 45.4).

The nature of the probouleutic functions of the Council is not contradicted by its only specific action of which a record has survived within the period between the reforms of Cleisthenes and those of Ephialtes.[90] On the occasion of his second occupation of Athens in the summer of 479 B.C., Mardonius dispatched a Hellespontine Greek named Murychides to the Athenians on Salamis to repeat the peace offer previously conveyed through Alexander of Macedon. Murychides submitted the offer to the Council, and one of the councilors, Lycides, moved "to accept the offer brought by Murychides and to submit it to the people."[91] We are not told whether the motion was ever put to a vote; if it was, it lost, and the other councilors, joined by outsiders, surrounded Lycides and stoned

---

87 See preceding note. On the manner of selection, see De Laix, *Probouleusis* 149–53; on the deme quotas, see Traill, *Organization* 1–24 and 56–58.

88 Arist. *Ath.Pol.* 62.3, with Busolt-Swoboda 1022 with n. 5. It is possible that only one term of office was permissible before 431 B.C.; see J. A. O. Larsen, *Representative Government in Greek and Roman History* (Berkeley and Los Angeles, 1955) 10–11. For the exclusion of thetes, see n. 64 above.

89 Rhodes, *AB* 209, seems to me to be right in believing that the only other powers the Council enjoyed before Ephialtes' reforms were limited disciplinary powers over its own members (ibid. 145–46), and possibly the *dokimasia* of its successors for the next year (ibid. 176–78, 209). De Laix, *Probouleusis* 22–23, goes too far in inferring from the oath in *IG* I³ 105 a limitation of larger earlier powers conferred upon the Council by Cleisthenes; cf. n. 90 below.

90 Rhodes, *AB* 194–99, has shown that neither the bouleutic oath nor *IG* I³ 105 can be used to reconstruct the powers of the βουλή before the reforms of Ephialtes.

91 Hdt. 9.5.1: τῶν δὲ βουλευτέων Λυκίδης εἶπε γνώμην ὥς οἱ ἐδόκεε ἄμεινον εἶναι δεξαμένους τὸν λόγον τόν σφι Μουρυχίδης προσφέρει ἐξενεῖκαι ἐς τὸν δῆμον.

him to death.[92] If constitutional inferences can be drawn from an account of a wartime situation, we may conclude that within the period 507/6–462/1 B.C. the Council was competent—and presumably already had the function—to receive foreign ambassadors and to deliberate on matters submitted by them;[93] that if a foreign proposal was accepted, it had to be referred to the people, that is to the Assembly, for ratification; and that in this case at least the refusal of the Council to entertain a foreign proposal ended the matter, so that it did not have to be submitted to the Assembly. The fact that only one other case is known in Athenian history in which the Council refused to make a probouleuma for referral to the Assembly[94] shows that this procedure was not the norm and could be taken only because the Council was confident of popular support. That it had such support in this instance is indicated by participation of non-members (οἱ ἔξωθεν) and their wives—no doubt the common people—in the stoning of Lycides and his family (Hdt. 9.5.2–3).

To sum up: even after the reforms of Cleisthenes the upper class retained effective control of the organs of government. The treasurers of Athena still had to be members of the highest property class, and the nine archons—and perhaps also the generals—of the highest two;[95] the archons, upon the expiration of their term of office, still became life members of the Council of the Areopagus,[96] whose broad and ancient powers gave it considerable control over the affairs of state.[97] All this Cleisthenes left substantially intact, but he provided against the arbitrary exercise of aristocratic power by letting no major decision or legislation be made or implemented without the approval of Council and Assembly.

A government in which a large representative Council and an Assembly of all citizens serve as counterweight and check to the

---

92   Id. 9.5.2. The same story is told of Cyrsilus in Dem. 18.204 and (dated somewhat earlier in the campaign of 480 B.C.) in Cic. *Off.* 3.11.48; cf. also Lycurg. *Leoc.* 122.

93   See Rhodes, *AB* 57–58 with 43 n. 3, citing ML, no. 52.12–14, and Dem. 19.185. A concern with foreign affairs at this time may also be inferred from the secret meeting that, so Diod. 11.39.5 alleges, Themistocles had with the Council before his departure on his Spartan embassy in 479/8 B.C.

94   Xen. *Hell.* 6.4.20.

95   Arist. *Ath.Pol.* 8.1 and 26.2, with Hignett, *HAC* 101–2 and 142, and with nn. 69, 71, and 76 above.

96   Cf. Hignett, *HAC* 94, 107, and 156.

97   Arist. *Ath.Pol.* 3.6, 4.4, 8.4, 23.1–2, 25.1, and 41.2; Plut. *Sol.* 19, with Rhodes, *AB* 202–6, and Martin "Kleisthenes" 28–29.

power of an aristocratic and wealthy ruling class is not yet a democracy. When Herodotus and others after him credit Cleisthenes with the establishment of a democracy at Athens,[98] they are right only to be extent that the Cleisthenic tribal reforms laid the foundations for the development of the fifth-century Athenian democracy as they knew it. The principle embodied in Cleisthenes' constitution is called *isonomia*—political equality between the ruling magistrates, who formulate political decisions, and the Council and Assembly, which approve or disapprove them. I have argued elsewhere that Cleisthenes may well have used *isonomia* as a catchword to win the people over to his reforms against the entrenched interests of the ruling class.[99] At the same time and in the same spirit, Cleisthenes may have been responsible for the adoption of *nomos* as the official term for "statute" to replace the older term, *thesmos*, in order to stress the democratic aspect of his reforms: namely, that no enactment was to be enforced unless its validity were first ratified by the people as a whole, regardless of social or economic status.[100] Just as the law on ostracism was contrived to let the people as a whole decide which of two major policies was to be adopted by temporarily banishing from the political scene the most prominent spokesman of one of them,[101] so the disappearance of *thesmos* from the official vocabulary of the new constitution indicates that imposition of laws by a ruling class was to give way to laws ratified by popular acceptance.

This means that to the right of the common people to elect their magistrates[102] Cleisthenes added through his revaluation of Council and Assembly the right to control the legislative process. This is an important step toward democracy; but it is not yet a full democracy, because the people still lacked a voice in the enforcement of the measures they had voted and had no control over the magistrates they had elected. So long as the Areopagus retained sole jurisdiction

98 Hdt. 6.131.1; Isoc. 15.232; Arist. *Ath.Pol.* 29.3.

99 Ostwald, *Nomos* 149–58. Cf. also P. Frei, " Ἰσονομία. Politik im Spiegel griechischer Wortbildungslehre," *MH* 38 (1981) 205–19.

100 Ostwald, *Nomos*, 158–60.

101 Martin, "Kleisthenes" 25–26; in general, see E. Vanderpool, *Ostracism at Athens*, Lectures in Memory of Louise Taft Semple, 2d ser., no. 6 (Cincinnati, 1970); R. Thomsen, *The Origin of Ostracism* (Copenhagen, 1972), esp. 115–42; and Ostwald, "The Reform of the Athenian State by Cleisthenes," *CAH* 4² (forthcoming).

102 See above, n. 2.

in crimes against the state and had exclusive control over the accountability of magistrates (*euthynai*), there could be no popular sovereignty. Cleisthenes does not seem to have been concerned with this issue. But it moved into the forefront of public concern soon after his reforms and was resolved in the following decades, chiefly through the reforms of Ephialtes.

FROM CLEISTHENES TO EPHIALTES

Jurisdiction in Crimes Against the State

There is some evidence that popular power was further increased soon after Cleisthenes' reforms by transferring the jurisdiction in some crimes against the state from the Areopagus to the *hēliaia* through a new application of the Solonian institution of *ephesis*. Under Solon *ephesis* was virtually an appeals procedure, but the literal meaning of the term is closer to "referral" than to "appeal"; hence, it was used from the fifth century on also to describe certain mandatory referrals from the jurisdiction of one tribunal to that of another for final disposition.[103] Although this use is not attested until 446/5 B.C.,[104] there are reasons to believe that the principle it embodied was first applied within the first decade of the fifth century.

To establish this, it is necessary to rehearse briefly the evidence for six much-discussed trials in Athens between about 493/2 and 462 B.C.[105]

1. *The trial of the tragedian Phrynichus*, about 493/2 B.C., for having written and performed his *Capture of Miletus* and thus having "reminded [the Athenians] of their own misfortunes." The defendant was fined one thousand drachmas and enjoined from any future performances of the play (Hdt. 6.21.2).[106]

---

103   MacDowell, *LCA* 30–32; cf. Rhodes, *CAAP* 160–62.

104   *IG* I³ 40 (= ML, no. 52) 74.

105   The most important recent discussions of these cases are W. von Wedel, "Die politischen Prozesse im Athen des fünften Jahrhunderts," *Bolletino dell' Istituto di Diritto Romano*, 3d ser., 13 (1971) 107–88, esp. 126–35; Rhodes, *AB* 199–200, and "Εἰσαγγελία" 104–5; Hansen, *Eisangelia* 19 and 69–71 (cases 1–5), and "Eisangelia: A Reply" 91.

106   Badian, "Archons" 15–16 n. 44, believes the attribution to 493 B.C. to be "highly unlikely" on the ground that "you can only remind people of what they

2. *The trial of Miltiades*, perhaps in the same year, for tyranny in the Thracian Chersonese, which resulted in his acquittal (Hdt. 6.104.2; Marcellin. *Vit. Thuc.* 13).[107]

3. *The trial of Miltiades*, in 489 B.C., for "deception of the Athenians" through the failure of his expedition against Paros. The prosecution, led by Xanthippus, demanded the death penalty, which was, however, reduced to a fine of fifty talents in consideration of the services he had rendered the state at Marathon and in the capture of Lemnos (Hdt. 6.136).

4. *The trial of Hipparchus*, son of Charmus, after 480 B.C., for treason, in which he was condemned to death *in absentia* (Lyc. *Leoc.* 117).[108]

5. *The trial of Themistocles*, perhaps about 471/0 B.C.,[109] which took place while he lived in Argos after his ostracism from Athens (Thuc. 1.135.2–3). Procedurally it was an *eisangelia* on the charge of treason in which Leobotes son of Alcmaeon served as chief prosecutor (Craterus *FGH* 342F11a–b). The verdict was permanent exile, which also meant that he could not be buried in Attic soil and may imply that he had been declared an outlaw and that his property had been confiscated.[110]

6. *The trial of Cimon* upon his return from Thasos in the late spring or early summer of 462 B.C.[111] on the charge of having accepted bribes from Alexander, king of Macedon. Although the

---

may be presumed to have forgotten, and it would take longer than a few months to forget the destruction of one of the greatest cities in the Greek world, if one felt ties of kinship with it." However, ἀναμνήσαντα does not necessarily presuppose a previous forgetting (this is shown by its use in the sense of "call to mind by association" at, e.g., Pl. *Phd.* 73c4–d10); and further, the penalty imposed on Phrynichus makes sense only if the wounds inflicted by the sack of Miletus were sufficiently fresh in Athenian minds. R. J. Lenardon, *The Saga of Themistocles* (London, 1978) 105–6, also prefers a later date.

107 The date 493 B.C. is suggested by a combination of Hdt. 6.41.4 with 104.1–2.

108 For the date, see U. von Wilamowitz-Moellendorff, *Aristoteles und Athen* (Berlin, 1893; repr.: Berlin, 1966) 1.114–15; A. R. Burn, *Persia and the Greeks* (London, 1962) 352.

109 R. J. Lenardon, "The Chronology of Themistokles' Ostracism and Exile," *Hist.* 8 (1959) 23–48, esp. 24–45; P. J. Rhodes, "Thucydides on Pausanias and Themistocles," ibid. 19 (1970) 387–400, esp. 396–99.

110 Thuc. 1.138.6 as interpreted by Busolt, *GG* 3.1.128 with n. 2.

111 P. Deane, *Thucydides' Dates: 465–431 B.C.* (Don Mills, Ont., 1972) 17–18, and E. Bayer and J. Heideking, *Die Chronologie des perikleischen Zeitalters*, Erträge der Forschung 36, (Darmstadt, 1975) 121–22.

prosecutors, among them Pericles, demanded the death penalty, Cimon was acquitted.[112]

Since we are not informed of any change in the judicial system between the reforms of Solon and those of Ephialtes, we should have expected either an archon or the Areopagus to have been the tribunal that heard and passed judgment in these cases, more probably the Areopagus, because in all of these cases the state was the injured party. However, if our sources can be trusted, neither agency gave any of the six verdicts: the δῆμος is credited with having passed judgment in the second trial of Miltiades (3) and in the case of Hipparchus (4); οἱ Ἀθηναῖοι passed judgment in the trials of Phrynichus (1) and Themistocles (5);[113] a δικαστήριον acquitted Miltiades at his first trial (2); and a δίκη and δικασταί are mentioned in connection with Cimon's trial (6). Though none of our sources is contemporary—they range from Herodotus (for three cases) and Thucydides (for one case) in the fifth century to Lycurgus in the fourth, Craterus in the third, and Plutarch in the late first century of our era—and though none of these authors evinces any particular penchant for the niceties of Athenian judicial procedure, the cumulative weight of the evidence they provide makes it remarkable that the Areopagus receives no mention in any of the six cases and that all point to trial by some kind of a popular court. In fact, the only judicial activity of the Areopagus of which we hear at this time consists of a story related by Aristotle (*Ath.Pol.* 25.3): Themistocles' alleged collaboration with Ephialtes against the Areopagus was motivated by a charge of collusion with the Persians (μηδισμός) on which Themistocles, himself a member of the Areopagus, was to have been tried before that body. That this story lacks any historical basis has long been recognized.[114]

How can this sudden appearance of popular jurisdiction be explained? Although the term *eisangelia* is used only in one of the cases under discussion, that of Themistocles (5), Hansen assumes

---

112   Arist. *Ath.Pol.* 27.1; Plut. *Cim.* 14.3–4, 15.1; *Per.* 10.6.

113   For Themistocles, this is suggested not only by Thuc. 1.135.3, but also by the fact that Craterus's collection of ψηφίσματα of Council and Assembly is the source of the information that Leobotes initiated an *eisangelia* against him (*FGH* 342 F11).

114   Wilamowitz, *Aristoteles* 1.140–42; Rhodes, "Εἰσαγγελία" 105 and *CAAP* 319–20; Hansen, "Eisangelia: A Reply" 91.

that five of six cases (he omits the case of Phrynichus [1] from his discussion) were handled by *eisangelia* to the Assembly and tried by that body, except that Miltiades' first trial and the case of Cimon were referred by the Assembly to a jury court.[115] This assumption is attacked by Rhodes because it leaves the role that Solon had assigned to the Areopagus in cases of *eisangelia* unexplained; Rhodes suggests himself that the case of Phrynichus (1) and the two charges against Miltiades (2 and 3) may have been heard by the *hēliaia* on appeal from an archon's verdict, that Hipparchus (4) was tried by some *ad hoc* procedure, and that the trials of Themistocles (5) and Cimon (6) took place before the Areopagus.[116] Three objections to Rhodes's view are that we know of no instance in which an individual archon was entrusted with jurisdiction in the kind of offences alleged to have been committed by Phrynichus and Miltiades, that it is hard to envisage on what basis an *ad hoc* procedure against Hipparchus should have been devised, and that it leaves unexplained why the Areopagus should not have been mentioned in the cases of Themistocles and Cimon. Hignett, whose solution, I believe, contains a kernel of historical plausibility, suggested that Cleisthenes enacted a law reserving to the people the final verdict in all cases involving the death penalty and that "those found guilty by the Areopagus on [the charge of attempting to subvert the constitution] could not be executed until the verdict had been confirmed by the ekklesia."[117] This seems to be essentially correct, except that there is no evidence that the law was enacted by Cleisthenes, that the only charge to which it applied was subversion of the constitution—unless we understand that expression in the wider sense of any crime against the state—and that necessarily the *ekklēsia* was to render the final verdict in cases of this sort.

Hignett bases his belief on an inscription of 410/09 B.C. that formed evidently part of the effort launched in the last decade of the fifth century to publish an authoritative law code by collecting and updating previously scattered and independent enactments. Although the stone is badly mutilated, there is general agreement among modern scholars that it contains legislation concerning the Council that incorporates, though not necessarily in their original form, regulations enacted at some indeterminable point between

115 Hansen, *Eisangelia* 69–71 (cases 1–5), repeated in "Eisangelia: A Reply" 91.
116 Rhodes, "Εἰσαγγελία" 105.
117 Hignett, *HAC* 154–55.

501/0 and 462/1 B.C.[118] The evidence for this rests on the identification as archaic of some intelligible words and phrases, foremost
among them the expression ὁ δῆμος ὁ ᾿Αθηναίων πληθύων, which
recurs at least eight times in the inscription, usually in the form ἄνευ
τõ δέμο τõ ᾿Αθεναίον πλεθύοντος (without a full meeting of the
Athenian people), and is paralleled only in two bronze inscriptions
from Olympia of the late sixth or early fifth century.[119] Moreover, an
astute epigraphical observation by D.M. Lewis has strengthened the
case that at least one of those passages in which this expression is
found is based on an early original.[120] Since none of the interpretations so far proposed for this unusual phrase is completely
satisfactory,[121] its meaning can be ascertained only by a fresh examination of the contexts in which it occurs.

118   *IG* I³ 105. The fundamental modern work on this inscription was done by
H. T. Wade-Gery, "Studies in Attic Inscriptions of the Fifth Century B.C., B. The
Charter of the Democracy, 410 B.C. = *I.G.* I² 114," *BSA* 33 (1932–33) 113–22. See
also Rhodes, *AB* 195–99, cf. 113; and De Laix, *Probouleusis* 23–24. Of earlier studies
the most instructive are P. Cloché, "Le Conseil athénien des Cinq Cents et la peine
de mort," *REG* 33 (1920) 1–50, esp. 28–36; Bonner-Smith 1.201–5; J. Sencie and W.
Peremans, "La Juridiction pénale de la Boulè à Athènes au début du Vᵉ siècle avant
J.-C.," *LEC* 10 (1941) 193–201 and esp. 329–37; Hignett, *HAC* 153–54; Larsen,
Representative Government 15–18. The dates proposed for the original version on
which this inscription depends range from the archonship of Hermocreon (Bonner-
Smith 1.340–45) to the time between 501/0 B.C. and Salamis (Cloché, "Conseil"
28–35), and from the first half of the fifth century (Rhodes, *AB* 198) to the reforms
of Ephialtes (H. Swoboda, "Über den Process des Perikles," *Hermes* 28 [1893] 597 n.
3); Sencie and Peremans believe ("Juridiction" 333–37) that *IG* I³ 105 is not based
on an earlier antecedent.
119   θοὰν ἐπιβαλὲν (line 41) and the phrase τάδε ἔδοχσεν (line 34) are usually and,
I believe, correctly taken as the other indications of archaic usage, adequately
discussed by Rhodes, *AB* 197. The δῆμος πληθύων is clearly legible in *IG* I³ 105.37,
42, 43, and 46, intelligible at 40, and convincingly restored at 25, 35, and 36. For the
parallels from Olympia, see E. Schwyzer, ed., *Dialectorum Graecarum Exempla
Epigraphica Potiora* (Leipzig, 1923), nos. 410 and 412, containing, respectively, the
phrases ἄνευς βολὰν καὶ ζᾶμον πλαθύοντα and σὺν βολᾶι (π)εντακατίον αϝλάνεος καὶ
δάμοι πλεθύοντι, with L. H. Jeffery, *The Local Scripts of Archaic Greece* (Oxford, 1961)
218 and 220 (nos. 5 and 9).
120   D. M. Lewis, "A Note on *IG* i² 114," *JHS* 87 (1967) 132, noticed that the
three pairs of vertical points in line 43 represent τõι of a damaged original, which the
mason could not read well enough to copy.
121   Cloché ("Conseil" 29 with n. 1 and 49) translated it "peuple réuni en
'assemblée plénière'" and believed that by the end of the fifth century this could
describe either the *dikastēria* or the Assembly. Against him, Sencie and Peremans
("Juridiction" 335–37) saw the expression as meaning "l'ensemble des citoyens" or
"le peuple 'en masse'" (as distinct from a meeting of the Assembly), whose
judgement was to replace that of the Four Hundred and the Five Thousand after
their fall in 410 B.C. Their view has found little acclaim, since it is hard to envisage

It has long been recognized that the inscription as a whole delineated the powers of the Council and those of the people from one another, affirming or extending the rights of the latter and limiting those of the former. In order to ascertain which of the rights given to the people may have been part of the presumptive original, we must, therefore, identify which rights the intelligible passages of the inscription assign to the δῆμος πληθύων, on the assumption that this expression was taken over from an archaic original. Three such rights can be recognized in the preserved remnants: without the δῆμος πληθύων "no war can be started or brought to an end;"[122] "no death penalty can be inflicted;"[123] and "no θοά [fine] can be imposed on any Athenian."[124] The right to declare war is clearly political and will have belonged to the δῆμος πληθύων in the form of the Assembly from very early times on.[125] The remaining identifiable rights are, on the other hand, judicial. The significance of the role of the *dēmos* in inflicting a θοά escapes us, since we do not know the exact meaning of the term. It may refer to any fine in excess of five hundred drachmas, which is mentioned in lines 31–32 as the limit to which the Council was empowered to impose fines;[126] but since the verb θοᾶν appears in connection with religious offences in the Hecatompedon decree (*IG* I³ 4B7 and 12), it is also plausible, though perhaps less likely, that the noun here denotes a penalty imposed for religious infractions. Despite this uncertainty, there can be no doubt either in this case or in the case of the right to inflict the death penalty that the δῆμος πληθύων is not the Assembly but a popular law court of some kind. The cases in which the δῆμος πληθύων could

---

how and by whom such a mass meeting would have been organized in an orderly manner. Rhodes (*AB* 197–98 with 197 n. 8) opts for the simpler interpretation "the people in assembly" to differentiate the Assembly from the Council, but this fails to take account of the fact that the usual term for "Assembly," ἐκκλησία, appears at least twice in the preserved text of the inscription (lines 53 and 54), leaving unanswered the question what the difference between ἐκκλησία and δῆμος πληθύων might be.

122 *IG* I³ 105.34–35: [ἄν|ευ τὸ δέμο τὸ Ἀθεναίον πλεθ]ύο̄[ντ]ος μὲ ἔγαι πόλεμον ἄρασθαι [μέτε καταλ]ῦ[σ]α[ι].

123 Ibid. 36: [ἄνευ τὸ δέμο τὸ Ἀθεναίον πλε̄]θύοντος μὲ ἔναι θαν[ά]τοι [ζεμι]-ο̄[σαι].

124 Ibid. 40–41: [ἄνευ τὸ δ]έμο τὸ Ἀθενα[ί]ο[ν] πλε|[θύο]ντος μὲ ἔγαι θοὰν ἐπι-βαλε̄ν ['Αθε]ναίον μεδὲ [ʰενί].

125 Busolt-Swoboda 1017 with n. 2; Rhodes, *AB* 113–14 with 113 nn. 3–5 and 114 n. 1.

126 Cf. [Dem.] 47.43.

have made use of its power to inflict the death penalty cannot have been cases of homicide, which had always been dealt with by the Areopagus in its judicial function and by the so-called ephetic courts, whose verdicts were not subject to appeal.[127] They must, therefore, have been cases that before the enactment of the original version of this regulation used to be heard by another tribunal. In other words, the purpose—or at least the effect—of this legislation must have been to transfer the final jurisdiction in cases in which conviction would entail the death penalty from another tribunal to the δῆμος πληθύων.

Which was the other tribunal? It cannot have been any of the archons' courts, since these had ceased to exist by 410 B.C. and since there are no indications that an individual archon ever had the right to pronounce the death penalty. Nor is it likely that it was the Council, since the Council never had the power to inflict the death penalty in its own right.[128] After the reforms of Ephialtes, the Council was the forum before which *eisangeliai* were normally initiated;[129] if the penalty prescribed for the alleged crime fell within the competence of the Council to impose, the case was judged as well as heard before the Council;[130] if, however, it exceeded the Council's authority to impose, the case was referred to the Assembly, which would then either assume itself the task of conducting the trial or, more usually, refer it to a *dikastērion*, which was, anyway, from the mid-fifth century on, regarded as representing the people as a whole.[131] However, since the Council acquired the authority to

127   See D. M. MacDowell, *Athenian Homicide Law in the Age of the Orators* (Manchester, 1963) chaps. 4–9.

128   See Rhodes, *AB* 179–207 and *CAAP* 477–78, 489–90, 537–38.

129   Against Hansen's view (*Eisangelia* 21–28) that *eisangeliai* for major public offenses were initiated before the Assembly whereas *eisangeliai* against magistrates were initiated before the Council, Rhodes, "Εἰσαγγελία" 108–14, has shown that even accusations first made in the Assembly were referred to the Council for a decision about their disposition.

130   [Dem.] 47.42.

131   Most clearly stated in Ar. *Vesp.* 590–91 and Lys. 13.35. For possible trial before the ἐκκλησία, see Lys. 28.9; for trial before a δικαστήριον, [Dem.] 47.43 and the cases cited by Rhodes, *AB* 167–68 with 167 nn. 7–8 and 168 nn. 1–4. For the *dikastēria* representing the people as a whole, see Rhodes, *AB* 169 with n. 5 and 197–98, and the works cited by Hansen, "*Demos*" 127 n. 1. Though Hansen seems to me to be right in arguing against a "delegation" of power from the *ekklēsia* to the *dikastērion* (p. 144), his disjunction of δῆμος and δικαστήριον fails to carry conviction. It is true that δῆμος refers in the fourth century almost exclusively to the *ekklēsia* and in only three instances to the *dikastēria* (p. 131), but Hansen's argument is weakened or invalidated in that by his own showing (p. 130) δῆμος refers to the *ekklēsia* in only about half of the six hundred instances, and then only in phrases such as ἐν τῷ δήμῳ,

receive *eisangeliai* not earlier than the reforms of Ephialtes,[132] the only tribunal likely to have been deprived of the final jurisdiction in cases involving the death penalty in the presumptive original of the legislation of 410 B.C. is the Areopagus in those crimes against the state for which Solon had given it jurisdiction. Moreover, since dikastic panels had not yet been established in the early fifth century, the δῆμος πληθύων to which final jurisdiction was assigned cannot have been the *dikastēria*, with which we are familiar from about the mid-fifth century on, but must have been the *dēmos* meeting either in its political capacity as *ekklēsia* or, more probably, in the judicial function as *hēliaia*, which Solon had instituted. The fact that the expression δῆμος πληθύων does not differentiate between those two functions suggests that the political function of the *dēmos* had not yet clearly been separated from the judicial at the time the original legislation was enacted, and it explains why in the late fifth century and in the fourth either the *ekklēsia* or a *dikastērion* appears as the tribunal to which the final verdict in crimes against the state was reserved.

Our reconstruction must remain a hypothesis, because there is no incontrovertible evidence to inform us how the Areopagus lost its final jurisdiction in those crimes against the state for which the death penalty could be inflicted upon conviction. Yet without the hypothesis that the inscription of 410 B.C. included legislation enacted in the late sixth or early fifth century we cannot explain why only popular jurisdiction and no verdict of the Areopagus is mentioned in any of the six trials for crimes against the state between about 493/2 and 462 B.C. that we discussed above.[133] After all, in at least three of the trials, the second trial of Miltiades (3), the trial *in absentia* of Hipparchus (4), and the trial of Cimon (6), the death penalty was

---

in conjunction with expressions signifying an election or a vote, or to contrast the βουλή with the Assembly. Since δῆμος is a more comprehensive term than either ἐκκλησία or δικαστήριον, including, as Hansen points out, the Athenian democracy and the Athenian state (p. 130), as well as the common people as distinct from the upper and middle classes (pp. 139–41), this result is not surprising: βουλή, ἐκκλησία, and δικαστήρια are all organs of the Athenian δῆμος, so that one would expect δῆμος, when used in a loose political sense, to be applied only to the most representative of these three and less in connection with such smaller bodies as βουλή and δικαστήριον. In other words, the result that δῆμος is more frequently associated with the Assembly and only rarely with the law courts does not mean that δικαστήρια were not regarded as representative of the people as a whole.

132　Rhodes, *AB* 201–7.
133　See above, pp. 28–30.

either demanded by the prosecution or actually pronounced, so that by the time the earliest of these cases was heard, Miltiades' second trial in 489 B.C., the Areopagus no longer had exclusive jurisdiction in crimes against the state, though our literary sources would lead us to believe it still did. And further, the penalty of one thousand drachmas imposed on Phrynichus (1) four years earlier, the charge of tyranny against Miltiades at his first trial (2), and Themistocles' condemnation to permanent exile for treason (5) suggest that crimes against the state for which heavy penalties other than death were provided had also been transferred from the Areopagus to a popular tribunal for final adjudication.

This hypothesis does not imply the complete exclusion of the Areopagus from any or all of these trials. The clause in *IG* I³ 105.36, [ἄνευ τō δέμο τō Ἀθεναίον πλε]θύοντος μὲ ἔναι θαγ[ά]τοι [ζεμι]ō̄[σαι], whose restorations are made certain by its context, contains merely the negative injunction that the δῆμος πληθύων must have a voice before the death penalty can be inflicted. It does not exclude the possibility that, in a way analogous to the *eisangelia* procedure after the reforms of Ephialtes,[134] charges of crimes against the state were initially aired before the Areopagus, as Solon had stipulated; but that, if a hearing before the Areopagus established that they had substance, and if the penalty upon conviction would be death (or probably likewise other severe fines or penalties), the case had to be referred by mandatory *ephesis* to a popular tribunal for final trial and verdict.

Support for this view is found in that it resolves a discrepancy in our sources for the trial of Themistocles (5). The charge of medism against Themistocles, which will have been technically a charge of treason, and the procedure of *eisangelia* used against him, which before the reforms of Ephialtes could only be initiated before the Areopagus, justify the general opinion that the Areopagus was the tribunal that tried him.[135] Moreover, this assumption seems corroborated by a tradition that, however untrustworthy in its details, associates him with Ephialtes in the attack on the Areopagus in 462/1 B.C.,[136] for Ephialtes' attack may well have been motivated in part by Themistocles' condemnation before the Areopagus.[137] Still, a trial

---

134   See nn. 129–31 above.
135   Rhodes, *AB* 199–200, "Εἰσαγγελία" 105, and *CAAP* 320; R. W. Wallace, "Ephialtes and the Areopagus," *GRBS* 15 (1974) 259–69, esp. 262 with n. 14.
136   Arist. *Ath.Pol.* 25.3; Isoc. 7 hypoth.
137   See Rhodes, *CAAP* 317.

before the Areopagus is hard to reconcile with the fact that the source of our information on Leobotes' *eisangelia* is the collection of popular decrees by Craterus (*FGH* 342F11a), which suggests that the Assembly was somehow involved in Themistocles' trial.[138] How it came to be involved can only be speculated. A plausible explanation for Craterus's inclusion of Leobotes' *eisangelia* in his collection is either that Leobotes moved in the Assembly that an *eisangelia* be laid before the Areopagus or, more probably, that the final verdict was passed by a popular tribunal because the powers of the Areopagus had already been so modified as to make referral (*ephesis*) to the δῆμος πληθύων mandatory in all cases involving the death penalty.[139]

The possible involvement of the Areopagus in the trial of Cimon (6) will be more fruitfully dealt with in the context of our discussion of *euthynai*. However, it is relevant to our present purpose because it corroborates the view that already before the reforms of Ephialtes political trials in which the death penalty would be inflicted upon conviction (Plut. *Per.* 10.6) were conducted before a popular court (δικασταί, Plut. *Cim.* 14.4), at least in the final instance.[140]

If our reconstruction is correct, Ephialtes' reforms will not have been so radical as is often assumed in the matter of the handling of crimes against the state, because they involved no more than the transfer of jurisdiction in the first instance from the Areopagus to the Council of the Five Hundred.[141] The main step will have been taken by legislation enacted earlier in the fifth century that had curtailed the jurisdiction of the Areopagus in making referral of all trials for crimes against the state to a popular tribunal mandatory when death or another heavy penalty would follow conviction. It had done so by applying the Solonian principle of *ephesis* from the decision of an archon, an enactment listed by Aristotle (*Ath.Pol.* 9.1) as one of the most populist parts of his reforms, to trial by the people. If the cases of Phrynichus (1) and of Miltiades (2) were regarded as crimes against the state, in which the Areopagus had jurisdiction, and if they were

138 This has prompted Hansen, *Eisangelia* 70, to assume that the whole proceedings took place before the Assembly.

139 For a different interpretation, which involves the rejection of Arist. *Ath.Pol.* 8.4 and 25.3–4 and attributes to Cleisthenes the institution of *eisangeliai* to be "heard by the Assembly or by the court" (which court we are not told), see Hansen, *Eisangelia* 17–20.

140 So Hansen, *Eisangelia* 71. J. T. Roberts, *Accountability in Athenian Government* (Madison, Wis., 1982) 55 assumes a dikastery without argument.

141 Rhodes, *AB* 201–7, esp. 202–5 and *CAAP* 316–17.

tried before the people, as we are told they were, we must assume that by about 493/2 B.C. a popular tribunal had to render the verdict in capital cases or cases involving another severe penalty.

One point in this interpretation requires further clarification. The document to which we owe our knowledge of the principle ἄνευ τοῦ δήμου τοῦ Ἀθηναίων πληθύοντος (*IG* I³ 105) constitutes the republication about 410/09 B.C. of earlier regulations concerning the βουλή, the Council. At the time of this republication, the kind of cases we have been discussing were handled by *eisangelia* before the Council of the Five Hundred. Does this entitle us to assume that an original version of this legislation limited the powers not of the Council of the Five Hundred but of the Areopagus? The term βουλή had been applied to the Council of the Areopagus long before it was ever applied to the Council of the Five Hundred and was still applied to the former at a time when it was more naturally associated with the latter.[142] Since the Council of the Five Hundred never had normally, so far as is known, the right to impose the death penalty,[143] it is not merely possible but probable that the experiences of 411 B.C. had made the reaffirmation of the powers of the people *vis-à-vis* the βουλή desirable by the reenactment of a law that had originally been devised to curtail the powers of the βουλή of the Areopagus.

This explanation may also help us understand a rather peculiar story preserved by Aristotle, according to which original punitive powers of the βουλή were curtailed when an otherwise unknown Eumelides from Alopeke prevented the execution of Lysimachus on the ground that "without the verdict of the jury court no citizen should be condemned to death. In a trial held before a jury court, Lysimachus was acquitted and received the nickname 'he who escaped the bastinado'; but the people deprived the Council of the power to impose the death penalty, imprisonment, and fines and enacted a law that any convictions or fines imposed by the Council for an offense should be brought before a jury court by the thesmothetai and that the vote of the jurors should be authoritative."[144] The story has been dismissed as fiction on the ground that

---

142   E.g., Lys. 3.1, 4.1, 7.1; Arist. *Ath.Pol.* 25.1, 2, and 3 with Rhodes, *AB* 206–7 and *CAAP* 320.

143   Rhodes, *AB* 179–207.

144   Arist. *Ath.Pol.* 45.1: ἡ δὲ βουλὴ πρότερον μὲν ἦν κυρία καὶ χρήμασιν ζημιῶσαι καὶ δῆσαι καὶ ἀποκτεῖναι. καὶ Λυσίμαχον αὐτῆς ἀγαγούσης ὡς τὸν δήμιον, καθήμενον ἤδη μέλλοντα ἀποθνήσκειν, Εὐμηλίδης ὁ Ἀλωπεκῆθεν ἀφείλετο, οὐ φάσκων δεῖν ἄνευ

the Council of the Five Hundred never had the powers with which this story credits it.[145] Yet the mention of two proper names, one of them very rare, the identification of a person by his demotic, and the likelihood that the incident was remembered for the etiology of a nickname give pause.[146] Eumelides' demotic creates the presumption that the incident does not antedate the reforms of Cleisthenes; any other chronological indication is missing. There seems therefore to be no good reason to reject the story as unhistorical. On the contrary, it may well be that the Council to which the story refers was originally the Areopagus, from which the Five Hundred had inherited these restrictions, and that it preserves the memory of the circumstances in which limitations had been placed on the Areopagus's jurisdiction in certain crimes against the state early in the fifth century; if that is so, the referral to the thesmothetai and the *dikastērion* of which Aristotle speaks may originally have been *ephesis* to the *hēliaia* in cases in which the defendant had been convicted by the Areopagus.

In short, an early fifth-century version of *IG* I³ 105 may be interpreted as extending to serious offenses against the state the principle of *ephesis*, which Solon had introduced at least for complaints heard in the first instance before an archon. Furthermore, by making *ephesis* in these cases obligatory, it designated the people as the final judge in all cases seriously affecting the state. Thus, in the sense that it made convictions by the Areopagus of offenders against the state subject to a compulsory final review by the people as a whole, the document represents an application to the judicial aspects of public life of the *isonomia* that Cleisthenes had instituted in the legislative sphere. Just as political *isonomia* implied that no legislative measure could be valid without the approval of the Assembly, so a judicial *isonomia* was introduced, either by Cleisthenes himself or soon after his reforms, in crimes against the state, in which the

---

δικαστηρίου γνώσεως οὐδένα τῶν πολιτῶν ἀποθνῄσκειν· καὶ κρίσεως ἐν δικαστηρίῳ γενομένης, ὁ μὲν Λυσίμαχος ἀπέφυγεν, καὶ ἐπωνυμίαν ἔσχεν ὁ ἀπὸ τοῦ τυπάνου, ὁ δὲ δῆμος ἀφείλετο τῆς βουλῆς τὸ θανατοῦν καὶ δεῖν καὶ χρήμασι ζημιοῦν, καὶ νόμον ἔθετο, ἄν τινος ἀδικεῖν ἡ βουλὴ καταγνῷ ἢ ζημιώσῃ, τὰς καταγνώσεις καὶ τὰς ἐπιζημιώσεις εἰσάγειν τοὺς θεσμοθέτας εἰς τὸ δικαστήριον, καὶ ὅ τι ἂν οἱ δικασταὶ ψηφίσωνται, τοῦτο κύριον εἶναι.

145 Rhodes, *AB* 179–207 and *CAAP* 537–40.
146 Kirchner, *PA* 9484 531 lists forty-eight Lysimachoi, but only five men named Eumelides are listed (5828–32), of whom only the one in this story (5829) comes from Alopeke; no other record of him survives.

verdict of the people as a whole acted as a counterweight to what had
been the sole jurisdiction by a body composed of the rich and well
born. Ephialtes' achievement was to complete the process by giving
the people full sovereignty in handling crimes against the state.

Accountability

We have no explicit testimony about changes in the *euthyna*
procedure between the reforms of Solon and those of Ephialtes, nor
do we even know with what frequency or regularity *euthynai* were
conducted within this span.[147] Still, since the Areopagus was
entrusted with the audit of magistrates, it is likely that some aspects
of its function were modified with the passage of the original version
of *IG* I³ 105. For if the charges aired at a *euthyna* will have been found
to have substance, the subsequent proceedings will have differed so
little from those in crimes against the state as to be indistinguishable
from them. If, for example, the penalty to be imposed on an
offending magistrate upon conviction would be death or another
severe penalty or fine, the case would have to be referred for final
judgment to the δῆμος πληθύων, presumably the *hēliaia*; if it was less,
the Areopagus could pass judgment in its own right. Of the six cases
of crimes against the state held in the early fifth century before the
reforms of Ephialtes, the second trial of Miltiades (3), for "deception
of the Athenians" in the wake of the failure of his expedition against
Paros, may well have resulted from his *euthyna*, since we know that
he was general at the time (Hdt. 6.104.1).[148] Still, no *euthyna*
proceeding is mentioned in our ancient sources.

Such a proceeding is, however, mentioned in the case of Cimon
(6), which was heard almost immediately before the reforms of
Ephialtes. Aristotle's statement that the trial arose from Cimon's
euthynai as general and that Pericles acted as prosecutor (*Ath.Pol.*
27.1) has with good reason been interpreted as meaning that Cimon
was tried before the Areopagus.[149] However, the occasion of the trial,
which has to be supplied from Plutarch, points in a different direction: Cimon was charged after his campaign against Thasos (465/4–
463/2 B.C.) with having been bribed by Alexander of Macedon to
refrain from attacking his country (*Cim.* 14.3–5), and Pericles was

147 The most comprehensive recent discussion of accountability is that of
Roberts, *Accountability*.
148 See above, p. 29.
149 Wallace, "Ephialtes" 262; Rhodes, *AB* 201 and 204, *CAAP* 335–36.

"appointed by the people" to act as one of his accusers (*Per.* 10.6). The nature of Pericles' appointment, when added to Plutarch's statements that the death penalty would have been inflicted upon condemnation (θανατικὴ δίκη, *Per.* 10.6) and that Cimon made his defense before δικασταί (*Cim.* 14.4), points to a trial before a popular tribunal,[150] although it does not rule out a trial before the Areopagus. Still, it is reconcilable with Aristotle's assertion that the trial arose from Cimon's *euthynai*: these may have been conducted before the Areopagus but referred for final disposition to a popular tribunal, either the Assembly or the *hēliaia*, when it became evident that the death penalty would follow conviction.

This reconstruction of Cimon's trial is supported by the measures soon taken by Ephialtes against the Areopagus. Cimon's acquittal (Plut. *Cim.* 15.1) does not argue against a trial before a popular tribunal but rather attests his popularity, which is also shown by his reelection as general for 462/1 B.C. (Thuc. 1.102.1) as well as by his success in making his policy of assisting the Spartan siege of Ithome prevail against the opposition of Ephialtes.[151] But at the same time it is clear that these successes added fuel to the desire of Ephialtes and his associates to strip the Areopagus of what political power it still exercised through its role in trials for crimes against the state and in the conduct of *euthynai*, presumably because it had used these powers in the interest of good relations with Sparta, at least in the cases of Themistocles (5) and Cimon (6).[152] We learn from Aristotle (*Ath. Pol.* 25.2) that two steps were involved in the reforms of Ephialtes. First he brought suits against many of the Areopagites for maladministration; after that, in the archonship of Conon, he initiated the reforms proper. The first step will have consisted in Ephialtes' and his associates' availing themselves of the right, granted by Solon to every citizen,[153] of lodging complaints against the incoming members of the Areopagus at their *euthynai*, held before the Areopagus upon the expiration of their archonships.[154] If the prosecutions resulting from these complaints had not been successful, Aristotle is not likely to have mentioned them as a prelude to the reforms. Since

---

150 See n. 140 above.
151 Plut. *Cim.* 16.8–10; Ar. *Lys.* 1137–43.
152 R. Sealey, *Essays in Greek Politics* (New York, 1967) 52–54; Martin, "Kleisthenes" 37–38; Wallace, "Ephialtes" 263.
153 See above, p. 12 with n. 38.
154 Wade-Gery, *Essays* 177; Rhodes, *AB* 204 n. 2 and *CAAP* 313–14.

they must have been successful, it is likely that the Areopagus itself did not pass the final verdict, but rather left it to a popular tribunal, the only other gremium that we know to have had jurisdiction in crimes against the state. In other words, the charges brought by Ephialtes and his associates will have been such that they made a referral to the *dēmos* for final disposition mandatory, and in the absence of Cimon in the Peloponnese with an army of four thousand hoplites (Ar. *Lys*. 1143), and with the thetes, who usually manned the fleet, left at home, Ephialtes will have had an easier time in obtaining convictions than Pericles had in the case of Cimon.[155] Thus, the prosecution of the incoming members of the Areopagus may have been a natural sequel to the prosecution of Cimon, and it helps explain why Pericles' name is frequently associated with Ephialtes' in the attack on the Areopagus.[156]

Thus, in the conduct of *euthynai*, too, Ephialtes' reforms appear less radical than is often supposed. If our reconstruction is correct, Solon had already given the right to any person so desiring to lodge complaints against a retiring magistrate before the Areopagus, though the Areopagus was presumably free to accept or reject the complaint. Next, the legislation contained in the original version of *IG* I³ 105 had already deprived the Areopagus early in the fifth century of the right to pass the final verdict in cases in which a severe penalty would follow conviction and had entrusted a popular tribunal with it. Still, the initiation of the *euthyna* procedure remained in the hands of the Areopagus, which could thus control which magistrates would and which would not be subjected to it. Ephialtes merely took the final step of eliminating the Areopagus from whatever role it had played before 462/1 B.C. in the conduct of the accounting,[157] and he probably in addition instituted the requirement that *euthynai* be regularly conducted upon the expiration of the terms of all magistrates, regardless of whether a complaint had been lodged against them, a measure that cannot have been introduced later than Ephialtes. In doing so, whatever his motives may have been, he removed control over the magistrates from a once-powerful aristocratic body and handed it to agencies constituted by the people as a whole.

155 See Hignett, *HAC* 196.
156 Arist. *Pol*. 2.12, 1274ᵃ7–8; Plut. *Per*. 9.5, *Mor*. 812d (*Praec. rei publ. ger*. 15).
157 Hignett, *HAC* 203–5; Sealey, *Essays* 52–54; Rhodes, *AB* 201, 204, and 210; Martin, "Kleisthenes" 32.

Scrutiny

Despite its putative antiquity, the scrutiny (*dokimasia*) of elected officials before they assumed their duties[158] is so poorly attested that probability and inferences drawn from fourth-century practices are our only guide to trace the development of the institution. Whether all magistrates were subjected to a *dokimasia* in Solon's times we do not know, and there is no explicit information that Ephialtes brought it under popular control. In the fourth century all magistrates, major or minor, whether chosen by lot or elected by a show of hands, had to undergo a *dokimasia*,[159] evidently in order to ensure that those whom the chance of the lot had elevated to office or who had been elected by only a segment of the population, such as deme or tribe, could satisfy the people as a whole that they were legally qualified to serve. The remarkable fact that all *dokimasiai* took place before a jury court but that different procedures were reserved for the *dokimasiai* of councilors and archons[160] enables us to conjecture that the latter were of greater antiquity and that the *dokimasia* of all other officials was introduced only after popular sovereignty had already been well established.

It is probable that the new councilors had never been scrutinized by any body other than the Council;[161] but in the case of the nine archons, Aristotle distinguishes three stages of development. In the earliest of these a negative verdict of the Council was final,[162] whereas in the second and third stages referral to a *dikastērion* was

158 We shall omit from consideration here some other *dokimasiai* with which the Council was entrusted probably only after the reforms of Ephialtes. These include the scrutiny of its own successors, of some, if not all, financial officers, possibly of the ephebes, of the cavalry, and of invalids entitled to state support; see Rhodes, *AB* 171–78, and pp. 50–51 below.

159 Arist. *Ath.Pol.* 55.2: Aeschin. 3.15 and 29. Of officials other than councilors and archons, we know of the δοκιμασία of generals (Lys. 13.10, 15.2), of taxiarchs ([Dem.] 40.34), of πάρεδροι (Arist. *Ath.Pol.* 56.1), of the ἐμπορίου ἐπιμελητής (Deinarchus 2.10), of overseers of public works (Aeschin. 3.14–15), and of ἀθλοθέται (Arist. *Ath.Pol.* 60.1).

160 Arist. *Ath.Pol.* 45.3, 55.2.

161 This is the natural conclusion to be drawn from the clause νῦν δὲ τούτοις ἔφεσίς ἐστιν εἰς τὸ δικαστήριον at *Ath.Pol.* 45.3, where τούτοις, "for the latter," seems to refer only to the nine archons but not to the βουλευταί. For a different view, see Rhodes *AB* 178. The only preserved speeches given at the δοκιμασία of a councilor, Lys. 16 and 31, were delivered before the Council and throw no light on the problem of the possibility of appeal.

162 Arist. *Ath.Pol.* 45.3: καὶ πρότερον μὲν ἦν ἀποδοκιμάσαι κυρία, with 55.2 as cited in n. 163 below.

not only permitted but mandatory, regardless of whether the archon-elect had or had not passed his scrutiny before the Council.[163] The difference between the second and third stages consists merely in a different voting procedure in the jury court. In case no charges were brought against the archon-elect, it was the original practice to have the court proceed at once to the casting of an affirmative vote without a hearing,[164] and the vote was cast by one juror on behalf of all. But this apparently left the door open to questionable deals between unscrupulous archons-elect and their possible accusers, and a vote of the entire court was thenceforth required.[165] Other fourth-century authors confirm that a double *dokimasia*, one before the Council and a second before a jury court, was required of all archons-elect,[166] but for its beginnings and the dating of its three stages we depend entirely on more or less plausible inferences.

One inference may be drawn from the fact that, apart from the councilors themselves, the nine archons were the only magistrates to be scrutinized by the Council. Scrutiny of the incoming members of the Council by their predecessors alone is in no way remarkable and, in view of the large number of five hundred new members it involved, in itself saddled the Council with rather a time-consuming task. But that the archons were singled out in this way and that theirs was the only magistracy to be subjected to a double *dokimasia*

163   Ibid.: νῦν δὲ τούτοις ἔφεσίς ἐστιν εἰς τὸ δικαστήριον, and 55.2: οἱ δ' ἐννέα ἄ[ρ]χοντες <δοκιμάζονται> ἔν τε τῇ βουλῇ καὶ πάλιν ἐν δικαστηρίῳ. καὶ πρότερον μὲν οὐκ ἦρχεν ὄντ[ιν'] ἀποδοκιμάσειεν ἡ βουλή, νῦν δ' ἔφεσίς ἐστιν εἰς τὸ δικαστήριον, καὶ τοῦτο κύριόν ἐστι τῆς δοκιμασίας.

164   This, I take it, is the meaning of *Ath.Pol.* 55.4: εὐθὺς δίδωσι τὴν ψῆφον.

165   Arist. *Ath.Pol.* 55.4. The precise meaning of ἄν τις πονηρὸς ὢν ἀπαλλάξῃ τοὺς κατηγόρους is difficult to determine: did the archon-elect bribe his prospective accuser not to say anthing or to make the case against him as weak as possible, as J. E. Sandys, ed., *Aristotle's Constitution of Athens*[2] (London, 1912) 217 with 117, in his note *ad loc.* seems to suggest? Or did the fact that in a δοκιμασία of an archon the prosecutor and the defendant were permitted to speak only once (see Lys. 31.16) make it possible for the accused archon-elect to evade the issues raised by the prosecutor? The latter is suggested by Lys. 26.3: διὰ βραχέων ἀπολογήσεσθαι, ἐπισύροντα τὰ πράγματα καὶ διακλέπτοντα τῇ ἀπολογίᾳ τὴν κατηγορίαν.

166   Dem. 20.90 mentions only the thesmothetai, but, as *Ath.Pol.* 45.3 and 55.2 show, what is true of them applies in this case also to the three senior archons. For a double δοκιμασία of the eponymous archon, see Lys. 26.6 and 8. I am not convinced by the argument of M. Just, "Die ἀποδοκιμασία der athenischen βουλή und ihre Anfechtung," *Hist.* 19 (1970) 132–40, that a double δοκιμασία of archons was not mandatory and took place only on the initiative of an official who had been rejected at his δοκιμασία before the Council.

suggests that the institution of scrutinizing them dates back to a period in which they enjoyed greater executive powers than they possessed in the fourth century and for most of the fifth, when more substantial powers rested in the hands of the generals. This means that a *dokimasia* of the nine archons is likely to have been first instituted earlier than the battle of Salamis and certainly before the reforms of Ephialtes;[167] if our interpretation of the *Constitution of Athens* (8.2) is correct, it may have begun in the pre-Solonian state as a scrutiny before the Areopagus, which retained its prerogative until Ephialtes transferred it to the Council of the Five Hundred.[168] In that case, a definitive negative vote by the Council, which represents the first stage in the development outlined in the *Constitution of Athens* (55.2), will refer to the Council of the Areopagus at least until the time of Solon. If the appeals procedure introduced by Solon (Arist. *Ath.Pol.* 9.1) could be used against a negative *dokimasia* of any archon-elect before the Areopagus, we shall have to posit after Solon a period of meaningful but not mandatory *dokimasia* before the *hēliaia* to have preceded the period in which confirmation by the jury court was a mere formality.

When are we, then, to assume the introduction of a mandatory double *dokimasia*, in which the Council gave its preliminary approval by a show of hands and the jury court cast the decisive ballot?[169] Since we are told that the vote of the jury was at first a mere formality in which one juror cast the vote for all (presumably only if the vote in the Council had been affirmative and if no prosecutor had appeared in court), the second phase of the *dokimasia* of archons-elect may have been made mandatory when the *dokimasia* before the courts of all officials, whether elected by a show of hands or by the lot, was first introduced and assigned to the thesmothetai as officers

167 Badian, "Archons" 21–27, has shown that the reform of 487/6 B.C. did nothing formally to weaken the *powers* of the archonship; but, as Martin, "Kleisthenes" 26–28, correctly points out, the supreme command of the military, which at Marathon had still rested with the polemarch, was by the time of Salamis in the hands of the generals (a sign perhaps of the increasing powers of the generals at the expense of the archons), and there was no institutional change until the reforms of Ephialtes.

168 So Rhodes, *AB* 178 and 205.

169 Arist. *Ath.Pol.* 55.4: οὕτω δίδωσιν ἐν μὲν τῇ βουλῇ τὴν ἐπιχειροτονίαν, ἐν δὲ τῷ δικαστηρίῳ τὴν ψῆφον. Cf. 55.2, where the δικαστήριον is κύριον τῆς δοκιμασίας. The doubts raised about the existence of a purely formal vote have been adequately dealt with by Rhodes, *AB* 177–78.

presiding over the *dikastēria*.[170] This is not likely to have happened until the reforms of Ephialtes.[171] That it was invariably a formality is hard to believe; but it is credible that, in cases where no charges had been brought before either the Council or the court, the court was satisfied that the Council had adequately fulfilled its task and cast a unanimous approving vote without a further hearing. Only when that system was abused—and the possibility of its abuse is mentioned as late as 382 B.C.[172]—was a real hearing before the *dikastērion* made obligatory, and this may have been at any point in the fourth century.

The possibility that a mandatory double *dokimasia* of archons-elect, before Council and jury court, was introduced by Ephialtes when he transferred the *dokimasia* from the Areopagus to the Council of the Five Hundred and extended at the same time the requirement of a *dokimasia* before a *dikastērion* to all elected officials receives a small measure of support from the kind of questions asked of the archon-elect before the Council, questions that, it is believed, were identical (except for minor modifications) with those asked of all other magistrates-elect at their *dokimasiai* before the thesmothetai and their *dikastērion*.[173] Though questions about the identity of father and mother of the archon-elect, of his paternal and maternal grandfathers, and of his own deme and that of his maternal grandfather (Arist. *Ath.Pol.* 55.3; Dem. 57.67) would be germane to establishing his Athenian citizenship at any time after Cleisthenes, the questions about his possession of an Apollo Patrōios and a Zeus Herkeios and the location of their sanctuaries point to a time when membership in a phratry constituted the prime—if not the sole—evidence for citizenship.[174] This suggests an antiquity for the *dokimasia* that may well antedate Solon, and only the Areopagus can have been entrusted with the conduct of the scrutiny down to the time of Ephialtes. We can feel confident only that scrutiny of councilors and of archons existed before Ephialtes; the date on which all other magistrates, too, had to submit to a *dokimasia*

---

170   Arist. *Ath.Pol.* 55.2; cf. Aeschin. 3.15 and 29. For the role of the thesmothetai, see *Ath.Pol.* 59.4 and Lys. 15.2.

171   So Hignett, *HAC* 207–8. Just, "Die ἀποδοκιμασία" 133 opts for this change as simultaneous with the admission of the zeugitai to the archonship in 457/6 B.C.

172   Lys. 26.3; see above, n. 166.

173   The evidence consists merely of Deinarchus 2.17 and Xen. *Mem.* 2.2.13, as interpreted by Lipsius, *ARRV* 273 with n. 12, and Harrison, *LA* 2.203; cf. also MacDowell, *LCA* 168.

174   See M. P. Nilsson, *Geschichte der griechischen Religion* 1³ (Munich, 1967) 556–57.

depends largely on the date we assign to the development of the jury courts, before whom it was conducted in the late fifth century and in the fourth. We shall have to discuss that problem in connection with the origin of the Athenian jury system (below, pp. 66–77). But the different treatment of councilors points to an earlier origin of the archons' scrutiny. In the case of the councilors, Solon in establishing the Council of Four Hundred (the predecessor of the Council of the Five Hundred) may have given it the right of examining its own successors in order to give it from the beginning a measure of independence from the Areopagus.[175] In the case of the archons, Solon may have made appeal from an adverse decision by the Areopagus to the *hēliaia* possible in order to prevent arbitrary interference by Areopagites with election results, thus taking the first step toward relaxing the absolute hold they had over the magistrates. That the scrutiny of the archons was, in the wake of the reforms of Ephialtes, not transferred to the jury courts can be explained by the fact that each of these was presided over by an archon, so that it would have been deemed more desirable to entrust the Council with the first step in that task and to use the *dikastēria* only to confirm or reject the findings of the Council. The net result, however, remained the same. By transferring the scrutiny of elected officials from the Areopagus to the Council of the Five Hundred and the jury courts, Ephialtes removed one further institution from aristocratic control and made it a factor in establishing popular sovereignty in Athens.

EPHIALTES, DEMOCRACY, AND THE ESTABLISHMENT OF THE JURY COURTS (*DIKASTĒRIA*)

The question when magistrates other than archons and councilors were first made subject to a *dokimasia* is closely linked to the development of the system of *dikastēria* in Athens. For while we have good evidence from the end of the fifth century and thereafter that all other magistrates, too, whether elected by a show of hands or by lot, had to undergo a *dokimasia* before a jury court,[176] there are no

---

175 Cf. the image of the two anchors in Plut. *Sol.* 19.1–2. See also n. 49 above.
176 The earliest surviving reference is to the ἀποδοκιμασία of Theramenes as general for 405/4 B.C. in Lys. 13.10. For the general requirement of δοκιμασία, see Aeschin. 3.15 and 29.

indications other than the establishment of *dikastēria* that can help us date the beginning of the institution of a general *dokimasia*. As we hope to show, both the *dikastēria* as jury panels representing the *dēmos* as a whole and the *dokimasia* of all officials not scrutinized by the Council are likely to have been instituted by or as an immediate consequence of the reforms of Ephialtes.

The development of the Athenian jury system is important not only for our understanding of the origin of a general *dokimasia*. We noted at the opening of this chapter that Aristotle regarded the *dikastēria* as the main repository of popular power in Athens,[177] and an examination of their origin will inevitably be linked to their role in making Athens a democracy. The foundations were laid by Solon. Consistent with his aim of curbing the arrogance of the upper classes without letting the commons become too powerful,[178] his institution of *ephesis* to a popular court constituted the first significant step toward popular power: the verdicts of rich and powerful magistrates were made subject to review before the *hēliaia*, and any concerned citizen was given the right to assume responsibility for bringing offenders against the state to justice.

Moreover, we have seen reason to believe that the original version of *IG* I³ 105 extended the power of the people early in the fifth century by making *ephesis* to the *hēliaia* mandatory in cases in which capital punishment or other severe penalties would follow conviction, thus depriving the Areopagus of final jurisdiction in major crimes against the state and in offenses uncovered in the course of the *euthynai* of a retiring magistrate.[179] Since these foundations had already been laid before Ephialtes enacted his program, his reforms constitute only the final and not very radical step in the formation of the Athenian democracy. For the content of these reforms we depend on the interpretation of one crucial passage in the *Constitution of Athens*. After the successful indictments of members of the Areopagus, we learn ἔπειτα τῆς βουλῆς ἐπὶ Κόνωνος ἄρχοντος ἅπαντα περιεῖλε τὰ ἐπίθετα δι' ὧν ἦν ἡ τῆς πολιτείας φυλακή, καὶ τὰ μὲν τοῖς πεντακοσίοις, τὰ δὲ τῷ δήμῳ καὶ τοῖς δικαστηρίοις ἀπέδωκεν (Then, in the archonship of Conon, he deprived the Council [of the Areopagus] of all those accretions by virtue of which it exercised

177 See above, pp. 5–6.
178 Solon, frr. 4.7–22, 32–39; 5; 36.18–25 West.
179 See above, pp. 40–42.

guardianship over the state, and he gave some of these to the Five Hundred and others to the people and the law courts).[180] Aristotle's terseness has left it to modern scholars to discover the precise nature of "those accretions by virtue of which it exercised guardianship over the state," and to determine which of these powers were assigned to the Council and which to "the people and the law courts." Two observations help us in obtaining an answer to the latter question. In the first place, it is worth noting that πεντακοσίοις alone is used of the Council of the Five Hundred, evidently in order to avoid confusion with the Council of the Areopagus, to whom βουλή is reserved here. Secondly, the μέν is answered by only one δέ, namely, the δέ before τῷ δήμῳ. This raises the possibility (but no more) that Ephialtes' legislation spoke only of οἱ πεντακόσιοι and of the δῆμος as recipients of new powers and that Aristotle added an epexegetic καὶ τοῖς δικαστηρίοις as an explanation of τῷ δήμῳ, but this possibility is strengthened by the fact that we know of no political powers previously held by the Areopagus that now devolved on the *ekklēsia*. Moreover, if this interpretation is correct, it will corroborate the view that as late as the reforms of Ephialtes the political and judicial powers of the *dēmos* had not yet been clearly demarcated from one another by the terms ἐκκλησία and ἡλιαία, respectively,[181] so that Aristotle's use of τοῖς δικαστηρίοις here is as anachronistic as it is in his account of Solon's reforms (*Ath.Pol.* 9.1; *Pol.* 2.12, 1273^{b}41 and 1274^{a}3–4). For, as we shall show later, the *dikastēria* developed only as a result of the reforms of Ephialtes as panels replacing the jurisdiction of the *hēliaia* and of individual archons.

The transfer of judicial powers in political cases from an aristocratic body, the Areopagus, to the Council of the Five Hundred, in which every deme of Attica was represented, to the Assembly, of which every adult male citizen was a member, and eventually to the jury courts, on which every adult male was eligible to serve, did not, to be sure, place executive power into the hands of the *dēmos*. The highest offices in the state remained the preserve of the higher property classes, and even the opening of the archonship to the zeugitai as of 457/6 B.C. (Arist. *Ath.Pol.* 26.2), which was a further

180 Arist. *Ath.Pol.* 25.2. Cf. also Plut. *Cim.* 15.2: Ἐφιάλτου προεστῶτος ἀφείλοντο τῆς ἐξ Ἀρείου πάγου βουλῆς τὰς κρίσεις πλὴν ὀλίγων ἁπάσας, καὶ τῶν δικαστηρίων κυρίους ἑαυτοὺς ποιήσαντες εἰς ἄκρατον δημοκρατίαν ἐνέβαλον τὴν πόλιν.
181 See above, p. 35.

step toward a more complete democracy, meant only that this office no longer ranked as a major magistracy. Still, by transferring jurisdiction in political cases from the Areopagus to popular organs, Ephialtes gave the *dēmos* an effective control over the executive offices that is tantamount to guardianship over the state; by extending to judicial proceedings the *isonomia* that Cleisthenes had given the people in legislative matters, he created popular sovereignty, which was justly called *dēmokratia*. How effective and how pervasive popular control was will emerge from a consideration of how the powers of which the Areopagus was stripped were distributed among the three chief organs of the democracy.

The Judicial Powers of the Council

Dokimasiai.   The functions that the Council of the Five Hundred inherited from the Areopagus have been so fully and competently discussed by P. J. Rhodes[182] that little more than a recapitulation of his findings is needed here. Rhodes believes that before the reforms of Ephialtes the Council possessed only two judicial functions: disciplinary power over its own members and the conduct of the scrutiny (*dokimasia*) of its successors.[183] Of the powers taken away from the Areopagus, the Council received the right to hear *eisangeliai* on high crimes against the state,[184] the *dokimasia* of archons,[185] and "some judical powers in connection with public officials," of which the supervision of the ten *pōlētai* (commissioners of public contracts) is the only function attributable with some confidence to the reforms of 462/1 B.C.[186] We know of three other kinds of *dokimasia* in which the Council was involved in the early fourth century: a *nomos* entrusted it with the examination of the cavalry;[187] it conducted the *dokimasia* of the ephebes after their registration by the demes;[188] and it checked, in accordance with a

---

182   Rhodes, *AB* chap. 4, esp. pp. 162–207.
183   Ibid. 144–47, 176–78, 179, 195, 204–5.
184   Ibid. 162–71, 199–201, 210.
185   Ibid. 176–78, 195.
186   Ibid. 211, cf. 169 n. 6; for the πωληταί, see ibid. 96.
187   For the involvement of the Council, see Xen. *Hipparchicus* 1.8 and 13; *Oec.* 9.15; and Arist. *Ath.Pol.* 49.1; for the νόμος see [Lys.] 14.8 and 10, and Lys. 16.13; cf. also [Lys.] 15.7, with Rhodes, *AB* 174–75. I do not follow Rhodes in interpreting the ὑμῶν of [Lys.] 14.10 as evidence that the *dokimasia* took place before a *dikastērion*.
188   Arist. *Ath.Pol.* 42.1–2, with Rhodes, *AB* 171–74, and Harrison, *LA* 2.205–7.

statute, the eligibility for a state grant of invalids whose property
was worth less than three minas.[189] Although general considerations make it likely that the Council had these same responsibilities
already in the fifth century and perhaps even as early as the reforms
of Ephialtes, our evidence does not go back that far. A speech
composed by Lysias (21.1) about 403/2 B.C. is our earliest testimony
of the *dokimasia* of ephebes before the Council, and a reference in
Aristophanes, apparently to another stage in the same proceeding,
enables us to push its date back as far as 422 B.C.[190] Similarly we
cannot assume that the grants to invalids examined by the Council
in the fourth century have anything to do with the grants to
disabled veterans with which Plutarch's sources credit Solon or
Peisistratus;[191] still, they are likely to have originated not later than
the welfare legislation of the Periclean age.

Crimes against the state. Of greater importance than these *dokimasiai* was the transfer from Areopagus to Council of the right to
hear *eisangeliai* in the first instance, because it put the disposition of
crimes against the state entirely into the hands of popular organs.[192]
A statement in Isocrates (15.314) suggesting that one of the chief
characteristics of this procedure was that it was initiated before the
Council is borne out for the fifth century even by those few cases
in which the first step was taken in the Assembly. Since the term
εἰσαγγελία and its verb εἰσαγγέλλειν refer in themselves to nothing
but a report made or information given, it seems that in the fifth
century εἰσαγγελία was not yet so strictly differentiated from the
kinds of "report" or "information," such as μήνυσις or φάσις, as it
was in the fourth; we know in fact one case in which the same
denunciation, made by Agoratus before the Council for conspiracy
shortly before the Thirty were installed in power, is first described
by the verb ἀπογράφει, then by εἰσαγγεῖλαι; and when it is repeated
in the Assembly, it becomes a μήνυσις.[193] According to Harpocra-

189　Arist. *Ath.Pol.* 49.4; Lys. 24.7 and 26, with Rhodes, *AB* 175–76.
190　Ar. *Vesp.* 578 seems to deal with an appeal before a *dikastērion* against
exclusion by the Council, a step not mentioned in Arist. *Ath.Pol.* 42.2. The relation
to this procedure of the *dokimasia* of orphans, mentioned in [Xen.] *Ath.Pol.* 3.4,
remains obscure.
191　Plut. *Sol.* 31.3–4.
192　The most important recent discussions of *eisangelia* are Hansen, *Eisangelia*
and "Eisangelia: A Reply"; and Rhodes, "Εἰσαγγελία." To these, add Roberts,
Accountability 15–17 and 21–24.
193　Lys. 13.30–31, 50, and 32.

tion, an *eisangelia* in major public offenses could be initiated before either the Council or the δῆμος, that is, the Assembly,[194] and we learn from Aristotle (*Ath.Pol.* 43.4) that at the principal Assembly meetings in each prytany one of the items on the agenda was to give a hearing to any person who might wish to bring forward an *eisangelia*. But significantly the Aristotelian passage appears in a chapter that outlines the duties of the Council, so that this item seems to be no more than an invitation to any citizen to come forward with any serious complaint about any aspect of the management of public affairs: it does not rule out the possibility that the juridical initiative still rested with the Council. Moreover, the only fifth-century case in which the term εἰσαγγεῖλαι is used of information first disclosed before an Assembly meeting not only happened during the extraordinary hysteria that followed the desecration of the herms and the profanation of the Eleusinian Mysteries in 415 B.C., but it also resulted in a vote that conferred full powers (αὐτοκράτωρ) upon the Council to deal with the situation.[195] In short, there is nothing to contradict the belief that in the fifth century the right first to hear *eisangeliai* belonged to the Council alone.[196]

But since the Council's jurisdiction was limited already in the fifth century to cases in which the maximum fine would not exceed five hundred drachmas, its power to pass judgment was limited to these cases.[197] However, as most offenses against the state will have called for a more severe punishment, the Council could either reject the information[198] or refer the case for final disposition either to a jury court or, less frequently, to the Assembly.[199] The option between jury court and Assembly will have been open to the councilors only after the institution of jury courts; this suggests that Ephialtes' legislation stipulated merely referral to the *dēmos*, which in 462/1 B.C. would still be the undivided *hēliaia*.[200] The criteria for determining to

194   Harp. s.v. εἰσαγγελία. The εἰσαγγελίαι for maltreatment, lodged before the archon, and εἰσαγγελίαι against the διαιτηταί (public arbitrators) before a jury, also mentioned by Harp., are not relevant to our present context.

195   Andoc. 1.14 and 27, referring to 11 and 15.

196   See n. 129 above.

197   The most explicit evidence is from the fourth century, [Dem.] 47.43, but *IG* I³ 105.31–32 and 78(= ML, no. 73).58 show that this limitation was valid also in the fifth century.

198   Its authority to do so is implied in Lys. 30.22.

199   See Rhodes, *AB* 168–71; Harrison, *LA* 2.56–58.

200   Rhodes, *AB* 168. Cf. above, p. 49.

which of these two tribunals a given case was to be referred are still controversial, since the ancient evidence is far from clear.[201]

In fact, it is even hard to determine to what kind of cases the *eisangelia* procedure was applicable in the fifth century. Although a νόμος εἰσαγγελτικός quoted by Hypereides (4.7–8) enables us to identify some of the crimes against the state that could be dealt with by *eisangelia* in the fourth century, there is no doubt that the list was in fact longer as well as less specific not only for the fourth century but *a fortiori* also for the fifth, "allowing εἰσαγγελίαι for ἄγραφα δημόσια ἀδικήματα ["crimes against the state for which no written legislation exists"] as well as for specific acts of treason and corruption."[202]

The eight fifth-century cases for which an *eisangelia* procedure is explicitly attested[203] bear out—to the extent that details are intelligible—that a great variety of offenses against the state was actionable by *eisangelia*, that the Council dealt with the complaint in the first instance, and that most cases were referred for final judgment to a jury court. The charges range from impiety (*asebeia*) to embezzlement, treason, and conspiracy;[204] in six cases we have information that the charge was officially first laid before the Council;[205] in three of the five cases in which a tribunal is named it is the jury court, and in only one, which also happens to be the only case against an incumbent general, the Assembly;[206] and the penalties, where specified, are death and confiscation of property, and, in the only case where the Council gives the final judgment, five hundred drachmas.[207] To these cases we may add what we learn about *eisangelia* in a

201 Hansen, *Eisangelia* 21–28, goes beyond the ancient evidence in assuming that most cases were tried before the Assembly and in his discussion of specific cases (for the fifth century, see esp. his cases 1 and 4–10 on pp. 69–74) too often merely assumes trial before the Assembly. Against this, Rhodes, "Εἰσαγγελία," esp. 106–8, with Hansen, "Eisangelia: A Reply," esp. 93–95.

202 Rhodes, *AB* 163–64 with bibliography on p. 162 n. 1, to which add: Harrison, *LA* 2.50–59; Hansen, *Eisangelia* 12–20; and the discussions cited in n. 192 above. The expression ἄγραφα δημόσια ἀδικήματα is attested only by Poll. 8.51, but similar descriptions are given by *Lex.Seg.* 244.14; Harp., *Lex.Rhet.Cantab.*, and *Suda* s.v. εἰσαγγελία; and schol. Pl. *Resp.* 8.565c.

203 See Appendix A.

204 Impiety: Appendix A, cases 1, 4, 5, and 6; embezzlement: case 3; treason: case 7; and conspiracy: case 8.

205 We lack that information for case 1; in case 4 the charge was first aired in the Assembly, but was immediately investigated by the prytaneis.

206 *Dikastērion* in cases 1, 3, and 7; Assembly in case 6. In case 2 the Council has the final verdict, but the penalty is no larger than five hundred drachmas.

207 Cases 6, 7, and 2.

statement of Aristotle's that may have been as valid for the period 462/1 to 403/2 B.C. as it was thereafter: "Further, private individuals have the right to lodge an *eisangelia* against any magistrate they wish for failure to apply the laws. Here, too, there is referral to the jury court, if the Council finds them guilty."[208] The right to hear these *eisangeliai*, concerned with the misconduct of magistrates rather than with major crimes against the state, may also have been among those transferred by Ephialtes from the Areopagus to the Council. The possibility of lodging complaints of this kind before the Areopagus may, as we have seen, have been instituted as early as Solon.[209] In assigning their hearing to the Council, Ephialtes, consistent with the rest of his reforms, took a further step in placing the control over the magistrates into the hands of an agency of the people as a whole.

A number of other procedures in crimes against the state of which we hear in the fifth century after Ephialtes resemble *eisangelia* in their being first aired before the Council and then referred by it to a jury court. We shall have occasion later to examine some of these in detail. For the moment we shall confine ourselves to the observations that in five of the known cases μήνυσις (information) is used of the initial complaint, and in one case ἔνδειξις (writ of indictment);[210]

---

208   Arist. *Ath.Pol.* 45.2: ἔξεστι δὲ καὶ τοῖς ἰδιώταις εἰσαγγέλλειν ἣν ἂν βούλωνται τῶν ἀρχῶν μὴ χρῆσθαι τοῖς νόμοις· ἔφεσις δὲ καὶ τούτοις ἐστὶν εἰς τὸ δικαστήριον, ἐὰν αὐτῶν ἡ βουλὴ καταγνῷ. On the significance, see Rhodes, *CAAP* 541–42.

209   See above, pp. 12–14.

210   The five cases of μήνυσις suggest that the incriminating information was given in return for immunity, and only the contexts make it clear that it was given before the Council. The earliest is the μήνυσις given by Menon against Phidias for embezzlement; the trial took place before the *ekklēsiā* (Plut. *Per.* 31.2). Three μηνύσεις were given in 415 B.C. against those alleged to have profaned the Mysteries: Teucrus's and Lydus's information was given before the Council (Andoc. 1.15, 17, and 27) and so was presumably that of Andromachus, which was part of the *eisangelia* of Pythonicus (ibid. 14, referring to 11–12); all these cases would normally have been referred for trial to a jury court (ibid. 23). The μήνυσις given by Menestratus in exchange for a promise of immunity just before the Thirty came to power is itself described by the verb εἰσαγγεῖλαι, although it was merely an extension of the *eisangelia* lodged before the Council by Agoratus (Lys. 13.55–56), for which see Appendix A, case 8. The only known case of *endeixis* in the fifth century, but after the restoration of the democracy in 403/2 B.C., is that of Andocides for having participated in the celebration of the Eleusinian Mysteries despite his alleged ἀτιμία (loss of civic rights). It resembles an *eisangelia* in that the illegal attendance had to be reported by the archon basileus to the Council, which referred the matter for trial to a jury court (Andoc. 1.111, with MacDowell's note *ad loc.*).

and that in only two cases the final verdict was given by the *ekklēsia* rather than a jury court.[211]

Euthynai. In order to ascertain what sort of cases of crimes against the state were referred by the Council to the Assembly and which to a jury court, we first have to investigate what role the Council played in the fifth century in the conduct of *euthynai* of which Ephialtes deprived the Areopagus. Our information about the procedures involved in this institution in the fifth century is so poor that we have to work our way backward on the basis of what we learn from Aristotle's *Constitution of Athens* for the fourth century.

Three boards of ten members each were involved in the fourth century in the *euthynai* of outgoing magistrates: *logistai* examined their financial ledgers; *euthynoi* investigated their general conduct of office; and if criminal charges resulted from the *euthynai*, then *synēgoroi* were entrusted with the prosecution. To be precise, there may have been four boards, for we know that the *logistai* were divided into two panels of ten members each. One of these, chosen by lot from among the members of the Council, examined the officials' accounts once during every prytany (Arist. *Ath.Pol.* 48.3; cf. Poll. 8.99). These were probably not directly involved in *euthynai*, except that their findings will have been made available to the other board of ten *logistai* chosen by lot from among all Athenian citizens (as were also the ten *synēgoroi*, who assisted them in prosecutions) to examine the financial accounts of all retiring officials within thirty days after the expiration of their terms of office (Arist. *Ath.Pol.* 54.2; Harp. s.v. λογισταὶ καὶ λογιστήρια).[212] Even officials who had not handled any public funds had to submit to this procedure (Aeschin. 3.22). At the examination any citizen had the right to lodge a complaint against an outgoing magistrate (ibid. 23); but even if no complaint was filed and no wrongdoing discovered, the *logistai* and their *synēgoroi* had to submit all the accounts they had scrutinized to a jury of 501 members for final disposition. Here they could prefer

211 The case of Phidias (see preceding note) and the case against the *hellēnotamiai* for embezzlement (Antiphon 5.69–70), where (*pace* Lipsius, *ARRV* 182 n. 16) ὑπὸ τοῦ δήμου is to be taken with παραδεδομένος; see L. Gernet, ed. and tr., *Antiphon: Discours* (Paris, 1923) 128 with n. 2.

212 There is, to the best of my knowledge, no evidence either for the fourth century or for the fifth for an election of *logistai* by the Assembly, as is asserted by Martin, "Kleisthenes" 32.

charges for embezzlement, bribery, or malversation against an offending magistrate. Conviction on the first two of these carried the mandatory penalty of ten times the amount involved, but conviction of misdemeanor merely required restitution of the simple amount (Arist. *Ath.Pol.* 54.2; *Lex. Rhet. Cantab.* s.v. λογισταὶ καὶ συνήγοροι). The decision of the jury was final and not subject to appeal (Dem. 18.250).

The functions of the *euthynoi* were in the fourth century B.C. subsidiary to those of the *logistai*. Like the *logistai*, they constituted a board of ten, but in their case each tribe contributed one member. Their selection, as well as that of the two assessors (*paredroi*) assigned to each, was by lot, and the context in which the selection is mentioned makes it likely that they were chosen by and from the members of the Council.[213] Their functions began only after the retiring magistrate's *euthyna* had been passed upon by the jury court and apparently consisted in hearing complaints about aspects of his administration other than those involving financial matters. At the assemblies of their tribes[214] they sat for three days after disposal of the case by the jury court each alongside the statue of the Eponymous Hero of his own tribe to accept in writing any charges against the retiring magistrate. If upon preliminary investigation they found the charge justified, they referred private complaints to the deme judges assigned to the tribe, the so-called Forty (Arist. *Ath.Pol.* 53.1); public complaints they referred to the thesmothetai, who, if they accepted the case, referred it for adjudication to a jury court, where the judgment of the jurors was final.[215]

The sparse evidence we have of *logistai* and *euthynoi* in the fifth

---

213   Arist. *Ath.Pol.* 48.4, with Wilamowitz, *Aristoteles* 2.234–35 with n. 14. The arguments brought against Wilamowitz's interpretation by Lipsius, *ARRV* 101 n. 190, and by O. Schulthess, "Λογισταί," *RE* 13. Band (1926) 1012, carry no conviction; cf. Busolt-Swoboda 2.1078.

214   Arist. *Ath.Pol.* 48.4, as restored by Kenyon, reads ταῖς ἀ[γορ]αῖς, which Wilamowitz, *Aristoteles* 2. 234–35 with n. 15, interpreted as "in den stunden des marktverkehrs." The influence of this interpretation (see, e.g., Busolt-Swoboda 2. 1078 with n. 3, and Rhodes, *CAAP* 561–62) has not been diminished by the fact that this meaning of ἀγορά is not attested anywhere. In view of that, it is preferable to adopt the meaning for which parallels are cited by Sandys, *Aristotle's Constitution*², in his note *ad loc.* For gathering places of the tribes, see E. B. Harrison, "Hesperides and Heroes: A Note on the Three-Figure Reliefs," *Hesp.* 33 (1964) 81 with n. 20 and the evidence cited there.

215   Arist. *Ath.Pol.* 48.4–5. The most important modern discussions are those of Busolt-Swoboda 2.1078–79; Hignett, *HAC* 203–5; and Harrison, *LA* 2.210–11.

century is, nevertheless, strong enough to enable us to assert that the function of the former was subordinate to that of the latter; this suggests a thorough reorganization of the audit system, probably in connection with the revision of the laws completed in 403/2 B.C. Only one board of *logistai* is known for the fifth century, but it had thirty members, chosen by and from the councilors, and its duties were mainly to keep accounts of the allied tribute and of sacred monies.[216] The only testimony for a role for the *logistai* in fifth-century *euthynai* is to be found in a fragment from Eupolis's *Poleis* whose humor depends on the assumption of such a role.[217]

With that our evidence for *logistai* in the fifth century is exhausted. If we compare it with what we learn of *logistai* in the fourth century, the following differences are striking: we do not learn the length of the term of office for which the *logistai* were chosen in the fifth century, although the likelihood that they were members of the Council suggests a term of one year; we do not know whether they were chosen by lot or by a show of hands; we hear of only one board of thirty instead of two panels of ten each; no *synēgoroi* are mentioned in connection with them; and, most important, we are not told that they could bring action against offenders before a *dikastērion*. In other words, the fifth-century *logistai* seem to have been keepers of the financial accounts of the state and nothing else, who could not even initiate on their own authority steps to enforce judicial action against those whose wrongdoing they may have uncovered.

Although the *euthynoi* are poorly attested in our fifth-century sources, our knowledge of their functions has been considerably enhanced by the work of M. Piérart.[218] Apart from the mention of a

216   First attested in 454/3 B.C.; see *ATL* 2, lists 1.1–4, 2.1, and 3.1, ML, p. 84. We next hear of them in the first Callias decree of 434/3 B.C., where the fact that they are to be convened by the Council to conduct a check of sums owed to the Other Gods suggests that they were members of it; see ML, no. 58A7–9 and 27. Next there is a financial account for the years 426/5–423/2 B.C. drawn up by an unspecified number of *logistai*, in which also the accounts received from their predecessors are mentioned (ML, no. 72, esp. 1, 54, 98, 99, 102, 107, and 109); and an inscription from ca. 449–447 B.C. assigns to an unspecified number of *logistai* the task of calculating the expenditures of Eleusinian *epistatai* in various localities of Attica: *IG* I³ 32.22–28.

217   Eupolis, fr. 223: ἄνδρες λογισταὶ τῶν ὑπευθύνων χορῶν, which obviously refers to judges of dramatic contests. I am unable to derive any information from Ar. *Av.* 318–26: ἄνδρε λεπτὼ λογιστά.

218   Piérart, "Les εὔθυνοι."

deme *euthynos* in the Skambonidai decree,[219] which permits merely the inference that the office as such was known in Attica before 460 B.C., we hear of them twice, once in a decree passed after 434/3 B.C. concerning funds pertaining to the cult of the Anake (Dioscuri),[220] and once in the decree of Patrocleides of 405 B.C. (Andoc. 1.78). In neither case is there any mention of their number, but it is of interest that in both documents they appear together with an unspecified number of assessors (πάρεδροι) and that the Anake decree makes it clear that they had the power to convict. The presence of the power of enforcement suggests that the *euthynoi* played a more decisive part in fifth-century audits than did the *logistai*; this conclusion is corroborated, despite much confusion and unreliability of details, by the general picture drawn by the lexicographers.[221]

The most reliable piece of evidence for the fifth century remains the decree of Patrocleides, which mentions officials subject to a *euthyna* among those to whom amnesty was granted after the battle of Aegospotami. The relevant passage runs καὶ ὅσων εὔθυναί τινές εἰσι κατεγνωσμέναι ἐν τοῖς λογιστηρίοις ὑπὸ τῶν εὐθύνων καὶ τῶν παρέδρων, ἢ μήπω εἰσηγμέναι εἰς τὸ δικαστήριον γραφαί τινές εἰσι περὶ τῶν εὐθυνῶν.[222] In addition to finding here a confirmation that the fifth-century *euthynoi* had power to convict, which their successors in the fourth century did not possess, we also learn that they had a different meeting place. Their hearings were held not at the tribe assemblies near the Eponymous Hero of each tribe, but in the "accounting offices." As Piérart has pointed out, this suggests that the *euthynoi* held their sessions in the fifth century in the same place

219   *IG* I³ 244.B7-12 and 15-21.
220   *IG* I³ 133.18-19: [---τοῖν 'A]νάκοιν ἐ εὐθυνόσ[θον] μ[υρίαις δρα-χμαῖς ℎέκαστος˙ ℎοι δὲ ε|ὔθυνοι καὶ ℎο]ι πάρℎεδροι κατ[αγι]γνο[σκόντον. . . . That demes had only one εὔθυνος in the fourth century is known from Myrrhinous (*IG* II² 1183.16), Eleusis (*REG* 91 [1978] 289-306, esp. 290-91, line 41), Halai Aixonides (*IG* II² 1174.15-16), Thorikos (*SEG* 26.136.57-62), and an unknown deme (*IG* II² 1216). I owe this information to the kindness of Dr. David Whitehead.
221   See especially Harp. s.v. εὔθυνοι; *Lexeis Rhetoricae* Bekker, p. 257.15-16; *BCH* 1 (1877) 153; Phot. s.v. εὔθυνος; Poll. 8.45 and 100; and schol. Pl. *Leg.* 12.945b, as discussed by Piérart, "Les εὔθυνοι" 552-58.
222   Andoc. 1.78: "And all those who have been convicted in the accounting offices by the *euthynoi* and their assessors to pay a fine as a result of their accounting, or against whom writs concerning their accounting have not yet come before the jury court."

in which, presumably, the *logistai* kept their records.[223] Why the decree of Patrocleides speaks of more than one λογιστήριον remains obscure. It may be that different λογιστήρια existed, perhaps to keep the accounts for different officials or perhaps for different tribes, or that—as often in the case of δικαστήριον—the plural of the place may simply refer to different occasions when sessions of the *euthynoi* and their assessors had been held in a single λογιστήριον. In any event, these circumstances, the reduction of the number of *logistai* from one panel of thirty in the fifth century to two panels of ten each by the fourth and the absence of any evidence for juridical power of the *logistai* in the fifth century, clearly show that important changes took place in the conduct of *euthynai* in the fourth century. That the *logistēria* were the places in which the *euthynoi* conducted their hearings in the fifth century permits the further inference that they may have needed ready access to the financial accounts, already investigated by the *logistai*, in conducting their *euthynai*. If this is true, we may conclude that in the fifth century the *euthynoi* and their *paredroi* were alone responsible for the conduct of hearings in the accounting procedure and that financial matters, prepared for them by the *logistai*, as well as general administrative matters fell within their competence. A measure of corroboration may be found in a passage in Lysias's speech *Against Nicomachus* (30.5), which, if it reflects the conditions before the reorganization of the *euthynai*, as it seems to, permits the inference that accounts checked in every prytany played a part in a general—presumably annual—procedure of εὐθύνας διδόναι that was not confined to financial matters. A similar relation between the activity of the *logistai* and the *euthyna* in the strict sense of the word is also suggested by the stipulations concerning the treasurers of the Other Gods in the first Callias decree—they are to inscribe their records on a stele and give an accounting to the *logistai* (λόγον διδόντον...πρὸς τὸς λογιστάς) of the balance on hand, receipts, and expenditures *per annum* before being subjected to their *euthynai*[224]—and corroborated to some small extent by the Eupolis fragment.[225]

223 Piérart, "Les εὔθυνοι" 551 and 564, where it is shown that [Lys.] 20.10 also describes the λογιστήριον as a place in which accusations concerning nonfinancial matters received a hearing, possibly in connection with *euthynai* of public officials.
224 ML, no. 58A24–27, cf. n. 216 above.
225 See above, n. 217.

We further learn from the decree of Patrocleides that written indictments (γραφαί) concerning the accounting could come before a jury court, and the μήπω in the relevant phrase indicates that this happened—or could happen—subsequent to the decision by the *euthynoi* and their assessors. In the fourth century, as we have seen, the *logistai* are described as the only body who "examine the financial accounts of those subject to an accounting and introduce the auditing procedure before the jury court."[226] Since we have found no evidence that they had any jurisdiction in the fifth century, it is unlikely that they performed a similar function then. This raises the question whether the *euthynoi* may have been empowered in the fifth century to initiate γραφαὶ περὶ τῶν εὐθυνῶν before a jury court. They certainly lacked this power in the fourth century, when they could indeed be instrumental in bringing before a jury court for a second time an outgoing magistrate whose accounts had already been passed upon by a jury if complaints concerning his conduct of nonfinancial public aspects of his administration had been brought before them. But they could only bring the case to the attention of the thesmothetai, who in their turn could do no more than either reject the case or bring the charges before a new session of the jury court.[227] Complaints of a private nature were in the fourth century not referred by them to a jury court, either, but to the deme judges.[228] Although the deme judges were an old institution, originally established by Peisistratus and reconstituted in 453/2 B.C. with a fixed number of thirty, which was increased to forty after the fall of the Thirty Tyrants,[229] we hear of no role they ever played in any part of the conduct of *euthynai* in the fifth century. That private matters did come up in fifth-century *euthynai* is confirmed by Antiphon (6.43). It seems, then, that the procedural distinction between public and private complaints received by the *euthynoi* in the fourth century did not obtain in the fifth.

The probability that the fourth-century *euthynoi* were chosen by and from members of the Council[230] suggests that they constituted a commission of the Council even in the fifth century.[231] In that case,

226 Arist. *Ath.Pol.* 54.2: οὗτοι γάρ εἰσι μόνοι <οἱ> τοῖς ὑπευθύνοις λογιζόμενοι καὶ τὰς εὐθύνας εἰς τὸ δικαστήριον εἰσάγοντες.
227 Ibid. 48.5, where the phrase ἐὰν παραλάβωσιν should be noted.
228 Ibid.
229 Ibid. 16.5, 26.3, and 53.1.
230 See n. 213 above.
231 So Piérart, "Les εὔθυνοι" 570 with n. 197.

their jurisdiction will have been subject to the same limitations as that of the Council as a whole, that is, they will not have been able to inflict fines in excess of five hundred drachmas and they will not have been authorized to inflict the death penalty ἄνευ τοῦ δήμου τοῦ Ἀθηναίων πληθύοντος as represented, at least in the late fifth century, by the jury courts.[232] Therefore, the γραφαὶ περὶ τῶν εὐθυνῶν mentioned in the Patrocleides decree may well be indictments arising from verdicts given by the *euthynoi* that, because of the magnitude of the penalty involved, were referred by them for final disposition to a jury court.[233] If then the *euthynai* were in the late fifth century entrusted to a commission of the Council, constrained by law to refer serious offenses for trial before a jury court, it may well be that it was Ephialtes who assigned this task to the Council. Does that mean that Ephialtes is also to be credited with the first creation of a board of *euthynoi*? Hignett believes that the *euthynoi* existed already before Ephialtes and were originally chosen from and by the members of the Areopagus.[234] But since there is no reason to believe that *euthynai* were regularly conducted for every magistrate at the end of his term of office,[235] it seems more probable that their appointment as new officials should have accompanied the regularization of the institution and that, in other words, it is more consonant with our evidence to attribute to Ephialtes the creation of *euthynoi* as members of the Council of the Five Hundred entrusted with the conduct of annual *euthynai* of retiring magistrates. It will then also have been Ephialtes who made mandatory the referral of serious offenses uncovered by the *euthynoi* to the popular law court.

It is probable but not certain that *synēgoroi* were also involved in the fifth century in bringing to trial offenses that had come to light in *euthynai*. The ten *synēgoroi* appointed from among the councilors to join the generals in the prosecution of Antiphon and his associates before a *dikastērion* after the fall of the Four Hundred were presumably appointed just for this occasion and did not constitute a regular board.[236] A similar appointment may be referred to by Aristophanes'

232   See Rhodes, *AB* 169 with n. 4; cf. also n. 131 above.

233   See Piérart, "Les εὐθυνοι" 570–71; and L. Gernet, "Notes sur Andocide," *Rev. Phil.*, 3d ser., 5 (1931) 308–26, esp. 309–10, as cited by Piérart.

234   Hignett, *HAC* 205.

235   See Arist. *Ath.Pol.* 8.4 and *Pol.* 2.12, 1274ᵃ15–17, as discussed above, pp. 12–13 with nn. 33 and 34.

236   [Plut.] *X orat.* 833f. See MacDowell, *Wasps* 198–99, who recognizes four different boards of *synēgoroi*.

mention in the *Wasps* of a ξυνήγορος who presses charges of treason or conspiracy before a jury court.[237] But elsewhere in the *Wasps*, as well as in the *Knights* and in the *Acharnians*, the context suggests that *synēgoroi* were active in *euthyna* proceedings, in which they brought charges not only of a financial nature before a jury court, and one passage intimates that they drew a salary of one drachma for their service.[238] How and by whom they were appointed we do not learn; in the absence of any indication to the contrary, it is therefore safe to assume that their functions and appointment were identical in the fifth with what we know about them for the fourth century (Arist. *Ath.Pol.* 54.2).

In sum, the Council inherited from the Areopagus through the reforms of Ephialtes the *dokimasiai* of archons and perhaps also of the cavalry, of ephebes, and of invalids;[239] the right to hear in the first instance *eisangeliai* and similar charges of crimes against the state;[240] and the conduct of *euthynai* to the extent that the *euthynoi*—and also the *logistai* and possibly the *synēgoroi*—were recruited from among its members.[241] It is remarkable that we hear of no involvement of the Council or its representatives in the conduct of the *euthynai* of generals after the reforms of Ephialtes except when such *euthynai* uncovered major crimes actionable by *eisangelia*; and even here participation of the Council is not so well attested as we should have wished. This problem brings us to the powers of the Areopagus that Ephialtes transferred directly to the *dēmos* in its political or judicial capacity, that is, as *ekklēsia* or *dikastērion*, respectively.

The Judicial Powers of the Assembly

There are good reasons why the *euthynai* of generals should have been handled differently from those of all other magistrates. They were the only major officials whom the laws permitted to succeed themselves for an indefinite number of years. A general might be away in the field or on some mission abroad when the *euthynai* of other officials were being conducted, or the nature of his task may have made interrupting it by a *euthyna* before it was completed

---

237   Ar. *Vesp.* 482, with MacDowell's note *ad loc.*

238   Ar. *Vesp.* 687–95 (with the reference to their pay at 691); *Eq.* 1358–61, and *Ach.* 676–718, with MacDowell (see preceding note).

239   See above, pp. 50–51.

240   See above, pp. 51–55.

241   See above, pp. 55–62, esp. 57 with n. 216, 60 with nn. 230–31, and 61–62.

undesirable. Therefore, a more flexible attitude to the time of his *euthyna* was called for, and it may have been thought that the stakes involved were too high to leave the accounting to any agency other than the *dēmos* as a whole. Moreover, his tenure was subject to interruption or termination at any time if the Assembly, dissatisfied with his conduct, decided to recall him. The *euthyna* that followed would in the fourth century have been tantamount to a trial anyway, because it was presented by the thesmothetai directly to a jury court without first passing through the hands of the *euthynoi* and their assessors (*paredroi*, Arist. *Ath.Pol.* 61.2).[242] If a general decided not to stand as a candidate for reelection or if he failed to be reelected, the presumption is that he would undergo his *euthyna* at the same time as all other outgoing officials.

In the fourth century, it was established practice to have on the Assembly agenda once every prytany the question whether the generals "are to be considered to be conducting their office well, and if the vote is adverse on anyone, they judge him in a jury court; if he is convicted, they fix his penalty or fine; if he is acquitted, he resumes his office."[243] Although this *epicheirotonia* procedure is not attested for the fifth century, we hear of a number of cases of generals recalled by vote of the Assembly for various kinds of misconduct during their terms of office and relieved of their commands. If this procedure, called *apocheirotonia* in the fourth century, was actually used against Themistocles in 479/8 B.C. for having taken bribes from the Spartans,[244] and if Cimon's *euthyna* in 463/2 B.C. was preceded by his recall by the Assembly for having accepted bribes to refrain from invading Macedonia,[245] the Assembly will have enjoyed this right already before the reforms of Ephialtes. That it used this right liberally in the remainder of the fifth century is securely attested.[246]

---

242 However, it is *a priori* likely that at some point the *logistai* had to pass on his financial accounts (Arist. *Ath.Pol.* 54.2), probably handing on their findings to the thesmothetai to present to the jury.

243 Arist. *Ath.Pol.* 61.2: ἐπιχειροτοντία δ᾽ αὐτῶν ἐστι κατὰ τὴν πρυτανείαν ἑκάστην, εἰ δοκοῦσιν καλῶς ἄρχειν· κἄν τινα ἀποχειροτονήσωσιν, κρίνουσιν ἐν τῷ δικαστηρίῳ, κἂν μὲν ἁλῷ, τιμῶσιν ὅ τι χρὴ παθεῖν ἢ ἀποτεῖσαι, ἂν δ᾽ ἀποφύγῃ, πάλι[ν] ἄρχει. That the ἐπιχειροτονία came up for discussion at the κυρία ἐκκλησία of every prytany and involved all magistrates is stated ibid. 43.4.

244 Diod. 11.27.3. The truth of this is open to doubt; however, W. K. Pritchett, *The Greek State at War, Part 2* (Berkeley and Los Angeles, 1974) 127–28 tends to believe this account.

245 See above, pp. 40–41.

246 A recall and/or deposition is specifically attested for Pericles in 430/29 B.C.

An answer to the question whether Ephialtes introduced any changes in the *euthynai* of generals depends on our interpretation of Cimon's trial in 462 B.C., the only *euthyna* against a general explicitly attested for the time before Ephialtes. We noticed already that Pericles was "appointed by the people" to be Cimon's prosecutor, that the trial took place before a popular law court, and that the death penalty would follow his conviction; we saw reason to believe that the case had been heard in the first instance before the Areopagus.[247] This proceeding cannot have been one of the regular annual *euthynai* to which all magistrates had to submit, if for no other reason than that a mandatory annual *euthyna* does not seem to antedate Ephialtes' reforms and because regular annual *euthynai* do not seem to have been mandatory for generals either in the fifth century or in the fourth. Still, there are two features in Cimon's *euthyna* that were changed or at least modified after 462/1 B.C. First, the Areopagus played no part in the later accounting procedure at all, and second, trial before the *hēliaia*—if we are correct in believing this was the popular law court before which Cimon was tried—gave way to trial before either a *dikastērion* or, less frequently, before the Assembly.

For our information on procedure after Ephialtes we depend on reports of twelve trials of generals in the fifth century; we are either told or have reason to believe that they were held in connection with these generals' *euthynai*.[248] Only in five of these cases do we know the body before which the trial was conducted. The cases of Pericles,

---

(Plut. *Per.* 35.4); for Xenophon, Histiodorus, and Phanomachus in 430/29 B.C. (Thuc. 2.70.4); for Alcibiades in 415 B.C. (ibid. 6.61.4–5); for Phrynichus and Scironides in 412/11 B.C. (ibid. 8.54.3); for Alcibiades and his fellow generals after Notium in 407/6 B.C. (Xen. *Hell.* 1.5.16; Lys. 21.6–7); and for the Arginusae generals (Xen. *Hell.* 1.7.1). Phormio may have been recalled for his *euthyna* in 428 B.C., and Pythodorus, Sophocles, and Eurymedon after their failure to conquer Sicily in 425/4 B.C.; see F. Jacoby, *FGH* 3b Suppl. 2.120, cf. 1.135–36.

247   Plut. *Per.* 10.6, *Cim.* 14.4, and Arist. *Ath.Pol.* 27.1, as discussed above, pp. 40–41.

248   The twelve cases are, with the most important testimonia given in parentheses:

    1.   Pericles for failing to capture Epidaurus (Thuc. 2.65.3–4, cf. 59.3; Plut. *Per.* 32.4, 35.3–5);

    2.   Xenophon, Histiodorus, and Phanomachus for failure to consult the authorities at home about the treatment of Potidaea in 430/29 B.C. (Thuc. 2.70.4);

    3.   Phormio for his command at Naupactus in 428/7 B.C. (Androt. *FGH* 324F8);

Paches, and Anytus were tried by a *dikastērion*;[249] the cases of Alcibiades and of the Arginusae generals were tried—or meant to be tried—before the *ekklēsia*. In none of these cases do we hear of the involvement of *euthynoi* or *logistai* in the proceedings. If we add to this *argumentum e silentio* the positive facts that the case of Alcibiades was procedurally an *eisangelia* lodged before the Council before it reached the *ekklēsia*[250] and that the proceedings against the Arginusae generals closely resemble an *eisangelia*,[251] we may conclude that these were not part of an ordinary *euthyna* and that, accordingly, in the fifth century, too, the *euthynai* of generals were normally conducted before a *dikastērion*. Only if the *euthyna* of a general uncovered

---

4. Paches for his command at Mytilene in 427/6 B.C. (Plut. *Nic.* 6.1; *Arist.* 26.5);

5. Laches for his command in Sicily in 426/5 B.C.(?) (Ar. *Vesp.* 240–44 with schol.; cf. Thuc. 3.115.6 with 103.3);

6. Pythodorus, Sophocles, and Eurymedon for failing to subdue Sicily in 425/4 B.C. (Thuc. 4.65.3);

7. Thucydides for his command at Amphipolis in 424/3 B.C. (Thuc. 5.26.5);

8. Alcibiades for participation in the profanation of the Mysteries in 415 B.C. (Thuc. 6.61.4–5; Plut. *Alc.* 22.4–5);

9. Phrynichus and Scironides for failure to capture Iasus in 412/11 B.C. (Thuc. 8.54.3);

10. Anytus for failure to rescue Pylos in 409/8 B.C. (Diod. 13.64.6);

11. Alcibiades and his fellow generals after the defeat at Notium in 407/6 B.C. (Xen. *Hell.* 1.5.16; Lys. 21.7–8, 14.38); and

12. The eight generals who had failed to rescue the shipwrecked after the battle at Arginusae (Xen. *Hell.* 1.7.1–35).

Of the twelve cases, *euthynai* are explicitly mentioned in connection with only three: the trials of Phormio (case 3) and Paches (case 4 ; Plut. *Nic.* 6.1) and the flight of Alcibiades after Notium (case 11; Lys. 14.38). No trial is explicitly or implicitly attested for four cases: the generals at Potidaea (case 2), Thucydides (case 7), Phrynichus and Scironides (case 9), and Alcibiades and his colleagues after Notium (case 11). Despite these gaps in our evidence, the principle of accountability of all public officials makes it necessary to assume that in all twelve cases the generals were liable to an accounting for their official acts, even if the term εὔθυνα is not explicitly mentioned; were to be given an official hearing in which the charges against them were aired and they were to be given a chance to respond, whether they availed themselves of that chance or not, as, for example, Thucydides (case 7) and Alcibiades (case 11) cannot have done; and were either acquitted or condemned at a hearing before a δικαστήριον, or had their cases transferred to be heard by the Assembly as an εἰσαγγελία.

249 So also the case of Laches, if any historical inferences can be drawn from Ar. *Vesp.* 240–44, and from the dog trial, ibid. 836–1008; see below, pp. 212–13 with n. 59.

250 See below, Appendix A, case 6 with n. 5.

251 See Hansen, *Eisangelia* 84–86 (case 66). We shall deal with this case in greater detail below, pp. 434–41.

offenses serious enough to warrant an *eisangelia* was the final verdict left to the Assembly, as it was also in the first half of the fourth century.[252] Incidentally, we know of two other cases, both of embezzlement, in which the Assembly passed the final judgment in the fifth century, the trial of Phidias in 438/7 B.C. and a trial of the *hellēnotamiai*, possibly in 440/39 B.C.[253] Why these cases were entrusted to the jurisdiction of the Assembly we do not know.

We may conclude, then, that Ephialtes left untouched the right of the Assembly to recall and depose the generals and that, in removing the Areopagus from any role in their *euthyna*, he may have made a regular *euthyna* of generals upon the expiration of their terms of office a mandatory institution to be conducted before the *dēmos* in its judicial capacity (*dikastērion*) without the intervention of *euthynoi*. He may also have given the *dēmos* in its political capacity (*ekklēsia*) jurisdiction over generals whose *euthynai* made them liable to an *eisangelia* procedure. Apart from that, the Assembly gained few powers from the reforms of Ephialtes. Although we know of one fifth-century case in which an *eisangelia* was first aired in the Assembly, the Assembly could take no judicial action without the *probouleuma* of the Council.[254] It was given no jurisdiction in the first instance at all, and it could pass a verdict only in such political cases as came to it by *ephesis* from the Council, including, in addition to *eisangeliai* arising from the *euthynai* of generals, some charges of having embezzled state funds, Apart from that, the Assembly was entitled to hear information that had been given to the Council by generals or taxiarchs in *eisangelia* cases,[255] and it could grant immunity from prosecution.[256]

The Development and Function of the Jury Courts (Dikastēria)

Our discussion has already shown in passing that by far the most extensive share of the powers by which the Areopagus had exercised

252   Lipsius, *ARRV* 188–91. Note that in the case of Agoratus, too, information (μήνυσις) against the generals and taxiarchs was to be presented to the Assembly (Lys. 13.32); cf. below, Appendix A, case 8.

253   See nn. 210 and 211 above. The trial of the *hellēnotamiai* is dated by its relation to an erasure in list 15 of the tribute lists; see *ATL* 1.184 with S. Dow, "Studies in the Athenian Tribute Lists. I," *CP* 37 (1942) 376–78 and B. D. Meritt, "The Early Athenian Tribute Lists," *CP* 38 (1943) 226–27.

254   See above, p. 52 with nn. 195 and 196.

255   See above, n. 252.

256   See the μήνυσις cases in n. 210 above, where immunity is voted by the Assembly for Menon (Plut. *Per* 31.2–3), for Andromachus (Andoc. 1.11), and for Menestratus (Lys. 13.55).

its guardianship over the state fell to the jury courts.[257] This was partly due to the limitations that had been placed on the jurisdiction of the Council, which the Council in its turn may have inherited from the Areopagus: all cases in which the penalty upon conviction was death or would exceed five hundred drachmas had to be referred for adjudication to a jury court, and the same was true of all *eisangeliai* with the exception of the few heard by the Assembly.[258] The *dikastērion* played an important part in the *euthynai* of all officials; in the fifth century, any irregularities uncovered by the *euthynoi* were tried before a *dikastērion*, and in the fourth it not only received from the *logistai* the financial report at the *euthyna* of an outgoing official, taking action where called for, but it also heard any allegation of public misconduct that had been brought against the magistrate before the tribal *euthynoi*[259] Moreover, in both the fifth century and in the fourth the jury court was alone responsible for hearing the *euthynai* of generals.[260] Its role in *dokimasiai* is reasonably certain in one respect: from the mid-fifth century on, perhaps beginning with the reforms of Ephialtes, it had to conduct a second obligatory *dokimasia* of archons who had already been scrutinized by the Council.[261] Did it also conduct in the fifth century the *dokimasiai* of all other officials? The answer to this question is closely tied to the question of the origin of the Athenian jury system.

We noted earlier that from the time before Solon the administration of justice was vested at Athens in the Areopagus and in the personal jurisdiction of the archons and that Solon created a new juridical forum in the *hēliaia* when he instituted the possibility of *ephesis* to the people meeting in a judicial capacity.[262] Neither the archon's jurisdiction nor the role of the *hēliaia* remained unaffected when Ephialtes stripped the Areopagus of all judicial powers except for cases of homicide, of wounding or poisoning with intent to kill, of arson, and for some religious matters. How long archons enjoyed their power to try cases in their own right is uncertain, but it is generally believed that they had lost it by the mid-fifth century.[263] By the fourth century their judicial functions, as well as those of any

257 Ar. *Vesp.* 590–91 remarks on this: ἔτι δ' ἡ βουλὴ χὠ δῆμος ὅταν κρῖναι μέγα πρᾶγμ' ἀπορήσῃ / ἐψήφισται τοὺς ἀδικοῦντας τοῖσι δικασταῖς παραδοῦναι.
258 See above, pp. 52–54.
259 See above, pp. 54–56 and 60–61.
260 See above, pp. 63–66.
261 See above, pp. 43–47.
262 See above, pp. 6–7 and 9–12 with n. 29.
263 See MacDowell, *LCA* 33 with n. 26.

other magistrates, were confined to conducting a preliminary hearing (*anakrisis*) to establish, by interrogating plaintiff and defendant, whether the case had sufficient substance to be brought before a jury court. If a magistrate decided that there was no case, he could refuse to let the matter come before the court; if he admitted the case, he would bring it before a *dikastērion* and himself preside over the trial.[264] Questions of law as well as of fact were decided by the jury alone, and the presiding magistrate had no right whatever to interject himself into its deliberations or to influence its vote.[265]

It is evident that this decline in the jurisdiction of the archons and of the other magistrates went hand in hand with the division of the *hēliaia* into a number of *dikastēria*, panels consisting of varying numbers of jurors, each of which represented the full judicial power of the *dēmos* as a whole.[266] From at least the mid-fifth century on, these panels were drawn from a pool of 6,000 jurors appointed for one year each.[267] What determined the number of 6,000, which is, incidentally, identical with the quorum required for a valid ostracism, is not known.[268] We are equally ignorant of the method by which they were chosen from among all eligible citizens. But we do know that the lot was used to assign each dikast or heliast—the terms were used interchangeably[269]—to the court of the magistrate in which he was to serve for the year.[270] The size of any given panel varied with the importance of the issue involved in the case to be tried. Only one case is known, the trial of Speusippus παρανόμων in 415 B.C., in which the entire complement of 6,000 jurors is said to have constituted the tribunal (Andoc. 1.17). Apart from that, a jury might range in size from 201 for claims of less than 1,000 drachmas[271]

---

264   See Harrison, *LA* 2.94–105; Hignett, *HAC* 223; Lipsius, *ARRV* 829–44; Bonner-Smith 1.283–93; MacDowell, *LCA* 239–42.

265   See Lys. 15.3–4.

266   Rhodes, *AB* 168–69. For Hansen's arguments against this, see above, n. 29 (2).

267   Arist. *Ath.Pol.* 24.3, confirmed by Ar. *Vesp.* 661–62 of 422 B.C.

268   Philochorus *FGH* 328F30; Plut. *Arist.* 7.6. For an interesting but unconvincing suggestion, see R. Meiggs, "A Note on the Population of Attica," *CR*, n.s., 14 (1964) 2–3.

269   Dem. 24.148–51.

270   Ar. *Vesp.* 303–6 and 1107–9. On the dikastic system, see J. H. Kroll, *Athenian Bronze Allotment Plates* (Cambridge, Mass., 1972), esp. 55–56, 91–93, 94–98, 99–104.

271   Arist. *Ath.Pol.* 53.3. The same number of jurors is also attested for a general's court sitting to hear appeals against having to undertake a trierarchy; see *IG* II² 1629.208.

to 2,500 jurors in an *eisangelia* procedure against a certain Pistias in the last quarter of the fourth century.[272]

How can this development be explained? When and under what circumstances did the jurisdiction of the magistrates come to an end, to give way to the most far-reaching popular control of the administration of justice the world has ever know? Wade-Gery may be right in dating in the period 469–462 B.C. the last known case in which a magistrate gave judgment in his own name.[273] That the *dikastēria*, which replaced the magistrates' jurisdiction as courts at the first instance, are directly descended from the *hēliaia* is too well known to be argued here.[274] But how did the change take place? Some modern scholars believe that it developed gradually and that "the old concept of the heliaea as a judicial session of the ecclesia lingered for some time after it had become normal for the heliaea to be divided into δικαστήρια."[275] The assumption on which this view is predicated, namely, that jurisdiction in the first instance by a magistrate existed for some time side by side with jurisdiction in the first instance by a *dikastērion*, is difficult to accept, because it leaves unexplained by what criterion some cases were assigned for adjudication to a magistrate and others to jury courts. The system of dividing the *hēliaia* into a number of *dikastēria* panels, varying in size with the importance of a given case, is too sophisticated to be ascribed to mere chance.

Some scholars have attributed the division of the *hēliaia* into *dikastēria* to an increase of judicial business that the growth of the Athenian empire and of its prosperity brought in its train.[276] If this had been the chief reason, one wonders whether the problem could have been solved more efficiently by the creation of new officials to take over some of the caseload that burdened the archons, as indeed was done when the thirty deme judges were instituted—or, more probably, reinstituted—nine years after the reforms of Ephialtes.[277]

---

272 Deinarchus 1.52. We learn from a scholion on Dem. 24.9 that an odd member was always added to juries to avoid a tie vote. For the size of juries, see H. Hommel, *Heliaia*, Philologus Supplement 19, Heft 2, (Leipzig, 1927) 78–83; and Harrison, *LA* 2.47–48.

273 Wade-Gery, *Essays* 182–86. Wade-Gery's arguments are accepted by ML, p. 68.

274 Cf. Hignett, *HAC* 216; Rhodes *AB* 168–69.

275 Rhodes, *AB* 168, approving (as also on p. 204 with n. 1) views of Sealey, *Essays* 46–52.

276 Bonner-Smith 1.221–23; Hignett, *HAC* 216–18; Sealey, *Essays* 48.

277 Arist. *Ath.Pol.* 26.3, cf. 16.5. For the increase of their number to forty after 403/2 B.C., see ibid. 53.1, with pp. 56 and 60 with n. 228 above.

In view of the fact that fourth-century authors, foremost among them Aristotle, see in the political power of the *dikastēria* the backbone of the Athenian democracy,[278] and since the *dikastēria* are mentioned most prominently as the beneficiaries of the powers of which Ephialtes deprived the Areopagus,[279] it makes more sense to explain the development of *dikastēria* by looking to the *hēliaia* not as a court of appeal from the verdicts of an archon but as a court of the second and final instance in cases that had been heard by the Areopagus in the first instance.

We know of no events or circumstances in Athens before 462/1 B.C. that could explain the development of *dikastēria* during the early part of the fifth century,[280] yet if the system of dividing the *hēliaia* into *dikastēria* panels, momentous as its consequences were, had been the creation of an individual, we should have expected tradition to preserve his name. Ephialtes' legislation mentioned only the Five Hundred and the *dēmos* — whose political functions (*ekklēsia*) had not yet been clearly differentiated from its judicial powers (*hēliaia*) — as recipients of powers taken from the Areopagus.[281] If that is so, he will not yet have envisaged *dikastēria* in the form in which we know them from the mid-fifth century on, and his term for the *hēliaia*, to which all major *eisangeliai* were henceforth to be transferred in the second instance, will have been δῆμος, which had been used to describe that forum in the original version of *IG* I³ 105. It would explain why later in the fifth century some *eisangeliai*, among them those arising from the *euthynai* of generals, would be heard before the *ekklēsia* whereas all others were tried before a *dikastērion*. In short, Ephialtes may well have specified the *dēmos* as the recipient of all those former powers for the Areopagus that he had not assigned to the Council.

In the face of little explicit evidence, the only method of assessing the achievement of Ephialtes is to compare the powers of the Areopagus before 462/1 B.C. with those it possessed after that date, thus creating the presumption that Ephialtes was responsible for the transfer of the ancient Areopagite powers found thereafter vested in Council, Assembly, and the jury courts.[282] This method is reliable for

278   E.g., Arist. *Ath.Pol.* 9.1, 41.2; *Pol.* 2.12, 1273ᵇ41–1274ᵃ7.
279   In addition to Arist. *Ath.Pol.* 25.2, see especially Plut. *Cim.* 15.2, *Per* 9.5.
280   The arguments for 487/6 B.C. for the introduction of *dikastēria*, proposed by Bonner-Smith 1.221–24, have been convincingly rejected by Hignett, *HAC* 217.
281   See above, pp. 48–49; cf. also Rhodes, *AB* 168.
282   See, e.g., Rhodes, *AB*, esp. 201–7; Martin, "Kleisthenes" 29–33.

the part played after 462/1 B.C. by the Council in *eisangeliai*, in the *dokimasia* of archons-elect, in the supervision of financial officials, and in the *euthynai* of outgoing magistrates. It is less certain when we wish to ascertain what powers he transferred from the Areopagus to the *dēmos*. Its role in *eisangeliai* and in other cases in which the penalty was death or exceeded five hundred drachmas seems to have been established already before the reforms of Ephialtes by the original of *IG* I³ 105; cases tried by mandatory referral to the *hēliaia* before 462/1 B.C. can have been referred for a final judgment to Assembly or *dikastēria* only after the *dikastēria* panels were already fully developed. The decree of Cannonus, mentioned by Xenophon (*Hell.* 1.7.20 and 34) and by Aristophanes (*Eccl.* 1089–90), presupposes that certain offenses against the Athenian people were to be tried before the *dēmos*. What these were we do not know; we can only assume that such offenses as were tried before the Assembly in the late fifth century were originally tried before the Areopagus as guardian of the state, and the same is presumably true of charges against persons alleged to have embezzled Athenian state funds. In both cases, we can only assume that Ephialtes at least laid the foundations for a transfer of jurisdiction.

The transfer of the conduct of *euthynai* and *dokimasiai* from the Areopagus to Council, Assembly, and the jury courts gave the people the most powerful instruments of popular control over public officials. The *euthyna*, which, as we have reason to believe, the Areopagus had conducted irregularly whenever it thought that an offense had been committed by a magistrate, now became a compulsory annual examination of every magistrate. It was made more effective by the creation of a board of *euthynoi*, assisted by thirty *logistai*, both chosen from and by the Council, so that the investigative work could be divided and entrusted to smaller and less cumbersome bodies that had the power to convict. Only for serious offenses will referral to the *dēmos* have remained mandatory.[283]

As we have seen, the *euthynai* of generals formed an exception both in the fourth century and in the fifth in that they were conducted before a *dikastērion*.[284] For the time before Ephialtes, our only evidence is the case of Cimon, which was tried only months before the reforms of Ephialtes. We have argued above that it took place before the *hēliaia*;[285] this presupposes for the time before

283   See above, pp. 57–62.   284   See above, pp. 62–66.
285   See above, p. 64.

Ephialtes that the *euthyna* was heard in the first instance before the Areopagus, where the prosecutor's demand for the death penalty made referral to the *dēmos* mandatory. If this analysis is correct, we should infer that the *euthyna* of generals did not differ from that of all other elected officials in the time before Ephialtes. Possibly the superior executive power that generals derived from their eligibility for an indefinite number of continuous terms created the belief that any offense committed by them in their official capacity was *ipso facto* a high crime against the state. Possibly, too, the fact that they were liable to recall by a vote of the Assembly, presumably preceded by a *probouleuma* of the Council, may have made the exclusion of these two bodies from the *euthyna* a more equitable procedure. But in any event, the significant fact remains that in their case the people were given the right to exercise unmediated control over the most powerful magistrates in the state. Cimon's εὔθυνα (Arist. *Ath.Pol.* 27.1) differed procedurally in no way from what would after 462/1 B.C. have been an *eisangelia* brought against a general as a result of his *euthyna* and conducted before the *dēmos* meeting as the *ekklēsia*. Since the normal *euthyna* procedure of generals cannot have been initiated before the creation of the *dikastēria*, it is possible that before Ephialtes *euthynai* of generals, too, were conducted only sporadically, when there was a serious complaint against them concerning high crimes against the state committed in discharging the duties of their office.[286] If this is so, Ephialtes' innovation may have consisted merely in making the *euthyna* of generals a regular and mandatory proceeding to be conducted either upon their recall or upon the expiration of their last term of office. Moreover, if we are correct in believing that any offenses uncovered in the course of the accounting would automatically be regarded as a crime against the state, Ephialtes may have bypassed a hearing before the *euthynoi* and have made the *dēmos* the court of first instance, since referral to it would have been a foregone conclusion. An alternative—namely, that the thesmothetai, who in the fourth century introduced the *euthynai* of generals into the jury courts (Arist. *Ath.Pol.* 59.2), were entrusted with that function either alone or with reference to the *hēliaia* from

---

286   It is possible, but not provable, that Miltiades' trial for ἀπάτη τοῦ δήμου in 489 B.C. (for which see above, p. 29, case 3) may in fact have arisen from his *euthyna* before the Areopagus, referred to the *dēmos* because of the capital gravity of the offense involved.

the beginning of the *stratēgia* on—is less likely since we know of no case in Athens in which archons were ever charged with the conduct of *euthynai*.

It has been argued above that the *dokimasia* of archons is likely to be a pre-Solonian institution, which was transferred by Ephialtes from the Areopagus to the Council, and that their mandatory second *dokimasia* before a jury court was introduced simultaneously with the compulsory *dokimasia* of all officials before a *dikastērion*.[287] That this cannot have happened before the reforms of Ephialtes is clear enough,[288] but the question whether it was due to Ephialtes himself or developed in the wake of his reforms is hard to answer. One consideration favors the attribution to Ephialtes himself: if one of Ephialtes' motives in depriving the Areopagus of its political powers was to advance an expansionist policy against the pro-Spartan and pan-Hellenic policies that Cimon had been pursuing with the support of the Areopagus,[289] Ephialtes will have wished to make sure of the general political orientation of elected officials whose views might be influential, especially of generals, before they entered upon their terms of office. An inquiry into the political views of elected officials is attested at *dokimasiai* in the late fifth century.[290] Could the tradition go back to Ephialtes himself? If it does, the terms in which his legislation couched it will have required any official, whether chosen by the lot or by show of hands, henceforth to pass a *dokimasia* before the *dēmos* prior to entering office. Since a *dokimasia* existed already only in the case of the archons, a formulation such as that proposed would at once account for the second compulsory *dokimasia* the archons had to undergo as well as the *dokimasia* to which henceforth all officials were to be subjected.

Such a formulation would also explain something else that was to be of considerably greater moment in the development of the Athenian democracy. In the chapter preceding its sketch of the reforms of Ephialtes, the *Constitution of Athens* enumerates among the people to whom the growing Athenian empire gave employment approximately 1,400 magistrates, 700 for domestic and 700 for

---

287 See above, pp. 43–47.
288 Cf. Hignett, *HAC* 207–8.
289 See Martin, "Kleisthenes" 36–40.
290 See Lys. 26.10 (cf. 16.3), 31.9 and 17, 13.10. See also G. Adeleye, "The Purpose of the *Dokimasia*," *GRBS* 24 (1983) 295–306.

overseas service.[291] Although these numbers look large, especially for a time as early as 462/1 B.C., Meiggs, while reserving some skepticism, keeps an open mind about the possibility of 700 magistrates for foreign service for the late 450s and early 440s.[292] If little Thespiae was governed by at least 90 magistrates toward the end of the third century B.C.,[293] the figure of 700 internal officials is not too large for imperial Athens; it has been convincingly demonstrated as accurate.[294]

The Areopagus will have had little difficulty in administering the hearing of *eisangeliai* in the first instance, the *dokimasiai* of the nine archons, and the *euthynai* of public officials, especially if the last had not yet been introduced as a regular procedure. But the situation will have changed when such responsibilities and their expansions or derivatives came under the *dēmos*'s control. The *dēmos* was entrusted with the annual *dokimasia* of all magistrates (Arist. *Ath.Pol.* 55.2; Aeschin. 3.15) and with a second compulsory *dokimasia* of the archons (Arist. loc. cit.) and the *euthyna* was extended to all officials and regularized to take place every year. Further, the *dēmos* was charged with the conduct of the obligatory hearing of all cases in which an official had been accused of a serious offense, conviction for which would bring the death penalty or a fine in excess of five hundred drachmas—and there must have been many such cases (Ar. *Vesp.* 587; Aeschin. 3.17–22)—and the conduct of the *euthynai* of generals fell to the *dēmos*. The *dēmos*, whether in its capacity as *ekklēsia* or as *hēliaia*, could not have taken over these functions without paralyzing the machinery of government at least during the period between the election of the new and the completed accounting of the old magistrates. A new device had to be found to expedite matters, and since any body that was to conduct the *euthynai* in the second instance had to have judicial power to inflict punishment, the device was found by dividing the *hēliaia* into a number of panels that could conduct several hearings concurrently, each panel being regarded as representative of the *dēmos* as a whole.[295] There is no evidence that Ephialtes—or, for that matter, the Archestratus associ-

291   Arist. *Ath.Pol.* 24.3: ἀρχαὶ δ' ἔνδημοι μὲν εἰς ἑπτακοσίους ἄνδρας, ὑπερόριοι δ' εἰς ἑπτακοσίους.

292   Meiggs, *AE* 215.

293   P. Roesch, *Thespies et la confédération béotienne* (Paris, 1965) esp. 22–24.

294   M. H. Hansen, "Seven Hundred *Archai* in Classical Athens," *GRBS* 21 (1980) 151–73.

295   See Hignett, *HAC* 216; Rhodes, *AB* 169; cf. above, n. 29.

ated with him in Aristotle's *Constitution of Athens* (35.2)—was responsible for the creation of a pool of six thousand jurors each year or for dividing them into panels of different sizes. There is no explicit evidence, either, that *dikastēria* panels were established in order to cope with the onerous new tasks Ephialtes imposed upon the *dēmos*. But there can be no doubt that the assignment to the *dēmos* of all *dokimasiai* and of all hearings arising from major complaints registered by any interested citizen at the now regular *euthynai* will have necessitated the creation of an organ for handling the new duties efficiently. As far as we know, individual magistrates were never entrusted with the control over or discipline of other state officials at any time in classical Athenian history. A division of the *hēliaia* into a number of *dikastēria* can have provided the answer to the problem, and since we hear of no other institution that handled these new duties from at least the late fifth century on, the reforms of Ephialtes provide the right occasion to explain how their creation became necessary.

It remains to find some explanation for the transfer of the archons' personal jurisdiction to the *dikastēria*, for which the archons in the fourth century merely conducted the preliminary examination (*anakrisis*) and over whose sessions they presided. There is no evidence to confirm or to deny the view that the transfer "is likely to have been a natural and gradual change rather than an abrupt and legally enforced reform" that, once completed, may have been confirmed by a law.[296] That it had been completed by 425/4 B.C. is virtually certain, since the tribute reassessment enacted in that year on the motion of Thudippus, empowering the generals to bypass all courts and bring suits arising from the collection of tribute directly before the Council, preserves the words τ]ὸν ἄλλον δικαστερίον. For this makes the restoration of the only "other" kind of law court that we know from Athens, the ἡλιαία, almost inevitable.[297] In short, more than one *dikastērion* must have existed alongside the *hēliaia* by 425/4 B.C. Earlier in the same decree there is mention of [h]ο πολέμαρ[χος, [τ]ἐι ἐλιαίαι, and τὸ[ν ἐ]λιαστὸν; if the restorations most recently accepted can be credited, the reference is to a preliminary investigation (*anakrisis*) that the polemarch and an εἰσαγωγεύς cho-

---

296   Rhodes, *AB* 204 with n. 1, referring to Sealey, *Essays* 46–52.
297   *IG* I³ 71.48–50. The reading [. . .ἄνευ τἐς ἐλιαίας καὶ τ]ὸν ἄλλον δικαστερίον was first proposed by B. D. Meritt and A. B. West, *The Athenian Assessment of 425 B.C.* (Ann Arbor, Mich., 1934) 43–63, esp. 46, 49–50, and 62.

sen by lot were to conduct in the same building, called ἡλιαία, in which the cases that were to be judged by the heliasts received their preliminary hearing.[298] This would mean that at this time the term ἡλιαία could refer to a building, as it certainly could in the fourth century,[299] as well as to a court distinct from "other *dikastēria*" that, we may presume, normally held its sessions in that building. This, plus the fact that ἡλιασταί are mentioned in the inscription, makes it unlikely that the *hēliaia* of 425/4 B.C. was the same kind of court— that is, the *dēmos* in its judicial capacity—as it had been before the reforms of Ephialtes, but rather that it was a *dikastērion* to which the name of the old Solonian institution had somehow become attached. Moreover, the fact that the only magistrates ever mentioned in connection with the *hēliaia* are the thesmothetai suggests that it was their *dikastērion* that fell heir to the ancient name, and what little evidence we possess suggests that this development had been completed by 446/5 B.C.[300]

If this entitles us to assume that the *hēliaia* had ceased to be the only popular court by 446/5 B.C. and had become merely the popular court that was presided over by the thesmothetai, some interesting inferences can be drawn. The thesmothetai were in the fourth century the only archons who had any connection at all with the conduct of *dokimasiai* and *euthynai*;[301] they were at that time also the magistrates whose task it was to determine the days on which sessions of the various courts were to be held, to assign the courts to the magistrates who needed them, and to allot jury panels for public

---

298   *IG* I³ 71.13–14: ἐσαγογέον δὲ hο λα]χὸν κα[ὶ h]ο πολέμαρ[χος ἀνακρινάντον τὰς δίκας ἐν τ] | ἐι ἐλιαίαι [καθάπερ τὰς δίκας τὰς ἄλ]λας τὸ[ν ἐ]λιαστὸν.

299   [Dem.] 47.12: ἡ μὲν γὰρ δίαιτα ἐν τῇ ἡλιαίᾳ ἦν. The testimonia on the Heliaia as a place are most readily accessible in R. E. Wycherley, *The Athenian Agora*, vol. 3: *Literary and Epigraphical Testimonia* (Princeton, N.J., 1957) 145–46, and in H. A. Thompson and R. E. Wycherley, *The Athenian Agora*, vol. 14: *The Agora of Athens* (Princeton, N.J., 1972) 62–65. Cf. also R. E. Wycherley, *The Stones of Athens* (Princeton, N.J., 1978) 35, 53, 54, and 59; and Hansen, "Athenian *Heliaia*" 15–27.

300   The earliest reference to ἡ ἡλιαία ἡ τῶν θεσμοθετῶν is in the Chalcis decree of 446/5 B.C., see ML, no. 52.71–76. That it was a δικαστήριον is shown by Antiphon 6.21 (419 B.C.), by Andoc. 1.28, and perhaps also by Ar. *Vesp.* 772 with 775. The decree of Cleinias on tightening the collection of the tribute perhaps for the year preceding that of the Chalcis decree may also have contained a reference to the ἡλιαία; see ML, no. 46.37–39. I see no reason to regard this with Rhodes, *AB* 168–69, as "perhaps the last active occurrence of the old sense of the word"; it may just as well refer to the court of the thesmothetai.

301   For the δοκιμασία, see Arist. *Ath.Pol.* 59.4; for the εὔθυνα, ibid. 59.2 and 48.5.

as well as private cases to the magistrates (Arist. *Ath.Pol.* 59.1 and 5). This is admittedly tenuous evidence for drawing inferences for the fifth century. Yet the coincidence of these functions does not make the suggestion outrageous that the thesmothetai may have been entrusted soon after the reforms of Ephialtes both with the formation of panels from the old *hēliaia* for purposes of conducting *dokimasiai* and of judging complaints registered at *euthynai*, and with the presidency over each of these panels. In their capacity as presiding officers the conduct of a preliminary examination may have been required of them, from which it would have been only a small step to make the same kind of procedure the rule for all cases that fell into the province of the thesmothetai. If this conjecture is correct, it may account for the fact that only the *dikastērion* of the thesmothetai continued to be called ἠλιαία when the old Solonian *hēliaia* had long fallen into desuetude. And once the principle of an archon's introducing cases into a court (as εἰσαγωγεύς) and presiding over a jury panel rather than being officially endowed with jurisdiction in his own right was established, it may have been eagerly accepted not only by the three senior archons but also by all other magistrates empowered to conduct trials; moreover, it may have afforded some protection against excessive complaints at the archons' own *euthynai* on the part of litigants who would have felt unfairly treated by an adverse judgment. For by passing the responsibility for a final verdict to a jury, the presiding magistrate will have been relieved of any onus that at an earlier period might have fallen upon him. The *dikastērion* as the representative voice of the *dēmos* as a whole now passed the final verdict in all cases public and private.

THE POLITICAL SOVEREIGNTY OF THE PEOPLE

The organs through which the Athenian democracy expressed itself are considerably older than the democracy itself. A popular Assembly in which all adult male citizens had the right to participate predates the reforms of Solon; a Council entrusted with preparing through its deliberations what business was to come before the Assembly is the creation of Solon; and Solon, too, constituted of all adult male citizens the *hēliaia* as a court of last resort, empowered to hear appeals from decisions handed down by the archons and, in political cases, by the Areopagus. Cleisthenes' *isonomia* gave Council and Assembly the exclusive right to legislate, and, by structuring the state on regional rather than on kinship principles, he shifted the basis of membership in the Council from kinship tribe to local deme, ensuring the proportional representation of every locality in Attica in this important body. The political power of the *hēliaia* was enhanced shortly after the Cleisthenic reforms when this court was given a role in the jurisdiction over crimes against the state.

But only after Ephialtes removed from the Areopagus those powers that had given it guardianship over the state and distributed them among Council, Assembly, and the popular law court in a way that necessitated the establishment of *dikastēria* can we fairly call Athens a democracy. Although the upper classes still retained a virtual monopoly of the generalship, all magistrates were henceforth answerable for their conduct in office not to a small group drawn from the upper classes but to those to whom they owed their election to office and those ultimately most affected by their official acts, the people as a whole. Because the *euthyna* was henceforth regular and not selective, no magistrate was exempt, and control by the people was established over all. That this could lead to excesses, injustice, and plain inefficiency is evident especially from the ease with which generals could be recalled and subjected to a *euthyna*, and the price paid is dramatized in Thucydides' description of Nicias's indecision, bred by fear of a *euthyna* during the Sicilian expedition. Institutionally, it can be seen in the leave granted every citizen to air even the smallest grievance against official misconduct at the magistrates' *euthyna*.

And yet Ephialtes or those who followed him built sufficient safeguards into the system to prevent it from getting out of hand. Although the Council as a whole may have been charged with the conduct of the accounting, it seems in fact to have delegated this task to a board of thirty financial accountants (*logistai*) who in the fifth century merely kept accounts and had no power to initiate judicial proceedings, and to a board of an undetermined number of general accounting officers (*euthynoi*) who did have the power to convict minor offenders but had to refer the cases of major offenders to a jury court. In other words, the popular control exercised by the Council was checked in that two specialized agencies were entrusted with the preliminary work, one with no judicial powers, the other with judicial authority only in cases of minor infractions. The smallness of both groups will have prevented emotionalism and gross inequity from taking over, and the final adjudication of serious offenses by a jury will have created a sufficiently long cooling-off period to make a fair hearing more likely. In short, every precaution was taken to observe due process and at the same time to ensure popular control over the accounting procedure.

Only in the *euthynai* of the most important executives of the government of fifth-century Athens, the generals, did the people assert their sovereignty directly, without the intervention of the Council and its *euthynoi*. A general was eligible to serve an indeterminate number of annual terms, and though we lack explicit evidence to prove it, in his case an annual *euthyna* was probably not mandatory. Since he might be serving in the field abroad or might be involved in sensitive diplomatic negotiations at the time of the annual *euthyna*, he had to render an account of his conduct of office only after a recall or failure to be reelected terminated his service. As he had been elected by the people as a whole and, in several cases, recalled by the Assembly, the *dēmos* reserved unto itself the right to hear his accounting. If the Council played any role in his *euthyna* at all—and there is no evidence that it did—its function will have been only probouleutic since it automatically referred the case to a jury court, and if any serious offense was uncovered, to the Assembly as a whole by a procedure that either was or closely resembled *eisangelia*. This, too, was due process, but its very openness left room for the emotionalism so often encountered in proceedings before the Athenian courts and in Athenian Assembly meetings, and in tense situations it invited the kind of abuse to which the generals of Arginusae were subjected.

A remarkable feature of political *dokimasiai* at Athens is that the competence of an official for the position to which he had been elected never became a subject of scrutiny. The questions to which he had to respond were designed to establish merely that he was an Athenian citizen, that he had discharged his private and his religious duties, and that he had met his financial and military obligations to the state.[302] In both the aristocratic and in the democratic state it was taken for granted that any citizen who had the proper legal creden-

---

302　See Arist. *Ath.Pol.* 55.3 and Dem. 57.67 as cited above, p. 46. Since maltreatment of parents, failure to perform military service, and nonpayment of public debts resulted in automatic ἀτιμία in the sense that the offender forfeited his right to address the Assembly (Aeschin. 1.28–29, with Harrison, *LA* 2.171–72 and 172–76), a reason for asking these questions may have been to ensure that the elected official had not lost his civil rights.

tials to be eligible could serve in the post to which he had been elected, regardless of whether his appointment had been by direct election or by the lot. However, it will have made a difference that after 462/1 B.C. *dokimasiai* were no longer conducted before the Areopagus but before the jury court, even of those magistrates, the archons-elect, who had already been scrutinized by the Council. The qualifications to serve were tested not before an aristocratic body but before a jury representing the people as a whole in a procedure from which no magistrate was exempt and in which any citizen, regardless of social or economic standing, had the right to step forward and bring charges against the elected official. We are told that no holds were barred in the questioning and that the aspirant might be called upon to justify any aspect of his life (Lys. 16.9; Dem. 21.111).

The jury courts gained more significant power from the reforms of Ephialtes than any other agency of government. Indeed, if our argument is correct, they owed their origin as panels of the *hēliaia* to Ephialtes' reorganization of *euthynai* and *dokimasiai*. Any serious problem arising in these procedures was left to the *dikastēria* for final settlement; all crimes against the state, with a few exceptions that were assigned to the Assembly, were left for final trial to the juries; and after the disappearance of the archons' jurisdiction, even all private cases, except those traditionally left to the Areopagus, were tried before the *dikastēria*. Surely, there is substance to the assertion of Solon's critics, quoted at the beginning of this chapter, that the *dikastērion*, "whose members are chosen by lot, is sovereign in all matters" (Arist. *Pol.* 2.12, 1274^{a}3–5).

There is an additional factor to account for the power and democratic character of the jury courts. The Athenian system made no provision for a public prosecutor, so that the initiative in prosecuting crimes against the state rested with individuals whose duty it was to investigate certain matters, as, for example, the *logistai* or *euthynoi*, or, more usually, with private individuals, who could, but need not, be aggrieved parties. Aristotle rightly singled out as one of the most democratic features of Solon's reforms the right given to any person who so desired to initiate proceedings against a wrongdoer (*Ath.Pol.* 9.1; Plut. *Sol.* 18.6), for in many cases this must have been the only resort a lowly victim of injustice could have had against a powerful offender. This right will have been especially valuable when the offending party was a public official. Before Solon only the victim himself seems to have been able to lodge a complaint before the Areopagus against unjust treatment sustained at the hands of a magistrate; in the fourth century any person could complain before the Council.[303] We know that any person, whether an interested party or not, could take such initiative in private suits in which the court of the eponymous archon had jurisdiction (Arist. *Ath.Pol.* 56.6); but as is to be expected, the prosecution of offenses against the state depended to a very large extent on the initiative of private individuals, and Aristotle makes a special point of this dependence in the *dokimasiai* and *euthynai* of magistrates (ibid. 48.4 and 55.4). Unquestionably, the possibility that anyone might bring a charge or appear as a witness at a *dokimasia* or *euthyna* hearing was a potent check against misuses of power on the part of public officials, and it was expected of a good citizen "to come to the defense of the city and its laws" (Aeschin. 1.2).

But of course the system was also open to great dangers. Not all accusations would be motivated by genuine moral indignation at wrongs committed against the state or by high patriotic sentiments. Many Athenians will have availed themselves of these opportunities to settle personal scores and to intimidate or even penalize a political opponent. And above all, the institution gave rise to the development of sycophants (συκοφάνται), that class of blackmailers and informers who specialized in prosecutions of cases in which an adverse decision of the jury would award a substantial part of the fine to the successful prosecutor. Both Aristophanes and the orators give us a vivid picture of how the sycophants flourished in the last quarter of the fifth century and throughout the fourth, despite the fact that by the late fifth century legislation had been enacted that imposed severe penalties on unsuccessful arbitrary prosecutions.[304] No doubt the sycophants were as odious to the Athenians as informers in any shape or form have been to any society in which they have appeared in the course of human history. How common the phenomenon

---

303 Contrast Arist. *Ath.Pol.* 4.4, ἐξῆν δὲ τῷ ἀδικουμένῳ πρὸ[ς τὴν τῶν] Ἀρεοπαγιτῶν βουλὴν εἰσαγγέλλειν, ἀποφαίνοντι παρ' ὃν ἀδικεῖται νόμον, with ibid. 45.2: ἔξεστι δὲ καὶ τοῖς ἰδιώταις εἰσαγγέλλειν ἣν ἂν βούλωνται τῶν ἀρχῶν μὴ χρῆσθαι τοῖς νόμοις.

304 See in general Bonner-Smith 2.39–74 and MacDowell, *LCA* 62–66; for the γραφὴ συκοφαντίας, see Lipsius, *ARRV* 448–51, esp. 449 n. 110. Doubts about its existence have been voiced by L. W. A. Crawley, "Γραφὴ συκοφαντίας," in B. F. Harris, ed., *Auckland Classical Essays Presented to E. M. Blailock* (Auckland and Oxford, 1970) 77–94.

actually was and how many of those whom the ancients reproached for their selfishness, greed, and slyness may in fact have been disinterested patriots we shall never know. There is no doubt that they brought a bad reputation to the justice administered in the jury courts as well as to the democracy as such. But we shall see later that some of the reasons for the allegations against them may not have been so high-minded as one might think.

The Athenian democracy is sometimes described as a form of government in which every citizen could rule and be ruled in turn and in which tenure of office was largely determined by the lot. But this is at best a half-truth, since only those magistrates were chosen by lot who had routine duties to perform; the important offices that required special political and diplomatic skills were filled by direct election, usually of members of rich and well-born families who had for generations given service to the state. As the "Old Oligarch" puts it: "To those offices that, if well managed, bring security to the whole people, and, if not well managed, danger, the common people do not demand to be eligible; they do not think that there is any need for them to have the lot make them eligible either to the general-ships or to the cavalry commands. For the common people realize that they stand to gain more by not holding these offices themselves and by letting the most competent men occupy them. But any office that brings pay or profit into the home, that the common people seek to hold" ([Xen.] *Ath.Pol.* 1.3). These words were of course written by an opponent of the Athenian democracy, who nevertheless admired its efficiency and consistency. There is no question that birth and wealth helped secure access to the important military, diplo-matic, and financial offices; in fact, only the wealthy and the well-born were normally elected to the major magistracies.[305] Yet anyone, regardless of provenance, experience, or wealth, could challenge these officials at their *dokimasiai* and at their *euthynai*, and the complaints against them would be heard and adjudicated by jurors chosen by lot from a pool of six thousand, also chosen by lot;[306] all citizens were eligible to serve as jurors and, if the impression conveyed by Aristophanes' *Wasps* can be credited, fifth-century juries consisted chiefly of old men from the lower classes to whom the

---

305 See Jones, *AD* 55, with the evidence cited in nn. 68 and 69.
306 Ar. *Vesp.* 661–62; Arist. *Ath.Pol.* 24.3 and 27.4.

prospect of earning some extra money by listening to juicy gossip proved irresistible.[307]

That these people should have been able to determine by their votes the fate of seasoned experts who, in most cases, will have served their city to the best of their abilities was indeed democratic; but it also opened the way for that criticism of the democracy with which we are most familiar from Plato, namely, that it "distributes a kind of equality to equal and unequal alike" (*Resp*. 8.558c5–6). As we shall see in a later chapter, the laws that made this state of affairs possible began in the last quarter or so of the fifth century to be regarded as introducing a leveling influence on the life of the state, a force imposing a tendency to conform to an establishment mentality dictated by the ignorant mob and stifling rather than nurturing the intelligence of the educated citizen. Other forces began to assert themselves against the *nomos* that had first paved the way for and then become the expression of the Athenian democracy.

---

307 Jones, *AD* 124 with n. 147, who, in addition to Ar. *Vesp*. 231 and 605ff. and *Eq*. 255, also cites [Xen.] *Ath.Pol*. 1.16–18 and Arist. *Ath.Pol*. 27.4.

CHAPTER TWO

Popular Sovereignty and Social Thought

CHANGES in the political structure of a state inevitably both reflect and induce changes in the way in which the society involved in these changes perceives itself. Athens is no exception: the growing political power of the Athenian *dēmos*, which we have traced in the preceding chapter, was accompanied by changes in social thought, social values, and social attitudes that, because they embodied the growing confidence of the Athenian people in its ability to fashion itself the norms by which it wanted to live, formed an integral part of popular sovereignty. To track down and define these thoughts, values, and attitudes can be more easily done for the fourth century, for which the orators and philosophers supply us with a wealth of direct and indirect information on details of Athenian life, than for the fifth century, for which the imaginative works of the dramatists constitute our most substantial source.[1]

One way we can gain some small insight into the effect that the growth of popular power had on Athenian social and political thinking in the fifth century is through the study of significant changes in language: "The suggestion that inquiries into the meanings of words merely throw light on words is false," writes H. L. A. Hart. "Many important distinctions, which are not immediately obvious, between types of social situation or relationships may best be brought to light by an examination of the standard uses of the relevant expressions and of the way in which these depend on a

---

1   K. J. Dover, *Greek Popular Morality in the Time of Plato and Aristotle* (Oxford, 1974), esp. 14–22.

social context, itself often left unstated."[2] The word νόμος (*nomos*) comes closest in Greek to describing the "types of social situation and relationships" of which Hart speaks, since the basic notion underlying it at all times in its history was that of a social norm accepted as valid and binding by those among whom it prevailed.[3] At the same time its adoption into the vocabulary of law and politics was a revolutionary step, probably first taken by Cleisthenes to consolidate his innovation of having reforms passed in Council and Assembly.[4] Through this innovation he substituted an ascending view of law for the descending view embodied in θεσμός (*thesmos*), which had theretofore regarded only the rules imposed by a lawgiver as imbued with public authority.[5] That this expansion of terminology reflects an incisive change in legal thinking goes without saying. But it is equally clear that it will have had repercussions on the nonlegal uses of νόμος, which continued to describe general social norms in the decades following Cleisthenes' reforms.

By tracing the history of νόμος and of its cognates from their earliest appearances to the end of the fifth century, we cannot, to be sure, discover in detail what effect the development of popular power had on Athenian social attitudes and social norms. Nevertheless, by confining our attention as much as we can to the significance and changing uses of the term in Attic authors and by resisting the temptation to include even Herodotus, despite the fact that his work remains the richest source available on *nomos* in the fifth century, we can hope to gain a general insight into that effect, which, as a companion piece to the development of political power, will help us understand the scope of popular sovereignty in Athens.

NOMOS BEFORE CLEISTHENES

A norm may be prescriptive or descriptive; it may be viewed, to borrow a felicitous distinction drawn by H. L. A. Hart, from the

---

2   H. L. A. Hart, *The Concept of Law*[3] (Oxford, 1972) vii.

3   See Ostwald, *Nomos*, 20–21, 54, and 55. I am here not concerned with its musical sense of "tune," nor with the geographical senses of "pasture," "abode," "district," etc., which it carries in its oxytone form.

4   Ibid. 157–60.

5   I borrow the useful terms "ascending" and "descending" from W. Ullmann, *A History of Political Thought: The Middle Ages* (Baltimore, 1965) 12–13, in full recognition of the different presuppositions on which this distinction rests in the Middle Ages.

internal perspective of the members of the group who are and feel themselves obliged to follow it or from the external perspective of an observer who is not or does not feel himself bound by the rule it imposes.[6] In other words, a norm is *prescriptive* when it is used as a means of legal or social control: it consists of rules that may or may not have been enacted by a particular person or group at a particular time in history; and it is viewed from the internal perspective only, its chief characteristics being that it is regarded as authoritative by those to whom it applies and that failure to conform with it is looked upon as a serious breach of the social order. Conformity is obligatory and enforced at least by social pressure and at most by penalties determined by authorities established for that purpose.[7] A *descriptive* norm, on the other hand, merely states the traditional form or customary pattern that a given practice follows without inviting thought about its origin: it is viewed primarily from an external perspective; deviations are noticed, to be sure, but are hardly envisaged as possible and are not regarded as a serious breach of the social order—in other words, a descriptive norm is not obligatory and hence does not serve as a means of legal or social control; social pressure for conformity is weak.[8]

If we were to try to apply the distinction between prescriptive and descriptive norms to the earliest uses of νόμος in Greek literature, we should find it too blurred to be useful. For example, when Hesiod says, ὥς κε πόλις ῥέζῃσι, νόμος δ' ἀρχαῖος ἄριστος (in whatever way a city sacrifices, the ancient rule is the best),[9] it is impossible to be sure whether νόμος describes a practice that people follow or a rule that

---

6   Hart, *Law*[3] 86–88.

7   For my present purposes, I prefer "prescriptive norm" to Hart's formulation of a similar phenomenon as "secondary rules of obligation" (*Law*[3] 91–96). Hart's explanation is geared more narrowly to the development of a purely legal system, in which these rules are designed to remedy deficiencies in what Hart defines as "primary rules of obligation." We shall see below that the very nature of obligation is fluid and uncertain in the case of νόμος.

8   My "descriptive norms" resemble Hart's "primary rules of obligation" (*Law*[3] 89–91); but though it is important for his purposes to exclude "custom" from his definition—"because it often implies that the customary rules are very old and supported with less social pressure than other rules"—a consideration of νόμος makes it imperative to include "custom" and the looser sense of obligation that it entails.

9   Porph. *Abst.* 2.18 (p. 148.16 Nauck) = Hes. fr. 322 M.-W. For the religious sense of ῥέζω, see Porph. ibid. and Hom. *Il.* 2.400, 8.250, 9.535, 10.292, 23.206; *Od.* 1.61, 3.5, 5.102, 9.553, 10.523, etc.; Pind. *Pyth.* 10.34; Soph. *Trach.* 288, etc. For the substance, see Xen. *Mem.* 1.3.1.

they are obliged to obey. Only the manner of sacrifice is addressed in the statement, and we have no clue whether νόμος is viewed from an internal or external perspective. Though the presence of ἄριστος (best) suggests that the ancient rule is merely preferred and not obligatory, we cannot be certain that those who conducted the sacrifice did not regard the weight of tradition as prescriptive.[10] Similarly in the νόμος of the plain to strip for sowing, plowing, and harvesting (*Op.* 388–92), the question whether it is a customary practice or a prescriptive rule does not seem to have occurred to Hesiod.[11] The same is true also of the νόμος established for men by Zeus (*Op.* 276–80): whereas animals, living as they do without δίκη (justice), devour one another, men have received δίκη, with which to order their lives.[12] Obviously, as applied to animals, νόμος connotes a fact, custom, or practice ascertained by an external observer; but in the case of men the obligation, if indeed it is an obligation, remains an abstract "ought," commended but not enforced by social pressures.[13]

This brings us to a second observation on the earliest uses of νόμος. It never seems to have occurred to anyone to inquire seriously into the origin in time of a given *nomos*. As a normative way of life, as a proper way of conduct, or as a norm of sacrifice, *nomos* exists as part of how the universe is constructed. There is no idea of development, no thought that there may have been a time when a given *nomos* did not yet exist. The only two early passages that may be construed as giving *nomos* a beginning in time, one of which we have just noted, name Zeus as its originator: in human terms this means that the norms of life have been decreed from time immemorial and for all time to come. These passages are statements affirming the validity and durability of the *nomos* concerned; they are not attempts to date it.[14]

10 Similarly in the case of νόμος in the Hecate hymn (Hes. *Theog.* 416–18), where we cannot tell whether κατὰ νόμον qualifies ἱλάσκηται, ἔρδων, or ἱερὰ καλά. For a similar ambiguity see Pherecydes of Syros, fr. 53 Kirk, Raven, and Schofield, and Hes. fr. 280.14 M.-W.

11 So also Archil. fr. 232 West, and Alc. fr. 72.6 L.-P., with Ostwald, *Nomos* 34 n. 6. Not much can be made of Alc. frr. 35.1, 129.25, and 181.1.

12 See M. Gagarin, "*Dikē* in the *Works and Days*," *CP* 68 (1973) 81–94, esp. 92 n. 58.

13 Cf. also Hes. *Theog.* 64–74, esp. 66, and Alcm. *PMG* fr. 40, with *Nomos* 21.

14 Hes. *Op.* 276–80; the other passage is Pherec. fr. 53 Kirk, Raven, and Schofield; cf. A. Kleingünther, Πρῶτος Εὑρέτης, Philologus Supplement 26, Heft 1 (Leipzig, 1933) 5: "Auf frühester Stufe sind die Götter der zeitlose Urgrund aller Dinge wie jedes menschlichen Wirkens."

All this changed when, presumably in connection with Cleisthenes' reforms, νόμος replaced θεσμός as the official term for "statute." It is true that semantically this was not a great step to take, because it merely extended a term from a more general social vocabulary to the language of law and politics.[15] But once the extension has been made, it had far-reaching consequences not only for the Athenian concept of law but also for Greek thinking about other social norms that had been expressed by νόμος in archaic times. A statute differs from the archaic *nomoi* in that it has a precise beginning in time, namely, the point at which its validity is authoritatively established by the legislative machinery of the state. At the same time, the fact that a statute has a beginning in time makes it possible to envisage a past in which it did not yet exist as well as future in which it will exist no longer. In short, when the general term for "social norm" became the official term for a specific enactment, its erstwhile absolute validity became relative: what had been timeless could become time-bound, and what had been immutable became changeable.

This development easily merged into the increasingly intellectual and man-oriented mainstream of Greek thinking in the fifth century, the earliest traces of which are preserved for us in Xenophanes' questioning of traditional religious and social values. The perception that *nomos* in the sense of "statute" has a beginning in time, that it is changeable and relative to the society that enacts it, soon began to affect also the other and older connotations of *nomos*. Norms and values of religious, social, and personal conduct, which had formerly been accepted without question as having existed forever and without change, were now also given a beginning in time and were, more often than not, attributed to human agents. The concomitant loss of an appeal to an absolute value eventually led near the end of the fifth century to a slackening of the bonds by which society is held together. The social value of *nomos* was no longer enduring and represented only what was regarded as valid and binding by a majority at a given time. It was exposed to corrosion, and new values emerged that, in the eyes of those who espoused them, had a higher claim to allegiance than did *nomos*.

A further consequence of the adoption of *nomos* as the official term for "statute" affected the ambivalence between prescriptive and

15   J. K. Davies in his review of Ostwald, *Nomos*, CR 87, n.s. 23 (1973) 226, and H. W. Pleket in his review of the same, *Mnemos.*, 4th ser., 25 (1972) 455–56.

descriptive norms that characterized *nomos* in the archaic period. As a secondary rule of obligation, a statute is by nature prescriptive: it tells people what they ought to do; it does not usually describe what they are doing. In becoming the official term for "statute," therefore, *nomos* automatically acquired prescriptive connotations, which were at best only latent in the archaic period, and this prescriptive element attached itself in its turn to the uses of *nomos* in other areas of human activity. Henceforth, νόμος tends to be used of rules as distinct from practices in religious, social, and behavioral matters, and new ways had to be found to express such practices as *nomos* had also connoted in the archaic period. A study of fifth-century vocabulary will show that the introduction of νόμος as "statute" created a rift between rule and practice, between prescriptive and descriptive norm, in all matters pertaining to social values and conduct.

NOMOS IN THE FIFTH CENTURY

This change in attitude and thinking can be traced clearly through the fifth-century uses of νόμος, and although no single factor can be isolated to account for it, there are indications that its leaven lay in the field of law and politics. For example, the verbs τιθέναι, καθιστάναι, and ποιεῖν denote in Greek from the earliest times the establishment, creation, or manufacture of anything; when associated with νόμος, these verbs usually serve as technical terms for "enact." Apart from the fact that this association is not attested before νόμος became the official term for "statute," the earliest and most frequent uses of this combination express the enactment of statutes. The earliest surviving example is found in the plaint of the Oceanids in the *Prometheus*, νεοχμοῖς δὲ δὴ νόμοις Ζεὺς ἀθέτως κρατύνει, which can only mean, "Zeus wields power with new laws without proper enactment,"[16] and presupposes that the expression νόμον τιθέναι was well established in Athens as a term denoting the enactment of statutes by the early 450s. The frequency of the combination of νόμος with verbs signifying enactment as well as its

16 Aesch. *PV* 150, discussed in greater detail in Ostwald, *Nomos* 43–44 with 44 n. 1. Although the authorship and date of the *PV* have recently again become a subject of scholarly controversy, I do not believe that a scientific solution to the problem can be found. The arguments for Aeschylean authorship martialed by C. J. Herington, *The Author of the "Prometheus Bound"* (Austin, Tex., and London, 1970), esp. 104–19, are less convincing than those against it by M. Griffith, *The Authenticity of the "Prometheus Bound"* (Cambridge, 1977), esp. 225–54.

early appearance creates the presumption that it was in the legal and political sphere that *nomos* first assumed the connotation of having a beginning in time.[17]

Soon after the mid-fifth century the notion of enactment at a specific time also spread to *nomoi* that had constituted primary rules of obligation. There are some instances outside Athens in which statutes may actually have instituted what we should regard as "customs,"[18] but it is not likely that statutes regulated the custom established by the Samians (ἐποιήσαντο νόμον) to offer cakes of sesame and honey at the festival of Artemis founded to save the Corcyrean boys from the fate awaiting them in Sardis (Hdt. 3.48.3), or the Odrysian custom (κατεστήσαντο νόμον) of receiving rather than giving gifts (Thuc. 2.97.4).[19] A beginning in time is the only feature that differentiates these from the pre-Cleisthenean *nomoi*; in other respects they are undifferentiated: they cannot be described as either descriptive or as prescriptive norms.

However, there is evidence that by the second half of the fifth century nonlegal enacted *nomoi* had in Athens also assumed the secondary sense, of prescriptive rule. In Euripides' *Alcestis* (57; 438 B.C.), in answer to Apollo's plea to postpone Alcestis's death on the grounds that older women get richer funerals than the young, Death rejoins that the enactment (τίθης) of this *nomos* would favor the rich. Ten years later, Theseus is presented in the *Hippolytus* as not wishing to heed the νόμος, earlier enacted (προύθηκας) by Hippolytus, that fathers ought to kill sons who violate their fathers' wives but instead

17   Political or legal νόμοι are associated with a form of τιθέναι (including the perfect passive, κεῖσθαι) in Soph. *Ant*. 480–81; Ar. *Ach*. 532, *Vesp*. 467, *Plut*. 914–15; Eur. *El*. 1268–69, *Cyc*. 338–39; and Thuc. 4.133.3, 5.63.4, 6.38.5, 54.6; with a form of καθιστάναι in Soph. *Aj*. 1247; Hdt. 2.177.2; and Ar. *Eccl*. 1041; and with ποιεῖν in Hdt. 1.29.1. Cf. also Hdt. 1.29.1–2, 2.136.2, 177.2.

18   For example, when Hdt. 1.82.7–8 tells us that after the battle of Thyreae the Argives ἐποιήσαντο νόμον to keep their heads shaved and to let their women wear no gold until Thyreae should be recaptured, the enforcement of the custom with a curse against anyone who would break it and the time limit set upon it leave room for the possibility that this custom was established by statute; see J. K. Anderson's review of Ostwald, *Nomos*, *CJ* 66 (1971) 369–71. This is less likely in the case of the Carian women (Hdt. 1.146.3) who retaliated for the slaughter of their parents νόμον θέμεναι not to eat with their husbands and not to call them by name, although oaths were taken to sanction the custom.

19   Cf. also the νόμος enacted by Danaus to call the Pelasgians "Danaans," Eur. fr. 228.8; the νόμος for husbands to kill unfaithful wives, for which Hecuba urges Menelaus to establish the precedent, Eur. *Tro*. 1031–32; and the νόμοι that prevent a man from marrying more than one wife, Eur. fr. 402.1.

as deciding to inflict exile on such a son as a worse punishment;[20] and Artemis cites a νόμος enforced by Zeus that enjoins the gods from opposing one another's designs in order to justify her failure to protect Hippolytus against Aphrodite.[21] The behavior of children toward their parents is at issue in νόμοι treated as enacted (καθισταίη) in the *Orestes* (892; 408 B.C.) and of fathers toward their sons in Aristophanes' *Clouds* (1421–26; 423 B.C.) By far the most striking example of this kind of usage is the question raised in the *Ion*: how can it be right that the gods who *wrote* νόμοι for men make themselves liable to the charge of lawless conduct?[22] Obviously, a passage such as this was not merely composed under the influence of a legal vocabulary but attests the impact of written legislation on thinking about the rules of moral conduct.

Norms regulating political conduct and relations between states were also thought of as capable of being enacted. In Thucydides, the Corinthians argue against the acceptance of Corcyra into the Athenian alliance by saying that this would enact (καθιστάναι) the rule— which, the Corinthians warn, might backfire against Athens—that abandonment of one ally opens the way to acceptance by the opposing side (1.40.4 and 6). Again, the Plataeans claim that the right of self-defense against an attacker is sanctioned by a universally established rule,[23] and the Athenians in the Melian Dialogue disavow being the authors of the enactment of the norm that power means domination, denying that they were the first to use it once it had been enacted.[24]

Rules of religious conduct appear as enacted *nomoi* in two Euripidean passages. In the *Supplices* (541; 423 B.C.) Theseus warns Adrastus against initiating the principle of leaving the dead un-

20 Eur. *Hipp.* 1046, referring to 1042–44. I now prefer W. S. Barrett's text and interpretation (*Euripides: Hippolytos* [Oxford, 1964] 357–58) to that I offered at *Nomos* 53 with n. 3, which was based on Murray's text.

21 Eur. *Hipp.* 1328. This νόμος is not given a beginning in time and no verb of enactment is associated with it; still, one cannot help feeling that Zeus is here thought of as a magistrate enforcing the statutes of his state.

22 Eur. *Ion* 442–43: πῶς οὖν δίκαιον τοὺς νόμους ὑμᾶς βροτοῖς / γράψαντας, αὐτοὺς ἀνομίαν ὀφλισκάνειν; cf. Ostwald, *Nomos* 48 with n. 1 and 91 with n. 1. Other relevant examples are Eur. *Ion* 1047, fr. 1091; Soph. *El.* 580–81; and Gorg. 82B11.21 DK⁶.

23 Thuc. 3.56.2: κατὰ τὸν πᾶσι νόμον καθεστῶτα. Cf. also Hdt. 7.8α1, where Xerxes describes himself as the heir rather than the author of the νόμος of Persian expansionism.

24 Thuc. 5.105.2: οὔτε θέντες τὸν νόμον οὔτε κειμένῳ πρῶτοι χρησάμενοι.

buried, and toward the end of the *Iphigeneia among the Taurians* (1458; after 412 B.C.) Athena bids Orestes to enact (θές) the ritual rule of having a sword put to a man's throat at the festival of Artemis at Halai.

Our discussion of enacted nonlegal *nomoi* in the fifth century has shown that although traces of the undifferentiated, archaic *nomos* remain alive to the end of the fifth century, by its second half, and especially in its last third, they had become decidedly more prescriptive than they had been before Cleisthenes. They tend to mark rules of conduct, compliance with which is expected, because they are enforced by social and moral pressures that will make neglect or breach perilous. This increased pressure toward conformity was instilled by the rising importance of the legal and political aspect of *nomos* in the wake of Cleisthenes' reforms, as is suggested by the emergence and use in the fifth century of the compounds νομοθετεῖν, νομοθέτης, νομοθεσία, and νομοθέτημα, presumably invented on the analogy of the older formation θεσμοθέτης.[25] The use of the verb in a religious context is preserved only once, and that by a non-Athenian;[26] in Athens it is used only of the enactment of statutes,[27] and when the sophist Antiphon employs it to describe social conventions, the context suggests that it is a rhetorical device to emphasize the indifference of *physis* to the arbitrary restraints enacted by men.[28] Similarly, the *nomen agentis* νομοθέτης (lawgiver)[29]

25 Ironically enough, the noun θεσμοθέτης is not attested before the early 450s, sc. in the Coinage decree (ML, no. 45, sec. [2]) and in the Chalcis decree (ibid., no. 52.75–76). The name as well as the institution must, however, certainly be pre-Solonian, and there is no good reason to doubt either Aristotle's statement (*Ath.Pol.* 3.4) that θεσμοθέται were instituted after the introduction of the annual archonship or the implication of Thuc. 1.126.8 that they were in existence by the time of Cylon's attempted *coup d'état*. See Hignett, *HAC* 76–77, and Ostwald, *Nomos* 174–75. The verb θεσμοθετέω, in its participial form and meaning "to serve as θεσμοθέτης," is not attested before the mid-fourth century B.C.; see Isae. 7.34 and [Dem.] 59.65.

26 Hdt. 2.41.6. Especially in view of the fact that this is the only surviving fifth-century use of the verb in a religious context, one wonders what its special point may be, since elsewhere Herodotus uses νομίζω to describe religious practices—e.g., at 1.131.2; 2.50.3, 51.1, and 63.4; 4.59.1 and 2, and 63. Does it mean that Herodotus believed the taboo formed part of a written ordinance?

27 [Andoc.] 4.3; Lys. 15.9 and fr. 87 Thalheim.

28 Antiphon, 87B44, A2.23–4.1 DK⁶, esp. 2.30–3.8: νενομοθέτηται γὰρ ἐπί τε τοῖς ὀφθαλμ[ι]οῖς, ἃ δεῖ αὐτοὺς ὁρᾶν καὶ ἃ οὐ δεῖ· καὶ ἐπὶ τοῖς ὠσίν, ἃ δεῖ αὐτὰ ἀκούειν καὶ ἃ οὐ δεῖ κτλ.

29 First in Antiphon 5.15; then Thuc. 8.97.2; Andoc. 1.82, 83, and 84; Lys. 1.31; 10.7 and 30; 11.4 and 11; 14.4; 30.2, 27 and 28; and 31.27.

and the abstract noun νομοθεσία (legislation)[30] invariably apply to the enactment of statutes. As for νομοθέτημα, Plato and Aristotle use it consistently of a specific legislative enactment,[31] but in its perhaps earliest surviving (though non-Athenian) occurrence, it describes a convention of speech as arbitrary,[32] possibly, as in the case of Antiphon, by a deliberate rhetorical borrowing from the language of law and politics.

It may be objected that our analysis has attached too much weight to the use of verbs that cannot be avoided when any kind of establishing is to be described. Yet the objection is answered because we have confined our attention to their association with νόμος, an association that does not begin until νόμος had become the official word for "statute." This makes it plausible that it was from the legal and political sphere that the idea of enactability at a specific time spread to other aspects of human life and thought. We have tried to show how the general trend of the fifth century to assign to mortals a higher degree of control over their world is reflected in the specific attribution to human initiative not only of the laws by which society is governed politically but also of its customs, behavioral norms, and, to a more limited extent, religious practices. Norms, which before Cleisthenes were thought of as having existed from time immemorial, now came to be regarded as having been enacted and as being enforceable in a way similar to that in which statutes are decided upon by a legislative agency. The social and religious norms of the last half of the fifth century presuppose a society in which written legislation is so much taken for granted that its standards can be applied to aspects of human life that are not normally regarded as capable of regulation by the acts of a legislature.

THE LANGUAGE OF RULE AND THE LANGUAGE OF PRACTICE

In addition to creating an awareness that norms of personal, social, and religious conduct could be regarded as enactable and thus as having a beginning in human time, the adoption of νόμος as the

---

30 Lys. 30.35. Cf. also [Hippoc.] *De decente habitu* 2 Heiberg.

31 Pl. *Resp.* 4.427b; *Politicus* 295e; *Leg.* 8.846c, 11.913c, and 12.957a; Arist. *Pol.* 5.8, 1308ᵃ14.

32 [Hippoc.] *De arte* 2 Heiberg: τὰ μὲν γὰρ ὀνόματα [φύσιος] νομοθετήματά ἐστιν, τὰ δὲ εἴδεα οὐ νομοθετήματα ἀλλὰ βλαστήματα.

official term for "statute" also created a distinction between rule and practice alien to the undifferentiated, timeless, and changeless *nomos* of the archaic period. We noted how νόμος in the course of fifth century came to be applied with decreasing frequency to social, behavioral, and religious practices and gradually came to define only those norms that prescribe the performance of acts or determine a mode of conduct. It became, consequently, necessary to find new ways to express the practices that νόμος had once covered, and a solution was found by coining the adjective νόμιμος (*nomimos*) and by using the verb νομίζω (*nomizō*), especially in its passive and participial forms, to express concrete customary practice, specific acts of personal behavior, and the performance of particular religious rites. It is to this development that we must now turn our attention.

Descriptive Social and Religious Norms

It may be no more than a quirk, an accident of survival, but it is a fact, nevertheless, that νόμιμος is not attested in the writings surviving from before the fifth century B.C. As the adjective of νόμος it can of course describe anything that is *nomos* in any of the various senses of the concept and regardless of whether a rule or a practice is the point at issue. But because in Greek adjectives are more flexible than nouns and permit a wider range of usage—they can not only modify nouns but can be used as nouns in their own right in any gender when preceded by the definite article—νόμιμος, as we shall see, gradually took over the areas νόμος was relinquishing and often became a suitable term when distinctions between legal-political and nonpolitical regulations had to be drawn.

Of particular interest in this connection is the νόμιμος ὅρκος (lawful oath) mandated in many pieces of legislation not only in Athens but also in other parts of the Greek world, often with the participle νομιζόμενος (*nomizomenos*) substituted for νόμιμος without any difference in meaning.[33] What precisely are the connotations of νόμιμος and νομιζόμενος when associated with oaths, curses, and imprecations? Oaths are public acts, usually political or legal in

33 Andoc. 1.98: τὸν νόμιμον ὅρκον to be sworn by all Athenians; Antiphon 5.90 and 96: τὸν νομιζόμενον ὅρκον to be sworn by the prosecutor in a διωμοσία before murder trials; cf. also the curse against those who break τοὺς ὅρκους τοὺς νενομισμένους in Ar. *Thesm.* 356–60 and the curse in [Lys.] 6.51. Outside Athens, see a judges' oath at Naupactus, ML no. 20.45; and an official imprecation from fifth-century Chios in Schwyzer, *Dialectorum Graecarum Exempla* no. 688C9: ἐπαράσθω κατ᾽ αὐτ[ō] ὁ βασιλεός, ἐπὴν τὰς νομ[α]ίας ἐπαρὰς ποιῆται.

nature, in which religious beliefs and practices are utilized for legal and political purposes—beliefs in that a divinity is invoked as witness to the truth of what is asserted, promised, or denied, and practices in that certain traditional formulas are used to give the oath validity. Different deities are invoked on different occasions, for different purposes, by different bodies or persons, and differently in different cities. In a passage in Euripides' *Medea*, Zeus is called "he who is worshiped as the steward of oaths for mortals";[34] the gods themselves invoke Gaia, Ouranos, and especially the waters of Styx in the Homeric poems;[35] and in the ephebic oath no fewer than eleven divinities are enumerated.[36] To prescribe the precise wording of the formula appropriate to each different kind of oath is not usually the business of the legislature but of those officials, lay or priestly, who have expert knowledge of what divinity needs to be invoked on a given occasion and of what the formulas, gestures, and rites are of which the oath, curse, or imprecation consists. The legislature can, therefore, usually do no more than demand that certain affirmations or promises be accompanied by an oath, but will leave it to specialists to decide what form the oath is to take and to administer it in the matter traditionally appropriate for the occasion (νόμιμος or νομιζόμενος).[37]

This brings us to the use of νόμιμος and various forms of νομίζω in other religious contexts. While νόμος in religious matters tends to refer in the fifth century to general regulations rather than to specific practices,[38] νόμιμος and the various forms of νομίζω, especially the participial νομιζόμενον, invariably refer to particular acts of worship

34 Eur. *Med.* 169–70: Ζῆνά θ' ὃς ὅρκων / θνητοῖς ταμίας νενόμισται.

35 *Il.* 15.36–39; *Od.* 5.184–86; *Hymn to Apollo* 84–86; cf. also *Il.* 2.755, 14.271; *Hymn to Demeter* 259; and *Hymn to Hermes* 519.

36 Tod, *GHI* 2, no. 204.17–19.

37 Note in this connection also the phrase ὀμνύντων δὲ τὸν ἐπιχώριον ὅρκον ἕκαστοι τὸν μέγιστον κατὰ ἱερῶν τελείων in the alliance of Athens with Argos, Elis, and Mantinea in 420 B.C. as reported by Thuc. 5.47.8. The point is obviously that each state has its own ὅρκιοι θεοί and formulas; and therefore, we may assume, a different ὅρκος is νόμιμος in each.

38 Of the sixty examples of religious νόμοι discussed in Ostwald, *Nomos* 40–43, only eleven refer unambiguously to a practice, and all these come from tragedy, which is less likely to reflect current usage than is prose: Soph. *Ant.* 519; Eur. *Supp.* 526–27; *Hel.* 800, 871, 1241–43, 1258; *IT* 35, 465, 958–60, 1458; and *IA* 734. In thirteen cases it is not clear whether the norm is prescriptive or descriptive: Hes. fr. 322 M.-W.; Aesch. *Supp.* 220; Soph. *Ant.* 287; Hdt. 2.36.1, 42.3; 3.16.4, 48.3; 6.58.2; Thuc. 2.52.4; Eur. *Supp.* 563; Ar. *Av.* 518; *Thesm.* 947, 1137; and in the remaining thirty-six cases the reference is clearly to prescriptive regulations.

or to specific beliefs. Examples are legion. Aeschylus, who uses νόμος to describe the customary worship of Hermes (*Suppl.* 220), is the earliest author to use νόμιμος to describe a set of specific religious acts when, in a rather difficult passage in the *Seven Against Thebes*, he seems to allude to marriage rites as νόμιμα.[39] A similar situation is envisaged when Jocasta in Euripides' *Phoenician Women* calls φῶς νόμιμον the torch carried by the groom's mother in the wedding ceremony.[40] In Euripides' *Helen*, the prohibition against burying on land those who have been drowned at sea is expressed by οὐ νομίζειν,[41] and in Thucydides the Plataeans call νόμιμα the ritual with which they annually honor the Spartans who fell in the battle of Plataea.[42] The sacrifice offered on the tenth day after the birth of a child is referred to as νομίζεται in Euripides' *Electra* (1126); prayers and sacrifices traditionally appropriate to the occasion on which they

39   Aesch. *Sept.* 333–35: κλαυτὸν δ᾽ ἀρτιτρόφοις ὠμοδρόπως / νομίμων προπάροιθεν διαμεῖψαι / δωμάτων στυγερῶν ὁδόν, which I translate: "It is lamentable for girls who have just come of age to traverse, plucked before ripeness, the road [that leads from] their hateful homes before the proper rites." I have quoted Page's text; but whatever we are to make of it, all editors and commentators seem to agree that νομίμων refers to the rites that must precede a proper marriage.

40   Eur. *Phoen.* 344–45. On the custom, see K. F. Hermann and H. Blümner, *Lehrbuch der griechischen Privatalterthümer*[3] (Freiburg and Tübingen, 1882) 274–75 with 275 n. 1; J. Heckenbach, "Hochzeit," *RE* 8. Band (1913) 2130; E. Pernice, *Griechisches und römisches Privatleben, Einleitung in die Altertumswissenschaft*, ed. A. Gercke and E. Norden, 2.1[4] (Leipzig and Berlin, 1932) 59; and W. Erdmann, *Die Ehe im alten Griechenland*, Münchener Beiträge zur Papyrusforschung und antiken Rechtsgeschichte 20 (Munich, 1934) 257–58. Peculiarly enough, all these scholars except Pernice mention only the torch carried by the bride's mother, and none of them cites either the present passage from the *Phoenissae* or the similar passage *Med.* 1027. That the groom's mother also carried a torch is corroborated by a mid-sixth-century shoulder lekythos in the Metropolitan Museum in New York (No. 56.11.1) by the Amasis Painter (see D. von Bothmer, "New Vases by the Amasis Painter," *Antike Kunst* 3 [1960] 71–80, esp. 73–74 with pl. 7) and by a red-figured cup by the Amphitrite Painter (second quarter of fifth century) in the Staatliche Museen in Berlin (No. 2530); see J. D. Beazley, *Attic Red-Figure Vase-Painters* 2[2] (Oxford, 1963) 831.20. (I am indebted to Professor J. Boardman for these last two references.) For forms of νομίζω to describe specific marriage rituals, see Hdt. 9.108.2 and Thuc. 2.15.5.

41   Eur. *Hel.* 1065; cf. 1262, 1270 (referring to 1267), 1277 (referring to 1275).

42   Thuc. 3.58.4. Cf. Soph. *El.* 327 and *OC* 1603, where νομίζεται is used of offerings to the dead. Cf. also Lys. 32.8, 12.96, and 2.9. For νομίζεται as referring to proper burial, see Eur. *IA* 1443, where I prefer England's emendation to the manuscript reading. For purification of the house after a funeral, see Antiphon 6.37. In Eur. *Alc.* 98–100, νομίζεται refers to the custom of placing lustral water for purification in front of a house of mourning. Cf. Hdt. 1.35.2, where τὰ νομιζόμενα describes the rites with which Croesus purifies Adrastus.

are offered are called τὰ νομιζόμενα;[43] and the same term is used of
religious contributions, such as those that a colony was expected to
send to festivals celebrated by its mother city (Thuc. 1.25.4), or the
part of the tribute exacted by Athens from its allies that was payable
to Athena and to the Other Gods.[44]

These passages show that the prescriptive connotations assumed
by *nomos* in the field of religion by the mid-fifth century made it
necessary to resort to expressions such as νόμιμα, νομιζόμενα, and
other forms of the verb νομίζω in cases in which practices were to be
described. One of the earliest occurrences of *nomima*, in the Praxiergidai decree,[45] suggests that religious *nomima* could be the subject of
a statutory enactment. The decree cites an oracle of Apollo as
assigning to the *genos* of the Praxiergidai the performance of certain
cultic tasks in the worship of Athena and of the Moirai, Zeus
Moiragetēs, Gē, and perhaps some other deities; but what is of
special interest is that the right to perform these *nomima* is here
confirmed and guaranteed by the secular organs of the state, Council
and Assembly, in the form of a decree (ψήφισμα), which in the fifth
century was no more than a form of legal and political statute
(νόμος).

The use of νόμιμα and forms of νομίζω to describe the secular
customs and institutions of society is poorly attested in Attic,
although νόμος in those writings that, we may assume, most faith-
fully mirror current usage, Attic prose and comedy, is well attested as
referring to the norms that underlie or prescribe customs or

---

43 Thuc. 6.32.1: εὐχὰς τὰς νομιζομένας, 6.69.2: σφάγια τὰ νομιζόμενα; Antiphon
5.82: ἱερὰ τὰ νομιζόμενα; cf. also <τὰ> νομιζόμενα ποιήσειν, in Lys. fr. 40 Thalheim,
and τὰ νομισθέντα, which the chorus of Eur. *Bacch.* 71 will sing in worshiping
Dionysus. Cf. also Eur. *IT* 471; Ar. *Plut.* 625, 682; Aesch. *Pers.* 498; Thuc. 3.82.8;
Eur. *Supp.* 731–33, fr. 839.6–7. For all these passages, see W. Fahr, ΘΕΟΥΣ
NOMIZEIN: *Zum Problem der Anfänge des Atheismus bei den Griechen*, Spudasmata 26
(Hildesheim and New York, 1969). Cf. also the use of νόμιμα for religious observances in general in Nicias's speech in Thuc. 7.77.2 (πολλὰ μὲν ἐς θεοὺς νόμιμα
δεδιῄτηται); in [Lys.] 6.16; and in the legal phraseology of the πρόρρησις, attested in,
e.g., Antiphon 6.34–36 and 40, εἴργεσθαι τῶν νομίμων, which prohibited a person
accused of murder from setting foot in the marketplace and in sanctuaries; see
Lipsius, *ARRV* 810 with n. 24.

44 *IG* I³ 21.4 (regulations imposed on Miletus in 450/49 B.C.): [τελὲν τὰ
ν]ομιζόμενα το[ῖς θεοῖς...]; and 49.15–16 (on financing the water supply of Athens
from the allied tribute): [ἐπειδὰν ℎε θεὸς ἔχς αὐτὸν λαμ]βάνει τὰ νομιζόμενα. Cf. also
Pherecrates, fr. 23.2, and Ar. *Plut.* 1185.

45 *IG* I³ 7.10–12. See also below, pp. 145–48.

institutions.[46] The distinction between the two can most neatly be illustrated by some examples from Herodotus, who, though not an Attic writer, may reasonably serve as a surrogate where good Attic evidence is not available. He frequently uses νόμαια (*nomaia*, an Ionic equivalent of νόμιμα) of specific social practices. He enumerates the wearing of Median attire, Egyptian cuirass, and the Greek practice of pederasty as proof of his contention that the Persians welcome foreign νόμαια (1.135); but the rule that the Magi are permitted to kill with their own hands any animals other than dogs or men is called a νόμος (1.140.3). The νόμαια of the Indian Padaioi include the killing and consumption of sick men by men and of sick women by women, as well as the sacrifice and consumption of the few that survive to old age (3.99). Of the Scythian Agathyrsoi we hear that they live very luxuriously, wear much gold, and have their wives in common in order to create a feeling of brotherhood among their children, but that they are close to the Thracians in all their other practices, τὰ ἄλλα νόμαια (4.104). The Amazons refused to follow their Scythian lovers to their homes on the grounds that their *nomaia* differed from those of Scythian women, and they specified their use of javelin and bow, as well as their practice of horsemanship, as distinguishing them from the pursuits of Scythian women, who stay in their wagons and prefer feminine activities to hunting (4.114.3). Herodotus also comments on the Egyptians' familiarity with Persian *nomima*, as an example of which he cites their knowledge of the rule (νόμος) not to let a bastard ascend the throne if a legitimate son exists (3.2.2).[47] Examples from Attic are Alcibiades' remark, reported by

---

46   I shall here treat as customary νόμος what I divided in *Nomos* into (a) way of life (21–22), (b) normal order of doing things (22–23), (c) normal way in which something is done (23–24), (d) mores of a social or political group (33–34), and (e) custom, social practice (34–37). If we retain these subjective and arbitrary distinctions for the moment, the following statistics may be of some interest: (a) of the six Attic passages discussed in *Nomos*, only one (Eur. *Hipp*. 98) is ambivalent (in the remaining five the norm is prescriptive); (b) all nine Attic passages refer to prescriptive rules; (c) of three Attic passages, all are prescriptive; (d) of thirty Attic passages, three in tragedy are possibly descriptive (Aesch. *Eum*. 693; Soph. *Ant*. 368; and Eur. *Bacch*. 484), whereas twenty-seven are prescriptive; (e) of the twenty Attic passages classified under this heading, three are ambivalent (Eur. *Or*. 571, fr. 346.1 and 4), and six seem to be descriptive (Eur. *Ion* 20, 25; *Heracl*. 292–93; and frr. 282.13, 469, and 530.9), and eleven prescriptive. On the basis of these figures, which, we must emphasise again, cannot be completely objective, fifty-five of sixty-eight passages, i.e., 80.9 percent, use νόμος in a prescriptive sense.

47   On the expression οὐ νόμος in this passage, see Ostwald, *Nomos* 24 with n. 1.

Thucydides (6.17.3), on the absence of the traditional type of farm-houses in Sicily with the words ἐξήρτυται οὔτε τὰ ἐν τῇ χώρᾳ νομίμοις κατασκευαῖς and the use of νομίζοντες with the dative in Pericles' Funeral Oration to describe the Athenian practice of celebrating games and sacrifices throughout the year and of living in tasteful homes (Thuc. 2.38.1).

In addition to religious and customary social practices, *nomima* also govern the conduct of individuals. Although the root νεμ- is associated with proper and improper conduct from the beginnings of Greek literature on, it appears in this sense in the pre-Cleisthenean period only in compounds[48] and in the impersonal passive of the verb νομίζω.[49] The fifth-century tragedians, beginning with Aeschylus, apply νόμος only to the norms that prescribe proper human conduct[50] but use νόμιμα and forms of νομίζω, usually combined with an expression of moral approbation, to describe the acts and practices of a person who conforms to these rules. The chorus in Sophocles' *Electra*, for example, motivates *nomima* by piety toward Zeus when it praises Electra for her acts of devotion to her father's memory,[51] and the chorus of Euripides' *Bacchae* associates *nomima* with εὐσεβεῖν and δίκη when it advocates a life of unquestioning piety and of honoring the gods, "casting out all modes of conduct that do not conform to justice."[52] Associations of *nomima* as acts of

---

48 E.g., εὐνομία in Hom. *Od.* 17.487, ἄνομος in Hes. *Theog.* 307.

49 Alc. fr. D13 L.-P.: φίλος μὲν ἦσθα κἀπ' ἔριφον κάλην / καὶ χοῖρον᾽ οὕτω τοῦτο νομίσδεται. The precise meaning of these lines is uncertain. A scholiast explains the invitation to dine on kid and pork as a proverb, and therefore Fahr, ΘΕΟΥΣ NOMIZEIN 11 translates the last three words "so sagt man es gewöhnlich"; the same reason is given by D. Page, *Sappho and Alcaeus* (Oxford, 1955) 295, for translating it "such is the way of the world." It seems more likely to me that the words refer to proper behavior: "You used to be my friend, and I used to invite you for kid and pork: that's the proper way to treat a friend."

50 See Ostwald, *Nomos* 24–26.

51 Soph. *El.* 1095–97: ἃ δὲ μέγιστ᾽ ἔβλαστε νόμιμα, τῶνδε φερομέναν / ἄριστα τᾷ Ζηνὸς εὐσεβείᾳ. The metaphor of winning the prize shows that acts and observances rather than rules are meant here. Since these observances are those that children owe to their parents (as G. Kaibel, *Sophokles Elektra* [Leipzig, 1896] 241, correctly noted), I prefer to classify them as acts of conduct rather than as religious obligations, even though they are prompted by a religious attitude.

52 Eur. *Bacch.* 1008–10: ἦμαρ ἐς νύκτα τ᾽ εὐαγοῦντ᾽ εὐσεβεῖν, τὰ δ᾽ ἔξω νόμιμα / δίκας ἐκβαλόντα τιμᾶν θεούς. This part at least of Murray's text seems fairly certain; for the difficulties in what precedes, see E. R. Dodds, *Euripides: Bacchae*[2] (Oxford, 1960) 202–5.

proper conduct with justice are also found in comedy[53] and in philosophy,[54] and in two dramatic passages forms of νομίζω express the conduct of a self-controlled person.[55] The moral connotations are carried in these passages by the verbal environment in which νόμιμα and the forms of νομίζω are placed; in themselves these terms are neutral. This comes out clearly in a passage from Aristophanes' *Wasps* in which Bdelycleon tries to allay Philocleon's skepticism about fighting the pankration protected by a θώραξ with the words οὕτω διηγεῖσθαι νομίζουσ' οἱ σοφοί.[56] Here personal habits are described without value judgment. But νόμιμον and νομίζω are also capable by themselves of carrying moral overtones when it is assumed that tradition has sanctioned a given mode of personal conduct. Examples can be found in Aristophanes' *Birds* (1450), where Peisthetaerus expresses his wish to give the Sycophant his wings χρηστοῖς λόγοις and thus turn him πρὸς ἔργον νόμιμον, or when Lysias accuses Peison ὅτι οὔτε θεοὺς οὔτ' ἀνθρώπους νομίζει, which can only mean "that he treats neither gods nor men with proper respect."[57]

Prescriptive Social and Religious Norms

The process by which νόμιμα, νομιζόμενα and other forms of νομίζω took over the earlier descriptive functions of *nomos* soon

53   Ar. *Thesm*. 675, where I prefer the Budé text: δικαίως τ' ἐφέπειν ὅσια καὶ νόμιμα.

54   The Anon. Iambl. 3.1 urges that skills acquired by hard work be used εἰς ἀγαθὰ καὶ νόμιμα and not εἰς ἄδικά τε καὶ ἄνομα. Cf. also Democr. 68B174 DK[6]: ὁ μὲν εὔθυμος εἰς ἔργα ἐπιφερόμενος δίκαια καὶ νόμιμα καὶ ὕπαρ καὶ ὄναρ χαίρει τε καὶ ἔρρωται καὶ ἀνακηδής ἐστιν.

55   Eur. *Stheneboea* 26, in D. L. Page, *Select Papyri* 3 (London and Cambridge, Mass., 1950) 128: οὐκοῦν νομίζω καὶ θανεῖν γε σωφρονῶν. The text is peculiar and the following line unmetrical, but I see no justification for Page's tentative translation, "Better, I think, that a man be virtuous, though he should die for it," since νομίζω is not usually construed with a participle; cf. R. Kühner and B. Gerth, *Ausführliche Grammatik der griechischen Sprache* 2.2³ (Hannover and Leipzig, 1904) 70. The context as well as the words demand the meaning "I regard it as right conduct to be self-controlled even as one dies." The Right Argument in Ar. *Nub*. (962) praises the good old upbringing ὅτ' ἐγὼ τὰ δίκαια λέγων ἤνθουν καὶ σωφροσύνη 'νενόμιστο. The opposite kind of life is condemned in Orestes' comments on the murder of Agamemnon near the end of Aesch. *Cho*. (1001–3): τοιοῦτον ἂν κτήσαιτο φιλήτης ἀνὴρ / ξένων ἀπαιόλημα κάργυροστερῆ / βίον νομίζων.

56   Ar. *Vesp*. 1196: "This is the way clever people usually tell the story." For the comic misunderstanding here, see MacDowell's note on line 1195.

57   Lys. 12.9. For the meaning, see Fahr ΘΕΟΥΣ ΝΟΜΙΖΕΙΝ 107–8; it is the addition of οὔτ' ἀνθρώπους that makes me classify this as a behavioral rather than a religious use of νομίζω.

went full circle. Accordingly as a number of specific acts may in themselves come to constitute a pattern of religious observance, custom, or behavior, the plurals τὰ νόμιμα and τὰ νομιζόμενα are found by the mid-fifth century also in a prescriptive sense, yet—and this is noteworthy—never in reference to the rules laid down by the statutes but always as norms of religious worship, of social conduct, and of interstate relations sanctioned by tradition and usage. In short, *ta nomima* came to be a collective expression, including in each nonlegal field all those regulations that cannot be enforced by a court of law but depend for their sanction upon social pressures.

We start with the use of νόμιμα in Thucydides' description of the Athenian occupation of Apollo's temple at Delium (4.97.2–3, 98.2). The Boeotian herald accuses the Athenians of having transgressed τὰ νόμιμα τῶν ῾Ελλήνων (the norms of the Greeks) and immediately proceeds to enumerate specifics: their fortification and occupation of the temple, its profanation, and the use of sacred lustral water for everyday purposes. In their reply to these charges the Athenians assert τὸν νόμον τοῖς ῞Ελλησιν εἶναι that sanctuaries belong to and are the responsibility of whoever has dominion over a land or any part thereof. Both the *nomima* and the *nomos* of the Greeks are prescriptive in character, but there is an obvious difference between them. Whereas the *nomos* to which the Athenians appeal is a general principle, the *nomima* of the Boeotian herald consist in specific acts that in this case have not been observed.

Religious practices in the fifth century were no longer *nomoi* but *nomima*, and religious *nomos* became prescriptive in character. These are remarkable indications that *nomos* was assuming greater prescriptive overtones. We have found some evidence that this development stood under the influence of the legal-political *nomos* in so far as even prescriptive religious regulations came to be expressed with greater frequency by νόμιμα or a form of νομίζω than by νόμος, apparently because νόμος had become increasingly associated with the secular statutes. For example, the rule prescribing the burial of the dead is included among the νόμιμα of the gods or of all Greece in Euripides' *Supplices* (19 and 311). Further, when this rule comes into conflict with the secular laws of the state, as it does in Sophocles' *Antigone*, a different vocabulary is employed to express the difference between the two norms. Antigone appeals to the ἄγραπτα κἀσφαλῆ θεῶν νόμιμα (the unwritten and unfailing norms of the gods) as the authority that bids her bury her brother; but what is remarkable is that she explicitly opposes this divine regulation to Creon's *nomoi*, that is, to his secular and transient injunctions, whose validity, she claims, pales before the ordinances of the gods. As if to drive home the point that her *nomima* are different from those of her opponent, she applies the adjective ἄγραπτα to them to indicate that, unlike the statutes of the state, the regulations sanctioned by the gods do not appear in written form.[58]

A similar development can also be observed in accounts of social customs. When the neuter plural adjective νόμιμα appears without a specific referent and in a general sense, its meaning often seems to come close to νόμος or νόμοι either in a collective sense as encompassing a group of practices or in the sense of a general rule from which specific practices are derived. And yet, even here there is a considerable difference between the two terms. The fact that νόμιμον is used of a specific practice makes its plural include all specifics—rules as well as practices—and thus assume a wider and more comprehensive meaning than νόμος or νόμοι.

Thucydides confines νόμος consistently to rules, mainly of the legal and political variety, and when he wants to express the customs, beliefs, practices, and traditions that make up the mores of a people, he resorts to νόμιμα. Thus in his account of the foundation of Himera: it was settled from Zancle, itself a colony of Chalcis, by Chalcidians and some Syracusan exiles; as a result its dialect developed into a mixture of Chalcidian and Doric elements, νόμιμα δὲ τὰ Χαλκιδικὰ ἐκράτησεν (6.5.1). In other words, despite its difference from its mother city in the dialect spoken, the customs and institutions of Chalcis, including of course practices as well as social conventions and laws, came to gain a stronger foothold in Himera than those of its Dorian contingent. Here the *nomima* are treated as a natural development; in the case of Gela, however, which was founded jointly by a Rhodian and a Cretan, Dorian *nomima* are spoken of as enacted,[59] and these Geloan *nomima* were, in their turn, given to Acragas when the people of Gela settled it as their colony.[60]

---

58   Soph. *Ant.* 454–55 against 449 and 452; see further below, pp. 148–61. For a similar contrast between the secular legal-political νόμος of the state and the prescriptive νομιζόμενον of religion, see Antiphon 6.4.

59   Thuc. 6.4.3: νόμιμα δὲ Δωρικὰ ἐτέθη αὐτοῖς.

60   Ibid. 4: νόμιμα δὲ τὰ Γελῴων δόντες. In poetry νόμος continued to be used in this wide sense, as, for example, in Eur. *El.* 234, where Orestes, still unrecognized by Electra, tells her that her brother as an exile οὐχ ἕνα νομίζων φθείρεται πόλεως νόμον, which J. D. Denniston aptly renders "uses the usages" in *Euripides: Electra* (Oxford, 1939) 77–78.

Language and *nomima* are joined also in Thucydides' list of the Athenian allies who participated in the Sicilian expedition. The Lemnians, Imbrians, the then-Aeginetans, and the then-Histiaeans are described as using the same dialect (φωνῇ) and the same νόμιμα as the Athenians (Thuc. 7.57.2). The use of a given language could in itself be considered conventional social behavior, or so the appearance of forms of νομίζω in several authors' works implies.[61]

On two occasions Thucydides presents the Athenians as accusing the Spartans of practicing only at home those institutions, laws, and customs that, according to Herodotus (1.65.5), Lycurgus's reforms had established as their νόμιμα. The Athenians reproach the Spartans for keeping their *nomima* uninfluenced by those of other peoples and for individually observing neither them nor those practiced (νομίζει) by the rest of Greece when they are abroad;[62] they also tell the Melians that the high moral standards of the Spartans in the observance of their *nomima* at home are not in evidence in their relations with other states.[63] Spartan institutions and social practices are also foremost in the mind of the Corinthians who argue at Sparta that unchanged *nomima* are excellent when a city enjoys peace but that constant planning is required when it is compelled to face many external problems.[64]

The social *nomima* we have discussed so far look descriptive rather than prescriptive in character because there is no indication of social or legal sanctions against transgression. We shall now turn to a number of such social *nomima*, which by implicitly or explicitly assuming the existence of penalties or sanctions against violation may more properly be regarded as prescriptive rules rather than as descriptions of fact. More often than not, the sanction is merely the

61 E.g., Soph. *El.* 691 and Lys. 10.17; among non-Attic authors, see Hdt. 1.142.3; 2.4.2, 42.4; 4.45.5, 183.4; 6.138.4; 7.192.2; Anaxagoras 59B17 DK[6]; and [Hippoc.], *Acut.* 6.

62 Thuc. 1.77.6: ἄμεικτα γὰρ τά τε καθ' ὑμᾶς αὐτοὺς νόμιμα τοῖς ἄλλοις ἔχετε καὶ προσέτι εἷς ἕκαστος ἐξιὼν οὔτε τούτοις χρῆται οὔθ' οἷς ἡ ἄλλη Ἑλλὰς νομίζει. For a similar use of νομίζω, see the Naupactian law (ML, no. 20), lines 24–26, τοῖς ḥυποκναμιδίοις νομίοις χρῆσται ḥόπος ἁ πόλις Ϝεκάστον νομίζει; and also Hdt. 4.106, where δίκην νομίζοντες is correctly interpreted by Fahr, ΘΕΟΥΣ ΝΟΜΙΖΕΙΝ 38, as "eine natürliche Rechtsordnung gebrauchen."

63 Thuc. 5.105.4: Λακεδαιμόνιοι γὰρ πρὸς σφᾶς μὲν αὐτοὺς καὶ τὰ ἐπιχώρια νόμιμα πλεῖστα ἀρετῇ χρῶνται· πρὸς δὲ τοὺς ἄλλους πολλὰ ἄν τις ἔχων εἰπεῖν ὡς προσφέρονται....

64 Ibid. 1.71.3: καὶ ἡσυχαζούσῃ μὲν πόλει τὰ ἀκίνητα νόμιμα ἄριστα, πρὸς πολλὰ δὲ ἀναγκαζομένοις ἰέναι πολλῆς καὶ τῆς ἐπιτεχνήσεως δεῖ.

shock of moral disapprobation that the reader is expected to experience at the thought of seeing these νόμιμα infringed; in other cases the nature of the penalty is made more explicit. Thus *nomima* of this kind often resemble legal or political *nomoi*, but they differ from them in that they describe behavioral patterns, which are not usually subject to legislation. In fact, the only political contexts in which these *nomima* appear are in those interstate relations that are not regulated by treaty but depend for their implementation on the moral sensibilities of the parties involved.

We begin with the first of these groups. When the chorus of Euripides' *Phoenician Women* speaks of Eteocles and Polyneices as οἱ μὴ νόμιμοι παῖδες, the point is not that they were illegitimately born but that the incest involved in their birth violates the norms of conduct accepted by society.[65] The kinds of sanction against transgression of these *nomima* are most explicitly stated by the sophist Antiphon: a person whose violation of the *nomima* goes undetected by those for whom they are binding gets away without feeling guilt and without penalty, but if he is found out he does not.[66] Feelings of guilt obviously are the sanction against the infraction of those *nomima* that are rules of social conduct subtly imposed upon the individual by social pressures of various kinds. Penalties, on the other hand, suggest that Antiphon has also in mind the transgression of rules upheld by specific stipulations of the statutes. It is noteworthy that when Pericles differentiates legal from social regulations, he calls them both νόμοι but differentiates their sanctions by ascribing the observance of the former to ἀκροάσει τῶν νόμων, "obedience to the statutes," whereas the latter are distinguished as ὅσοι ἄγραφοι ὄντες αἰσχύνην ὁμολογουμένην φέρουσιν (Thuc. 2.37.3). In other words, Thucydides cannot call these social rules νόμοι *tout court*, but

---

65   Eur. *Phoen*. 814–17 (OCT): οὐ γὰρ ὃ μὴ καλὸν οὔποτ᾽ ἔφυ καλόν, / οὐδ᾽ οἱ μὴ νόμιμοι / †παῖδες ματρὶ λόχευμα, μίασμα πατρός᾽ / ἢ δὲ συναίμονος ἐς λέχος ἦλθεν.† This obviously corrupt passage has never been emended satisfactorily. The sense, however, seems fairly clear: it is the incest of their mother and the pollution of parricide committed by their father that makes the sons μὴ νόμιμοι. It is grammatically also possible to take μίασμα πατρός in apposition to λόχευμα and interpret the birth of the sons as constituting a pollution of the father. But the point, first made by A. C. Pearson, ed., *Euripides: Phoenissae* (Cambridge, 1909) 140, that μίασμα is always used in connection with bloodshed rules out this interpretation, and the introductory οὐ γὰρ ὃ μὴ καλὸν οὔποτ᾽ ἔφυ καλόν shows the alternative interpretation to be correct.

66   Antiphon 87B44, A2.3–9 DK[6]: τὰ οὖν νόμιμα παραβαίνων ἐὰν λάθηι τοὺς ὁμολογήσαντας καὶ αἰσχύνης καὶ ζημίας ἀπήλλακται᾽ μὴ λαθὼν δ᾽ οὔ.

has to identify them as "unwritten" to differentiate them from the statutes.

Some *nomima* of this kind are applicable to mankind as a whole, for example, the rule that in the normal course of events all men have to suffer and die,[67] or, again, Gylippus's exhortation to his troops before the battle in the harbor of Syracuse to regard it as a νομιμώτατον (*nomimōtaton*) to sate to the full one's anger against an enemy (7.68.1), or Archidamus's prayer to the local gods before beginning the siege of Plataea to grant success to those who are seeking their revenge νομίμως, that is, in conformity with the norms of political conduct (2.74.2). But in two other Thucydidean passages, the *nomima* apply only to Greek states in their dealings with one another. In the first of these, the Plataeans tell their Spartan judges that they surrendered to them οὐ τοιάνδε δίκην οἰόμενοι ὑφέξειν, νομιμωτέραν δέ τινα ἔσεσθαι,[68] and in the second, a little later in the same speech, the Plataeans argue that it would be an offense against τὰ κοινὰ τῶν Ἑλλήνων νόμιμα (the common norms of the Greeks) if the Spartans were to kill them or hand them over to the Thebans (3.59.1).

Since the κοινὰ τῶν Ἑλλήνων νόμιμα in the last passage are in substance identical with the νόμος τοῖς Ἕλλησι in the preceding chapter (3.58.3), it is worth examining the possible reasons for the difference in terminology. The run of the Plataean argument in chapter 58 leaves no doubt that *nomos* is a rule of interstate relations, to which they appeal. The chapter opens with a plea to heed the gods invoked during the Persian Wars to sanction the Hellenic alliance to which Sparta and Plataea had been parties. The Plataeans next plead for the safety of their persons with the argument that they surrendered voluntarily and refer in this connection in passing to ὁ νόμος τοῖς Ἕλλησι as prohibiting the slaying of those whose surrender has been voluntary; finally, they point to the benefactions rendered by Plataea to the Greek cause during the Persian Wars and especially to

---

67 Lys. fr. 53.4 Thalheim: τὸ μὲν γὰρ ἀποθανεῖν ἢ καμεῖν νομίμως κοινὸν ἡμῖν ἅπασιν ἐστί.

68 Thuc. 3.53.1, "in the belief that they would not be subjected to a trial of this kind, but to one which would adhere more closely to traditional rules of procedure." That this is meant by νομιμωτέραν is shown by the explanation in the next paragraph: προκατηγορίας τε ἡμῶν οὐ προγεγενημένης ᾗ χρὴ ἀντειπεῖν (ἀλλ᾽ αὐτοὶ λόγον ᾐτησάμεθα) τό τε ἐπερώτημα βραχὺ ὄν, ᾧ τὰ μὲν ἀληθῆ ἀποκρίνασθαι ἐναντία γίγνεται, τὰ δὲ ψευδῆ ἔλεγχον ἔχει. Cf. the use of νενόμισται to describe proper trial procedure at Antiphon 4α1.

the honors the Plataeans still bestowed upon the Spartans fallen in the battle of Plataea (Thuc. 3.58.3). This νόμος becomes τὰ κοινὰ τῶν Ἑλλήνων νόμιμα when, at the opening of chapter 59, the Plataeans turn the arguments established in chapter 58 into a plea for the kind of actions they hope the Spartans will take or refrain from taking: they want their lives spared, because killing them would be detrimental to Sparta's reputation and would constitute an offense on the grounds just stated.[69] It would be a violation of τὰ κοινὰ τῶν Ἑλλήνων νόμιμα, both of Spartans' ancestors and of Sparta's benefactors, to destroy the Plataeans, who have not wronged Sparta, simply to please Plataea's Theban enemies.[70] In other words, the rule prescribing the treatment of prisoners is a *nomos*, but when its implementation is the point at issue, *nomima* is used to emphasize the action required by the *nomos*.[71]

Related to these *nomima* are two passages in which the singular, νόμιμον, closely associated with forms of νομίζω, describes a conventional belief (tantamount to a social rather than a political rule) from which certain actions are presumed to follow, although the *nomimon* refers only to the rule without envisaging subsequent action. In Thucydides (3.9.1), the Mytilenean ambassadors begin their address to the meeting of the Peloponnesian League at Olympia by appealing to τὸ καθεστὸς τοῖς Ἕλλησι νόμιμον, which they identify as the belief that those who switch from one alliance to another in time of war, however welcome they may be to their new allies, are regarded by them (νομίζοντες) as traitors to their former friends and are therefore held (ἡγοῦνται) in little esteem. The second passage, from Euripides' *Bacchae*, is of considerably greater interest because it

69   See the note on τάδε at 3.59.1 in Classen-Steup[3] 3 (Berlin, 1963) 121.

70   Thuc. 3.59.1: οὐ πρὸς τῆς ὑμετέρας δόξης, ὦ Λακεδαιμόνιοι, τάδε, οὔτε ἐς τὰ κοινὰ τῶν Ἑλλήνων νόμιμα καὶ ἐς τοὺς προγόνους ἁμαρτάνειν οὔτε ἡμᾶς τοὺς εὐεργέτας ἀλλοτρίας ἕνεκα ἔχθρας μὴ αὐτοὺς ἀδικηθέντας διαφθεῖραι.

71   This is a convenient place to subjoin some social rules expressed by forms of νομίζω: in Aesch. *Eum.* 32, the Pythia speaks of rules, accepted by all Greeks, determining the sequence in which consultants are admitted to the Delphic Oracle as πάλῳ λαχόντες, ὡς νομίζεται; ibid. 423, the Furies tell Athena that they pursue the murderer ὅπου τὸ χαίρειν μηδαμοῦ νομίζεται, sc. to a place whose norms preclude joy; in Ar. *Nub.* 498, Strepsiades is informed by Socrates of the rules for entering the Thinking Shop γυμνοὺς εἰσιέναι νομίζεται; and the invitation to dine at the Prytaneion was extended to the ambassadors from Egesta in 458/7 B.C. [ἐς τὸν] νομιζόμενον χρόνον (ML, no. 37.15).

relates the νόμιμον not only to νομίζω but also to νόμος and therefore is perhaps better discussed in full:

οὐ
γὰρ κρεῖσσόν ποτε τῶν νόμων
γιγνώσκειν χρὴ καὶ μελετᾶν.
κοῦφα γὰρ δαπάνα νομίζειν ἰσχὺν τόδ' ἔχειν
ὅ τι ποτ' ἄρα τὸ δαιμόνιον,
τό τ' ἐν χρόνῳ μακρῷ νόμιμον
ἀεὶ φύσει τε πεφυκός.[72]

The νόμοι here prescribe both beliefs and practices as is shown by their association with the verbs γιγνώσκειν and μελετᾶν. The verb νομίζειν followed by the infinitive ἔχειν indicates that the strength of the divine is a belief; that this belief has validity is established by predicating of the divine both the length of time through which it has been laid down as a specific νόμιμον by the νόμοι mentioned before and the eternity for which it has existed in nature. Since the νόμοι explicitly prescribe beliefs as well as practices, we may assume that τὸ νόμιμον describes the divine as an object of belief as well as of worship.

In the description of individual conduct, too, νόμιμος and the various forms of νομίζω came to assume the connotation of rule as νόμος became so closely associated with the (written) statutes that the adjectival forms were required to differentiate behavioral from political and legal rules. This is seen particularly in the fifth-century prose writers, that is, those authors who are more likely to reflect current usage than the more elevated language of poetry. Thucydides uses the expression εἴ τί που ἐξεδεδιήτητο τῶν καθεστώτων νομίμων in his account of the Spartan investigation into the *paranomia* of Pausanias (1.132.2) to indicate possible infringements of the Spartan code of conduct; Antiphon uses the phrase συγχεῖν τὰ νόμιμα three times in his third *Tetralogy* (4α2 and 6; β7) to indicate violations

---

72 Eur. *Bacch*. 890–96: "For one must never attempt to gain insights or to perform acts that go beyond the laws. For it is a light expense to believe that there is strength in whatever is the divine, [the divine that has been] both an object of belief throughout a long period of time and is forever rooted in nature." My interpretation of these lines is essentially the same as that of Dodds, *Bacchae*[2] 189–90, except that he seems to take lines 895–96 as depending on νομίζειν, whereas I take them in apposition to τὸ δαιμόνιον. See also the discussion in Fahr, ΘΕΟΥΣ ΝΟΜΙΖΕΙΝ 62–63, and in J. Roux, *Euripide: Les Bacchantes* 1–2, Bibliothèque de la Faculté des Lettres de Lyon 21 (Paris, 1970–72) 521–23.

of the rules governing proper human conduct, and in his speech *On the Murder of Herodes* (5.7) he once describes his request to the jury to pay more attention to the matter than to the manner of his speech as νομίμως καὶ ὁσίως ἔχουσα, that is, as conforming to both human and divine rules of conduct.[73]

The last step in this development, a return to *nomos* in the sense it had now assumed, came late in the fifth century and began in the area of behavioral norms. *Nomimos* came itself to be tinged with the statutory connotations of *nomos* and was henceforth used also to describe persons or acts that "conform to the statutes," a meaning it retains throughout the fourth century: a person is *nomimos* when he is law-abiding,[74] an act is *nomimos* when it is consonant with what written treaties or laws stipulate.[75]

THE MEANING OF *ENNOMOS*

It will be convenient to defer a statement of the general conclusions to be drawn from our examination of *nomimos* and the forms of *nomizō* until we can integrate them with the results of an inquiry into the meaning of two further *–nomos* compounds that are first found in the fifth century and that show in peculiar ways of their own the impact of the legal-political sense of *nomos* on fifth-century Athenian social thought. *Ennomos* and *paranomos* do not appear until the fifth century, when, in adjectival, adverbial, verbal, and nominal

73   I have found examples of νομίζω in relation to rules only in Ar. *Nub.* 1416–20, where both Pheidippides and Strepsiades refer using passive forms of νομίζω to the rule that permits a father to beat his son; and in *Av.* 1344–50, where the same rule is at issue when Parricide wants to participate in the νόμοι of the birds, because among the birds strangling and biting one's father καλὸν νομίζεται, and where this is confirmed by Peisthetaerus's statement that ἀνδρεῖόν γε πάνυ νομίζομεν for a nestling to beat his father.

74   See Antiphon 2β12 and [Andoc.] 4.40. The use of νόμιμος to describe a personal quality is surprisingly rare; among the many passages cited in F. Ast, *Lexicon Platonicum* 2² (Leipzig, 1908) s.v. νόμιμος, there are only four in which it has this sense: *Hp.Ma.* 285b6, *Grg.* 504d2, *Resp.* 7.539a3, and *Minos* 321b1; in Xenophon it occurs in this sense only at *Hell.* 4.4.3, *Cyr.* 1.6.27, *Mem.* 1.2.41, 4.4.13 and 17.

75   Thuc. 1.85.2, where it refers to the arbitration clause of the Thirty Years' Peace of 446/5 B.C.; cf. ibid. 1.78.4, 140.2, 145; and 7.18.2. That the treaty was a written document is shown by the expression τῶν ἀγράφων πόλεων at 1.40.2 as well as by the mention by Paus. 5.23.4 of a bronze stele on which the treaty was inscribed in front of the statue of Zeus near the Bouleuterion at Olympia. For the treaty as a whole, see Bengtson, *SVA* 2², no. 156. For early uses of νόμιμος in reference to the statutes, see especially Antiphon 5.9, 14 (cf. 6.2), 85, and 94.

forms, they describe, respectively, adherence to and transgressions of *nomos*. Though it may simply be an accident that no form of these expressions has survived from before the fifth century, we are justified in regarding this lack as telling rather than as accidental. Since adherence and transgression can refer only to rules and not to acts or practices, ἔννομος and παράνομος are not likely to have been coined until the adoption of νόμος as the technical term for "statute" had given *nomos* a primarily prescriptive sense. Thus the *nomos* expressed is always prescriptive, but it appears first in nonlegal contexts—*ennomos* significantly only in poetry—before prose passages of the late fifth century use it exclusively to describe adherence to statutes or treaties.

We shall pass over the earliest instances of ἔννομος, preserved in three Pindaric passages, since they come from outside Attica.[76] In Attica, ἔννομος is first found in three passages in Aeschylus's *Supplices*. In one of these the compound is clearly derived from the geographical νομός (region, district) and refers to the inhabitants of Egypt, who were shocked at the sight of Io.[77] The second and third passages are interesting because they provide us with the earliest association of ἔννομος with δίκη in contexts in which religious and behavioral norms are at issue. Part of the epirrhema in which the Danaids plead with Pelasgus to grant them asylum in Argos consists of a debate whether religious and moral or political *nomoi* should carry greater weight (348–437). The Danaids warn the king that he may incur the wrath of Zeus Lord of Suppliants if he should disregard the plea of anguished mortals οἳ τοῖς πέλας προσήμενοι / δίκας οὐ τυγχάνουσιν ἐννόμου.[78] In response the king raises possible legal objections to their admission based on Egyptian law (νόμοι),[79] and the Danaids react with a further appeal to justice and reverence for the gods (395–96), reminding him again of the watchful eye of Zeus: ἀμφοτέροις ὁμαίμων τάδ᾽ ἐπισκοπεῖ / Ζεὺς ἑτερορρεπής, νέμων

---

76 Pind. *Pyth.* 9.56–58 (474 B.C.); *Ol.* 7.84 (464 B.C.); and *Paean* 6.181–83 Snell³ (467 B.C.?). The χθονὸς αἶσα ἔννομος of the first passage is probably best derived from the geographical νομός rather than from νόμος, whereas the term in *Ol.* 7 probably refers to the orderly way Boeotian games are organized, and in *Paean* 6 to the musical sense of νόμος = "tune."

77 Aesch. *Supp.* 565: βροτοὶ δ᾽ οἳ γᾶς τότ᾽ ἦσαν ἔννομοι.

78 Aesch. *Supp.* 383–84, "who sit as suppliants at their neighbors' door without obtaining the justice prescribed by the norms."

79 Ibid. 387–91, discussed in Ostwald, *Nomos* 58–59.

εἰκότως / ἄδικα μὲν κακοῖς, ὅσια δ' ἐννόμοις.⁸⁰ In the first of these passages the description of δίκη as ἔννομος seems to imply that the admission of suppliants constitutes a norm of proper behavior, adherence to which is the essence of righteous moral action; in the second passage (which marks, incidentally, the earliest use of ἔννομος to describe a personal quality) a relation with δίκη is negatively established by opposing the ἔννομοι to those to whom Zeus assigns ἄδικα. Here too the norms observed look like purely social rules, which prescribe a certain kind of behavior, yet their explicit association with Zeus Lord of Suppliants adds a religious sanction to these behavioral norms. In short, the νομος-element of ἔννομος is in these two passages opposed to rather than associated with the legalpolitical sense of *nomos*.⁸¹ Similarly, when Oedipus taunts Teiresias with the words οὔτ' ἔννομ' εἶπας οὔτε προσφιλῆ πόλει / τῇδ', ἥ σ' ἔθρεφε, τήνδ' ἀποστερῶν φάτιν,⁸² it is not the violation of a statute that is at stake, but what seems in Oedipus's view to be an abnormal, inexplicable, and unpatriotic kind of behavior.

In the five fifth-century prose passages in which ἔννομος is found, however, the νομος-element invariably embodies the legal or political sense of the noun. When in his speech at the congress of Gela Hermocrates accuses the Athenians of hiding their imperialistic ends speciously (εὐπρεπῶς) behind ὀνόματι ἐννόμῳ ξυμμαχίας,⁸³ he alleges that Athenian alliances with states such as Leontini⁸⁴ are no more

80 Ibid. 402–4: "Related in blood to both sides, Zeus watches these proceedings with impartial balance, fairly meting out [the fruit of] unjust acts to the wicked and [the fruit of] their pious acts to those who adhere to his norms."

81 A combination of ἔννομος and δίκη is also found in Eur. *Phoen.* 1650–51, where it also straddles the border between a religious and a behavioral sense: when Creon regards as morally justified (δικαίως) his intention of leaving Polyneices' corpse for the dogs to devour, Antigone objects that justice of this kind does not conform to the demands of traditional religious observance (οὐκ ἔννομον... τὴν δίκην). At Aesch. *Cho.* 483–85, the δαῖτες ἔννομοι βροτῶν refer to observance of religious norms, sc. to traditional funerary banquets.

82 Soph. *OT* 322–23: "You have said things that neither conform to rules of normal conduct nor show affection for this city, which nurtured you, in that you deprive it of this information."

83 Thuc. 4.60.1: τάς τε ἁμαρτίας ἡμῶν τηροῦσιν ὀλίγαις ναυσὶ παρόντες, καὶ ὀνόματι ἐννόμῳ ξυμμαχίας τὸ φύσει πολέμιον εὐπρεπῶς ἐς τὸ ξυμφέρον καθίστανται. The allusion in τὸ φύσει πολέμιον is presumably to the ethnic differences between Ionians and Dorians, which had in the past led to wars between Sicilian states; cf. 3.86.2–4. What Hermocrates seems to fear is that a recurrence of such wars will invite the Athenians to realize their imperialistic designs upon the whole of Sicily by intervening on the pretext of helping their Ionian kinsmen.

84 See Thuc. 3.86.2–3 with ML, no. 64 of 433/2 B.C., and also the Athenian alliance with Rhegium of the same year, ML, no. 63.

than a legal justification for gaining a foothold in Sicily preparatory to finding a pretext on ethnic grounds for an attack on Sicily as a whole.[85] Whereas ἔννομος here signifies adherence to the terms of a treaty, it refers to the observance of the statutes of a particular city in Athenagoras's charge that the ambition for public office on the part of young Syracusans is οὐκ ἔννομον, apparently because it violates a Syracusan statute that set a minimum age for eligibility to office (Thuc. 6.38.5). The adverb ἐννόμως appears in a similar sense in two passages in Lysias to express conformity with the laws of Athens. In the speech *For the Soldier* it refers to a specific law, which had been read into the speech just before.[86] In the peroration of the speech *Against Nicomachus* (30.35), on the other hand, where it is part of an appeal to the jurors that the constitution will be administered ἐννόμως if they condemn those who are trying to invalidate the legislative process (νομοθεσίαν), it is not a specific statute to which adherence is commended but the entire body of Athenian laws as such; ἐννόμως is here used as the opposite of παρανόμως, an opposition to which we shall now turn.

THE MEANING OF *PARANOMOS*

The opposition between ἔννομος and παράνομος is strikingly illustrated by a passage in Thucydides, the importance of which warrants our quoting it in full. It forms part of the Theban reply to the Plataeans' allegation against the Thebans before the Spartan commission:

παρενόμησάν τε οὐ προπαθόντες ὑφ' ἡμῶν, μίσει δὲ πλέον ἢ δίκῃ κρίναντες καὶ οὐκ ἀνταποδόντες νῦν τὴν ἴσην τιμωρίαν· ἔννομα γὰρ πείσονται καὶ οὐχὶ ἐκ μάχης χεῖρας προϊσχόμενοι, ὥσπερ φασίν, ἀλλ' ἀπὸ ξυμβάσεως ἐς δίκην σφᾶς αὐτοὺς παραδόντες. ἀμύνατε οὖν, ὦ Λακεδαιμόνιοι, καὶ τῷ τῶν Ἑλλήνων νόμῳ ὑπὸ τῶνδε παραβαθέντι, καὶ ἡμῖν ἄνομα παθοῦσιν ἀνταπόδοτε χάριν δικαίαν ὧν πρόθυμοι γεγενήμεθα.[87]

85 Gomme (*HCT* 3.515 on 4.60.1), who favors the interpretation here given over the scholiast's suggestion that there existed a natural enmity between the Athenians and the Sicilians as a whole, does not go far enough when he calls the Athenians "the natural defenders of the Ionians"; the point surely is that the alliance will be the legal pretext for Athenian intervention, though φύσις is the real bond with which the Athenians will wish to explain their imperialistic designs.

86 Lys. 9.12; for the νόμος applicable ἐάν τις ἀρχὴν ἐν συνεδρίῳ λοιδορῇ, see ibid. 6 and 9.

87 Thuc. 3.67.5-6: "They transgressed in that, though not provoked by us, their decision was prompted by hatred rather than by a judicial verdict and in that

Of the words underlined ἔννομα is the one most readily interpreted from the context alone as referring to the (anticipated) outcome of the present legal proceedings, to which the Plataeans submitted voluntarily by treaty (ἀπὸ ξυμβάσεως);[88] its meaning is, therefore, "in conformity with the treaty." The *nomos* conformed to is, in other words, legal or political *nomos*, which is also involved in the other fifth-century prose passages discussed above. The context further shows that these ἔννομα are in some way treated as the opposite of both παρενόμησαν at the beginning and the ἄνομα at the end of the passage quoted; but as we shall see, the opposition is not a direct one, because the νομος-element in παρενόμησαν and ἄνομα does not have a narrowly legal-political sense.

I have argued elsewhere that ἀνομία, ἄνομος, and ἀνομέω denote lawless conduct—that is, the concept is the opposite of *eunomia*, which describes orderly conduct—and that its νομος-element refers to the normal and proper conduct of an individual.[89] If this is correct, the Theban complaint at the end of our passage is not directed at a specific offense perpetrated by the Plataeans but against their conduct as such. Conduct, of course, manifests itself in a number of acts, which may or may not be specified in a given context; but the point of the concept is that the perpetrator of such acts has characteristics that place him outside the pale (ἀ-) of what is generally regarded as acceptable behavior (νόμος).

In order to understand παρενόμησαν in our passage, it is necessary to rehearse in some detail the facts underlying the debate between the Plataeans and the Thebans as reported by Thucydides in his own person.[90] Upon the invitation of some power-thirsty Plataeans, the Thebans had occupied Plataea without provocation at night in the spring of 431 B.C. At the first shock of surprise, the Plataeans agreed to their demand to join the Boeotian League and forsake their alliance with Athens. But when they realized how small the Theban

---

they are not now [willing to] pay a penalty equal to what they have done. For what they will suffer will be in conformity with legal procedure, not, as they allege, as people stretching out [suppliant] hands on the battlefield, but as people who have subjected themselves by compact to legal proceedings. Accordingly, Lacedaemonians, vindicate the law of the Greeks, which these men have violated, and pay us a just recompense for the lawless treatment to which we have been subjected in return for services we gladly rendered."

88   Cf. ibid. 52.1–3 and 53.1.
89   See Ostwald, *Nomos* 85–94, esp. 88, for the passage under discussion.
90   See Thuc. 2.2–5, 71–78, and 3.20–24 and 52.

contingent was, they counterattacked and took most of the Thebans prisoner. The fate of these prisoners formed the subject of negotiations between the Plataeans and the approaching main body of a Theban army. Upon promise that their prisoners would be spared, the Thebans withdrew. The Plataeans, in violation of their promise, proceeded to butcher them. The following summer a Peloponnesian army joined a Theban force in investing Plataea and offered to lift the siege on condition that the Plataeans switch their allegiance to the alliance against Athens. Upon their refusal hostilities began, in which the Plataeans managed to hold their own for three years; they were finally compelled by lack of food to capitulate in the summer of 427 B.C. on condition that they would submit to the judgment of a Spartan commission, which would punish only the guilty (τοὺς ἀδίκους). This tribunal was the one before which the Plataeans pleaded (3.53–59) and from which the Thebans obtained permission to rebut the Plataean arguments (3.61–67).

Objectively speaking, there are here, as in most Thucydidean situations, rights and wrongs on both sides. But it is naturally in the interest of the Thebans to shift the burden of guilt from themselves onto the Plataeans. They do this by first representing the Plataeans as having accused the Thebans of *paranomia* (a term that, curiously enough, does not occur in any form in the Plataean speech) and then turning the tables on them. Accordingly, they begin by paraphrasing the Plataean version of the Theban attack—πόλιν γὰρ αὐτοὺς τὴν ἡμετέραν καταλαμβάνοντας ἐν σπονδαῖς καὶ προσέτι ἱερομηνίᾳ (3.56.2)—as παρανόμως γὰρ ἐλθεῖν ἡμᾶς ἐν σπονδαῖς καὶ ἱερομηνίᾳ ἐπὶ τὴν ὑμετέραν πόλιν.[91] They then proceed to place upon the Plataean traitors, who invited them into the city, the true burden of their attack with the words οἱ γὰρ ἄγοντες παρανομοῦσι μᾶλλον τῶν ἑπομένων (3.65.2), a phrase that in its turn parodies an earlier statement of the Plataeans in which they had attributed their alliance with Athens to Spartan initiative.[92] We may stop here for a moment to consider the precise meaning of παρανόμως and παρανομοῦσι in these passages. Each time a specific act is described: at 65.1 it is the Theban attack upon Plataea, and at 65.2 the traitorous action of the Plataean subversives. What *nomos* did these actions violate? That the

91 Thuc. 3.65.1: "For they allege that we went against your city contrary to law at the time of a treaty and during a festival season."

92 Ibid. 55.4: ἃ δὲ ἑκάτεροι ἐξηγεῖσθε τοῖς ξυμμάχοις, οὐχ οἱ ἑπόμενοι αἴτιοι εἴ τι μὴ καλῶς ἐδρᾶτο, ἀλλ' οἱ ἄγοντες ἐπὶ τὰ μὴ ὀρθῶς ἔχοντα.

Theban attack violated the terms of the Thirty Years' Peace is indicated by ἐν σπονδαῖς, but that παρανόμως includes more than the legal-political *nomos* is shown by the inclusion also of ἱερομηνίᾳ, which adds a religious dimension to the offense. Similarly, because παρανομοῦσι parodies a statement of the Plataeans, it seems less likely to describe a violation of Plataean *nomoi* against treason than to criticize the behavior of the citizens in question. In short, these two passages permit us to draw the tentative conclusion that the παρανομ- stem describes specific acts of transgression against *nomoi* that, although they may include specific legal-political stipulations, have at the same time a wider, more general range.

The next step in the Theban argument is the assertion that the Plataean slaughter of their prisoners took place παρανόμως because the prisoners surrendered voluntarily and received the promise that they would be spared (3.66.2). Again, the argument echoes one the Plataeans made earlier, when they based their appeal to the Spartans to spare them on the fact that they had submitted of their own free will (3.58.3). Nothing legal or political is here involved; the *nomos* transgressed enjoins the keeping of promises and the humane treatment of persons who have voluntarily surrendered to the enemy in battle. It is a moral or behavioral code that has been violated, and the context confirms this. In the preceding clause the Thebans had also complained that the Plataeans broke a ξύμβασις, an "undertaking" or "agreement", to join the Boeotian cause, but the breach of this ξύμβασις is explicitly excluded from the term παρανόμως when the Thebans concede that those of them who died in the mêlée resulting from the breach κατὰ νόμον τινὰ ἔπασχον (suffered in conformity with some kind of law). Thus παρανόμως is confined to the wanton slaughter of the prisoners and describes a violation of a moral rather than of a legal or political code.

After calling attention to the impertinence of the Plataeans, who though having committed three wrongs (τρεῖς ἀδικίας) nevertheless charge the Thebans with transgression (παρανομῆσαι) yet refuse to pay the penalty for their own misdeeds (3.66.3), the Thebans finally launch a countercharge of *paranomia* in the passage quoted at the beginning of our discussion: "They transgressed [παρενόμησαν] in that, though not provoked by us, their decision was prompted by hatred rather than by a judicial verdict and in that they are not now [willing to] pay a penalty equal to what they have done" (3.67.5). In neither case is the transgression concerned exclusively with the breach of a treaty: the Plataean allegation was directed against the unprovoked attack by the Thebans and not primarily at the breach of the Thirty Years' Peace; similarly the transgression with which the Plataeans are charged consists in the unprovoked slaughter of the Theban prisoners without judicial proceedings and in their refusal to take the fair punishment they have coming to them. That the latter is the thrust of the Theban argument is corroborated by their appeal to the Spartans: ἀμύνατε οὖν, ὦ Λακεδαιμόνιοι, καὶ τῷ τῶν Ἑλλήνων νόμῳ ὑπὸ τῶνδε παραβαθέντι.[93] It is not aimed at the violation of a clause in a treaty or of a specific law but of the norms of behavior expected of Greeks to spare the lives of those who voluntarily surrender in fighting.

We are now in a position to sum up what the five uses of the adverb and verb, respectively, in the Theban speech have taught us about the use of *paranomos*. In every case the transgression consists in specific acts, but the *nomos* violated does not necessarily involve a treaty or statute and does not even necessarily refer to a specific political or religious injunction. It is rather a broad general code prohibiting, in the cases mentioned, an unprovoked attack, an invitation to foreign troops to occupy one's city, and the slaughter of prisoners who have surrendered voluntarily. In short, the *nomos* violated constitutes a general code of behavior, which may involve— but is not limited to—observance of specific legal-political or religious injunctions. It takes for granted the existence of a frame of reference (e.g., ὁ τῶν Ἑλλήνων νόμος) within which a code that ought to have been observed was in fact violated. If this definition is correct, we must posit a certain amount of overlap between *paranomia* and *anomia*, especially in view of the fact that the Thebans conclude this part of their speech (3.67.6) with a reference to the lawless treatment (ἄνομα) they have suffered. Still, there does seem to be a difference between the two concepts: *paranomia* constitutes a specific violation of a code that the perpetrator recognizes (or ought to recognize) as binding for himself, whereas *anomia* is stronger, since it describes an act or an attitude that denies the existence of such a code altogether.

The meaning of *paranomia* as the violation of a general code of the existence of which the perpetrator is or ought to be aware is

---

93   Ibid. 67.6: "Come to the defense, Lacedaemonians, of the law of the Greeks, which they have transgressed."

confirmed by all its other uses in fifth-century Attic. The occupation of the Pelargikon by the rural population gathered into the city during the Peloponnesian War was considered by the Athenians unlawful (παράνομον) because an ancient curse and a Pythian oracle had forbidden it (Thuc. 2.17.1–2), and the Athenian occupation of Apollo's temple at Delium was regarded as an act of *paranomia* by the Boeotians because it infringed τὰ νόμιμα τῶν Ἑλλήνων.[94] The return from exile of the Spartan king Pleistoanax was regarded as unlawful (παρανομηθεῖσαν) by those who believed that it had been effected by bribing the Delphic oracle (Thuc. 5.16.1).[95]

It would be tedious to discuss or even mention all the numerous passages in which *paranomia* consists in the violation of a code of social conduct. An instructive summary is provided by a discussion of its use by several authors in describing the person to whom it was applied most frequently in the fifth century: Alcibiades.

Lysias attacks Alcibiades' ancestors for their sexual excesses, their incest with sisters and daughters, their profanation of the Mysteries and the mutilation of the herms, and he sums up the register of their sins thus: καὶ περὶ πάντας τοὺς θεοὺς ἠσεβήκασι καὶ εἰς ἅπασαν τὴν πόλιν ἡμαρτήκασιν, ἀδίκως καὶ παρανόμως καὶ πρὸς τοὺς ἄλλους πολιτευόμενοι καὶ πρὸς σφᾶς αὐτοὺς διακείμενοι, οὐδεμιᾶς τόλμης ἀπεχόμενοι, οὐδὲ ἔργου δεινοῦ ἄπειροι γεγενημένοι.[96] The association with πολιτευόμενοι and διακείμενοι[97] shows that παρανόμως characterizes the conduct of Alcibiades' family, and the list preceding it specifies the actions in which the disposition manifested itself. In short, they are charged not with the violation of specific statutes but with offending against the moral and political standards accepted by the city.

From Thucydides we learn that Alcibiades was feared by the

94 Ibid. 4.98.6 with 97.2; cf. p. 101 above.

95 Not much can be made of Lys. fr. 89 Thalheim, μὴ παρανομεῖν ἀλλ' εὐσεβεῖν, or of a tragic fragment preserved in Stobaeus 1.3.39, οὐδεὶς παρανομῶν πρὸς θεοὺς ἐχέγγυος, beyond stating that the infraction is religious in nature. In Eur. *Bacch.* 997–1000, Pentheus's outbursts against the new worship and even the very divinity of Dionysus (242–45) are characterized as emanating from παρανόμῳ ὀργᾷ, which is at the same time an act of unjust judgment (ἀδίκῳ γνώμᾳ).

96 Lys. 14.42: "And they have profaned all the gods and committed offenses against the whole city in that they showed injustice and lawlessness in their public relations with their fellow citizens and in their private relations with one another, refraining from no audacity and involved even in outrageous acts."

97 For the association of παρανόμως with a form of πολιτεύω, see Lys. 26.5; for an association with διατεθέντες, see ibid. 9.17–18.

multitude because of τὸ μέγεθος τῆς τε κατὰ τὸ ἑαυτοῦ σῶμα παρανομίας ἐς τὴν δίαιταν καὶ τῆς διανοίας ὧν καθ' ἓν ἕκαστον ἐν ὅτῳ γίγνοιτο ἔπρασσεν.[98] The juxtaposition of παρανομίας and διανοίας indicates that a disposition toward unconventional and offensive behavior is meant here, and no doubt his extravagant way of living beyond his means, particularly his expensive penchant for horse breeding alluded to in the preceding section (6.15.3), is meant to illustrate his παρανομία. Later in the same book, Thucydides identifies this ἐς τὰ ἐπιτηδεύματα οὐ δημοτικὴν παρανομίαν as the source of the popular suspicions of his involvement in the desecration of the Mysteries and of the herms as a step toward his aim of subverting the democracy (6.28.2). In both instances specific activities are cited as manifestations of Alcibiades' character, and in both cases the *nomos* transgressed is not a specific statute but the general norms of conduct governing Athenian social life.[99]

A specific target of Alcibiades' opponents is his conduct in sexual matters, his adultery, and his wife stealing, which are characterized as violence (βιαιότης) and *paranomia* ([Andoc.] 4.10). He is accused of having taken off for Abydos upon attaining his majority in order to learn from the local women ways of activating the lawlessness (παρανομία) and self-indulgence that were already part of his character (Antiphon, fr. 67 Thalheim). An illustration is given in pseudo-Andocides' description of Alcibiades' treatment of a Melian girl he purchased after having himself recommended that the captured Melians be sold into slavery. The son he had by her was born παρανομωτέρως Αἰγίσθου (more lawlessly than Aegisthus) because he was born of a woman enslaved by an act of Alcibiades, whose father and relatives he had killed, and whose city he had annihilated ([Andoc.] 4.22, cf. 23). In arguing for the ostracism of Alcibiades, the speaker alludes to another peculiarly interesting case of sexual *paranomia*: Cimon's ostracism is attributed to the παρανομία he displayed in committing incest with his sister (ibid. 33). The question of historical accuracy does not concern us here, and the context does not provide an answer to the question whether παρανομία in the

98   Thuc. 6.15.4, "the magnitude of his personal lawlessness in his manner of living and the grandeur of his designs, which pervaded every single enterprise in which he was engaged."

99   Cf. also [Andoc.] 4.30, where παρανομία is coupled with δωροδοκία as marking his conduct at Olympia, and where the lavish gifts extorted from the people of Ephesus, Chios, and Lesbos are cited as specific examples.

Cimon passage is to be taken as an act or as a trait of character. But what is certain is that it does not describe the violation of a statute. For apart from the fact that ostracism was not a penalty for criminal offenses, Athenian law permitted marriage between brother and sister, provided that they were not of the same mother, and it is possible that Cimon and Elpinice had different mothers.[100] It is, therefore, an offense against the social norms of Athens or perhaps even those accepted by all Greeks.[101] Similarly, the ostracisms of Alcibiades' paternal and maternal grandfathers are adduced as evidence that they were the παρανομώτατοι of their times, yet more restrained and more just than their grandson (ibid. 34). No specific transgressions are enumerated, but, as in the case of Cimon, their offenses must have been against general social norms rather than against specific statutes, else the moral terms σωφρονέστεροι and δικαιότεροι would not be appropriate in a comparison of their conduct with that of Alcibiades. It is, therefore, an opposition of just and restrained persons (not of law-abiding citizens) with transgressors (παρανομοῦντες) that is used in the final appeal to the jury to make the punishment of Alcibiades a deterrent for others (ibid. 40).

Alcibiades is only the most outstanding example of a person of whom *paranomia* is predicated. The fact that ἀνομία and its cognates never appear to characterize his behavior seems to indicate that his transgressions are viewed as violations, but not as absolute denials, of social norms. Among other eminent persons, Pausanias is said by Thucydides to have aroused Spartan suspicions τῇ τε παρανομίᾳ καὶ ζηλώσει τῶν βαρβάρων μὴ ἴσος βούλεσθαι εἶναι τοῖς παροῦσι, and they investigated εἴ τί που ἐξεδεδίῃτητο τῶν καθεστώτων νομίμων.[102] The context makes it more likely that παρανομία describes a trait of character than acts of misdemeanor collectively, but it clearly shows that the code violated consists of moral and social norms rather than of statutes, and in the sequel the dedication of the Delphic tripod in his own name is cited as a specific example of his *paranomia*.

----

100   Harrison, *LA* 1.22 with n. 3, citing Nep. *Cim.* 1.2; cf. also Plut. *Cim.* 4.6 and 8, and Eup. fr. 208, cited ibid. 15.4, and Ath. 13.589e. Cf. also Davies, *APF* 302–3, who inclines to the view that Elpinice was the full sister of Cimon.

101   Cf. Δισσοὶ Λόγοι 90.2, 15 DK⁶ (vol. 2, p. 408): τοὶ δὲ Πέρσαι κοσμεῖσθαί τε ὥσπερ τὰς γυναῖκας καὶ τὼς ἄνδρας καλὸν νομίζοντι, καὶ τᾶι θυγατρὶ καὶ τᾶι ματρὶ καὶ τᾶι ἀδελφᾶι συνίμεν· τοὶ δὲ Ἕλλανες καὶ αἰσχρὰ καὶ παράνομα.

102   Thuc. 1.132.2, "by his lawlessness and his copying of the barbarians that he was unwilling to accept the living conditions at home as everyone else did. . . whether he had in his style of living departed from the established code of conduct." For νόμιμα here, see above, p. 107.

We need not pursue this aspect of *paranomia* any farther, and rather may broach the question that is the goal of this part of our discussion: what influence did the adoption of *nomos* as "statute" have upon *paranomos* and its various forms? As we shall see, the facts that the compound does not appear before the second half of the fifth century and that most of the passages discussed come from the same prose authors who use the concept also with political and legal connotations show that contravention of the statutes is not the only—and not even the dominant—idea associated with *paranomia*. In other words, the chronological overlap of legal and nonlegal usages is more extensive in the case of *paranomos* than in the case of any other νομος-compound.

The truth of this is shown strikingly when we consider the use of the concept in relations between states, which were in ancient Greece not regulated by a written code of international law or convention analogous to, for example, the Geneva Conventions in modern times, but either by *ad hoc* treaties or by general religious or moral norms of conduct expected to be observed by all parties. We have already had occasion to examine the use of adverb and verb in several passages in the speech of the Thebans against the Plataeans[103] and concluded that, although the breach of a treaty—the Thirty Years' Peace—was involved in two of the passages, the offense was also directed against religious convictions and constituted, in addition, an unprovoked attack (Thuc. 3.65.1 and 66.3); that in two other passages the transgression consisted in the wanton slaughter of prisoners who had surrendered voluntarily (66.2 and 67.5); and that παρανομοῦσι once describes the action of citizens who invited foreign troops to occupy their own city in order to realize their own personal political ambitions (65.2). The same unprovoked attack upon Plataea is described by Thucydides as a παρανόμημα against the arbitration clause of the Thirty Years' Peace when he relates the Spartan deliberations preceding the occupation of Deceleia in 414/13 B.C. (7.18.2) No offense against religious sensibilities is mentioned here, and the matter seems to be regarded as a specific violation of a specific clause of a treaty; the same is true later in the same chapter, when the Athenian attacks on Epidaurus and Prasiae, as well as their raids from Pylos, are called a παρανόμημα against the arbitration clause in the Peace of Nicias (ibid. 18.3). That the rare noun παρανόμημα should be applied to specific violations of specific

103   See above, pp. 111–15.

clauses of a treaty is not surprising in view of the fact that nouns in
-μα are usually *nomina rei actae*.[104] But even here the offense is not
conceived of in purely legal-political terms, for a clause that intervenes between the two passages quoted explains the Spartan belief
that their failures at Pylos and elsewhere were a punishment of sorts
(εἰκότως δυστυχεῖν) for the παρανόμημα their allies committed; the
natural inference is thus that they also expected a divine punishment
to follow the present Athenian παρανόμημα.[105]

All other fifth-century uses of the παρανομ- stem that reflect the
legal and political sense of *nomos* refer to the statutes of a particular
city rather than to treaties between states. More often than not it is
impossible to determine whether the norm violated is a (written)
statute or the (unwritten) mores of society. For example, when
Thucydides (3.82.6) ascribes the cohesion of the Corcyrean factions
to their desire κοινῇ τι παρανομῆσαι, only the wording of the context
suggests that the statutes are the object of transgression, and these
seem not to be any specific statutes but the whole body of the
established laws of Corcyra. The legal offense is at the same time a
moral offense. This is also true of Pericles' statement in the Funeral
Oration (Thuc. 2.37.3) that fear prevents the Athenians from transgression—διὰ δέος μάλιστα οὐ παρανομοῦμεν—for the fear has as its
object not only the incumbent magistrates and the statutes that
afford redress to the injured but also unwritten *nomoi* that bring
shame upon the offender in the eyes of the community. Again, in the
question in Lysias's speech *On the Olive Tree*—πότερον δέ μοι κρεῖττον
ἦν, ὦ βουλή, δημοκρατίας οὔσης παρανομεῖν ἢ ἐπὶ τῶν τριάκοντα;[106]—
παρανομεῖν clearly refers immediately to the statute protecting
sacred olive trees, but, as the context shows, it also implies that it was
easier under the Thirty to act unjustly (ἀδικεῖν), that is, to offend
against the moral code, than it was under the democracy.

In the case of other violations of a specific statute, it remains
uncertain whether παρανομέω is meant to characterize the act committed or the conduct of the person who committed it. For example,
in the speech *Against Alcibiades* attributed to Andocides (4.21), the
speaker calls Alcibiades τὸν τοιαῦτα παρανομοῦντα for having
assaulted Taureas, the choregus of the boys' chorus that competed

---

104   E. Schwyzer, *Griechische Grammatik*[2] 1 (Munich, 1953) 522.
105   Thuc. 7.18.2 with Gomme-Andrewes-Dover, *HCT* 4.394.
106   Lys. 7.27: "Was I in a better position to break the law under the democracy
or under the Thirty?"

against a chorus led by Alcibiades, and for having chased him out of the theater during the performance. The law violated and the events themselves are indeed described by the speaker, but in terms that leave important questions unanswered both about the precise circumstances of the ejection and about the legal stipulations that were violated: κελεύοντος δὲ τοῦ νόμου τῶν χορευτῶν ἐξάγειν ὃν ἄν τις βούληται ξένον ἀγωνιζόμενον, οὐκ ἐξὸν ἐπιχειρήσαντα κωλύειν, ἐναντίον ὑμῶν καὶ τῶν ἄλλων Ἑλλήνων τῶν θεωρούντων καὶ τῶν ἀρχόντων ἁπάντων παρόντων <τῶν> ἐν τῇ πόλει τύπτων ἐξήλασεν αὐτόν.[107] That Taureas was—or was alleged to be—an alien is unlikely, even if he is not identical with Andocides' relative of the same name.[108] One should rather think that either Taureas or Alcibiades challenged the citizenship (and thus the right to compete) of one of the members of the opposing chorus, and that thereupon a fight broke out, in the course of which Taureas was violently ejected. If that was the case, the offense may have consisted in Alcibiades' ejecting the chorus leader rather than the alien member of his own or of Taureas' chorus, an interpretation that is supported by Demosthenes' account of the same incident (21.147). Yet Demosthenes also states that Taureas's ejection did not at the time of the incident constitute a violation of the relevant law, since it had not yet been enacted. The law of Demosthenes' time prescribed definite procedures for challenging, with a view to ejection, the citizenship of a chorus member (ibid. 56–57 cf. 8–9); though the procedure may have been different in the late fifth century, one cannot imagine that none existed at all. This would suggest that Alcibiades' transgression consisted in using force in place of the proper legal process to eliminate an alleged foreigner and that, in short, his action violated both a statute and the norms of decent behavior.[109]

107 [Andoc.] 4.20: "For though the law permits the removal of any member of a chorus from the competition if he is an alien, and though it is not permissible to stop someone who has made the attempt, he drove him off with blows in the presence of you and of all the other Greeks who had come to attend and with all the magistrates in the city present."

108 Andoc. 1.47; see K. Fiehn, "Taureas," *RE* 2. Reihe, 4. Band (1932) 2536–37. The identity of this Taureas with Andocides' relative is assumed by Davies, *APF* 29.

109 Alternatively, it is possible that his offense violated the οὐκ ἐξόν clause of the statute. But it is by no means clear whether ἐπιχειρήσαντα in that clause refers (a) to the person who attempted the ejection, sc. that it was "forbidden to resist any attempt at such ejection" (so Maidment), or (b) to the person who attempted to participate in the performance, sc. that the law "interdit de l'arrêter quand il a commencé" (so Dalmeyda). Since linguistic usage favors (a), it is possible that

There is an ambiguity also about Nicomachus's accusation as a παρανομήσας in Lysias 30.6. Earlier in the speech the charges against Nicomachus had been specified as his having taken four years rather than the assigned thirty days to complete his job as ἀναγραφεὺς τῶν νόμων, his having disobeyed orders specifying which texts he was to publish, and his not having submitted to an annual audit of his actions as was expected of magistrates; it is for these misdeeds that the jurors are now exhorted to punish him (30.2–5). But since no acts are specified, and since Nicomachus's extraordinary appointment probably excused him from the annual *euthyna* of magistrates,[110] it seems that the transgressions enumerated are not of a kind for which Nicomachus would have been legally liable and that the participle is used merely to denigrate his character by insinuating unsubstantiated legal-political offenses.

We shall forego a detailed discussion of three uses of παρανομέω in Lysias[111] and of some uses of adverb and adjective by Thucydides, Andocides, and Aristophanes,[112] because it would not give us any new insights. Instead we shall concentrate on a rather detailed examination of Antiphon's speech *On the Murder of Herodes*, in which *paranomia* plays a central and very interesting part. This speech,

---

Alcibiades' transgression of the law consisted in resistance to Taureas's attempt to eject a foreign member from Alcibiades' chorus.

110 See R. S. Stroud, *Drakon's Law on Homicide*, University of California Publications in Classical Studies 3 (Berkeley and Los Angeles, 1968) 25 with n. 29.

111 The three Lysianic passages describe specific transgressions of specific provisions: at 26.7, the convocation of a jury for conducting a *dokimasia* on a day when it was παρὰ τοὺς νόμους to do so is described as παρανομῆσαι. Regardless of whether they were written or not, the violated νόμοι here are specific regulations. The two passages in the speech *Against the Corn Dealers* (22.13 and 17) refer to the violation of a statute that limited to fifty *phormoi* the amount of grain that could be bought up (ibid. 5–6).

112 It is uncertain what law is being broken in Thuc. 4.132.3, where the Spartans employed Spartiates to administer some cities conquered by Brasidas in the north. A scholion to Thuc. 4.132.3 suggests ὡς οὐκ ὄντος νομίμου ἐξάγειν τοὺς ἡβῶντας ἢ οὐκ ὄντος νομίμου ἄρχοντας καθιστάνειν ταῖς πόλεσι τοὺς ἡβῶντας, ἀλλὰ τοὺς προβεβηκότας καθ' ἡλικίαν and glosses παρανόμως as ἤγουν παρὰ τὸ καθεστὸς ἔθος. Gomme's suggestion, *HCT* 3.623, that παρανόμως may refer to Brasidas's broken promise to leave Acanthus, Torone, and Scione free does not commend itself, since a broken promise is in itself not an act of *paranomia*. Andocides (1.8) in protesting that the *endeixis* against him was made παρανόμως no doubt refers to the decree of Isotimides; Aristophanes' objection to the ἰχθυοπώλου χειρὶ παρανομωτάτῃ probably protests a violation of the νόμος ἀγορανομικός (fr. 387.10), cf. Theophr. *ap.* Harp. s.v. κατὰ τὴν ἀγορὰν ἀψευδεῖν, which cites a relevant law; see also Dem. 20.9 and Hyp. *Athenog.* 14 with Lipsius, *ARRV* 93–94 n. 155.

delivered at some time between 416/15 and 414/13 B.C.,[113] contains altogether seven passages in which a form of *paranomos* appears as verb, adverb, adjective, or noun. Since all these passages are concerned with a single issue, we shall first have to place them into their contexts. The speech is for the defense of a Mytilenean, Euxitheos, who has been accused of murdering an Athenian, Herodes, in the course of a voyage. The peculiar feature of the case is that Herodes' relatives prosecuted Euxitheos as a κακοῦργος (felon) instead of initiating the appropriate δίκη φόνου (action for murder) against him. Why they did so is not quite clear,[114] but the fact that Euxitheos was not an Athenian certainly had something to do with it, even if Euxitheos found it in his interest not to make too much of his alien status. A δίκη φόνου was tried before the Areopagus; although we lack specific information on the subject, it may be that the original purpose of the statute prescribing this procedure was to protect the community against blood guilt incurred by one of its members and that an action for murder could not, therefore, be used against an alien. It is equally possible that the prosecution may have feared that the elaborate formalities preceding a δίκη φόνου might not be completed before a new archon basileus would take office, so that new proceedings would have to be initiated under his successor. Meanwhile, Euxitheos might have escaped, since he could remain free on bail. In any event, by charging Euxitheos as a κακοῦργος, his adversaries were able to secure his summary arrest and detention (*apagōgē*) by the Eleven until the trial, which was conducted before a jury court; and since it was up to the jurors to accept or reject the penalty proposed by the prosecution (Antiphon 5.10), it could be death under the one procedure just as much as under the other (ibid. 59, 71). The choice of this procedure in place of a δίκη φόνου is not only one of the chief lines of argument on which Euxitheos relies for his acquittal, but it also forms the basis of his charge of *paranomia* against his accusers.

Immediately after his opening request for a fair hearing, Euxitheos begins his defense by charging that the acts of his prosecutors

113   K. J. Dover, "The Chronology of Antiphon's Speeches," *CQ* 44 (1950) 44–60, esp. 44–48 and chronological table on p. 55.

114   The following remarks owe much to the clear and sensible discussion of K. J. Maidment, ed. and tr., *Minor Attic Orators* 1 (London and Cambridge, Mass., 1941) 150–57. Cf. also M. H. Hansen, *Apagoge, Endeixis and Ephegesis against Kakourgoi, Atimoi and Pheugontes: A Study in the Administration of Justice in the Fourth Century B.C.* (Odense, 1976) 124–25.

are παρανομώτατα καὶ βιαιότατα and spring from their βιαιότης καὶ παρανομία (Antiphon 5.8). He substantiates this by arguing that the κακούργων νόμος is applicable only to thieves and footpads but not to murderers and that each different offense has its own different procedure laid down for prosecution (ibid. 9–10). Next, two formal aspects of the manner of prosecution chosen are attacked. The solemn oath required of prosecutors as well as of witnesses in murder trials was evaded in dealing with the case by apagōgē, and this evasion—παρελθὼν τοὺς κειμένους νόμους—is branded by Euxitheos with the words καὶ ἡγῇ χρῆναι αὐτοῖς τὴν σὴν παρανομίαν κρείσσω γενέσθαι αὐτῶν τῶν νόμων and is later described by the verb παρανομεῖς.[115] The other formal aspect of the apagōgē attacked as παρανομώτατα is that it denied Euxitheos his right (κατὰ τὸν νόμον) to furnish the three sureties required to permit his release on bail, despite the fact that no foreigner was ever refused release on bail by those charged with the apagōgē of κακοῦργοι, that is, by the Eleven (ibid. 17). Nothing more is said about paranomia until the peroration, in which Euxitheos pleads for a proper trial for murder ἐν ᾧ ταῦτα νομίμως πράξεθ' ἃ νῦν ὑμᾶς παρανόμως πείθουσιν οἱ κατήγοροι ψηφίσασθαι and in which the prosecutors will have to swear the prescribed oath (τὸν νομιζόμενον ὅρκον) and περὶ ἐμοῦ κατὰ τοὺς κειμένους νόμους διαγνώσεσθε, καὶ ἐμοὶ οὐδεὶς λόγος ἔσται ἔτι, ἐάν τι πάσχω, ὡς παρανόμως ἀπωλόμην.[116]

What can we learn from all this about the kind of nomos Euxitheos alleges to have been violated? That the violation of statutes is involved is clear beyond a doubt, but what written statutes does he claim have been broken by the prosecution? Surely, it is unlikely that the Athenian statutes made the δίκη φόνου the mandatory and only permissible procedure against a suspected murderer; on the contrary, the broad and vague legal use of κακοῦργος[117] suggests that the term could provide an appropriate weapon with which to proceed against a foreigner suspected of the murder of an Athenian. In short, it is not a specific law that is alleged to have been violated, but the laws as a whole, which prescribe different procedures for trying different

115   Antiphon 5.12: "And you think that your violation of the laws should carry greater weight with the court than the laws themselves." See also ibid. 15.

116   Ibid. 94, "in which you will do legally what my prosecutors are trying to persuade you to do illegally," and 96: "You will arrive at a decision about me in conformity with the established laws, and I shall have no further argument, if it goes against me, that I was illegally condemned to death."

117   See Lipsius, ARRV 78 with n. 104, 320, and Hansen, Apagōgē 36–48.

kinds of crime and which are said to have reserved the ἀπαγωγὴ κακούργων for thieves and footpads (Antiphon 5.9–10). The argument is, therefore, based on analogy: a statute directed at thieves and footpads, Euxitheos asserts, is not a suitable instrument for prosecuting an alleged murderer. The same is true of the insinuation that the present proceedings have been chosen to avoid the oath mandatory in murder cases. Again, no specific statute has been violated, but the use of a procedure other than that customary against murderers is sufficient to charge the opposition with *paranomia* (ibid. 12, 15). No illegal act is involved, but a violation of the procedure prescribed for cases of murder is alleged. And finally, the denial of bail is attacked as παρανομώτατα by appeal to precedent, that is, to the general practice of extending bail to foreigners who can provide the required sureties (ibid. 17); no stature is adduced to show that granting bail is mandatory in the present case.

The way Euxitheos uses παράνομος and its congnates is remarkably close to the way in which the genitive plural of the adjective is used in the legal expression *graphē paranomōn*, an institution first attested about the same time as Antiphon composed *On the Murder of Herodes*.[118] H. J. Wolff's study of the *graphē paranomōn* has shown convincingly "dass man den Begriff des παράνομον in einem weiten Sinn verstand und augenscheinlich schon frühzeitig nicht mehr, vielleicht sogar zu keiner Zeit, nur auf offenkundige Widersprüche zum unmittelbaren Wortlaut bestehender Gesetze bezog," but rather that a ψήφισμα or νόμος was regarded als παράνομον, "wenn sie mit den politischen Grundprinzipien der demokratischen Staatsordnung oder mit den tragenden Institutionen der Gesellschaftsordnung unvereinbar schienen."[119] In Antiphon's speech it is a point in the legal rather than in the political or social order that is being transgressed, but the violated *nomos*, like the *nomos* indicted in a *graphē paranomōn*, is not a specific statute but the legal system as a whole.

118 I do not of course mean to imply that Euxitheos tried to intimate that his opponents were making themselves liable to prosecution under the γραφὴ παρανόμων by having used ἀπαγωγὴ κακούργου as an expedient in a murder case. γραφαὶ παρανόμων were applicable only against legislative proposals or, as in Andoc. 1.17, against individuals acting in their official capacity as members of a legislative body.

119 H. J. Wolff, *"Normenkontrolle" und Gesetzesbegriff in der attischen Demokratie*, Sber. d. Heidelberg. Ak. d. Wiss., Philos.-hist. Kl. 1970, 2. Abh. (Heidelberg, 1970) 45–67, quotations from pp. 46 and 65.

Wolff's evidence necessarily comes mainly from the fourth-century orators,[120] but his examination of two late fifth-century *graphai paranomōn* shows that from its very inception the *nomos* violated by a specific act was not a particular statute but the legal or political system as such.[121] The earliest attested case[122] is the one that Andocides' father, Leogoras, brought successfully against a certain Speusippus, who in his capacity as Council member had handed him and others over to the jurors for having been present at the profanation of the Mysteries at the house of Pherecles (Andoc. 1.17, 22). What was παράνομον about Speusippus's action we do not know. Wolff may be right in interpreting it, on the basis of Leogoras's denial ever to have visited the house of Pherecles (ibid. 22), as the act of indicting a person who was not even present when the crime was committed. But there is no evidence for his assertion: "Also kein Angriff auf die Rechtsgrundlage des Beschlusses, sondern schlichtes Abstreiten der eigenen Mittäterschaft, d.h. der bei der Beschlussfassung unterstellten Tatsachen, und auch dieser nur, soweit sie Leogoras persönlich betrafen."[123] We simply do not know whether or not Speusippus's action violated a statute, and only the natural presumption that Leogoras alone of all those denounced with him indicted Speusippus *paranomōn* suggests that the indictment had a basis broader than a formal legal offense.

A situation that combines features of Euxitheos's argument with Leogoras's case against Speusippus is found in Xenophon's account of the treatment of the generals after the battle of Arginusae, including in particular Euryptolemus's attempt to issue a summons

120   For a list of all known γραφαὶ παρανόμων down to 322 B.C., see Hansen, *PAUP* 28–43.

121   It is worth noting in this connection that the indictment is not called a γραφὴ παρανομίας, a fact that seems to corroborate our view that παρανομία is a disposition of character, which cannot of course be actionable. In this respect the γραφὴ παρανόμων differs from most (but not all) γραφαί and δίκαι, which use the genitive singular of the crime alleged both of adjectives and—most frequently—of nouns.

122   Neither the date nor the facts underlying Antiphon's speech against the general Demosthenes are known; [Plut.] *X orat.* 833d.

123   Wolff, *"Normenkontrolle"* 48. Wolff goes beyond the evidence when he draws from this the general conclusion that "das juristisch noch ungeschulte und daher unvollkommen differenzierende Denken des 5. Jahrhunderts wird den Ratsentscheid, welchem infolge Fehlens ihrer tatbestandlichen Voraussetzungen die gesetzliche Grundlage faktisch abging, einem von vornherein widergesetzlich ergangenen Beschluss ohne weiteres gleichgesetzt haben."

against Callixenus for having drafted an illegal proposal (παράνομα συγγεγραφέναι)[124] that treated as a judicial procedure what had been no more than a deliberative meeting of the Assembly and wanted a verdict passed without a preceding trial. The case resembles that of Speusippus in being directed at an action taken by a member of the Council but differs from it in that the matter did not even enter into the initial stages because of intimidation by the mob and its leaders. Under these circumstances we cannot be certain whether the charges against Callixenus would have been the same as those included in Euryptolemus's speech if the matter had come to a trial. If they had been the same, we have, as in Euxitheos's argument, a wrong procedure branded as παράνομον, except of course that Euxitheos was tried under a law he believed was not applicable in his case, whereas the generals did not get the proper trial at all to which the law entitled them.[125] In any event, Euryptolemus mentions no specific positive statute that Callixenus's motion may have violated; this further corroborates Wolff's contention that the *nomos* transgressed in an act *paranomōn* consists in the fundamental principles of the democratic constitution and in the social institutions, including positive statutes, that embody them—it refers to the legal and social system as a whole and not to a particular statute.[126]

Once we realize that this the thrust of the *graphē paranomōn* we understand why its abolition—or at least suspension—was one of the first acts of the commissioners appointed in 411 B.C. as a prelude to the establishment of the oligarchy of the Four Hundred,[127] for

---

124 Xen. *Hell.* 1.7.12. The use of συγγεγραφέναι is peculiar, since the term is usually applied to reports submitted by specially appointed commissions (e.g., *IG* I³ 78.3; Andoc. 1.96; Xen. *Hell.* 2.3.2; Arist. *Ath.Pol.* 29.2, 30.1) and not to προβουλεύματα submitted to Council and Assembly. Does the word imply that Euryptolemus charged Callixenus with having submitted as a motion of the Council something concocted by himself? The fact that we are told at 1.7.14 that some prytaneis refused to put the motion to a vote suggests that this may indeed have been the case and may have been at least one factor in a possible charge against Callixenus. The fact that Callixenus's motion is introduced at sec. 9 with the words εἰς ἣν ἡ βουλὴ εἰσήνεγκε τὴν ἑαυτῆς γνώμην Καλλιξένου εἰπόντος τήνδε is no argument against the possibility that Euryptolemus and his friends challenged the motion as παράνομα in the belief that it did not represent the γνώμη of the majority of the councilors but was entirely manufactured by Callixenus; note Xenophon's words at *Hell.* 1.7.12: παράνομα φάσκοντες συγγεγραφέναι.

125 Xen. *Hell.* 1.7.5, οὐ γὰρ προυτέθη σφίσι λόγος κατὰ τὸν νόμον, and 25, ἀκρίτους παρὰ τὸν νόμον.

126 Wolff, "Normenkontrolle" 49–50.

127 Thuc. 8.67.2; Arist. *Ath.Pol.* 29.4

without its elimination the thoroughgoing constitutional reform envisaged by the decree of Pythodorus would have been impossible to enact. Wolff's conclusions also contribute to an understanding of the adverb in three passages in Lysias. In the latest of these, the reading and context are equally problematic. That the speech *On the Confiscation of the Property of Nicias's Brother* is spoken in a case of *apographē* by the defense and not by the prosecution is now generally agreed.[128] For that reason the speaker's complaint, that this constitutes the second attempt at confiscating his paternal estate, cannot have contained the phrase παρανόμων φεύγοντος τοῦ αὐτοῦ ἀνδρός, which is found in the manuscripts, and the emendation παρανόμως, first proposed by Reiske,[129] seems inevitable. For surely, τοῦ αὐτοῦ ἀνδρός can in the context refer only to the speaker and his late father, Eucrates, whose property is involved, and the suit against him is not a *graphē paranomōn*. Blass believed that the statute violated is the law against double jeopardy, the text of which is preserved in Demosthenes;[130] but since Lysias's text seems to apply the term παρανόμως not only to the present suit but to both, and since the speaker bases his plea less on specific statutes than on the services rendered by Nicias and his brothers to the democracy (18.1–12) and on hints that his conviction would violate the amnesty decree,[131] it seems preferable to interpret the adverb as signifying a violation of the social and political order as a whole.

The remaining two passages come from the speech *Against Eratosthenes*. In the first of these, Eratosthenes' position as one of the five *ephoroi* allegedly appointed by the oligarchical clubs after the defeat of Aegospotami is called παρανόμως ἄρχειν (12.48; cf. 43–44); in the second, Lysias appeals to the judges that, even if they were to exact a penalty παρανόμως from Eratosthenes and his associates instead of judging them κατὰ νόμον, the penalty would not be commensurate with the crimes they committed against the city (ibid. 82). That Eratosthenes' position was a violation of the Athenian legal and political system as a whole rather than of a specific statute goes without saying, for his appointment was to an office not provided for

128 Blass, *AB*² 1.525–26; Gernet-Bizos, *Lysias* 2² 26–27; and K. J. Dover, *Lysias and the Corpus Lysiacum* (Berkeley and Los Angeles, 1968) 5 and 7.
129 Lys. 18.14 (Budé text); cf. also Lipsius, *ARRV* 116 n. 253; παρὰ νόμον, proposed by Taylor, is another possible emendation.
130 Blass, *AB*² 1.526 with n. 1, citing Dem. 24.54, 20.147, and 18.224.
131 Lys. 18.15 with Gernet-Bizos, *Lysias* 2² 33 n. 2.

by the (unwritten) constitution and was made by *hetairoi* and not by a properly and legally constituted electorate. Similarly, in the second passage the violation of the legal system as a whole is at issue, for in the context παρανόμως is antithetical to the legal procedure (κατὰ τὸν νόμον) to which Eratosthenes is being subjected—in contrast to his own slaughter of innocent people without due process (ἀκρίτους)—so that it must be the Athenian legal system as such, with whatever provisions for due process its constituent laws might have, that would be bypassed if Eratosthenes' punishment were not to be determined in duly constituted court proceedings.

SUMMARY AND CONCLUSIONS

We set out to show in this chapter how the political changes that brought popular sovereignty to Athens in the fifth century went hand in hand with changes in social attitudes and values. The path chosen to demonstrate this relationship has involved us in so much detailed philological discussion and analysis that it is now time to take stock of the general conclusions that have emerged.

In the belief that *nomos*, its cognates, and its compounds constitute the most characteristically Greek nexus of concepts of social norms, we chose it as the most sensitive barometer from which changes in Athenian social thought can be read. We noted that archaic, pre-Cleisthenic *nomos* states a timeless, unchangeable pattern observable in religious usages, in the daily activities that people perform, and in the norms that determine or ought to determine their way of life. People such as Hesiod's brother may have strayed away from the pattern, but the pattern itself is taken for granted and is never questioned. It is not only a standard but *the* standard accepted for all social behavior; the question how it can or cannot be enforced does not arise, because the possibility that alternative standards may exist is not envisaged.

However easily *nomos* may have lent itself to being applied to the norms of political life, its adoption as the official term for "statute" in the course or in the wake of the reforms of Cleisthenes brought with it dramatic and far-reaching changes over the next decades. The Council and Assembly, through which Cleisthenes had enacted his reforms, were henceforth to be the organs authorized to formulate, ratify, and promulgate the *nomoi* by which Athens was to be governed; *nomos* thus became the instrument in which the people of

Athens asserted their sovereignty over their own legal and political affairs. At the same time, the elements of timelessness and immutability, expressed in archaic times by the fact that only gods were credited with the establishment of *nomoi*, were overshadowed by the idea that human agents now became the authors, formulators, enacters, and enforcers of a *nomos* that could no longer be taken for granted as a perennial pattern of human existence. The determination of what is valid and authoritative in political affairs became the province of man, or, rather, of men, since *nomos* implies also the general acceptance of what has been enacted.

These effects did not stay confined to the sphere of law and politics. The norms of religious and social conduct that *nomos* embodied in the archaic period now take on an increasingly prescriptive color. No longer do they describe common practices, but they lay down rules that are expected to be observed. The same verbs of enactment that are commonly applied to laws are now also found connoting the setting of religious, social, and behavioral precedents and the establishment of customs. Social and religious norms are thus not only given a beginning in time, that is, they are not only removed from the category of the timeless and immutable, but they are also infused with a human sanction analogous to the popular authority that sanctions the enactment of statutes.[132] *Nomos* when used without a modifier carried with it the notion of popular authority in the second half of the fifth century; this is driven home by a few passages in which the adjective ἄγραφος (unwritten) is attached to those prescriptive norms to which a speaker attributes a value superior to that of the political and legal *nomoi* of the state.[133] In short, *nomos* tends to assume after the Cleisthenean reforms the connotation of a prescriptive norm, enforceable when passed by Council and Assembly and contributing a social pressure to regulate religious, social, and personal conduct in conformity with what was taken to be the consensus of the sovereign people.

As *nomos* thus came to be progressively more closely associated with prescriptive norms, other ways had to be devised to express the descriptive aspect of archaic *nomos*. It is significant that for this purpose no attempt seems to have been made to coin new concepts from different roots but that ways were found to adapt the stem νεμ- to the new needs. The adjective *nomimos*, which is not attested

132   See above, pp. 90–92.
133   Soph. *Ant.* 453–57; Thuc. 2.37.3; [Lys.] 6.10; on the point of political authority, cf. also the law in Andoc. 1.85 and 87.

before the fifth century B.C., seems to have been used in Athens from at least 467 B.C. to express in its neuter singular forms particular religious, social, and behavioral practices; its plural *nomima* was employed either to treat these practices collectively or to describe a general principle underlying them.[134] An alternative device was to use various forms of the verb *nomizō* in describing social and religious norms. From this we may infer, first, that in the course of the fifth century *nomimos* came increasingly to take over the connotation of practices and specific acts for which *nomos* had done service in the archaic period, evidently in direct proportion and response to the prevailing identification of *nomos* with prescriptive norms. This is corroborated by the second observation, namely, that those prescriptive norms or principles underlying specific acts that are called *nomima* are found only in religious, social and behavioral contexts, never in matters of law and politics. In other words, in *nomima*, *nomizomena*, and similar expressions we find another way of differentiating rules of conduct from those *nomoi* enacted by the state, especially in contexts in which it was important to distinguish legal and political from other norms. Expressed in Hart's terms, as *nomos* was increasingly attached to secondary rules of obligation, *nomimos* and *nomizō* were pressed into service to describe the primary rules that had formerly also been expressed by *nomos*. At the same time, however, the retention of the νεμ- stem attests the close relationship felt to prevail between political, social, and religious rules.

This development is primarily true of Athens, and in Athens first and foremost of current and official usage. There is strong evidence that *nomos* not only assumed predominantly prescriptive overtones but further, developed more and more toward the exclusive meaning of "statute." Again, this process is more easily perceivable in those authors whose works reflect current usage than in the elevated language of the tragedians. Still, even the tragedians from Aeschylus to Euripides apply νόμος with increasing frequency to legal and political ordinances, statutes, and regulations. The earliest surviving use of νόμος as "statute" is in Aeschylus;[135] Sophocles has νόμος six

---

134   The earliest use of νόμιμα in Athens occurs in Aesch. *Sept.* 334 (467 B.C.), where it describes the wedding ritual; outside Athens its first appearance is earlier and in a legal sense in the founding instrument of Naupactus by the East Locrians, which ML, no. 20, date between 500 and 475 B.C.

135   Aesch. *Supp.* 387-91, of 464/3 B.C., with Ostwald, *Nomos* 43, 44, 58-59, and 120. So also in *PV* 149-50, 402-3.

times in the legal-political sense, mostly referring to Creon's edict in the *Antigone*;[136] and Euripides has it in eighteen passages (scattered over ten plays), in fifteen of which it occurs with implicit and in three with explicit reference to written enactments.[137] These figures may not be impressive in their relation to other uses of νόμος by the three tragedians,[138] but they do assume significance when we compare them to the twenty passages, out of a total of fifty-two, in which νόμος means "statute" in Aristophanes; all of these refer to or assume a background of written legislation,[139] to say nothing of at least eight other passages that treat other kinds of *nomoi* as if they were enactable statutes.[140] Moreover, the earliest extant Attic prose writer uses νόμος exclusively in the sense "statute,"[141] and Thucydides applies the term only to rules, never to practices, and uses it in a legal or political sense in at least twenty-two passages.[142] In fifth-century Attic inscriptions νόμος is rare, but when it appears it almost invariably carries the sense "statute";[143] the same is true of all the uses of νόμος in the orator Antiphon, and the meaning "statute" seems to underlie all its uses in the sophist Antiphon;[144] with rare exceptions it has this sense exclusively in the preserved writings of Andocides[145] and of Lysias.[146]

136   Soph. *Ant.* 382, 449, 481, 847; *Aj.* 1247; and *OC* 548.

137   Implicit in Eur. *Heracl.* 141, 963; *Andr.* 176; *Hec.* 291; *HF* 1322; *El.* 1268–69; *IT* 3ε, 277, 586, 970, 1189; *Ion* 1250–56; *Or.* 941; *Cyc.* 338; and fr. 597. Explicitly written in *Hec.* 864–67; *Supp.* 433; and *Ion* 442.

138   I count altogether 20 occurrences of νόμος in Aeschylus, 37 in Sophocles, and 101 in Euripides.

139   Ar. *Ach.* 532; *Nub.* 1185; *Vesp.* 467; *Av.* 1038–39, 1346, 1353–54, 1650, 1655–56, 1660; *Thesm.* 361–62; *Ran.* 761–64; *Eccl.* 759, 762, 944, 1022, 1041, 1049, 1056, 1077; and *Plut.* 914.

140   See above, pp. 90–92.

141   [Xen.] *Ath.Pol.* 1.9, 10, 18; and 3.2.

142   Thuc. 1.77.1; 2.35.1, 37.1 and 3, 39.4, 53.4; 3.37.3, 45.3 and 7, 46.4, 70.5 and 6; 4.38.1, 133.3; 5.49.1, 63.4, 66.2–3; 6.14, 38.5, 54.6; 8.53.2, 76.6.

143   The relevant documents are discussed in Ostwald, *Nomos* 34 n. 1, 41–42, 50–51; cf. also 44–46 and 167–70, esp. 168 n. 2, for the influence of Athenian usage on the empire. I modify my statement with an "almost" only because there is more probability than certainty that the νόμοι in the Samian decree (ML, no. 94.15) and the Colophonian νόμος (*IG* I³ 37.43) existed in statutory form.

144   For the orator Antiphon, see the 70 passages cited in F. L. van Cleef, *Index Antiphonteus*, Cornell Studies in Classical Philology 5 (Ithaca, N.Y., 1895); for the sophist, see 87B44 A1.18–19, 24, 28–29; 3.22; 4.3–4; 5.29–30; 6.2–3, 7 DK⁶.

145   Of the 76 passages cited in L. L. Forman's *Index Andocideus Lycurgeus Dinarcheus* (Oxford, 1897) only the νόμος of the Kerykes, mentioned at 1.127, does not seem to apply to the state as a whole.

146   The only exceptions among the 130 passages cited in D. H. Holmes, *Index*

Moreover, concomitant with this development, a change is observable in the meaning of *nomimos*. Its use in the late fifth century is no longer confined to religious, social, and behavioral matters, but it also becomes the adjectival representative of νόμος in the sense "statute": it describes persons or acts that "conform to the laws." This sense, which *nomimos* retains as its primary connotation throughout the fourth century, is attested for the first time no earlier than 432 B.C.[147] and predominates in the speeches of Antiphon, Andocides, and Lysias, more commonly describing acts and attitudes than a personal quality. The tone of moral approval inherent in *nomimos* in its nonlegal senses, where it was often conjoined with expressions of just, reverent, self-controlled, and wise conduct,[148] carried over also into its association with the statutes.[149] That a person who is law-abiding or whose conduct conforms to the statutes is commended is not surprising; but it means that the laws established by the sovereign people contributed to setting a moral standard for society: conformity with and obedience to the enactments of Council and Assembly tend to become the marks not merely of the good citizen but also of the good person. The sovereign people sets the norms not only for political but also for moral conduct.

What is true of *nomimos* applies even more strongly to *ennomos*. Here the dividing line between legal and nonlegal connotations, that is, between secondary and primary obligations, coincides with the use of the term in prose and poetry, respectively. Fifth-century poetry, in which ἔννομος appears earlier than it does in prose, uses it exclusively in nonlegal contexts to describe adherence to the source of norms, to a way of life, or to the norms of religion[150] and to give moral approbation to adherence to a religious or moral code of

---

Lysiacus (Bonn, 1895), are the Ἑλληνικὸς (πάτριος) νόμος prescribing the burial and mourning of those fallen in battle at 2.9 and 81 and the ἄγραφοι <νόμοι> καθ' οὓς Εὐμολπίδαι ἐξηγοῦνται at [6].10.

147 In Archidamus's speech at Thuc. 1.85.2 (cf. n. 75 above), delivered in 432 B.C., if for the sake of argument we assume that Thucydides either reports the *ipsissima verba* of Archidamus or recorded them soon after they were spoken; cf. Gomme, *HCT* 1.252–55.

148 See above, pp. 99–100 with nn. 51–56.

149 The most signal example of this is Socrates' equation of τὸ νόμιμον with τὸ δίκαιον reported in Xen. *Mem.* 4.4.12–25 and 6.5–6.

150 Aesch. *Cho.* 483–85; cf. also Pind. *Pyth.* 9.56–58, *Ol.* 7.84, *Paean* 6.181–83 (?).

conduct.[151] In fifth-century prose, on the other hand, its dependence on νόμος in the sense "statute" is evident from the beginning: ἔννομος never has a meaning other than that of conforming to statutes or treaties, a sure indication that it entered into current usage at a time when the legal-political use of *nomos* had become dominant. It cannot be mere coincidence that this sense is first found in Thucydides, the same author whose writings also attest the earliest use of νόμιμος as an adjectival representative of νόμος meaning "statute." In relations between states it designates abiding by the terms of a treaty (Thuc. 3.67.5, 4.60.1), and within a city-state it means adherence to specific legal stipulations (6.38.5; cf. Lys. 9.12). One passage in Lysias (30.35) stands out because the law observed is not a specific statute but the whole body of Athenian law. In this respect *ennomos* is the exact opposite of the legal-political sense that *paranomos* begins to assume toward the end of the fifth century, especially when *paranomos* identifies one of the politically most potent *graphai* of the Athenian law code. But *ennomos*, unlike *paranomos*, never strays in its use in prose from the narrowly legal sense of *nomos*; like *nomimos* it carries the overtones of moral commendation that it has in poetry,[152] suggesting again that conformity with the political will of the people was a strong formative influence on the moral norms of the Athenian democracy in the last quarter of the fifth century.

The same conclusion emerges even more powerfully from our study of *paranomos*, a term that signifies lack of conformity with norms of every sort, even when these are conceived of as including the statutes enacted by the state. The fact that *paranomos*, unlike *ennomos*, has a verbal and two nominal forms in addition to adjective and adverb makes it capable of differentiating acts that violate a norm from character traits more precisely than *ennomos* can. Both the personal quality of παρανομία and the παράνομα perpetrated by a person possessing this quality are usually accompanied by an enumeration of specifics. However, these specifics are more frequently infringements of a general *nomos* than of its specific stipulations. In Thucydides, Euripides, and Lysias, adjective, noun, and verb describe transgressions of the code of religious conduct taken as a whole;[153] the moral code is violated by παράνομα or παρανόμως in

---

151 Aesch. *Supp.* 383–84; Eur. *Phoen.* 1651; Soph. *OT* 322–23.
152 See above, pp. 109–11.
153 Thuc. 2.17.2, 4.98.6, and 5.16.1; Eur. *Bacch.* 997; Lys. fr. 89 Thalheim.

Euripides, Thucydides, Aristophanes, and Lysias;[154] and παράνομοι offend by their παρανομία the social sensibilities of their fellow citizens.[155]

Moral overtones remain even when the παρανομ- stem first appears in a legal-political sense in Thucydides. In relations between states it expresses not merely the breach of specific terms of a specific treaty, but, as we saw in the speech of the Thebans against the Plataeans, it also has moral and religious overtones, expressing disapproval of transgressions of a *nomos* valid for all Greeks (Thuc. 3.65–66, 67.6). These overtones are not entirely absent even when Thucydides (7.18.2–3) uses παρανόμημα to describe the breach of the arbitration clause of the Thirty Years' Peace by the Peloponnesian League and the violation of a similar clause in the Peace of Nicias by the Athenians, inasmuch as the Spartans regarded their own subsequent misfortunes as a (divine?) punishment for their own offense and expected the Athenians to suffer similar consequences for theirs. Similarly, in internal affairs, even violations of no more than a specific statute[156] affect also the moral code as such ([Andoc.] 4.21), and the violation is certainly treated as moral when it is against the political and legal system of the state as a whole.[157]

The date at which such offenses against the legal and political system and the institutions and statutes embodying it first became actionable through the *graphē paranomōn* is not known.[158] The earliest datable evidence is Leogoras's case against Speusippus in 415 B.C.,[159] and the fact that about the same time Antiphon made an extensive use of the institution in his speech *On the Murder of Herodes*, but without lodging or threatening to lodge a formal *graphē*

154 Eur. *Med*. 1121; Thuc. 8.108.4–5; Ar. *Thesm*. 684, *Plut*. 415, 967; Lys. 3.37, 9.17–18, 26.5.

155 See especially the passages on the conduct of Alcibiades, Pausanias, and others cited on pp. 116–18 above.

156 Thuc. 4.132.3; Ar. fr. 387.10; Andoc. 1.8; Lys. 22.13 and 17, 26.7.

157 Thuc. 2.37.3, 3.82.6; Lys. 7.27, 30.6.

158 The dates suggested range from Solon (Wilamowitz, *Aristoteles* 2.193–94) to the revision of the laws of 403/2 B.C. (U. Kahrstedt, "Untersuchungen zu athenischen Behörden," *Klio* 31 [1938] 21–25), with the majority of scholarly guesses favoring the reforms of Ephialtes (bibliography in E. Gerner, "Παρανόμων γραφή," *RE* 18. Band [1949] 1281, and in Wolff, "Normenkontrolle" 18 n. 33).

159 Andoc. 1.17 and 22. Wolff "Normenkontrolle" 15–16, reluctantly rejects C. F. Smith's suggestion (*Thucydides* 2 [London and Cambridge, Mass., 1930] 75 n. 1) that Diodotus alludes to the γραφὴ παρανόμων in Thuc. 3.43.4–5; cf. also Gomme's commentary *ad loc*. that the action "is doubtful at this date."

paranomōn, supports the view that this procedure had by 415 B.C. been so recently instituted that its full legal possibilities were as yet unexplored.[160] Through its institution strong social or political disapproval of a specific enactment could be translated into a kind of legal action; this was to prove a potent political weapon in the fourth century. The *nomos*, however, whose transgression it sought to punish was not necessarily one specific statute but statutes or institutions that were thought to embody a general consensus of values and that found their first political expression in the adoption of *nomos* as the new official term for "statute" in Cleisthenes' reforms. It is true that the *graphē paranomōn* could in the fourth century be lodged only against legislative proposals[161] and not against private acts committed by individuals that were believed to violate the established order; still, the *nomos* that the *graphē paranomōn* envisaged is the same as that embodied in the nontechnical uses of *nomos*, which encompasses not only specific statutes but the entire social order, including its religious, moral, and political norms. By protecting these norms, the *graphē paranomōn* gave a statutory guarantee for their inviolability; it could invoke a positive legal *nomos* against violations of *nomos* in a broader sense. The control over social as well as political norms was firmly placed into the hands of the sovereign people, acting, but acting under the law, through Council, Assembly, and the jury courts.

160   MacDowell's note on Andoc. 1.17, cited with approval by Wolff, "*Normenkontrolle*" 22 n. 48.

161   I use this vague term to cover both new ψηφίσματα and new νόμοι, although, as Wolff, "*Normenkontrolle*" 45–60, has shown, we have evidence of its use only against proposed ψηφίσματα. Cf. the list of all the known cases in Hansen, *PAUP* 28–43.

CHAPTER THREE

Popular Sovereignty and the Control
of Religion

RELIGION was for the Greeks not a matter of individual conscience but was of vital concern to the community. It was free from
dogma, and a concept of "faith" was alien to it. Before the sophists,
there was no belief in the gods in the Christian sense of the term:
θεοὺς νομίζειν describes the performance of ritual acts, predicated on
the unchallenged assumption that the gods exist and demand
veneration.[1] The knowledge of how the gods were to be worshiped
was in the hands of priests and priestesses who did not constitute a
separate caste as they did in many Near Eastern societies but held
their positions by virtue of having been born into noble families that
had hereditary control of the most important priesthoods, usually
from time immemorial. The state never interfered in their handling
of cultic and ritual matters; but since the gods were regarded as the
guarantors of the stability of the social order, and since their displea-
sure would disturb it, the state through its customs, laws and secular
institutions tried to enforce and protect divine worship to ensure that
the public interest would suffer no harm by neglecting the gods.
That the nature of state regulation of religion underwent a change
concomitant with the decline of aristocratic control and the rise of
popular power goes without saying.[2]

In the preceding chapter, in our discussion of how the political
changes due to Cleisthenes' reforms affected Athenian social think-

1   Fahr, ΘΕΟΥΣ ΝΟΜΙΖΕΙΝ 153–68.
2   The standard discussion of this problem is D. D. Feaver, "Historical Development in the Priesthoods of Athens," *YClS* 15 (1957) 123–58.

ing, we noted that they had an impact also on religious attitudes. Like social customs, religious rites began to be thought of as having had an identifiable beginning in historical time; as in the case of social conduct, linguistic distinctions were made between descriptive practice and prescriptive norm, and devices were found to differentiate legal-political from religious norms and practices. We shall now turn from formal to more substantive consequences of the political development of popular sovereignty on the administration of Athenian religious life.

Cleisthenes' reforms neither affected the control of religious cults traditionally left to noble families (*genē*) and phratries to administer nor changed these families' tenure of the priesthoods "in the ancestral way."[3] His grouping of demes into trittyes had, to be sure, eliminated or at least reduced what political power noble families had been able to exercise through their control of local cults;[4] but the reforms neither spelled the removal of noble families from their priesthoods and cults nor put an end to the use of cult control for political ends. Religion had always been one of the state's concerns in Athens, just as it was in all other Greek cities. At least since Solon the state published calendars of sacrifices, revising which was still part of Nicomachus's duties at the end of the fifth century (Lys. 30.17–20). Presumably from pre-Solonian times on, a state official, the archon basileus, was entrusted with administering cults and religious festivals in which the state had an interest, though their ritual conduct was left to gentilician priests (Arist. *Ath.Pol.* 57.1); other cults and festivals were part of the responsibilities of the eponymous archon (ibid. 56.3–5). Probably from the earliest times on, disputes among *genē* or priests about priesthoods and their perquisites were adjudicated by the archon basileus (ibid. 57.2); and it is likely, though we lack concrete evidence, that the state had always given some financial support to certain religious functions[5] and had taken a hand in defining the duties of some cult officials, such as those of the

---

3   Arist. *Ath.Pol.* 21.6: τὰ δὲ γένη καὶ τὰς φρατρίας καὶ τὰς ἱερωσύνας εἴασεν ἔχειν ἑκάστους κατὰ τὰ πάτρια. For a convenient list of the foremost cults administered by the *genē*, see Nilsson, *Geschichte* 1³ 709.

4   D. Lewis, "Cleisthenes" 30–39.

5   According to the *Antattikistes* (86.20 Bekker), Solon's *axones* spoke of the Genesia as a ἑορτὴ δημοτελής, which, if true, is the earliest testimony for such expenditure. On the development of the Genesia, see F. Jacoby, "Γενέσια: A Forgotten Festival of the Dead," *CQ* 38 (1944) 65–75, and H. W. Parke, *Festivals of the Athenians* (London, 1977) 53–54. For the meaning of δημοτελής, see *Lexeis Rhetoricae* 240.28 Bekker.

Eumolpids and Kerykes for the cult of Demeter at Eleusis.[6] So it is not surprising that Cleisthenes established new religious cults to give cohesion to the newly created political groupings of the state.[7] What is noteworthy, however, is that these new priesthoods were not filled by the nobility but were open to all Athenians and that thereafter priests for all new cults were chosen by lot, usually for a limited term, from among all Athenians.[8]

In addition, there are indications that in the decades following the reforms of Cleisthenes the state injected itself in unprecedented ways into cults controlled by the *genē*. The evidence is hard to interpret because we know so little about the extent of state control over gentilician cults before Cleisthenes. The inscriptions on which our knowledge depends for the fifth century are often fragmentary and only rarely provide a clue whether a given regulation replaces an earlier measure or introduces controls where none had existed before. Within the decade after Cleisthenes' reforms, we have a decree of Council and Assembly (*IG* I³ 5) specifying the preliminary sacrifices to be offered by *hieropoioi* of the Eleusinia at the Eleusinion to Gē, to Hermes, to the Graces, to Poseidon, to Artemis, to Telesidromus, to Triptolemus, to Pluto, to Dolichus, and to the Two Goddesses. As early as 485/4 B.C. we find the state imposing a fine of one hundred drachmas on the priestesses on the Acropolis and their attendants if they make a storehouse on the Acropolis or bake for themselves in the oven (?) and the same fine on the treasurers if they fail to enforce this regulation.[9] A number of decrees from the 460s and 450s indicate state interference in the Eleusinian Mysteries. The earliest of these permits the Athenians to begin to expend the sacred funds of the Eleusinian goddesses for an indefinite period, just as they expend the funds of Athena on the Acropolis. This decree entrusts

---

6 For the evidence, see Nilsson, *Geschichte* 1³ 663–67.

7 For deme cults, see J. D. Mikalson, "Religion in the Attic Demes," *AJP* 98 (1977) 424–35; a trittys cult (possibly of a Cleisthenic trittys) is attested by *IG* I³ 255, of ca. 430 B.C.; see F. Sokolowski, *Lois sacrées des cités grecques*, École française d'Athènes, Travaux et mémoires, 18 (Paris, 1969) no. 11; and for tribal cults, see U. Kron, *Die zehn attischen Phylenheroen*, Mitteilungen des Deutschen archäologischen Instituts, Athenische Abteilung, Beiheft 5 (Berlin, 1976).

8 See Feaver, "Development" 136–37. The best-known example is probably the appointment of a priestess of Athena Nike by lot from among all Athenian women ca. 448 B.C.; see *IG* I³ 35.2–6 (= ML, no. 44).

9 *IG* I³ 4B. 13–17: [τὰς] ἱερέα[ς] τὰς ἐμ πόλει · καὶ τ|ὰς ζακόρος [μὲ ἑ χεν οἴ]κεμα ταμιεῖον · ἐμ πόλει · μ|εδὲ hιπνε[ύεσθαι· ἐὰν δέ τις τ]ούτον τι δρᾶι · εὐθύ|νε[σθαι hεκατὸν] · δραχμέ[σι καὶ] τὸς ταμίας · ἐὰν ἐ ό|σ[ι εὐθύνεσθαι] hεκατὸν δραχμέ[σι.

the administration of the funds to presumably publicly appointed ἱεροποιοί, who receive a daily payment of one-half obol from each initiate for their services (*IG* I³ 6C.6–14). Further, the Kerykes and Eumolpids are ordered to conduct initiations individually; if they initiate in groups a fine of one thousand drachmas is to be imposed on them (ibid. 26–31). More remarkable still is a decree moved from the floor of the Assembly about 449–447 B.C. that created a new board of state overseers with financial powers to be exercised in the Eleusinian sanctuary itself. These new *epistatai* are to "be in charge of the monies of the Two Goddesses in the same way as those in charge of the works on the Acropolis were to oversee the temple and the statue; they cannot decline the office on oath; those chosen are to approach the Council if they discover any debts owed to the Two Goddessess, to give information and to exact payment; their term of office shall be one year, the oath of office to be sworn between the two altars at Eleusis, and men are to be chosen every year on the same terms; they are also to be in charge of the yearly offerings received by the Two Goddesses and are to retrieve any loss of which they are informed."[10] The Praxiergidai decree, with which we shall deal in detail below, also survives from this period;[11] a little later, the state legislated the appointment of a priestess and the constuction of a temple of Athena Nike;[12] and about 422 B.C. it regulated the offering of first fruits at Eleusis.[13]

These are a few examples of state interference in religious affairs during the fifth century B.C. The state intervenes mainly in fiscal matters and prescribes some of the more secular duties and perquisites of various religious functionaries. No attempt is made to meddle in ritual, although some regulations may have affected the conduct of religious rites. Yet all these decrees show that the secular and political authority of the people now regulates administrative aspects of the religious life of the state.

We cannot extrapolate from this disparate epigraphical evidence a secular encroachment on religion. But scattered literary references indicate that the state's increasing interference bred conflicts and tensions. Situations arose in the fifth century in which the state's

10   *IG* I³ 32.10–22. The attempt of H. B. Mattingly, "Athens and Eleusis: Some New Ideas," in ΦΟΡΟΣ: *Tribute to B. D. Meritt* (Locust Valley, N.Y., 1974) 97–101, to date this decree in 426/5 B.C. does not affect the point made here.

11   *IG* I³ 7, as discussed below, pp. 145–48.

12   See n. 8 above.

13   *IG* I³ 78 (= ML, no. 73).

legitimate claims clashed with the equally legitimate prerogatives of religious organs that remained the preserve of old noble families. Here, too, the evidence cannot support a coherent development; but it does give us four vignettes, one from the time shortly before Ephialtes' reforms, two from the two decades thereafter, and one from the end of the fifth century, in which we can with some confidence identify stages of a secular, democratic encroachment on gentilician cultic authority. To them we shall now turn.

AESCHYLUS'S *SUPPLICES*: THE STATE PROTECTS RELIGION

One of the central themes of Aeschylus's *Supplices* is the clash between the right of sanctuary (*asylia*), based on a religious appeal to kinship, and the secular interest of the state, which is likely to be involved in war if it grants asylum. It is as difficult in this play as in any other Greek tragedy to ascertain what historical realities the tragic conflict may embody,[14] but it is surely safe to assume that its issues reflect concerns close to the Athenian audience of 464/3 B.C., when the play won first prize at its first performance.[15] Even the

14 The most recent discussions of the *Supplices* have concentrated more on the external relations of Athens and Argos (particularly on the presence of Themistocles in Argos about the time of the first production of the play) than on internal developments in Athens itself. The relevant contributions are thoroughly discussed by A. F. Garvie, *Aeschylus' Supplices: Play and Trilogy* (Cambridge, 1969) 141–62, who concludes that there is no reliable internal evidence, political or nonpolitical, for dating the play. A connection of the play with the flight of Themistocles and Athenian-Argive relations is posited, not always convincingly, by A. J. Podlecki, *The Political Background of Aeschylean Tragedy* (Ann Arbor, Mich., 1966) 42–62, esp. 52–60, on the basis of W. G. Forrest, "Themistokles and Argos," *CQ*, n.s., 10 (1960) 221–41; see the skeptical comments of Lenardon, *Saga* 38–39, and of J. L. O'Neil, "The Exile of Themistokles and Democracy in the Peloponnese," *CQ*, n.s., 31 (1981) 335–46, esp. 342.

15 The date is attested by the external evidence of *POxy.* 2256.3. It has been unconvincingly contested by F. Stoessl, *Die Hiketiden des Aischylos als geistesgeschichtliches und theatergeschichtliches Phänomen*," Sber. d. Österr. Ak. d. Wiss., Philos.-hist. Kl. 356 (Vienna, 1979), esp. 7–25, who argues for 475 or 474 B.C. as the date of the original performance. The much-disputed question whether it is the Athenian or Argive constitution that forms the background of the *Supplices* (see U. von Wilamowitz-Moellendorff, *Aischylos Interpretationen* [Berlin, 1914] 11; A. Diamantopoulos, "The Danaid Tetralogy of Aeschylus," *JHS* 77 [1957] 220–29, esp. 223–24; Podlecki, *Political Background* 49–50) is therefore irrelevant for our purposes, especially since the dependence of the Argive democracy upon the Athenian model in the *Supplices* has been shown by C. Gülke, *Mythos und Zeitgeschichte bei Aischylos*, Beiträge zur klassischen Philologie, ed. R. Merkelbach, Heft 31 (Meisenheim am Glan, 1969) 65, 67–70.

figure of the Argive ruler, Pelasgus, whose presence the exigencies of the myth demand,[16] is far from impairing the democratic process at the core of the play.[17] Rather, Pelasgus glorifies democracy: his insistence on consulting the people (365–69, 397–401, 483–88, 517–19) counters the Danaids' belief that the king alone must decide on their asylum (370–75), and the people as a whole make the final decision to accept the suppliants in full awareness of the possible dire consequences for the state (600–624).

Aeschylus takes great pains to define the legal issues inherent in the situation.[18] At the opening of the play the Danaids describe their exile as voluntary and not as the result of legal or political action against them in their native Egypt: they have incurred no blood guilt in avoiding an undesired marriage.[19] Why they are averse to marriage—whether out of a reluctance to marry their cousins or out of a general dislike of wedlock—is not mentioned in the play and is, therefore, not germane to the problem of their supplication.[20] The decisive points in their plea for asylum at Argos are their refusal to be forced into marriage against their will[21] and their descent from Io, through whom they are tied to Argos by bonds of kinship. The latter, they believe, obliges Argos to grant them asylum (274–324), and Pelasgus recognizes the justice of their claim (325–26).

Yet acknowledging the right to asylum is not tantamount to granting asylum, especially since such a grant may involve Argos in a war against the sons of Aegyptus (341–42). Before submitting this weighty issue to the popular assembly for a decision, the king wants

16   On this point, see P. Burian, "Pelasgus and Politics in Aeschylus' Danaid Trilogy," WS, n.s., 8 (1974) 5–14.

17   The absence of any constitutional conflict in the Supplices and its emphasis on democratic procedures has been seen most clearly by V. Ehrenberg, "Origins of Democracy," Hist. 1 (1950) 515–48, esp. 517–24.

18   The following is much indebted to the sensitive analysis of the legal issues by B. Daube, Zu den Rechtsproblemen in Aischylos' Agamemnon (Zurich and Leipzig, 1938) 74–87.

19   Aesch. Supp. 6–10: οὔτιν' ἐφ' αἵματι δημηλασίαν / ψήφῳ πόλεως γνωσθεῖσαι, / ἀλλ' αὐτογενῆ φυξανορίαν, / γάμον Αἰγύπτου παίδων ἀσεβῆ τ' / ὀνοταζόμεναι. For the meaning of αὐτογενής see Daube, Rechtsprobleme 78 with n. 33.

20   See S. Ireland, "The Problem of Motivation in the Supplices of Aeschylus," RhM 117 (1974) 14–29.

21   Aesch. Supp. 37–39: πρίν ποτε λέκτρων ὧν θέμις εἴργει / σφετεριξάμενοι πατραδέλφειαν / τήνδ' ἀεκόντων ἐπιβῆναι, and 227–28: πῶς δ' ἂν γαμῶν ἄκουσαν ἄκοντος πάρα / ἁγνὸς γένοιτ' ἄν; Cf. also the avoidance of βία as a motivation of the popular decree at line 943.

to be convinced of the justice of the Danaids' cause. Their response to his demand sharply defines the opposing principles of the conflict. The Danaids invoke the protector of suppliants, Zeus Hiktaios (i.e., Hikesios), to protect them: τὸν ὑψόθεν σκοπὸν ἐπισκόπει / φύλακα πολυπόνων / βροτῶν οἳ τοῖς πέλας προσήμενοι / δίκας οὐ τυγχάνουσιν ἐννόμου· / μένει τοι Ζηνὸς ἱκταίου κότος / δυσπαράθελκτος παθόντος οἴκτοις.[22] What is significant here is not merely their appeal to the wrath of Zeus Hikesios, which will fall on those who disregard supplication, but the fact that his wrath is said to be provoked by a violation of δίκη ἔννομος. The relation here between Zeus and Dikē (Justice) is as close as the one we find in Hesiod;[23] this is corroborated by the personification in the next strophe (395): to violate δίκη is to offend Zeus. But what is the relevance of the adjective ἔννομος? Even in this context alone it clearly does not refer to adherence to the secular statutes of the state, as its association with δίκη and Zeus shows.[24] It rather seems to describe here those norms of conduct and those religious attitudes that will constrain a neighbor reverently to accept a suppliant at his door.[25] In short, the adjective suggests that to ignore the protection given by Zeus is from a religious point of view an unlawful treatment of justice. Thus the Danaids sidestep Pelasgus's initial question, whether justice was on their side from the beginning (343–44), by diverting the king's attention to a religious view of the justice their present situation demands. They equate a rejection of their plea with an offense against religious law.

Pelasgus, however, in response insists upon observing the secular law of the state. He asks the Danaids to demonstrate that their exile does not violate the *nomoi* of their native Egypt: εἴ τοι κρατοῦσι παῖδες Αἰγύπτου σέθεν / νόμῳ πόλεως, φάσκοντες ἐγγύτατα γένους / εἶναι, τίς ἂν τοῖσδ' ἀντιωθῆναι θέλοι; / δεῖ τοί σε φεύγειν κατὰ νόμους / τοὺς οἴκοθεν, / ὡς οὐκ ἔχουσιν κῦρος οὐδὲν ἀμφὶ σοῦ.[26] His purpose

22 Ibid. 381–86: "Look to him who watches from on high, the protector of much-afflicted mortals, who sit as suppliants at their neighbors' door without obtaining the justice prescribed by the norms: surely the wrath of Zeus Lord of Suppliants awaits them, a wrath that cannot be averted by sufferers' laments."
23 On this relation, see F. Solmsen, *Hesiod and Aeschylus* (Ithaca, N.Y., 1949) 214, and Gagarin, "*Dikē* in the *Works and Days*," 81–94.
24 See above, pp. 109–10.
25 Cf. Soph. *OT* 322–23; Eur. *Phoen.* 1650–51; and the religious overtones in ἐννόμοις at Aesch. *Supp.* 404.
26 Aesch. *Supp.* 387–91: "If the sons of Aegyptus get power over you [by appealing to] the law of the state, asserting that they are your nearest kin, who

in raising the legal issue is clearly to gain assurance that any war the admission of the suppliants might entail will be a just one. Yet the very fact that he raises it means that he envisages the possibility that secular law might override the religious considerations upon which the Danaids base their case.

The Danaids' agitated response shows that Aeschylus intended the two passages quoted above as a statement of the two kinds of law that have come into conflict. The suppliants have no patience with the ˙king's legal niceties but merely implore him to take Dikē as his ally and judge the issue on the basis of reverence for the gods (392–96); by reminding him that Zeus assigns ἄδικα μὲν κακοῖς, ὅσια δ' ἐννόμοις (404), they attach a higher value to obedience to religious law than to obedience to the laws of the state. The dilemma Pelasgus and the state of Argos face is thus stated unequivocally. Pelasgus feels that he does not have the right to resolve the issue by himself and refers the decision to the people as a whole, especially since a decision in the Danaids' favor might involve the state in war (357–58).[27]

The issue of war and peace links the *Supplices* firmly to the

---

would be willing to resist them? Surely you must plead in your defense in accordance with the laws of your native land that they have no authority over you." The substantive issue underlying this question remains somewhat obscure. As far as we know from Athenian law of the fourth century, a father had sole and absolute authority over his daughter, and he exercised this authority until he gave her personally or by will in marriage to a husband, to whom then the authority would pass. To the evidence cited in Ostwald, *Nomos* 59 with n. 3, add Harrison, *LA* 1.19, 30–32 with 32 n. 1, 74, and 108–11. Under these circumstances it is peculiar that nowhere in the play is Danaus treated as κύριος over his daughters. He is, to be sure, described as the girls' πατὴρ καὶ βούλαρχος καὶ στασίαρχος, who initiated their flight to Argos (11–18), but if he had been their κύριος his refusal to give his daughters in marriage to the sons of Aegyptus would have been decisive; that he refused consent is clearly stated by ἄκοντος in line 227. Evidently, then, Danaus's refusal did not end the matter, and the tenor of the *Supplices* leads to the inference that the flight was necessitated by the violent reaction of the sons of Aegyptus to Danaus's refusal to permit the marriage. If this reasoning is correct, Pelasgus's question about the κῦρος of the sons of Aegyptus over the Danaids as their next of kin according to Egyptian law can refer only to the situation after Danaus's death. However, since Danaus is still alive, it is odd that Pelasgus should raise the question of κῦρος in this form at this juncture.

27 Aesch. *Supp.* 398–99, οὐκ ἄνευ δήμου τάδε / πράξαιμ' ἄν, reiterating thoughts he expressed at 366–69. On the progression of the supplication and its end in the grant of metic status, see J. Gould, "Hiketeia," *JHS* 93 (1973) 74–103, esp. 89–90.

historical realities of the fifth century. The original version of the document of about 410/09 B.C. that, as we saw earlier, affirmed the powers of the δῆμος πληθύων *vis-à-vis* the Council also included the stipulation that no war could be declared or terminated without the approval of the popular Assembly.[28] Pelasgus's referring the decision about the admission of the Danaids to the people of Argos thus conforms closely to Athenian constitutional procedure, even though the immediate issue is not a declaration of war but the resolution of the conflict between the religious law and its secular consequences, including a determination of the suppliants' status under Egyptian law and a risk of war.

The decision of the Argive people, as communicated by Danaus (605–24), to admit the Danaids as legally resident aliens (μετοικεῖν, 609) and to protect them against any attack foreign or domestic (611–12) therefore places the Argives squarely in support of the religious law. According to Danaus's report, their vote was taken under the impact of Pelasgus's reminder that, as the girls had protested to him, failure to admit suppliants would incur for Argos "the mighty wrath of Zeus Hikesios" and afflict the city with a "double pollution of strangers and citizens alike."[29] The secular authority thus resolves the conflict by adopting the demands of religion as its own policy, ratified in the form of a decree.[30] The democratic state has become the protector of religion.

THE PRAXIERGIDAI DECREE: THE *GENOS* SUBMITS TO THE STATE

Despite its fragmentary nature and extensive restorations the Praxiergidai decree (*IG* I³ 7) provides us with considerable information not easily available from any other source on how secular and religious authority were related. For dating the decree the lettering is, unfortunately, the only criterion available, and on its basis we can

28   *IG* I³ 105.35. See above, pp. 33–34 with n. 122.
29   Aesch. *Supp.* 615–20, esp. 616–17, ἱκεσίου Ζηνὸς κότον / μέγαν προφωνῶν, and 618–19, ξενικὸν ἀστικόν θ' ἅμα / λέγων διπλοῦν μίασμα. The latter is well explained by a scholion on the passage: διπλοῦν καθὸ καὶ ξένους ὄντας παρορῶμεν καὶ συγγενεῖς δειχθέντας οὐκ ἐλεοῦμεν.
30   The opening words of Danaus's report, ἔδοξεν 'Αργείοισιν (605), are obviously modeled on the formal opening of Athenian decrees; cf. also line 601: δήμου δέδοκται παντελῆ ψηφίσματα.

say no more than that it was enacted shortly before the middle of the fifth century, probably about 460–450 B.C.[31] The preserved parts of the inscription leave no doubt that it contains a decree duly passed by Council and Assembly (line 1) and to be published on the Acropolis behind the "ancient temple" (lines 5–6). That it contains religious regulations applying to the *genos* of the Praxiergidai is shown in the unrestored parts of the inscription by the phrases τἔς θε<ὦ> κατὰ τὰ πάτρι[α (8), [τά]δε ho 'Απόλλων ἔχρεσεν (10), [Μοί]ραις, Διὶ Μοιρ<α>γέτει, Γ[ἔι (12), and πάτρια Πραχσ[ιεργίδαις (13). We shall, therefore, not go far wrong in assuming that the πάτρια in this inscription refer to traditional norms and usage relative but not necessarily confined to religious matters, ratified in this instance by a popular decree. The fragmentary nature of the text makes it difficult to identify the substance of these *patria*. It is fairly certain that they sanctioned using funds from the treasury of the Goddess to publish this decree (lines 7–9), presumably because it concerned her worship. But we have no way of knowing what the πάτρια Πραχσιεργίδαις were, though they were probably enumerated in lines 13ff., or what was given to whom κατὰ τὰ πάτρια in lines 18–19. The last decipherable κατὰ τὰ πάτρια phrase seems to require the archon to hand over the keys to the closed temple to the Praxiergidai (20–23).[32] Thus duties of state officials in religious matters are the only identifiable acts sanctioned by τὰ πάτρια in this inscription, and probability suggests that some ritual duties, the specifics of which are lost, were confirmed as *patria* for the Praxiergidai.

The preamble of the decree, if correctly restored, gives us some help toward understanding the nature of these *patria*. If the decree

---

31 The most reliable text is that of D. M. Lewis, *IG* I³ 7, whose discussion "Notes on Attic Inscriptions," *BSA* 49 (1954) 17–21, is fundamental. For a different text, with full bibliography, see Sokolowski, *Lois*, no. 15, reproduced in part in *SEG* 25, no. 10. A date in the period 470–450 B.C., accepted by J. M. Paton, ed., *The Erechtheum* (Cambridge, Mass., 1927) 449–50, A. E. Raubitschek, *Dedications from the Athenian Acropolis* (Cambridge, Mass., 1949) 323, and Lewis, seems more reasonable than a date in the second half of the fifth century, accepted by Sokolowski, *Lois*, no. 15. A date in the 420s, advocated by H. B. Mattingly, "The Financial Decrees of Kallias," *Proceedings of the African Classical Associations* 7 (1964) 37, has been rightly rejected by R. Meiggs, "The Dating of Fifth-Century Attic Inscriptions," *JHS* 86 (1966) 86–98, esp. 98 n. 44.

32 Though reserving judgment on Lewis's restorations of lines 20 and 21, as also of 24 and 25, I prefer his reading of line 22 to Sokolowski's κατὰ τὰ πάτρ[ια τὸν ἔναρχο]ν ἄρχοντα, since ἔναρχος is not only redundant but also unattested in Attic usage.

records [τὲν μαντεί|αν τõ θ]εõ καὶ τὰ πρό [τερον αὐτοῖς ἐφσεφισμένα] (3–4), we may conclude that the *patria* of the Praxiergidai of lines 13ff. had been confirmed on an earlier occasion by a vote of Council and Assembly. That the earlier version had ever been published in a written form is unlikely, because the present decree is published at the request of the Praxiergidai (3): if the original decree had already been published, there would have been no need to request publication now.

The first part of the decree, however, containing an oracle of the God, had presumably been neither published nor formulated before its inclusion in the present decree. The oracle quoted is likely to be recent and may have been what prompted the Praxiergidai to request Council and Assembly to publish a comprehensive document ratifying all the religious functions of the *genos* for the cult of Athena. The functions defined by the oracle seem recent from the wording of the first clause as restored by Lewis (10–12): in contrast to the *patria* in the second part of the decree (13ff.), the rules that are to govern the furnishing of a robe to the Goddess and the preliminary sacrifice to the Moirai, Zeus Moiragetēs, and Gē are not sanctioned by ancient traditions but are established as *nomima* on the authority of Apollo's oracle.[33] This suggests that the new regulation is being differentiated from tradition by the adjectival form νόμιμα, used in order to distinguish the religious measure the oracle propounds from the secular legal *nomos-psēphisma* that in the present instance guarantees it.[34]

To sum up: with the help of the restorations proposed by D. M. Lewis, we can assert that the Praxiergidai decree constitutes the democracy's secular legislative ratification of two kinds of religious regulations applying to the functions of the *genos* of the Praxiergidai. There are, in the first place, new regulations called *nomima*, for which the oracle of Apollo is mentioned as the source; and there are, second, the *patria* applicable to the Praxiergidai, which derive their sanction from tradition, but which, it seems, had been confirmed by a secular popular vote on an unspecified earlier occasion. On this earlier occasion, however, the popular decree had not been published in writing, and it may well be, therefore, that the recent oracle

33 I prefer Lewis's reading in line 10, γ[όμιμα Πραχσιεργίδαις], to Sokolowski's ἄ[μεινον Πραχσιεργίδαις].

34 See above, pp. 101–2.

prompted the Praxiergidai to ask secular authority to confirm all their priestly duties in relation to the cult of Athena. Why they should have felt the need to have their religious functions confirmed in this fashion we do not know. Lewis has surmised that the decree constitutes "an implied assertion by the *demos* that even the oldest privileges depend on the will of the people," and this cannot be far from the truth.[35] But it is perhaps useful to carry speculation one step farther. When added to the fact that the new regulations of the present decree derive from an oracle of Apollo and are published at the Praxiergidai's request, the fact that the Council and Assembly had earlier voted to confirm the *patria* of the *genos* suggests that a dispute about their functions had erupted between the *genos* and (we may assume) the state about the nature or extent of their prerogatives. Apparently the oracle was consulted to settle the matter, and the Praxiergidai requested publication so that if any doubt about their prerogatives should arise in the future, the dispute might be settled by reference to a written document. The state complied; but as the last preserved line of the inscription (25) indicates, it also imposed a fine for noncompliance with the new regulation. In short, the *genos* submits at its own request some of its religious prerogatives to the control of the state, and the state insists on enforcing its control even against the *genos*.

SOPHOCLES' *ANTIGONE*: THE FAMILY COLLIDES WITH THE STATE

The conflict between secular and religious law in Sophocles' *Antigone* differs from what we witnessed in Aeschylus's *Supplices* as well as from what we inferred from the Praxiergidai decree. In contrast to the *Supplices*, the positions of the opposing sides in the *Antigone* are already taken, so that the play explores rather than develops them; and whereas in Aeschylus's play the suppliants'

---

35 D. Lewis, "Notes," 19. The substance of the functions guaranteed to the Praxiergidai in this decree is impossible to determine. We know from Plut. *Alc.* 34.1 that the Praxiergidai were in charge of the ritual of the Plynteria festival, which involved the removal, cleansing, and replacement of the robe of the sacred image of Athena; cf. also Xen. *Hell.* 1.4.12. For the details of this festival, see L. Deubner, *Attische Feste* (Berlin, 1932; repr.: Darmstadt, 1969) 17–22; L. Ziehen, "Πλυντήρια," *RE* 21. Band (1951) 1060–65; Parke, *Festivals* 152–55; E. Simon, *Festivals of Attica: An Archaeological Commentary* (Madison, Wis., 1983) 46–48; and for the role of the Praxiergidai in it, J. von Geisau, "Praxiergidai," *RE* 22. Band (1954) 1761. Since this

religious claims of kinship were considered in making the political decision to admit them, in the *Antigone* the comparative disregard of kinship obligations by the state and of political obligations by the family constitutes a large part of the tragic momentum. Moreover, the issue in the *Antigone* is not drawn between the state and a *genos*, as it is in the Praxiergidai decree, but between the state and the family (*oikos*). It concerns not public duties but the private obligation of honoring the dead by according them burial.

Yet despite these differences the *Antigone* may reliably indicate the attitudes toward secular and religious authority in the Athenian democracy more than two decades after the first performance of Aeschylus's *Supplices* and approximately a decade after the Praxiergidai decree.[36] The conflicts in the *Antigone* between political obligations imposed by the state's *nomoi* and religious obligations incumbent upon the family may thus reflect tensions that had become acute in Athens after the reforms of Ephialtes.[37] The structure of the play as a whole will require less attention than the terms in which the

festival was celebrated on 25 Thargelion (Plut. *Alc*. 34.1 with Deubner, *Feste* 18) and since Θαργελι-- is legible in line 20 of our inscription, it is probable that their functions at the Plynteria form at least part of the content of this decree. On the other hand, the possibility cannot be excluded that the inscription refers to the new peplos offered to Athena at the Panathenaia or that it contains more general regulations concerning the religious functions of the clan. Cf. Ziehen, "Πλυντήρια" 1063.

36   The date 442 B.C., widely accepted as one of the more secure dates of Sophocles' extant plays, is based on the statement of Aristophanes of Byzantium in his hypothesis to the *Antigone* that Sophocles' election as a general in the Samian campaign of 441/0 B.C. was the direct result of his success with the *Antigone*; cf. Fornara, *ABG* 48–49. Some scholars, including W. M. Calder III, "Sophokles' Political Tragedy, *Antigone*," *GRBS* 9 (1968) 389–407, esp. 389–90 with n. 2, prefer 443 B.C., on the ground that Sophocles was chairman of the *hellēnotamiai* in 443/2 B.C. (*IG* I³ 269.36) and too busy to write plays. I find it easier to believe with V. Ehrenberg, *Sophocles and Pericles* (Oxford, 1954) 135–36, that the interval between the performance of the play and election to the generalship was very short than to believe that the tasks of the chairmanship of the *hellēnotamiai* were too exacting.

37   The recognition of this polarity is one of the most valuable insights of Ehrenberg, *Sophocles*, esp. chap. 7, who tends, however, to overemphasize the religious outlook of Sophocles. For a more balanced view of the subtle interplay of political and religious motives in both Creon and Antigone, see B. M. W. Knox, *The Heroic Temper: Studies in Sophoclean Tragedy* (Berkeley and Los Angeles, 1964) chaps. 3 and 4, esp. pp. 75–90 and 91–102, to whom the following discussion is much indebted; cf. also E. Eberlein, "Über die verschiedenen Deutungen des tragischen Konflikts in der 'Antigone' des Sophokles," *Gymnasium* 68 (1961) 16–34, and D. A. Hester, "Sophocles the Unphilosophical. A Study in the *Antigone*," *Mnemos.*, 4th ser., 24 (1971) 11–59.

conflicting secular and religious obligations are staged and the points at which they clash with one another.

It cannot be mere accident that of the thirty-eight occurrences of νόμος in the seven surviving plays of Sophocles almost one-half—eighteen—are found in the *Antigone*, a small but perhaps not insignificant statistical indication that *nomos* is more central to the *Antigone* than to any other Sophoclean play. *Nomos* is the mainstay of the city, and throughout the play not only Creon but also Antigone, Ismene, and the chorus regularly apply the word to the legitimate authority that rests in Creon's hands.[38] The most explicit statement of the nature of *nomos* comes early in the drama in what has sometimes been called Creon's "inaugural" speech. After arguing the legitimacy of his accession to power (173–74), Creon asks the chorus, the citizens of Thebes, to suspend judgment about his personality, thinking, and decision-making ability until his authority and legislative capacity (νόμοι) have been tested.[39] His conduct of office will be guided by such rules (νόμοι, 191) as that he will not be daunted in laying down the policies best for the state as a whole (178–81) and that he himself and his fellow citizens will put the welfare of the country ahead of other bonds (182–83). He invokes all-seeing Zeus as his witness that he will not keep silent when the security of the land is threatened and that he will never regard a public enemy as his personal friend, since for salvation one must look to the homeland: its stability is a precondition for forming personal bonds (184–90). The Athenians of Sophocles' own day will have accepted this statement as an outline for properly constituted authority, as is indicated by the chorus's assertion that it is inherent in Creon's power to make full use of his authority (νόμῳ δὲ χρῆσθαι παντί) concerning both the living and the dead (213–14) and by Ismene's remark early in the play that transgressing the legitimate decree and the legitimate powers of the ruler does violence to *nomos*.[40] Demosthenes (19.247–48) still approved of it a century later.

---

38 On the use of νόμος in *Ant.*, see also the sensitive remarks of J. Dalfen, "Gesetz ist nicht Gesetz und fromm ist nicht fromm. Die Sprache der Personen in der sophokleischen Antigone," *WS*, n.s., 11 (1977) 5–26, esp. 9–14.

39 Soph. *Ant.* 175–77: ἀμήχανον δὲ παντὸς ἀνδρὸς ἐκμαθεῖν / ψυχήν τε καὶ φρόνημα καὶ γνώμην, πρὶν ἂν / ἀρχαῖς τε καὶ νόμοισιν ἐντριβὴς φανῇ. For the meaning of νόμοι here, see Ostwald, *Nomos* 29 with n. 2.

40 Soph. *Ant.* 59–60, on which Knox, *Heroic Temper* 63, aptly remarks: "The word τυράννων emphasizes the absolute power of Creon, conferred on him by the

From the principles thus outlined Creon derives the content of his edict—introduced as ἀδελφὰ τῶνδε (192)—according to Eteocles, who fell defending Thebes, full funeral honors but denying them to Polyneices, who had tried to lay waste his native city (192–210). The appropriateness of this edict and its legality is acknowledged for the case of Eteocles even by Antigone (σὺν δίκῃ. . .καὶ νόμῳ, 23–24). The Athenian audience probably so regarded it also for the case of Polyneices: an Athenian *nomos* prohibited burying traitors in Attic soil,[41] although some qualms (not articulated in the play) may have been felt about Creon's prohibition of any burial for Polyneices at all. Still, the edict is regarded as a *nomos* not only by Creon himself (449, 481, 663) but also by the chorus (213, 382) and even by Antigone (452, 847). It is not without significance that the chorus, on seeing Antigone arrested, comments on the legality of the arrest and on the folly of Antigone's defiance (382–83).

Moreover, Creon knows that in championing the cause of the city he also champions the cause of its gods. In his first line he gives the gods credit for having safely brought the city through its crisis (162); he invokes Zeus as upholder of the city's safety (184); and his judgment against the body of Polyneices is motivated at least in part by his view that Polyneices aimed to destroy the sanctuaries and the *nomoi* of the gods.[42] *Nomos* remains the characteristic watchword for the state's authority even when Creon cites that authority to bolster his own personal standing in the face of Antigone's opposition. For in his encounter with his son, Haemon, he puts violence to the *nomoi*

---

polis in the emergency, and at the same time, by its plural form, generalizes the expression and thus lessens the suggestion that he is a 'tyrant.' The word 'vote' (ψῆφον) suggests that Creon's proclamation is no capricious gesture but the expression of a deliberate policy. . .and it also, with its democratic associations, hints that Creon speaks for the whole body of the citizens. The word κράτη, another generalizing plural, emphasizes the fact that Creon has the full power of the state at his command, and the phrase 'in violence to the law' marks Antigone's attempt as criminal."

41 Xen. *Hell.* 1.7.22; cf. Thuc. 1.138.6 and Lycurg. 1.113 with Lipsius, *ARRV* 379. See also the lengthier discussion of this issue by Hester, "Sophocles" 19–21.

42 Soph. *Ant.* 199 and esp. 284–87, with my comments at *Nomos* 41 n. 2. The religious element in Creon's stance is ignored by J. de Romilly, *La Loi dans la pensée grecque* (Paris, 1971) 29–34, who sees the conflict between Creon and Antigone in such simple terms as "l'État aurait une exigence et la conscience morale ou religieuse une autre" (p. 29); Creon stands for "une législation d'ordre purement politique, qui s'accorde mal aux impératifs religieux ou moraux" (p. 30) and Antigone for a "forme de loi non écrite—la plus haute, la plus pure, qui est la loi d'ordre religieux" (p. 31).

on the same level as transgression and as trying to give orders to those in power; authority, he claims, must be obeyed in matters small and great, just and unjust, in order to avoid the evils of anarchy (663–67, 672). In short, it is fair to say that *nomos* in the *Antigone* is on the side of Creon as the legitimate ruler of Thebes: throughout most of the play the Theban people accept the authority of *nomos* and regard as obligatory the rules *nomos* establishes; Creon can invoke *nomos* even when, driven to the extreme of identifying the city with himself, he assumes the posture of a tyrant (736, 738). His eventual fall, which affects his family and himself rather than the city, is not a blow against *nomos*. It merely compels him to view the "established laws"—τοὺς καθεστῶτας νόμους—from a perspective wider than that of his own authority (1113–14). His fall does not damage the *nomoi* of the state.

From this it is clear that Antigone's cause involves opposition to *nomos*. Her law is not the law of the city but her own: she has lived αὐτόνομος, a law unto herself (821). Her temper is self-willed, an αὐτόγνωτος ὀργά (875), not the social temper required for life in the city (ἀστυνόμους ὀργάς, 355–56). She acknowledges Creon's edict as νόμος (452, 847) and accepts it as it applies to Eteocles (24); but the rule of her own conduct is to honor her outlawed brother, fully aware that in doing so she has defied her fellow citizens (βίᾳ πολιτῶν, 907; cf. 79) but knowing also that, unlike a husband or a child, a brother cannot be replaced (908, 914). Except in a single line (519), about which we shall have more to say presently, Antigone never appeals to *nomos* as sanctioning her cause. This is the more remarkable because in the *Ajax* the *nomoi* of the gods are invoked as demanding Ajax's burial against the *nomoi* of the established authorities, who want to forbid it.[43]

The most explicit statements of the principles that sanction Antigone's opposition come in her speech in response to Creon's question καὶ δῆτ' ἐτόλμας τούσδ' ὑπερβαίνειν νόμους;—"So you really had the nerve to transgress these laws?" (449)—and in the dialogue that follows her speech and Creon's (450–525). Antigone begins her speech by objecting that Creon's νόμοι (452) were not proclaimed by Zeus or by the Justice (Dikē) that dwells with the gods below (450–51), suggesting that she accepts the authority of these two divinities

---

43   Soph. *Aj.* 1130–33 and 1343 for the δαιμόνων or θεῶν νόμοι, and 1073 and 1247 for the νόμοι represented by Menelaus and Agamemnon.

as superior to Creon's. But Creon had earlier invoked Zeus as his witness (304) to stress his determination to enforce his edict; and later in the play, even as Antigone is on her way to her rocky chamber, the chorus reminds her that in her daring she has fallen against the high pedestal of Justice.[44] Evidently, her Zeus is not the Zeus of the city but, presumably, the Zeus of the family, Ζεὺς ἑρκεῖος or Ζεὺς ξύναιμος, whom Creon later repudiates (487, 658–59), and her Dikē is not the Justice of the city, but one that dwells in the realm of the dead and sanctions her defiance (921). The injunctions of these divinities she describes as ἄγραπτα κἀσφαλῆ θεῶν νόμιμα (454–55); this expression deliberately differentiates them from the *nomoi* of the state, to which Antigone cannot appeal because they are on Creon's side. Like Creon's *nomoi*, the gods' *nomima* are prescriptive, but the obligation they impose is, in Antigone's view, higher and stronger than what the laws of the state impose. This is evident not only because they are unfailing, sanctioned by the gods, and eternal[45] but also because they are "unwritten," for what is unwritten tends to stand higher in the Greek scale of values when it is contrasted with what is written.[46] Sophocles doubtless knew as well as we do that Creon's *nomoi* were no more written than Antigone's *nomima*, since there was no written legislation in the heroic age. But by calling Antigone's *nomima* "unwritten," he shows that they are to be viewed against the background of written legislation, the form in which the *nomoi* of the state were normally promulgated in Athens by the time the *Antigone* was performed. That in the immediate context Antigone contrasts her *nomima* with Creon's likewise unwritten κηρύγματα only strengthens this view, and it shows at the same time that Antigone regards Creon's edict as less secure and less permanent than

---

44   Soph. *Ant.* 853–55: προβᾶσ᾽ ἐπ᾽ ἔσχατον θράσους / ὑψηλὸν ἐς Δίκας βάθρον / προσέπεσες, ὦ τέκνον, πολύ. With Jebb, I prefer the προσέπεσες of the Laurentianus and the Parisinus to Pearson's προσέπαισας.

45   Ibid. 457, κοὐδεὶς οἶδεν ἐξ ὅτου ᾽φάνη, with my comments in "Was There a Concept ἄγραφος νόμος in Classical Greece?" in E. N. Lee, A. P. D. Mourelatos, and R. M. Rorty, eds., *Exegesis and Argument: Studies in Greek Philosophy Presented to Gregory Vlastos* (Assen, 1973) 70–104, esp. 85 with n. 48.

46   I have dealt with this aspect of the *Antigone* in "Was There a Concept ἄγραφος νόμος?" 83–86. For the higher valuation of the unwritten, see, e.g., Aesch. *Supp.* 942–49; Thuc. 2.37.3, 43.3; [Lys.] 6.10; Xen. *Mem.* 4.4.19; Dem. 18.275, 23.70; Pl. *Leg.* 7.793a–b; and Arist. *Rh.* 1.13, 1374ᵃ20–28. When the actual or implied contrast is with ἀναγεγραμμένος, as it is, for example, in Thuc. 1.40.2 and in Andoc. 1.85–87, ἄγραφος has a neutral or lower valuation.

the principles to which she adheres. For though she has just acknowledged the edict as νόμοι (452), she now looks on her νόμιμα as opposing the mere proclamations of a herald, announcements whose authority is derivative, that say one thing today and another tomorrow.[47] It is remarkable that no other generic term than νόμιμα is used in the *Antigone* to describe the principle of her defiance; this shows, as we have seen,[48] that νόμιμα came to describe religious laws as νόμος came increasingly to be associated with political and legal regulations in the course of the fifth century. Only once does Antigone refers to her laws as νόμοι, and that is when, toward the end of her verbal sparring with Creon, she adds the sanction of Hades to her cause—in order to indicate, it seems, that her νόμιμα are no less valid than Creon's νόμοι (519).

The content of Antigone's *nomima* must be gleaned from statements by Antigone and by others scattered over all parts of the play. The term itself is of little help, because unlike νόμος with its frequent appearances, νόμιμα occurs only once in the play. Yet the main outlines are clear. They are of course the rules that bid her bury Polyneices so that he may obtain such honor (τιμή) among the dead below as Creon has already accorded to Eteocles (23–30) and such as she herself had accorded to her father and mother before (900–904). She feels this obligation all the more keenly in the case of Polyneices because, with her parents dead, a brother is irreplaceable.[49] Honoring the dead constitutes at the same time an honor demanded by the gods below; Antigone herself repeatedly says so (77, 521, and 921; cf. also 749), and Teiresias confirms this as an objective truth (1070–71). For that reason, Antigone regards the burial of Polyneices as an act of piety (σέβειν, 511; εὐσέβεια, 924 and 943) and noble (καλόν) even if it involves her own death (72–75)—especially since failure to accom-

---

47   Of course there was no way other than by proclamation that Creon's edict could have been promulgated, and it may be argued that the term κηρύγματα is not intended as a devaluation of Creon's νόμοι. Still, it remains noteworthy that though both Creon (192, 203, 447) and Antigone (27, 34, 450, 461) use forms of the verb κηρύσσω to describe the promulgation, the noun is given only to Antigone (8, 454) and stands here to create a contrast with her ἄγραπτα νόμιμα. (The κήρυγμα at 162 refers merely to the announcement of an Assembly meeting.)

48   See above, pp. 97 and 101–2.

49   Soph. *Ant.* 908–12 and esp. ἐκπροτιμήσασα at 913. The νόμος on which she predicates this preference at lines 908 and 914 has nothing to do with either Creon's νόμος or Antigone's νόμιμα, but, as noted above, p. 152, merely constitutes the rule that guides her conduct in general without implying the higher sanction of either the state or the gods.

plish it would bring divine punishment upon her head (458–62).

What is more, as Knox has shown, Antigone's *nomima* are sanctioned by family ties rather than by ties with the city.[50] This is, in the first instance, the basis of her appeal to Ismene to assist her. In the first line of the play she addresses Ismene as αὐτάδελφον κάρα and a little later reminds her of the obligations noble birth imposes (38) and calls failure to comply an act of treason against their brother (45–46), which she will not countenance (80–81). Faced with Creon, she emphasizes three times that she will not leave unburied her mother's son (466–68), who is her own brother (503–4),[51] sprung from the same womb (511). Even Creon's edict will not keep her from what is "her own" (48), and despite his mockery of the blood bond (658–59) she joins her own people in death (893).[52]

In what terms are we meant to envisage the issue that separates Creon and Antigone? To pose the question in this manner does not imply that we are trying to pass judgment on the *Antigone* as a work of dramatic art, for the play is not a conflict of personified principles.[53] We are using the tragedy as a historical document rather than as a literary monument, on the assumption that it reflects broad concerns that agitated—or could agitate—the Athenians about 440 B.C. The issue is not simply one of religion against the state, in which Antigone is completely right and Creon completely wrong;[54] religious considerations are part of both Creon's and of Antigone's cause:[55] even Antigone acknowledges in her final speech a religious

---

50　Knox, *Heroic Temper* 76–82.

51　It is remarkable that the rare compound αὐτάδελφος, which does not occur in any of the other surviving Sophoclean plays, is found three times in *Ant.* (1, 503, 696). Equally remarkable is the frequency with which αὐτόχειρ occurs in *Ant.* (172, 306, 900, 1175, 1315), and especially its use at 1175–76, where the response of the chorus leader to the Messenger's report indicates that the term can refer equally to Haemon or to his father. In the other surviving plays of Sophocles, αὐτόχειρ is found three times in *OT* (231, 266, 1331), twice in *El.* (955, 1019), and once each in *Aj.* (57) and *Trach.* (1194).

52　Knox, *Heroic Temper* 80–82, trenchantly observes that φίλος "in Antigone's speeches...always refers to the blood relationship." Less cogently, Dalfen, "Gezetz" 25–26, sees in Antigone's φιλεῖν a more general other-directed sentiment.

53　This point is well made by Hester, "Sophocles."

54　This is the view of G. Müller, *Sophokles: Antigone* (Heidelberg, 1967), esp. p. 11; cf. the review by B. M. W. Knox, *Gnomon* 40 (1968) 747–60.

55　For Creon, see above, p. 151 with n. 42; for Antigone, pp. 152–54. I see no evidence in the play for the assertion of R. Bultmann, "Polis and Hades in Sophocles' *Antigone*," in *Essays Philosophical and Theological* (London, 1955) 22–35, esp. 25–26 (originally published in 1936), that Creon's false piety is pitted against the true piety of Antigone.

sanction in Creon's case when she admits that her own pursuit of piety laid her open to the charge of impiety.[56]

The issue is not one of the individual against the state, either. Nowhere in the play does Antigone champion any personal rights of her own; she always predicates the righteousness of her cause on the family's obligation to bury its dead. For the same reason, we cannot attribute to the Sophoclean Antigone the protest of the individual against tyranny, which Anouilh made the theme of his version of the story. As we have shown above, Creon starts out as a constitutional ruler, whose convictions, far from being tyrannical, conform to the principles of the Athenian democracy; *nomos*, which he upholds, included in contemporary Athens the injunction against burying a traitor in the soil of his homeland.[57] If in prohibiting the burial of Polyneices altogether he exceeds what the law requires, that excess is motivated by a patriotism fanned by the danger from which Thebes has just escaped; it does not mark him as a tyrant. The tyrannical behavior he exhibits in the course of the play against Antigone, Haemon, and Teiresias results from his anger at Antigone's defiant attitude, which pushes him into too strong an assertion of an authority constitutionally his. Sophocles meant us to see him in this perspective: the explanations or mitigating circumstances attendant upon Creon's flare-ups make it impossible to regard Creon as a tyrant *tout court*. His anger first bursts out when he is faced with Antigone's defiance and the provocative manner in which it is thrown at him.[58] Creon's reaction is equally strong: he speaks of her as a slave (479), threatens to curb her arrogance and wanton mockery (480–83), and implicates Ismene in her guilt (486–92). In his encounter with Haemon, his initial insistence on obedience to properly constituted authority as the only alternative to anarchy (663–76) will have sounded tyrannical to the audience only from the point at which Creon treats the city as his personal property (734–61, esp. 738). And even this is somewhat mitigated when, almost immediately thereafter, he absolves Ismene from guilt (771) and changes his sentence against Antigone from death by stoning (36) to confinement in a rocky vault (773–80). Similarly, his attitude toward Teiresias

---

56 Soph. *Ant.* 923–24: ἐπεί γε δὴ / τὴν δυσσέβειαν εὐσεβοῦσ' ἐκτησάμην. She shows the same awareness early in the play when she refers to her projected burial of Polyneices as ὅσια πανουργήσασα (74).

57 See above, p. 151 with n. 41.

58 Cf. the chorus leader's comments at 471–72.

changes from courtesy and respect to wild accusations of conspiracy and treason for profit when he feels the pressure against his authority mounting unbearably (1033–63), but immediately thereafter he does what no other Sophoclean hero ever does: he gives in and tries— unsuccessfully, it turns out—to undo the damage he has caused (1095–1114).[59] Under these circumstances, it is difficult to see him portrayed as a tyrant by Sophocles.

It rather seems that the issue between Creon and Antigone is meant to be seen as a conflict between the obligation to the state as embodied in its *nomos*, which includes state religion and here also the law prohibiting the burial of traitors in Attic soil, and the obligation incumbent upon families (*nomima*) to fulfill certain religious duties toward their members. The desirable state of affairs in the city seems to be that articulated by the chorus at the end of its "Ode on Man": νόμους γεραίρων χθονὸς / θεῶν τ᾽ ἔνορκον δίκαν, ὑψίπολις (honoring the laws of the land and the justice of the gods, to uphold which oaths are sworn, high is the city, 368–70).[60] The disjunction of the νόμους...χθονός from the θεῶν...ἔνορκον δίκαν suggests that there is a difference between the two prerequisites for a flourishing city.[61] That the "laws of the land" are primarily political is not open to doubt.[62] The interpretation of θεῶν ἔνορκον δίκαν, from which they seem to be differentiated, is more difficult. It is a

59 Cf. Knox, *Heroic Temper* 74–75 with n. 22.

60 With Müller, *Sophokles: Antigone* 86 and 95, and Jebb, *ad loc.*, I prefer Reiske's γεραίρων to the manuscript reading, παρείρων, which Knox, *Heroic Temper* 185 n. 46, wants to retain. But I am inclined to accept Knox's arguments (ibid. 185 n. 47) that ὑψίπολις carries the dual meaning "the city stands high" and "the man stands high in his city." For a searching analysis of the place of this ode in the play, see H. Gundert, "Grösse und Gefährdung des Menschen. Ein sophokleisches Chorlied und seine Stellung im Drama (Sophokles, Antigone 332–375)," *Antike und Abendland* 22 (1976) 21–39.

61 It is peculiar that most scholars, including Hester, "Sophocles" 27 (with full citations of his predecessors), worry only whether the chorus is condemning Creon or Antigone or both. They fail to draw the most natural inference from the theme of the ambivalence of the human condition as such (sc. not merely the condition of Thebes as depicted in the play), which characterizes this stasimon, namely, that in the lines quoted we have a statement of the most favorable (ὑψίπολις) condition of man in his society, followed in lines 370–75 by a statement of the least favorable (ἄπολις) condition. If lines 368–75 contain a criticism at all of either Creon or Antigone, it can only be left for the audience to infer from the general picture. On this point, see the remarks of G. Bona, "ὑψίπολις e ἄπολις nel primo stasimo dell' *Antigone*," *Riv.Filol.*, 3d ser., 99 (1971) 129–48, esp. 144–48.

62 Müller, *Sophokles: Antigone* 86, makes the interesting point that χθονός is chosen deliberately in preference to πόλεως "weil χθών sowohl das Land im

divinely sanctioned system of justice, whose transgression will result in retribution: this is clear from the very meaning of δίκη.[63] As such it will include but also transcend the laws of the state. The truth of that will emerge from a consideration of Sophocles' use of ἔνορκον to modify δίκαν and the consequences of that use in the scene that follows.

In the only other two passages in which ἔνορκος is found in extant tragedy, both from Sophocles' *Philoctetes* (72, 811), the adjective describes a person bound by an oath, a sense not suitable here. But two fourth-century passages are illuminating. The first stipulation of Plato's agrarian legislation in the *Laws* contains a prohibition against moving boundary stones: βουλέσθω δὲ πᾶς πέτρον ἐπιχειρῆσαι κινεῖν τὸν μέγιστον ἄλλον πλὴν ὅρον μᾶλλον ἢ σμικρὸν λίθον ὁρίζοντα φιλίαν τε καὶ ἔχθραν ἔνορκον παρὰ θεῶν. τοῦ μὲν γὰρ ὁμόφυλος Ζεὺς μάρτυς, τοῦ δὲ ξένιος, οἳ μετὰ πολέμων τῶν ἐχθίστων ἐγείρονται.[64] A stone boundary marker is here described as ἔνορκος (because it has been consecrated by an oath sworn in the name of the gods and witnessed by Zeus) to indicate that the boundary it marks must be respected on pain of terrible retribution by Zeus. The adjective, in other words, does not here describe the person who has taken an oath but the object the oath has promised to respect. We thus get a meaning appropriate to the passage in the *Antigone*: the θεῶν δίκα is ἔνορκος because men have taken an oath to uphold it.

Under what circumstances and to what effect the oath may be

---

politischen Sinn als auch den Bereich der Toten unter der Erde bedeuten kann." But the conclusion he draws from this (p. 87) gives the expression a too one-sidedly religious sense. To the extent that the soil is included in the laws of the land, χθονός surely also implies that it would be desecrated by the burial of a traitor.

63 Gagarin, "*Dikē* in the *Works and Days*," and "*Dikē* in Archaic Greek Thought," *CP* 69 (1974) 186–97, stresses the political and legal (rather than moral) character of δίκη in Greek literature down to 480 B.C. That this connotation is still present in the passage under discussion seems likely: in view of the secular and human connotations of νόμος in the *Antigone*, a distinction from νόμους in this context suggests that θεῶν δίκα constitutes a divinely sanctioned system of justice, whose existence must be recognized and honored if the city is to flourish. The only moral consequence of its existence is that it demands obedience no less than the laws of the state do.

64 Plato, *Leg.* 8.843a1–5: "Let every person wish to try to move the biggest stone that does not mark a boundary rather than a small stone that separates friend's land from foe's, established by an oath sworn in the name of the gods. Zeus the Protector of Kin is the witness to the one, and Zeus the Protector of Strangers witness to the other, who when aroused bring with them the bitterest wars."

assumed to have been taken can partly be inferred from a rather verbose passage in the first Demosthenic speech against Aristo-geiton.[65] This passage is of special interest to the *Antigone* because it too relates ἔνορκος to δίκη:

καὶ τὴν ἀπαραίτητον καὶ σεμνὴν Δίκην, ἣν ὁ τὰς ἁγιωτάτας ἡμῖν τελετὰς καταδείξας Ὀρφεὺς παρὰ τὸν τοῦ Διὸς θρόνον φησὶ καθημένην πάντα τὰ τῶν ἀνθρώπων ἐφορᾶν, εἰς αὐτὸν ἕκαστον νομίσαντα βλέπειν οὕτω ψηφίζεσθαι, φυλαττόμενον καὶ προορώμενον μὴ καταισχῦναι ταύτην, ἧς ἐπώνυμός ἐστιν ὑμῶν ἕκαστος ὁ ἀεὶ δικάζειν λαχών, πάντα τὰ ἐν τῇ πόλει καλὰ καὶ δίκαια καὶ συμφέροντα [φυλάττων καὶ] ταύτην τὴν ἡμέραν παρακαταθήκην ἔνορκον εἰληφὼς παρὰ τῶν νόμων καὶ τῆς πολιτείας καὶ τῆς πατρίδος.[66]

The immediate reference of ἔνορκος is of course to the heliastic oath, in which, in Demosthenes' time, the jurors swore to "cast their vote in accordance with the laws and the decrees of the Athenian people and of the Council of the Five Hundred" (Dem. 24.149–51). But the fact that its object is here metaphorically described as "a trust the juror has sworn to preserve" enables us to take the oath as covering a wider area. For the trust has been given not only by the *nomoi* but also by the community (*politeia*) and by the fatherland; it includes not merely what the laws have laid down but all that is good, just, and beneficial in the city; and it has been placed under the auspices of a universal power, Dikē who sits by the throne of Zeus. From this we may infer that it is more than an oath to enforce the secular *nomoi* of the state; it is rather an oath promising to uphold Dikē in all her manifestations in the life of the community, including the due performance of religious rites by families and individuals. Still, it might be argued, ἔνορκος in this context describes only an oath sworn by the jurors, whereas the *Antigone* passage would suggest an oath by which all Athenians are bound. To this, one may reply that

---

65 There is general agreement that the speech was composed but never delivered, in the late fourth century B.C. Blass, *AB*[2] 3.1.408–17, believed that Demosthenes was its author; recent scholarship, however, has cast doubt on this belief; see de Romilly, *Loi* 155–58.

66 [Dem.] 25.11: "You must cast your vote in the belief that inexorable and solemn Dikē, who, as Orpheus, who has instructed us in the most holy mysteries, tells us, sits beside the throne of Zeus and supervises all the affairs of men, is watching each and every one of you; you must be on your guard and see to it not to disgrace her from whom each one of you, whenever the lot falls on him, derives his name as dikast, because he [is guarding] whatever is good, just, and beneficial in the city [and] has on this day received from the laws, from the constitution, and from the fatherland a trust that he is sworn to preserve."

although Harpocration's statement that all Athenians swore the heliastic oath at Ardettos is hard to believe,[67] it probably was annually sworn by the six thousand Athenians eligible for service as jurymen (Isoc. 15.21), who probably were thought of as representing the Athenian people as a whole.[68] And further, the ephebic oath, which was sworn by all male Athenians, contained the promise to protect the ancestral cults.[69]

The Demosthenic passage, exhorting the jurors to regard Dikē who sits beside the throne of Zeus, makes it seem no mere coincidence that Antigone in her defense against Creon invokes the sanction of "Zeus and the Dikē that dwells with the gods below" for the ἄγραπτα νόμιμα on which she bases her defiance of Creon's edict (450–51). This similarity makes it plausible that the θεῶν ἔνορκος δίκα of the preceding stasimon (369) is meant to point forward to the Justice on which Antigone will rest her claim. If this is so, the phrase will express the "justice of the gods that the flourishing city [or: "the man flourishing in the city," ὑψίπολις] is sworn to uphold," which does indeed include the *nomoi* of the state but also encompasses religious obligations incumbent upon the family, among them the burial of the dead—obligations that the state, too, is sworn to respect.

If this interpretation is correct, the desirable state of affairs is described by the chorus (368–69) as one in which both the laws of the land and the fulfillment of all obligations imposed by the justice of the gods (or: due to the gods) are observed. This means that Creon and Antigone each honor the obligations that their situations demand of them: as the constitutional representative of the state Creon has no choice but to enforce the *nomos* prohibiting the burial of a traitor in Theban soil; as a sister Antigone has no choice but to bury her brother. The tragic conflict is the result of Sophocles' envisaging a situation in which two equally strong and valid obligations are set on a collision course and destroy their champions. As the chorus sees, it is also an eternal and universal *nomos* that whatever has tremendous importance does not come into the life of mortals without disaster.[70] Under the pressure of the consequences of having

---

67 Harp. s.v. Ἀρδηττός; cf. *Suda* s.v. ἡλιαστής.

68 See Hignett, *HAC* 216; Rhodes, *AB* 169.

69 The promise καὶ τιμήσω ἱερὰ τὰ πάτρια is found in all literary and epigraphical versions of the ephebic oath; see Stob. 43.48; Poll. 8.105–6; and Tod, *GHI* 2.204.16.

70 Soph. *Ant.* 611–14: τό τ᾽ ἔπειτα καὶ τὸ μέλλον / καὶ τὸ πρὶν ἐπαρκέσει / νόμος ὅδ᾽ οὐδὲν ἔρπει / θνατῶν βιότῳ πάμπολύ γ᾽ ἐκτὸς ἄτας.

tried to enforce his edict, Creon is forced to yield and to learn that the νόμιμα of the family form part of the καθεστῶτες νόμοι the state must uphold (1113–14). In pursuing its more secular tasks, the *nomos* of the state must not lose sight of the *nomima* administered by the family for its own members.

The *Antigone* is the product of a powerful poetic and dramatic imagination. But like all products of the imagination it is based on historical reality and addresses itself to issues that would engage the interest of a contemporary audience. We cannot be confident at this distance that we are able to identify these issues, but we cannot go far wrong, either, if we see the play as drawing attention to the dangers to which a state exposes itself by applying its *raison d'état* too rigidly, oblivious to other factors that give cohesion to society.

THE CASE OF ANDOCIDES: THE *NOMOS* OF THE STATE OVERRIDES "ANCESTRAL LAW" (*PATRIOS NOMOS*)

We saw earlier in this chapter scattered evidence for state interference in the fifth century in the administration of the Eleusinian Mysteries, whose cult was the traditional prerogative of the Eumolpids and Kerykes.[71] Such interference was sometimes the result of conflict between secular and religious authority, as we can see from the trial of Andocides in the autumn of 400 B.C.[72]

The charge against Andocides was that earlier in the year he had illegally participated in the celebration of the Eleusinian Mysteries in violation of the decree of Isotimides, which barred him from all access to the holy places and the agora of Athens because of his implication in the profanation of the Eleusinian Mysteries in 415 B.C. (Andoc. 1.71; [Lys.] 6.9 and 24). A subsidiary charge against him, which is of primary interest to us here, was that he had deposited a suppliant's bough on the altar of the Eleusinion at Athens, an act prohibited by law during the celebration of the Mysteries. Andocides' chief accuser was a certain Cephisius, whose reputation for upright behavior was not the best ([Lys.] 6.42). We can therefore believe Andocides' charge that Cephisius had been suborned by Callias (a member of the *genos* of the Kerykes and himself,

71 See pp. 138–40 above.
72 For the date, see MacDowell, *Andokides* 204–5.

as the *dāidouchos*, an important functionary of the Eleusinian cult),[73] who had personal reasons for wishing Andocides to get out of his way.

The information (*endeixis*) that Andocides had illegally participated in the Eleusinian Mysteries had already been lodged by Cephisius before the archon basileus, who in accordance with established procedure had conveyed it to the prytaneis. The prytaneis in their turn had summoned the archon basileus to report the matter to a meeting of the entire Council, which in accordance with Solonian law had to be convened in the Eleusinion at Athens on the day after the celebration of the Mysteries. The prytaneis had asked the archon basileus to ensure that Andocides and Cephisius would be available at the Eleusinion (Andoc. 1.111). The time and place of meeting suggests that the Council was by statute convened on this occasion to hear the report of the archon basileus on the celebrations[74] and, presumably, reports of other cult officials also. This would explain the presence of Callias at the Council meeting clad in his ceremonial robe as *dāidouchos*.

As the proceedings opened, Callias pointed out that a suppliant's bough had been deposited on the altar. A herald was dispatched to those waiting outside, among whom were Andocides and Cephisius, to ask who had deposited a bough; when no response was forthcoming, the herald returned to the assembled Council to report that fact (Andoc. 1.112). Understanding the sequel requires a close interpretation of Andocides' narrative:

Ἐπειδὴ δ' ἔλεγε τῇ βουλῇ Εὐκλῆς ὅτι οὐδεὶς ὑπακούοι, πάλιν ὁ Καλλίας ἀναστὰς ἔλεγεν ὅτι εἴη νόμος πάτριος, εἴ τις ἱκετηρίαν θείη ἐν τῷ Ἐλευσινίῳ, ἄκριτον ἀποθανεῖν, καὶ ὁ πατήρ ποτ' αὐτοῦ Ἱππόνικος ἐξηγήσατο ταῦτα Ἀθηναίοις, ἀκούσειε δὲ ὅτι ἐγὼ θείην τὴν ἱκετηρίαν. ἐντεῦθεν ἀναπηδᾷ Κέφαλος οὑτοσὶ καὶ λέγει· "Ὦ Καλλία, πάντων ἀνθρώπων ἀνοσιώτατε, πρῶτον μὲν ἐξηγῇ Κηρύκων ὤν, οὐχ ὅσιον <ὂν> σοι ἐξηγεῖσθαι· ἔπειτα δὲ νόμον πάτριον λέγεις, ἡ δὲ στήλη παρ' ᾗ ἕστηκας χιλίας δραχμὰς κελεύει ὀφείλειν, ἐάν τις ἱκετηρίαν θῇ ἐν τῷ Ἐλευσινίῳ. ἔπειτα δὲ τίνος ἤκουσας ὅτι Ἀνδοκίδης θείη τὴν ἱκετηρίαν; κάλεσον αὐτὸν τῇ βουλῇ, ἵνα καὶ ἡμεῖς ἀκούσωμεν." ἐπειδὴ δὲ ἀνεγνώσθη ἡ στήλη κἀκεῖνος οὐκ εἶχεν εἰπεῖν ὅτου ἤκουσεν, καταφανὴς ἦν τῇ βουλῇ αὐτὸς θεὶς τὴν ἱκετηρίαν.[75]

---

73   See Xen. *Hell.* 6.3.3, and Arist. *Rh.* 3.2, 1405ª 16–22, with MacDowell, *Andokides* 10–11, and especially Davies, *APF*, no. 7826 (Kallias III).

74   Cf. P. Foucart, *Les Mystères d'Éleusis* (Paris, 1914) 231–32.

75   Andoc. 1.115–16: "When Eucles [the herald] told the Council that there was

Of the three points made by Callias and answered one by one by Cephalus, presumably a member of the Council at this time and a supporter of Andocides (Andoc. 1.150), the one concerning the identity of Andocides as the alleged perpetrator of the deed need not concern us here. Further, the question whether or not the Kerykes had the right to give authoritative interpretations (ἐξηγεῖσθαι) of the laws governing the sacred affairs of Eleusis, though interesting in its own right, is only of peripheral importance for our purposes.[76] What is of interest to us is that Callias's appeal to a *patrios nomos* is successfully overruled by Cephalus's appeal to a law inscribed on a stele near the altar of the Eleusinion.

What is the relation between these two laws? From a substantive point of view both deal with the same offense, namely, the deposition of a suppliant's bough at the Eleusinion in Athens during the celebration of the Mysteries at Eleusis; they disagree only about the penalty. The *patrios nomos* demands the death penalty without a trial: the circumstances in which Callias appeals to it suggest that in his opinion the Council upon having heard accuser, accused, and perhaps witnesses could order the immediate execution of the offender. The stele, however, demands merely a fine of one thousand drachmas, no doubt to be imposed only after a proper trial before a jury court, since the Council had no authority to impose so high a fine. But this does not mean that Callias is rebuked simply for having misquoted the law on the stele: the two laws are different in kind, because their sources are different. Whereas Cephalus points to a

---

no response, Callias stood up once more and said that there was an ancestral law to the effect that if someone deposits a suppliant's bough in the Eleusinion, he should be put to death without trial, and that his father Hipponicus had once given this interpretation to the Athenians; he further stated that he had heard that I had deposited the suppliant's bough. At that point Cephalus, who is present here, jumped up and retorted, 'Callias, you are the most unholy of men. In the first place, you give an official interpretation despite the fact that you belong to the Kerykes and it is not your religious right to interpret. Second, you cite an ancestral law, but the stele by which you are standing prescribes a penalty of one thousand drachmas for anyone who deposits a suppliant's bough in the Eleusinion. Third, from whom did you hear that Andocides deposited the bough? Summon him for the benefit of the Council, so that we too may hear.' When the text on the stone was read and he was unable to say from whom he had heard this information, it was evident to the Council that he had deposited the suppliant's bough himself."

76 On the problem, see F. Jacoby, *Atthis: The Local Chronicles of Ancient Athens* (Oxford, 1949) 18–19, 26–27, 244–245 n. 46; and J. H. Oliver, *The Athenian Expounders of the Sacred and Ancestral Law* (Baltimore, 1950) 18–23.

written text, presumably drafted and sanctioned by the legislative authority of the state, Callias bolsters the authority of his law by calling it "ancestral" (*patrios*) and by referring to an appeal his father, Hipponicus, made to it on an earlier occasion, when Hipponicus too was presumably acting in his capacity as *dāidouchos*, that is, as a high functionary of the Eleusinian cult. Moreover, the existence of Cephalus's law in written form shows that it was—or could be—known to any person who was tempted to deposit a suppliant's bough on the altar. But the *patrios nomos* was not assumed to be generally known, else Callias could have appealed to something more substantial than an earlier exegesis given by his father.[77] The possible conflict is, accordingly, not between a secular and a religious law but between two religious laws, one sanctioned by the authority of the state, the other a *patrios nomos* that contained cult regulations administered by functionaries of the Eleusinian Mysteries.

Before raising the question about the nature of such *patrioi nomoi*, we ought to investigate the possibility that the conflict may have been one of written against unwritten laws. We know from other passages in Andocides' speech that after the revision of the laws was completed in 403/2 B.C., a law was passed prohibiting for the future the use of any ἄγραφος νόμος, that is, any law that had not been incorporated into the new code.[78] Was Callias's *patrios nomos* one of these, and did the stele to which Cephalus pointed contain a new law that had been substituted for it? The impression that Cephalus's appeal would have overruled Callias suggests that this may indeed have been the case. Still, there is cause to doubt this interpretation. We cannot expect Andocides himself to have argued that not only the decree of Isotimides but also Callias's *patrios nomos* had been invalidated by the law of 403/2 B.C. If he had done so, he would have acknowledged the applicability of the law on the stele to his case, whereas in fact he denied having committed the sacrilegious act altogether. Still, there is no reason to believe that ancestral laws for

77 It seems, however, that familiarity with the πάτριος νόμος could be assumed in the case of initiates, else Andocides' accusers could not have stated that the Two Goddesses confused him so as to deposit the suppliant's bough in ignorance of the law (1.113: ὅτι αὐτῷ με τὼ θεὼ περιαγάγοιεν ὥστε θεῖναι τὴν ἱκετηρίαν μὴ εἰδότα τὸν νόμον, ἵνα δῶ δίκην), a point substantiated perhaps by Meletus's speech, [Lys.] 6.3: ἀδύνατον δὲ καὶ ὑμῖν ἐστι...ἢ κατελεῆσαι ἢ καταχαρίσασθαι ᾿Ανδοκίδῃ, ἐπισταμένοις ὅτι ἐναργῶς τὼ θεὼ τούτω τιμωρεῖτον τοὺς ἀδικοῦντας.

78 Andoc. 1.85 and 87: ἀγράφῳ δὲ νόμῳ τὰς ἀρχὰς μὴ χρῆσθαι μηδὲ περὶ ἑνός. For the meaning, see Ostwald, "Was There a Concept ἄγραφος νομος?" 91–92.

internal cult administration, which had been promulgated as occasion arose by members of the *genē* officially in charge, were as a group included among the ἄγραφοι νόμοι of 403/2 B.C.[79] Cult regulations will have retained even after 403/2 B.C. an existence independent of the laws of the state; they will not have been published, but probably knowledge of them was the preserve of the priests in charge. This will have been true especially in the case of a cult like the Eleusinian Mysteries, which was open only to initiates sworn not to divulge the secrets of their worship. Yet there are indications that the enforcement of penalties for major ritual breaches had passed largely into the hands of the state by the end of the fifth century. This is borne out by a close examination of the terms in which Cephalus's objection is couched. He interprets Callias's reference to the *patrios nomos* as an exegesis, but he raises no objection to the exegesis given on an earlier occasion by Callias's father. Hipponicus's exegesis, to be sure, must be included in the general charge that a Keryx was not allowed to give an official interpretation of the sacred law; still, Cephalus does not contest the fact that exegesis may be made by appropriate officials in certain cases before the Council, and if there had been an objection to Hipponicus's exegesis at the time when he made it, Callias would probably not have referred to his father's interpretation at all. In other words, we may conclude that although authoritative exegesis could be given only by someone other than a Keryx, other Eleusinian functionaries did on occasion cite before the state authorities relevant religious laws accepted as valid. However, Cephalus's citation of the written law dealing with the same offense makes it probable that this particular *patrios nomos* had been superseded by state law in the course of the revisions of 403/2 B.C. It looks, therefore, as if some of the ancestral laws of the Eleusinian cult had been incorporated in a modified form into the written code of 403/2 B.C. and no longer depended upon exegesis. If this is so, Callias was overruled not merely because he belonged to the wrong *genos* but because he cited what had formerly been a sacred law to be applied through exegesis but had by this time been changed and published under the authority of the state.

79 So also K. Clinton, "The Nature of the Late Fifth-Century Revision of the Athenian Law Code," in *Studies in Attic Epigraphy, History, and Topography Presented to Eugene Vanderpool*, Hesperia Supplement 19 (Princeton, 1982) 27–37, esp. 35–36, who unnecessarily believes that Andocides omitted a crucial clause, "if there is a written law concerning the same matter," from his citations at 1.85 and 87. His arguments against ἄγραφος meaning "unpublished" do not carry conviction.

What had been the relation of the laws administered by the Eleusinian priesthood to the laws of the state before 403/2 B.C.? Some light is thrown on this question as well as on the general content of Callias's *patrioi nomoi* by the speech made on this occasion by one of Andocides' prosecutors, Meletus, who was himself a member of the Eumolpid *genos*.[80] The mutilated text, the sanctimonious tone, and the lack of organization and of cogent argumentation, often remarked on by commentators,[81] make it difficult to relate specific statements to the charges against Andocides. It is, therefore, no more than plausible that the deposition of the suppliant's bough and Callias's intended use of it are in the speaker's mind: according to the speaker, Pericles believed in cases of impiety "one should use not only the written laws that deal with them but also the unwritten ones, on the basis of which the Eumolpids expound, which no one yet had the authority to annul or the daring to contradict, and they do not even know who enacted them. His belief was that in this manner these people would pay the penalty not only to men but also to the gods."[82] The prestige of Pericles is invoked to lend an air of authority to an appeal to a set of laws that differ from the written laws of the state in that they are unwritten (ἄγραφοι) and form the basis of exegesis by the Eumolpids. This suggests that the statement is intended to support Callias's appeal to the *patrios nomos* against Cephalus's appeal to the law inscribed upon the stele (Andoc. 1.115–16). Moreover, by stating that "no one yet had the authority to annul or the daring to contradict" them, the speaker seems to exempt these unwritten laws of the Eumolpids as a group from the laws that the legislation of 403/2 B.C. had declared invalid (ἄγραφος). In short, the laws of the Eumolpids are not ἄγραφοι as that term applied to the

---

80 [Lys.] 6.54. For his possible identity with Meletus, the prosecutor of Socrates, see Dover, *Lysias* 79–80. A more agnostic view is expressed by H. Blumenthal, "Meletus the Accuser of Andocides and Meletus the Accuser of Socrates: One Man or Two?" *Philol.* 117 (1973) 169–78.

81 See, for example, Gernet-Bizos, *Lysias* 90: "L'analyse n'en est pas très facile, parce qu'il n'y a guère de composition là-dedans. Le ton général est celui d'une piété déclamatoire; le thème continuel, celui de l'indignité religieuse de l'accusé."

82 [Lys.] 6.10: μὴ μόνον χρῆσθαι τοῖς γεγραμμένοις νόμοις περὶ αὐτῶν, ἀλλὰ καὶ τοῖς ἀγράφοις, καθ' οὓς Εὐμολπίδαι ἐξηγοῦνται, οὓς οὐδείς πω κύριος ἐγένετο καθελεῖν οὐδὲ ἐτόλμησεν ἀντειπεῖν, οὐδὲ αὐτὸν τὸν θέντα ἴσασιν· ἡγεῖσθαι γὰρ ἂν αὐτοὺς οὕτως οὐ μόνον τοῖς ἀνθρώποις ἀλλὰ καὶ τοῖς θεοῖς διδόναι δίκην. I have discussed some aspects of this passage in "Was There a Concept ἄγραφος νόμος?" 89–91; cf. also below, Appendix B, pp. 530–32.

laws excluded from the completed code of 403/2 B.C. (Andoc. 1.85, 87). Although the mention of the Eumolpids here may be construed as a silent admission that Cephalus was correct in denying the Kerykes the right to authoritative exegesis (Andoc. 1.116), the speaker seems nevertheless intent on supporting the substance of the *patrios nomos* Callias had tried to introduce into the case and on strengthening Callias's appeal by emphasizing the need to "pay the penalty not only to men but also to the gods."

I have tried to show elsewhere what the nature of these Eumolpid laws may have been and have argued that they had to be identified as ἄγραφοι or πάτριοι (or simply as πάτρια) in order to differentiate them from the statutes of the state.[83] We can learn a little more about them and their relation to the laws of the state from the writ of impeachment (*eisangelia*) issued against Alcibiades for his alleged participation in the profanation of the Eleusinian Mysteries in 415 B.C. and preserved verbatim by Plutarch. Though Alcibiades' offense is described as a violation of "rules and regulations established by the Eumolpids, Kerykes, and the priests of Eleusis,"[84] it is important to note that none of these Eleusinian functionaries was involved either in bringing the charges against Alcibiades, or in accepting the complaint, or in trying the case. The charge was brought by Thessalus son of Cimon, who did not belong to the Eleusinian priesthood;[85] since the procedure took the form of an *eisangelia*, the initial complaint was lodged before the Council and was referred by the Council for trial before the Assembly.[86] In short, although the Eleusinian priesthood was the source of these νόμιμα and καθεστηκότα, their enforcement rested with the state.

The circumstances in which the *eisangelia* against Alcibiades was lodged in 415 B.C. were different from those surrounding the *endeixis* against Andocides in 400 B.C. Yet in both cases the issue was a violation of Eleusinian cult regulations—called τὰ νόμιμ α καὶ τὰ

83 Ostwald, "Was There a Concept ἄγραφος νόμος?" 90–91. That πάτριοι νόμοι are not invariably laws of this nature is shown by the statement at [Lys.] 6.8–9, εὖ γὰρ ἐπίστασθε, ὦ ἄνδρες ᾿Αθηναῖοι, ὅτι οὐχ οἷόν τε ὑμῖν ἐστιν ἅμα τοῖς τε νόμοις τοῖς πατρίοις καὶ ᾿Ανδοκίδῃ χρῆσθαι, where the context leaves no doubt that the decree of Isotimides as well as the νόμοι of the Eumolpids are subsumed under the term πάτριοι νόμοι.

84 Plut. *Alc.* 22.4: παρὰ τὰ νόμιμα καὶ τὰ καθεστηκότα ὑπό τ᾿ Εὐμολπιδῶν καὶ Κηρύκων καὶ τῶν ἱερέων τῶν ἐξ ᾿Ελευσῖνος.

85 See Davies, *APF*, no. 8429 XIII (C).

86 See above, p. 65 with n. 250.

καθεστηκότα in one case and ἄγραφοι <νόμοι> or πάτριος νόμος in the other—and in the cases of Alcibiades and of Callias's appeal to the *patrios nomos* the interests of Eleusis were (or were to be) enforced by the state, acting through the Council. This suggests that the speaker of the pseudo-Lysianic *Against Andocides* ([Lys.] 6.10) could do no more than exhort the jury to consider the ἄγραφοι <νόμοι> καθ' οὓς Εὐμολπίδαι ἐξηγοῦνται in arriving at their verdict as well as the written laws against impiety: he could promise himself a moral but not a legal effect from his appeal. By the end of the fifth century, therefore, although a distinction between the ritual law of the priestly families and the law of the state was still very much alive and was reflected in differences in terminology, ritual laws were enforced by the secular authorities of the state.

We can go even a step farther. Plutarch reports that after Alcibiades was convicted and his property confiscated, "they voted in addition that all the priests and priestesses should pronounce a curse on him; only Theano, daughter of Menon from Agryle, is said to have objected to the decree, saying that she had become a priestess to utter prayers, not curses."[87] It is not clear from the text whether the curse was voted by the Assembly or by a law court, or, to put it differently, whether it was ordered as a political action independently of the trial or whether it was part of the verdict given by the jury. The problem can be solved by assuming that Alcibiades' trial took place before the Assembly, whose verdict would be indistinguishable from a vote. But in either case, we find an organ of the state prescribing a course of action to a religious authority. It is possible but not demonstrable that the curse was voted under the influence of a Eumolpid exegesis, although Theano's refusal shows that voting the curse was an unusual step to take.[88] The Council did on occasion

---

87 Plut. *Alc.* 22.5: ἔτι καὶ καταρᾶσθαι προσεψηφίσαντο πάντας ἱερεῖς καὶ ἱερείας, ὧν μόνην φασὶ Θεανὼ τὴν Μένωνος Ἀγρυλῆθεν ἀντειπεῖν πρὸς τὸ ψήφισμα, φάσκουσαν εὐχῶν, οὐ καταρῶν ἱέρειαν γεγονέναι. That only the priests of the Eleusinian cult are meant here is clear from ibid. 33.3 and from the likelihood that Theano was a priestess of Demeter and Kore; see Toepffer, *Genealogie* 96–97 n. 2.

88 The mention of Theano's name seems to guarantee the authenticity of Plutarch's statement. A curse pronounced against participants in the profanation of the Mysteries and in the desecration of the herms is also described in awe-inspiring detail in [Lys.] 6.51, καὶ ἐπὶ τούτοις ἱέρειαι καὶ ἱερεῖς στάντες κατηράσαντο πρὸς ἑσπέραν καὶ φοινικίδας ἀνέσεισαν, κατὰ τὸ νόμιμον τὸ παλαιὸν καὶ ἀρχαῖον, where the speaker tries to create the impression that this curse had implicated Andocides by following it immediately with the statement ὡμολόγησε δὲ οὗτος ποιῆσαι. No

act favorably on the advice of Eumolpid priest, as is shown by a report in *Against Andocides* ([Lys.] 6.54) of an incident that happened two generations earlier. When the Council was deliberating whether a Megarian who had committed an act of impiety should be tried or summarily executed—interestingly enough the same penalty Callias's *patrios nomos* demanded—the hierophant Diocles son of Zacorus successfully intervened, advising[89] that an example should be made of the case by putting the man on trial before a jury court. We are not told whether the verdict of the court was more lenient on that occasion. Still, the story provides us with a further example that earlier in the fifth century, too, religious regulations had to be enforced through the agencies of the state. However, it is not until the completed revision of the laws that the supremacy of the written law of the state over the *patrioi nomoi* of individual cults is unequivocally attested.

POPULAR SOVEREIGNTY AND RELIGION

It is time to take stock of the conclusions we have reached about the relation of secular to religious authority in the fifth century B.C. The absence of a caste of priests or of a professional priesthood and the hereditary tenure of the major priesthoods by the noble *genē* obviated the outbreak of major conflicts between secular and religious authority in the aristocratic state. Tensions seem to have set in when Cleisthenes' reforms undermined the gentilician monopoly in religious affairs by reducing the exploitation of cult control for political purposes and by opening the new priesthoods of deme cults, trittys cults, and tribal cults to the lot. At the same time, the legislative powers given to the people in political matters were increasingly used to create popular control over administrative functions in old gentilician cults.

We have tried to trace a development by recognizing four mile-

---

preceding vote is mentioned and the language is manipulated—κατὰ τὸ νόμιμον τὸ παλαιὸν καὶ ἀρχαῖον–to suggest that a curse of this kind was a venerable, traditional procedure. This lack of specificity leads me to believe that Meletus is attempting to implicate Andocides by innuendo in the punishment meted out to Alcibiades fifteen years before and that Plutarch's account has a greater claim to historical accuracy.

89 I am not sure what significance, if any, is to be attached to the fact that [Lys.] 6.54 uses συνεβούλευσε rather than ἐξηγήσατο: possibly Diocles was a member of the Council at this time or at least appeared before it to testify.

stones on the way to the people's assertion of sovereignty in religious matters. Aeschylus's *Supplices* crystallizes a situation in which the secular interest of the state may clash with the dictates of kinship and religion. The conflict is resolved by the magnanimity and piety of the people in assembly, embodying the sovereign element of the state, shouldering religious obligation as part of its political responsibilities, and freely extending the secular protection of religious claims, regardless of consequences. A decade later the Praxiergidai decree reveals a slightly tougher attitude. If we are right in positing that a conflict about the prerogatives of the clan preceded the enactment of the decree, we may see its enactment as a recognition by the *genos* of the people's sovereignty but we may also see it as a demand for a guarantee from the secular power that the rights of the *genos* will be respected. The response of the state leaves no doubt that it believes in exercising its sovereignty over the rights of the clan, for it enforces adherence to the terms of the agreement by imposing penalties for noncompliance.

The *Antigone* does not deal with a problem of foreign policy, as does the *Supplices*; nor does it deal, as does the Praxiergidai decree, with functions traditionally assigned to the *genos* by the state. And yet the problem of the clash between secular authority and religious demands upon the family, between the νόμοι χθονός and the θεῶν δίκα, make the *Antigone* part of the same general complex of secular popular sovereignty coming into conflict with familial religious obligations. If our interpretation of that conflict is correct, the *Antigone* asserts the validity of both, but its treatment of Creon warns of the danger to a state too rigid duly to consider divine demands whose implementation belongs to the family. Not by voluntary acquiescence, as in the Praxiergidai decree, but through the consequences of unbending secularism the state is compelled to acknowledge the religious obligations of the family as part of the καθεστῶτες νόμοι (1113) it has sworn to uphold. Is it possible that in the *Antigone* Sophocles meant to warn against the dangers inherent in too secular an interpretation of the power of the state? Did he try to apply the brake of religious conservatism to the secularism that by 440 B.C. had grown vastly with the development of the Athenian empire, a secularism to which Thucydides provides the most eloquent testimony?

The time separating these three documents is shorter than that between them and the trial of Andocides; strictly speaking, that comes just after the end of the period this book sets out to explore. If Sophocles' *Antigone* permits us to infer that in the 440s the authority of the *nomoi* of the state could still be questioned by appeal to the *nomima* of the family, the events of the late fifth century show the unquestioned dominance of the laws of the state over those ritual laws whose guardianship lay in the hands of the priestly families. The sovereignty of the people in religious administration was more firmly and more explicitly established by the end of the fifth century than it had ever been before. But it had been established by law, not arbitrarily.

Part II

OPPOSITION TO POPULAR SOVEREIGNTY

CHAPTER FOUR

The Prelude

FROM CLEISTHENES TO PERICLES

One of the remarkable facts of human history is that the Athenians attained popular sovereignty with a minimum of bloodshed and internal upheaval. This does not mean that Athens was free from stresses and strains that might on occasion manifest themselves in violent acts; but it does mean that major reforms put an end to internal conflict rather than were born of it. Solon's reforms, we are told, resolved a long-standing strife between the upper and the lower classes. But the agreement of the contending parties had caused his appointment as "mediator and archon" with a mandate to enact constitutional and legal reforms; and though these did not eliminate dissatisfaction, Solon's measures were accepted by both sides and remained a keystone in the Athenian political system for well over three centuries.[1] Cleisthenes' reforms were born of his struggle with Isagoras; what violence they entailed was initiated by Isagoras's summoning Spartan help to cut short the Cleisthenic program. The resistance that Council and people offered was directed against foreign intervention; but the reforms themselves were duly voted into existence by the people, and the durability they gave to the political structure of Athens for the next two centuries testifies to their general acceptance.[2] Ephialtes, to be sure, met a violent death

1 Arist. *Ath.Pol.* 5.2 (cf. 2.1); Plut. *Sol.* 14.
2 Hdt. 5.66, 69.2–70. 2, 72.1–2; Arist. *Ath.Pol.* 20.2–3.

175

after his reforms and possibly as a result of them.[3] Still, the reforms themselves were free from violence: due process was observed in the judicial prosecutions of members of the Areopagus that preceded them, and the reforms were enacted by the votes of Council and Assembly.[4] Until the Thirty came to power, we know of no attempt to invalidate them (Arist. *Ath.Pol.* 35.2).

All this does not mean that there was no opposition to popular government or to the policies it pursued. From the first half of the fifth century we have reports of two attempts to overthrow the democracy, but in neither case does an aversion to popular government as such seem to have been the motive, to say nothing of an attempt to establish an oligarchy.

For the earlier of these attempts Plutarch is our only source. Shortly before the battle of Plataea, he tells us, "some men of great wealth from distinguished families, impoverished by the war and seeing all their power and recognition in the city evaporating with their wealth while others won honors and office, secretly forgathered in a house at Plataea and conspired to overthrow the rule of the people and, if that should fail, to sabotage the cause and to betray it to the barbarians."[5] The historical accuracy of this account has been doubted by some modern scholars,[6] but the fact that the name of one of the ringleaders identified by Plutarch appears on ostraka of the 480s from the Kerameikos suggests that the story deserves to be taken seriously.[7] But to accept Plutarch's story as an account of treasonous activities does not mean that we have to accept the

---

3   Diod. 11.77.6; Plut. *Per.* 10.7–8 reports that "enemies had suborned Aristodicus of Tanagra" (also named by Arist. *Ath.Pol.* 25.4) to kill him. Cf. also Antiphon 5.68 and [Pl.] *Axioch.* 368d. The arguments of D. Stockton, "The Death of Ephialtes," *CQ*, n.s., 32 (1982) 227–28, against the reliability of the evidence on Ephialtes' death carry no conviction.

4   Arist. *Ath.Pol.* 25.2 and 4 with Rhodes, *CAAP* 314–15; Diod. 11.77.6.

5   Plut. *Arist.* 13.1: ἄνδρες ἐξ οἴκων ἐπιφανῶν καὶ χρημάτων μεγάλων πένητες ὑπὸ τοῦ πολέμου γεγονότες καὶ πᾶσαν ἅμα τῷ πλούτῳ τὴν ἐν τῇ πόλει δύναμιν αὐτῶν καὶ δόξαν οἰχομένην ὁρῶντες, ἑτέρων τιμωμένων καὶ ἀρχόντων, συνῆλθον εἰς οἰκίαν τινὰ τῶν ἐν Πλαταιαῖς κρύφα καὶ συνωμόσαντο καταλύσειν τὸν δῆμον· εἰ δὲ μὴ προχωροίη, λυμαίνεσθαι τὰ πράγματα καὶ τοῖς βαρβάροις προδώσειν.

6   E.g., C. Hignett, *Xerxes' Invasion of Greece* (Oxford, 1963) 321 with n. 2. It is accepted by E. Will, "Deux livres sur les guerres médiques et leur temps," *Rev. Phil.*, 3d ser., 38 (1964) 79 n. 1.

7   For the Agasias ostraka, see F. Willemsen, "Ostraka," *Ath.Mitt.* 80 (1965) 100–26, esp. 108–10, and "Die Ausgrabungen im Kerameikos," *Arch.Delt.* 23, part 2, no. 1 (1968) 24–32, esp. 28. According to R. Thomsen, *The Origin of Ostracism* (Copenhagen, 1972) 94 and 101 n. 285, forty-three ostraka inscribed "Agasias

motives it ascribes to the conspirators as historical. Men who lost their possessions to the Persian ravages of Attica in 480 B.C. may well have been convinced that Salamis had not been so decisive a calamity for the Persians as it turned out to be and may have been sufficiently fainthearted before the battle of Plataea to wish to come to terms with the Persians in order to enjoy their property in peace. Many Greek states had taken this step in 480 B.C., and in the years between 487 and 480 B.C. the "friends of the tyrants" in Athens, against whom the law of ostracism is said to have been originally directed, may in fact have been men who preferred accommodation with Persia to preparations for further hostilities.[8] The presence of Agasias's name among the ostraka of the 480s suggests that he may have been a prominent partisan of peace with Persia, and Plutarch's story makes it credible that he made one last, desperate attempt to obtain it before Plataea. But it does not mean that he was opposed on ideological grounds to having a democratic government run the affairs of Athens. Quite apart from the fact that the expression κατάλυσις τοῦ δήμου cannot antedate the reforms of Ephialtes,[9] it is hard to see what opponents of the official policy against Persia would have gained by depriving Council and Assembly of whatever power was theirs in 479 B.C. It is more likely that they merely wanted to oust those who were winning honors and office and were getting ready to fight at Plataea.

The second attempt to overthrow the democracy of which we hear between the time of Cleisthenes and of Pericles deserves to be taken more seriously, especially because it took place within a few years after the reforms of Ephialtes established the democracy. We

---

Arximachou" or "Agasias Lamptreus" were found. The fact that Plutarch uses the spelling "Agesias" and assigns him to Acharnae is no obstacle to the identification, especially since he says (*Arist.* 13.3) that Agesias's fellow conspirator Aeschines belonged to Lamptrae: the two demotics may well have been transposed by Plutarch or his source. I am indebted to F. D. Harvey of the University of Exeter for drawing my attention to this material, which he has now made accessible in "The Conspiracy of Agasias and Aischines (Plutarch, Aristeides 13)," *Klio* 66 (1984) 58–73.

8 Arist. *Ath.Pol.* 22.6. Note in this connection especially the Callias ostraka, discussed by Thomsen, *Origin* 97–99, but with the caveat of D. M. Lewis, "The Kerameikos Ostraka," *ZPE* 14 (1974) 1–4, esp. 3, which is not invalidated by G. M. E. Williams, "The Kerameikos Ostraka," *ZPE* 31 (1978) 103–13, esp. 105–6 and 112–13.

9 It is no less out of place in 479 B.C. than it is in Arist. *Ath.Pol.* 8.4 in connection with the Solonian reforms. See above, p. 8 with n. 17.

learn from Thucydides that in 458/7 B.C., during the first Peloponnesian War, the Spartan army in Boeotia was secretly encouraged to attack Athens by some Athenians "who hoped to put an end to popular rule and to the building of the Long Walls." At the same time Thucydides ascribes the Athenian decision to take the field against the Spartans partly to "a suspicion that there was an attempt to overthrow the rule of the people."[10] The fact that the desire to put an end to popular rule is bracketed with opposition to building the Long Walls affords us some insight into the identity of the conspirators and their motives. The erection of the Long Walls connecting Athens with the Piraeus will have been opposed by rich landowners who realized that their construction would seal Athenian dependence on the sea and that in case of war this would mean abandoning their fields to the land army of an invading enemy.[11] Their fears came to a head just before the battle of Tanagra, when their lands were actually endangered; and that danger might have caused them to seek Spartan assistance in ousting the democratic government, which favored and depended upon the development of sea power.

The Long Walls, further, were crucial in Athenian relations with Sparta. The Spartans regarded the building of an earlier set of walls as the Athenians' first hostile act toward them after the Persian Wars (Thuc. 1.89.3–92), and the dismantling of the Long Walls was looked upon as one of the most humiliating peace conditions Sparta inflicted on the Athenian democracy to end the Peloponnesian War (Xen. *Hell.* 2.2.20, 23; Plut. *Lys.* 15). If we hear of no Athenian voices raised against the initial affront to Sparta, the probable reason is that a great majority of Athenians supported Themistocles in his declaration of Athenian independence of Sparta (Thuc. 1.91.5–7). But with the eclipse of Themistocles' power, the leadership of the allied effort against the Persians fell to Cimon, who both personally admired Sparta and firmly believed in a policy of cooperation between the two powers.[12] Themistocles' ostracism, not later than 471/0 B.C.,[13]

---

10   Thuc. 1.107.4–6: τὸ δέ τι καὶ ἄνδρες τῶν 'Αθηναίων ἐπῆγον αὐτοὺς κρύφα, ἐλπίσαντες δῆμόν τε καταπαύσειν καὶ τὰ μακρὰ τείχη οἰκοδομούμενα.... νομίσαντες δὲ ἀπορεῖν ὅπῃ διέλθωσιν ἐπεστράτευσαν αὐτοῖς, καί τι τοῦ δήμου καταλύσεως ὑποψίᾳ.

11   Meiggs, *AE* 99.

12   Plut. *Cim.* 10.8, 14.4, 15.4, 16.1–3 and 10. For the opposition of Themistocles and Cimon, based on both personal and political grounds, see Plut. *Them.* 5.4, 20.4, 24.6; *Arist*, 25.10; *Cim.* 5.5, 10.8, 16.2.

13   For the date, which has only the weak warrant of Diod. 11.55.1, see A. J. Podlecki, *The Life of Themistocles* (Montreal and London, 1975) 197–98; Lenardon,

shows that the pursuit of the war against Persia had made Athenian policy toward Sparta a major internal issue, which his ostracism resolved in favor of good relations between the rival cities.[14]

These good relations began to deteriorate within five years of Themistocles' banishment, as is apparent from the Spartan promise to support the revolt of Thasos by invading Attica (Thuc. 1.101.1-2) and from Cimon's trial (in which Pericles was the chief prosecutor) after his *euthyna* for his conduct of the Thasian campaign.[15] His acquittal at that time, allegedly obtained by his professing admiration for Sparta (Plut. *Cim*. 14.4, 15.1), his reelection as general for 462/1 B.C. (Thuc. 1.102.1), and his success in persuading the Athenians to accede to the Spartan request for help against the helots at Ithome over the opposition of Ephialtes (Plut. *Cim*. 16.8-10) indicate the strength of the Athenians' desire for good relations with Sparta.

According to Plutarch, Ephialtes enacted his reforms during Cimon's absence, and Cimon tried to reverse them upon his return from the Peloponnese.[16] But the reversal of the Athenian attitude toward Sparta, which was sealed with Cimon's ostracism in 461 B.C., is more easily explained by dating Ephialtes' reforms soon after Cimon's return from the Spartans' abrupt dismissal of the Athenian force at Ithome[17] and by relating those reforms to the support that the Areopagus had given to Cimon and his policies at the time of his *euthyna*.[18] Ephialtes' reforms had the effect of establishing the sovereignty of the people in political affairs, but that does not mean this was their intent. His primary purpose may well have been to outflank those who had been most effective in supporting Cimon's now-discredited policy of "giving a higher priority to the interests of

---

Saga 106-7, 120-21; and J. F. Barrett, "The downfall of Themistocles," *GRBS* 18 (1977) 291-305, esp. 305.

14 See G. L. Cawkwell, "The Fall of Themistocles," in B. F. Harris, ed., *Auckland Classical Essays Presented to E. M. Blailock* (Auckland and Oxford, 1970) 39-58.

15 See above, pp. 40-42.

16 Plut. *Cim*. 15 with Meiggs, *AE* 89 with n. 3.

17 Thuc. 1.102.3-4 with de Ste. Croix, *OPW* 179 n. 43.

18 See above, p. 41 with n. 152. I am not convinced by the arguments of J. R. Cole, "Cimon's Dismissal, Ephialtes' Revolution and the Peloponnesian Wars," *GRBS* 15 (1974) 369-85, esp. 380, that Cimon engineered his own dismissal from Ithome with Spartan connivance in order to oppose the anti-Spartan policy of Ephialtes at home.

Sparta than to the expansion of his own country"[19] by depriving them of their power to conduct the audit of generals. Further, he probably wanted to ensure that pro-Spartan sentiments would not be an obstacle to continued Athenian expansion.[20] This view is the more likely because we hear of no contemporary opposition to the reforms on such grounds as that they gave too much power to the people; Cimon's ostracism in the following year suggests that the issue between him and Ephialtes revolved around Athenian policy toward Sparta and not around ideological principles concerning the structure of the Athenian state.[21]

However strong the anti-Spartan sentiment in Athens may have been as a result of the rebuff at Ithome, conservative elements resented Ephialtes' attack on what they conceived of as the ancient powers of the Areopagus more strongly than they lamented its effect of establishing popular sovereignty. This is clear from what Plutarch (*Cim*. 15.3) reports about Cimon's reaction to the reforms and as well from a tradition preserved by Diodorus that Ephialtes was assassinated for his attack on the Areopagus.[22]

The plot to enlist Spartan help to overthrow popular rule at the time of Tanagra is therefore best taken as indicating that conservative Athenians continued to resent the curtailment of Areopagite power for several years after the reforms of Ephialtes and that they had therefore come to oppose the extension of popular power to which Ephialtes' program had given rise. Ephialtes' measures had polarized the internal politics of Athens: on one side, Cimon's foreign policy of friendship with Sparta had coalesced with a conservative internal policy symbolized by the Areopagus; on the other, an expansionist, sea-oriented, and anti-Spartan foreign policy had come to be associated with increased popular control over the magistrates by the organs and institutions of the new democracy. Fear for the security of their lands in case of war will have led some extremists to regard the

19 Plut. *Cim*. 16.9–10. The relevant expression (Critias 88B52 [DK⁶]) runs: τὴν τῆς πατρίδος αὔξησιν ἐν ὑστέρῳ θέμενον τοῦ Λακεδαιμονίων συμφέροντος.

20 Cf. Martin, "Kleisthenes" 33–38, esp. 38: "Solange der Areopag die Beamten kontrollierte und solange er bestrebt war, mit Sparta in gutem Einvernehmen zu bleiben, waren der athenischen Expansion Grenzen gesetzt. Meine These ist, dass Ephialtes dem Areopag die Kontrolle der Magistrate mit der Absicht entzog, diese Grenzen zu beseitigen."

21 Plut. *Cim*. 17.3 relates the ostracism to anti-Spartan sentiment after Ithome; cf. *Per*. 9.5, where, however, μισόδημον is bracketed with φιλολάκωνα.

22 See n. 3 above.

construction of the Long Walls less as marking undue increase in the political power of the people than as manifesting a further and perhaps fatal deterioration in Athenian-Spartan relations, which could be repaired if Sparta were induced to help oust the regime responsible for the anti-Spartan policy of Athens. If this interpretation is correct, genuine antidemocratic sentiment among the conspirators seems secondary to fear for their lands and to a desire for Sparta's friendship. The conspiracy's primary motive was not opposition to the government of Athens or to the principles it embodied, nor either, certainly, a desire to establish an oligarchy.

We learn of no other attempts to overthrow the government in the period between Cleisthenes and Pericles. If there were any, they are likely to have arisen, as the conspiracies before Plataea and Tanagra did, from a fear for the security of property that led aristocratic landowners to oppose a foreign policy the people and their leaders supported. Such conspiracies probably would not have been based on ideological antagonism to popular rule *per se*; for had such a sentiment existed at large, our sources would surely have preserved traces of opposition to the measures by which popular power was established and enlarged during this period. We hear of no protest against the inclusion of the *hēliaia* in trying crimes against the state; nor of any objection to the right of every citizen, however humble, to participate in the discussion of public policies and to contribute by his vote to shaping them; nor either of any outcry, even after the reforms of Ephialtes, against nobly born officials' having to submit themselves to panels of simple citizens, who did not match them in distinction, for scrutiny and audit. Of course we should not expect any protests to come from the common people, who were the chief beneficiaries of these developments, but we might have expected to hear demands from among them for more (or more far-reaching) rights than were already theirs. In fact we hear of nothing of the kind, and more remarkably still, until the death of Pericles we hear of no complaints from the upper classes against the masses' increasing political rights.

PERICLEAN DEMOCRACY AND ITS OPPOSITION

Internal Policy

Although we know more about the Periclean age than about any period in Greek history before it, our knowledge of its internal affairs is subject to peculiar encumbrances. The most serious of these is that our most detailed information comes from our latest and least reliable source, Plutarch. A second difficulty is that our best and most reliable source, Thucydides, offers no more than a few general remarks on the internal policies of Pericles (2.65.3–9). Third, and least troublesome, our best source on life in Periclean Athens, the *Constitution of the Athenians* wrongly ascribed to Xenophon and commonly known as the "Old Oligarch" (although its author was probably neither),[23] draws an excellent picture of Athenian society as seen through the keen eyes of a disenchanted member of the upper classes, but it is rather short on political information and gives no specific account of Pericles and his policies.

Pericles made only two known contributions to the political development of popular sovereignty. The more important of these was the introduction of pay for jury service, which is likely to have come early in his career, certainly before the ostracism of his chief political antagonist, Thucydides son of Melesias.[24] The amount of the pay was small; two obols a day was "little more than bare subsistence,"[25] but it assured even the poorest Athenian he would not completely forfeit the day's earnings if he wished to participate in calling elected officials to account. The second measure attributed to Pericles is the citizenship law of 451/0 B.C., by which citizens' rights were bestowed only on those who could prove that both their parents were citizens of Athens.[26] We need not here enter into the vexing problem of the motive underlying its enactment,[27] but its minimum effect will have been to give the people as a whole the

---

23   E. Lévy, *Athènes devant la défaite de 404*, Bibliothèque des Écoles Françaises d'Athènes et de Rome 225 (Paris, 1976) 273–75 with bibliography on p. 273 n. 1, has new and convincing arguments for its composition in 431 or 430 B.C. Cf. E. Will, "Un Nouvel Essai d'interprétation de l'*Athènaiôn Politeia* pseudo-Xénophontique," *REG* 91 (1978) 77–95, esp. 91–95. With the majority of modern scholars I believe that the treatise must have been composed before Brasidas's expedition of 424 B.C. and after the outbreak of the Peloponnesian War. There can be little doubt that the conditions it reflects are those prevailing in the years immediately preceding as well as immediately following the death of Pericles.

24   Arist. *Pol.* 2.12, 1274ᵃ 8–9; *Ath.Pol.* 27.4, where the motive for its introduction, namely, competition with Cimon's munificence, suggests an early date; cf. Hignett, *HAC* 342–43.

25   Scholl. Ar. *Vesp.* 88, 300; cf. Jones, *AD* 50 with n. 43.

26   Arist. *Ath.Pol.* 26.4; Plut. *Per.* 37.3, Ael. *VH* 6.10; cf. *Suda* s.v. δημοποίητος.

27   On this problem, see Rhodes, *CAAP* 331–35, and especially J. K. Davies, "Athenian Citizenship: The Descent Group and the Alternatives," *CJ* 73 (1977–8) 105–21.

power of determining who was and who was not to enjoy citizenship and the privileges that went with it (including pay for public service) instead of leaving the final decision in this matter to the demes.[28]

In the Funeral Oration, Thucydides has Pericles define democracy as a form of government "run with a view to the interests of the majority, not of the few."[29] Democracy, in this view, does not define those who govern but those to whose welfare the government of the state is geared; the *dēmos*, in this context, is not the people as a whole but its largest constituent, the πλείονες, the masses. This statement is a true reflection of Pericles' internal economic policy. We know few details about the history of state pay in Athens and cannot be sure of the extent of Pericles' responsibility for the pay of the councilors, army, navy, ambassadors, and supervisors of public works, which is attested from the 430s on.[30] But if it is correct to infer from the institution of pay for jurors and from the citizenship law that Pericles wished to ensure both that all classes, especially the lower classes, would participate to the maximum in the democratic process and that the people as a whole would control questions of citizenship, it is likely that he approved of pay for other public services also.

Moreover, Pericles initiated a policy of spending public revenues, mainly from the allied tribute, to give employment and entertain-

28 C. Patterson, *Pericles' Citizenship Law of 451–50 B.C.* (New York, 1981) 104–7.

29 Thuc. 2.37.1: καὶ ὄνομα μὲν διὰ τὸ μὴ ἐς ὀλίγους ἀλλ' ἐς πλείονας οἰκεῖν δημοκρατία κέκληται. That this is the correct interpretation of οἰκεῖν ἐς was already seen by J. G. Sheppard and L. Evans, *Notes on Thucydides*[2] (London, 1870) 190. Their observation invalidates the view taken of δημοκρατία by Kinzl, "Δημοκρατία" 117–27, 312–26, esp. 316–18, as "der Zustand einer auf die Mehrheit gegründeten Regierungs- bzw. Verwaltungs- (nicht aber Herrschafts-) form (nicht aber die Form selber)."

30 For the evidence, see G. F. Hill, *Sources for Greek History between the Persian and Peloponnesian Wars*, ed. R. Meiggs and A. Andrewes (Oxford, 1951) Index II.3.5. For jury pay, see Arist. *Pol.* 2.12, 1274ᵃ 8–9; *Ath.Pol.* 27.4. That hoplites and sailors guarding Potidaea in 428 B.C. were paid one drachma per day (plus one drachma for the hoplite's ὑπερέτης) is attested at Thuc. 3.17.4, and the same rate of pay is attested for sailors in the Sicilian campaign at Thuc. 6.31.3, suggesting that this was the normal rate of pay (differently Gomme, *HCT* 2.275) and that its introduction goes back to at least the days of Pericles. To what extent the rates agreed upon by Athens, Argos, Mantineia, and Elis for the pay of hoplites, light-armed troops, archers, and cavalrymen can be regarded as normal is unknown; see Thuc. 5.47.6. On the introduction of pay for military service in Athens, see W. K. Pritchett, *Ancient Greek Military Practices Part 1*, University of California Publications in Classical Studies 7 (Berkeley and Los Angeles, 1971) 3–29, esp. 7–24.

ment to the urban masses and at the same time to make Athens a worthy cultural center of the empire it controlled. Although most of our information comes couched in the hostile valuations Plutarch preserves, its factual basis can hardly be questioned. There was not only the impressive building program, which gave work to an impressive number of craftsmen and laborers (*Per.* 12.5–6), but also the organization of shows, feasts, and processions for the entertainment of the public,[31] the annual dispatch of sixty triremes on eight-month missions to provide paid work for crews, and the settlement of cleruchs and colonists in many parts of the empire. By such programs Pericles "relieved the city of its idle mob, whom leisure had turned into busybodies, solved the needs of the people, and sent among the allies settlers to inspire them with fear and to provide a garrison to inhibit revolt" (*Per.* 11.4–6).

Under these circumstances the masses are unlikely to have felt slighted by the few political disabilities from which they still suffered. The admission of the zeugitai to the archonship from 457/6 B.C. on (Arist. *Ath.Pol.* 26.2) may have given the masses hope that in time all offices in the state would be open to all citizens, but even this hope was not essential for their happiness. In the absence of a fully paid civil service, any ambition for high office will have been tempered by the knowledge that it involved personal sacrifice and personal expense. As the Old Oligarch puts it, "To those offices that, if well managed, bring security to the whole people and, if not well managed, danger, the common people do not demand to be eligible; they do not think that there is any need for them to have the lot make them eligible either to the generalships or to the cavalry commands. For the common people realize that they stand to gain more by not holding these offices themselves and by letting the most competent men occupy them. But any office that brings pay or profit into the home, that one the common people seek to hold" ([Xen.] *Ath.Pol.* 1.3). The people's vote in Council and Assembly constituted real power, as did also their right to elect the higher magistrates; and Pericles' policy of paid jury service made the people's power to control the elected magistrates also more palpable than it had been before. No policy could be implemented without the people's approval, and at the same time they were freed from the responsibilities of implementation and could hold executive officials accounta-

31   Cf. also [Xen.] *Ath.Pol.* 1.13, 2.9–10, 3.8.

ble if anything went awry. And the policies they would approve would of course be those of Periclean imperialism, which brought them economic prosperity; that Pericles belonged to a higher social class may have made a difference to his fellow aristocrats, but it will have made no difference to the common people.

Aristocratic Opposition

The popular appeal of Pericles' policies, his haughty bearing and personal charisma, and perhaps also the fact that he likened the empire to a tyranny gave rise to the suspicion already in his lifetime that he was aiming at sole, tyrannical rule.[32] It was especially on these grounds that opposition to his power developed, first among the upper classes and, in the 430s, among those who felt his policies threatened the religious structure of the state.

The most serious opposition Pericles had to face is associated with Thucydides son of Melesias.[33] The grounds on which Thucydides attacked Pericles are difficult to ascertain; our knowledge depends almost exclusively on three chapters of Plutarch's *Pericles* so filled with anachronisms, patently false historical information, and moralistic cant that a recent study has rejected their evidence as the worthless creation of a postclassical rhetorician.[34] But this is too radical a solution for a real historical problem: however garbled and moralizing Plutarch and his source may be, the issues that arose between Pericles and Thucydides cannot be pure invention and remain recognizable enough for us amid all the confusion to give them at least historical plausibility.

According to Plutarch (*Per*. 11.1–2), Thucydides was put up by the aristocrats "to curb Pericles' power and prevent it from altogether becoming a monarchy"; this was to be achieved by consolidating the upper classes, which had previously "been scattered and mixed up with the people," into a solid counterweight to the masses in order to restore balance in the state. Aristotle confirms that Thucydides was indeed a spokesman (*prostatēs*) for the upper classes, variously

32 Some of the contemporary evidence is mentioned by Plut. *Per*. 16.1; cf. also 7.4, 8.3, *et passim*. See also Thuc. 2.65.8–10, 63.2; Ar. *Ach*. 530–39; Diod. 12.38.2–39.3.

33 Arist. *Ath.Pol*. 28.2; Plut. *Per*. 6.2, 8.5 (cf. *Mor*. 802c), 11, 14.1–3, 16.3; *Nic*. 2.2; schol. Ar. *Vesp*. 947; Aristeides 46 ὑπὲρ τῶν τεττάρων (ed. G. Dindorf, vol. 2 [Leipzig, 1829] 159–60) with schol. (ibid. 3.446–47); cf. also Satyrus, fr. 14 (*FHG* 3.163).

34 A. Andrewes, "The Opposition to Perikles," *JHS* 98 (1978) 1–8.

identified as εὐγενεῖς, γνώριμοι, or εὔποροι, against the populist cause Pericles espoused (*Ath.Pol.* 28.2). Aristotle's further information that Thucydides was related to Cimon by marriage (ibid.) would be pointless if his policies were not thought of as in some way continuing Cimon's; Plutarch's repetition of this statement (*Per.* 11.1), with the addition that Thucydides was less warlike than Cimon but more of a speaker and politician, suggests that Thucydides' distinction lay in internal affairs rather than in external or military exploits.[35]

One wonders how the aristocrats may have "put up" Thucydides "in opposition" (ἀντέστησαν ἐναντιωσόμενον, Plut. *Per.* 11.1) to Pericles, considering that there were no party political organizations in ancient Athens,[36] and how he may have gone about "separating [the nobility] from the rest and uniting them into one."[37] The statement becomes more intelligible, however, if we consider that later tradition credited Thucydides' opposition with beginning a polarization of the state into democratic and oligarchical camps, which became a serious problem after the death of Pericles.[38] The minimum core of historical truth in chapter 11 of Plutarch's *Pericles* is, therefore, that Thucydides made his mark as the spokesman for the social class that viewed Pericles' manipulation of the masses with alarm, believing he was using them as a stepping stone toward absolute personal power. There is no indication of antagonism toward the democratic institutions of Athens as such; no attempt was made to set up oligarchical institutions in their place.

The cause-and-effect relationship (διό, *Per.* 11.4–6) Plutarch posits between Thucydides' opposition and Pericles' publicly financed employment and entertainment of the masses is ludicrously anachronistic. Many of the measures Plutarch's account attributes to reaction against Thucydides must have followed rather than preceded his ostracism in 444 or 443 B.C.[39] Nevertheless, we may infer

35   For this reason I do not believe with Andrewes, "Opposition" 5, that Plutarch's source excluded any achievements of Thucydides in external affairs; there simply were none worth mentioning.

36   See Connor, *New Politicians* 24 n. 36.

37   Plut. *Per.* 11.2 with Andrewes, "Opposition" 2.

38   Plut. *Per.* 11.3. F. J. Frost, "Pericles, Thucydides, Son of Melesias, and Athenian Politics before the War," *Hist.* 13 (1964) 385–99, argues more suggestively than convincingly that the rift Plutarch attributed to Thucydides' opposition to Pericles actually reflects the attacks by Cleon and his like on the aristocratic establishment, as prefigured by the attacks on Pericles' associates in the 430s. Nothing so specific can be assumed, especially since we know little of such attacks by Cleon.

39   Andrewes, "Opposition" 2–4, 6–7.

the existence of a credible tradition regarding Pericles' populist measures as a tactic to satisfy his personal political ambitions by using public funds to outspend his aristocratic opposition, which Plutarch identifies with Thucydides but Aristotle identifies with Cimon (*Ath. Pol.* 27.3–4).

Of the populist measures the building program sustained the heaviest attack, and Plutarch (*Per.* 14.3) intimates that opposition to it led to Thucydides' ostracism. Scholars agree that Thucydides spearheaded the opposition, but there is no agreement what part of it in particular he attacked.[40] Plutarch presents Pericles as vulnerable on three interrelated scores: his financial policies were giving the Athenian people a bad reputation among the Greeks for overbearing and tyrannical conduct (*Per.* 12.1–2); for the beautification of Athens he had diverted from Delos monies exacted from the allies for use against Persia (ibid. and 14.1);[41] and he was spoiling the masses by his policy of state pay for public works and for public service (9.1–3, 11.4–6, 12.4–6; cf. Pl. *Grg.* 515e). Plutarch (*Per.* 14.1) associates Thucydides and his group only with opposition to squandering allied funds on the masses, but it is hard not to identify them also with the unnamed enemies who objected to the diversion of allied tribute into the building program (12.1–2). The nature of Thucydides' concern with allied funds must remain a matter of conjecture. There is no reason to believe that he was a sentimental panhellenist who supported the allies on principle, nor is there any indication that either he or any other member of the upper classes objected on principle to levying tribute from the allies for the benefit of Athens.[42] What he seems to have been concerned about, as a close study of Plutarch's text has shown, was the use made of tribute revenues in defiance of Greek and especially of allied opinion.[43] The respect he enjoyed among some allies is attested by Plato (*Meno* 94d). On the tenuous basis of his relation to Cimon by marriage, and in view of the Athenians' major problems when he led the opposition to Pericles, we may guess that he shared with some Spartans on

40 See Andrewes, "Opposition" 2.

41 Meiggs, *AE* 133, believes that this argument could not have been made after the Peace of Callias since it assumes "that the allies still think that they are paying tribute for operations against Persia." But this is not a necessary inference: the point may well be that the tribute originally levied against Persia—and still being levied— was misused for the building program.

42 Meiggs, *AE* 157, and Andrewes, "Opposition" 4–5.

43 H. D. Meyer, "Thukydides Melesiou und die oligarchische Opposition gegen Perikles," *Hist.* 16 (1967) 141–54, esp. 146–51.

occasion a genuine concern that the imposition of tribute and the punishment meted out for revolt should not deprive a Greek state of its *autonomia*, as it had done in Thasos and Aegina.[44] He may have had no objection to using tribute to rebuild Athenian temples, but he may have found an impressive number of adherents, especially among upper-class Athenians, who regarded forcible exaction of tribute for that purpose and the "enslavement" of allies for failure to pay as excessive treatment of a Greek state (Plut. *Per.* 11.3).

Our investigation so far has shown that the mode of exercise of popular power was not an issue between Thucydides and Pericles; Thucydides was concerned with what excessive influence Pericles acquired by catering to the masses and with how Athens was humiliating other Greek states by exploiting them for the benefit of the Athenian mob. But the mode of the exercise of popular power is very much on the mind of another aristocratic opponent—or, more precisely, critic—of the Periclean democracy, the Old Oligarch, who wrote his *Constitution of the Athenians* toward the end of Pericles' career.[45] Unlike Thucydides, he was not an active politician; and the purpose for which he composed his work remains obscure.[46] Nothing is known about the author, but we can infer that he belonged to the Athenian upper class from his negative, though often admiring, comments on Athenian democracy and from his consistent use of pejorative and laudatory adjectives to describe the lower and upper classes, respectively.[47] If he propounds any thesis at all, it is that, its glaring shortcomings notwithstanding, the Athenian democracy works too consistently and too well to produce a group of disfranchised malcontents strong enough to overthrow it ([Xen.] *Ath.Pol.* 3.12–13). Consequently, the treatise is a piece of analysis rather than an invitation to induce change by political action. It names no

44   See M. Ostwald, *Autonomia: Its Genesis and Early History* (Chico, Calif., 1982) 40–41.

45   See n. 23 above.

46   The suggestions offered range from a private letter addressed by an Athenian oligarch to a Spartan sympathizer (so E. Hohl, "Zeit und Zweck der pseudoxenophontischen *Athenaion Politeia*," *CP* 45 [1950] 26–35) to a set piece in a theoretical debate (W. G. Forrest, "An Athenian Generation Gap," *YClS* 24 [1975] 37–52, esp. 43–45). On the problem, see M. Treu, "Ps. Xenophon: D. Πολιτεία Ἀθηναίων," *RE* 2. Reihe, 9. Band (1967) 1962–73.

47   For his identity as an Athenian, see H. Frisch, *The Constitution of the Athenians* (Copenhagen, 1942) 90, but it remains doubtful whether the treatise was written in Athens or in exile; see A. Lesky, *A History of Greek Literature*, tr. J. Willis and C. de Heer (New York, 1966) 453–54.

leading politicians, neither Pericles nor any other popular leader. It is largely devoted to describing what factors account for the strength of Athenian society, and its criticisms are so tempered with explanations why things are the way they are that as criticism it is less cutting than resentful.

The Old Oligarch's specific attacks are social and economic rather than political. Behind his antagonism lurks little more than a wistful regret that power has passed into the hands of the wrong people, who lack the style that had characterized the old, aristocratic ruling class; it thus reminds us of the plaints of Theognis about his native Megara a century earlier. The Old Oligarch is upset that the wretched masses (οἱ πονηροί) are better off than the decent citizens (οἱ χρηστοί, 1.1) and that they enjoy a privileged position (1.4); he charges them with being more interested in their private profit than in the good of the state (1.3); and he objects to their ignorance, disorderliness, and mischievousness (1.5). Their indiscipline has had its effect in the bad manners of slaves and of resident aliens, who can no longer be distinguished from Athenians in appearance or attire and even have the nerve to talk back to free citizens (1.10–12). The masses' lack of education makes them reject athletic and cultural pursuits, which had once been the hallmarks of aristocratic society, to indulge instead in the kind of singing and dancing for which they get paid from the liturgies levied upon the rich (1.13), or to build for themselves more palaestras, changing rooms, and bathing facilities than are available to the upper classes (2.10), and to have more holidays than are good for them (2.9; 3.2, 4, 8).

Underlying these criticisms is a tone of strong moral disapprobation: "The best element is universally opposed to democracy" (ἔστι δὲ πάσῃ γῇ τὸ βέλτιστον ἐναντίον τῇ δημοκρατίᾳ, 1.5). The main reasons adduced to support this contention revolve about a concern for justice. The best social elements pay "painstaking attention to decency" (ἀκρίβεια δὲ πλείστη εἰς τὰ χρηστά) and are least prone to indiscipline and dishonesty (1.5). But in a democracy, the commons are more interested in their own freedom of action than in an orderly and law-abiding life (1.8); and the jury courts render expedient rather than just verdicts (1.13), geared, in cases involving allies, to preserving democrats and destroying their opponents (1.16)—who, interestingly enough, are never referred to as "oligarchs" but always as "the better sort" (χρηστοί, βελτίους, ἀγαθοί) or "the rich" (πλούσιοι). The ideas here set forth prefigure the policy Diodotus advocates toward the allies in Thucydides (3.47).

The tacit assumption that class interests are fixed and immutable pervades the Old Oligarch's thinking. They make tensions between the upper and lower classes inevitable (1.2, 2.20), except that occasionally a member of the lower class may be found who is not populist in outlook (2.19) or a member of the upper classes is depraved enough to prefer life in a democratic state to that in an oligarchical state (2.20).[48] Thus for the author the social, economic, and moral faults he censures in the Athenian democracy inhere of necessity in its structure; this explains why he has no real complaint about the political and judicial functioning of the Athenian democracy. All he says is that the Council and the jury courts labor under too heavy a caseload to operate efficiently and that even bribes are inadequate to procure proper service (3.1–6).

Class divisions and the structural defects they import into a democracy also determine the nature of external relations. The Athenian *dēmos* harasses and prosecutes the upper classes among the allies, the πλούσιοι καὶ χρηστοί, because it knows that their strength would spell an end to imperial rule. The Athenian upper class feels solidarity with its allied counterpart, aware that the preservation of the "best" element (τοὺς βελτίστους) in allied states will support them, too (1.14–2.19). For the same reason, the Athenians support the inferior social elements in cases of allied revolts: they know that they can count on their good will but can expect only hostility from the upper classes (3.10–11). And finally, we are told that alliances and treaties among oligarchical states are more enduring than among democratic states, since a large body can more easily disavow a treaty's obligations than a small group can (2.17).

Is there any hope for reform? In the author's view the answer is no. He has his idea of what a good state will look like: "If you are looking for government by good laws, you will first of all see that the most capable enact laws for them; then the decent men will

48 The text at 2.19–20 is difficult and subject to misinterpretation: καὶ τοὐναντίον γε τούτου (sc. that the lower classes feel threatened by the goodness of the upper classes) ἔνιοι, ὄντες ὡς ἀληθῶς τοῦ δήμου, τὴν φύσιν οὐ δημοτικοί εἰσι. Bowersock's translation (Loeb, 1971), "On the other hand, some persons are not by nature democratic although they are truly on the people's side," makes nonsense of the context and of the Greek. For, as the following paragraph (2.20) shows, ὄντες . . . τοῦ δήμου refers to the social class to which a person belongs, while δημοτικός— here as well as normally—applies to social or political sympathies. Translate: "And, to be sure, there are some cases in which the opposite is true, namely, that men who in fact belong to the common people are not populist by natural inclination."

discipline the wretches; the decent men will deliberate in the Council about the city and will not let madmen be members of the Council, make speeches, or be members of the Assembly. Surely, good measures such as these would very quickly reduce the masses to slavery" (1.9). Obviously this kind of state cannot be attained under a democracy: "One can find many ways for making the condition of the state better, but to find ways sufficient to make it better while maintaining it as a democracy is not easy, except, as I just suggested, to add a little here and take away a little there" (3.9). In short, good government can be had only from the upper classes, but we are told neither what their government would look like nor whether it would be able to maintain the empire (which the Old Oligarch is not inclined to give up) without retaining the institutions of the Athenian democracy. We are left, then, with the picture of a democracy politically capable of preserving its institutions against any attempts, however morally desirable, to overthrow it (3.12–13) and resented by a member of the upper classes for the social and economic benefits it brings to the masses.

Religious Opposition

The Old Oligarch speaks with the voice of an aristocrat hostile but largely resigned to the realities of the Athenian democracy, to which there had been no effective political opposition since the ostracism of Thucydides. A different kind of resistance, aimed more at Pericles' person and perhaps predicated on the fear that his policies might lead to war,[49] arose in the early 430s after Thucydides' ostracism and almost immediately upon the completion of the Parthenon. In contrast to the aristocratic opposition, it seems to have been informed mainly by religious scruples and by an intense dislike of the foreign intellectuals with whom Pericles had surrounded himself, and it took advantage of the judicial institutions of the democracy in its attempt to curb Pericles' power.

There were two proceedings against Pericles in the 430s. The facts of the later one are fairly clear: he was recalled and deposed from his generalship in 430/29 B.C. for having failed to capture Epidaurus; he was put on trial presumably as a result of his *euthyna*, and a fine of

---

49 This seems to me the most sensible interpretation of the charges that Pericles started the war to extricate himself from personal difficulties, mentioned as early as Ar. *Ach*. 515–39 and *Pax* 605–18 and preserved mainly in Diod. 12.38.2–39.3, Aristodemus *FGH* 104F1.16, and Plut. *Per*. 32.6.

between fifteen and fifty talents was imposed on him. Various ancient authors name Cleon, Simmias, and Lacratidas as his accusers;[50] but the tribunal that tried him is not identified, and we are not told what the formal charges were.[51] The relation of this trial to earlier proceedings against Pericles and his associates had been obscured by Plutarch's confused narrative; but it has now been clarified by the demonstration that Dracontides' motion against Pericles, which led to his prosecution, was part of the Phidias affair and that the alleged trials of Aspasia and Anaxagoras were also closely related to it.[52] All these proceedings took place in the short period from 438/7 to 437/6 B.C., and all exhibit in common an appeal to the religious sensibilities of the Athenian people, to which, as Sophocles had pointed out a few years earlier in his *Antigone*, the secular policies of the state were vulnerable.[53]

Phidias was tried in 438/7 B.C. for having embezzled some of the gold and ivory appropriated to him for his chryselephantine statue of Athena.[54] All our sources suggest that his trial was engineered by enemies of Pericles who according to Plutarch suborned one of Phidias's associates, Menon, to lodge an information (*mēnysis*) against Phidias in return for immunity (*adeia*) for himself. The

---

50 Plut. *Per.* 35.4–5; cf. Diod. 12.45.4, who attributes the charge to war-weariness on the part of the Athenians and gives eighty talents as the amount of the fine. [Dem.] 26.6 and *Suda* s.v. τάλαντον give the fine as fifty talents. This is presumably the occasion referred to by Thuc. 2.65.3–4 (cf. ἔτι δ' ἐστρατήγει, 2.59.3), a passage that like Diod. 12.45.5, also attests his reelection as general. Cf. above, Chap. 1, n. 248, case 1.

51 Pl. *Grg.* 515e–516a mentions a trial for embezzlement (κλοπή) to which Pericles was subjected toward the end of his life; he was convicted and almost condemned to death. As Gomme, *HCT* 2.182–83, points out, the charge of embezzlement "looks like an echo of the charge against Pheidias, in which Perikles was involved." That his accusers proposed the death penalty is as likely for 430 B.C. as for the earlier trial.

52 See F. J. Frost, "Pericles and Dracontides," *JHS* 84 (1964) 69–72, and "Pericles, Thucydides" 385–99, esp. 392–97; G. Donnay, "La Date du procès de Phidias," *Ant.Class.* 37 (1968) 19–36; and especially J. Mansfeld, "The Chronology of Anaxagoras' Athenian Period and the Date of His Trial," part 1, *Mnemos.*, 4th ser., 22 (1979) 39–69, and esp. part 2, ibid. 23 (1980) 17–95, whose chronological framework is here adopted. A similar chronology is adopted without argument by Roberts, *Accountability* 59–62.

53 Brought out by Mansfeld, "Chronology," part 2, 76–80. However, I see no warrant to assume with Mansfeld a *hetaireia* or a combination of *hetaireiai* as the source of these attacks. On Sophocles' *Antigone*, see pp. 148–61 above.

54 Philochorus *FGH* 328F121 (= schol. Ar. *Pax* 605); Diod. 12.39.1–2; Aristodemus *FGH* 104F1.16; and Plut. *Per.* 31.2–5. For the accuracy of Philochorus's date, see Donnay, "Date"; and especially Mansfeld, "Chronology," part 2, 40–47, 69–70.

people complied with Menon's request for immunity, and Phidias was prosecuted in the Assembly (*Per.* 31.3). This rather unusual choice of a tribunal may be due to the fact that the funds alleged to have been embezzled were sacred: Diodorus reports that the same Assembly meeting that ordered Phidias's arrest also implicated Pericles, ordering his prosecution for theft of sacred objects (ἱεροσυλία) because he had been a supervisor (*epistatēs*) of the work on the Parthenon (12.39.1–2).[55] We can accept the relation between the two cases even if the accusation against Pericles was made at a later Assembly meeting. Although Pericles was also serving as general at the time he functioned as supervisor,[56] the tenor of the decree a certain Dracontides proposed in the Assembly suggests that it was a demand for a *euthyna* on Pericles' administration as an *epistatēs*, preparatory to an *eisangelia* to be lodged against him. Under this decree Pericles' accounts of monies disbursed were to be deposited with the prytaneis; a trial was to be conducted on the Acropolis, that is, on ground sacred to Athena; and the judges were to take their ballots from the altar, that is, from a sacred place.[57] We know too little about Dracontides to do more than guess at his motives for attacking Pericles. He had been a councilor in 446/5 B.C. and had presided over the Assembly meeting at which the Chalcis decree was passed (ML, no. 52.2), and he was one of the generals dispatched to Corcyra in 433/2 B.C. (ML, no. 61.20), but these facts tell us nothing about his political stance in 438/7 B.C. However, since his name is not uncommon in the branch of the Eteobutad *genos* that held the hereditary priesthood of Athena Polias,[58] religious motives may well have played a part in his action.

Dracontides' motion did not, however, have its desired effect. Hagnon, the father of Theramenes and a staunch supporter of

---

55   That Pericles was an *epistatēs* at that time is confirmed by Philochorus *FGH* 328F121. That this (rather than Diodorus's ἐπιμελητής) was the correct title is shown by, e.g., ML, no. 54A(2).3 and B1. See Donnay, "Date" 32–34.

56   Although we have no list of generals for 438/7 B.C., this year is one of the fifteen in which, according to Plut. *Per.* 16.3, Pericles held that office continuously.

57   Plut. *Per.* 32.3. That this procedure envisages an accounting of disbursements made for a religious purpose, which would have no place in the proceedings of 430/29 B.C., is rightly stressed by Donnay, "Date" 33–34 with 33 n. 65. For analogous procedures, Donnay cites Dem. 18.134, where in a trial before the Areopagus the ballots were taken from an altar, and the Demotionidai decree (*IG* II² 1237.17–18, 29, and 82–83), where the votes on the accreditation of purported phratry members are to be taken from an altar; cf. also [Dem.] 43.14.

58   See Davies, *APF* 173 with 169.

Periclean policies,[59] offered an alternative by moving that Pericles be tried by a jury of 1,500, either for embezzlement and bribery or for petty malversation (Plut. *Per*. 32.4). The significance of this was first seen by Swoboda: by removing the trial from the Acropolis and by eliminating the sacred ballots, Hagnon wanted to see the trial conducted in an ordinary, secular jury court; and by adding the charge of petty malversation to embezzlement and bribery, to which Dracontides had evidently confined his charges, he broadened the basis of inquiry to include not merely Pericles' culpability in the embezzlement with which Phidias had been charged but also the probity of Pericles' official conduct overall, both as general and as *epistatēs*.[60] The purpose of requiring a large jury may have been to give Pericles a more equitable hearing; and the three counts proposed, which are precisely those on which the *logistai* and their *synēgoroi* were to conduct the audits of all public officials in the fourth century (Arist. *Ath.Pol*. 54.2),[61] suggest that the trial examined Pericles' administration as a whole. Hagnon did not propose a trial before the Assembly; Pericles therefore was probably not tried in an *eisangelia* procedure arising from his conduct as general. That is why the Assembly had jurisdiction in the case of the private citizen Phidias but not over his *epistatēs*.[62] In short, by countering Dracontides' proposal with a regular *euthyna* procedure, Hagnon avoided the religious issues. What the outcome of Pericles' trial was we do not know. Possibly the fine that the ancient sources associate with his *euthyna* as general in 430/29 B.C. was actually imposed upon his conviction for embezzlement at this time, especially in view of Phidias's conviction, presumably on the same charge.[63] But whatever the outcome was, it did not prevent Pericles' reelection as general for the following year.[64]

The trials of Aspasia and Anaxagoras, which were thinly disguised attacks against Pericles on religious grounds, are dated by Plutarch "about the time" of the Phidias affair (περὶ τοῦτον τὸν χρόνον, *Per*. 32.1). Recent scholarship has shown that there are less serious objections to a date between 438 and 436 B.C. than to either Dio-

59   Ibid. 227–28.
60   Swoboda, "Process" 536–98, esp. 556–60.
61   See above, pp. 55–56.
62   See above, p. 66 with nn. 252 and 253.
63   See above, n. 50.
64   See above, n. 56. Mansfeld, "Chronology," part 2, 70–76, believes that Pericles was either acquitted or convicted of only petty malversation (ἀδικίου).

dorus's connection between the prosecutions of Phidias and Anaxagoras and the outbreak of the Peloponnesian War (12.38–39) or a relation of these cases to the presumed return of Thucydides from exile.[65] Although it makes for a rather crowded sequence of events, Mansfeld's argument offers persuasive reasons for believing that the proceedings against Aspasia and Anaxagoras were staged to support the religious thrust of Dracontides' measure against Pericles himself.[66] It is noteworthy that in both cases a charge of impiety (*asebeia*) was brought against one of Pericles' personal friends who was a foreigner and, more important, a member of his intellectual entourage. Evidently the religious establishment was beginning to feel threatened by the foreign intellectuals who were flocking to the imperial city and were welcomed by its leaders.

The trial of Aspasia, which Plutarch mentions before the case of Anaxagoras, and which Diodorus-Ephorus does not mention at all, is so poorly attested that some scholars doubt it ever took place.[67] Our knowledge depends almost exclusively on Plutarch's statement that the comic poet Hermippus prosecuted her for impiety and for procuring free women for Pericles (*Per.* 32.1); only his story that Pericles defended her and that his tears moved the jurors to acquit (32.5) is also attested elsewhere.[68] Too little is known about Hermippus for us to guess at his motives; the fact that he was a comic poet does not imply that his prosecution was in reality only an attack on Aspasia in one of his comedies.[69] Nor can we simply reject Plutarch's information entire because some of it may preserve mere gossip that Aspasia acted as a procuress for Pericles; such a charge may have been related to the laws denying adulterous women and prostitutes access to sacred places.[70] What does give pause is that whereas Plutarch speaks of Aspasia's trial before an ordinary jury court (δικαστῶν, *Per.* 32.5) Anaxagoras, though presumably also charged with impiety, was subjected to an *eisangelia* proceeding.[71]

---

65   See Frost, "Pericles, Thucydides" 396–97; Donnay, "Date" 28–30 with n. 41; Mansfeld, "Chronology," part 2, 34–40, 76–80.

66   Mansfeld, "Chronology," part 2, 76–80.

67   Donnay, "Date" 29; K. J. Dover, "The Freedom of the Intellectual in Greek Society," *Talanta* 7 (1975) 24–54, esp. 28 with nn. 6 and 7.

68   Plutarch himself cites Aeschines Socraticus as his source; Ath. 13.589e cites the Socratic Antisthenes as his.

69   Against Dover, "Freedom," 28 with nn. 6 and 7.

70   [Dem.] 59.85–86, 113–14; Isae. 6.50.

71   It is of course possible that an *eisangelia* was also the basis for Aspasia's trial and that Plutarch simply does not detail the steps preceding the actual trial.

The action against Anaxagoras is the earliest *eisangelia* of which we know, and it may well have been the first prosecution ever in Athens on the charge of impiety. According to Plutarch, it was initiated by a decree moved by Diopeithes stipulating that "an *eisangelia* be lodged against those who do not pay the customary respect to the divine or who teach doctrines about celestial phenomena"; this is said to have been aimed at casting suspicion on Pericles through Anaxagoras.[72] We are told neither what judicial steps the decree prescribed nor what happened to Anaxagoras as a result. According to Plutarch, Pericles helped him escape from Athens (*Per*. 32.5); according to Satyrus, he was prosecuted by Thucydides (no doubt the son of Melesias is meant) and was condemned to death *in absentia*. According to Sotion, his accuser was Cleon; Pericles, his defender; and the penalty, exile and a fine of five talents. And according to Hieronymus, Pericles produced him so sick and emaciated before a jury court that he was acquitted.[73]

Of greater interest to us than the fate of Anaxagoras is what Diopeithes' decree reveals about the nature of the opposition to Pericles. Neither a decree nor a definition of the charge or of the procedure to be pursued would have been needed if legislation against similar offenses had already existed. Plutarch's text does not attach the label "impiety" (*asebeia*) to Diopeithes' decree. But that Diopeithes meant the offense to be so classified is evident from Plutarch's bracketing it with the charge against Aspasia (which he explicitly called a δίκη ἀσεβείας, *Per*. 32.1) as well as from Diodorus's report that Anaxagoras was accused of "impiety against the gods" (12.39.2). Plutarch's assertion that Pericles was the real target of Diopeithes' attack is made credible by the close relation between the statesman and this philosopher, which is amply attested.[74] Thus the

---

72 Plut. *Per*. 32.2: εἰσαγγέλλεσθαι τοὺς τὰ θεῖα μὴ νομίζοντας ἢ λόγους περὶ τῶν μεταρσίων διδάσκοντας. The arguments against the authenticity of this decree advanced by Dover, "Freedom" 39–40, fail to carry conviction; they are based on the silence of other ancient sources and on the *a priori* assumption that the decree may have been fabricated on the basis of "fulminations attributed to Diopeithes in a comedy." Hansen, *Eisangelia*, ignores the case completely.

73 D.L. 2.12 and 14. On the trial see von Wedel, "Prozesse" 139–40. Dover, "Freedom" 31–32, doubts that a trial took place at all and concludes from the conflicting evidence that "we have to deal...with ancient ideas about what must have happened, ideas generated by a historical attitude which is itself rooted in the condemnation of Socrates." However, the authenticity and date of the trial have now been firmly established by Mansfeld, "Chronology," esp. part 2, 80–84.

74 Pl. *Phdr*. 269e–270a, *Alc. I* 118c; Isoc. 15.235; D. L. 2.12 and 13; Diod. 12.39.2; Plut. *Per*. 4.6, 6.1–2, 16.7–9, 32.2–3.

decree does not merely evince a fear of the corrosive influence of Anaxagoras's doctrines on the traditional religion, but it shows further, that offended sensibilities among the democratic establishment had exposed Pericles to censure on religious grounds because of his association with the philosopher.[75]

In order to gauge Diopeithes' interest in the attack, we have to examine briefly in what respect he may have regarded Anaxagoras as culpable. The answer hinges to a large extent on the interpretation of νομίζοντας, which we ambivalently rendered "pay the customary respect" in quoting Diopeithes' decree. We observed earlier that νομίζω and its related forms may express the performance of customary practices;[76] when applied to things divine, this means participation in traditional worship. There is no evidence either to support or to reject the view that Anaxagoras opposed or did not participate in the conventional prayers, sacrifices, or other celebrations of the gods. But νομίζω may also describe a conventional belief in the reality of something,[77] and in this respect Anaxagoras was vulnerable. We learn from Plato (*Ap.* 26d) and Xenophon (*Mem.* 4.7.6–7) that his doctrine that the sun was a fiery stone offended the religious sensibilities of some Athenians; several later authors give this theory as the reason for his indictment,[78] and there is no reason to disbelieve them. On the contrary, since Diopeithes directed his decree against τοὺς τὰ θεῖα (rather than τοὺς θεούς) μὴ νομίζοντας and since he brackets Anaxagoras's teachings about celestial phenomena (περὶ τῶν μεταρσίων) with this offense, it seems indeed this tenet of Anaxagoras's natural philosophy that made the religious majority feel threatened.

What other information we possess about Diopeithes makes him precisely the kind of person who would spearhead such a drive against an intellectual.[79] He was a divine of sorts, possessed with an

75 E. Derenne, *Les Procès d'impiété intentés aux philosophes à Athènes au Vme et au IVme siècles avant J.-C.*, Bibliothèque de la Faculté de Philosophie et Lettres de l'Université de Liège 45, (Liège and Paris, 1930) 41, associates with the trial of Anaxagoras what should also be associated with Diopeithes' larger motive as reported by Plutarch. The view that Diopeithes was not a democrat has been laid to rest by W. R. Connor, "Two Notes on Diopeithes the Seer," *CP* 58 (1963) 115–18, esp. 115–16; cf. also Frost, "Pericles, Thucydides" 397–98.

76 See above, pp. 97–99.

77 This is taken by Derenne, *Procès* 217–23 to be the only meaning of the verb in connection with the gods. But Fahr, ΘΕΟΥΣ ΝΟΜΙΖΕΙΝ, esp. 160–62 and, for the decree of Diopeithes, 162–63, has shown that the two meanings may blend.

78 Sotion *ap.* D. L. 2.12; Joseph. *Ap.* 2.265; Plut. *Mor.* 169f (*De superst.* 10).

79 For a full discussion of Diopeithes' character and activities, see Derenne, *Procès* 19–21.

evangelistic fervor for which he was thought slightly crazy,[80] and he may have had an interest in politics. He appears to have been a friend of Nicias's and he may have introduced the first Methone decree.[81] He had a crippled hand, which was not immune to taking bribes (Ar. *Eq*. 1085, with schol.), but we do not know whether this allegation was prompted by his religious or by his political activities. The Methone decree indicates that his political activity cannot have begun later than about 430 B.C. Aristophanes' reference to him in the *Birds* shows that he was still alive in 414 B.C.; and if he is the same oracular expert whom the Spartans consulted in choosing the successor to Agis, he was still active as late as 402/1 B.C.[82] It would not be out of character for such a person early in his career to safeguard the religious majority by proposing that an *eisangelia* procedure, designed to deal with crimes against the state, be used against a natural philosopher. It is more surprising and more indicative of a latent popular opposition to Pericles that Diopeithes had a large enough following to get his decree passed and to have Anaxagoras summoned before a court. Thus, far from opposing the principle of popular sovereignty, Dracontides and Diopeithes as guardians of the traditional religion mobilized secular instruments in voicing their opposition to Pericles.[83]

80   Ar. *Av*. 988, where he is bracketed with Lampon, and schol., which also cite Phrynichus, fr. 9; Telecleides, fr. 6; and Ameipsias, fr. 10. For his fervor, see also *Vesp*. 380 with schol.
81   Scholl. Ar. *Eq*. 1085, *Vesp*. 380, *Av*. 988; ML, no. 65.4–5.
82   Xen. *Hell*. 3.3.3; Plut. *Ages*. 3.6–7; *Lys*. 22.10–11. For the date, see G. L. Cawkwell, "Agesilaus and Sparta," *CQ*, n.s., 26 (1976) 62–84, esp. 63 n. 8.
83   See Appendix B, below.

CHAPTER FIVE

The Polarizations of the 420s

SOCIAL AND POLITICAL POLARIZATION

"But those who came after him were persons of rather the same caliber one as the other, and in striving each to become the first they changed things so as to hand over to the people and its whims even the affairs of state" (Thuc. 2.65.10). With these words, Thucydides signals the change in the temper of Athenian politics that set in after the death of Pericles, a change he does not define except by recording its results. The same change is also noted by Isocrates (8.126–27; cf. 75), who attributes it simplistically to the fact that, like Aristides, Themistocles, and Miltiades before him, Pericles was devoted to the interest of the people rather than to his own enrichment and was thus a better man than such of his successors as Hyperbolus and Cleophon. Some modern scholars doubt the reality of the change, however, and attribute the perception of it to the social and intellectual provenance of our sources;[1] others regard it as real and explain it as consisting in Cleon's perfection of new political techniques originated by Pericles, looking to the state as a whole, and especially to the commons, for such support as had been sought from a narrower circle of political "friends" (φίλοι) earlier in Athenian history.[2] Both propositions ring both true and false: no doubt our contemporary sources, especially Thucydides and Aristophanes, were biased against the politicians, especially Cleon, who were most influential in Athens after the death of Pericles; no doubt, too, their domestic programs and their policies toward the allies were in most

1 M. I. Finley, "Athenian Demagogues," *Past and Present* 21 (1962) 3–24.
2 Connor, *New Politicians* 87–136.

respects a continuation of Periclean policies. Yet even after due allowance for bias in our sources is made, Athenian political life still seems to have changed enough for us to regard the death of Pericles as the dividing line between two different political styles. The new style involved a new relationship between politician and people, but we lack the evidence to judge whether it implied the rejection of the old: Aristophanes may be showing mere animus when he calls the men with whom Cleon surrounded himself "flatterers" rather than "friends."[3]

Change was to a large extent dictated by the exigencies of war. Pericles' policy of gathering the entire population of Attica into the city created congested living conditions, which in turn had important effects on the morale of the evacuated (Thuc. 2.13.2, 16.2–17.3). What political consequences this congestion had can only be guessed. People who had been unable to attend Assembly meetings because they lived too far from the city will now have participated, making the attendance larger than it had been in peacetime; they will have taken a more immediate interest than before in elections, Council meetings, and jury selections, especially because many evacuees will have now been deprived of their usual occupations. They will have expected public support to compensate for what they had lost and will have demanded a greater say in administrative matters to make sure that they got it (Arist. *Ath.Pol.* 27.2). Their resentment about their condition exploded with remarkable force against Pericles when the plague broke out, but it will have erupted on many more occasions than we hear of[4] and will have injected a keener and more strident emotional element into public debate than had prevailed before. Pericles' intelligence and psychological and political insight prevented unreason from dominating policy, and his prestige made his voice heard above the discontent (Thuc. 2.65.1, 4–5, 8–9). Yet even he could not prevent the dispatch of ambassadors to Sparta to sue, against his advice, for peace, though his policy was vindicated by the rebuff they received from the Spartans (ibid. 59.2).

Pericles' prestige was based on the military and political leadership he had given as one of the ten generals, the highest elected officers in Athens. Unlike his colleagues, he was reelected year after

3 See J. K. Davies' review of Connor, *New Politicians*, in *Gnomon* 47 (1975) 374–78, esp. 377–78.

4 Thuc. 2.16.2, 59.2, 65.2. For reflections of it, see Ar. *Ach.* 33–36, *Eq.* 805–9, *Pax* 632–35.

year after the ostracism of Thucydides son of Melesias in 444/3 B.C. Since none of the generals elected after his death could even approximate his political genius, the generalship lost most of its political significance, and the decisive political influence in the state came to be wielded by men whose style, breeding, and social class transformed the Athenian democracy. The term "demagogue," by which modern scholars refer to these political leaders, originally lacked in Greek the pejorative connotations it has in modern languages:[5] δημαγωγός, its verbal cognate δημαγωγέω, and its cognate abstract noun δημαγωγία simply denote leadership of the people; though that usually has a democratic or populist bias,[6] it may be practiced even by oligarchs.[7] Moreover, the contemporary evidence that Pericles' political successors were called "demagogues" is not very strong;[8] it is much more likely that they were known as προστάται τοῦ δήμου.[9] Reverdin has compiled a list of eight who were identified as προστάται τοῦ δήμου in their own lifetime: Cleon, Hyperbolus, Androcles, Cleophon, Archedemus, Thrasybulus, Archinus, and Agyrrhius;[10] various others are identified in other sources.[11] This uncertainty about what precisely the contemporary terminology was makes it more convenient to retain the conventional appella-

5   The pejorative connotations of "demagogue" are probably due to Aristotle's use of δημαγωγός, especially in Pol. 4.4, 1292ᵃ4–38, to describe a politician who both creates and is created by a democracy in which the will of the people is superior to law, who can maintain his own position only by flattering the masses. For a full discussion of this and other relevant passages, as well as their historical antecedents, see R. Zoepffel, "Aristoteles und die Demagogen," Chiron 4 (1974) 69–90, esp. 71–75, and her conclusion "dass hier die Theorie das historische Urteil beeinflusst hat" (p. 75). For a similar conclusion and an attempt to redress the historical balance by demonstrating that the demagogues were "a structural element in the Athenian political system," see Finley, "Demagogues," esp. 19.
6   E.g., Thuc. 4.21.3, 8.65.2; Ar. Eq. 191–93 (where ἔτι in line 192 indicates that there is nothing wrong with δημαγωγία in itself), 217–18; Ran. 423–25.
7   So, e.g., at Arist. Pol. 5.6, 1305ᵇ22–28, with Zoepffel, "Aristoteles" 73–74.
8   It is exhausted with the five passages referred to in n. 6 above.
9   προστάτης at Thuc. 3.75.2, 82.1; 4.46.4, 66.3; 6.35.2; 8.89.4; Ar. Eq. 1128, Pax 684, Eccl. 176 (in a different sense also in Ran. 569 and Plut. 920). προστασία at Thuc. 2.65.11 and 6.89.4. Forms of προΐστημι at Thuc. 2.65.5; 3.11.7, 70.3, 82.8; 6.28.2, 89.6; 8.17.2, 65.2, 75.2, 81.1, 90.1 (of oligarchs); Ar. Eq. 325, Vesp. 419. Cf. the combination of the two terms in Arist. Ath.Pol. 28.1: προεστήκει τοῦ δήμου...ἀεὶ διετέλουν οἱ ἐπιεικεῖς δημαγωγοῦντες. On the relation of the two terms in general, see O. Reverdin, "Remarques sur la vie politique d'Athènes au Vᵉ siècle," MH 2 (1945) 201–12, esp. 204 with n. 22.
10   Reverdin, "Remarques," 204 with nn. 13–20.
11   Scholl. Ar. Eq. 129–32, for example, alone mention Eucrates, Callias, and Lysicles.

tion, "demagogues," for Pericles' political successors, provided that we use the term descriptively and without any of the pejorative connotations it assumed after Aristotle.

Inasmuch as a demagogue was a *prostatēs tou dēmou*, he held no official position. He was merely a private individual who by force of his personality and his rhetorical ability managed to persuade the people in Council and Assembly to support the measures and policies he favored. Since his was no official position, he could not himself be held accountable at a *euthyna* for the effects of his proposals as all public officials were; on the contrary, he was free to bring actions against public officials at their *euthynai* for having failed to carry out what he had proposed. The demagogues tended to avoid holding high public office themselves: of the eight fifth-century demagogues listed by Reverdin, we can be certain only that Cleon and Thrasybulus ever held a generalship.[12] Demagogues' influence was strongest as speakers in the Assembly and, above all, as prosecutors in the jury courts, where they seem to have been especially active at trials arising from the *euthynai* of elected officials. As we shall see, this activity did not exactly serve to enhance their popularity, especially as they were themselves not subject to an accounting.

The demagogues did not come from the lower classes. Cleon's father, Cleaenetus, owned a tannery worked by slaves; he was prosperous enough to undertake an important liturgy at the Dionysia of 460/59 B.C.[13] The upper-class status of Cleophon's father, Cleidippides, is attested by his election as general in command of the first expedition against Mytilene, in 428 B.C., and by his earlier candidacy for ostracism, perhaps on the same occasion on which Thucydides son of Melesias was exiled.[14] Hyperbolus's pros-

---

12 See Fornara, *ABG* 59–62 and 68–69. The evidence that Hyperbolus was a general is weak; see F. Camon, "Le Cariche pubbliche di Iperbolo," *Giornale Italiano di Filologia* 16 (1963) 46–59, esp. 46–48 and 58, who tends to accept it. The generalship attributed to Cleophon in schol. Ar. *Ran.* 679 is of even more dubious authenticity; see Fornara, *ABG* 70 with n. 126. The problem of what official positions, if any, he may have occupied in the course of his political career is not touched upon by R. Renaud, "Cléophon et la guerre du Péloponnèse," *LEC* 38 (1970) 458–77.

13 Schol. Ar. *Eq.* 44; *IG* II² 2318.34, with Davies, *APF*, no. 8674.

14 E. Vanderpool, "Kleophon," *Hesp.* 21 (1952) 114–15, with Thuc. 3.3.2. For the Cleophon ostraka, see Thomsen, *Origin* 76 with nn. 115 and 117, 93, and 100; for a recent attempt to gain an objective perspective, see B. Baldwin, "Notes on Cleophon," *Acta Classica* 17 (1974) 35–47.

perity is shown by the fact that he was a trierarch, but it is likely that he had made his own fortune by operating a lamp factory.[15]

Because these demagogues derived their wealth from manufacture and industry, they were looked down upon by the landed aristocracy, who had virtually monopolized high office, influence, and power until the death of Pericles.[16] Since they lacked the ready-made support that centuries of prominence had given the landed aristocracy through its old social and religious organizations and through an elaborate network of intermarriages, these new politicians had to look for new avenues to political power and influence; they found them in the Council, Assembly, and jury courts, where certainly since Ephialtes and probably since Cleisthenes every citizen had an equal right to be heard.[17] Conversely, thanks to the use the demagogues made of them, Council, Assembly, and jury courts became more potent instruments of political power than they had been before. The demagogues and not the generals were now manipulating the organs of popular sovereignty: Nicias, like the demagogues not a member of the landed aristocracy but unlike the demagogues accepted by it,[18] was elected general almost continuously from 427/6 to 413/12 B.C., yet he was politically overshadowed first by Cleon and then by Alcibiades.[19] Before Pericles' death, the generals contributed in Council and Assembly to shaping the policy they were responsible for implementing; after 429/8 B.C. the Assembly took a more active part in determining policy. The con-

---

15   Ar. *Thesm.* 837, with Camon, "Cariche" 51–53; see Davies, *APF*, no. 13910.

16   Connor, *New Politicians* 154–58, aptly suggests distinguishing the two classes as καλοὶ κἀγαθοί and ἀγοραῖοι, respectively, even if these terms are poorly attested. However, apart from Hyperbolus there is no evidence that the ἀγοραῖοι were *nouveaux riches* (Connor, p. 155): Connor himself disproves this explicitly for Dieitrephes, and implicitly in his remarks on Cleon and Cleophon (pp. 158–63).

17   J. D. Lewis, "Isegoria at Athens: When Did It Begin?" *Hist.* 20 (1971) 129–40, wants to attribute the basic institution of ἰσηγορία to Solon, its extension to Cleisthenes; G. T. Griffith, "Isegoria in the Assembly at Athens," in *Ancient Society and Institutions: Studies Presented to V. Ehrenberg* (Oxford, 1966) 115–38, opts for the time between the reforms of Ephialtes and 457/6 B.C.; A. G. Woodhead, "Ἰσηγορία and the Council of 500," *Hist.* 16 (1967) 129–40, accepts Griffith's date for the Assembly, but sees the roots of general ἰσηγορία in Cleisthenes' reform of the Council.

18   See Davies, *APF*, no. 10808, with Arist. *Ath.Pol.* 28.3 and 5.

19   He was general continuously from 427/6 to 421/0 B.C. and again from 418/17 until his death, in 413 B.C.; see Fornara, *ABG* 56–65. For Cleon, see Thuc. 4.28; for Alcibiades, Plut. *Alc.* 15.1.

duct of generals was openly attacked by men who had no responsibility to implement what had been voted (Thuc. 4.28.5) and who, moreover, used the third instrument of popular sovereignty, the jury courts, to make sure at the *euthynai* that popular policy had been carried out successfully; and the Assembly became the forum to which generals submitted their conflicting policies for decision (5.45–46.3; 6.8.3–24.2).

"Of all these people you shall personally be lord and master, and also of the marketplace, the harbors, and the Pnyx. You will tread the Council under foot; you will clip the generals; you will imprison people, arrest them, taste sex in the Prytaneion."[20] This is Cleon's heritage as a demagogue as it is promised to the Sausage Seller in Aristophanes' *Knights*: he will control the sources of Athenian prosperity and the source of political power, the Pnyx, where the Assembly meets; he will be able to bully the Council and cut the generals down to size in the jury courts at their accounting. The importance of these organs of the Athenian democracy and the amount of business they handled was enormous ([Xen.] *Ath.Pol.* 3.1–5), and Cleon exploited them to the full (Ar. *Eq.* 395–96). As merchants and industrialists the demagogues had a special interest in finances, control over which lay mainly in the hands of the Council.[21] We know that Cleon and Hyperbolus exerted some of their influence in their terms as councilors.[22]

Two financial measures can be plausibly attributed to Cleon's membership in the Council in 428/7 B.C. He challenged the knights' claim to a state subvention to which they were entitled, probably on the grounds that they had failed to go out against the Peloponnesian invasion of Attica; and it may have been at his instigation that the *eisphora*—a capital property tax levied in emergency situations on Athenians and resident aliens, which Pericles had

20   Ar. *Eq.* 164–67: τούτων ἁπάντων αὐτὸς ἀρχέλας ἔσει, / καὶ τῆς ἀγορᾶς καὶ τῶν λιμένων καὶ τῆς πυκνός· / βουλὴν πατήσεις καὶ στρατηγοὺς κλαστάσεις, / δήσεις, φυλάξεις, ἐν πρυτανείῳ λαικάσεις. For the meaning of λαικάζειν, see H. D. Jocelyn, "A Greek Indecency and Its Students: Λαικάζειν," *PCPS* 206, n.s. 26 (1980) 12–66, esp. 34–36.
21   Rhodes, *AB* 88–113.
22   For Cleon, see Ar. *Eq.* 774; for Hyperbolus, Plato Com. frr. 166–67, *IG* I³ 82.5 and 85.6, with H. Swoboda, "Hyperbolos," *RE* 9. Band (1914) 256; see also Camon, "Cariche" 53–55 and 58.

been reluctant to levy—was first imposed, to help defray the cost of the siege of Mytilene.[23] In addition, there are indications that Cleon was behind two decrees that tried to squeeze the last drop of tribute from the allies. After the Panathenaia of 426/5 B.C. Cleonymus moved a more rigorous enforcement of tribute collections in the future: a local citizen was to be appointed in each city as *eklogeus*, to be held personally responsible that all tribute owed by his city be properly collected; the *hellēnotamiai* were to present to an assembly after the payment of the annual tribute at the Dionysia a list of cities fully paid up, partially paid up, and defaulting; and five men were to be sent to exact the debt from the defaulters (ML, no. 68.5–9, 12–15, 15–17). Worse was to come in the decree of Thudippus a year later, which assessed a total tribute in excess of 1,460 talents, an amount twice as large as that calculated for 428 B.C.[24] On pain of severe penalties, tributes were to be assessed in the future punctually at the Great Panathenaia (ML, no. 69.26–33); to implement collection, ten assessors (τάκται) were to be appointed by the Council (8–12); a new court of one thousand jurors was to hear any allies' complaints about their assessment (16); and the final figure was to be ratified by the Council (17–20). That Cleonymus and Thudippus acted as friends

---

23 Cleon's boast at Ar. *Eq*. 774–75, ἡνίκ' ἐβούλευον σοὶ χρήματα πλεῖστ' ἀπέδειξα / ἐν τῷ κοινῷ, dates his tenure before the production of *Eq*. in 424 B.C. A more precise date can be conjectured on the basis of *Eq*. 225–26, which speaks of the hatred one thousand Athenian knights harbored against Cleon. A scholiast's comment on these lines, ingeniously emended by C. W. Fornara, "Cleon's Attack against the Cavalry," *CQ*, n.s., 23 (1973) 24, quotes Theopompus to the effect that Cleon challenged the state subvention (κατάστασις) to which they were entitled and accused them of desertion. Busolt, *GG* 3.2.994–96 n. 6, believed that Cleon as *hellēnotamias* for 427/6 B.C. tried to withhold the κατάστασις from the knights because they had failed to take the field against the Peloponnesian invasion of Attica in 427 B.C.; and he relates the failure of that attempt to the five talents the knights made Cleon cough up in Ar. *Ach*. 6–7 (cf. also 300–301). However, since there is no evidence that Cleon ever served as *hellēnotamias*, it makes more sense to relate Cleon's challenge to his membership in the Council, which was charged with the *dokimasia* of the cavalry (see above, p. 50 with n. 187). Therefore his opposition to the knights will also antedate the *Acharnians* (425 B.C.) and may well belong to 428/7 B.C., the year in which the *eisphora* was first introduced, possibly on his initiative (Gomme, *HCT* 2.278–9); see Thuc. 3.19 with Mciggs, *AE* 318 with n. 4. The question whether πρῶτον means that this was the first *eisphora* ever or the first in the Peloponnesian War need not concern us here; for the various interpretations given, see R. Thomsen, *Eisphora: A Study of Direct Taxation in Ancient Athens* (Copenhagen, 1964) 14–15, and 145–46 for Thomsen's own view.

24 ML, no. 69.20–22 with pp. 193–94 and Meiggs, *AE* 325.

and agents of Cleon[25] can be inferred from the severe and impatient tone of their decrees, and especially of Thudippus's: deadlines were peremptorily laid down for all officials involved in assessment and collection (ML, no. 69.9, 11, 20, 33–36); harsh fines and penalties, including loss of civic rights and confiscation of property, were imposed for noncompliance at every stage (9–10, 11–12, 15, 28–31, 31–33, 35–38). True, the allies were given an opportunity to protest the amount assessed, but if we can take any cue from Aristophanes' *Wasps*, the Athenian juries will not have inclined to leniency.

A tough policy bordering on brutality toward the allies may also be related to Cleon's membership in the Council for 428/7 B.C., although it is attested only by his speech on the fate of the Mytileneans in the Assembly. Cleon begins with the comment that a democracy is incompetent to rule others, intimating that relations with the allies cannot be handled democratically, and he advocates the harshest and most drastic means to intimidate the Mytileneans and to deter others from revolting (Thuc. 3.37.1–40.7, 36.2; Diod. 12.55.8–9). By a narrow margin the implementation of this policy was averted in the case of Mytilene, but it was not averted when Cleon proposed the same reprisals against Scione two years later (Thuc. 4.122.6, 5.32.1). The same attitude can be detected in Aristophanes' parodies of Cleon's suspicions of allied revolts and of his ambitions to extend the sway of the Athenian *dēmos* over the whole of Greece (Ar. *Eq.* 236–38, 797–800). That it was shared by other demagogues is indicated by Aristophanes' reference to Hyperbolus's scheme of dispatching one hundred triremes to conquer Carthage.[26]

Cleon appears to have served a second term as councilor in 425 B.C.[27] Thucydides reports that the Spartan offer of peace after Pylos was turned down on Cleon's insistence that, in addition to surrendering her troops on Sphacteria, Sparta cede Nisaea, Pegae, Troezen, and Achaea to Athens.[28] Since this demand cannot have

25   For Cleonymus, see ML, p. 188; and Meiggs, *AE* 317. For Thudippus, see ML, pp. 194–95 and 196–97; and Meiggs, *AE* 317.

26   Ar. *Eq.* 1303–4. The scheme may have been seriously entertained: similar designs are attributed to Alcibiades by Thuc. 6.15.2 and 90.2 and are taken seriously by Hermocrates at 6.34.2; cf. 6.88.6. Camon, "Cariche" 46–48, takes the Aristophanes passage as evidence for Hyperbolus's generalship, perhaps in 425/4 B.C.

27   Two nonconsecutive memberships of the Council were constitutionally permissible; see Arist. *Ath.Pol.* 62.3 with Rhodes, *CAAP* 696, and Hignett, *HAC* 152 with n. 3 and 228 with n. 3.

28   Thuc. 4.21.3–22.2; Philochorus *FGH* 328F128; cf. also Ar. *Eq.* 792–96.

been made in the Assembly,[29] and since it was the Council's function to receive foreign ambassadors,[30] Cleon is likely to have made his point as a member of the Council. An unyielding policy of war to the finish is characteristic of other demagogues also: Hyperbolus is said to have displayed as councilor a similar intransigence about the Peace of Nicias,[31] and Cleophon is credited with this policy after the battle of Cyzicus in 410 B.C. and again four years later after the Athenian victory at Arginusae.[32]

Cleon made political use of the Council also as a private citizen: before that body he laid an action against Aristophanes for "having ridiculed magistrates, both elected by lot and by a show of hands, as well as Cleon, in the presence of foreigners" in the *Babylonians* at the City Dionysia in 426 B.C.[33] What precisely the charge was is hard to tell; the scholiast on the *Acharnians* (378) speaks of ἀδικία εἰς τοὺς πολίτας and of a γραφὴ ξενίας. The latter is hardly credible, unless we assume that Cleon introduced in his formal charge against Aristophanes a slanderous accusation of foreign birth, a very common maneuver in Athens against one's enemies at that time and one made with gusto by all comic poets, including Aristophanes himself.[34] What may be hiding behind the expression ἀδικία εἰς τοὺς πολίτας is a charge for crimes against the people under the decree of Cannonus, ἐάν τις τὸν τῶν Ἀθηναίων δῆμον ἀδικῇ, which was subject first to a *probouleuma* of the Council.[35] This tallies with what we learn about Cleon's charge against Aristophanes: the initial accusation was lodged with the Council, which could either quash it or refer it for trial to a judicial body. Aristophanes' acquittal apparently means that the Council quashed it (Ar. *Ach*. 381–82).

Although this is the only specific record we have of Cleon's use of the Council in political litigation, several passages in Aristophanes'

29   This is shown by the fact that Cleon demands a discussion of the Spartan offer in the Assembly at Thuc. 4.22.2. Philochorus's statement that the Assembly turned down the peace offer refers possibly to a meeting different from that in which Cleon demanded open discussion; see Jacoby, *FGH* 3b Suppl. 1. 501–3.

30   Rhodes, *AB* 211 with pp. 43 and 54.

31   See n. 22 above. Cf. Ar. *Pax* 681–84, 921, 1319.

32   Philochorus *FGH* 328F139; Diod. 13.53.1–2; Arist. *Ath.Pol*. 34.1 with Ar. *Ran*. 1532 and schol.; Lys. 13.7–12 and 30.10–14.

33   Ar. *Ach*. 377–82, esp. 379 and schol. on 378, 502–3 with schol.

34   For the demagogues as the butt of that charge, see below, p. 215 with nn. 68–71.

35   Xen. *Hell*. 1.7.20 with Lipsius, *ARRV* 186–87.

Knights make sense only if taken as parodies of Cleon's frequent use of the Council as a law court to suppress suspected conspiracies (*Eq*. 624–82) or in *phasis* procedures in pursuit of his financial policies.[36] A threat of wholesale denunciations (*eisangeliai*?) for alleged treasonous dealings with the enemy, including intrigues with the Boeotians, may well refer to the delicate negotiations going on about that time with the Theban exile Ptoeodorus to overthrow the oligarchy in his home state and establish a democracy in its place.[37]

Cleon's penchant for using the Assembly as a political instrument, parodied in the *agōn* of the *Knights* (710, 725–835), is amply attested as historical. We have already noted it in his speech on the fate of the Mytileneans and in his insistence that the Spartan peace offer after Pylos be submitted to the Assembly,[38] which he probably proposed because he felt confident that he could have his way more easily in a mass meeting and because he aimed to embarrass and humiliate the Spartans in the eyes of their allies (Thuc. 4.22.2–3). A few weeks later, Cleon chose an Assembly meeting as the occasion for his attack on Nicias's command at Pylos; as a result Nicias yielded his command to him (Thuc. 4.27.5–28.3; Plut. *Nic*. 7.2–5). Moreover, Cleon's successful harassment of Pericles, which first put him into the political limelight, may well have taken place in the Assembly.[39] Hyperbolus, too, is said to have first come to prominence in the Assembly as a young man in the 420s and to have preferred the Assembly as the forum of his political activity, especially after Cleon's death;[40] the Assembly was also where Cleophon, drunk and wearing his breastplate, shattered all hopes for peace after the victory at Arginusae with his impassioned proposal that Sparta surrender all the cities under her dominion (Arist. *Ath.Pol*. 34.1 with Ar. *Ran*. 1532 and schol.).

The demagogues' favorite forum, however, was the jury courts. Through their functions in *dokimasiai*, *euthynai*, and *eisangeliai*, these were the most potent expression of popular sovereignty in political affairs. Every citizen, regardless of social standing, was eligible to serve on them, and any citizen was entitled to have his objections

---

36 Ar. *Eq*. 300–302 with Lipsius, *ARRV* 309–16, esp. 310–11 and 314 with n. 20.

37 Ar. *Eq*. 475–79 and 485–87 with Thuc. 4.76.2–5.

38 See above, pp. 206–7.

39 Plut. *Per*. 33.8, quoting Hermippus, fr. 46.

40 Cratinus, fr. 262, perhaps of 428–426 B.C.; Eup. fr. 238; Ar. *Pax* 679–84.

against the election of a high official heard at the *dokimasia*, to air his complaints about an official's administration at the *euthyna*, or to lodge an *eisangelia* before the Council.[41] Although Ephialtes had laid the foundations of these powers some forty years before, they attained their full growth only in the 420s, largely, we may assume, through the agency of the demagogues. For even though known demagogues are explicitly linked with only a few of the specific cases of which we hear, their activity in the jury courts is too richly attested to leave any doubt about the uses they made of this institution. The reasons for that activity are clear.

We observed earlier that Athens had no public prosecutor and that Solon gave the right to any citizen to initiate legal action on behalf of an injured party, leaving it to private individuals to bring crimes against the state and misconduct of elected officials to justice.[42] The rewards offered for information of wrongdoing against the state[43] opened the door to the worst kind of malicious prosecution by men intent on settling personal scores and invited others, hopeful of winning the rewards to which the law entitled them, to snoop into the lives of their fellows, especially of elected officials who had public funds to administer. It can be no accident that ancient Greek has a word only for a person of this kind and for his activity, συκοφάντης and συκοφαντεῖν; no technical term exists for disinterested, public-spirited prosecution.[44] Since we depend on comic poets for most of our information on activities of this kind in the fifth century, we must expect a more liberal use of the term *sykophantēs* and its cognates than the historical situation would have warranted, especially when prominent political figures are involved. And the

41 See above, Chap. 1, "Jurisdiction in Crimes against the State."

42 See above, pp. 80–81.

43 In a successful *phasis* the informer received one-half of the property confiscated from the accused or one-half of the fine imposed on him, and in an *apographē* the successful accuser could be awarded three-quarters of the property confiscated; see Lipsius, *ARRV* 310–11 and 299–308, esp. 308 n. 27. While we have this information only for the fourth century, it is unthinkable that no analogous institution existed in the fifth.

44 Though etymologically a συκοφάντης is beyond doubt a person who "brings figs out into the open," the significance and origin of the term are unknown. The word μηνυτής, which is also translated "informer," describes a person who provides information of any kind: his motives are not necessarily public-spirited and his information is not necessarily geared to initiating prosecution. Note that the lack of a term for public-spirited prosecution does not imply failure to recognize the phenomenon at, e.g., Ar. *Plut.* 850–950, esp. 898–950. For various conjectures, see J. O. Lofberg, *Sycophancy in Athens* (Menasha, Wis., 1917) vii–viii.

existence only of a pejorative term indicates also the targets of such prosecutions: obviously the wealthy upper classes resented and maligned those who took legal action against them, however patriotic their motives for prosecution may have been.

The use of informers against the subject allies is explicitly attested by the Old Oligarch, who adds that their main targets were the wealthy citizens of allied states ([Xen.] *Ath.Pol.* 1.14-16). Their activities can be inferred from the coinage decree of about 450-446 B.C. which permits "anyone who wishes" to initiate proceedings against offenders before the ἡλιαία τῶν θεσμοθετῶν (ML, no. 45[2]); from the Cleinias decree of 447 B.C.(?), which leaves any Athenian or ally free to lodge a writ before the prytaneis against persons tampering with the collection of tribute (ML, no. 46.31-35); from the oath exacted from the Chalcidians in 446/5 B.C. to denounce to the Athenians any future attempt at secession;[45] or from Cleonymus's decree of 426 B.C., which empowers any inhabitant of an allied city to bring a charge of treason against any fellow citizen who attempts to obstruct the collection of tribute (ML, no. 68.42-46). Thus the law left much scope to the activity of volunteer informers; and if we consider that, in addition, Athens assumed jurisdiction over her allies in cases involving loss of civic rights, exile, or confiscation of property,[46] we may conclude that Athenian citizens had more opportunities than we know of to ferret out infractions of Athenian laws and regulations.[47] In fact, without such information Athens would not have been able to subject her allies to the control she needed in order to maintain her empire.[48] The Sycophant in Aristophanes' *Birds* wants wings to commute faster between Athens and the islands: having obtained an islander's conviction, he wants to confiscate his property before the condemned man can return home.[49] Tenos boasts in Eupolis's *Poleis* (fr. 231) that

45 ML, no. 52.24-25; cf. also the Eretria decree, *ATL* 2.D16.10-11.
46 Most explicitly attested in the Chalcis decree, ML, no. 52.6-10 and 71-74.
47 For an exemplary treatment of the matters discussed here, see G. E. M. de Ste. Croix, "Notes on Jurisdiction in the Athenian Empire," parts 1 and 2, *CQ*, n.s., 11 (1961) 94-112 and 268-80, esp. 268-72.
48 I omit from consideration here such wartime informers as Carystion of Samos (Ar. *Vesp.* 281-83 with schol. on 283); pro-Athenians, such as Peithias of Corcyra (Thuc. 3.70); and fifth columnists, for whom see L. A. Losada, *The Fifth Column in the Peloponnesian War*, Mnemosyne Supplement 21, (Leiden, 1972).
49 Ar. *AV*. 1410-69, with the comments of de Ste. Croix, "Notes," part 2, 270 and 279-80.

she has many sycophants to offer, and the Sausage Seller's allegation in Aristophanes' *Knights* (438) that Cleon has ten talents from Potidaea may mean that he has obtained the money by informing against a Potidaean, or that he has blackmailed a Potidaean into paying him this fantastic bribe in return for not informing against him, or, most likely, that he has taken a bribe for not pressing charges against the generals who accepted the surrender of Potidaea.[50] Rich Thracians were shaken down by being haled before Athenian courts on the presumably trumped-up charge of conspiracy with the enemy commander Brasidas (Ar. *Vesp.* 288–89; *Pax* 639–40).

Demagogues' manipulation of the jury courts is attested mainly in general terms by the comic poets. Aristophanes wrote the *Wasps* to parody Cleon's use of the juries, and the *Knights* abounds with Cleon's writs, threats of prosecutions for desertion and embezzlement, and requests for patronage of his cronies.[51] Hyperbolus's love of litigation is recorded in *Acharnians* (846–47 with schol.), *Knights* (1358–63), *Clouds* (874–76), and *Wasps* (1007) and will have received its share of attention in the comedies written about him by Eupolis, Hermippus, Leucon, and Plato Comicus, of which little evidence is preserved.[52] The jurors' appreciation of the business Cleon gave them is expressed in the *Wasps* (197, 409–14), and that they were kept very busy is attested not only by Aristophanes.[53]

The most intense judicial activity of the demagogues will have been in *eisangeliai* and in cases resulting from *euthynai*, especially from those of generals. Of the eight known cases of *eisangelia* between the reforms of Ephialtes and the end of the fifth century, only one, the case of Anaxagoras, belongs to the period before the death of Pericles; most of the rest are not earlier than 415 B.C.[54] The figures are even more striking for trials arising from the *euthynai* of

---

50   G. Gilbert, *Beiträge zur innern Geschichte Athens im Zeitalter des peloponnesischen Krieges* (Leipzig, 1877) 122–23.

51   Ar. *Eq.* 305–6, 441–44, 1256 (Phanus, for whom see also *Vesp.* 1220, where Theorus and Aeschines are mentioned as other cronies; cf. *Vesp.* 42 and 459 with MacDowell's notes).

52   The only surviving evidence is Eup. fr. 181 (from the *Maricas*).

53   Ar. *Nub.* 207–8, *Pax* 505, *Av.* 39–41; [Xen.] *Ath.Pol.* 1.16–18, 3.2–7; Thuc. 1.77.1. Prosecutions of Nicias by Hyperbolus and of Alcibiades by Cleophon are mentioned by Himerius 36.18 Colonna; cf. Phot. *Bibl.* 377a (ed. R. Henry, *Photius: Bibliothèque* 6 [Paris, 1971] 126). But since this information is not corroborated by any other source and no details are given, it is of doubtful value.

54   See Appendix A below. Sotion's note that Cleon prosecuted Anaxagoras (D.L. 2.12) is hardly credible.

generals: of the thirteen cases known, only the trials of Cimon and of Pericles are earlier than the 420s; more than half the rest took place in the 420s alone.[55] Only rarely do our sources preserve the names of accusers in *euthyna* proceedings. Plutarch (*Per.* 35.5) cites Idomeneus as having named Cleon as one of Pericles' accusers, presumably at the latter's *euthyna*, for his failure at Epidaurus in 431/0 B.C. Peisander is named by Thucydides as the accuser of Phrynichus, and presumably also of Scironides (8.54.3). Conversely, in some cases that have the name of an accuser attached to them, we can at best surmise the nature of the charge: Hyperbolus's main activity is said to have been as *synēgoros* in trials arising from *euthynai*, but no details are known.[56] Cleon's activity in this respect is shown by several references in Aristophanes' *Knights*: he threatens the Sausage Seller, "I will smear you if you serve as general" (288); he likes to investigate officials liable to the audit (τοὺς ὑπευθύνους), recalling them from as far as the Chersonese for that purpose, especially if they are rich (258–65); such maneuvers gave him and other demagogues considerable power over generals (164–67) and over other elected officials.[57] We have already mentioned Cleon's possible involvement in the *euthyna* of the generals who accepted the surrender of Potidaea.[58] In Aristophanes' *Wasps*, the famous trial of the dog Labes in Philocleon's own private court has long been recognized as a thinly disguised parody of Laches' trial before a heliastic court for embezzlement during his generalship in Sicily in 426/5 B.C., in which prosecution Cleon had some kind of interest.[59]

55 For Cimon, see above pp. 40–42, 63–64; for Pericles, see above, pp. 191–92. A list of the twelve cases other than Cimon's is given above, Chap. 1, n. 248.

56 Ar. *Eq.* 1358–63; cf. *Ach.* 846–47 with schol., and *Vesp.* 1007.

57 Cf. Antiphon 6.43: Φιλοκράτης γὰρ οὑτοσί ἑτέρους τῶν ὑπευθύνων ἔσειε καὶ ἐσυκοφάντει, τούτου δὲ τοῦ βασιλέως, ὅν φασι δεινὰ καὶ σχέτλια εἰργάσθαι, οὐκ ἦλθε κατηγορήσων εἰς τὰς εὐθύνας.

58 See p. 211 with n. 50 above.

59 Ar. *Vesp.* 240–44, 836–1008. The nature of the charge can only be inferred from the dog trial itself and is not explicitly stated; see MacDowell's note on *Vesp.* 896, and Jacoby, *FGH* 3b Suppl. 1.500. That it is a heliastic court is attested in line 891 and that it is presided over by a thesmothetes in line 935. The fact that *Vesp.* was not produced until three years after the event has been used as an argument against the historicity of Laches' trial and acquittal at his *euthyna* in 425 B.C.; see Jacoby, *FGH* 36 Suppl. 1.500–501, accepted by H. D. Westlake, "Athenian Aims in Sicily, 427–424 B.C.," *Hist.* 9 (1960) 385–402, esp. 402 n. 67 (reprinted in *Essays on the Greek Historians and Greek History* [Manchester, 1969] 101–22, esp. 122 n. 67), and by MacDowell on *Vesp.* 240. But there is no reason why a famous trial should not have been parodied in comedy three years later, especially if it had resulted in an acquittal,

It must be emphasized that practically all the information on the use Cleon and other demagogues made of Council, Assembly, and jury courts comes from hostile sources. Like all extant classical authors, both Aristophanes and Thucydides belonged to the upper classes, and although they need not inevitably have shared all its prejudices, they could not help taking their own background for granted. Their background not only contributed to the judgments they have passed on to us but also governed the selection of the information for which we depend on them. Moreover, we cannot expect Aristophanes to have cherished warm feelings for the man who took him to court for his production of the *Babylonians*, nor can we expect Thucydides to have been an uncritical admirer of a system that exiled him for his failure as general at Amphipolis. This explains to some extent why in the five instances he discusses of impeachments of generals "his treatment of the impeached generals is favorable; in more than one case he is open in siding with the generals; and in no instance does he support the citizens who voted for impeachment."[60] The bias is real, but it seems born less of a malicious and partisan desire to suppress facts than of an ingrained conviction that the fickle mob is not a suitable instrument for formulating public policy.[61]

---

so that no old wounds would be opened. MacDowell's comment that "the future tense in 240 shows that Lakhes had not yet been tried when the *Wasps* was performed" makes no sense at all, except on the strange assumption that Aristophanes could not be as free with his dates as with his other inventions. M. Landfester, "Beobachtungen zu den *Wespen* des Aristophanes," *Mnemos.* 4th ser., 29 (1976) 26–32, esp. 31–32, takes certain features of the comic setting of the dog trial too literally when he concludes that Cleon was the accuser of Laches in 425 B.C. and secured his conviction. Only the silence of Thucydides and of other sources speaks against a *euthyna* of Laches having led to his trial and acquittal in 425 B.C. and thus against the assumption that this is the historical basis of the parody. Whatever the historical facts may be, *Vesp.* proves that there was or had been political enmity between Cleon and Laches in 423/2 B.C. and that Cleon did use or could have used the jury courts at that time to cultivate his political image as watchdog for the people (*Eq.* 1017, 1030; *Vesp.* 895, 970, 1031; *Pax* 313). Whether greed was Cleon's motive (*Vesp.* 241) we cannot tell; it is just as likely—and perhaps more so—that Cleon opposed Laches for his willingness to make peace with Sparta (Thuc. 4.118.11, 5.43.2).

60 Roberts, *Accountability* 134. She discusses the cases of Pericles, of the Potidaea generals, of Sophocles, Pythodorus, and Eurymedon, of Phrynichus and Scironides, and Thucydides' own case (see above, Chap. 1, n. 248, cases 1, 2, 6, 7, and 9) to prove this point on pp. 124–35 and Plutarch's treatment of the case of Paches (4) on pp. 136–41.

61 See the comments on the fickleness and emotionalism of the masses at Thuc. 2.65.4; 4.28.3; 6.24.3–4, 60, 63.2; 8.1.4, 89.4.

Prejudice against the demagogues is manifested in a number of ways. For example, it is peculiar that unlike their predecessors as popular leaders the demagogues are frequently identified by their professions. None of the earlier *prostatai tou dēmou* listed in Aristotle's *Constitution of Athens* (chap. 28) is given a profession: we are not told how Solon, Peisistratus, or Cleisthenes made his living, nor do any of our sources make a point of the economic background of Xanthippus, Themistocles, Ephialtes, or Pericles. It rather seems to be taken for granted that they derived an income from family estates or some other agricultural form of family capital. Moreover, no ancient source identifies the professions of Nicias and Theramenes, the two political opponents of the demagogues Aristotle enumerates. This is surprising in the case of Nicias, whose wealth, as we know from other sources, was not derived from landed agricultural estates but from silver mines and from slaves he leased out.[62] But when it comes to Cleon, Hyperbolus, and Cleophon, ancient authors—and not only comedians—never tire of pointing out that they were, respectively, a tanner, a lampmaker, and a lyremaker,[63] usually implying that they themselves made or sold (or both made and sold) their products. This was not so in fact, at least in the cases of Cleon and Cleophon, as has already been noted;[64] but such an image was no doubt cultivated by the demagogues themselves. In order to enhance their political standing with the masses, they constantly professed to be committed to the interests of the common people[65] and sometimes even claimed lower-class origin.[66]

This also explains why the upper classes despised the demagogues as ἀγοραῖοι, "men of the marketplace." The Athenian agora was the main industrial quarter of Athens as well as the place where people would usually congregate; one would draw attention to the source of

---

62   Xen. *Vect.* 4.14; Plut. *Nic.* 4.2; cf. Xen. *Mem.* 2.5.2. For his wealth in general, see Thuc. 7.86.4; Lys. 19.47; and Plut. *Nic.* 3.1, 11.2, and 15.2.

63   For Cleon, see, e.g., Ar. *Eq.* 44, 47, 136, *et passim*; *Nub.* 581; *Vesp.* 38. For Hyperbolus, see Cratinus, fr. 196; Ar. *Eq.* 739 and 1304 with schol., 1315; *Nub.* 1065 with schol.; *Pax* 690 and schol. 681 and 692. For Cleophon, see Andoc. 1.146; Aeschin. 2.76; Arist. *Ath.Pol.* 28.3; scholl. Ar. *Thesm.* 805 and *Ran.* 681. In general, see V. Ehrenberg, *The People of Aristophanes*² (Oxford, 1951) 120–23. On the wealth of the demagogues, see Connor, *New Politicians* 151–58.

64   See above, p. 202 with nn. 13–14.

65   See, e.g., Ar. *Eq.* 763–85; *Ran.* 569–71; and Cleon's penchant for posing as watchdog of the people parodied in Ar. *Eq.* 1017 and 1030; *Vesp.* 895, 970, and 1031; and *Pax* 313.

66   See id. *Eq.* 335–39, Plato Com. fr. 219.

a demagogue's economic and political influence by calling him *agoraios*.[67]

The upper classes' social contempt for the demagogues comes out most strongly in their denigration as foreigners or as slaves or both. For reasons unknown to us, Cleon is consistently called a Paphlagonian in Aristophanes' *Knights*.[68] Hyperbolus is dubbed a Lydian or a Phrygian;[69] his father is falsely given the foreign name Chremes and is called a slave so as to brand Hyperbolus as a foreigner and even a non-Greek.[70] Cleophon is alleged to have been a slave who obtained his citizenship by fraud.[71]

There may have been genuine, substantive reasons for upper-class animosity. There is certainly strong evidence that Cleon at some point unsuccessfully tried to make life difficult for the knights, perhaps by attempting to withhold the state subventions to which they were entitled.[72] But the attacks of the upper classes are less commonly aimed at such substantive grievances than at personalities and style, an indication that, as in the case of the Old Oligarch, resentment that a lower social class held the effective power in the state may lie at the root of the criticism we find in the comedians and in Thucydides. Only rarely in the 420s do elected officials come under such sharp attack as the chorus in Eupolis's *Dēmoi* (fr. 117) leveled at them in 412 B.C.; in the *Knights*, for example, first performed in 424 B.C., though the generals Nicias and Demosthenes are presented as slaves to Dēmos, Aristophanes reserves his most stinging barbs not for them but for Cleon, who, having just become general for the first time, is introduced as the newest acquisition and the biggest bully among Dēmos's slaves (Ar. *Eq.* 1–5). The action of the play does not, however, involve Cleon's recent election as general but the question of succession in popular leadership

---

67   Ar. *Eq.* 1234–48; cf. 181, 218, 293, 410, 500, and 636. On the significance of ἀγοραῖος, see Connor, *New Politicians* 154–55 with n. 39.

68   H. Dunbar, *A Complete Concordance to the Comedies and Fragments of Aristophanes* (Oxford, 1883) lists twenty-five uses of the noun in *Eq.* and one at *Nub.* 581. Possibly Cleon employed Paphlagonian slaves in his tannery or the nickname was due to Cleon's "blustering" (παφλάζω); see *Eq.* 919 and *Pax* 314.

69   A Lydian in Plato Com. fr. 170, a Phrygian in Polyzelus, fr. 5.

70   Schol. Ar. *Vesp.* 1007 (=Andoc. fr. 5 Blass); Theopompus *FGH* 115F95; Plato Com. frr. 166–67, with Davies, *APF* 517.

71   Aeschin. 2.76. Note also Andocides' disgust (1.146) that Cleophon occupied his house while he was in exile. See also Ar. *Ran.* 679–82 with scholl. on 679, 681, and 1532; Plato Com. fr. 60; Ael. *VH* 12.43.

72   See above, p. 205 with n. 23.

(δημαγωγία). The qualifications required for political power are listed as low birth, being a habitué of the marketplace, having no inhibitions, and not being a member of the upper class (ibid. 181–86): "Popular leadership no longer comes from cultured men with respectable manners but has passed into the hands of the ignoramus and the crook."[73] The identity of the vocabulary here with that of the Old Oligarch's description of the two classes shows that the attack comes from the same quarter. But whereas the Old Oligarch had predicated disreputable qualities of the masses, they are here used to describe the demagogues.[74] A recipe for demagoguery is appended: "Stir up and make a batch of mincemeat of all affairs of state and get the people over to your side by continually adding a dash of cookbook phrases as a sweetener. You have the other prerequisites for demagoguery: a coarse voice, low birth, and you hang about the marketplace. That's all you need for a public career."[75]

This brings us to the personal and social characteristics the upper classes imputed to the demagogues. The most terse and comprehensive critique of Cleon's manners is Aristotle's: "He was the first to shout from the speaker's platform, to use vile language, and to harangue with his cloak girt up about him, whereas all others spoke in an orderly manner."[76] It would be surprising if it were true that no one before Cleon ever shouted from the speaker's platform or ever used vile language, and it would be difficult to explain the influence Cleon had over the masses if the manners criticized here had been found universally reprehensible by Cleon's contemporaries. Since we learn that Cleon was "rough and heavy against the upper classes and subjected himself to the masses in order to win their favor,"[77] Aristotle's emphasis on the vulgarity of his manners tends to imply an aristocratic tradition that instead of finding substantive fault with

73   Ar. *Eq.* 191–93: ἡ δημαγωγία γὰρ οὐ πρὸς μουσικοῦ / ἔτ' ἐστὶν ἀνδρὸς οὐδὲ χρηστοῦ τοὺς τρόπους, / ἀλλ' εἰς ἀμαθῆ καὶ βδελυρόν.

74   Apart from the use of χρηστοί and πονηροί to describe the upper and the lower classes, respectively, see esp. [Xen.] *Ath.Pol.* 1.5 and 7 for ἀμαθία and 1.13 and 2.9–10 for cultural pursuits.

75   Ar. *Eq.* 214–19. It is impossible to do justice in English to the constant punning on recipes for sausage, especially to the phrase καὶ τὸν δῆμον προσποιοῦ (215), which, in addition to meaning "get the people over to your side" also means "and put in the fat."

76   Arist. *Ath.Pol.* 28.3. On the contrast with other speakers, cf. Aeschin. 1.25; on this aspect of the criticism of demagogues, see Connor, *New Politicians* 132–34.

77   Plut. *Mor.* 807a (*Praec. rei publ. ger.* 13): τραχὺς ὢν πρὸς τοὺς ἐπιεικεῖς καὶ βαρὺς αὖθις ὑπέβαλλε τοῖς πολλοῖς πρὸς χάριν ἑαυτόν. Cf. *Nic.* 2.2–3.

Cleon's policies expressed mere resentment by attacks upon his personal style and the style of politicians who depended, as he did, on the organs of popular sovereignty for their success. This is not to deny that Cleon and others actually did possess at least some of the unpleasant characteristics attributed to them. For example, his voice is so persistently the target of Aristophanes' barbs that it must indeed have been unusually loud and raucous,[78] perhaps sufficiently so to intimidate both the rich and the poor (Ar. *Eq.* 223–24). But the preoccupation with such externals and the sparse criticism of his substantive policies suggest social prejudice as a primary motivation. The same will be true of the rhetorical peculiarities Eupolis attributes to a politician named Syracosius, who is said to have proposed a decree prohibiting comic writers from attacking individuals by name.[79] Aristotle's charge that Cleon "used vile language" (ἐλοιδορήσατο) may be derived from the recurrent charge of "shamelessness" (ἀναίδεια) that contemporaries hurled at Cleon[80] or possibly from Thucydides' description of him as "the most violent citizen."[81] Moral vilification is not lacking: Aristophanes (*Eq.* 392, 296, 297–98; *Vesp.* 592–93) accuses him and other popular leaders of, among other things, reaping other people's harvests, stealing, perjury, and cowardice; and Thucydides goes so far as to describe Cleon's death, quite wantonly and unnecessarily, as a coward's.[82]

There are indications that hidden beneath these social and personal slurs lay a real and deep upper-class resentment of Cleon's populist methods and a genuine fear that they could become ominous for the state. Gomme has demonstrated that even Thucydides, scrupulous though he was, let his bias against Cleon so distort his narrative of events that Cleon's successes and creditable exploits are shown in a bad light.[83] In the Mytilene debate, Thucydides is content to let the events and Cleon's speech create their own impression in the reader, except that he lets the expression βιαιότατος τῶν πολιτῶν

---

78 Ar. *Ach.* 381; *Eq.* 137 with schol., 256, 275–76, 286–87, 311; *Vesp.* 35–36, 1034; *Pax* 314; fr. 636.

79 Eup. fr. 207; cf. also schol. Ar. *Av.* 1297, and Phrynichus, fr. 26.

80 Ar. *Eq.* 277, 324–25, 409, 1206; reflected perhaps also in the βδελυρία καὶ τόλμα of Plut. *Nic.* 2.2.

81 Thuc. 3.36.6; βιαιότατος τῶν πολιτῶν. Cf. also the ascription of Hyperbolus's ostracism to πονηρίαν καὶ αἰσχύνην τῆς πόλεως at 8.73.3.

82 Thuc. 5.10.9 with Gomme's note *ad loc*.

83 A. W. Gomme, "Thucydides and Kleon," in *More Essays in Greek History and Literature* (Oxford, 1962) 112–21.

(3.36.6) "anticipate the evidence," as Gomme discreetly puts it. But not so in the case of Sphacteria: Cleon's successfully breaking the deadlock is presented as the result of his knaveries and prevarications. Thucydides portrays Cleon as having acted because his motives in opposing peace were under suspicion (4.27.3), as having proposed the expedition because he feared that the results of the fact-finding mission on which he was to be sent would be embarrassing to him (4.27.4), and as having led the expedition not because of the vacillations of Nicias but because public pressure made it impossible for him to back down from a lightly and foolishly made proposal (κουφολογία, 4.28). The Athenians are represented as happy that they could not lose anything by accepting Cleon's scheme: they would be rid either of Cleon or of the deadlock with the Spartans (4.28.5). "Every detail is, we need not doubt, true," Gomme aptly comments, "and the proportion given to them will also be correct in that they loomed large at the moment of that assembly and filled men's minds; but from the historian we might have had something more, in order that all these things might be seen in their right perspective"[84]— especially, we might add, in view of the singular and unexpected success with which Cleon fulfilled his promise.

Thucydides' treatment of Cleon's campaign against Brasidas in Thrace is hardly any different. The narrative of the demagogue's success is brusquely interrupted by the statement that Cleon "was placed in a position in which he had to do what Brasidas expected. His soldiers became restive at sitting still and began to discuss his leadership, comparing the incompetence and softness he would evince with the kind of experience and daring on the other side, and remarking how unwilling they had been to leave home to join his expedition" (Thuc. 5.7.1–2). Nothing prepares the reader for this demoralization among Cleon's troops, and it becomes the motivation for Cleon's command to march toward Amphipolis. In other words, Thucydides' narrative deprives Cleon of credit for an important initiative that must in fact have been his, especially in the light of the excessive confidence attributed to him in the sequel. In the battle that follows, though Cleon dies no less honorably than Brasidas, he is said to have been killed by the spear of a Myrcinian peltast as he started to flee (5.10.9), whereas the larger part of the following chapter (5.11.1) is devoted to a description of the honors

84   Ibid. 113.

accorded to the body of Brasidas.[85] Surely, one would have expected in Thucydides that such hostility would have had some basis more solid than mere upper-class bias against a *prostatēs tou dēmou*.

Cleon's policy of war to the finish was one of the major substantive issues on which he had to face opposition not only from the upper but also from the lower classes. The chorus of Acharnian charcoal burners is still intent on fighting the war to its bitter end in 425 B.C.;[86] a year later, however, the *Knights* challenges Cleon's professed love for Dēmos because he had rejected the peace offer Archeptolemus brought from the Spartans at the time of Pylos (Ar. *Eq.* 792–96; cf. Thuc. 4.21.3, 22.2), and only after Cleon's defeat can the reformed Dēmos get the thirty-year peace the demagogue had withheld from him (*Eq.* 1388–95). Evidently, the attitude of the people had changed within the year. Thucydides articulates the upper-class opposition to Cleon's war policy, alleging that the unpopularity of this policy was the demagogue's primary motive for attacking those then in charge of the conduct of the Pylos campaign (4.27.3); further, the historian is convinced that only the deaths of Cleon and of Brasidas made peace possible (5.16.1).[87] Moreover, both he and Aristophanes invariably describe Cleon's known opponents as responsible men who were willing to entertain reasonable peace offers from the Spartans: Laches, Cleon's target as parodied in the dog trial in the *Wasps*, was the man on whose motion the one-year truce with Sparta was concluded in the spring of 423 B.C. (Thuc. 4.118.11); he was among those who negotiated and signed the Peace of Nicias in 421 B.C. (Thuc. 5.43.2, 19.2); and he was a signatory of the fifty-year alliance with Sparta thereafter (Thuc. 5.22.3, 24.1). Nicias, whose encounter with Cleon over the command at Pylos is

85   Cf. also Thucydides' obituary on Cleon and Brasidas at 5.16.1: καὶ ἐτεθνήκει Κλέων τε καὶ Βρασίδας, οἵπερ ἀμφοτέρωθεν μάλιστα ἠναντιοῦντο τῇ εἰρήνῃ, ὁ μὲν διὰ τὸ εὐτυχεῖν τε καὶ τιμᾶσθαι ἐκ τοῦ πολεμεῖν, ὁ δὲ γενομένης ἡσυχίας καταφανέστερος νομίζων ἂν εἶναι κακουργῶν καὶ ἀπιστότερος διαβάλλων.

86   Ar. *Ach*. 215–17, 223–32, 289–91, and 299–301. Whether the dislike of Cleon expressed at 300 reflects genuine popular sentiment in 425 B.C. or merely Aristophanes' personal bias is impossible to say. On *Ach*. as a war play, see W. G. Forrest, "Aristophanes' *Acharnians*," *Phoenix* 17 (1963) 1–12.

87   For Cleon's warmongering in general, see Ar. *Pax* 637, and argum. 1 to *Pax*: τὸ δὲ κεφάλαιον τῆς κωμῳδίας ἐστὶ τοῦτο· συμβουλεύει 'Αθηναίοις σπείσασθαι πρὸς Λακεδαιμονίους καὶ τοὺς ἄλλους Ἕλληνας. οὐ τοῦτο δὲ μόνον ὑπὲρ εἰρήνης 'Αριστοφάνης τὸ δρᾶμα τέθεικεν, ἀλλὰ καὶ τοὺς 'Αχαρνεῖς καὶ τοὺς 'Ιππέας καὶ 'Ολκάδας, καὶ πανταχοῦ τοῦτο ἐσπούδακεν, τὸν δὲ Κλέωνα κωμῳδῶν τὸν ἀντιλέγοντα καὶ Λάμαχον τὸν φιλοπόλεμον ἀεὶ διαβάλλων.

immortalized by Thucydides (4.27.5–28.5), is said to have taken Cleon's death as a signal to begin working for peace with such dedication that the treaty eventually concluded bore his name already in antiquity.[88]

The most intense resentment of the upper classes was reserved for Cleon's use of the jury courts, because through them many of their number had become his victims. Moreover, since success in the courts required the cooperation of large bodies of jurors, whose support had to be enlisted through persuasive oratory, and since the majority of jurors were likely to come from the lower classes, the upper classes tended to regard themselves as victims of class prejudice and came to look upon the common people as the tool of the demagogues. This sentiment is expressed strongly in general terms in Aristophanes' *Knights* and *Wasps*.

The opposition to Cleon is defined in the *Knights* as consisting of one thousand noble cavalrymen who hate Cleon (no doubt because of the treatment they had received from him in 428/7 B.C.),[89] of upper-class citizens, of the intelligent among the spectators, and even of the divinity.[90] It is put into high relief by the vulgarity of Cleon's reaction: he turns to the audience as if they were jurors, reminding them of their pay, which he had increased to three obols, claiming that their livelihood depends on his bawling, indifferent though it is to right and wrong, and blindly charging his attackers with conspiracy.[91]

Upper-class hostility evoked by courtroom tactics of this kind is reflected in almost every line of the *Wasps*, where the main antagonists are by their very names identified as "loving Cleon" and "loathing Cleon," respectively, for his use of the jury courts. The fact that Philocleon is depicted as a lively and lovable character and his son, Bdelycleon, is a rather stiff and humorless voice of reason does not contradict this view, for part of the serious thrust of Aristophanes' argument is that even so attractive an old man as Philocleon can be so

---

88 Thuc. 5.16.1 and 43.2; Plut. *Nic.* 9.4–9, esp. 9.9; and *Alc.* 14.2. For Nicias as signatory also of the one-year truce and of the peace and alliance that bear his name, see Thuc. 4.119.2, 5.19.2 and 24.1 with 22.3.

89 See above, pp. 204–5 with n. 23.

90 Ar. *Eq.* 225–29. The crucial expressions are ἱππῆς ἄνδρες ἀγαθοὶ χίλιοι, τῶν πολιτῶν οἱ καλοί τε κἀγαθοί, τῶν θεατῶν ὅστις ἐστὶ δεξιός, κἀγὼ μετ' αὐτῶν χώ θεὸς ξυλλήψεται.

91 Ibid. 255–57: ὦ γέροντες ἡλιασταί, φράτερες τριωβόλου, / οὓς ἐγὼ βόσκω κεκραγὼς καὶ δίκαια κἄδικα, / παραβοηθεῖθ', ὡς ὑπ' ἀνδρῶν τύπτομαι ξυνωμοτῶν.

perverted by the courts and by demagogic use of them that he enjoys the exercise of arbitrary power, that he is vindictive, and that he feels shattered if he cannot convict a defendant.[92] What mitigates the comic poet's attack is that the representatives of the two social classes are, incongruously, father and son, and that by the end of the play the son has succeeded in persuading his father to channel his energies into less harmful, social pursuits.

Still, we have already seen that the resentment of the upper classes against Cleon and other demagogues rested on solid foundations, especially on their use of the courts at the *euthynai* of elected officials. In the *Acharnians* (703–12) we get a pathetic picture of the patron saint of the upper classes, Thucydides son of Melesias, being pummeled in his old age by Cephisodemus and Euathlus, presumably at his *euthyna*;[93] we have already mentioned the trial of Laches, at which Cleon instigated the jurors to vent their fury against the respectable old gentleman.[94] On stage, jurors exult in the power they wield over the high and mighty at their *euthynai* (Ar. *Vesp*. 548–58) and in the fact that they are themselves answerable to no one (ibid. 587), or rich members of the upper class are said to be recalled from service in Thrace or the Chersonese to face trial on fabricated charges (Ar. *Vesp*. 288–89; *Eq.* 261–63). Thucydides (4.65.3–4) intimates that the three generals returning from campaigning in Sicily in the summer of 424 B.C. were unjustly accused of taking bribes not to subdue the island and were condemned to exile and to a fine, respectively, merely because the Athenians were unrealistic enough to believe that there could be no obstacle to their success. If, as Gomme suggested, Cleon and his friends "were the men so elated with success, so convinced that all things were possible to Athens, that they thought that only incompetence and dishonesty could explain the failure in Sicily,"[95] it is likely that they were responsible for accusation and conviction, although it is strange that Thucydides should not mention that detail.

92   On Philocleon's character and on the treatment of the law courts see the remarks of K. J. Dover, *Aristophanic Comedy* (London, 1972) 125–31.

93   Only the title ξυνήγορος at Ar. *Ach*. 705 and 715 suggests that Thucydides' trial was a consequence of a *euthyna*, but what office he may have occupied between his return from exile in 433/2 B.C. and the performance of the *Acharnians* in 425 B.C. we do not know.

94   Ar. *Vesp*. 242–44 and the entire proceeding against the dog Labes, ibid. 836–997. See above, p. 212 with n. 59.

95   Gomme, *HCT* 3.527.

The most attractive victims for *euthynai* trials were the wealthy. Rich simpletons who had no lower-class connections and who liked to stay out of trouble are presented in comedy as Cleon's favorite target (Ar. *Eq*. 264–65). A special incentive for attacking Laches is said to be that he has pots of money (Ar. *Vesp*. 241). Appeals for conviction are made to juries on the grounds that confiscating the property of the accused will increase the revenue from which the jurors can get paid (Ar. *Eq*. 1358–60). No wonder the rich and the proud felt intimidated before the courts (Ar. *Vesp*. 622–30), and no wonder Aristophanes prides himself on having taken up the cause of those members of the upper class (ἀπράγμονες) who have become victims of Cleon's affidavits, summonses, and subpoenas.[96]

Greedy self-enrichment is given as the most pervasive motive for Cleon's penchant for *euthyna* trials. In the *Knights* (259–60) he is said to be squeezing officials liable to the audit to explore the possibilities for sycophancy, examining which figs are raw and which ripe for the plucking, and he is accused of stripping the audit stalk of its juiciest sprouts and gulping them down, helping himself with both hands to public monies (Ar. *Eq*. 823–27). He is supposed to have taken a bribe from Potidaea;[97] he is also said to have extorted money from other allies (Ar. *Eq*. 801–2, 1032–34; *Vesp*. 666–79; *Pax* 644–47) for his own profit, while sanctimoniously arguing that the sums exacted would benefit Athens (*Eq*. 1226; *Vesp*. 666–68)—for example, from the very Mytileneans for whose death he had agitated at the time of the revolt, presumably to persuade the Assembly to ameliorate the conditions that it had imposed.[98] Or, again, the Milesians are said to have promised Cleon a talent in return for securing no increase in their tribute assessment (*Eq*. 930–40). Cleon may have been sensitive to such charges, as is suggested by his countercharge against Aristophanes for having maligned the city in the presence of foreigners;[99] we know that the allies appeared as stigmatized slaves in the *Babylonians* in 427/6 B.C. (Ar. frr. 64, 88, 97).

To arrive at an objective evaluation of Cleon's policies and influence is difficult if not impossible for us, because none of the

---

96   Ar. *Vesp*. 1037–42. The terms mentioned are ἀντωμοσίαι, προσκλήσεις, and μαρτυρίαι. For ἀπράγμονες as a description of the upper classes, see V. Ehrenberg, "Polypragmosyne: A Study in Greek Politics," *JHS* 67 (1947) 46–67, esp. 53 and 55–56.

97   See above, p. 211 with n. 50.

98   Ar. *Eq*. 832–35 with Gilbert, *Beiträge* 143–44.

99   See above, p. 207 with n. 33.

surviving contemporary literature has anything positive to say about him and because later authors depend for their judgments on the evaluations of his contemporaries. The charges Cleon and other demagogues made against members of the upper classes are invariably presented as unsubstantiated, frivolous, and malicious. Comedy abounds in parodies of demagogues as sycophants and attests their prevalence by frequent punning on words meaning "fig" (σῦκον, ἰσχάς) and on φάσις;[100] expressions such as διαβάλλω and διαβολή (slander) are frequently used instead of more sober expressions for "accusation" when Cleon's activities in the law courts are at issue.[101] Of the twenty-one uses of the διαβαλ- stem in the extant plays of Aristophanes, fourteen occur in plays written in Cleon's lifetime, and all fourteen have to do with Cleon's activities.[102] Obviously, the possibility that a successful prosecutor might profit from cases in which the verdict could lead to confiscation of property exposed litigious demagogues to the charge of sycophancy, especially if they prosecuted wealthy men (Ar. *Vesp.* 240–44, 288–89, 626–27; *Eq.* 258–65; Antiphon 6.43), without giving due weight to the consideration whether any such prosecutions had substance or merit. The fact—too often overlooked—that we know of no political or legal action taken against Cleon for his policies must give us pause: we know of no trial to which he was subjected as the result of a *euthyna*, nor of any attempt to recall him from his command in Thrace.

Moreover, there is surprisingly little criticism of the one institutional contribution Cleon made to the development of popular sovereignty: the increase and perhaps also expansion of state pay for public service, which Pericles had instituted to help every adult male citizen exercise his right to participate in the affairs of state.[103] Cleon is credited with raising the jurors' pay from two obols a day to three, probably in 425 or 424 B.C.;[104] and in his lifetime, too, the *synēgoroi*, who brought charges arising from the audits of elected officials, received a daily stipend of one drachma (Ar. *Vesp.* 691). We do not

100   For explicit parodies of sycophants, see, e.g., Ar. *Ach.* 818–35, 910–51, and *Plut.* 850–950; for a list of puns, see Lofberg, *Sycophancy* 20.
101   Ar. *Ach.* 380, 502, and 630; *Eq.* 7, 45, 64, 262, 288, 486, 491, 496, 711, 810; *Vesp.* 950.
102   Of the remaining seven, four describe Euripides' treatment of women (Ar., *Thesm.* 390, 411, 1169, and 1214), but the remaining three have little general significance (id. *Pax* 643; *Av.* 1648; and *Plut.* 204).
103   See above, Chap. 4, n. 30.
104   See scholl. Ar. *Vesp.* 88 and 300, with Meiggs, *AE* 331 with n. 1. The *terminus ante quem* is established by *Eq.* 255; cf. also ibid. 904–5.

know when this pay was first instituted, and we do not know, either, how early the pay for archons and councilmembers was introduced: we first hear of it in 411 B.C., when they are exempted from the earliest recorded opposition to the principle of pay for public office.[105]

If we can trust even a fraction of what Aristophanes has to say against Cleon in the *Knights* and in the *Wasps*, there will have been some justice in the charge that the demagogues slandered their victims, though it remains doubtful that what we learn is the whole truth. Similarly, there may be some truth in Aristophanes' allegation that this "watchdog of the people" was quick to charge others with conspiracy at the slightest sign of animosity against him,[106] especially with conspiracy to establish a tyranny.[107] Such charges presumably had less ground in 422 B.C. than they had in the wake of the desecration of the herms and the profanation of the Mysteries in 415 B.C. (Ar. *Av*. 1074; *Lys*. 619, 630; *Thesm*. 338–39, 1143), after which Thucydides and Andocides also attest a very real fear of tyranny and oligarchy.[108]

The political polarization that increased the power of the demagogues in the 420s, complemented by a concomitant erosion of the prestige of the upper classes, affected in turn the aristocracy's view of the *dēmos* and its ability to exercise sovereign power in Athens. An ambivalent attitude toward the common people and their capacity for self-government is graphically shown in two estimates of Pericles' leadership appearing only one generation apart. Thucydides attributes the effectiveness of Pericles' administration to his ability to keep the commons in check without making them feel suppressed; to the power he derived from their respect for his stature, for his political intelligence, and for his incorruptibility; and to the leadership he was able to give because he had preserved his own integrity in the quest for power and was therefore so esteemed that, far from having to say what the people wanted to hear, he could afford even to face their anger by opposing their wishes.[109] Not many

---

105   Thuc. 8.65.3, 67.3, 69.4; Arist. *Ath.Pol*. 29.5.
106   See Ar. *Eq*. 236, 257, 452, 475–79, 628, and 862; *Vesp*. 345, 482–83, 953.
107   Id. *Vesp*. 417, 463–507, esp. 474, 487, 488–99, 502, and 507.
108   Thuc. 6.27.3, 28.2, 53.3, 60.1, 61.1–3; Andoc. 1.36.
109   Thuc. 2.65.8: αἴτιον δ' ἦν ὅτι ἐκεῖνος μὲν δυνατὸς ὢν τῷ τε ἀξιώματι καὶ τῇ γνώμῃ χρημάτων τε διαφανῶς ἀδωρότατος γενόμενος κατεῖχε τὸ πλῆθος ἐλευθέρως, καὶ οὐκ ἤγετο μᾶλλον ὑπ' αὐτοῦ ἢ αὐτὸς ἦγε, διὰ τὸ μὴ κτώμενος ἐξ οὐ προσηκόντων τὴν δύναμιν πρὸς ἡδονήν τι λέγειν, ἀλλ' ἔχων ἐπ' ἀξιώσει καὶ πρὸς ὀργήν τι ἀντειπεῖν.

decades after this estimate was composed, Plato made Socrates argue against Callicles that by introducing pay for public service Pericles had corrupted the Athenians into becoming lazy, cowardly, talkative, and greedy.[110] Both are judgments by members of the upper class, and both treat the commons as an object that can be either kept in check or corrupted by the leadership they get; neither author suggests that any good can come out of the commons if they are left to their own devices. For Thucydides, however, their response to leadership is important: Pericles' leadership was willingly accepted because he dealt with the commons ἐλευθέρως (freely; without inhibition) and because their regard for him (ἀξίωσις) was an important element in the status he enjoyed (ἀξίωμα), which enabled him so to deal with them. But for Socrates in Plato's *Gorgias* the commons are like animals that Pericles corrupted instead of tamed. The very fact of introducing pay for public service seems to be sufficient to condemn the same leadership Thucydides was able to praise for its integrity and intelligence.

Interestingly enough, the charge that Pericles corrupted the people by instituting pay for jurors is not found earlier than the *Gorgias*, that is, it is not found at all in the extant writings of the fifth century B.C.[111] Although similar objections may have been voiced against Pericles by such contemporaries as Thucydides son of Melesias, resentful of the religious, economic, and political effects of the building program,[112] the bitterness of the fourth-century charges is best explained as originating from criticism first leveled by the upper classes not at Pericles for instituting jurors' pay but at the demagogues for their manipulation of the jury courts. In the fifth century the masses are faulted for gullibility and fickleness: corrupt politicians exploit these weaknesses for their own ends, but there is no suggestion that the demagogues' actions or methods corrupted the masses. The Old Oligarch, for example, condemns a system in which the lower classes fare better than the upper, because the

---

110 Pl. *Grg.* 515e: ἀλλὰ τόδε μοι εἰπὲ ἐπὶ τούτῳ, εἰ λέγονται ᾿Αθηναῖοι διὰ Περικλέα βελτίους γεγονέναι, ἢ πᾶν τοὐναντίον διαφθαρῆναι ὑπ᾿ ἐκείνου. ταυτὶ γὰρ ἔγωγε ἀκούω, Περικλέα πεποιηκέναι ᾿Αθηναίους ἀργοὺς καὶ δειλοὺς καὶ λάλους καὶ φιλαργύρους, εἰς μισθοφορίαν πρῶτον καταστήσαντα.

111 Arist. *Ath. Pol.* 27.4 attributes the charge to τινες, explaining it on the grounds κληρουμένων ἐπιμελῶς ἀεὶ μᾶλλον τῶν τυχόντων ἢ τῶν ἐπιεικῶν ἀνθρώπων. Cf. also Plut. *Per.* 9.1–3, where the charge, attributed to ἄλλοι πολλοί (contrasted with Thucydides), is more virulent and moralistic.

112 See above, pp. 185–91.

commons are ignorant, undisciplined, and mischievous; he does not say that they have been made so by their leaders ([Xen.] *Ath.Pol.* 1.1, 1.5). But he also admires the system for the efficiency with which it achieves what it has set out to do: his complaint about the jury courts is not that the judges are corrupted by the pay they receive but that they care more for what is to the people's advantage than for what is just (ibid. 1.13).

Aristophanes goes even farther when he presents the common people, both in the *Knights* and in the *Wasps*, as amenable to reason and capable of correction and improvement. True enough, they do let themselves be duped by demagogues into meting out harsh treatment to the allies from which the demagogues would stand to gain most;[113] and they can be seduced by the allies, who would feel constrained to cultivate Council, Assembly, and jury courts, the agencies directly involved in assessing and receiving payment of the tribute,[114] so as to obtain the most favorable terms for their states (cf. Thuc. 3.11.7; ML, no. 52.25–27). Elsewhere Aristophanes shows the Athenians bamboozled by the flattery of allied ambassadors into unnecessary concessions about tribute payments (*Ach.* 633–45); or they are taken in by demagogues promising rule over the entire Greek world, from the Black Sea to Sardinia, whence will come revenue to maintain and increase the jurors' stipend—though in reality the demagogues will keep control over the money in their own hands and give the people just enough to stay poor and dependent.[115]

But if someone can show the people that they have been deceived by unscrupulous leaders, they can come back to their senses. Two passages toward the end of the *Knights* are particularly instructive in this respect. Though they are informed by comic fantasy, the underlying sentiment rings true. In a lyrical interlude the chorus of aristocratic knights ends its reproach of Dēmos for his gullibility with the remark, "You do have a mind, but it has gone off on a trip" (Ar. *Eq.* 1119–20). But Dēmos claims to have been affecting simple-mindedness merely to catch the popular leaders stealing and then

---

113 Note Bdelycleon's question at Ar. *Vesp.* 519–20; ἐπεὶ δίδαξον ἡμᾶς, ὦ πάτερ, / ἥτις ἡ τιμή 'στί σοι καρπουμένη τὴν Ἑλλάδα, which introduces his debate with Philocleon, ibid. 548–724.

114 For the evidence, see Rhodes, *AB* 89–91.

115 Ar. *Vesp.* 698–712, *Eq.* 797–809; cf. also Hyperbolus's expansionist schemes against Carthage, ibid. 1302–4.

pounce on them: "I watch them every time they steal without letting on that I see them, and then I make them vomit up again whatever they have stolen from me by using the funnel of the juror's urn as a probe" (ibid. 1121–30, 1141–50). These remarks are hardly in keeping with the character of Dēmos earlier in the play, or, for that matter, with any serious attempt either by Aristophanes or by his contemporaries to describe the qualities of the common people. It is certainly diametrically opposed to the charge of ignorance (ἀμαθία) the Old Oligarch levelled against them. Yet it is not likely that Aristophanes would have drawn this utopian picture, or would have produced comedies at all, if he had regarded the masses as hopelessly corrupt or hopelessly stupid.

The same is true of the second passage, at the very end of the play, in which the Sausage Seller parades the product of his reeducation. Dēmos is shocked and ashamed when reminded that he used to succumb to flattery and voted to increase pay for public service rather than to build new triremes; he promises henceforth to disregard the threats hurled at jurors by *synēgoroi*; he will throw the *synēgoroi* into the pit; he will pay the sailors and will permit no draftdodging.[116] Although the scene provides an interesting and important comment on what Aristophanes regarded as right and wrong about the priorities of the democratic institutions of Athens, it can hardly be taken at face value as a realistic prescription for reform. But two points in it can, I think, be taken seriously. First of all, Dēmos's reform is presented as the restoration of an ancient state of affairs, a return to the Athens of Aristeides, Miltiades, and the days of Marathon (Ar. *Eq.* 1323–34, 1387). Aristophanes adopts the stance of a *laudator temporis acti*, who believes that political and social standards were higher in the past than they are at present. The second point tells us where the blame for that lies. When Dēmos experiences shame at his erstwhile shortcomings, the Sausage Seller comforts him by saying, "Don't worry; you are not to blame, but those who deceived you."[117] We cannot be sure that Aristophanes meant this view to be taken seriously, but since there is no hint in any of his works that he believed the common people to be corrupt past all help, it is possible that, like Thucydides, he regarded them as capable of responding to good leadership.

116 Ar. *Eq.* 1316–83, esp. 1340–49, 1350–55, 1358–65, 1366–68, and 1369–71.
117 Ibid. 1356–57: ἀλλ' οὐ σὺ τούτων αἴτιος, μὴ φροντίσῃς, / ἀλλ' οἵ σε ταῦτ' ἐξηπάτων.

Similar sentiments are still alive in the fourth century. Aristotle thinks that Cleon corrupted the people with his bulldozer tactics (ταῖς ὁρμαῖς) in the Assembly; he also condemns Cleophon and Callicrates for having introduced payment for attendance at public festivals (διωβελία) and approves the death sentence later passed on them: "For even if the masses are deceived, they later usually hate those who have induced them to do things that are not good."[118]

Though it may be true that one can't fool all the people all the time, it is also true that a large segment of the upper classes believed the masses did let themselves be fooled for a considerable time because they were gullible and an easy prey to flattery. The Sausage Seller in the *Knights* (214–16) is told that he will have no trouble in winning them over: all he needs to do is to stir up and make mincemeat of everything and then put in a dash of cookbook platitudes to make the dish palatable. In the parabasis of the *Acharnians* (634–40), Aristophanes claims with comic exaggeration and bombast that because of him the Athenians are no longer deceived by the speeches of foreigners and no longer swell with open-mouthed pride when allied ambassadors try to soften them with flattery. The people's gullibility sometimes explains a clever speaker's success. According to Dicaeopolis, Attic farmers are so delighted at hearing themselves and Athens praised, regardless of how false the praise may be, that any charlatan can sell them down the river (Ar. *Ach*. 370–74). In the *Wasps* Bdelycleon tells his father that all a politician has to do to get elected is profess himself champion of the cause of the people; after that, he can fill his own pockets and laugh at the gullibility of those who believe they are ruling Athens but are actually his servants and slaves.[119]

There is one final charge made against the commons, and presumably not by the upper classes alone: they are unpredictable. This charge can take a variety of forms. We have already noted Thucydides' observation of the people's sudden change in attitude toward Pericles, of their emotional encouragement of Cleon to accept the command at Pylos relinquished by Nicias, and above all of their excitement at the events surrounding the Sicilian expedition.[120] Their unpredictability comes out more gently but no less decisively

118 Arist. *Ath.Pol.* 28.3: εἴωθεν γὰρ κἂν ἐξαπατηθῇ τὸ πλῆθος ὕστερον μισεῖν τούς τι προαγαγόντας ποιεῖν αὐτοὺς τῶν μὴ καλῶς ἐχόντων.
119 Ar. *Vesp.* 515–20 and 666–68; cf. also *Eq.* 46–57 and 1340–49.
120 See above, p. 213 with n. ɔ1.

in Aristophanes. In the *Knights* (736-40) the affections of Dēmos are said to be as unreasonable and as injudicious as those of a lover: he turns down the advances of gentlemen and gives himself to lampsellers and leatherworkers. In other plays the people are too quick to arrive at decisions and equally prone to changing them again (Ar. *Ach*. 630, 632; cf. *Eccl*. 797-98). But the criticism is not malicious: the failings of Dēmos are part of the natural condition of old age; he is a gruff little old man who has the temper of a peasant, chews voting beans, is irascible and a little hard of hearing (Ar. *Eq*. 40-43; cf. *Ach*. 375-76). Elsewhere in the *Knights* (801-4) the cloud of war prevents the people from seeing through Cleon and his misdeeds; the pressures on them, their needs, and concern for their pay make them gawk at him with mouths agape. The masses are victims of forces they cannot control, but they are not base in character.

THE GENERATION GAP AND THE SOPHISTS

In a stimulating paper published in the wake of the student unrest of the late 1960s, W. G. Forrest drew attention to a "generation gap" that began to show in Athens in the 420s.[121] Tension between the young and the old exists in all times; but the way it set in and dominated the internal social and political life of Athens in the course of the Archidamian War is so unprecedented in Athenian history that we are justified in treating it as a further feature of the polarization of society we have been discussing. Equally noteworthy is the tendency to find the old, regardless of the social class to which they belong, portrayed as staunch supporters of the institutions of the Athenian democracy, while the young, usually members of the upper classes, are presented as at odds with the aims and methods of the democratic establishment and the demagogues who manipulate it. The dominance of older men in home affairs in wartime is not surprising, for they are exempt from military service, in which the young and those in their prime are enlisted. What does require explanation is the high visibility on the domestic scene of so many young men of the upper classes, whom we should expect to see serving in the field.

The peculiar structure of the Athenian armed services is presumably the single most important factor in accounting for this phenom-

121 Forrest, "Generation Gap."

enon. Athens fought the Peloponnesian War primarily on or from the sea, but the upper classes saw naval service only as generals or trierarchs; they were exempt even in emergencies from such menial tasks as rowing (Thuc. 3.16.1). Generals and trierarchs will have been comparatively few in number and will have been mainly older and more seasoned members of the upper classes; the young will have stayed closer to home as members of the land forces, the cavalry, and the home guard while their coevals of the lower class will have been away at sea rowing in the Athenian fleet. Reliable numbers are hard to come by: Thucydides (2.13.6–9) reports that at the outbreak of the Peloponnesian War Athens had a force of 13,000 hoplites to take the field and an additional hoplite force of 16,000 from the oldest and youngest age groups (citizen and metic) for home-guard duty, 1,200 cavalrymen, 200 of whom were probably mounted archers, 1,600 archers, and 300 triremes.[122] On the assumption that the complement of each trireme included 10 *epibatai* (marines), all of whom were citizens of hoplite status, and 170 rowers, an indeterminate majority of whom will have been citizen thetes, the contribution of the lowest class to the armed forces of Athens will have been more than half the total—that is, greater than that of the total of the three upper property classes taken together.[123] If these military figures can serve as a guideline for inferences about the political life of Athens, we may surmise that less than half the adult citizen population was regularly available for attendance at the Assembly and for service on juries, that the lowest class will have been represented primarily by its oldest members, and that younger men on the political scene at home would be mainly of the upper class. This is precisely the impression Aristophanes conveys.

What we learn from Aristophanes and others about the interests, sympathies, and aspirations of these two groups indicates that in part because of their social provenance, the young were beginning deli-

---

122   See Gomme, *HCT* 2.33–43, and M. H. Hansen, "The Number of Athenian Hoplites in 431 B.C.," *SO* 56 (1981) 19–32.

123   On the πλήρωμα of an Athenian trireme in the fifth century, see J. Taillardat, "La Trière athénienne et la guerre sur mer aux Vᵉ et IVᵉ siècles," in Vernant, ed., *Problèmes* 183–205, esp. 199–200; for the hoplite status of the *epibatai*, see also B. Jordan, *The Athenian Navy in the Classical Period*, University of California Publications in Classical Studies 13 (Berkeley and Los Angeles, 1975) 195–200; Dover, *HCT* 4.310, believes that they were usually thetes. The forces other than the navy add up to 21,800 men, while the total naval manpower consists of 60,000 men.

berately to cultivate a stance in opposition to political and social norms that, as we observed earlier, had hardened over the years since the reforms of Cleisthenes into the prescriptive rules of a democratic establishment.[124] Three of Aristophanes' earliest preserved plays are constructed around this conflict, and a fourth contains an elaborate reference to it. The chorus of young aristocrats in the *Knights* comes to help old Dēmos against the pernicious influence of Cleon (Ar. *Eq*. 225–26, 731); in the *Clouds* the thrifty old farmer Strepsiades has been ruined by the extravagances of his son, Pheidippides, who loves horses and affects aristocratic airs and tastes (Ar. *Nub*. 41–55, 61–77); in the *Wasps*, Bdelycleon tries to cure his old father of his addiction to the jury courts (Ar. *Vesp*. 87–135 *et passim*); and the parabasis of the *Acharnians* (676–718) contains a long complaint about the indignities to which the young subject the old.

The older generation found the jury courts the democratic institution closest to their hearts. They looked to Cleon as their protector and guide, because his penchant for litigation gave them employment and the pay for serving as jurors that they believed was their due for services they had rendered Athens in the field.[125] Cleon realized how dependent they were on him and could therefore appeal to their loyalty at need (Ar. *Eq*. 255–57). The young were also active in the jury courts; but whereas the old appeared only as jurors, the young are shown as cronies or imitators of the demagogues and as functionaries of the court. Like the demagogues, they seem to have regarded the courts merely as stepping stones toward political prominence. We encounter them as sycophants against wealthy allies (Ar. *Vesp*. 1096; *Av*. 1430–31) and as *synēgoroi* in *euthyna* trials; there they collected twice as much pay as a juror, however late they appeared in court—though they could make a juror forfeit his three obols if he came late (Ar. *Vesp*. 686–95). The names of two young *synēgoroi* have come down to us, Cephisodemus and Euathlus, at least one of whom secured the conviction of Thucydides son of Melesias when he was a weak old man.[126] Nothing further is known of Cephisodemus, but Euathlus's prowess as a prosecutor is attested elsewhere in Aristophanes (*Vesp*. 592; fr. 411). He is possibly identical

124 See above, pp. 129–36.
125 Ar. *Eq*. 41, *Vesp*. 240–44 and 1117–21; Com. Adesp. fr. 11.
126 Ar. *Ach*. 703–12, esp. 705 and 710, and *Vesp*. 946–48. The text does not make clear whether Euathlus was involved in this prosecution.

with the rich young pupil of Protagoras who is said to have been involved in a lawsuit about the fee due his master.[127] If we can infer from Euathlus's wealth that he belonged to the upper classes, he will have shared their political outlook as little as did Cleon, but rather, like Cleon, he will have used the courts to promote his own political career. Both he and Cephisodemus proceeded ruthlessly enough against such venerable old aristocrats as Thucydides son of Melesias for Aristophanes to venture the suggestion that henceforth young prosecutors ought to be used only against the young and old prosecutors against the aged (Ar. *Ach*. 676–718, esp. 714–18).

All this suggests that young men like Cephisodemus and Euathlus did not spring from the landed aristocracy but, like Cleon, Hyperbolus, and Cleophon, from families who had acquired their wealth through industry or commerce. In fact, Hyperbolus himself is said to have been still young when he started his career in the Assembly,[128] and Cleon, we are told, surrounded himself with a gang of young merchants willing to do his bidding and "play" ostracism in his behalf (Ar. *Eq*. 852–57). Moreover, there are general complaints about young men being too eager in their ambition to occupy positions of influence and importance (Eup. frr. 100, 121, 310). Like the demagogues, they are alleged to be stealing the tribute that the older generation's wars had brought to Athens and to be securing for themselves the most remunerative and least hazardous jobs in the army (Ar. *Vesp*. 1099–1101; *Ach*. 600–606). Like the demagogues, too, they are often associated with the agora, the marketplace,[129] as if to mark their origins in the industrial and mercantile classes.

But unlike the demagogues, the young, whether from landed or industrial families, seem to have shown no sympathy for the *dēmos* and its leaders. This is clearly intimated by the chorus in the *Wasps* (887–90) and by the dislike of Cleon evinced by the young aristocratic chorus of the *Knights* (225–26, 731). The same picture emerges from Euripides' *Supplices*: although Theseus, the democratic Athenian statesman *par excellence* in the play, is presented as young (190–91), much more emphasis is placed on the young nobility who

---

127 D. L. 9.54 and 56; Quint. 3.1.10; Aul. Gell. *NA* 5.10. If he was of humble birth (ἀγεννής), as is suggested by the *Suda* s.v. Εὐάθλους δέκα and by schol. *Ach*. 710 he must have been rich enough to afford the fee of one hundred mnai charged by Protagoras according to D. L. 9.52. Quint. 3.1.10 speaks of ten thousand denarii.

128 Cratinus, fr. 262; Eup. fr. 238.

129 Ar. *Eq*. 1373–83; *Nub*. 991; cf. also above, pp. 214-15 with n. 67.

misled Adrastus into attacking Thebes in defiance of the prophecy of Amphiaraus. Their "love of being honored makes them foment wars unjustly, destroying their fellow citizens, one in order to lead an army, another to get power into his hands to use indiscriminately, and a third to make a profit, without regard for the harm suffered by the masses."[130] The picture drawn here might almost be a sketch of Alcibiades, more indifferent than opposed to the interests of the people in the pursuit of his personal objectives. But we know of others, too, to whom Euripides' description might apply—for example, Phaeax, who like his contemporary Alcibiades came from an old and distinguished family.[131] His father may have been a general; his nephew, called, like Phaeax's father, Erasistratus, may have been one of the Thirty Tyrants.[132] This tenuous evidence conveys the impression that Phaeax came from the upper class and that his family was far from enthusiastic about Athenian democratic institutions. There is other evidence to this effect: Phaeax allegedly participated in the intrigues that led to the ostracism of Hyperbolus in 416 B.C. (Plut. *Nic.* 11.10; *Alc.* 13), and Aristophanes hints that the young nobles supported him enthusiastically for using his considerable rhetorical talents to keep the noisy mob in check.[133] Yet he headed the embassy that the Athenians sent to Sicily in 422 B.C. in hopes of organizing an expedition against Syracuse in order to save the *dēmos* of Leontini from its upper-class opponents (Thuc. 5.4.1–5). Evidently, an Athenian's antipathy to democratic institutions in his home state did not yet preclude his supporting democratic regimes abroad and had not yet taken on the oligarchical coloring it was to assume in 411 B.C. Things seem to have been different outside Athens. Athenagoras's speech shows that the young members of the upper class in Syracuse were closely identified with oligarchical interests in 415 B.C., only a few years after Phaeax's mission (Thuc. 6.38.5–39.2).

We do not know whether and, if so, how antidemocratic nobles were organized in Athens in the 420s. But we do know that gatherings of young men of the upper classes, however innocent in nature, were suspected by Cleon and his supporters of harboring conspirato-

130 Eur. *Supp.* 232–37. That the young men belong to the ὄλβιοι is indicated in lines 238–39.

131 See Plut. *Alc.* 13.1, with Davies, *APF*, no. 13921.

132 D. L. 2.63; Antiphon, frr. 57–59 Thalheim; and Xen. *Hell.* 2.3.2, as discussed by Gomme, *HCT* 3.633–34.

133 Ar. *Eq.* 1377–80. On his rhetorical ability, see also Eup. fr. 95: λαλεῖν ἄριστος, ἀδυνώτατος λέγειν, "long on form but short on substance."

rial designs against the established order. In his first words in the *Knights*, Cleon accuses the young nobles of conspiracy against the *dēmos* (Ar. *Eq.* 236; cf. 257), and the rest of the play is replete with Cleon's charges that they are conspiring against the state (ibid. 452, 476, 478, 628, 862). The word ξυνωμότης (conspirator) and its cognates are applied throughout the play only to young nobles suspected of conspiracy against the state; these words are found again in this sense in the *Wasps* but, with two insignificant exceptions, not elsewhere in the surviving plays of Aristophanes.[134] In the *Wasps* they occur—either by themselves or with allegations of aspiring to tyranny—only in charges that the chorus of aged democratic jurors hurls at Bdelycleon (Ar. *Vesp.* 345, 483; cf. 417, 464, 487) and in Bdelycleon's disquisition on the recklessness of such accusations.[135]

The close association of these charges with Cleon—him alone in the *Wasps* and together with his supporters in the *Knights*—must make us wary of inferring from them that in the 420s young men were organizing to subvert the democracy. Aristophanes' Cleon is prone to making such extravagant allegations that one cannot be sure where reality is being parodied and where pure fantasy has set in. Moreover, the fact that these charges link conspiracy with tyranny but not with oligarchy makes it rash to infer the existence at this time of oligarchical clubs, as a number of scholars have done.[136] Bdelycleon's speech teaches us that the common people, upon whom Cleon's influence will have been strongest (Ar. *Vesp.* 488–507), widely believed such rumors because they were instinctively suspicious of the personal ambitions of rich young dandies who milled about the marketplace and made clever speeches in the Assembly.[137] But there is no reason to suppose that they suspected them of organizing a coup to establish an oligarchy in Athens.

Aristophanes portrays the older generation as embodying the traditional values of the Athenian democracy: we have to think only

---

134   The exceptions are *Lys.* 182 and 1007, where they refer to the heroine's plot.

135   Ar. *Vesp.* 488 and 507, in both instances combined with tyranny; cf. also 495, 498, and the slave's joke at 502. Philocleon accuses the dog Labes of conspiracy at 953.

136   E. g., G. M. Calhoun, *Athenian Clubs in Politics and Litigation*, Bulletin of the University of Texas 262, Humanistic Series 14 (Austin, Tex., 1913) 8 n. 7 and 144 n. 4; and F. Sartori, *Le Eterie nella vita politica ateniese del VI e V secolo a.C.* (Rome, 1957) 75–76.

137   See Ar. *Eq.* 1373–83; *Nub.* 991.

of Dicaeopolis and the chorus of charcoal burners in the *Archarnians* (397, 607–17; 176–85, 209–22), of Dēmos in the *Knights* (40–43 *et passim*), of Strepsiades in the *Clouds* (129, 263, 358, 513–14, 746, 1304), of Philocleon and the chorus of jurors in the *Wasps* (133, 245–48, 728, *et passim*), and of Peisthetaerus and Euelpides in the *Birds* (255–57, 320–21). Socially, the old are simple, unpretentious folk. Dicaeopolis is a farmer who yearns to return to the land because he hates the city; Dēmos is a farmer by birth and in temper; and Strepsiades looks back with longing to the days before his marriage, when he could enjoy a farmer's life, "moldy with dirt and dust, flopping down as I pleased, teeming with bees, sheep, and olive-cakes."[138] Against this backdrop, the new ways cultivated by the young are criticized as not conforming to the values of the democratic establishment. Strepsiades' aristocratic wife, an Alcmaeonid, has nothing on her mind but perfume, saffron, French kissing, spending money, gourmet food, and sex (Ar. *Nub*. 46–55). His son, Pheidippides, takes after his mother's side of the family: he wears his hair long, dreams of nothing but horses, and spends money wildly on horses and racing chariots, driving his father to the edge of bankruptcy (ibid. 14–16, 797, *et passim*). Both in the *Clouds* and in the *Wasps* father and son affect allegiance to different social classes. Whether this reflects a common situation in Athens or whether it is merely a comic device to highlight the generation gap we cannot tell.

We do know that the fancy ways of the young shocked the simple older generation. For example, young men took up the ancient custom of wearing their hair long; but whereas the more old-fashioned among their elders tied up their hair in a bun and held it in place with a cicada-shaped clasp,[139] the young wore it loose in the Laconian style, to the disgust of their elders.[140] Older Athenians also took exception to their assuming Laconian mannerisms in dress and

138 Ar. *Ach*. 32–33; *Eq*. 40–43; *Nub*. 43–45.
139 Ar. *Eq*. 1331; *Nub*. 984; Thuc. 1.6.3.
140 Ar. *Eq*. 1121; *Nub*. 14, 348–50, 1101; *Vesp*. 466, 474–76, 1068–70; *Av*. 1281–82; *Lys*. 561; Plato Com. fr. 124. See C. Ehrhardt, "Hair in Ancient Greece," *Classical News and Views* 15 (1971) 14–19, esp. 15–17, who fails to see, however, that long hair was only objectionable on young men of the upper classes. At Ar. *Eq*. 580, the young knights implore the audience not to begrudge them their long hair after the war. Cf. also *Lys*. 16.18, where Mantitheus pleads at his *dokimasia* in the late 390s not to hold it against him that he wears his hair long.

in sexual behavior,[141] sometimes attributed to the influence of the sophists with whom they studied (Ar. *Nub*. 332, 895–96; *Av*. 911). Other mannerisms of the young that their elders disliked are summed up in Bdelycleon's attempt toward the end of the *Wasps* (1122–1264) to spruce up his father: he tries to persuade him to exchange his old, worn cloak for a tunic of Persian material from Ecbatana, to wear Laconian shoes so as to "walk like the rich," and to talk cleverly, engage in name dropping, watch sports, take up hunting, and learn to conduct himself at a drinking party.

Such a life could be maintained only at a cost offensive to thrifty old democrats. They came to look upon the younger generation as softies, addicted more to baths, perfumes, and drinking bouts than to the old manly virtues that had won Athens her eminence in the Greek world.[142] They looked back to the days of Marathon and reminisced over their escapades at Byzantium, when men were still men, when they fought the Mede, when they laid the foundations for the tribute the young were now stealing to meet their expenses.[143] They recalled with admiration the wealthy upper classes who had then led the state and the armed forces; they felt the present leaders were nothing but young sexual perverts who enjoyed having a general's robe flap about their ankles (Eup. frr. 100, 117). The old no longer had the strength they once did, but what was still left had to be used to keep the young in check (Ar. *Ach*. 676–91; *Vesp*. 1060–70). Times had changed: the values of the democratic establishment were being threatened and undermined by the younger generation.

A further dimension of the polarization of the old and the young was to have momentous consequences. The aged jurors in the *Wasps* contrast the victories they won over the enemy at sea with the preoccupations of the young, who they allege are more interested in clever talk than in action and only worry about who will be their next victim in the law courts.[144] We have seen evidence of this in the

141　Ar. *Vesp*. 475–76. For pederasty as a Spartan trait, see also Ar. fr. 338, and for its spread among the upper classes, see *Vesp*. 687, 1070; *Ran*. 739–40; Eup. fr. 100; Com. Adesp. frr. 12–14.

142　Ar. *Eq*. 1373–83; *Nub*. 835–37, 991; fr. 216; Pherecrates, frr. 2 and 29; Hermippus, fr. 76; Com. Adesp. fr. 375. For a comprehensive account, see Ehrenberg, *People*[2] 99–108.

143　Ar. *Ach*. 695–96; *Vesp*. 235–39, 1096–1101.

144　Ar. *Vesp*. 1091–97, esp. 1094–97: οὐ γὰρ ἦν ἡμῖν ὅπως / ῥῆσιν εὖ λέξειν ἐμέλλομεν τότ᾽, οὐδὲ / συκοφαντήσειν τινὰ φροντίς.

persuasive talents of Cephisodemus and Euathlus as accusers and in the admiration clever young men had for the rhetorical prowess of Phaeax.[145] Rhetoric came into its own in Athens in the 420s because of the importance public speaking had come to assume in trying to sway Council, Assembly, and the juries, where power was exercised. The demand for rhetorical teaching was filled by the sophists, whose following consisted largely of ambitious young men of the upper classes.

"A man who has a policy but does not explain it clearly is in the same situation as one who has none in mind" (Thuc. 2.60.6). Effective speaking combined with political intelligence and an incorruptible love of country is for the Thucydidean Pericles a prime requisite for statesmanship. Rhetorical excellence came, if we can trust tradition, as a natural gift to Pericles. Plutarch (*Per.* 4) names two musicians and two natural philosophers as his teachers, but no rhetorician. Themistocles, the only pre-Periclean statesman about whose oratorical prowess reports have come down to us from antiquity, also had no rhetorical training. Thucydides (1.138.3) remarks on the swift and keen intelligence with which he could fathom a situation and expound it to others. Plutarch, emphasizing Themistocles' natural endowments over against any formal training, says the statesman emulated Mnesiphilus, a worthy example in that he was "neither a rhetorician nor one of the so-called natural philosophers, but one who had made his own what was then called "wisdom" [σοφία], which was actually political acumen and practical insight: these he preserved as a heritage from Solon."[146] There is no indication, either, that Cleon, the most successful speaker of the early 420s, had received any training in rhetoric. On the contrary, he may well have owed his success to a native vulgarity in speech and delivery that made the masses feel he was no more educated than they were.[147] Yet the lesson he could impart, namely, that effective public speaking was an important avenue to power, will not have been lost on ambitious young men, who now actively sought training in the skill of which Cleon was a natural, even if uncouth,

145 See above, pp. 231–33.
146 Plut. *Them*. 2.6. At Hdt. 8.57–58, Mnesiphilus is credited with having advised Themistocles to engage the Persians at Salamis.
147 See above, pp. 216–17. Cf. also his anti-intellectual remarks at Thuc. 3.37.3–5 and 3.38.3–4.

practitioner.[148] The supply to fill this demand was not slow in coming. The men who provided it are known as "sophists."

The impact that the sophists had on Athenian life from the 420s on was prefigured by the arrival in Athens of Protagoras of Abdera in 433 B.C., an event immortalized by the Platonic dialogue bearing his name.[149] The flurry his visit evoked, so vividly depicted at the opening of Plato's *Protagoras*, shows that his reputation had preceded him, almost certainly because he was the first man to identify himself as a professional *sophistēs*.[150] Obviously Protagoras would not have called himself a sophist if the term had had for him the derogatory connotations it was to assume in the fourth century,[151] although his statement that his predecessors identified their profession differently "because they feared the odium of the name" (316d) shows that Plato imputed to him an awareness of a pejorative meaning. However, if the comparatively rare occurrence of the noun in the surviving fifth-century writings reliably attests its usage, σοφιστής from its earliest appearance (Pind. *Isthm.* 5.28) describes a person endowed with some special skill or expertise that—and this nuance is important—he activates so as to make a contribution to the life of his society. It is used of poets, of musicians and rhapsodes, of

148   To cite but a few Aristophanic passages to illustrate these points: at *Eq.* 634–38 the Sausage Seller prays for rhetorical qualities such as are usually attributed to Cleon; at *Ach.* 370–74 Dicaeopolis states how smooth patriotic talk fools the farmers; at *Vesp.* 1174–96 Bdelycleon wants to teach his father the kind of speech to use in the presence of learned and sophisticated men; and at *Nub.* 1399–1405 Pheidippides glories in the power his newly acquired skill has given him; for the potential of that skill, see the speech of Wrong, ibid. 1036–78, esp. 1040, 1056–59, 1077–78. For a general statement on the good old times of the Persian Wars, when action mattered more than smooth forensic talk, see *Vesp.* 1094–1101.

149   That this was neither Protagoras's first visit to Athens nor his last is shown by a reference to an earlier visit—perhaps in connection with the foundation of Thurii in 444/3 B.C.—at Pl. *Prt.* 310e and by a mention of him by Eup. fr. 146 as present in Athens at the time of the performance of his *Kolakes* in 422/1 B.C.; see J. S. Morrison, "The Place of Protagoras in Athenian Public Life (460–415 B.C.)," *CQ* 35 (1941) 1–16, esp. 2–3, and J. A. Davison, "Protagoras, Democritus, and Anaxagoras," *CQ*, n.s., 3 (1953) 33–45, esp. 37–38. But the tone and setting of Plato's *Protagoras* leave no doubt that the visit of 433 B.C. was the most decisive for its impact on Athenian society. J. Walsh, "The Dramatic Dates of Plato's *Protagoras* and the Lesson of *Arete*," *CQ*, n.s., 34 (1984) 101–6, believes that the *Protagoras* conflates the visits of the 430s and the 420s. In general, see Kerferd, *SM* 15–23.

150   Pl. *Prt.* 309d–312b, esp. 311e; 317b, 349a. The reference at *Meno* 92a to ἄλλοι πάμπολλοι, οἱ μὲν πρότερον γεγονότες ἐκείνου [sc. Πρωταγόρου], οἱ δὲ καὶ νῦν ἔτι ὄντες does not indicate that anyone called himself a σοφιστής before Protagoras.

151   Among the countless passages that could be cited, see esp. Pl. *Soph.* 231d–232a; Xen. *Mem.* 1.6.13; Arist. *Soph. El.* 1.1, 165ᵃ21–23.

diviners and seers, of a statesman such as Solon, a religious leader such as Pythagoras, and of figures such as Prometheus or Eurystheus, whose contrivances brought pain and misery.[152] Conspicuously absent from this list are the so-called natural philosophers (φυσικοί), thinkers such as Thales, Anaximander, Anaximenes, Heraclitus, Parmenides, and Empedocles, who were referred to as *sophistai* only from the fourth century on, presumably by an extension of the term to cover all σοφοί.[153] Protagoras appears deliberately to have wanted to distance himself from them: in Plato's portrait he claims to be carrying on the tradition of the poets Homer and Hesiod, of the religious leaders Orpheus and Musaeus, of physical trainers such as Iccus of Tarentum and Herodicus of Selymbria, and of the music (μουσική) teachers Agathocles and Pythocleides of Ceos; but he pointedly disassociates himself from the teaching of arithmetic, astronomy, geometry, and literature (μουσική) other sophists dispensed.[154] Of course Protagoras wanted to impart his knowledge of human concerns to other human beings; he did not wish to gain a scientific knowledge of the physical universe only for his own satisfaction. He wanted to be a σοφιστής, not merely a σοφός, in the sense that he wanted to do something with his wisdom.[155] This, surely, is one of the reasons why the *homo mensura* sentence stood at the opening of one of his works (D.L. 9.51): what is and what is not

152   This list is adapted from G. B. Kerferd, "The First Greek Sophists," *CR* 64 (1950) 8–10, esp. 8, where the relevant passages are cited. For Prometheus, see Aesch. *PV* 62 and 944; for Eurystheus, Eur. *Heracl.* 993.

153   Xen. *Mem*. 1.1.11 applies σοφισταί to the natural philosophers as such; Pl. *Meno* 85b uses it of geometricians, and Isocrates enumerates, among others Anaxagoras, Damon (15.235), Anaximander, Empedocles, Ion, Alcmaeon, Parmenides, Melissus, and Gorgias (15.268). A possible exception is Diogenes of Apollonia: if we can trust Simplicius (*Comm. in Arist. Graeca* 9 ed. H. Diels [Berlin, 1882] 151.25–26) he wrote a tract πρὸς φυσιολόγους in which he labeled them σοφιστάς.

154   Pl. *Prt.* 316d–e, 318d–e. The contradiction of embracing some teachers of μουσική though rejecting others is not as glaring as it may seem, because the term covers all activities over which the Muses preside. Of Agathocles and Pythocleides we know that they taught instrumental music; we can only guess what μουσική the other sophists taught: the context suggests that it was a specialized kind of literary or musical theory.

155   For this sense of the -της suffix, see P. Chantraine, *La Formation des noms en grec ancien* (Paris, 1933) 313; cf. also E. Benveniste, *Noms d'agent et noms d'action en indo-européen* (Paris, 1948) 56. That Protagoras himself stressed this aspect of his activity is shown by his statement at 317b: καὶ ὁμολογῶ τε σοφιστὴς εἶναι καὶ παιδεύειν ἀνθρώπους, καὶ εὐλάβειαν ταύτην οἶμαι βελτίω ἐκείνης εἶναι, τὸ ὁμολογεῖν μᾶλλον ἢ ἔξαρνον εἶναι.

are established by common-sense human experience, not by abstruse speculations about the structure of the universe.[156]

Protagoras defined his pedagogical aims as to impart "sound judgment [εὐβουλία] in personal affairs, to enable a person to run his own household in the best way, and in the affairs of the city to make his contribution to public affairs most effective in action and speech." He concurs with Socrates' description of his activity as the teaching of the "art of citizenship" or "political science" (πολιτικὴ τέχνη).[157] The political aspect of his teaching is defined in Plato's *Theaetetus* (167c–d): "Whatever sorts of thing seem just and honorable to a particular city are in fact [just and honorable] for it, as long as it so regards them." This statement not only sanctions the social and political conditions current and accepted in any given city at any particular time, but it also implies an attitude of *laisser vivre* toward any other city to which different things seem just and honorable and suggests that changes in any current state of affairs can legitimately be introduced, provided that they are agreeable to the citizens. Changes are thus predicated not on the truth but on better perceptions of what is just and honorable for a given state. According to Protagoras the aim of a *sophistēs* is to educate his students to speak well enough to effect such changes in the societies in which they live.[158]

This principle seems to have formed the basis of Protagoras's rhetorical teachings, though what specifically these teachings were

156 So E. Kapp in his review of H. Langerbeck, ΔΟΞΙΣ ΕΠΙΡΥΣΜΙΗ, *Gnomon* 12 (1936) 70–72, and Kerferd, *SM* 85–89.

157 Pl. *Prt.* 318e–319a. Cf. Kerferd, *SM* 132–36.

158 Pl. *Tht.* 167a4–6: οὕτω δὲ καὶ ἐν τῇ παιδείᾳ ἀπὸ ἑτέρας ἕξεως ἐπὶ τὴν ἀμείνω μεταβλητέον· ἀλλ᾽ ὁ μὲν ἰατρὸς φαρμάκοις μεταβάλλει, ὁ δὲ σοφιστὴς λόγοις. Ibid. 167c2–d1: τοὺς δέ γε σοφούς τε καὶ ἀγαθοὺς ῥήτορας ταῖς πόλεσι τὰ χρηστὰ ἀντὶ τῶν πονηρῶν δίκαια δοκεῖν εἶναι ποιεῖν. ἐπεὶ οἷά γ᾽ ἂν ἑκάστῃ πόλει δίκαια καὶ καλὰ δοκῇ, ταῦτα καὶ εἶναι αὐτῇ, ἕως ἂν αὐτὰ νομίζῃ· ἀλλ᾽ ὁ σοφὸς ἀντὶ πονηρῶν ὄντων αὐτοῖς ἑκάστων χρηστὰ ἐποίησεν εἶναι καὶ δοκεῖν. κατὰ δὲ τὸν αὐτὸν λόγον καὶ ὁ σοφιστὴς τοὺς παιδευομένους οὕτω δυνάμενος παιδαγωγεῖν σοφός τε καὶ ἄξιος πολλῶν χρημάτων τοῖς παιδευθεῖσιν. Most modern scholars agree that there is no reason for Plato to have seriously misrepresented Protagoras's beliefs either in *Prt.* or in *Tht.* Plato's respect for Protagoras is attested at *Meno* 91d–e and emerges also from the general tone of *Prt.*; at *Tht.* 165e and 166c–d he is careful to be fair to Protagoras's views, indicating that the account at 165e–168c "is fairly reproducing the standpoint of the historic Protagoras" (F. M. Cornford, *Plato's Theory of Knowledge* [London, 1935] 72), and he takes equally great care at 168c2–5, 169d10–e5, and 172b6–7 to dissociate Protagoras from the criticisms and modifications of his doctrine at 169d–172b. For a contrary view, see J. McDowell, ed. and tr., *Plato: Theaetetus* (Oxford, 1973) 172–73.

is hard to ascertain. Diogenes Laertius reports (9.51) that Protagoras was the first to maintain that any argument on any issue admits of counterargument; this makes sense if we bear in mind that for Protagoras no issue can be true or false. If that is so, "sound judgement" (εὐβουλία) will consist in marshaling arguments for commending or rejecting a given course of action for a given society under a given set of circumstances, and consequently the teaching of the *sophistēs* will consist in the formulation of what kind of arguments suit what kind of circumstances. That this was indeed the content of Protagoras's rhetorical training seems confirmed by a passage in Plato's *Euthydemus* (286b–c) that attributes to his school the doctrine that there is no contradiction between truth and falsehood, as there obviously cannot be if different views differ only in being better or worse for a given situation. The emphasis on which course of action is more commendable than another will have been interpreted by Protagoras's contemporaries and by later generations as an indifference to truth and falsehood in the discussion of a given issue, and we find in Aristotle the criticism that he "presented the weaker argument as stronger" (τὸν ἥττω δὲ λόγον κρείττω ποιεῖν, *Rh*. 2.24, 1402ᵃ 22–28). If this expression is Protagoras's own, it may well also be reflected in the argument between Right and Wrong in Aristophanes' *Clouds*. Moreover, it is likely that two books entitled *Contradictions* ('Αντιλογίαι) and one entitled *Eristics* (Τέχνη ἐριστικῶν), listed among his published works by Diogenes Laertius (9.55), contained his rhetorical precepts and that his well-attested interest in language and in the structure of speech springs from his rhetorical principles.[159]

If our interpretation is right, Protagoras's originality in proclaiming himself a sophist will have consisted in expounding a philosophy that could be applied to the daily social and political life of the state and in giving at the same time training in rhetoric as the corollary of his philosophy. The fact that his pupils would be able to derive not only political but also material profit from his instruction explains another first attributed to him by our sources: he was the first to demand pay for his teaching.[160] Although we are told that he permitted his students to challenge his fee and pay only what value

---

159 E.g., Pl. *Phdr*. 267c; *Crat*. 391c; Arist. *Soph.El*. 1.14, 173ᵇ17–25; D. L. 9.53–54. On these problems, see Kerferd, *SM* 84–92.

160 Pl. *Prt*. 349a; D. L. 9.52; Philostr. *VS* 1.10.4; schol. Pl. *Resp*. 600c.

they attached to his instruction,[161] he was believed to have earned more money than Phidias and ten other sculptors together (Pl. *Meno* 91d).

This in turn meant that only the wealthy could afford Protagoras. Plato makes him admit as much in stating that the most influential men, whom he identifies with the wealthiest, are best able to give their sons the maximum of education (*Prt.* 326c). Socrates alludes to the high cost of Protagoras's services when he introduces his young friend Hippocrates to the master: "He comes from a great and prosperous family, and in natural talent he seems a match for anyone his age" (316b). Similarly, the *Protagoras* is set at the house of the aristocrat Callias. This wealthy young Athenian spent large sums to study with sophists (*Ap.* 20a; *Cra.* 391b–c); he is presented in this dialogue as the host of Protagoras, Hippias, Prodicus, and a number of young upper-class Athenians (*Prt.* 314e–316a).

Protagoras was so far as we know the only person who identified himself as a *sophistēs*. From the time of Plato the term was applied loosely to a number of men who appeared in Athens from the 420s on primarily as teachers of rhetoric. We have no secure list of their names: modern scholars, dependent on an erratic and usually hostile ancient tradition, do not agree who should be called a sophist, because the ancient criteria for such identification remain obscure. But comprehensiveness is unnecessary for our purposes; it will suffice to mention the men most widely regarded as sophists— Gorgias, Prodicus, Hippias, Antiphon, and Thrasymachus—and to address ourselves to the question of what they had in common with one another and with Protagoras to deserve being given the same label. The most obvious observations to be made are that regardless of what other interests they showed or taught all sophists were primarily concerned with rhetoric and argumentation[162] and that all charged a fee for their instruction.[163] Moreover, as with Protagoras,

---

161   Pl. *Prt.* 328b–c. Cf. also n. 127 above.

162   This point, which forms the thesis of H. Gomperz, *Sophistik und Rhetorik* (Leipzig and Berlin, 1912), has been emphasized again by E. L. Harrison, "Was Gorgias a Sophist?" *Phoenix* 18 (1964) 183–92, esp. 190–91 with nn. 40–42. This does not imply that they were not interested in matters other than rhetoric: on the contrary, Hippias is credited with an impressive array of intellectual pursuits at Pl. *Hp.Ma.* 285b–e and elsewhere, and Cic. *De or.* 3.32.128 speaks of interest in natural philosophy on the part of Prodicus, Thrasymachus, and Protagoras; but there is no indication that any of these interests entered into the instruction given by these sophists except incidentally.

163   On this point, see E. L. Harrison, "Gorgias a Sophist?" 191 with nn. 44–46.

their appeal was chiefly to young men from wealthy upper-class families,[164] and like him most were itinerant, traveling from city to city to give courses of lectures and coming to Athens as foreigners, sometimes accompanied by their students.[165] In this last respect they will have resembled other artists and intellectuals who had been attracted to the imperial city—"the capital of wisdom of Greece," as Hippias of Elis called it (Pl. *Prt.* 337d)—ever since the days of Pericles. But unlike Protagoras, the sophists coming to Athens from the 420s on were not philosophers who propounded a consistent doctrine on the nature of man and society. If they can be regarded as Protagoras's heirs at all, it is because they developed the teaching of rhetoric, which was for Protagoras no more than an offshoot, however important, of his "art of citizenship" (πολιτικὴ τέχνη).

The impact of these teachers on Athenian life is most effectively summed up in general terms in Plato's *Gorgias*, which is named for the earliest of those sophists who first came to Athens as ambassadors from their states. Gorgias was dispatched by his native city of Leontini in 427 B.C. to negotiate a request for an alliance and ships against Syracuse,[166] Neither the fragments surviving from his writings nor the picture Plato draws of him suggests that he studied or taught anything other than rhetoric, but of that art he was an acknowledged master, respected as such by Plato;[167] any speculative or social thought we find embedded in his fragments or in reports about his writings is put into the service of rhetoric and shows no

---

164 See the definition of the sophist as νέων καὶ πλουσίων ἔμμισθος θηρευτής at Pl. *Soph.* 231d, and in general, *Theages* 121d; *Phlb.* 15d–16b. From *Grg.* 463e and 466a it is clear that Polus is a young man, and at 487c Socrates claims to have overheard a discussion between Callicles and his rich young friends Teisander, Andron, and Nausicydes (for their identities, see E. R. Dodds, *Plato: Gorgias* [Oxford, 1959] 282) on the desirable extent of philosophical studies; Prodicus is said in Philostr. *VS* 1.12 to have tracked down rich young aristocrats to be his pupils. On this aspect, see also C. Corbato, *Sofisti e politica ad Atene durante la Guerra del Peloponneso*, Università degli Studi di Trieste, Istituto di Filologia Classica 4 (Trieste, 1958) 16–24.

165 Pl. *Ap.* 19e–20c; *Ti.* 19e; *Euthyd.* 271c. For students accompanying them, see, e.g., *Prt.* 315a; *Grg.* 487a.

166 Diod. 12.53.2; cf. Thuc. 3.86.3. See also Pl. *Hp.Ma.* 282b–c, where mention is made also of embassies on which Prodicus was dispatched from his native Ceos, and ibid. 281a for foreign missions by Hippias. The doubts of Dodds, *Plato: Gorgias* 6–7 that Gorgias was regarded as a sophist have been convincingly removed by E. L. Harrison, "Gorgias a Sophist?" 183–92; cf. also Kerferd, *SM* 44–45.

167 On this point, see the sane observations of Dodds, *Plato: Gorgias* 9–10.

intrinsic interest in philosophy.[168] He seems to have been of too good a conventional moral character to have understood the revolutionary moral and political consequences of his teaching. But that his teaching did have such consequences, which Plato with the benefit of hindsight regarded as corrosive, is brilliantly shown in the *Gorgias*. Plato deserves more credence as a philosopher than as a historian, and his views are colored by his own belief in moral absolutes; yet the dialogue rings true if we read it as a keen-eyed perception of yet another polarization in the 420s, to wit, a split between a set of new intellectual values that the sophists introduced into Athenian life and the old, established ethos of the Athenian democracy.

The moral influence of the sophists is imaginatively depicted in Socrates' progression from discussion with Gorgias to discussion with Polus; its political effect is demonstrated in the brilliant portrait of the practical politician Callicles. That the last of these was Plato's focus is obvious from the length of Socrates' discussion with Callicles: it is twice as long as his discussion with Polus and three and one-half times as long as his argument with Gorgias, who nevertheless gives the title to the work.[169] The fact that Plato has Gorgias stay as a guest in Callicles' home (447b) and that it is Callicles who introduces Socrates to Gorgias is similarly significant: in short, Plato saw a linear relation between the best rhetorical teaching available in Athens in the 420s and the kind of politician it produced.

Gorgias is treated with respect, but his teaching is presented as hollow and self-contradictory. He regards the art of rhetoric as amoral because it can be used both for good ends and for bad, but he also advocates death or exile for those who practice it immorally (457b–c); and yet, further, he claims that morality (τὰ δίκαια) is a sufficiently important prerequisite for the practice of rhetoric that he

168 H. Gomperz, *Sophistik* 1–35 may have overemphasised this point, but its substance has to the best of my knowledge not yet been refuted. Even his connection with Empedoclean doctrine at Pl. *Meno* 76c is less philosophical than rhetorical; see R. S. Bluck, *Plato's Meno* (Cambridge, 1961) 251 and 252–53. Similarly, the aim of his celebrated treatise περὶ τοῦ μὴ ὄντος ἢ περὶ φύσεως (Sext. Emp. *Math*. 7.87) was merely "to show that, by the sort of arguments that Parmenides used, it was as easy to prove 'it is not' as 'it is'" (Guthrie, *HGP* 3.194); that he needs not to be taken seriously as a philosopher has been shown by J. M. Robinson, "On Gorgias," in E. N. Lee, A. P. D. Mourelatos, and R. M. Rorty, eds., *Exegesis and Argument: Studies in Greek Philosophy Presented to Gregory Vlastos* (Assen, 1973) 49–60. His philosophy is taken seriously by Kerferd, *SM* 95–98.

169 The discussion with Gorgias comprises twelve Stephanus pages (449c–461b), that with Polus twenty (461b–481b) and that with Callicles forty-five (482c–527e).

teaches it to any who come to him as pupils without previous knowledge of it (459c–460c).

Socrates' discussion with Polus, one of Gorgias's young pupils who aspires to become a teacher of rhetoric himself and has written a textbook on the subject,[170] has a dual purpose. It demonstrates that rhetoric is no systematic art (τέχνη) at all but merely an empirical knack of treating people the way they like to be treated (κολακεία, 462c–466a), and it presents a young sophist's view of the practical political benefits that can be derived from his craft (466b). There is no need for us here to rehearse the complex arguments by which Socrates tries to convert Polus to what is ultimately an apolitical position, that it is better to be the victim than the perpetrator of injustice. What is of interest is that Polus praises the orators for the tyrannical power they can wield to kill or banish anyone they wish and confiscate his property (466b–c); his ideal happy man is the Macedonian king Archelaus, whose road to power was paved with the most heinous crimes. Success, in Polus's opinion, justifies such crimes; that he is unjust does not mean that he is not happy (470d–472d). Socrates concedes that Polus's view is shared by most Athenians and foreigners and that it can be defended with the rhetorical devices one uses to sway a jury (471e–472b), but he dissociates himself from such ethics utterly (473e–476a). Plato could not have shown more clearly how he thought the kindly old gentleman's narrow rhetorical teaching affected the political thinking of his successors. The effect Plato believed it had on the practical politicians of Athens is depicted in his painstaking portrayal of Callicles, Socrates' chief Athenian interlocutor in the dialogue.

Unless new evidence unexpectedly appears, we shall never be certain whether Callicles was a historical person, though there are ample grounds for believing he existed. If he did, Plato's genius can be credited with having identified him as the most intelligent and formidable example in politics of the consequences of Gorgias's rhetorical teaching. If he did not, Plato's imaginative powers must be admired for the creation of a complex composite character made up of the most salient traits of the young aristocratic Athenian intellectuals who flocked to the sophists out of political ambition in the 420s and later.[171] What is beyond doubt is that Plato made him a creature

170 For the professional training given by the sophists (ἐπὶ τέχνῃ), see also Pl. *Prt.* 315a; on Polus's textbook, see *Grg.* 462b–c.
171 On the question of Callicles' historicity, see Dodds, *Plato: Gorgias* 12–13; Guthrie, *HGP* 3.102.

of flesh and blood: his deme is Acharnae (495d); he comes from the upper class (512d); he has had a decent education (487b); his friends come from good families—they include Andron (487c), who was also attracted to the sophists and who prosecuted Antiphon, Archeptolemus, and Onomacles for treason after the overthrow of the Four Hundred, though he had himself been one of their number in 411 B.C.[172]—and he is a lover of Demos son of Pyrilampes (481d), Plato's stepfather, who was certainly a historical person and a member of the upper class.[173]

Callicles is a man of paradoxes. His powers of speech and an explicit reference to his education clearly indicate that he had undergone rhetorical training, presumably at the feet of Gorgias, who was now his houseguest. Yet he despises as "worthless" those Socrates identifies as sophists, who claim to educate men for a life of virtue (520a), and he attacks the study of philosophy by grown men as "ridiculous" (484c–486c). This is not likely to be intended as a slur against Gorgias: we learn earlier in the dialogue (459c–460c) that Gorgias teaches morality only to those who have no previous knowledge of it, and Callicles will surely not have been one of these; and the *Meno* (95b–c) contains a disclaimer that Gorgias ever professed to be teaching virtue.[174] Callicles' denunciations, rather, seem to show that he regards himself as a practical orator-politician who has outgrown any teaching to which he has been subjected in the past—he has arrived as an *homme d'affaires*. This view is consistent with the statement that he has embarked on a political career only recently (515a), which means, if we are to take the dramatic date of the *Gorgias* seriously, shortly before 427 B.C.

There is a paradox also about Callicles' political position. Modern scholars debate whether he was a democrat, an oligarch, or an advocate of tyranny;[175] but the question cannot be answered in these terms, simply because the evidence is contradictory—as we should expect it to be in an age unfamiliar with the party-political commitment we know in most modern states. His eagerness never to oppose

---

172 [Plut.] *X Orat.* 833e; Harp. s.v. Ἄνδρων. He is present among Hippias's audience in Pl. *Prt.* 315c.

173 Ar. *Vesp.* 98 shows that Demos was admired as καλός in 422 B.C.; see MacDowell's note *ad loc.* on biographical details on him and his father.

174 In this connection note the observation of E. L. Harrison, "Gorgias a Sophist?" 186–87 with n. 21, that distinctions between ῥητορική and σοφιστική are not drawn clearly in the *Gorgias*.

175 See G. B. Kerferd, "Plato's Treatment of Callicles in the 'Gorgias,'" *PCPS* 200, n.s. 20 (1974) 48–52, who regards him as a democrat.

the desires either of his lover, Demos, or of the Athenian *dēmos* (481d) has been interpreted as identifying him as a democrat, and support for this view has been seen in his admiration for the great statesmen of the heyday of the Athenian democracy, especially Pericles (515c–e). But his great speech reveals that he is anything but a democrat: he despises the masses as nothing but an obstacle to the self-realization of the superior man. No part of his speech addresses the problem of what constitutes good government or what form of government is the most desirable. If any political aim can be inferred from what he says, it is tyranny or, more correctly, the pursuit of absolute power. For unlike Darius, whom Herodotus (3.82) makes advocate one-man rule as the best form of government for his country, Callicles seeks in political activity nothing but the fulfillment of his own insatiable lust for power: his is a personal, not a political, goal.

The paradox of Callicles' politics suggests that he caters to the people's whims not because he believes in the principle of popular sovereignty but because he thinks that one can attain power only by manipulating the despicable rabble. He is a direct descendant of the demagogues whom Thucydides (2.65.10) censured for surrendering even the affairs of state to the whims of the people in their striving each to be at the top. But whereas the demagogues seem to have avoided the responsibilities of office, Callicles' reluctance to contradict the people is geared, so we may infer, to gaining their support in his attempt to concentrate all executive power in his own hands and be answerable to no one.

The context of Callicles' forthright and brilliant exposition of his views (487a–b) shows that Plato regarded them as the political consequence of sophistic teaching. He divides Callicles' speech into two parts, separated by Socrates' searching examination of the first (486d–491e). The second part (491e–492c), which contains Callicles' account of the absolute ruler as the happiest of men, is of less interest to us than the first (482c–486d, esp. 482e–484c), in which he seeks to discredit the principle of popular sovereignty with arguments based on an opposition of *nomos* to *physis*:

I believe that those who establish *nomoi* are the weak, who constitute the majority. What they establish as *nomoi*, what they praise, and what they disapprove of is determined in relation to themselves and to what suits their own advantage. In order to intimidate the stronger among their fellowmen, who are capable of getting more than an equal share, and in order to prevent them from getting it, they say that taking more than one's share is disgraceful and unjust, and they define wrongdoing as seeking to have more than everyone else. For they are satisfied with an equal share, I think, because they are inferior. That is the reason why *nomos* censures seeking to have more than most other people as unjust and disgraceful, and why they call it wrongdoing. But, in my opinion, it is *physis* itself that declares what really is just, namely, that the better has more than the worse, and the more capable more than the less capable. It manifests the truth of this in many instances: among all other living things and in entire states and families of men it shows that what is just has been determined by the fact that the stronger rules over and has more than the weaker. What standard of justice but this made Xerxes undertake his expedition against the Greeks, and his father against the Scythians? One could enumerate countless other examples. Actions of such men as these, I think, are informed by the *physis* of what is just, and, by Zeus, by a *nomos* of *physis*—but, I dare say, not by the *nomos* we enact.[176]

Though the philosophical significance of this speech has often been explored,[177] some points on Callicles' use of νόμος and φύσις have not yet been adequately noted. He begins by accusing Socrates of having trapped Polus with an argument from what is true νόμῳ but not φύσει. "Law" and "nature" fall short of paraphrasing the norms here opposed to one another; the opposition is between "conventional belief" and "actual fact." These meanings prevail until just before the central passage, which we quoted: the point is that by the standard of actual fact suffering wrong is more disgraceful, worse, and more slavish than doing wrong, which is worse only in terms of conventional belief (483a2–b4). However, the association of νόμῳ with ἀδικεῖν (483a8), which has both a legal and a

---

176 Pl. *Grg.* 483b–e: ἀλλ᾽ οἶμαι οἱ τιθέμενοι τοὺς νόμους οἱ ἀσθενεῖς ἄνθρωποί εἰσιν καὶ οἱ πολλοί. πρὸς αὑτοὺς οὖν καὶ τὸ αὑτοῖς συμφέρον τούς τε νόμους τίθενται καὶ τοὺς ἐπαίνους ἐπαινοῦσιν καὶ τοὺς ψόγους ψέγουσιν· ἐκφοβοῦντες τοὺς ἐρρωμενεστέρους τῶν ἀνθρώπων καὶ δυνατοὺς ὄντας πλέον ἔχειν, ἵνα μὴ αὐτῶν πλέον ἔχωσιν, λέγουσιν ὡς αἰσχρὸν καὶ ἄδικον τὸ πλεονεκτεῖν, καὶ τοῦτό ἐστιν τὸ ἀδικεῖν, τὸ πλέον τῶν ἄλλων ζητεῖν ἔχειν· ἀγαπῶσι γὰρ οἶμαι αὐτοὶ ἂν τὸ ἴσον ἔχωσιν φαυλότεροι ὄντες. διὰ ταῦτα δὴ νόμῳ μὲν τοῦτο ἄδικον καὶ αἰσχρὸν λέγεται, τὸ πλέον ζητεῖν ἔχειν τῶν πολλῶν, καὶ ἀδικεῖν αὐτὸ καλοῦσιν· ἡ δέ γε οἶμαι φύσις αὐτὴ ἀποφαίνει αὐτὸ ὅτι δίκαιόν ἐστιν, τὸν ἀμείνω τοῦ χείρονος πλέον ἔχειν καὶ τὸν δυνατώτερον τοῦ ἀδυνατωτέρου. δηλοῖ δὲ ταῦτα πολλαχοῦ ὅτι οὕτως ἔχει, καὶ ἐν τοῖς ἄλλοις ζῴοις καὶ τῶν ἀνθρώπων ἐν ὅλαις ταῖς πόλεσι καὶ τοῖς γένεσιν, ὅτι οὕτω τὸ δίκαιον κέκριται, τὸν κρείττω τοῦ ἥττονος ἄρχειν καὶ πλέον ἔχειν. ἐπεὶ ποίῳ δικαίῳ χρώμενος Ξέρξης ἐπὶ τὴν Ἑλλάδα ἐστράτευσεν ἢ ὁ πατὴρ αὐτοῦ ἐπὶ Σκύθας; ἢ ἄλλα μυρία ἄν τις ἔχοι τοιαῦτα λέγειν. ἀλλ᾽ οἶμαι οὗτοι κατὰ φύσιν τὴν τοῦ δικαίου ταῦτα πράττουσιν, καὶ ναὶ μὰ Δία κατὰ νόμον γε τὸν τῆς φύσεως, οὐ μέντοι ἴσως κατὰ τοῦτον ὃν ἡμεῖς τιθέμεθα.

177 Most recently by Kerferd, *SM* 117–20.

moral meaning, imperceptibly pulls *nomos* toward the sense of "statute," and this sense remains dominant in the sequel. This is clear from the noun's association with τίθεσθαι (enact: 483b5, 7); but it is noteworthy that the enactment of statutes is grammatically coordinated with standards of praise and disapproval (483b7–8), evidently in order to leave no doubt that the enactment of *nomoi* is envisaged as part of a social order and its mores. This social order is said to be relative: the people have determined it "in relation to themselves" and "to their own advantage" (483b5–6). Further, it embraces the principle of equality (τὸ ἴσον) not as an ideal but as a defensive weapon contrived by the masses against superior individuals (483c1–6).

The qualities Callicles attributes to *nomos* make it the embodiment of the principle of popular sovereignty as we have discussed it in Chapters 1 and 2. It includes the power vested in the people as a whole to make laws, to establish conventions, and to determine what social norms and mores are to prevail. But it is presented as an establishment norm, which demands conformity and brooks no disagreement: what matters is the advantage of the people and not the superiority (in whatever sense that word may be taken) of any person. This establishment morality Callicles attacks in the sequel by increasingly identifying *nomos* in the sense of "statute" with τὸ ἄδικον (injustice) while simultaneously associating its opposite, *physis*, with τὸ δίκαιον (justice, 483c7–d5); in the end, he praises Xerxes and Darius as having acted κατὰ φύσιν τὴν τοῦ δικαίου, "according to the nature of what is just" (483e2), in their attacks on Greece because they exemplified the principle that right is on the side of superiority. Moreover, right is paradoxically described as νόμος ὁ τῆς φύσεως—the statute of *physis*—and in order to make it explicit that this is a paradox, to be taken metaphorically, Callicles adds, "but, I dare say, not by the *nomos* we enact" (483e3–4).

The paradox of the expression νόμος ὁ τῆς φύσεως is brought home by an examination of *physis* in the sense in which Callicles seems to use it. We already noted that it stands for "actual fact" as opposed to the mere "conventional belief" inherent in the meaning of *nomos*. Callicles implies that its priority can be ascertained by simple observation of facts both in the animal kingdom and among men (483c9–d6). He infers from the fact that "the better has more than the worse, and the more capable more than the less capable" and that "the stronger rules and has more than the weaker" that it is right that this should be so. In short, the main contrast he seems to see between *nomos* and *physis* as norms is that the former is relative, manmade, and therefore mutable and arbitrary, whereas *physis* is absolute, constant, and unchangeable.[178] The paradox in the expression νόμος ὁ τῆς φύσεως consists accordingly in its positing a changeable norm of an immutable reality, treating the latter as if it were subject to human control. Callicles has no clear idea in what the superiority sanctioned by *physis* consists, and he is rightly attacked by Socrates for having none (488b–491e), but that need not concern us here, because it is more germane to a study of Plato's reaction to sophistic doctrines than of the consequences of sophistic teaching in the 420s. What is of interest to us is that although his speech is an imaginative, artistic recreation in about 387–385 B.C.[179] of views held by a young aristocratic Athenian political activist a generation earlier, it is the most cogent ancient evidence we possess of the polarizing influence of sophism on Athenian life.

INTELLECTUAL POLARIZATION: *NOMOS*, *PHYSIS*, AND *NOMOS-PHYSIS*

The Establishment Mentality

The *nomos-physis* antithesis that appears full-blown in Callicles' speech is the direct outcome of new attitudes toward popular sovereignty that developed probably under the influence of the sophists; it can first be noticed in the 420s. Until about the mid-fifth century the absolute validity of *nomos*, the embodiment of the concept of popular sovereignty, remained unquestioned, and, if we can draw reliable inferences from our rather sparse evidence, its religious dimensions were extended in the establishment of new cults and in the regulation of old ones by the Assembly.[180] We observed that an act of the people is required to admit suppliants in Aeschylus's *Supplices* and that the people ratify the cultic prerogatives of the Praxiergidai.[181]

---

178 There is a certain similarity between Callicles' view on the relation of νόμος and φύσις and that of [Hippoc.] *Vict.* 1.11: νόμος γὰρ καὶ φύσις, οἷσι πάντα διαπρησσόμεθα οὐχ ὁμολογεῖται ὁμολογεόμενα· νόμον μὲν ἄνθρωποι ἔθεσαν αὐτοὶ ἑωυτοῖσιν, οὐ γινώσκοντες περὶ ὧν ἔθεσαν, φύσιν δὲ πάντων θεοὶ διεκόσμησαν. τὰ μὲν οὖν ἄνθρωποι διέθεσαν οὐδέποτε κατὰ τωὐτὸ ἔχει οὔτε ὀρθῶς οὔτε μὴ ὀρθῶς· ὅσα δὲ θεοὶ διέθεσαν αἰεὶ ὀρθῶς ἔχει· καὶ τὰ ὀρθὰ καὶ τὰ μὴ ὀρθὰ τοσοῦτον διαφέρει. The chief difference is the absence of the gods from Callicles.

179 See Dodds, *Plato:Gorgias* 24–30.

180 See above, pp. 139–41.

181 See above, pp. 141–48.

Outside Athens, Heraclitus exemplifies a similar attitude when he derives all human *nomoi* from the one, which is divine, and accordingly prescribes that "the people must fight for their *nomos* as for their walls" (22B114 and 44 DK⁶).

At the same time there was also an incipient realization that the same *nomoi* do not prevail universally. We find this as early as Aeschylus, who tends to treat religious *nomoi* as universally recognized[182] but also believes that *nomoi* can be infringed by gods[183] and weakened by men (*Eum.* 690–94). Likewise he supposes the *nomoi* of the Egyptians not only know a different Hermes but also lay down legal rules that may differ from those prevailing in Argos (*Supp.* 220, 387–91). The awareness that different *nomoi* are valid among different societies is most manifest in Herodotus; and Protagoras drew the corresponding political conclusion, namely, that whatever seems to be just and honorable to a city is just and honorable for it as long as it adheres to its convictions.[184]

Doubts about the absolute validity of *nomos* began around the mid-fifth century, but they were initially confined to philosophy and science and had no political repercussions.[185] Empedocles, for example, accepts common parlance (νόμος) when he speaks of "birth" and "death," despite his knowledge as a philosopher that they are really only mixture and separation.[186] Democritus opposes ἐτεῇ to νόμῳ: knowledge of the truth that only atoms and void are real does not prevent him from accepting "color," "sweet," and "bitter" as part of ordinary speech (νόμος).[187] In the Hippocratic treatise *On the Sacred Disease*, τὸ ἐόν is opposed to νόμος in the assertion that the diaphragm (φρένες) is not the seat of the intellect.[188] And Herodotus speaks of the peninsula on which Persia, Assyria, and Arabia are situated as being generally (νόμῳ) but wrongly taken to end at the Arabian Gulf (4.39.1). In all these cases, *nomos* describes conven-

---

182   E.g., Aesch. *Supp.* 241–42, 673; *Cho.* 400; *Eum.* 576.

183   E.g., id. *Eum.* 171–72; 778–808; *PV* 148–51, 402–3.

184   See above, p. 240.

185   For the antecedents of these doubts in antitheses such as word/deed, name/reality, and appearance/being, see Heinimann, *NP* 42–58.

186   Emp. 31B9 DK⁶, esp. line 5: ἦ θέμις <οὔ> καλέουσι, νόμῳ δ' ἐπίφημι καὶ αὐτός.

187   Democr. 68B125 DK⁶, cf. B9 νόμῳ χροιή, νόμῳ γλυκύ, νόμῳ πικρόν, ἐτεῇ δ' ἄτομα καὶ κενόν.

188   [Hippoc.] *Morb.Sacr.* 17.1, in H. Grensemann, ed. and tr., *Die hippokratische Schrift "Über die heilige Krankheit"* (Berlin, 1968) 86.

tional belief, which is found wanting by scientific thinking or research; νόμος is the nominal representative of νομίζειν in the sense of holding a common but false opinion.[189]

An opposition to political *nomos* is not in evidence before the late 440s, when Sophocles' Antigone challenges the monopoly of the state's *nomoi* by claiming an equal validity for the *nomima* of family religion.[190] But her challenge only demands equal recognition for a different set of norms; the validity itself of the state's *nomoi* is not in question in the play. Even at a later time, when its validity had begun to erode, a deep respect for *nomos* remains ingrained in Athens: it is praised as the preserver of the state,[191] as a guarantor of freedom,[192] and as a bulwark against tyranny;[193] even adversity is no excuse for disregarding the *nomoi* (Eur. fr. 433). It is credited with all those qualities in which the Athenian democracy took pride: *nomos* is the basis of the state's social as well as legal norms (Thuc. 2.37.3); it knows no class distinctions in the administration of justice (ibid. 2.37. 1; Eur. *Hec*. 291–92) and guarantees justice in state and society;[194] it gives freedom of speech to rich and poor alike (Eur. *Supp*. 435–36). But, peculiarly enough, it is not explicitly associated with democracy before the fourth century B.C.[195]

Moreover, the valuation of written laws changed in the course of the fifth century. Aeschylus made a special point in his *Supplices* (946–49; cf. 387–91) that the vote of the Argive assembly to admit the Danaids was "not inscribed on tablets," perhaps to contrast it with the (written?) *nomoi* of the Egyptians, which had caused the suppliants to flee from their native land. And Pericles in his Funeral Oration rated the social norms, ἄγραφοι νόμοι, as high as (if not higher than) the statutes as the basis for the Athenian democracy. But in the 420s a peculiar ambivalence set in. In the *Supplices*, in 422 B.C., Euripides has Theseus attribute to written *nomoi* the equal

---

189   See, e.g., Xenoph. 21B2.11–14 DK[6]; Parm. 28B6 DK[6] esp. line 8; Anaxag. 59B17 DK[6] and the Hippocratic treatises *Aër* 7 (*ad fin.*), *Vict*. 1.4.2, *Morb.Sacr*. 1.30–31, *Acut*. 56.1, *De arte* 2.

190   See above, pp. 148–61.

191   Eur. *Supp*. 312–13, cf. Soph. *Ant*. 663–76.

192   Eur. *Supp*. 438; cf. Hdt. 7.104.4–5.

193   Eur. *Supp*. 429–32; Ar. *Vesp*. 463–67; Thuc. 3.62.3.

194   Gorg. 82B11a30 DK[6]; Eur. *Hec*. 799–801; *Supp*. 433–38; frr. 252 and 1049.1–2; Soph. *Ant*. 23–25; *OC* 913–14 and 1382.

195   First in Ar. *Eccl*. 944–45 (392 B.C.). The *locus classicus* for the association is Aeschin. 3.6.

justice and equal freedom of speech rich and poor alike enjoyed in Athens.[196] Yet two years earlier he had Hecuba class written laws along with material possessions, fortune, and social pressures as inhibiting the freedom to act according to one's own judgment (Eur. *Hec*. 864–67). Of course the statements are made in different plays; it would be foolish to accuse Euripides of contradicting himself, or even to believe that either one statement or the other represented his personal views. But if both statements were made in public performances, then the Athenian audience was willing to listen to both, presumably because they were used to hearing the pros and cons of written legislation discussed.

It is not difficult to account for the simultaneous currency of both views. Written law is the more democratic of the two; it enables all literate members of the community to ascertain what rules society expects them to follow and what risks they take if they transgress them. It respects no distinction between persons: written legislation makes it harder to discriminate between rich and poor, noble and commoner. At the same time, since the written text is fixed, it is less easily changed and is therefore less subject to political whim. Yet this very immutability can be an encumbrance: too rigid an adherence to the letter of the law or too stubborn a resistance to adapting it to altered circumstances can result in an establishment mentality, narrow in outlook, intolerant of change, and prone to using law to constrain rather than to promote the freedom of the individual.

Such a mentality began to develop in Athens in the early 420s, as is seen in the speech Thucydides assigns to Cleon in the debate about Mytilene:

The most shocking thing of all is if none of our decisions will be firmly fixed, and if you fail to realize that a state is stronger when it enforces inferior laws [*nomoi*] that are inviolable than when it has good laws that lack authority. Ignorance with discipline is more useful than cleverness with indiscipline; compared with the more intelligent, the less educated people generally run a state better. The former want to project an image of being smarter than the laws [*nomoi*] and want to have the last word in any public discussion, as if there could be no more important matter on which to disclose their opinion. As a result, they generally bring disaster to the state. But those who feel diffident about their own insight are content to be less informed than the laws [*nomoi*] and to be less competent to find fault with

196   Eur. *Supp*. 433–38; cf. also Gorg. 82B11a30 DK⁶.

the argument of a sensible speaker. As they are impartial judges rather than competitors, their verdict is usually right.[197]

It is instructive to compare Cleon's speech with the very similar remarks attributed to Archidamus before the declaration of war: "We [Spartans] have become warlike and men of sound judgment through our sense of orderliness: warlike, because respect for others is the primary element in discipline, just as self-reliance is the primary element in self-respect; and we have sound judgment because we are brought up too uneducated to despise the laws and too severely disciplined not to obey them."[198] What sounds in Archidamus's statement like an ethos ingrained in Spartan society becomes for Cleon an attempt to preserve the system—simply because it is a system—against attacks that he fears are based on superior intelligence. Cleon sees the system's preservation in a leveling conformity unconcerned with quality. By the early 420s, that is, a democratic establishment mentality had developed in Athens, a mentality most clearly expressed about a decade later in Alcibiades' explanation to the Spartans of the vagaries of his own past policies: "Since the state had a democratic regime, it was necessary by and large to go along with prevailing conditions."[199]

Attic usage in this period bespeaks a growing establishment cast of mind. The substantive forms of *nomimos* had originally taken on a descriptive sense for social and religious norms as that meaning was being relinquished by *nomos*, but about 430 B.C. *nomimos* began to assume prescriptive connotations. This implies that the enactments of the sovereign people were regarded as also setting a moral

197 Thucydides 3.37.3-4: πάντων δὲ δεινότατον εἰ βέβαιον ἡμῖν μηδὲν καθεστήξει ὧν ἂν δόξῃ πέρι, μηδὲ γνωσόμεθα ὅτι χείροσι νόμοις ἀκινήτοις χρωμένη πόλις κρείσσων ἐστὶν ἢ καλῶς ἔχουσιν ἀκύροις, ἀμαθία τε μετὰ σωφροσύνης ὠφελιμώτερον ἢ δεξιότης μετὰ ἀκολασίας, οἵ τε φαυλότεροι τῶν ἀνθρώπων πρὸς τοὺς ξυνετωτέρους ὡς ἐπὶ τὸ πλέον ἄμεινον οἰκοῦσι τὰς πόλεις. οἱ μὲν γὰρ τῶν τε νόμων σοφώτεροι βούλονται φαίνεσθαι τῶν τε αἰεὶ λεγομένων ἐς τὸ κοινὸν περιγίγνεσθαι, ὡς ἐν ἄλλοις μείζοσιν οὐκ ἂν δηλώσαντες τὴν γνώμην, καὶ ἐκ τοῦ τοιούτου τὰ πολλὰ σφάλλουσι τὰς πόλεις· οἱ δ' ἀπιστοῦντες τῇ ἐξ αὑτῶν ξυνέσει ἀμαθέστεροι μὲν τῶν νόμων ἀξιοῦσιν εἶναι, ἀδυνατώτεροι δὲ τοῦ καλῶς εἰπόντος μέμψασθαι λόγον, κριταὶ δὲ ὄντες ἀπὸ τοῦ ἴσου μᾶλλον ἢ ἀγωνισταὶ ὀρθοῦνται τὰ πλείω.

198 Id. 1.84.3: πολεμικοί τε καὶ εὔβουλοι διὰ τὸ εὔκοσμον γιγνόμεθα, τὸ μὲν ὅτι αἰδὼς σωφροσύνης πλεῖστον μετέχει, αἰσχύνης δὲ εὐψυχία, εὔβουλοι δὲ ἀμαθέστερον τῶν νόμων τῆς ὑπεροψίας παιδευόμενοι καὶ ξὺν χαλεπότητι σωφρονέστερον ἢ ὥστε αὐτῶν ἀνηκουστεῖν.

199 Id. 6.89.4: ἅμα δὲ καὶ τῆς πόλεως δημοκρατουμένης τὰ πολλὰ ἀνάγκη ἦν τοῖς παροῦσιν ἕπεσθαι.

standard for society.[200] About the same time *ennomos*, which began its career in exclusively nonlegal contexts in poetry, entered prose as a term of moral commendation for obedience to the statutes; not very much later *paranomos*, which had always denoted a transgression of social norms of any kind, began to be used of actionable offenses.[201] A final indication that an establishment mentality came to inform *nomos* at this time can be seen in how nonlegal norms were beginning to be spoken of as if they were legal enactments, sometimes, but not always, in jest. Artemis in Euripides' *Hippolytus* (428 B.C.) speaks of a *nomos* preventing one god from interfering in the province of another; in Aristophanes' *Clouds* (423 B.C.) Pheidippides treats the *nomos* that fathers beat their sons as if it were an enacted statute; and in Euripides' *Ion* (after 412 B.C.) we are told that no *nomos* prevents a person from treating his enemies ill, and the gods are said to have established norms of human conduct through written legislation.[202]

Nomos and the Intelligentsia

Athenian intellectuals began almost immediately to react against this rigidity. A sensitive comparison of the use of *nomos* in Herodotus and Thucydides has shown that, though the differences in meaning between the two authors are insignificant, Herodotus never questions the obligation that *nomos* imposes, whereas for Thucydides "the useful" is a more potent norm of political action than *nomos*, especially in the exercise of superior power.[203] Among the voices questioning the validity of *nomos*, we have already mentioned Hecuba's in Euripides; she speaks of it as inhibiting free judgment (*Hec.* 864–67). To this example we can add the praises of a new life, free from the constraints of *nomos* here on earth, that the chorus sings in Aristophanes' *Birds* (755–59) and the happiness the Cyclops expresses that he can indulge his appetites because he lives unencumbered by the *nomoi* complicating human life (Eur. *Cyc.* 336–46). In Euripides' *Ion*, not only are we told that the observance of *nomos* depends on the circumstances and persons involved (1045–47), but there are complaints that the gods who "write" laws for men behave

---

200   See above, p. 133 with n. 147.

201   See above, pp. 133–35.

202   Eur. *Hipp.* 1328; Ar. *Nub.* 1421–26; Eur. *Ion* 1047 (cf. fr. 1091), 442–43. All these passages are discussed in Ostwald, *Nomos* 26, 36–37, 48, and 91.

203   J. Herrman, "Nomos bei Herodot und Thukydides," *Gedächtnisschrift Hans Peters* (Berlin, 1967) 116–24.

themselves lawlessly and that it is not right for *nomos* to permit unjust men to find protection at an altar.[204] Elsewhere in Euripides, a Greek *nomos* is criticized for attaching too high a value to athletic contests (fr. 282.13–15), and in Aristophanes' *Clouds*, Wrong prides itself on its cleverness in having invented the idea of contradicting established notions of law and justice (1039–40).

Other values are recognized, measured against which *nomos* is seen as deficient. Pericles in his Funeral Oration distinguishes the Athenian warrior from the Spartan in that the former's character rather than the *nomoi* of his society make him courageous (Thuc. 2.39.4), and a Euripidean fragment (597) prefers good character as more reliable than the law. Diodotus in his reply to Cleon gives effective administration of the allies a higher rating than the rigors of the laws (Thuc. 3.46.4). Nobility conferred by birth and wealth is regarded as merely conventional (νόμῳ) and unreal in comparison with god-given nobility, which consists in good sense and intelligence (Eur. fr. 52.8–10). The force of circumstances (ἀνάγκη) is also sometimes recognized as a more potent norm than *nomos* (Eur. *Hec*. 846–49; *Or.* 486–88).

Thucydides' account of the plague shows that these are not mere intellectual exercises but reflect serious threats to the established social order. The historian tells us that then no fear of the gods or law of men inhibited lawless behavior and that the laws governing burial of the dead were widely ignored (2.52.4, 53.4). Greed (πλεονεξία) as a possible motive for transgressing *nomos* is mentioned by the Athenians in their speech before the Lacedaemonian Congress (1.77.3) and as an actual motive by Thucydides as narrator in his description of the revolt at Corcyra (3.82.6). The plays of Euripides abound in criticisms of the social order as embodied in *nomos*: in social matters we find in his *Ino* a criticism of the law enjoining monogamy (fr. 402), and in his *Andromeda* he laments as existing only by law (νόμῳ) the disabilities unjustly suffered by illegitimate children (fr. 141); in political matters, he presents as cruelly rigid the Taurian *nomos* according to which arriving strangers are sacrificed to Artemis (*IT* 1189), and he calls the maltreatment of an enemy a demand of *nomos* (fr. 1091).

That these and similar criticisms of the *nomoi* should have emanated from the Athenian intelligentsia is consistent with the attacks

---

204   Eur. *Ion* 442–43 (cf. *HF* 777–78; *IA* 1089–97), 1312–13.

to which such men were subjected by the democratic establishment. In the 430s the prosecution of Anaxagoras was a barely disguised attack on Pericles' personal power, launched probably by men who resented the growing secularism of the state under his leadership. It is difficult otherwise to explain why the charge should have been impiety against Anaxagoras as well as against Aspasia, and why it should have been Phidias's alleged embezzlement of sacred funds that Pericles' opposition used to hound him.[205] But the attacks against intellectuals in the 420s were entirely different in character. In the first place, they were as a rule not directed against individuals for their undue influence over public officials; second, they tended to be voiced by members of the establishment, who felt their own positions threatened; and third, clever speakers were their main target.

Cleon provides the most explicit example of such an attack in the second debate about Mytilene, which we had occasion to quote at some length earlier.[206] Whereas Thucydides had presented Pericles in the Funeral Oration extolling discussion as an indispensable preliminary to action and stating that in Athens boldness is not based on ignorance but on calculation (2.40.2–3), he has Cleon inveigh against discussion as creating indecision, which will make it impossible for a democracy to exercise imperial control (3.37.1–3). A decision once made must not be questioned, even if it is bad; a *nomos* once made must not be challenged. The disciplined ignorant who probe no farther are the mainstay of the state; its antagonists are the clever, the intelligent, and the smart: they are filled with a sense of the importance of what they have to say, and their true concern is not the state but competition with one another in displaying their oratorical prowess, reducing the Assembly to spectators at a sophistic exhibition.[207] In other words, the rigid democratic establishment believes it has most to fear from those endowed with superior intelligence and superior education; included in that group are sophists and the orators they train.[208]

205 See above, pp. 191–98.

206 See above, pp. 253–54.

207 Thuc. 3.37.4–38.7. The deprecating expressions include δεξιότης, ξυνετώτερος, σοφώτερος, δεινότης; ἀγωνισταί, ἀγώνων ἆθλα, θεαταὶ λόγων, σοφιστῶν θεαταί. Terms of commendation are ἀμαθία, σωφροσύνη, φαυλότεροι, ἀδυνατώτεροι.

208 The Sausage Seller's dislike for orators in Ar. *Eq.* 358 (λαρυγγιῶ τοὺς ῥήτορας καὶ Νικίαν ταράξω) is attributed to Cleon in Plut. *Nic.* 4.7.

The ideal establishment democrat is seen, however jocularly, in Aristophanes' description of the demagogues as uneducated, low-class, and ignorant (*Eq.* 191–93). When the Old Oligarch criticizes the lower classes for their ignorance, indiscipline, and lack of education, regarding himself as belonging to the clever aristocrats,[209] he uses Aristophanes' terms but views them from the opposite perspective, switching the positive and negative prefixes. If any further evidence is needed that the teaching and activity of the intellectuals was blamed for eroding the validity of the traditional *nomoi*, we may recall Pheidippides' jubilant cry after completing his studies at Socrates' Thinking School: ὡς ἡδὺ καινοῖς πράγμασιν καὶ δεξιοῖς ὁμιλεῖν, / καὶ τῶν καθεστώτων νόμων ὑπερφρονεῖν δύνασθαι.[210] Thinking, cleverness, and novelty in the individual are held in greater esteem than the conventional norms of society. What is more, the new values are those of the upper-class young, who are said to have absorbed them from the teaching of the sophists.

Yet enthusiasm for the new learning is not matched by love for those who dispense it. When Strepsiades first broaches the subject of enrolling his son in the Thinking School, Pheidippides reacts with strong aversion because he fears he will be ridiculed by his horsey friends for associating with wretched humbugs and barefoot sallow-faces (Ar. *Nub.* 102–25). Ambivalent feelings toward Protagoras are attributed to young Hippocrates (Pl. *Prt.* 312a); serious and influential politicians are said to be reluctant to leave written speeches behind, afraid that future generations will brand them as sophists (Pl. *Phdr.* 257d); such stalwarts of the democratic establishment as Laches and Anytus express revulsion against the sophists (Pl. *Lach.* 197d; *Meno* 91c). Most surprising of all, Callicles, whose own speech bristles with intellectual brilliance, calls "worthless fellows" those who claim to be educating people toward excellence (Pl. *Grg.* 519e–520a).

Callicles' reaction is particularly surprising if we remember that he is a friend and pupil of Gorgias, who was commonly regarded as a sophist, and that his speech brought the criteria of *physis* to bear upon the traditional values represented by *nomos*: from whom did he

---

209 [Xen.] *Ath.Pol.* 1.5–7. The relevant terms are ἀμαθία, ἀταξία, ἀπαιδευσία, δεξιωτάτους καὶ ἄνδρας ἀρίστους.

210 Ar. *Nub.* 1399–1400: "How pleasant it is to be familiar with the latest clever things and to be able to soar so high in thought as to look down on the established laws."

learn the arguments from *physis* if not from the sophists? After all, many sophists were said to combine the teaching of rhetoric with the teaching of natural science. Explicit testimony to that effect is found in the scientific activities Aristophanes (*Nub.* 94–99; cf. 112–18) attributes to Socrates' Thinking School and in Socrates' analysis in the *Apology* of the charges his hidden accusers leveled against him, to wit, that he is a "smart man [σοφὸς ἀνήρ] who thinks about the things that are in midair, who has conducted research into whatever is beneath the earth, and who makes out the weaker argument to be the stronger."[211]

But there are other indications that rhetoric and natural science could both be taught by the same people. The interest in correct linguistic usage with which Prodicus is credited[212] may have been part of his teaching of rhetoric;[213] whether this was also true of the scientific pursuits in which he engaged we cannot tell.[214] Of Hippias we are told not only that he taught astronomy, geometry, arithmetic, grammar, literary criticism, and various other subjects in addition to rhetoric,[215] but we are also given a hint in a late but credible source how his polymathy was related to his teaching of rhetoric. According to Philostratus, "he introduced these subjects into his discourses,"[216] which probably means his learning was not a disinterested study but was intended to give his pupils a general education to draw on when making their public speeches. Moreover, since neither he nor any of the other sophists is credited with any original doctrine concerning the physical universe,[217] it is reasonable to assume that not only for Hippias but for the other sophists, too, teaching natural science—though perhaps not scientific investiga-

211   Pl. *Ap.* 18b; cf. also 19b. At 23d Socrates remarks that such charges, including θεοὺς μὴ νομίζειν, are leveled κατὰ πάντων τῶν φιλοσοφούντων, a sign that the Athenian public made no attempt to differentiate sophists from philosophers.

212   Pl. *Cra.* 384b, *Euthyd.* 277e; cf. *Prt.* 337a–c, 340a, *Meno* 75e, *Lach.* 197b and d, *Chrm.* 163b–d.

213   Id. *Ap.* 19e, *Hp.Ma.* 282c; Xen. *Mem.* 2.1.21–34 with Philostr. *VS* 1.12. Only the first of these passages and reports enumerating Theramenes (Ath. 5.220b; schol. Ar. *Nub.* 361) and Isocrates (Dion. Hal. *Isoc.* 1) among his students suggest teaching activity; the remaining passages attest public performances (ἐπιδείξεις).

214   Ar. *Nub.* 360–61; cf. also schol. Ar. *Av.* 692 and *Suda* s.v. Πρόδικος.

215   Pl. *Hp.Ma.* 285b–d, *Hp.Mi.* 368b–d; Philostr. *VS* 1.11. For his rhetoric, largely epideictic, see Pl. *Ap.* 19e; *Hp.Ma.* 281a, 286a; *Hp.Mi.* 363c.

216   Philostr. *VS* 1.11: ἐσήγετο δὲ ἐς τὰς διαλέξεις.

217   The only possible exception is Hippias, whom Procl. *In Euc.*, pp. 272 and 356 Friedlein, credits with the discovery of the quadratrix curve (τετραγωνίζουσα); but the attribution is doubtful. See Guthrie, *HGP* 3.283–84.

tion—was subordinate to teaching rhetoric, which was their primary concern. This assumption is consistent with the fact that such contemporary natural philosophers as Anaxagoras, Democritus, and Diogenes were not tarred with the same brush as the sophists; it is consistent also with Protagoras's aversion to the technical professional training in arithmetic, astronomy, geometry, and literature that other sophists gave—if his aversion means that the natural philosophers of Protagoras's day took their subject matter more seriously than the political education of their pupils.[218]

Physis versus Nomos

The assumption that natural philosophy was only ancillary to the teaching of rhetoric will also help us explain how in the 420s *physis* came to be the most formidable and durable opponent of *nomos*. We have so far examined the antithesis of these two terms only in Callicles' great speech in Plato's *Gorgias*, where the early political impact of that antithesis on Athens is imaginatively recreated in the hindsight of a time when its worst effects were past. An examination of its antecedents has to start with the observation that *physis* was not the earliest opponent to enter the field against *nomos*: in philosophy and science other values, such as ἐτεῇ, or τὸ ἐόν, or simply a fact, were regarded as containing a greater degree of truth from about the mid-fifth century on.[219] By the time *physis* came in, *nomos* had already begun to be suffused in politics with a rigid, establishment mentality. Who first conceived the idea that it would be an effective weapon against *nomos*, and when was it first so used? It may be stated at the outset that there is not a shred of evidence that it originated with any of the sophists known to us. Protagoras, the first sophist, had indeed had something to say about both *nomos* and *physis*, but he had nowhere related them to one another;[220] nor is there any relation between the two in Gorgias or in Thrasymachus. In fact, the only sophists thought to have had any interest at all in this antithesis are Hippias of Elis and Antiphon. If we could trust Plato's dramatic dates, we would have to call Hippias's statement the earliest preserved testimony, since it occurs in the *Protagoras* (337c–d),

218   See above, p. 239 with n. 154.
219   See above, pp. 251–52.
220   For Protagoras's discussion of νόμος, see Pl. *Prt.* 325c–326d; he uses φύσις exclusively of the native endowment of an individual, both mental and physical; see ibid. 323c–d and 351a–b, and Protag. 80B3 DK⁶.

whose dramatic date is 433 B.C. But we cannot have such faith; in addition, Hippias's rather sanctimonious pronouncement seems trite: the intellectual interests shared by those assembled in Callias's house, he says, make them relatives, kinsmen, and fellow citizens of one another by nature (*physei*) but not in law (*nomōi*), because the natural kinship between like and like is violated by the tyranny of *nomos*. Such facile contrivance presupposes that the antithesis had long been naturalized by the dramatic date Plato's Hippias uses it. To be sure, Hippias was alive and presumably active in 433 B.C. and thus might have made this statement then; but he was also considerably younger than Protagoras and seems to have survived Socrates, so that such a statement might have been made at any time in the last quarter of the fifth century.[221] Similar considerations apply to Antiphon's treatise *On Truth*, which contains the most elaborate surviving fifth-century disquisition on *nomos* and *physis*. Even if he was not identical with the politician and orator of the same name, who died in 411 B.C. and was probably born about 470 B.C., they were certainly contemporaries.[222] Yet it is hard to imagine his work standing at the beginning rather than at the height of the *nomos-physis* controversy, and a date in the late 420s, which is commonly accepted for his work, cannot be wide of the mark.[223] These criteria are admittedly subjective, but we have no others to guide us.

If the sophists provide no answer, it is tempting to look for the origin of the antithesis in the Hippocratic tract *Airs, Waters, Places*, which, if it was composed about 430 B.C. as it is thought to have been, will contain the earliest surviving juxtaposition of *nomos* and *physis*.[224] Yet as Heinimann has convincingly shown, *nomos* and *physis* complement rather than contradict one another in this treatise: both are drawn upon to explain the qualities peculiar to different peoples as due either to their social traditions or to their natural environments, and the two concepts are so far from being antithetical that in one case *nomos* even develops into *physis*.[225] The opposition of the two terms, which is essential in their "sophistic" usage, is

---

221 For Hippias's dates, see Guthrie, *HGP* 3.280–81 with n. 3.
222 For Antiphon's identity and dates, see below, pp. 359–64.
223 See Heinimann, *NP* 141–42.
224 Ibid. 13–41, 170–80, and 106–9.
225 [Hippoc.] *Aer.* 14 and 16. For the νόμος becoming φύσις, see ibid. 14, where the custom of the Macrocephali to shape the head of a newborn infant resulted in the course of time in children being born with elongated skulls. See Heinimann, *NP* 26–28.

still absent. A more likely initiator of the antithesis would be Archelaus, the only natural philosopher Athens produced, who is said to have been a pupil of Anaxagoras and a teacher of Socrates.[226] The doxographic tradition attributes to him the belief τὸ δίκαιον εἶναι καὶ τὸ αἰσχρὸν οὐ φύσει, ἀλλὰ νόμῳ.[227] But, to say the least, it is extremely doubtful that this paraphrase contains the terms in which Archelaus couched a moral doctrine. There is, rather, reason to believe that in addition to physical views adapted from Anaxagoras, Archelaus had a theory of cultural development much like the view Plato attributes to Protagoras, seeing the development of social norms of right and wrong as taking different paths in different societies. In other words, Archelaus may have regarded the *nomoi* of each state as determined not by an absolute standard, like natural phenomena, but by the notions of right and wrong prevailing in each state. In that event, later authors more conversant with the *nomos-physis* antinomy will have paraphrased this theory into what has come down to us.[228]

Because no sophist, medical writer, or even natural philosopher can be credited with the invention of the *nomos-physis* antithesis, and because at its first surviving occurrence, in Aristophanes' *Clouds* (1075–78) in 423 B.C., it is already an instrument of social criticism, we may more profitably assume that it was already in the air by the late 430s and early 420s and inquire in what contexts *physis* is found as a countervalue to *nomos* as a social and political norm. There is substance to our assumption, because our evidence comes not so much from the speculations of sophists or philosophers, but from Aristophanes, Euripides, and Thucydides. Though it is often alleged that these authors reflect sophistic influences, the basis for that allegation is no more concrete than that they evince in comparison with earlier authors such as Aeschylus, Pindar, and Herodotus a new spirit of inquiry and challenge to established values; this is assumed to have originated after the mid-fifth century in intellectual circles such as those in which Pericles will have moved or those we

226   D. L. 2.16 and 23; Porph. *FGH* 260F11; Sext. Emp. *Math.* 9.360; *Suda* s.v. Ἀρχέλαος. On the unreliability of the tradition, see L. Woodbury, "Socrates and Archelaus," *Phoenix* 25 (1971) 229–309.

227   D. L. 2.16: "Things are just or disgraceful not by nature but by conventional belief." Cf. also *Suda* s.v. Ἀρχέλαος.

228   Heinimann, *NP* 111–14. The problem is ignored by Guthrie, *HGP* 2.339–44 and 3.51–52 with n. 1.

encounter in their liveliest depiction in Plato's *Protagoras*.[229] The fact that the origin remains hypothetical does not make the spirit any less real.

The most noteworthy feature of this opposition for our present purposes is the fact that in the 420s *physis* for the first time begins to enter into discussions of social, behavioral, and political issues. Heinimann has shown that earlier authors had used *physis* to describe the coming-to-be of things; the true being of natural phenomena; the provenance or physical appearance of a person or thing; the normal state or behavior of the sea, rivers, snakes, bulls, the human brain, the sheen of the stars, and so on; as well as the innate, unschooled, native endowment of a person, which for Pindar constitutes his essence and determines his achievement, or the basic normal state of the human body, with which the medical writers were concerned.[230] The native endowment of a person, both mental and physical, was still the only meaning of *physis* for Protagoras.[231] This does indeed remain an important meaning in the 420s and later: Thucydides has Pericles speak of the envy aroused when people hear an exaggerated account of achievements surpassing their own native capacities (2.35.2) and has him exhort the women of Athens to achieve no less than their capabilities allow (2.45.2; cf. 3.74.1); the sufferings brought by the plague were beyond human capacity to endure (2.50). But the historian also speaks about the native capacities of specific individuals: he praises the strength of Themistocles' *physis*, which he sees manifested in his ability to form judgments "on the basis of his native insight, having received no previous instruction or later explanation" (1.138.3); he has Alcibiades when defending himself against Nicias ascribe his own success against the Spartans to youth and "seemingly abnormal madness" (6.17.1). In Aristophanes' *Clouds* Socrates asks Strepsiades whether speechmaking is part of his natural endowment (486; cf. *Vesp.* 1281–83).

From this it is but a small step to ascribe moral or other personal qualities to *physis*. Hippolytus attributes his chastity (τὸ σωφρονεῖν) to his inborn character (ἐν τῇ φύσει),[232] and Alcibiades finds the envy

---

229 For the character of this new spirit, it is sufficient to refer to J. H. Finley, Jr., "Euripides and Thucydides," *HSCP* 49 (1938) 23–68, and F. Solmsen, *Intellectual Experiments of the Greek Enlightenment* (Princeton, 1975).

230 Heinimann, *NP* 89–98.

231 Protag. 80B3 DK⁶; Pl. *Prt.* 323c–d, 351a–b.

232 Eur. *Hipp.* 79–80; cf. also *Bacch.* 314–18, where Teiresias ascribes female chastity to *physis* and not to constraints imposed by Dionysus.

his fellow citizens feel at the splendor of his public services "natural" (Thuc. 6.16.3). *Physis* becomes the true character of a man, to which he must not be false;[233] and if he is himself good, his works will follow his nature (Ar. *Thesm*. 165–67). Different people have different *physeis* (Eur. *IA* 558–60; fr. 494), and this makes it necessary to treat them differently (id. frr. 759, 812.4–9). The *physis* of one may be hateful and savage (*Med*. 103, 1343); another's may be noble, mean-spirited, intelligent, genial, or as changeable as Theramenes'.[234] Even different groups of people may be characterized each by a common *physis*: in one context women are said to be susceptible to flattery, impertinent in another (Ar. *Lys*. 1037; *Thesm*. 531–32); the Athenians are variously said to be very smart, excellent, changeable, hard to control, desirous of being pleased, and vindictive when disappointed.[235]

Moreover, questions are raised whether congenital qualities of character are inherited and whether they can change. Theonoë in Euripides' *Helen* (998–1004) wants to preserve the pious disposition she has inherited from her father;[236] in the *Electra* (368–70) Orestes is bewildered by the φύσεις βροτῶν because he has seen a son of a noble father turn out a nothing, whereas good offspring have come from bad parents. The question whether the *physis* of an individual can be changed receives different answers. Hecuba, perhaps somewhat optimistically, believes that no misfortune can change a noble *physis* (Eur. *Hec*. 592–99), and an unknown speaker in Euripides' *Antiope* (fr. 206) has faith that no fair-sounding words can prevail over *physis* and what is right. Elsewhere, *physis* is regarded as capable of improvement: the chorus of Aristophanes' *Wasps* (1457–61) believes that it is difficult but not impossible to change one's *physis* by exposure to the views of others; the chorus of the *Clouds* (510–17, esp. 515–17) wishes Strepsiades luck as he, at his age, subjects his *physis* to the pursuits of new-fangled wisdom.

Yet learning rather than producing an improvement can also be opposed to *physis*; in that case, "nature" connotes what is home-grown, spontaneous, untutored, and untampered-with. We have seen an example of this in Thucydides' description of Themistocles'

233   Eur. frr. 963.4–5, 634. The most extensive dramatic treatment of this conception of *physis* is Soph. *Phil*., for which see M. Nussbaum, "Consequences and Character in Sophocles' *Philoctetes*," *Philosophy and Literature* 1 (1976–77) 25–53, esp. 43–49.

234   Eur. *IA* 1410–11; Eur. fr. 617; Ar. *Nub*. 877, 1187; *Ran*. 540–41.

235   Ar. *Ran*. 700, 1115–16; *Eq*. 518; Thuc. 7.14.2 and 4, 48.4; cf. Ar. *Pax* 607.

236   Cf. Eur. fr. 75.

character (1.138.3), where it is also said that the statesman's achievements cost him a minimum of exertion (μελέτη); a further example is the Corinthian claim (1.121.4) that their own natural (φύσει) self-confidence is greater than any the Athenians can attain by instruction (διδαχῇ) and that through their own exertions (μελέτη) in naval warfare they will neutralize the advantage the Athenians have in knowledge. On the other hand, a natural disposition (*physis*) can also be treated as corruptible: for example, excessive devotion to the pleasures of song can corrupt a man's *physis* by making him neglect his own affairs and those of his city (Eur. fr. 187); or, conversely, the passions and appetites inherent in *physis* can set an individual at odds with himself when they overrule his rational judgment.[237]

We now pass on to a *physis* to which all men are equally subject, which does not manifest itself differently in different individuals. Thucydides explicitly so describes it in his account of *stasis* (civil strife) in Corcyra: "Many harsh experiences befell the cities as they became embroiled in faction, experiences that arise and will always occur as long as human *physis* remains the same, but more or less intensely and different in kind, depending on the turns taken by the events."[238] It includes the immutable rule that all mortals must die and must put up with every manner of affliction and disaster (Eur. *Alc.* 780–84; *Or.* 1–3; cf. fr. 757.5–9). But it also exhibits less dire qualities, which will finally bring us to the use of the term as the counterpoint of *nomos* and other entrenched social and political values. The earliest exposition of this dichotomy is in the appeal of Wrong in Aristophanes' *Clouds*:

> πάρειμ' ἐντεῦθεν εἰς τὰς τῆς φύσεως ἀνάγκας.
> ἥμαρτες, ἠράσθης, ἐμοίχευσάς τι, κᾆτ' ἐλήφθης.
> ἀπόλωλας· ἀδύνατος γὰρ εἶ λέγειν. ἐμοὶ δ' ὁμιλῶν
> χρῶ τῇ φύσει, σκίρτα, γέλα, νόμιζε μηδὲν αἰσχρόν.[239]

---

237 Eur. fr. 840: λέληθεν οὐδὲν τῶνδέ μ' ὧν σὺ νουθετεῖς, / γνώμην δ' ἔχοντά μ' ἡ φύσις βιάζεται. Peculiarly enough, Phaedra expresses a similar sentiment at *Hipp.* 377–85, asserting it is not the *physis* of rational judgment that makes us act badly, but the fact that indolence or pleasure prevents us from doing what rational judgment bids.

238 Thuc. 3.82.2: καὶ ἐπέπεσε πολλὰ καὶ χαλεπὰ κατὰ στάσιν ταῖς πόλεσι, γιγνόμενα μὲν καὶ αἰεὶ ἐσόμενα, ἕως ἂν ἡ αὐτὴ φύσις ἀνθρώπων ᾖ, μᾶλλον δὲ καὶ ἡσυχαίτερα καὶ τοῖς εἴδεσι διηλλαγμένα, ὡς ἂν ἕκασται αἱ μεταβολαὶ τῶν ξυντυχιῶν ἐφιστῶνται.

239 Ar. *Nub.* 1075–78: "I shall now proceed to the needs of nature: you've gone wrong, you've lusted, you've committed a little adultery, and then you've been

The "needs of nature" (φύσεως ἀνάγκας) in this passage are of course sexual urges. Their full indulgence is commended as "natural" (χρῶ τῇ φύσει), however much they might offend conventional morality and even break the law against adultery—which permitted the injured husband to kill the offender on the spot if caught in the act.[240] That Wrong promises its followers to overcome the obstacles of convention and legality by teaching them rhetoric is of only secondary importance at the moment. What is of interest to us is that *physis* is affirmed as a force stronger than conventional morality, here expressed by νόμιζε, and that no external social forces ought to be permitted to prevent its free expression. Here νόμιζε clearly represents *nomos* as the opponent of *physis*: earlier in the scene Wrong claims to have been the first to conceive the idea of contradicting the *nomoi* and regulations of justice.[241] We might remark in passing that the uninhibited sexual expression of *physis* here runs directly counter to the sexual restraint attributed to the individual's *physis* in Euripides' *Hippolytus* (79–80) and *Bacchae* (314–18). This raises the question whether it is possible to resist *physis* at all. A fragment from an unknown play of Euripides suggests that to wish to prevail over nature is sheer folly (fr. 904), and another, from his *Phoenix* (fr. 810), that no amount of fostering care will ever make the bad good.

Physis and the Athenian Intelligentsia

The *Clouds* shows that *physis* has arrived as an instrument of that kind of social criticism of which Euripides is the foremost Athenian exponent. The tone is set by a fragment (920) from an unidentified play: ἡ φύσις ἐβούλεθ', ᾗ νόμων οὐδὲν μέλει (nature willed it, unconcerned as it is for the laws). The antithesis with *nomos* is taken for granted; *physis* is a stronger, perhaps even more valid, force in human life than the norms prevailing in society. But *nomos* is not necessarily alone opposed to *physis*: the conventional attitude toward bastard children, for example, condemned by an appeal to *physis*, is called

---

caught. You're ruined because you're not capable of making a speech. But if you attach yourself to me, do as nature bids you, skip, laugh, make shamelessness your *nomos*."

240 See MacDowell, *LCA* 124–25.

241 Ar. *Nub.* 1039–40: ὅτι πρώτιστος ἐπενόησα / τοῖσιν νόμοις καὶ ταῖς δίκαις τἀναντί' ἀντιλέξαι.

nomos in one play and *onoma* (mere name) in two others.[242]

It is impossible to do justice to Euripides' social criticism in the present context. We shall confine our discussion to a passage that shows more clearly than any other how *physis* can champion the cause of the underdog to prove that reality belies his appearance and the regard in which he is commonly held. The sterling qualities of the poor farmer his sister married so baffle Orestes in Euripides' *Electra* that he questions the relation between real and apparent nobility (367–90). After observing that a noble father may have worthless children and vice versa, he wonders by what criteria true worth should be judged and rejects in turn wealth, poverty, and valor in arms as appropriate measures. The answer at which he finally arrives is interesting both for what Orestes commends and for what he rejects. The criterion for true nobility regards the company a man keeps and the character he displays:[243] they are noble who run their own affairs and those of the state well.[244] Orestes rejects judgment on the basis of family prestige, which he attributes to opinionated vacuity, or of mere physical prowess.[245] The significance of this is reinforced later in the play, when Electra vaunts over the body of Aegisthus: "You used to boast that you were one whose strength lay in his money; but money is with us only for a brief moment or not at all: it is our innate character [*physis*] that remains steadfast, not our money. For character is always with us and helps us overcome adversity, but when prosperity comes with injustice and stupidity, it flies out of the house after flourishing but a short time."[246] Here wealth is opposed to *physis*; in the earlier passage wealth, poverty, and family prestige were. *Physis* alone has a permanence and a

242 Eur. fr. 141: ἐγὼ δὲ παῖδας οὐκ ἐῶ νόθους λαβεῖν· / τῶν γνησίων γὰρ οὐδὲν ὄντες ἐνδεεῖς / νόμῳ νοσοῦσιν· ὅ σε φυλάξασθαι χρεών. But cf. fr. 168, ὀνόματι μεμπτὸν τὸ νόθον, ἡ φύσις δ' ἴση, and fr. 377: μάτην δὲ θνητοὶ τοὺς νόθους φεύγουσ' ἄρα / παῖδας φυτεύειν· ὃς γὰρ ἂν χρηστὸς φύῃ, / οὐ τοὔνομ' αὐτοῦ τὴν φύσιν διαφθερεῖ.

243 Eur. *El*. 385, τοὺς εὐγενεῖς, 390: ἐν τῇ φύσει δὲ τοῦτο κἀν εὐψυχίᾳ.

244 Ibid. 384–87: τῇ δ' ὁμιλίᾳ βροτοὺς / κρινεῖτε καὶ τοῖς ἤθεσιν τοὺς εὐγενεῖς; / οἱ γὰρ τοιοῦτοι καὶ πόλεις οἰκοῦσιν εὖ / καὶ δώμαθ'.

245 Ibid. 381–84: οὔτ' αὖ δοκήσει δωμάτων ὠγκωμένος, / ἐν τοῖς δὲ πολλοῖς ὤν, ἄριστος ηὑρέθη. / οὐ μὴ φρονήσεθ', οἳ κενῶν δοξασμάτων / πλήρεις πλανᾶσθε. Also 387–89: αἱ δὲ σάρκες αἱ κεναὶ φρενῶν / ἀγάλματ' ἀγορᾶς εἰσιν. οὐδὲ γὰρ δόρυ / μᾶλλον βραχίων σθεναρὸς ἀσθενοῦς μένει.

246 Ibid. 939–44: ηὔχεις τις εἶναι τοῖσι χρήμασι σθένων· / τὰ δ' οὐδὲν εἰ μὴ βραχὺν ὁμιλῆσαι χρόνον. / ἡ γὰρ φύσις βέβαιος, οὐ τὰ χρήματα. / ἡ μὲν γὰρ αἰεὶ παραμένουσ' αἴρει κακά· / ὁ δ' ὄλβος ἀδίκως καὶ μετὰ σκαιῶν ξυνὼν / ἐξέπτατ' οἴκων, σμικρὸν ἀνθήσας χρόνον.

reality, which status symbols and other external social trimmings lack: intelligence is on the side of *physis*; only the stupid and empty-headed attach value to transitory externals.[247]

Social criticism, especially the criticism of wealth, is in Greek literature at least as old as Solon (fr. 15 West), but it is not until the 420s that *physis* appears as the yardstick measured against which wealth is found wanting. How can its emergence as an instrument of social criticism be explained? There is no evidence that any of the early sophists, with the possible exception of Hippias and Antiphon, displayed any interest in the polemical use of *physis* at all. But since Prodicus and Hippias are credited with scientific pursuits ancillary to their teaching of rhetoric,[248] it is likely that they injected *physis* into social criticism, at least to the extent that their rhetorical teaching included the theory and practice of argumentation.[249] However, though the sophists may have stimulated the Athenians to apply physical doctrines to the critique of society, their own knowledge of *physis* was derivative. A more direct access to it was available through the *physikoi*, the natural philosophers, especially Anaxagoras, Democritus, and Diogenes of Apollonia (on the Black Sea?), who had been attracted to the imperial city. Athenian familiarity with their work is attested for the last third of the fifth century.

The impact of Anaxagoras on Athenian life is best attested. His philosophical activity in Athens began in the archonship of Callias, in 456/5 B.C., and he remained there for twenty-seven years.[250] That he gave formal instruction other than an occasional public lecture is unlikely. Pericles and Euripides are mentioned most prominently among his pupils. In the case of Euripides this need mean no more than that Anaxagoras's influence was seen in numerous passages in his plays;[251] but frequent Anaxagorean echoes in the tragedies point

247 Cf. also id. fr. 495.40–43, from the lost *Melanippe*, where the naturally courageous and just are called nobler than opinionated vacuity.

248 See above, pp. 259–60.

249 See above, p. 242 with n. 162. See also C. J. Classen, "The Study of Language Amongst Socrates' Contemporaries," in C. J. Classen, ed., *Sophistik*, Wege der Forschung 187, (Darmstadt, 1976) 215–47.

250 D. L. 2.7, citing Apollodorus *FGH* 244F31 and Demetrius of Phaleron *FGH* 228F2. For the problems raised by these data, see Mansfeld, "Chronology," part 1, 39–69; see also above, pp. 194–98.

251 Euripidean passages attesting his studies under Anaxagoras are cited in D. L. 2.10; schol. Pind. *Ol.* 1.91; Satyr. *Vit.Eur.* frr. 37 I–38 I (in G. Arrighetti, ed., *Satiro: Vita di Euripide*, Studi Classici e Orientali 13) [Pisa, 1964], with commentary on pp. 105–10); scholl. Eur. *Or.* 982 and *Tro.* 884; Diod. 1.7.7 and 38.4; Cic. *Tusc.*

to personal acquaintance between the two.[252] For Pericles, there is not only the testimony of his relations with Anaxagoras, including the attack on Anaxagoras because of their closeness,[253] but also an illuminating passage in Plato's *Phaedrus* that shows how the influence of a natural philosopher on a statesman was envisaged:

All the important skills must be supplemented by some light discussion and high speculation about nature [*physis*], for that, it seems, is the source of a high level of thinking and of a polished performance. In fact, this is what Pericles acquired to supplement his native talent: when he came across Anaxagoras, who, I think, was the right kind of man, he filled himself with speculation on nature, proceeded to [an understanding of] the nature [*physis*] of mind and mindlessness, which were the major preoccupation of Anaxagoras, and derived from that what was suitable for the art of speaking.[254]

Thucydides is another member of the upper classes who is said to have attended lectures of Anaxagoras (Marcellin. *Vit. Thuc.* 22), Aeschines Socraticus is said to have mentioned Philoxenus son of Eryxis, and Ariphrades, the brother of the harp-singer Arignotus, as disciples of Anaxagoras (Ath. 5.220b). Both these men were prominent enough to have become the butt of Aristophanes' humor: Philoxenus is ridiculed as a κατάπυγων, effeminate, and a glutton;[255] Ariphrades is credited with inventing a sexual practice described as γλωττοποιεῖν in the *Wasps* and depicted in greater detail elsewhere.[256] The choice of γλωττοποιεῖν to describe Ariphrades' sexual habits indicates that he was also well known as a public speaker,[257]

3.14.30; Vitr. 8 praef. 1. For the relationship alone, see also Strab. 14.1.36 C645; Alexander Aetolus *ap.* Aul. Gell. 15.20.8; Γένος Εὐριπίδου II and III Arrighetti.

252 See Guthrie, *HGP* 2.323–25.

253 Pl. *Alc. I* 118c; Isoc. 15.235; D. L. 2.12 and 13; Diod. 12.39.2; Plut. *Per.* 4.6, 6.1–2, 16.7–9 and 32.1–2.

254 Pl. *Phdr.* 269e–270a: πᾶσαι ὅσαι μεγάλαι τῶν τεχνῶν προσδέονται ἀδολεσχίας καὶ μετεωρολογίας φύσεως πέρι· τὸ γὰρ ὑψηλόνουν τοῦτο καὶ πάντη τελεσιουργὸν ἔοικεν ἐντεῦθέν ποθεν εἰσιέναι. ὃ καὶ Περικλῆς πρὸς τῷ εὐφυὴς εἶναι ἐκτήσατο· προσπεσὼν γὰρ οἶμαι τοιούτῳ ὄντι Ἀναξαγόρᾳ, μετεωρολογίας ἐμπλησθεὶς καὶ ἐπὶ φύσιν νοῦ τε καὶ ἀνοίας [*sic* BT] ἀφικόμενος, ὧν δὴ πέρι τὸν πολὺν λόγον ἐποιεῖτο Ἀναξαγόρας, ἐντεῦθεν εἵλκυσεν ἐπὶ τὴν τῶν λόγων τέχνην τὸ πρόσφορον αὐτῇ.

255 Ar. *Nub.* 686; *Vesp.* 84; *Ran.* 934; cf. Eup. fr. 235. The charge of gluttony is not attested before the fourth century: see Arist. *EE* 3.2, 1231ᵃ15–17 (cf. *EN* 3.10, 1118ᵃ32–33); [*Pr.*] 28.7, 950ᵃ3; Plut. *Mor.* 668c (*Quaest. conv.* 4.4) and 1128b (*An recte dictum sit latenter esse vivendum* 1); Ath. 1.6b, 6.239f, 241e; Ael. *VH* 10.9.

256 Ar. *Eq.* 1274–89; *Vesp.* 1275–83, esp. 1283; *Pax* 883; *Eccl.* 129. See the ingenious article of E. Degani, "Arifrade l'anassagoreo," *Maia* 12 (1960) 190–217.

257 Cf. Degani, "Arifrade" 215. This seems confirmed by *Eccl.* 129.

and the fact that he is called θυμοσοφικώτατος (Ar. *Vesp.* 1280) may be an indication that he had also been schooled by the sophists. If that is the case, and in view of the fact that his brother Arignotus is described as an accomplished harp-singer (id. *Eq.* 1278–79; *Vesp.* 1278), it is probable but not provable that he came from a prosperous family.[258] Gorgias's disciple Polus, too, is credited by Socrates with expertise in Anaxagoras's philosophy (Pl. *Grg.* 465d). Finally, there is the rather tenuous relation between Anaxagoras and Socrates: there is no evidence that Socrates ever heard Anaxagoras lecture in person, but the *Apology* and the *Phaedo* attest, respectively, to the existence of his works in published form and to public readings of them being available in Athens, and to Socrates' interest in them.[259] In short, the impact Anaxagoras had on Athens survived him.

We have considerably less evidence about the activity of the Athenian Archelaus, and what survives is indirect, late, and of doubtful authenticity. What little we know of his physical doctrines lends credibility to reports that he was a pupil of Anaxagoras,[260] but he also formulated a theory of the origins of human society, which seems to have followed the same general lines as that attributed to Protagoras[261] and which caused later doxographers to attribute—erroneously, I believe—a moral theory based on the *nomos-physis* antinomy to him.[262] Of his connections in Athens the most reliably attested is that with Cimon, to whom he addressed an elegy upon the death of his wife, Isodike (Plut. *Cim.* 4.1, 10). That he was a friend and teacher of Socrates is credible, even though the significance of their relation eludes us;[263] that Euripides was his pupil is asserted

---

258 Degani, "Arifrade" 216–17, interprets his appellation as πονηρός as meaning that he was not a noble. That is not a necessary inference, because it is also possible that πόνηρός is used here in a moral rather than a social sense and because he may have been disparaged as belonging to the industrial rather than the agricultural upper class.

259 Pl. *Ap.* 26d tells us that the books were available at the low price of one drachma; *Phd.* 97b–c has Socrates report on his attendance at a public reading.

260 D. L. 2.16, who also says ἐκλήθη φυσικός, παρὸ καὶ ἔληξεν ἐν αὐτῷ ἡ φυσικὴ φιλοσοφία; *Suda* s.v. Ἀρχέλαος also calls him φυσικός, but not the last; Simplicius's commentary on Arist. *Ph.* 1.2, 184b15 (*Comm. in Arist. Graeca* 9.27.23–24); August. *De civ. D.* 8.2. For his physical doctrine, see 60A4–18 DK⁶.

261 Hippol. *Haer.* 1.9.6 with Guthrie, *HGP* 2.340.

262 See above, p. 262 with nn. 226–28.

263 See n. 226 above.

only by very late testimony and may be due to confusion with Anaxagoras.[264]

The most trustworthy witness of Democritus's presence in Athens is his own celebrated statement: "For I came to Athens and no one knew me."[265] In view of his serene but shy scholarly character, this is less likely to be a complaint than an expression of satisfaction at having escaped the social adulation accorded to celebrities in the big city.[266] It seems to be corroborated by the extraordinary absence of any reference to students he may have had or of any mark he left on contemporary Athenian literature, possibly because his stay was too short and no more than a stopover on trips said to have taken him as far as Egypt, Persia, the Red Sea, India, and Ethiopia.[267] For these reasons we would be rash to do more than state what we can glean from his fragments about the rule of *physis* in social and political matters, assuming that some of these may reflect thoughts current in Athens in the last third of the fifth century.[268]

It may be only an accident of survival that the noun *physis* is preserved only once in Democritus's scientific fragments (68B168 DK⁶), where it seems to refer to the atoms. But it is remarkable that none of its many occurrences in the ethical fragments seems to have any relation to the atoms, except perhaps in the statement that "some people, ignorant of the dissolution of mortal *physis*, but conscious of their bad conduct in life, labor for the whole time of their lives disturbed and fearful and invent fictional accounts of the time after their death,"[269] a statement that may prefigure the Epicurean belief in the mortality of the soul as a basis for ethics.[270] It is more noteworthy still that the value of *physis* is muted in the ethical fragments: true, Democritus prefers the self-sufficient self-reliance of *physis* over the hope of generous fortune (68B176), but he also

264 *Suda* s.v. 'Αρχέλαος; Γένος Εὐριπίδου III Arrighetti.
265 D. L. 9.36 (= 68B116 DK⁶); cf. also Cic. *Tusc.* 5.36.104, and Val. Max. 8.7 ext. 4, who adds that he stayed there for several years.
266 So Guthrie, *HGP* 2.349 n. 2.
267 D. L. 9.35; Clem. Al. *Strom.* 1.15.69.
268 For the authenticity of the ethical fragments, see F. K. Voros, "The Ethical Fragments of Democritus: The Problem of the Authenticity," Ἑλληνικά 26 (1973) 193–206.
269 Democr. 68B297 DK⁶: ἔνιοι θνητῆς φύσεως διάλυσιν οὐκ εἰδότες ἄνθρωποι, συνειδήσει δὲ τῆς ἐν τῷ βίῳ κακοπραγμοσύνης, τὸν τῆς βιοτῆς χρόνον ἐν ταραχαῖς καὶ φόβοις ταλαιπωρέουσι, ψεύδεα περὶ τοῦ μετὰ τὴν τελευτὴν μυθοπλαστέοντες χρόνου.
270 There is, however, no evidence for such an influence; see Cic. *Nat.D.* 1.33.93, where Epicurus is said to have been *ingratus* to Democritus.

seems to believe that training in childhood in addition to *physis* is required to make people think and that constant practice is more conducive to excellence than *physis* is (68B183 and 242). He even regards it as a function of teaching to transform human nature (*physis*), a view not encountered elsewhere in Greek antiquity;[271] and in the only juxtaposition of *nomos* and *physis* in his works, he suggests that people have so absorbed into their way of life (νομίζον) the selfless desire for procreation (which they share "by nature and some ancient arrangement" with all other living beings) that unlike the animals they also derive enjoyment from their offspring.[272] Thus, if Democritus's theories left any mark on social criticism in Athens, they more likely did so by virtue of his ethical than of his physical doctrines.

There is some indication that the physical doctrines of Diogenes of Apollonia, a contemporary of Anaxagoras, may have had some influence on Athenian thinking in the 420s, even though there is no evidence that he ever visited Athens.[273] The only possible original for Socrates' apostrophe to Air in Aristophanes' *Clouds* as encompassing the earth and keeping it suspended, and as the seat of intelligence and divinity,[274] is Diogenes' theory that "what has intelligence is what men call 'air', and that all men are governed by it and that it rules all, for I believe that it is god, affects everything, disposes everything, and inheres in everything."[275] At the very least, Diogenes' theories were familiar enough in Athens to be parodied in comedy. Still, the exploitation of scientific doctrine for popular entertainment makes it likely that Diogenes' theories reached the Athenians rather through the rhetorical teaching of the sophists, who were well-known public figures, than through direct contact with Diogenes.

271 Democr. 68B33: ἡ φύσις καὶ ἡ διδαχὴ παραπλήσιόν ἐστι. καὶ γὰρ ἡ διδαχὴ μεταρυσμοῖ τὸν ἄνθρωπον, μεταρυσμοῦσα δὲ φυσιοποιεῖ. Contrast Thuc. 1.121.4.

272 Id. B278: ἀνθρώποισι τῶν ἀναγκαίων δοκεῖ εἶναι παῖδας κτήσασθαι ἀπὸ φύσιος καὶ καταστάσιός τινος ἀρχαίης. δῆλον δὲ καὶ τοῖς ἄλλοις ζώοισι· πάντα γὰρ ἔκγονα κτᾶται κατὰ φύσιν ἐπωφελείης γε οὐδεμιᾶς εἵνεκα. ... ἡ μὲν φύσις τοιαύτη πάντων ἐστὶν ὅσσα ψυχὴν ἔχει· τῷ δὲ δὴ ἀνθρώπῳ νομίζον ἤδη πεποίηται, ὥστε καὶ ἐπαύρεσίν τινα γίγνεσθαι ἀπὸ τοῦ ἐκγόνου.

273 D. L. 9.57. Guthrie, *HGP.* 2.362–63, dates his activity between 440 and 423 B.C.

274 Ar. *Nub.* 227–33 with Dover's notes on 230–33, 264–66, 627.

275 Diog. Apoll. 64B5 DK⁶: καί μοι δοκεῖ τὸ τὴν νόησιν ἔχον εἶναι ὁ ἀὴρ καλούμενος ὑπὸ τῶν ἀνθρώπων, καὶ ὑπὸ τούτου πάντας καὶ κυβερνᾶσθαι καὶ πάντων κρατεῖν· αὐτὸ γάρ μοι τοῦτο θεὸς δοκεῖ εἶναι καὶ ἐπὶ πᾶν ἀφῖχθαι καὶ πάντα διατιθέναι καὶ ἐν παντὶ ἐνεῖναι. The same view is thought by some to have influenced Eur. *Tro.* 884; see Heinimann, *NP* 130 with n. 17.

It is time to summarize what we have discovered about the new learning in vogue especially among young upper-class Athenians in the 420s. Novel attitudes and beliefs grew up in opposition to the traditional values of the Athenian democracy, which had become the stale property of an aging, rigid establishment. For a price only the well-to-do could afford, sophists promised to provide the disenchanted younger generation with rhetorical and other training, wherewith political, social, and personal power could supposedly be attained and maintained through the organs of the Athenian democracy. But the teaching of the sophists in its turn drew on the thinking of natural philosophers to find in the immutable principles of nature a stick with which to beat the constraints of the establishment's manmade *nomoi*.

We have made the development of the *nomos-physis* controversy the main and most convenient basis for our account of the content of the new learning, insofar as that can be identified and described. By and large, *nomos* identifies the conventions, traditions, and values of the democratic establishment, which the older generation tended to regard itself as guarding; arguments from *physis* were marshaled by an intelligentsia that took shape in the Periclean age and from the late 430s attracted the allegiance of young aristocrats. But there are also other categories in which the polarization becomes apparent. Beginning with the Old Oligarch, Attic social and political discourses reserve terms signifying intellectual excellence to characterize the aristocracy, whereas terms signifying the opposite describe the defenders of the democratic establishment. The Old Oligarch uses δεξιός and σοφία only of the upper class (1.6, 7, 9) and ἀμαθία and ἀπαιδευσία (1.5, 7) of the lower; ξύνεσις and δεινότης are foremost among the expressions later writers added to the social vocabulary to describe the intellectuals, with σωφροσύνη occasionally used to flatter the common people.[276] Euripidean plays are full of these terms, and his characters outdo one another in showing their cleverness in argumentation.[277] Aristophanes' *Clouds* as a whole, but especially in its contest between Right and Wrong, bears eloquent testimony to the social polarization that the new intellectualism brought about *vis-à-vis* the old, traditional values.

---

276 All these terms (except ἀπαιδευσία, for which see 3.42.1) can be found in Cleon's speech regarding Mytilene in Thuc. 3.37.4–38.7; see n. 207 above.

277 This aspect of Euripides has been admirably treated by Solmsen, *Intellectual Experiments*, esp. chaps. 1 and 2.

RELIGION AND RATIONALISM: THE FEAR OF ATHEISM

The trials of Anaxagoras and Protagoras indicate that religion stood most to fear from the new intellectual currents. If Anaxagoras's assertion that the sun is a fiery stone gained currency, it would detract from the sun's divinity and thus from its worship,[278] and for his statement Anaxagoras had been subjected to an *eisangelia* by Diopeithes.[279] For professing an agnostic suspension of belief in the gods, Protagoras (80B4 DK[6]), we are told, was expelled from Athens, and his books were burned in the agora.[280] Evidently, the questions he raised were too disconcerting, too prone to undermine the public worship of the gods.

Neither Anaxagoras nor Protagoras can be called atheists in the strict sense of the term, which for us as well as for fourth-century and later Greeks denotes the denial of the existence of the gods altogether.[281] There is no evidence that either of these philosophers was labeled an *atheos* in his lifetime. And yet, presumably because of the convictions for which they were tried, both appear in Hellenistic and Roman lists of *atheoi*.[282] Such lists also include the names of other fifth-century writers likewise not marked as *atheoi* by their contemporaries but whose views ran counter to the conventional piety of the late fifth century. We may infer that their inclusion goes back to opposition they encountered from the religious majority in their own lifetimes.[283] Apart from the trials of Anaxagoras and

---

278　See W. Burkert, *Griechische Religion der archaischen und klassischen Epoche* (Stuttgart, 1977) 146, 192, 272–73, 349.

279　See above, p. 197.

280　See below, Appendix B, p. 532 with n. 19.

281　On the shift of the meaning of ἄθεος from "forsaken by the gods" to "forsaking the gods," see L. Woodbury, "The Date and Atheism of Diagoras of Melos," *Phoenix* 19 (1965) 178–211, esp. 208; Fahr, ΘΕΟΥΣ NOMIZEIN 15–17, 107, 138–39.

282　According to Diels, *Dox.Graec.* 58–59, the original catalogue of atheists was compiled by Cleitomachus of Carthage, head of the Academy from 127/6–110/09 B.C. The best-known such lists are to be found in Sext. Emp. *Math.* 9.50–55 and *Pyr.* 3.218, Aët. 1.7.1–2 (*Dox.Graec.* 297–98), and Gal. *Hist.Philos.* 35 (*Dox.Graec.* 617–18); cf. also Cic. *Nat.D.* 1.1.2. For Anaxagoras, see Irenaeus 2.14.2 (=59A113 DK[6]); for Protagoras, see Sext. Emp. *Math.* 9.55.

283　A. Dihle, "Das Satyrspiel 'Sisyphos,'" *Hermes* 105 (1977) 28–42, esp. 32–33, believes that philosophical atheists of the fourth century B.C. interpreted relevant fifth-century texts as atheistic in order to give their own views an ancestry. However, they would not have been able to do so if these texts had not already been earmarked as hostile by the upholders of conventional religiosity.

Protagoras, we know of active opposition only in the case of Diagoras of Melos.

Diagoras's name appears prominently on all lists of atheists, but the earliest evidence for this epithet does not go back beyond the first century B.C.[284] The reason for his prominence is clear: he is said to have so maligned the Mysteries that many would-be initiates did not go through with their initiations. The Athenians therefore published on a bronze stele a proclamation, the text of which is said to have been preserved by Craterus and copied by Melanthius, promising one silver talent to anyone who would kill Diagoras or two silver talents to anyone who would bring him alive to Athens.[285] Diodorus (13.6.7) assigns to 415/14 B.C. his report that Diagoras, slanderously charged with impiety and fearing the people, fled from Attica and that thereupon the Athenians proclaimed a reward of one silver talent to anyone who would kill him. This date is confirmed not only by the mention of the archon Charias in the garbled version of the incident preserved by Mubaššir[286] but also by Aristophanes' unmistakable parody of the proclamation against Diagoras in the *Birds*, first performed in 414 B.C.[287]

What precisely Diagoras's offense against the Mysteries was we are not told in any ancient source. Aristophanes' *Frogs* (320) shows that the Athenian public still remembered it as an especially heinous violation a decade after the proclamation. Six years later Andocides' opponent used Diagoras as an example in a way that brings us a little closer to understanding what crime he may have perpetrated. The speaker charges Andocides with an impiety more heinous than what Diagoras committed, for whereas the latter showed his impiety "in speech concerning rites and celebrations not his own, Andocides acted impiously concerning the rites in his own city" ([Lys.] 6.17).

---

284   See the lists enumerated in n. 282 above. He is first called an atheist in Cic. *Nat.D*. 1.23.63 and Diod. 13.6.7. The following account is indebted to the fundamental works of F. Jacoby, *Diagoras ὁ Ἄθεος*, Abh. d. Deutschen Ak. d. Wiss. Berlin, Kl. f. Sprachen, Literatur und Kunst 1959, no. 3 (Berlin, 1959), and of Woodbury, "Date," where a bibliography of earlier works can be found in n. 1; see also T. G. Rosenmeyer, "Notes on Aristophanes' *Birds*," *AJP* 93 (1972) 223–38, esp. 232–38.

285   Scholl. Ar. *Av*. 1073 and *Ran*. 320; Melanthius *FGH* 326F3 and Craterus *FGH*342F16.

286   Most accessible in Jacoby, *Diagoras* 4–5. Jacoby's own date of 433/2 B.C., however, has been convincingly refuted by Woodbury, "Date" 192–95.

287   Ar. *Av*. 1072–78. [Lys.] 6.17–18 refutes the contention of Rosenmeyer, "Notes", that the entire tradition of Diagoras's outlawry and the price on his head is unhistorical because it rests only on this product of Aristophanes' imagination.

This shows that Diagoras had made some kind of public statement that was regarded as particularly offensive because it came from a foreigner (who, we may assume, did not even enjoy metic status at Athens) and perhaps also because he made the statement at a time when young Athenian intellectuals from the upper classes had been discovered illicitly performing—and thus profaning—the Mysteries. We know that the profaners were put on trial for impiety, but there is nothing in the tradition to suggest that Diagoras was ever subjected to a judicial proceeding.[288] On the contrary, what evidence there is speaks against a trial: since our knowledge of the measures taken against him comes from Craterus, it appears that the Assembly decreed him an outlaw, put a price on his head, and pressured the people of Pellene, to whom he had fled, to extradite him (scholl. Ar. *Av.* 1073 and *Ran.* 320). Further, the absence of judicial terms in all our sources in the description of the measure taken against him and the consistent use of forms of κηρύττω and its compounds suggest that the document known to Melanthius and Craterus was a resolution of the Assembly, not the verdict of a jury court. If the proclamation was preceded by a trial, it will have been conducted *absente reo*.[289]

However offensive Diagoras's disparagement of the Mysteries may have been, it does not constitute evidence of atheism in the later sense, of denying the existence of the gods. Still, Diagoras seems to have been known in Athens as an enlightened poet considerably before the proclamation against him. Aristophanes' reference to Socrates as a "Melian" in connection with the doctrine that Zeus had been supplanted by Dinos (pot, *Nub.* 828–30) is generally taken as indicating that Diagoras was well known—and perhaps even present—in Athens when the *Clouds* was produced in 423 B.C. But it indicates also that Diagoras was reputed to have absorbed enough Ionian science, presumably from the sophists, to have been tarred in Athens with the same brush as Anaxagoras.[290] If he enjoyed that reputation as early as 423 B.C., any derogatory statement he may

288   Against Derenne, *Procès* 64–70, and Jacoby, *Diagoras* 17.38; correctly in MacDowell, *LCA* 201 with n. 451.

289   See Diod. 13.6.7 and Mubaššir, as cited by Jacoby, *Diagoras* 19 with n. 139. Cf. also Woodbury, "Date" 195, who concludes from the use of the perfect ἐκκεκήρυκται in schol. *Av.* 1073 that Diagoras had been in Athens but fled before the proclamation was voted.

290   A tradition of Ionian influence survives also in the statement in *Suda* s.v. Διαγόρας Τηλεκλείδου that Democritus bought him as a slave and made him his pupil.

have made against the Mysteries in 415 B.C. will have evoked a strong reaction on the part of the religious establishment, as we see in the proclamation, and will explain why fear of the people made him leave Athens before it was issued (Diod. 13.6.7).

Diagoras's reputation for atheism rested on something offensive he had said and the political response it evoked. Prodicus's inclusion in Hellenistic lists (Sext. Emp. *Math*. 9.51–55) seems due to his questioning the existence of the traditional gods. The story that he was forced to drink the hemlock in Athens, condemned on a charge of having corrupted the young,[291] is too obviously modeled on the fate of Socrates to deserve credence:[292] it merely attests an ancient view that some thought his influence as pernicious as Socrates'.

If atheism involves simply the refusal to believe in the existence of the gods traditionally venerated by a society, Prodicus was indeed an atheist.[293] But as Albert Henrichs has shown, Prodicus was no theologian; his denial of the traditional gods was only a by-product of his study of the correct meaning and usage of words, in which his rhetorical teaching had involved him. The origin of accepted divinities he may have placed in a general context of the development of civilization, just as Protagoras had prefaced his social theory with an account of the origin of human civilization.[294] Prodicus seems to have seen two phases in the development of religion. In the first, ancient men (οἱ παλαιοί) venerated as gods all those primary natural forces on which their sustenance and well-being depended: sun and moon, rivers and springs, and the like.[295] In the second, divinity was extended to the great human benefactors of the past, whose skills had provided mankind with shelter or taught them the preparation of foodstuffs—bread or wine, for example, whose givers were now

---

291 Schol. Pl. *Resp.* 600c; *Suda* s.v. Πρόδικος.

292 See Derenne, *Procès* 56, and Dover, "Freedom" 41–42.

293 *PHerc.* 1428, fr. 19.12–16, ὑ]πὸ [τ]ῶγ . ἀνθρώπων νομιζομένους θεοὺς οὔτ' εἶναί φησιν οὔτ' εἰδέναι, with A. Henrichs, "Two Doxographical Notes: Democritus and Prodicus on Religion," *HSCP* 79 (1975) 93–123, esp. 107–15. For the meaning of εἰδέναι in this fragment, see id., "The Atheism of Prodicus," *Cronache Ercolanesi* 6 (1976) 15–21.

294 See above, p. 259 with nn. 212 and 213, and Henrichs, "Two Notes" 111–12 n. 67.

295 The clearest statement is that of Sext. Emp. *Math.* 9.18 (84B5 DK⁶): Πρόδικος δὲ ὁ Κεῖος "ἥλιον" φησί "καὶ σελήνην καὶ ποταμοὺς καὶ κρήνας καὶ καθόλου πάντα τὰ ὠφελοῦντα τὸν βίον ἡμῶν οἱ παλαιοὶ θεοὺς ἐνόμισαν διὰ τὴν ἀπ' αὐτῶν ὠφελίαν, καθάπερ Αἰγύπτιοι τὸν Νεῖλον." Cf. also Phld. *De pietate* 9.7 (=84B5 DK⁶) as discussed by Henrichs, "Two Notes" 115–23, and Cic. *Nat.D.* 1.42.118.

identified as Demeter and Dionysus, respectively.[296] Whether such an outlook deserves to be identified as atheism *tout court* remains moot. Prodicus's denial of the existence of the traditional gods, his assertion that they were merely deified men, may indeed have been combined with the expectation that intelligent men such as himself should refuse them traditional worship. Still, the benefactions they had bestowed were real and lasting: would Prodicus have objected if simple folk continued to recognize their indebtedness by worshiping them? Or would he have disapproved of intellectuals who against their better knowledge encouraged divine worship by the masses in the interest of promoting a spirit of cohesion and piety in society?[297]

No statement has survived to suggest that Prodicus worked out the social consequences of his theology, so our questions must remain unanswered. But there is contemporary or nearly contemporary evidence strong enough to enable us to affirm that, whatever his views on the gods may have been, at least some upper-class Athenians to whom the maintenance of traditional piety was important respected and admired him, and perhaps even the people in general did also. His frequent visits to Athens in official as well as nonofficial capacities (Pl. *Hp.Ma.* 282c) made him sufficiently well known for Aristophanes to refer in respectful terms to his scientific learning and judgment in the *Clouds* (423 B.C.), the *Tagenistai* (422 B.C.), and the *Birds* (414 B.C.).[298] These will also have been the occasions on which he met and taught the younger members of the upper classes for pay, as all sophists did.[299] Fun could be poked at his innocent idiosyncrasies and at his deep, resounding voice; yet he was widely respected as a learned man and as a good teacher,[300] who counted not only Theramenes but also Socrates among his pupils and friends.[301] Nev-

---

296 The only evidence that this constituted a second phase is contained in *PHerc*. 1428, cols. ii–iii, as interpreted by Henrichs, "Two Notes" 115–23. In the light of it, the sequel to our quotation from Sext. Emp. *Math*. 9.18 (see preceding note) makes more sense: καὶ διὰ τοῦτο τὸν μὲν ἄρτον Δήμητραν νομισθῆναι, τὸν δὲ οἶνον Διόνυσον, τὸ δὲ ὕδωρ Ποσειδῶνα, τὸ δὲ πῦρ Ἥφαιστον καὶ ἤδη τῶν εὐχρηστούντων ἕκαστον. Cf. also Cic. *Nat.D*. 1.15.38 and Min. Fel. *Oct*. 21.2, with Guthrie, *HGP* 3.239–41.

297 See Guthrie, *HGP* 3.239–41, and Henrichs, "Atheism" 18 and 20–21.

298 Ar. *Nub*. 361, *Av*. 692, and fr. 490, as discussed by Dover, *Clouds* liv–lvi.

299 Pl. *Hp.Ma.* 282c; *Ap*. 19e; *Cra*. 384b; Xen *Symp*. 4.62. The quality of his lecture (or course of lectures?) varied with the amount of pay he received for it; fifty drachmas seems to have been his top fee; see Pl. *Cra*. 384b and Arist. *Rh*. 3.14, 1415^{b}12–17.

300 Pl. *Prt*. 315d–e; cf. also *Symp*. 177b; *Tht*. 151b; Xen. *Mem*. 2.1.21 and *Symp*. 4.62.

301 Pl. *Meno* 96d; *Chrm*. 163d; *Hp.Ma.* 282c. For Theramenes, see Ath. 5.220b and schol. Ar. *Nub*. 361.

ertheless, when Plato attributes to such an upright, old-fashioned aristocrat as Laches the disparaging remark that Prodicus's talents are more fit for a sophist than for a political leader (Pl. *Lach*. 197d) we see that the admiration for him was not universal. But it is significant that nothing disparaging is said about any of Prodicus's religious beliefs and that Laches regards him in the same light as he regards other sophists. In short, his religious convictions were no more detrimental to his reputation among his contemporaries than Xenophanes' will have been in his time. But his inclusion among the list of *atheoi* a century or two later permits the inference that his views were considered subversive by the contemporary religious majority.[302]

To Euripides more than to any other author we are indebted for our knowledge that unconventional ideas about the gods had gained wide currency and opposition thanks to the sophists' popularization of Ionic science. What Euripides' own views were we cannot know; we merely know the views of the characters in his plays and can infer from them that they were sufficiently familiar to his contemporary audience to be dramatically useful and to lead to success in tragic competition. But though Euripides' plays are good evidence for ideas current in Athens in the late fifth century, his strong predilection for dramatic use of the intellectual questions of his time makes it hard to believe that he accepted conventional piety with the same resigned acquiescence as his contemporary Sophocles seems to have. However, some modern scholars have inherited from ancient critics the tendency to credit Euripides personally with the opinions his characters express, an error that earned Euripides inclusion in the Hellenistic list of *atheoi*.[303]

Euripides' close involvement with the intellectual circles of his time is reflected in the student-teacher relationships his late biographers establish for him with Anaxagoras, Prodicus, Protagoras, and Socrates.[304] Although such statements cannot be taken at face value, they attest an awareness even in antiquity of the historical fact that

302 See n. 283 above.

303 See Aët. 1.7.1–2 and Gal. *Hist.Philos*. 35 (*Dox. Graec*. 297–98 and 617–18); cf. also Lucian, *Iupp.Trag*. 41 and Plut. *Mor*. 756b–c (*Amat*. 13).

304 For the relationship with Anaxagoras, see above, pp. 268–69 with n. 251; for Prodicus, see Γένος Εὐριπίδου II Arrighetti; Aul. Gell. *NA* 15.20.4; *Suda* s.v. Εὐριπίδης; for Protagoras, see Γένος Εὐριπίδου II; for Socrates, who is also said to have contributed to the writing of some Euripidean plays, see Satyr. *Vit.Eur*. fr. 38 IV and 29 I Arrighetti; D. L. 2.18, citing Telecleides frr. 39–40 (also cited in Γένος Εὐριπίδου II), Callias, fr. 12, and Ar. fr. 376; Aul. Gell. *NA* 15.20.4 and *Suda* s.v. Εὐριπίδης.

these thinkers influenced Euripidean tragedy.[305] Since modern scholars have long recognized that his influence exposed Euripides to the same charges as the sophists,[306] it will suffice here to identify briefly (and not exhaustively) some Euripidean passages that may have been regarded by later generations as suffused with the same atheism as they suspected in the natural philosophers and sophists.[307]

Euripides' criticism of the gods of traditional religion is of special interest since it exhibits different phases, each showing traces of contemporary thought that struck later generations as atheistic. His early plays show that his criticism was born of his concern for social justice: a speech in the *Philoctetes* (413 B.C.) alleges that seers manipulate people by persuasion, falsely claiming to have clear knowledge of divine matters (fr. 795); and a long extract from the *Bellerophon* (before 425 B.C.) rejects the existence of the heavenly gods on the grounds that wicked and impious tyrants prosper and small god-fearing states fall victim to more powerful impious states (fr. 286). The ambiguity of Hecuba's famous cry (425 B.C.) ἀλλ' οἱ θεοὶ σθέ-νουσι χὠ κείνων κρατῶν / νόμος· νόμῳ γὰρ τοὺς θεοὺς ἡγούμεθα / καὶ ζῶμεν ἄδικα καὶ δίκαι' ὡρισμένοι was first recognized by Heinimann.[308] The affirmation of divine power in the first of these lines is immediately undercut by the statement that the gods are controlled by norms, the precise nature of which we are not told; the following two lines suggest that this affirmation has no sanction beyond the human conventions that require gods for establishing social norms. Some scholars have seen traces of Protagoras or Archelaus in these lines;[309] others, of Prodicus and Critias.[310] But the parallels are too vague to enable us to say more than that Euripides was steeped in the same spirit as the thinkers of his age.

305   M. R. Lefkowitz, "The Euripides *Vita*," *GRBS* 20 (1979) 187–210, goes too far in her attempt to debunk the biographical tradition.

306   Euripides' association with Anaxagoras and Socrates probably accounts for the unlikely story that he was prosecuted for impiety by Cleon; see Satyr. *Vit.Eur*. fr. 39 X Arrighetti, perhaps related to the charge of impiety that according to Arist. *Rh*. 3.15, 1416ᵃ28–35, came up in an *antidosis* proceeding that a certain Hygiainon brought against Euripides. See Dover, "Freedom" 29 and 42.

307   The following remarks are much indebted to Dihle, "Satyrspiel" 33–35 and R. Scodel, *The Trojan Trilogy of Euripides*, Hypomnemata 60 (Göttingen, 1980).

308   Eur *Hec*. 799–801: "For the gods are strong and the *nomos* [law] that controls them; for by *nomos* [conventional belief] do we believe in the gods and define the rules of right and wrong by which we live." See Heinimann, *NP* 121–22.

309   U. von Wilamowitz-Moellendorff, *Aus Kydathen*, vol. 1 of *Philologische Untersuchungen* (Berlin, 1880) 49, as cited by Heinimann, *NP* 122 n. 33.

310   E.g., Fahr, ΘΕΟΥΣ ΝΟΜΙΖΕΙΝ 64–65 with 97–101.

This morally based questioning of the gods recedes in Euripides' later works, giving way to a more ontological attitude. At the same time, a greater affinity with the thought of the Ionian scientists seems to be grafted onto his interest in sophistic topics. This can be seen in Hecuba's outcry in the *Trojan Women* (415 B.C.): ὦ γῆς ὄχημα κἀπὶ γῆς ἔχων ἕδραν, / ὅστις ποτ' εἶ σύ, δυστόπαστος εἰδέναι, / Ζεύς, εἴτ' ἀνάγκη φύσεος εἴτε νοῦς βροτῶν, / προσηυξάμην σε.[311] Echoes of Diogenes (64B5DK[6]), of Heraclitus, of the atomists, and of Anaxagoras's concept "mind" have been detected in this passage,[312] but the religious turn given to their ideas is entirely Euripides'. It is not concerned with the morality or immorality of the gods, but it questions the existence of the traditional gods by searching for their reality in the powers underlying natural phenomena. A similar sentiment is expressed at the opening of the *Wise Melanippe*, which is of about the same date as the *Trojan Women*: Ζεὺς ὅστις ὁ Ζεύς, οὐ γὰρ οἶδα πλὴν λόγῳ.[313] This line is said to have caused such an uproar in the theatre that Euripides was compelled to change it.[314] But no other passage will have made Euripides more vulnerable to the charge of atheism than the speech of Sisyphus in the satyr play of the same name, performed as part of the same tetralogy as the *Trojan Women*, in 415 B.C. Sextus Empiricus, to whom we owe the fragment, attributes it to Critias as evidence of his atheism, but the work of Albrecht Dihle has removed any lingering doubts that it does not belong to Euripides.[315]

A considerable variety of parallels to the views of contemporary scientists and sophists can be and has been detected in the forty-two lines preserved.[316] It is difficult to attach a name to the theory with which the fragment opens, namely, that men originally lived "beast-

---

311 Eur. *Tro*. 884–87: "You who are the stay of the earth and have your seat on the earth, whoever you are, hard to guess and hard to know, Zeus, whether you are nature's necessity or mortals' mind, I invoke you."

312 See Heinimann, *NP* 130–31, and Guthrie, *HGP* 2.310, 379, 479 n.3.

313 Eur. Fr. 480: "Zeus, whoever Zeus is, for I know him only by report."

314 Plut. *Mor*. 756b–c (*Amat*. 13); cf. also Lucian, *Iupp.Trag* 41.

315 Sext. Emp. *Math*. 9.54. However, Aët. 1.6.7 and 7.2 (*Dox.Graec*. 294 and 298) assigns some of the verses cited by Sextus to Euripides. For Dihle, see n. 283 above, accepted by Scodel, *Trilogy* 122–37. D. Sutton, "Critias and Atheism," *CQ*, n.s., 31 (1981) 33–38, does not accept Dihle (though he does not argue against him, either) but rightly states that Dihle merely shifts the problem of atheism from Critias to Euripides.

316 The following is based on the text in B. Snell, *TGrF* 43F19; some of Dihle's emendations ("Satyrspiel" 41–42) have been accepted. For a discussion of sources, see also Scodel, *Trilogy* 127–28.

like and disorganized" (1–2); it appears already around the mid-fifth century and is found with increasing frequency in the last quarter of the century, though not in any other extant systematic discussion of the origins of civilization.[317] The invention of laws (*nomoi*), contrived to curb and discipline the excesses of the wicked and establish justice as a tyrant (5–8), is curiously enough not attributed to an individual lawgiver, but, as in the account Plato assigns to Protagoras (*Prt.* 324a–b, 325a–b, 326c–d), to enactment by "mankind" (*anthrōpoi*). What is credited to a "shrewd man wise in judgment" is the invention of religion, which is of interest to us here. Its purpose was to inhibit secret wrongdoing in action, speech, or thought by instilling the fear of an immortal, powerful, all-hearing, all-seeing divinity, from whom no thought is hidden (9–11, 14–15, 16–24). In giving this account, the wise man, we are told, "concealed the truth with a deceitful speech" (24–26), adding that the gods live in a place where they would most scare and benefit men at the same time: the sky, with its thunder and lightning, but also with its sun and rain (27–36). "In this manner," the fragment concludes, "I think some person first persuaded mortals to believe that there exists a race of divinities" (41–42).

If we look for comparable ideas in the surviving contemporary writings of the late fifth century, we shall discover that the atheism expressed by Sisyphus either is a new conclusion based on contemporary ideas or constitutes a different and more extreme form of atheism than any we have so far encountered. The notion that the law (*nomos*) cannot inhibit natural human drives is also found in the sophist Antiphon (87B44, A1.12–2.23 DK⁶); but unlike Sisyphus (5–8), Antiphon gives no thought to the origin of law at all and takes its existence for granted. However, like Sisyphus (11), he recognizes that it does not provide a safeguard against secret wrongdoing (A2.3–23), but the conclusions the two authors draw from this are diametrically opposed. For Antiphon this deficiency is again simply taken for granted and explained as inherent in the artificial character of *nomos*, which constitutes a barrier to the free play of the necessary course of nature (A1.23–25, 2.26–30, 4.1–8); the gods do not enter the argument at all. For Sisyphus the laws enforce social justice (6), and when they prove inadequate to that task their deficiency

---

317 Heinimann, *NP* 148–49, cites Eur. *Supp.* 201ff., Trag. Adespot. fr. 470, Aesch. *PV* 443f. and 456ff., and Diod. 1.8.1.

becomes the explanation of the invention of religion by a man of genius (9–16).

The idea that religion is a human invention can also be found in Democritus (68B30 DK⁶): "A few intelligent men raised their hands to the place we Greeks now call 'air' and said, 'Zeus considers[?] all things; he knows, gives, and takes away everything, and he is king over all.'" We do not know what place, if any, this fragment occupied in Democritus's theology; but the thought it expresses is sharpened in the *Sisyphus* fragment, where the invention of the gods is attributed to a single "shrewd man wise in judgment" (12) not as intended to explain the majesty of the universe but to manipulate his less intelligent or more gullible fellow citizens into being more law-abiding. In short, the cognitive purpose of Democritus has been transformed into a socially or politically useful tool. Similarly with another piece of Democritean wisdom: Sextus Empiricus (*Math.* 9.24) informs us of Democritus's belief that the notion of the gods was implanted in primitive man by the experience of celestial phenomena, such as thunder, lightning, thunderbolts, formation of the constellations, and eclipses of sun and moon, and by the fear this engendered. In the *Sisyphus* fragment the same phenomena are also associated with fear of the gods, but only in order to account for the wise man's placing the gods in heaven—the locale of these phenomena—in order to maximize fear of the gods (28) and harness it to socially and politically useful purposes (37–40).

Finally, there is an analogy with Prodicus in Sisyphus's mention of the benefits human derive from the celestial bodies and phenomena, especially sun and rain.[318] But whereas Prodicus was concerned with explaining the origin of popular religion by the awe people felt in the face of these benefactions, Sisyphus not only puts this awe pragmatically into the service of his social and political aims, emphasizing fear rather than admiration[319] but also, in doing so, undermines belief even in philosophical gods, for which the doctrines of Prodicus and Democritus may still have left room. After all, there is an objective reality underlying the worship of Demeter and Diony-

318 Compare *TGrF* 43F19.30–31 and 34–36 with Prodicus in Phld. *De pietate* 9.7 and Cic. *Nat.D.* 1.42.118 (=84B5 DK⁶). It is worth noting that Sisyphus refers to the sun as λαμπρὸς ἀστέρος μύδρος at line 35, which may well reflect Anaxagoras's view; see 59A2, 3, 19, 20a DK⁶. Cf. Pl. *Ap.* 26d; Xen. *Mem.* 4.7.7; D. L. 2.12. Cf. also Euripides' use of the same doctrine at *Or.* 982 and fr. 783 (from *Phaeton*).

319 Compare [Critias]'s φόβους (29 and 37) versus Prodicus's ἀγα[σθέντας ἐκθειάσαι] (*PHerc.* 1428 fr. 19.19–20 with Henrichs, "Two Notes" 107, 115–23).

sus in Prodicus's theology, and for Democritus the awe inspired by meteorological phenomena is real;[320] Sisyphus's divinity is purely the contrivance of a human genius, stripped of any vestiges of anthropomorphic personality. He is all mind and perception (17–21), a vindictive, disembodied master spy (22–24) maintaining order and discipline in human society.

Passages like this will have contributed to shaping Euripides' reputation as an atheist, which was first attested within a few years after his Trojan trilogy (Ar. *Thesm*. 450–51).[321] Though presumably based on contemporary opinion, this reputation is even less deserved than that of his alleged unpopularity.[322] But it does bear witness to the same profound concern with the phenomenon of religion that we encounter in the *Bacchae*, where we find Euripides' great attempt to reconcile the establishment's popular religion to the enlightenment's theology.

The *Bacchae* is neither the palinode of a converted atheist nor a renewed defiant denunciation of evils wrought by religion.[323] Euripidean characters in the 420s express ideas and themes from earlier plays now welded into new and more profound thoughts about religion and the gods. This is not the place to attempt to define the nature of these thoughts; their essential point has been well captured by Jeanne Roux: "It is not a matter of knowing whether the gods are good or bad, just or unjust, in the light of human morality, but of knowing whether they exist and, if they do, how man ought to conduct himself toward them in order to attain happiness and prosperity."[324] Questions raised by human morality are of lesser moment than recognition of the existence of the gods and acceptance, for better or for worse, of the worship they demand. We shall consider two passages showing how in the *Bacchae* Euripides transformed contemporary thought to express his peculiar religiosity.

The first of these is spoken by Teiresias in his first encounter with Pentheus. The aged seer tries to convince Pentheus to accept the

---

320   See above, pp. 277–78 with n. 296, and p. 283.

321   See above, n. 303.

322   On this point, see P. T. Stevens, "Euripides and the Athenians," *JHS* 76 (1956) 87–94.

323   Dodds, *Bacchae*² xl–xlii.

324   Roux, *Bacchantes* 41.

worship of Dionysus, arguing that his cult will spread through the whole of Greece:

> δύο γάρ, ὦ νεανία,
> 275 τὰ πρῶτ' ἐν ἀνθρώποισι· Δημήτηρ θεά—
> γῆ δ' ἐστίν, ὄνομα δ' ὁπότερον βούλῃ κάλει·
> αὕτη μὲν ἐν ξηροῖσιν ἐκτρέφει βροτούς·
> ὃς δ' ἦλθ' ἔπειτ', ἀντίπαλον ὁ Σεμέλης γόνος
> βότρυος ὑγρὸν πῶμ' ηὗρε κεἰσηνέγκατο
> 280 θνητοῖς, ὃ παύει τοὺς ταλαιπώρους βροτοὺς
> λύπης, ὅταν πλησθῶσιν ἀμπέλου ῥοῆς,
> ὕπνον τε λήθην τῶν καθ' ἡμέραν κακῶν
> δίδωσιν, οὐδ' ἔστ' ἄλλο φάρμακον πόνων.
> οὗτος θεοῖσι σπένδεται θεὸς γεγώς,
> 285 ὥστε διὰ τοῦτον τἀγάθ' ἀνθρώπους ἔχειν.[325]

The closeness of this passage to concepts of early Greek science and to the thought of Prodicus has often been noted but is rarely stated in detail. Greek science is reflected in the significant opposition of dry and wet, which can be traced back as far as Hesiod and informs practically all Presocratic thinking about the nature of the physical universe.[326] Considerably more striking, however, is the similarity to Prodicus's two phases in the development of religion.[327] The similarity goes even farther: if we can credit Sextus Empiricus (*Math.* 9.18), Prodicus believed in the identity of Demeter and bread and of Dionysus and wine, a point that becomes in Teiresias's speech an avowed indifference whether "earth" or "Demeter" is the proper name for the goddess (276) and results in identifying Dionysus with his product (284).

---

325   Eur. *Bacch.* 274–85: "For two things, young man, are first among mortals: the goddess Demeter—she is the earth, call her by either of these names you wish. She nurtures men by way of dry food. He who came afterward, Semele's offspring, invented, to balance it, the wet drink of the grape cluster and introduced it to mortals. It puts an end to the pain men suffer, whenever they are filled with the flow that comes from the vine, and it gives sleep to make them forget the ills besetting them by day: there is no other drug against their suffering. Having become a god, he is poured as a libation to the gods, so that it is through him that men have all good things."

326   The best discussion of this problem is still that of C. H. Kahn, *Anaximander and the Origins of Greek Cosmology* (New York, 1960) 126–33, 159–63.

327   See above, pp. 277-78 with nn. 295 and 296.

Yet Euripides puts a stamp of his own on Prodicus's view: Demeter, whom Prodicus seems to have regarded as a human deified for discovering how to make bread from grain, becomes in Euripides one of the primary divinities. This is suggested by the opposition of wet and dry that opens Teiresias's argument, and it seems corroborated by the indifference to her name, recalling a similar indifference to divine nomenclature in the *Trojan Women* and the *Wise Melanippe*.[328] Not quite consistently with this, Dionysus seems still to belong to Prodicus's second phase. This is indicated by the statements that "he came afterward" (278), that he is Semele's offspring (278), that he "invented" the wet drink of the grape cluster whereas Demeter "nurtures" directly (277), and that he "became" a god (284), and by his being explicitly named a benefactor to mortals (285). But here again Euripides adds a peculiar twist. Prodicus concluded that the gods of popular tradition do not exist; in Euripides his arguments are made by a spokesman for the religious establishment, whom we would expect to represent the attitude of conventional piety toward the nature of Dionysus and toward the problem of admitting his worship into Thebes. If that was Euripides' intent in composing this scene, a strange spokesman Teiresias turns out to be: he uses an argument originally formulated to deny the existence of the conventional gods to show that they—or at least Dionysus—are real enough to deserve recognition and worship. His proof consists in the pragmatic enumeration of some of the benefits derived for men from wine, more a philosophical than a popular theology. However, one of the benefits is that Dionysus, "having become a god, is poured as a libation to the gods" (284). The recipients of these libations must be the gods of traditional religion, since there cannot be any others whom this sacrifice is likely to honor. This means that Dionysus holds an important key to the performance of traditional worship: as a god he contributes to swaying the good will of the gods of popular religion to our favor.

This strange fusion of philosophical and conventional elements is deliberate, as is shown in the rest of Teiresias's speech. In the immediate sequel, his rationalistic, etymological explanation of the story that Zeus hid Dionysus in his thigh (286–96) is contrived to show that there is a reality underlying an otherwise incredible story; following that, the entrance of "the god" into the body is given as

328　See above, p. 281 with nn. 311 and 313.

the source of the seer's craft, in which the "manic" (*maniōdes*) results in the "mantic" (*mantikē*, 298–313).³²⁹ Is this transformation of philosophical atheism into a part of traditional religion to be taken as characterizing the attitude of Athenian aristocrats whose stewardship of religious cults had been influenced by sophists? If it is, the dry, abstract tone of Teiresias's disquisition, often remarked on by commentators,³³⁰ may well be intended as a foil to the stark reality of the divine presence that will be demonstrated in the rest of the play.

A tension between attempts to comprehend life through the intellect and through direct experience of the divine stands at the heart of Euripidean religiosity in the *Bacchae*. It is most strikingly expressed in the question posed at the beginning of two identical stanzas in the stasimon between Dionysus's persuasion of Pentheus to become a voyeur and Pentheus's appearance in Bacchic garb: τί τὸ σοφόν;—"What is the wise thing?" (877, 897). That this question dominates the play as a whole has long been seen.³³¹ Throughout, its common contemporary connotation of intellectual keenness is pitted against another connotation, which sees in the simple, unquestioning surrender to the god a higher wisdom: τὸ σοφὸν δ' οὐ σοφία / τό τε μὴ θνητὰ φρονεῖν—"The wise thing is not wisdom, nor is it wisdom to think thoughts that are not mortal" (395–96). The wisdom of the intellect is consistently found wanting. Dionysus decides to punish Thebes because Cadmus's daughters believe the story of Semele's mating with Zeus was merely their father's *sophisma* (clever trick) to protect their sister's reputation (30). Cadmus regards Teiresias as *sophos* (179, 186), but the seer's true wisdom does not go beyond a general recognition that human wisdom is nothing in the eyes of the gods and that the *sophon* of the sharpest human mind cannot countervail against timeless traditions;³³² his own understanding of the nature of divinity is, as we saw, infected with some of the same intellectualism he condemns as *sophon* in Pentheus (266).

329   Dodds's attempt (*Bacchae*² *ad loc.*) to make Prodicus's doctrine less "atheistic" has been adequately answered by Henrichs, "Two Notes" 110 n. 64.

330   So, e.g., Dodds, *Bacchae*² 91.

331   E.g., by Dodds, *Bacchae*² xlii, 92, 121, 186–88, 204–5, 219; and G. S. Kirk in the commentary on his translation of the *Bacchae* (Englewood Cliffs, N. J., 1970) 45, 96–97, 118.

332   Eur. *Bacch.* 200–203: οὐδὲν σοφιζόμεσθα τοῖσι δαίμοσιν. / πατρίους παραδοχάς, ἅς θ' ὁμήλικας χρόνῳ / κεκτήμεθ', οὐδεὶς αὐτὰ καταβαλεῖ λόγος, / οὐδ' εἰ δι' ἄκρων τὸ σοφὸν ηὕρηται φρενῶν.

Pentheus is of course the chief representative of the human wisdom that the course of the action shows to be deficient in the face of Dionysiac wisdom. Euripides brings this out by the frequent use of *sophon* in an ambivalent sense in the *agōn* scenes between Pentheus and Dionysus. Pentheus's failure to understand the account the fettered Dionysus gives of himself makes Dionysus describe the gulf that separates them with the words δόξει τις ἀμαθεῖ σοφὰ λέγων οὐκ εὖ φρονεῖν—"A person saying wise things to an ignorant man will give the impression of having no sense at all" (480). Pentheus looks upon Dionysus's explanations as *sophismata* (489). In the next episode Dionysus, having just freed himself, resolves to meet Pentheus's anger with calmness: "For it is the part of a wise man to practice a well-controlled temper" (641). He attributes true inner calm to the wisdom that springs from the cult Pentheus condemns as excessively emotional; this point is driven home a few lines later when Pentheus predicates "cleverness" (*sophon*) of Dionysus's escape, whereas Dionysus claims to be *sophos* where it really matters (655–56). Pentheus's tragic end is foreshadowed when he praises Dionysus as wise for proposing to dress him up as a woman (824) and when Dionysus approves of his investigating the spot where the orgies are taking place as wiser than immediately hunting down the worshipers (839).

What the play commends as true wisdom is fully expressed only in the choral lyrics, especially in the third stasimon. The first stasimon, to be sure, differentiates from the *sophon* true *sophia* (the only occurrence of the noun in the *Bacchae*), which consists in a quiet life confined to thinking mortal thoughts (389–96) and which promises a life of happy contentment "that wisely withholds mind and thought from superior men" and is willing to "accept whatever the mass of simple folk practices and considers as the norm" (425–32). But only in the third stasimon (just before Pentheus embarks on the errand from which he will not return), do the question τί τὸ σοφόν;—"What is the wise thing?"—and its answer appear:

890   οὐ
γὰρ κρεῖσσόν ποτε τῶν νόμων
γιγνώσκειν χρὴ καὶ μελετᾶν.
κοῦφα γὰρ δαπάνα νομίζειν ἰσχὺν τόδ' ἔχειν,
ὅ τι ποτ' ἄρα τὸ δαιμόνιον,

895 τό τ' ἐν χρόνῳ μακρῷ νόμιμον
ἀεὶ φύσει τε πεφυκός.[333]

We have quoted these lines before to show how the *nomoi* that demarcate the limits of human endeavor imply beliefs as well as practices and how the *nomimon* regards the divine as an object both of belief and of worship. If this is so, the *sophon* will resolve the conflict between intellectual and traditional religion by demanding a fusion of the two that at the same time offers a religious resolution of the tension between *nomos* and *physis* imported into Athenian thought ·by sophistic teaching. The *nomoi* include the πάτριοι παραδοχαί, the ancestral traditions—which, as Teiresias had asserted (200–203), will resist any human *sophon*—as well as the norms and practices of the common simple folk (430–33).[334] But they will also include Teiresias's feeble attempt to reconcile the enlightened views of Prodicus with conventional piety, so long as the traditional worship of the gods is not adversely affected. It will not cost the intellect much, this passage assures us, to recognize the divine strength underlying the natural phenomena of our experience— meaning, I presume, that whether or not we identify Demeter with earth or Dionysus with wine, the ἰσχύς (strength) manifested in the very existence of earth and wine demands recognition and worship. The combination of this recognition and the worship it entails will then not only be sanctioned as a *nomimon* hallowed by long tradition, but it will also be grounded in the nature (*physis*) that the human intellect can explore.

Seen in this light, the ending of the *Bacchae* is not a statement on the horrors of religion—*tantum religio potuit suadere malorum* is frequently cited by scholars who believe that it is—but on the dire consequences of the intellect's failure to acknowledge the reality of divine power. It stands in a direct line of development with the tragic perception of Medea and of Phaedra, that life is subject to forces against which rationality cannot prevail.[335] Here as in earlier plays Euripides is concerned with and affected by problems the natural philosophers raised and the sophists popularized. But as in the

333   Ibid. 890–96. Cf. above, pp. 106–7 with n. 72, where a translation is provided.
334   See Dodds, *Bacchae*² 129–30, 189.
335   Eur. *Med*. 1079–80; *Hipp*. 380–402.

Sisyphus fragment, he is no longer content to measure the gods by the standard of human morality. In the *Bacchae* Euripides came to grips with the phenomenon of religion itself and concluded that the reality underlying it is the object of traditional religion and philosophical inquiry alike. Euripides' attempt to reconcile *nomos* and *physis* in the religious sphere remains unique in fifth-century thought. But it left a less lasting impression on his contemporaries and on later generations than the fact that he openly grappled with problems raised by thinkers whose views were branded as atheistic because they were believed to undermine the traditional worship of the gods.

CHAPTER SIX

Popular Sovereignty and the Intellectual: Alcibiades

IF Callicles was not a historical person but was created in Plato's powerful imagination to embody the corruption with which sophistic education had tainted Athenian politics, Plato's model in provenance, training, political purpose, and political method may well have been Alcibiades.[1] Alcibiades came from old aristocratic Athenian stock.[2] He cannot have been more than four or five years old, when his father, Cleinias, died in the battle of Coroneia in 447/6 B.C.[3] Alcibiades and his brother became the wards of their mother's cousin Pericles,[4] presumably according to the terms of Cleinias's will and because of the close personal and political ties between Cleinias and Pericles.[5]

In the thirteen years Alcibiades spent at Pericles' house, until he was old enough to serve in the army at Potidaea,[6] Pericles' power

1 For Callicles, see pp. 245–47 above.
2 According to Isoc. 16.25, he was a Eupatrid on his father's side and an Alcmaeonid on his mother's; according to Pl. *Alc. I* 121a–b, Plut. *Alc.* 1.1, and Didymus *ap.* schol. Pind. *Nem.* 2.19, he traced his descent back to Ajax. For details, see Davies, *APF* 10–12, 15–18.
3 Alcibiades was born "not later than 452" (so Andrewes, *HCT* 4.48–49) or perhaps a year later (so Davies, *APF* 17–18, who dates the birth of his younger brother, Cleinias, between 449 and 446 B.C.).
4 Isoc. 16.28; Pl. *Alc. I* 104b and 112c, *Prt.* 320a.
5 See ML, no. 46 with pp. 120–21 and Davies, *APF* 16, 18. Axiochus, Cleinias's brother, who would normally have been expected to assume the guardianship, may have been excluded as too young or as morally too unreliable; cf. Hatzfeld 29 with nn. 2 and 3.
6 Pl. *Symp.* 219e–220e; Isoc. 16.29; Plut. *Alc.* 7.3–5 with Hatzfeld 62–66 and Andrewes, *HCT* 4.48–49.

and with it the glory of Athens were at their zenith. Even if Pericles devoted no more attention to Alcibiades' upbringing than he did to the education of his own sons, Alcibiades will have spent his most impressionable years in a milieu that exposed him to the best intellects and greatest artists of his time. We know the names of two of his formal teachers: according to Plato, Pericles assigned "the most useless" of his household slaves, a superannuated Thracian named Zopyrus, to be his tutor; there is a tradition that he received instruction also from Antiphon's father, the sophist Sophilus.[7] Moreover, his presence with Critias at the house of Callias, easily mingling with the sophists there assembled in 433 B.C. (Pl. *Prt.* 316a), indicates that he had moved in the highest social and intellectual circles even before he left Athens for the campaign at Potidaea. About the same time began his friendship with Socrates, which is the best-attested influence on his intellectual development, although later apologists for Socrates claim that their relations had cooled by the time Alcibiades had gained political prominence.[8]

Alcibiades' assets were probably sufficient to make him eligible for cavalry service, but he served as a hoplite at Potidaea; he earned the prize of valor (*aristeia*), which our sources assure us should by rights have gone to Socrates.[9] At Delium he served with the cavalry.[10] In the eight years between these two battles he became a public enough figure in Athens to be identified with the young men to whom the sophists dispensed their new learning. In a dialogue between an old man and his fashionably educated son in Aristophanes' *Banqueters* (427 B.C.), the young man uses a neologism his father attributes to Alcibiades (Ar. fr. 198.6); two years later the *Acharnians* links him with Cephisodemus and Euathlus, the brash young prosecutors of Thucydides son of Melesias (Ar. *Ach.* 716).[11] But there is no evidence that Alcibiades was himself involved in political prosecutions of public officials at this or any other time. There is some evidence,

7   Pl. *Alc. I* 122b, cited also in Plut. *Alc.* 1.3 and *Lyc.* 16.6. We do not know whether this Zopyrus is identical with the physiognomer mentioned in Cic. *Fat.* 5.10–11 and *Tusc.* 4.37.80 as having disparaged Socrates. For Sophilus, see [Plut.] *X orat.* 832c.

8   Pl. *Symp.* 213e–214a, 219e–221b, *Prt.* 309a; *Alc. I* 135d; Xen. *Mem.* 1.2.12, 24; cf. also Plut. *Alc.* 4.1–4, 6.1, 7.3–6. For a sensitive evaluation of the development of their relationship see Hatzfeld 32–58, esp. 51–58.

9   Pl. *Symp.* 219e–220e, Plut. *Alc.* 7.3–5 (who says ἔτι δὲ μειράκιον ὤν) with Hatzfeld 65 and n. 3.

10   Pl. *Symp.* 220e–221c, Plut. *Alc.* 7.6 with Hatzfeld 65–66.

11   See pp. 231–32 above.

however, of his association with Cleon's financial policies. The speech *Against Alcibiades*, which has come down to us among the works of Andocides, states that Alcibiades was one of ten men appointed to revise the tribute assessment for the allies and that he doubled the contribution exacted from each city ([Andoc.] 4.11). The occasion to which this refers is most likely Thudippus's decree of 425/4 B.C. (passed with Cleon's blessing shortly after the Athenian success at Sphacteria), which stipulated the appointment of ten assessors (*taktai*) by the Council.[12] Is Alcibiades likely to have been one of them? The only reason to reject the statement of pseudo-Andocides is that a person twenty-five years of age was too young to be appointed to any office at that time.[13] But though appointment to office of anyone under age of thirty was unusual,[14] we know of no statutory limitation that prevented it, and further, Alcibiades was an unusual person, whose years had not prevented his ability from coming to public attention before 425/4 B.C.[15]

If Alcibiades owed this appointment at so early an age to his vocal support of Cleon's financial policy, he may also have supported Cleon in rejecting the Spartan peace overtures after Sphacteria[16] and thus in making continued levies for the war a necessity. We have no information whether the flush of Cleon's recent victory also caused Nicias to support this policy. But since he had been at odds with Cleon over the issue of Sphacteria (Thuc. 4.27.5; Plut. *Nic.* 7.2), he may have favored peace even at this juncture.

The peace Nicias favored could not be struck until death had removed Cleon and Brasidas from the scene (Thuc. 5.16.1; cf. Ar. *Pax* 262–86). Although Cleon's mantle as a warmonger fell to Hyperbolus, if we can trust Aristophanes (*Pax* 681–84, 921, 1319), the political arena was now dominated by Nicias and Laches, patriots and solid citizens of the Athenian democracy. Their sterling qualities are immortalized in Plato's *Laches* (named, strangely enough, after the less distinguished of the two), where we also learn (186c) that they were older than Socrates, that is, that they were born before 469 B.C. Thus they will have been about fifty when the peace for which they had worked was concluded. Neither of them seems to

---

12 ML, no. 69.8–12 and Meiggs, *AE* 325–27 with pp. 205–6 above.
13 So Andrewes, *HCT* 4.49.
14 See Hignett, *HAC* 224.
15 Hatzfeld 68–69 believes the story.
16 Thuc. 4.41.3–4; cf. also Ar. *Pax* 635–67 with schol. on 665 (=Philochorus *FGH* 328F128).

have been so dynamic a leader as the Athenians had found in their contemporaries Pericles and Cleon, and neither could rival Alcibiades either in social status or in political acumen.

Nothing is known of Laches' provenance, which may (but need not) indicate that he was not a member of an old and distinguished aristocratic family. The generalships to which we know he was elected for 427/6, 426/5, and 418/17 B.C. he seems to have earned by his own personal qualities and perhaps by his nonagricultural wealth.[17] We are better informed about Nicias, although his antecedents too remain obscure. His prominence will to a large extent have been due to his wealth, which he accumulated through mining interests and spent lavishly on public liturgies, especially as choregus and for religious purposes:[18] "His economic background is that of the slave-owning demagogues like Kleon and Hyperbolos rather than that of the landowner Perikles."[19] And yet, he was accepted by the upper classes in a way Cleon and the demagogues were not.[20] We learn from Plutarch (*Nic*. 2.2) that in his earliest commands he had been associated with Pericles as general and that after Pericles' death the upper classes supported him as a counterweight to Cleon's influence, while he had at the same time the good will of the people. If this is correct, the mutual dislike between him and Cleon will have been based on differences in temperament and policy rather than on social class and will have come into the open considerably earlier than when we first hear about it, in connection with the Pylos affair.[21] Not much love will have been lost, either, between Laches and Cleon—especially if, as we believe, the dog trial in Aristophanes' *Wasps* is based on accusations Cleon leveled when Laches was tried after the *euthyna* for his generalship in Sicily.[22]

In addition to these personal reasons, the military situation after Pylos will have inclined even so devoted a soldier as Laches to join Nicias in opposing Cleon's intransigent policy of war to the finish.

---

17 Thuc. 3.86.1, 103.3; 5.61.1. For his wealth, see Ar. *Vesp*. 241.
18 Davies, *APF* 403–4; cf. also Plut. *Nic*.4.1.
19 Davies, *APF* 404.
20 See Arist. *Ath.Pol*. 28.5, where he is bracketed with Thucydides son of Melesias and Theramenes: καὶ περὶ μὲν Νικίου καὶ Θουκυδίδου πάντες σχεδὸν ὁμολογοῦσιν ἄνδρας γεγονέναι οὐ μόνον καλοὺς κἀγαθούς, ἀλλὰ καὶ πολιτικοὺς καὶ τῇ πόλει πάσῃ πατρικῶς χρωμένους.
21 Thuc. 4.27.5–28.3, esp. 27.5, ἐχθρὸς ὢν καὶ ἐπιτιμῶν, with Gomme's note *ad loc*.
22 See above, pp. 212–13 with n. 59.

But their joint efforts could not win the Athenian people over until Cleon was dead: although Laches succeeded in moving a one-year truce with Sparta in 423 B.C., it took another two years until Nicias, with his support, could get the peace and the alliance with Sparta accepted.[23]

ARGOS: POPULAR SOVEREIGNTY MANIPULATED

The reasons why the Peace of Nicias was stillborn and was little more than a chance for both sides to regroup for renewed hostilities—which as Thucydides intimates could be deferred but not averted—need not concern us here.[24] What does concern us is how Athenian politics were affected by the gradual breakdown of the peace and by Alcibiades' rise to prominence. Thucydides' account of the complex diplomatic situation in Greece after 421/0 B.C. is remarkable: the reciprocal relation between the form of government prevailing in a given state and its external relations receives an emphasis it had not had in his earlier narrative. To be sure, in the wake of the Mytilenean revolt Diodotus had proposed a policy of supporting the *dēmos* in the allied cities in order to prevent defection (Thuc. 3.47), and after the Corcyrean revolt oligarchical and democratic factions in the smaller states turned for support to Sparta and Athens, respectively (3.82.1); but after 421/0 B.C. such relations assume unprecedented ideological dimensions and become a counter in the policy and diplomacy of all Greek states. While Athens and Sparta remain the strongholds of democracy and oligarchy, respectively, democracy and oligarchy are transformed into political principles in smaller states, each with its partisans intent on enlisting the aid of either Athens or Sparta to oust the opposition on ideological grounds. The phenomenon of ideological *stasis* (internal discord) was beginning to spread from Corcyra and Megara to the rest of the Greek world.

A minor but significant barometer of this change is that Thucydides uses expressions denoting democratic or oligarchical government, which occur only rarely in the earlier part of his work, with increasing frequency in his account of events after the Peace of

23   Thuc. 4.118.11, 5.43.2 with Gomme, *HCT* 3.605, 4.87.
24   On this point and on the interstate relations between 421 and 416 B.C., see R. Seager, "After the Peace of Nicias: Diplomacy and Policy, 421–416 B.C." *CQ*, n.s., 26 (1976) 249–69.

Nicias.[25] Substantively, the change becomes visible at once after the Peace of Nicias when the Corinthians instigate the Argives to entrust the negotiations of the proposed alliances "to a few men with full powers, so that no negotiations be conducted with the popular Assembly, lest any failure to persuade the Assembly to accept a given ally become known."[26] The advice is prudent and was wisely taken by the Argive democracy, yet it is significant that an oligarchical state, Corinth, sees fit to point out to Argos this shortcoming in a democratic government and equally significant that the Argive Assembly reserved for itself the right to conduct such negotiations with Athens or Sparta, should need arise (Thuc. 5.28.1). Further, the fact that Argos was democratically governed is given as one reason why democratic Mantinea and her allies were so quick to accept the Argive overtures for an alliance (5.29.1), and similarly, oligarchical Boeotia and Megara are reluctant to join the alliance because they believe the Argive democracy would be less useful to them than the Lacedaemonian form of government (5.31.6). A year later, in the summer of 420 B.C., the fact that Athens was democratically governed was one reason why Argos sought an alliance there rather than with Sparta (5.44.1). And when two years after that, in the winter of 418 B.C., the Spartans wanted to conclude a peace treaty with Argos, they employed as their agents Argives hostile to democracy, who were interested in using an alliance with Sparta to overthrow the Argive government. They succeeded in doing so with Spartan help after the Spartans had tightened the oligarchy at Sicyon (5.76.2, 81.2). But the Argive oligarchy proved of short duration: the commons ousted the oligarchs by force of arms, and when Sparta failed to respond immediately to their friends' appeal, the commons turned to Athens for help. This consisted at first in dispatching Athenian carpenters and stoneworkers to help in fortifying Argos; but at the beginning of the summer of 417 B.C., twenty Athenian ships arrived in Argos, and their commander proceeded at once to arrest three hundred Spartan sympathizers and deport them to offshore islands under Athenian control. The Athenian commander was Alcibiades (5.82.2–6, 84.1).

25 δημοκρατέομαι does not occur before 5.27, but is found eleven times thereafter; ὀλιγαρχέομαι and ὀλιγαρχικός are only found after 5.27, the former five times, the latter twice. Of the twenty instances of δημοκρατία, only six precede but fourteen follow 5.27; and of the thirty-four occurrences of ὀλιγαρχία only three are earlier than 5.27.

26 Thuc. 5.27.2: ἀποδεῖξαι δὲ ἄνδρας ὀλίγους ἀρχὴν αὐτοκράτορας καὶ μὴ πρὸς τὸν δῆμον τοὺς λόγους εἶναι, τοῦ μὴ καταφανεῖς γίγνεσθαι τοὺς μὴ πείσαντας τὸ πλῆθος.

However important ideology may have become in local politics, it was not among the factors that had secured Alcibiades this appointment. According to Thucydides,

When the relations of the Lacedaemonians toward the Athenians had grown so far apart, those men in Athens who wanted the peace treaty rescinded lost no time in pushing their policy. Foremost among them was Alcibiades son of Cleinias, a man who, though in age he would have been regarded as still young at that time in any other city, was respected because of the social standing of his ancestors. In his view it was better to side with the Argives, but the main reason for his opposition was a temperament that brooked no competitor, because the Lacedaemonians had negotiated the peace through Nicias and Laches without paying attention to him as still too young and without respecting the ancient *proxenia* that once existed between them and his family. Though his grandfather had renounced it, he was thinking of renewing it by cultivating the Spartan prisoners from Sphacteria.[27]

This, Thucydides' first mention of Alcibiades, comes in his account of the winter of 421/0 B.C. At that time Spartan opponents of the peace, who had been elected ephors, initiated a policy that made Argos the central issue in the struggle between the two superpowers and led to Sparta's impressive victory at Mantinea two years later (in which Laches lost his life; Thuc. 5.36–74). Not a word is said about Alcibiades' military or diplomatic qualifications,[28] none about any political principles that may have prompted him, and even considerations of what was the most advantageous policy for Athens to follow at this juncture are given only second billing. "A temperament that brooked no competitor" (φρονήματι φιλονικῶν) is the mainspring of his actions. Like Cleon, he pursued a war policy that

27 Ibid. 43.1–2: κατὰ τοιαύτην δὴ διαφορὰν ὄντων τῶν Λακεδαιμονίων πρὸς τοὺς Ἀθηναίους, οἱ ἐν ταῖς Ἀθήναις αὖ βουλόμενοι λῦσαι τὰς σπονδὰς εὐθὺς ἐνέκειντο. ἦσαν δὲ ἄλλοι τε καὶ Ἀλκιβιάδης ὁ Κλεινίου, ἀνὴρ ἡλικίᾳ μὲν ἔτι τότε ὢν νέος ὡς ἐν ἄλλῃ πόλει, ἀξιώματι δὲ προγόνων τιμώμενος· ᾧ ἐδόκει μὲν καὶ ἄμεινον εἶναι πρὸς τοὺς Ἀργείους μᾶλλον χωρεῖν, οὐ μέντοι ἀλλὰ καὶ φρονήματι φιλονικῶν ἠναντιοῦτο, ὅτι Λακεδαιμόνιοι διὰ Νικίου καὶ Λάχητος ἔπραξαν τὰς σπονδάς, ἑαυτὸν κατά τε τὴν νεότητα ὑπεριδόντες καὶ κατὰ τὴν παλαιὰν προξενίαν ποτὲ οὖσαν οὐ τιμήσαντες, ἣν τοῦ πάππου ἀπειπόντος αὐτὸς τοὺς ἐκ τῆς νήσου αὐτῶν αἰχμαλώτους θεραπεύων διενοεῖτο ἀνανεώσασθαι.

28 Modern scholars have given widely divergent evaluations of Alcibiades' abilities, ranging from the unqualified admiration of M. F. McGregor, "The Genius of Alcibiades," *Phoenix* 19 (1965) 27–46, to the questioning of the influence Thucydides assigned to him in P. A Brunt, "Thucydides and Alcibiades," *REG* 65 (1952) 59–96, esp. 59–65, and to the challenge of Thucydides' judgment of Alcibiades and the almost complete devaluation of Alcibiades by E. F. Bloedow, *Alcibiades Reexamined*, Historia Einzelschrift 21 (Wiesbaden, 1973).

made Nicias his enemy; but unlike Cleon, he wanted to carry on the war not in the hope of wresting better conditions from Sparta by prolonged fighting but out of a young aristocrat's personal pique at having been cheated of the prestige he believed was due him despite his tender years.

Aristophanes' charges of bribery and greed notwithstanding, Cleon seems to have been genuinely concerned to implement a policy he regarded as good for his city. His horizon was limited by his background: as a businessman and industrialist he saw that Athens needed steady revenues to mount a major war effort against Sparta, and he pursued his financial policies with all the ruthlessness, relentlessness, and crudity with which nature had endowed him, oblivious of other values and often unaware of the political or diplomatic consequences of his proposals. For better or for worse, he contributed more than anyone before him to the full development of popular sovereignty in Athens. By his native oratorical and theatrical ability he managed to rally the masses to his support in the Assembly and in the jury courts. They trusted him because, unlike the members of the upper classes, they stood to lose nothing by his policies; they felt that they could control the magistrates without foregoing a day's pay, and they knew that Cleon would see to it that even delicate diplomatic negotiations would not be kept secret from them (Thuc. 4.22.1–2). He was one of them, and they were as suspicious as he was of anyone (especially young men from the upper classes) who projected an image of being smarter than the *nomoi*, whose unchanged preservation was an article of faith for Cleon.[29]

Alcibiades not only wished to seem smarter than the established *nomoi*, but wanted to be in fact superior to them. He had a reputation for *paranomia* in his personal conduct, and his womanizing had drawn the attention of comic poets perhaps even before his participation in the Potidaea campaign.[30] As if to contrast him with Cleon, Thucydides when introducing him singles out his youth and aristocratic origins. Cleon had long championed the old mainstays of the Athenian democracy, who filled the juries he kept so busy;[31] Alcibia-

---

29   Thuc. 3.37.4: τῶν τε νόμων σοφώτεροι βούλονται φαίνεσθαι; cf. also Ar. *Nub.* 1399–1400: ὡς ἡδὺ καινοῖς πράγμασιν καὶ δεξιοῖς ὁμιλεῖν / καὶ τῶν καθεστώτων νόμων ὑπερφρονεῖν δύνασθαι.

30   See above, pp. 116–18. Pherecrates, fr. 155, οὐκ ὢν ἀνὴρ γὰρ Ἀλκιβιάδης, ὡς δοκεῖ, / ἀνὴρ ἁπασῶν τῶν γυναικῶν ἐστι νῦν, is dated Edmonds before Alcibiades' twentieth birthday on the basis of its content; cf. also Eup. *Kolakes* fr. 158, of 421 B.C., and Com. Adesp. fr. 3–5, which refer to his seduction of Agis's wife in 415 B.C.

31   See pp. 208–12 and 231–32 above.

des would have been regarded as young ἐν ἄλλῃ πόλει: in any other city the fact that Alcibiades was just old enough to be elected to public office would have prevented him from becoming politically influential so quickly as he did. We are reminded of Athenagoras's rebuke to the young men of Syracuse for aspiring to high office contrary to the statutes (Thuc. 6.38.5). In Athens, however, youth was no obstacle, especially to an ambitious young man from an old aristocratic line. Alcibiades was an aristocrat, whereas Cleon belonged to the milieu of manufacturers, whom the old families despised; the younger man was distinguishing himself in the cavalry at Delium about the same time that Cleon's difficulties with the knights were providing Aristophanes with the subject of a comedy (*Eq.* 225–26, 730–31). Alcibiades' policies may have resembled Cleon's, but his motive was different; part of his resentment that Nicias and Laches had been chosen by the Spartans as intermediaries for the peace may have been provoked merely by his sense that they, too, were his social inferiors.

Unbounded personal ambition is also what Thucydides sees as Alcibiades' motive for opposing Nicias on the subject of the Sicilian campaign: "He wished to oppose Nicias not only because he had general political differences with him, but because Nicias had disparaged him, and especially because he wanted to be general. He hoped that thanks to him Sicily and Carthage as well would be captured and that success in this campaign would at the same time enhance his personal wealth and reputation."[32] Again, personal pique against Nicias, combined with a consuming ambition for personal glory, produces a war policy with objectives such as were attributed earlier to Hyperbolus only in comic fantasies (Ar. *Eq.* 1303; cf. 174). Not a trace of concern for the good of the state enters into Alcibiades' thinking; the state becomes a tool to be used or rejected as suits his purposes at any time. Unlike Cleon, who accomplished most of his purposes in the Council or at the *euthynai* of outgoing officials, Alcibiades operated almost exclusively in the Assembly. To gain prominence by destroying others in the courts was not his style; he preferred to outshine others by the grand scale on which he thought and acted. His extravagant living, his penchant for horses and the

32 Thuc. 6.15.2: ἐνῆγε δὲ προθυμότατα τὴν στρατείαν Ἀλκιβιάδης ὁ Κλεινίου, βουλόμενος τῷ τε Νικίᾳ ἐναντιοῦσθαι, ὤν καὶ ἐς τἆλλα διάφορος τὰ πολιτικὰ καὶ ὅτι αὐτοῦ διαβόλως ἐμνήσθη, καὶ μάλιστα στρατηγῆσαί τε ἐπιθυμῶν καὶ ἐλπίζων Σικελίαν τε δι' αὐτοῦ καὶ Καρχηδόνα λήψεσθαι καὶ τὰ ἴδια ἅμα εὐτυχήσας χρήμασί τε καὶ δόξῃ ὠφελήσειν.

victories he won with them, his personal beauty, and his intellectual brilliance are too well attested to require discussion. Only the Assembly supplied him a large enough audience to dazzle with his charisma, one before which to outmaneuvre his opponents and to get measures approved from which he stood most to gain. But that made him no more a believer in democracy or in democratic processes than Callicles. On that issue, Thucydides puts what seems a forthright statement into his mouth when, disgraced in Athens, he offers his services to the enemy. At the time of Mantinea, he explains, his support of democracy was merely due to his family's traditional aversion to tyrants. He tries to ingratiate himself with the Spartans by defining as *dēmos* anything opposed to despotic power; aversion to tyranny, he claims, has conferred upon his family προστασία τοῦ πλήθους, "leadership of the masses." Furthermore, democracy demands conformity, but his political leadership was characterized by the attempt to be more moderate than the radicals, whom he blames for his exile. Contrary to them,

We gave leadership to the people as a whole, because we thought it right to preserve the form of government under which our city had attained the peak of its greatness and freedom, the form we had inherited, though as intelligent people we realized what democracy is—I more than anyone, because I have more reason to revile it. However, nothing new can be said about what everyone agrees is madness, and to change it did not seem to us a safe course to take when you, our enemy, were standing at the gates. (Thuc. 6.89.3–6)

The Athenian democracy was for Alcibiades not an article of faith but a condition to be recognized in his political calculations, and the *dēmos* an instrument to be manipulated for furthering his political ambitions.

In his first political act in Thucydides he deceives the Spartan ambassadors and the Athenian Assembly at the same time in order to frustrate Nicias's policy of preferring Spartan friendship to an alliance with Argos.[33] The substantive merits of this preference and the arguments by which Alcibiades made the Spartans a party to his deception[34] are less germane to our present purposes than Alcibiades' methods: whereas Cleon in the summer of 425 B.C. believed that he could more easily effect a rejection of peace with Sparta by an open

33   Thuc. 5.45–46.3; cf. Plut. *Nic.* 10.4–8.
34   For a discussion of these questions, see Andrewes, *HCT* 4.51–52.

discussion before the Assembly (Thuc. 4.22.1–2), Alcibiades thought he would better serve his purposes by deceiving the Assembly. Cleon had indeed objected to a second debate about Mytilene, but we know of no instance in which he obstructed open democratic debate as Alcibiades did, and that primarily for the internal political reason of driving a wedge between the Spartans and Nicias.[35]

However inevitable renewed hostilities between Athens and Sparta after the Peace of Nicias appeared to Thucydides as he wrote his account of the period between 421 and 415 B.C., it will have been clear to the Athenians then living that Alcibiades' policy envisaged a resumption of hostilities with Sparta, whereas Nicias's aim was to preserve the hard-won peace at any cost short of dishonor. This emerges clearly from the sequel to Alcibiades' deception: although Nicias had been deceived along with the rest of the Athenians, he still insisted that efforts to maintain friendly relations with Sparta should continue unabated, and he managed to stall Alcibiades' aim by proposing that ambassadors, himself among them, be dispatched to Sparta to try to resolve differences that arose in implementing the peace. But when the embassy returned without having succeeded in separating the Spartans from the Boeotians, having obtained no more than the vague promise Nicias exacted that Sparta would abide by the terms of the peace, Nicias's stock fell in Athens (Thuc. 5.46): Alcibiades was elected general for 420/19 B.C., and on his initiative an alliance for one hundred years was concluded with Argos, Mantinea, and Elis.[36]

Alcibiades' political triumph over a seasoned senior public official who had already held at least six generalships by the time he was elected to his first can be explained by the contrast of the two personalities. Nicias' experience seemed dull and staid in contrast to Alcibiades' youth, dash, and color. Alcibiades was entering the political stage in a flash; Nicias had earned his spurs the hard way, serving with Pericles before getting a command of his own,[37] and not until the fifth year of the war did he rise to prominence, taking Minoa in the summer of 427 B.C. (Thuc. 3.51.1). The campaigns he conducted annually thereafter were successful, though his leadership seems to have been competent rather than inspiring. His only failure was inability to coerce Melos into becoming a member of the

---

35 Cf. Thuc. 3.37–38 with 5.45.3.
36 Plut. *Alc.* 15.1, *Nic.* 10.9, with Thuc. 5.46.5–47, 52.2.
37 Plut. *Nic.* 2.2: κἀκείνῳ συστρατηγῆσαι καὶ καθ' αὑτὸν ἄρξαι πολλάκις.

Athenian empire in the summer of 426 B.C. (3.91.1–3), though Nicias can hardly have won acclaim by willingly ceding his command at Pylos to a man with little military experience who succeeded where he had not (4.27.5–28.4). And yet, Thucydides is no doubt correct in describing him as the most successful military leader alive in Athens in 422/1 B.C. His appraisal of Nicias's motives for wanting to negotiate peace with Pleistoanax sounds equally correct: "While his record was still clean and his reputation intact, he wished to preserve his good fortune; he wanted a moment of rest from hardships for himself and for his fellow citizens; he wanted to leave his name to posterity as that of a man who had ended his days without endangering the state. He thought that he would attain this end by taking no risks and by entrusting his life to chance as little as possible, convinced that peace would afford a situation free from risks" (5.16.1). Similar motives are attributed to his preferring friendship with Sparta over alliance with Argos.[38] Thoughtful deliberation, cautious rather than aggressive, was less likely to spark imagination of a democratic Assembly than bold and imaginative schemes rationally and persuasively presented by a young man in a hurry.

The relations between Nicias and Alcibiades took an unexpected turn when Hyperbolus proposed, probably in 417/16 B.C., that the issue between Nicias's policy of peace and Alcibiades' policy of war be decided by ostracism.[39] We know too little about Hyperbolus to understand his motives. His social standing was, like Cleon's, based on industrial success, in his case as a manufacturer of lamps.[40] Like

---

38   Thuc. 5.46.1, where the phrase διασώσασθαι τὴν εὐπραγίαν echoes διασώσασθαι τὴν εὐτυχίαν of 16.1.

39   I do not propose here to reopen the discussion of the date of Hyperbolus's ostracism but will confine myself to a few observations and justification of my preference for the winter of 417/16 B.C. I agree with Hatzfeld 106–18 that the ostracism preceded Alcibiades' expedition to Argos, assigned by Thucydides to the summer of 416 (5.84.1 with *HCT* 4.155), but that it followed the alliance between Sparta, Argos, and Mantinea, which was accomplished by early spring 417 B.C. (see *HCT* 4.149, on Thuc. 5.81.2). However, whereas Hatzfeld (109) assumes early 417 B.C. for the ostracism, I am persuaded by the arguments of A. G. Woodhead, "I.G., I², 95, and the Ostracism of Hyperbolus," *Hesp.* 18 (1949) 78–83, that Hyperbolus's ostracism and exile cannot be earlier than the spring of 416 B.C.; and I believe that this date can be reconciled by inclusive counting with A. E. Raubitschek's interpretation of Theopompus *FGH* 115F96, "Theopompos on Hyperbolos," *Phoenix* 9 (1955) 122–26, which assigns six years to Hyperbolus's popular leadership after Cleon's death rather than to the duration of his exile. As Thucydides 5.82–83 shows, the situation in 417/16 B.C. was still fluid enough to put in question the success of the Argive democrats and the Spartan measures against them.

40   See p. 214 with n. 63 above.

Cleon, he had been politically most active before the jury courts.[41] Although he is said to have addressed the Assembly when still under age,[42] before Cleon's death his public service consisted only in performing the liturgy as a trierarch and in his appointment by lot as *hieromnēmōn*.[43] After Cleon's death he was probably a councilor in 421/0 B.C., when he proposed legislation reorganizing the celebration of the Hephaestia (*IG* I³ 82.5), and he may well have held the same office again four years later.[44] If we contrast this kind of public career with that of Alcibiades, who on the strength of his personality and aristocratic background burst into the limelight by privately negotiating with Sparta and Argos and by his subsequent election to a generalship as early as was legally feasible, it is clear that Hyperbolus was small fry, who would be outclassed as a popular leader as soon as Alcibiades would appear on the political scene.

We do not know what policy Hyperbolus favored before the battle of Mantinea in the summer of 418 B.C. But since the Athenian defeat there and the subsequent alliance between Sparta and Argos (Thuc. 5.76–81) had demonstrated the failure of both Nicias's policy of accommodation with Sparta and Alcibiades' policy of enlisting Argos on the Athenian side against Sparta, it may well have been at this point—that is, before the results of the democratic counterrevolution in Argos and Spartan reaction to it had become clear (5.82–83)—that Hyperbolus proposed an ostracism to determine which policy enjoyed popular support. Whether or not Plutarch (*Alc.* 13.4–8; *Nic.* 11.4) is right in asserting that Hyperbolus hoped to get rid of either Nicias or Alcibiades in order to have to cope with only one rival for political power, he will have had no difficulty in persuading the Athenian Assembly that only an ostracism could prevent the harm that could come to the state through the clash of two personalities as opposed in character and in policy as Nicias and Alcibiades.[45]

41 See Ar. *Ach.* 846–47 with schol; *Eq.* 1358–63; *Nub.* 874–76; *Vesp.* 1007, as cited above, Chap.5 n. 56.

42 Cratinus, fr. 262 and Eup. fr. 238 with F. Camon, "La Demagogia di Iperbolo," *Giornale Italiano di Filologia* 15 (1962) 364–74, esp. 364–67.

43 Eup. fr. 195, cf. fr. 192; Ar. *Thesm.* 837–45, with Davies, *APF* 517, and Camon, "Cariche" 49–51, 51–53; Ar. *Nub.* 623–25 with Dover, *Clouds* lxxx–xcviii.

44 *IG* I³ 85, dated by Woodhead ("I.G., I²,95" 78–83) to 417 B.C. It is possibly to this tenure of a seat in the Council that Plato Com. *Hyperbolus* frr. 166–67 refers.

45 The role Phaeax is alleged to have had in the ostracism remains a mystery. His involvement is recorded by Plutarch in *Alc.* 13.1–3 and 8, who in *Nic.* 11.10 attributes this tradition to Theophrastus; moreover, a speech *Against Alcibiades*, purporting to have been delivered on the occasion of this ostracism but probably a

However, he had failed to calculate that dislike of him would prove a bond strong enough between Nicias and Alcibiades for them to put aside their political differences. That Alcibiades took the initiative in their negotiations (Plut. *Alc*. 13.7) shows that he had more to fear from an *ostrakophoria* and that he was more imaginative than Nicias in unscrupulously manipulating the instruments of the Athenian democracy for his own ends. Nicias will have been more than willing to listen to his overtures, since his humiliation at Sparta had left him apprehensive of his fellow citizens' feelings toward him (Thuc. 5.46.5). The desired result was achieved: Hyperbolus became the victim of the ostracism he had proposed.[46] But the crucial political question for which ostracism had been devised, namely, which of two contradictory and mutually exclusive views should be adopted as the policy of the state, remained unresolved. The institution of ostracism did not survive its manipulation for personal political ends; it was never again used to gauge public sentiment about alternative policies.

The immediate political success of this maneuver is shown by Nicias's and Alcibiades' reelection as generals for 416/15 B.C. soon after Hyperbolus had been ostracized.[47] But in external politics,

---

fourth-century forgery that found its way into the works of Andocides, was ascribed to Phaeax already in antiquity. A possible explanation is that Phaeax received in the ostracism a sufficient share of the scatter vote to have been remembered in an ancient tradition.

46　Plut. *Nic*. 11.5 suggests that Nicias and Alcibiades pooled their *staseis* to drive Hyperbolus into exile. Those *staseis* are generally assumed to be identical in structure with the ἑταιρία in which according to Plut. *Alc*. 13.8 the followers of Phaeax were organized. These groups are mentioned together with *synōmotai* in [Andoc.] 4.4: see Calhoun, *Clubs* 136–40, esp. 137–38; Hatzfeld 110–18; Sartori, *Eterie* 79–83. If this is correct, it would constitute the earliest evidence for the existence of the *hetaireiai*, which were to play a prominent part in the oligarchical revolutions of 411 and 404 B.C.: see Thuc. 8.54.4, 65.2; Arist. *Ath.Pol*. 34.3. However, there is neither evidence nor reason to assume that the *staseis* of Nicias and Alcibiades were tightly knit organizations. They are more likely to have been coteries of followers, whose nuclei will have consisted of personal friends and boon companions but will also have included a wider circle of like-minded citizens whose political support could be counted on; among these it would be let known that Nicias and Alcibiades were in and Hyperbolus out. I find it difficult to accept the suggestion of B. Baldwin, "Notes on Hyperbolus," *Acta Classica* 14 (1971) 151–56, esp. 154, that Hyperbolus was ostracized for proposing an expedition against Carthage, since that proposal was made, if at all, before 424 B.C.; see Ar. *Eq*. 1302–4.

47　The reelection can be inferred from Thuc. 6.8.2; that both were generals in 417/16 B.C. is shown id. 5.83.4, and 84.1, the latter with Diod. 12.81.2 and Andrewes, *HCT* 4.155.

Hyperbolus's ostracism led to an eclipse of Nicias's policy and a victory for Alcibiades': even before the beginning of their new term two major offensives were launched, designed to strengthen the Athenians' hand in anticipation of eventually resuming direct hostilities with Sparta. Alcibiades' immediate involvement is attested only for the intervention in Argos, an attempt to secure the democracy by banishing three hundred Spartan sympathizers to islands controlled by Athens (Thuc. 5.84.1; Diod. 12.81.2–3). A more momentous step followed hard upon that intervention—the attack on Melos, immortalized by Thucydides.

MELOS: THE POLITICS OF *NOMOS-PHYSIS*

Thucydides' account is our most extensive and reliable document for the Melian expedition, but it is peculiar in a number of ways. For one thing, whereas its design and execution breathe the spirit of the anti-Spartan warmongering characteristic of Alcibiades at this time, Thucydides does not associate him with the expedition at all, suppressing even what scant information about its end we gather from other sources, namely, that Alcibiades spoke in favor of the motion to have all male Melians put to death and all women and children sold as slaves ([Andoc.] 4.22; Plut. *Alc.* 16.6). Even more strangely, Thucydides leaves the attack almost completely unmotivated, preferring to make it a showpiece of the problems of imperialism.[48] It was more than merely an arbitrary exercise of imperialist tyranny, as is clearly indicated by Thucydides' own report that six Chian and two Lesbian ships joined the Athenian fleet of thirty and that the allies, particularly the islanders among them, supplied more hoplites to the enterprise than did the Athenians.[49] Therefore, the allies must have had solid reasons of their own to join the expedition, and the Athenian leadership will have had good

48 On this point, see especially A. Andrewes, "The Melian Dialogue and Perikles' Last Speech," *PCPS* 186, n.s. 6 (1960) 1–10. The only hint at an explanation is the elliptical statement of Thuc. 5.84.2, ἔπειτα ὡς αὐτοὺς ἠνάγκαζον οἱ Ἀθηναῖοι δῃοῦντες τὴν γῆν, ἐς πόλεμον φανερὸν κατέστησαν, which is likely to refer to Melos's relations with Athens in the wake of Nicias's attack in 426 B.C. but still leaves the present expedition unmotivated; see Andrewes, *HCT* 4.156–57.

49 Thuc. 5.84.1, where the Athenian hoplite contingent consists of 1,200 men; the allies and islanders contributed 1,500. However, the addition of 300 archers and 20 mounted archers makes the combined Athenian force slightly larger than that of the allies.

reasons to target Melos in implementing an aggressive policy against the Peloponnesians. What these reasons may have been is impossible to determine with any assurance;[50] but Nicias, his peace policy notwithstanding, may have acquiesced in the plan—perhaps as a price exacted by Alcibiades for joining forces with him against Hyperbolus—because Nicias's failure to reduce Melos in 426 B.C. was the one blotch on his military record.[51]

The interest of the Melian expedition and its relevance to our discussion of Alcibiades lie in the dialogue between Athenian and Melian representatives that Thucydides reports in direct speech. He remarks in his narrative that such a dialogue did take place before the commencement of hostilities (5.84.3), and this is not open to doubt. Similarly there is no reason to reject Thucydides' assertion (ibid.) that the meeting was held *in camera* at the Melians' insistence and despite the Athenians' desire to address the assembled people. Nor are there good grounds to concur with later scholars (the first among them being Dionysius of Halicarnassus) who doubt that the Melian Dialogue reflects the issues discussed on that occasion.[52] It is hard to believe that so passionately factual and accurate an author as Thucydides should in this instance have abandoned his professed principle of

50　Thuc. 2.9.4 names Melos and Thera as the only Cycladic islands that did not fight on the Athenian side in the Peloponnesian War, and an Athenian attempt under Nicias, reported at 3.91.1–3, to coerce Melos into the Athenian alliance in the summer of 426 B.C. was unsuccessful. The fact that a year later Melos was assessed a tribute of fifteen talents (ML, no. 69.65), which was apparently never paid, may be explained by the assumption that the list was drafted at a time when there were still hopes and expectations that the subjugation was imminent. Not much can be made of a Melian contribution of twenty silver mnai to a Spartan war chest early in the Peloponnesian War, see ML, no. 67, side, lines 1–7. The arguments of M. Treu ("Athen und Melos und der Melierdialog des Thukydides," *Hist.* 2 [1953–54] 253–73, and "Athen und Karthago und die thukydideische Darstellung," ibid. 3 [1954–55] 58–59) and of A. E. Raubitschek ("War Melos tributpflichtig?" ibid. 12 [1963] 78–83) that Melos was liable to pay tribute before 416 B.C. have been laid to rest by W. Eberhardt ("Der Melierdialog und die Inschriften ATL A9 und IG I²97 +," ibid. 8 [1959] 284–314), Andrewes (*HCT* 4.156), and E. Buchner ("Die Aristophanes-Scholien und die Frage der Tributpflicht von Melos," *Chiron* 4 [1974] 91–99).

51　The statement by the scholl. on Ar. *Av.* 186 and 363 that Nicias reduced the Melians by starving them into submission cannot be correct, as has been shown by Andrewes, *HCT* 4.190, and by Buchner, "Aristophanes-Scholien" 92–94.

52　Dion. Hal. *Thuc.* 41.395–96 (Usener-Radermacher). Recent discussions: H. L. Hudson-Williams, "Conventional Forms of Debate and the Melian Dialogue," *AJP* 71 (1950) 156–69, esp. 167–68; J. de Romilly, *Thucydides and Athenian Imperialism*², tr. P. Thody (Oxford, 1963) 273–74; and H. D. Westlake, *Individuals in Thucydides* (Cambridge, 1968) 317 n. 1; cf. id. "Thucydides and the Uneasy Peace—A Study in Political Incompetence," *CQ*, n.s., 21 (1971) 315–25, esp. 316 n. 2.

reporting in speeches "what was demanded by each given situation, keeping as close as possible to the general thrust of what was actually said" (1.22.1) and have passed off his own philosophical speculations as a substantively true account of the main issues the Athenians and Melians discussed.[53] This does not mean, of course, that Thucydides did not exploit the situation to emphasize what he considered noteworthy about imperialism; we need not deny that his powerful mind filtered and interpreted events and structured his text accordingly. It merely means that Thucydides would not have so used the Melian Dialogue if the stances and arguments on either side had no basis in history.

The fact that the meeting was held *in camera* makes the question who Thucydides' informants may have been particularly pertinent, even if it cannot be answered except in general terms. The sophistic cast of the arguments, which has long been recognized,[54] suggests that the Athenian representatives belonged to the social milieu that had been schooled by the sophists. Comparing their arguments with those of the Cleon-Diodotus debate, one sees that the imperialism Cleon and other demagogues had pursued in the Archidamian War had now been appropriated by the new, aristocratic generation of intellectuals, who had aligned themselves with the aggressive policy of Alcibiades.

The problem of how what is morally right (τὸ δίκαιον) is to be measured against the public interest (τὸ ξυμφέρον) dominates both the debate over the treatment to be meted out to the Mytileneans and the argument between Melians and Athenians; the *nomos-physis* polarity is brought into both discussions, as is the role of necessity (ἀνάγκη) in human affairs.[55] To show that these terms formed part of

53 Cf. J. A. Grant, "A Note on the Tone of Greek Diplomacy," *CQ*, n.s., 15 (1965) 261–66, esp. 266 n. 2; M. Amit, "The Melian Dialogue and History," *Athenaeum*, n.s., 46 (1968) 216–35, esp. 225–26; D. Gillis, "Murder on Melos," *Rend.Ist.Lomb.* 112 (1978) 185–211, esp. 194–96. On the problematic points, see the sane observations of Andrewes, *HCT* 4.182–88.

54 For the sophistic antecedents of the dialogue, see Hudson-Williams, "Forms"; for sophistic features in its structure, see C. W. Macleod, "Form and Meaning in the Melian Dialogue," *Hist.* 23 (1974) 385–400, esp. 387–96.

55 The following is an incomplete list of relevant passages in Thucydides. τὸ δίκαιον and related terms: Cleon at 3.38.1, 39.1, 3, 6, 40.3,4; Diodotus at 3.44.1, 4, 47.5; Melians at 5.86, 90, 104; Athenians at 5.89, 105.4, 107. τὸ ξυμφέρον, ὠφέλιμον, and related terms: Cleon at 3.37.3, 38.1, 40.2, 4; Diodotus at 3.44.2, 3, 47.5; Melians at 5.90, 92, 98, 106; Athenians at 5.91.2, 105.4, 107. νόμος and νόμιμα: Cleon at 3.37.3, 4; Diodotus at 3.45.3, 7, 46.4; Athenians at 5.105.2, 4. φύσις and related

the stock-in-trade of sophistic teaching, it is necessary to refer only to the argument between Right and Wrong in Aristophanes' *Clouds* (esp. 1036–45 and 1068–82). But there are telling differences between the two debates in Thucydides' account. In the Mytilenean debate, Cleon advocates a brutal deployment of imperial power on the basis of arguments from *nomos* and what is right, and in opposition Diodotus argues from *physis* and the public interest. For Cleon a city is strong only so long as its laws remain unchanged, and these laws, represented by the Assembly's earlier decision, demand as both right (δίκαια) and in the public interest a harsh punishment of the wrong (ἀδικία) done by the Mytileneans.[56] For Diodotus no law is adequate to inhibit the fallibility of human nature (ἀνθρωπεία φύσις) or to halt human nature once it has embarked upon its course; the issue is not whether the Mytileneans were right or wrong but what policy best serves the public interest, and fearsome laws are less in the public interest than is cultivating the allegiance of the common people in allied states in order to quash incipient revolts.[57] In the Melian Dialogue, however, ruthless exercise of imperial power is entirely predicated on *physis*, a concrete political application of Democritus's belief that "ruling belongs by nature to the stronger."[58] The aim is not so much to preserve the empire as to extend it. From the beginning the Athenians exclude arguments from justice, because "what is right is decided in human reckoning when the pressure that can be exerted by the two sides is equal, but what is possible is achieved by those who have superior power and is acquiesced in by the weak."[59] Like Diodotus, the Athenians combine arguments from public interest with arguments from *physis* (Thuc. 5.91.2). Their perspective on *physis*, however, is radically different from Diodotus's. For he envisaged the *physis* of the allies as making their attempts at revolt inevitable, but the Athenians at

---

terms: Cleon at 3.39.5; Diodotus at 3.45.3, 7; Athenians at 5.103, 105.2. ἀνάγκη and related terms: Cleon at 3.39.2, 7, 40.3, 6; Diodotus at 3.45.4; Athenians at 5.89, 99, 105.2; Melians at 5.104.

56   Thuc. 3.37.3; 38.1; 39.1, 3, 6; 40.4.
57   Ibid. 44.1, 2, 3, 4; 45.3, 7; 47.5.
58   Democritus 68B267 DK[6]: φύσει τὸ ἄρχειν οἰκήιον τῷ κρέσσονι.
59   Thuc. 5.89: δίκαια μὲν ἐν τῷ ἀνθρωπείῳ λόγῳ ἀπὸ τῆς ἴσης ἀνάγκης κρίνεται, δυνατὰ δὲ οἱ προύχοντες πράσσουσι καὶ οἱ ἀσθενεῖς ξυγχωροῦσιν. Note how much farther this statement goes than an analogous statement on pity by Cleon at 3.40.3: ἔλεός τε γὰρ πρὸς τοὺς ὁμοίους δίκαιος ἀντιδίδοσθαι, καὶ μὴ πρὸς τοὺς οὔτ᾽ ἀντοικτιοῦντας ἐξ ἀνάγκης τε καθεστῶτας αἰεὶ πολεμίους.

Melos think only of the *physis* of the imperial power: nothing can inhibit it. This harks back to the statement of the Athenian ambassadors at Sparta before the outbreak of the Peloponnesian War, ascribing the growth of the Athenian empire to the natural human impulse toward dominion over others.[60]

Though it is the most frequently quoted part of the Melian Dialogue, the central passage in which these views on *physis* are expressed remains worth quoting because it gives imperialism a theological dimension not in evidence in any earlier discussion in Thucydides. In response to the Melians' express faith that divine fortune will not favor the Athenians over them, since they are god-fearing people arrayed against unjust attackers (5.104), the Athenians reply:

When it comes to divine benevolence we do not believe that the event will have us fall short of it. For neither our judgments nor our actions are beyond the pale of what humans believe about the divine and of what they want of one another. In the case of the gods we hold it as an opinion and in the case of men as a certainty that in all circumstances a constraint of nature prompts them to exercise dominion wherever they have control. We did not establish this as a law and we were not the first to use it once it had been enacted; we took it over as a present reality and will leave it behind as a reality forever after: we are using it in the knowledge that you as well as anyone else who had accumulated as much power as we have would do the same. Thus, as regards the divinity, probability does not make us fear that we shall be worse off than you.[61]

The view that this passage anticipates Callicles' might-makes-right doctrine in Plato's *Gorgias* (483c–484c) has long been proved wrong.[62] What the Melian Dialogue asserts is that the drive to rule is grounded in nature and that its growth is inevitable (ὑπὸ φύσεως ἀναγκαίας); when the Athenians proceed to call this a "law" (*nomos*) they do so with tongue in cheek, obviously realizing that an inevita-

---

60   Id. 1.76.3: χρησάμενοι τῇ ἀνθρωπείᾳ φύσει ὥστε ἑτέρων ἄρχειν.

61   Id. 5.105.1–3: τῆς μὲν τοίνυν πρὸς τὸ θεῖον εὐμενείας οὐδ' ἡμεῖς οἰόμεθα λελείψεσθαι· οὐδὲν γὰρ ἔξω τῆς ἀνθρωπείας τῶν μὲν ἐς τὸ θεῖον νομίσεως, τῶν δ' ἐς σφᾶς αὐτοὺς βουλήσεως δικαιοῦμεν ἢ πράσσομεν. ἡγούμεθα γὰρ τό τε θεῖον δόξῃ τὸ ἀνθρώπειόν τε σαφῶς διὰ παντὸς ὑπὸ φύσεως ἀναγκαίας, οὗ ἂν κρατῇ, ἄρχειν· καὶ ἡμεῖς οὔτε θέντες τὸν νόμον οὔτε κειμένῳ πρῶτοι χρησάμενοι, ὄντα δὲ παραλαβόντες καὶ ἐσόμενον ἐς αἰεὶ καταλείψοντες χρώμεθα αὐτῷ, εἰδότες καὶ ὑμᾶς ἂν καὶ ἄλλους ἐν τῇ αὐτῇ δυνάμει ἡμῖν γενομένους δρῶντας ἂν ταὐτό. καὶ πρὸς μὲν τὸ θεῖον οὕτως ἐκ τοῦ εἰκότος οὐ φοβούμεθα ἐλασσώσεσθαι.

62   Most cogently by de Ste. Croix, *OPW* 14–15 with n. 30.

ble fact of nature is not the product of human legislation. In the Mytilene debate, Diodotus ventures a sophistic contrast of *nomos* and *physis* in his argument that the "human nature" (*anthrōpeia physis*) causing an allied state to defect cannot be suppressed by legislation (Thuc. 3.45.7). The Athenians at Melos recast the *nomos-physis* dichotomy to make human *nomoi* look futile and ridiculous when faced with the natural impulse to assert superior power.

One may further observe how deeply the Athenian arguments at Melos were steeped in sophistic teaching. The epistemological difference between opinion (δόξῃ) and certain belief (ἡγούμεθα σαφῶς) is used to make the human intellect a more reliable guide to action than belief in the divine. The gods, so the Athenians suppose, are no less constrained than men are to follow the dictates of *physis*. There is no evidence of atheism here, but the passage is suffused with an anthropocentric agnosticism similar to what we encountered among the *atheoi*, especially in the teachings of men such as Protagoras and Prodicus.[63] Therefore, if we are correct in believing that the Melian Dialogue is based in tone and substance on arguments the Athenians and Melians used in their conference before hostile actions were taken, we may infer that the Athenian ambassadors had sat at the feet of the sophists, that they were members of the upper class who had been young in the 420s and had sufficient wealth to pay high fees for their instruction. Thucydides does not name them, but if he shared their social standing and educational background, one of the Athenian participants may have been his informant—perhaps even Alcibiades himself, whose position as general at the time will have made him directly or indirectly privy to the proceedings.[64]

This conjecture gains credibility if we look at the generals in charge of the Melian campaign. We know that both Cleomedes son of Lycomedes and Teisias son of Teisimachus belonged to old and wealthy Athenian families.[65] Both are likely to have been young in 416 B.C.: Cleomedes' father was probably the Lycomedes who died in battle about 424 B.C.;[66] Teisias was about the same age as Alcibia-

63   See above, pp. 274–90, esp. 274 and 277–79.
64   For Alcibiades as one of Thucydides' informants, see Brunt, "Thucydides," esp. 65–81.
65   Thuc. 5.84.3; ML, no. 77.29–30, 32. It is likely that both were *pentakosiomedimnoi*: it is possible that Cleomedes' uncle Archestratus was *tamias* of Athena in 429/8 B.C. (*IG* I³ 297.13, 322.36); cf. Davies, *APF* 346. Teisias's father had held the same position in 444/3 B.C. (*IG* I³ 455.15–16).
66   *IG* I² 949.14 with Davies, *APF* 347.

des, perhaps a little younger. Just before the Olympic Games of 416 B.C., that is, about the time the Melian expedition began,[67] Alcibiades purchased Argive horses in Teisias's name. Since Thucydides dates the Argive expedition immediately before the Melian campaign, Alcibiades probably bought the horses during this stay in Argos; the Olympic Games at which he gave out the horses as his own were probably held in July, when Teisias was already busy with the operations before Melos.

A taste for expensive horses and the wealth to satisfy it was not the only characteristic Teisias shared with his friend Alcibiades. Teisias was married to the sister of Charicles, who was active as a councilor and investigator (*zētētēs*) against the suspected oligarchs of 415 B.C., was exiled after the fall of the Four Hundred, and later became one of the Thirty Tyrants.[68] Especially in view of this marriage connection, Teisias's service as councilor under the Thirty (Isoc. 16.43) indicates in him the same unprincipled, opportunistic "realism" that characterizes Alcibiades, which points in both their cases to sophistic training. Teisias's assignment as one of the generals against Melos thus strongly suggests Alcibiades' influence behind the scenes, and it may ironically have given Alcibiades the opportunity to cheat his friend out of an Olympic victory with his Argive horses. At the same time, the probability that Teisias at least had a hand in selecting the ambassadors sent to Melos, if he was not himself one of them, explains the amoral and highly intellectualized justification of imperialism that we find in the Melian Dialogue.

Any apprehensions Nicias may have had about the Melian campaign would have been allayed by the appointment of Cleomedes as Teisias's colleague: his roots were in an old Athenian family distinguished by loyal service to the Athenian democracy. He was

67 For the details, see Davies, *APF* 501–3. Briefly, we know from Isoc. 16.1 and 49 that Alcibiades was alleged to have entered in his own name at the Olympic Games of 416 B.C. a team of horses he had purchased from the city of Argos in Teisias's behalf. The accounts of the same event in [Andoc.] 4.26–27, Diod. 13.74.3, and Plut. *Alc.* 12.3 name Diomedes (and not Teisias) as the defrauded person. The ingenious conjecture of R. Münsterberg, "Zum Rennstallprocess des Alkibiades (Isokrates περὶ τοῦ ζεύγους)," in *Festschrift Theodor Gomperz* (Vienna, 1902) 298–99, has resolved the discrepancy by reference to the tradition that the horses owned by the people of Argos were direct descendants of the mares that Heracles brought from Diomedes to Eurystheus (Diod. 4.15.3–4): the genitive of provenance "of Diomedes" was misinterpreted at some point in the tradition as a genitive of the possessor, and the true owner was, accordingly, Teisias.

68 Isoc. 16.42 with Davies, *APF* 502–3, and MacDowell, *Andokides* 87.

probably the grandson of one of the trierarchs at Artemisium (Hdt. 8.11.2) and possibly a nephew of the Archestratus who was an associate of Ephialtes, a general at Potidaea in 433/2 B.C., and a treasurer of Athena in 429/8 B.C.;[69] he may have been the cousin of Chaereas son of Archestratus, who, on service with the *Paralus*, was a democratic loyalist in 412/11 B.C. and commanded land forces at Cyzicus in 410 B.C.[70] Though such family associations would not prove that Cleomedes' politics were democratic, they would at least suggest so, and as well that he was appointed for some of the same reasons Nicias was chosen along with Alcibiades to lead the Sicilian expedition. Cleomedes' appointment would thus have gone some way in making Nicias acquiesce in the campaign against Melos. Nevertheless, in planning as in execution, the Melian expedition represents a victory of the policy advocated by enlightened young aristocrats over the peace policy of an older generation of patriotic democrats.

SICILY: THE *PERIPETEIA* OF POPULAR SOVEREIGNTY

"A contest of young warmongers against elderly peacemakers":[71] so Plutarch describes the political situation in Athens in 416 B.C., which prompted Hyperbolus's call for an ostracism. It is even more applicable to the situation a year later, when Egesta's appeal for help against Selinus reawakened the Athenians' desire to conquer Sicily: for the first time the polarizations that had developed since the death of Pericles threatened to split the state in two.

We shall never know exactly what prompted the Athenians at this time to use the pretext of their alliance with Egesta to further Alcibiades' expansionist designs. When that alliance was contracted is uncertain. The earlier of the proposed dates, 458/7 or, less probably, 454/3 B.C., is epigraphically likely but cannot provide a historical context;[72] the later date, 421/0 or, more probably, 427/6–

---

69   Arist. *Ath.Pol.* 35.2; Thuc. 1.57.6; *IG* I³ 297.13, 322.36; ML, no. 52.70; all with Davies, *APF* 346–47.

70   Thuc. 8.74.1, 86.3; Diod. 13.49.6, 50.7, 51.2, with Davies, *APF* 346–47.

71   Plut. *Nic.* 11.3: ὡς δ' ἁπλῶς εἰπεῖν, νέων ἦν καὶ πολεμοποιῶν ἅμιλλα πρὸς εἰρηνοποιοὺς καὶ πρεσβυτέρους.

72   *IG* I³ 11.1–2 with ML, no. 37 and pp. 80–82, and Bengston, *SVA*² 2.41–42, both with bibliography. Cf. also B. D. Meritt and H. T. Wade-Gery, "The Dating of Documents to the Mid-Fifth Century,"Part 1, *JHS* 82 (1962) 67–74, and Part 2, ibid. 83 (1963) 100–117; and R. Meiggs, "The Dating of Fifth-Century Attic Inscriptions," ibid. 86 (1966) 86–98.

426/5 B.C., though unsatisfactory on epigraphical grounds, dovetails well with other information we have on Athenian involvement in Sicily in the 420s and provides a better historical explanation for Egesta's appeal to Athens in 415 B.C.[73]

Shortly before the outbreak of the Peloponnesian War, in 433/2 B.C., the Athenians renewed alliances with Rhegium and Leontini originally concluded eleven years earlier to protect the newly founded colony of Thurii.[74] No doubt they did this in order to have Western allies capable of preventing the Syracusans from supplying their Dorian kinsmen in the Peloponnese with grain, troops, and military supplies in case of war.[75] The fact that the renewal of both treaties was moved by Callias, presumably the son of Calliades, shows that these apprehensions were shared by the upper-class intelligentsia: Callias's cultural ties to the West are attested by the instruction he received around 450 B.C. from Zeno of Elea, the pupil of Parmenides, for which he paid one hundred minas.[76] He doubtless was among the intellectuals who about this time opened their doors to Protagoras and other sophists.

Relations with Sicily took a new turn when, in the late summer of 427 B.C., Leontini invoked the alliance of 433/2 B.C. to request Athenian help against Syracuse. Athenian manpower and material strength had been at that time depleted by the recent reduction of

---

73 The date 418/17 B.C. was first advocated by H. B. Mattingly, "The Growth of Athenian Imperialism," *Hist.* 12 (1963) 257–73, esp. 267–69, with arguments that won the support of J. D. Smart, "Athens and Egesta," *JHS* 92 (1972) 128–46; and T. E. Wick, "A Note on the Date of the Athenian-Egestan Alliance," ibid. 95 (1975) 186–90, and "Athens' Alliances with Rhegion and Leontinoi," *Hist.* 25 (1976) 288–304, esp. 288 with nn. 1–6, and "The Date of the Athenian-Egestan Alliance," *CP* 76 (1981) 118–21. Mattingly himself, however, opted for 421/0 B.C. in "Athens and the Western Greeks: c. 500–413 B.C.," in *Atti del I Convegno del Centro Internazionale di Studi Numismatici*, AIIN Supplement 12–14 (Rome, 1969) 201–21, esp. 205 n. 7 and 213–18, with arguments stronger on the historical (pp. 212–13) than on the epigraphical side. A. S. Henry, "The Dating of Fifth-Century Attic Inscriptions," *CSCA* 11 (1979) 75–108, esp. 101–2, regards the epigraphical evidence as inconclusive. D. W. Madsen and M. F. McGregor, "Thucydides and Egesta," *Phoenix* 33 (1979) 233–38, have plausibly interpreted Thuc. 6.6.2 as indicating that an old alliance of 458/7 was renewed by Laches between 427/6 and 426/5 B.C.

74 ML, nos. 63 and 64 with commentary; D. M. Lewis, "The Treaties with Leontini and Rhegion," *ZPE* 22 (1976) 223–25; Wick, "Alliances" 290–98.

75 See Westlake, "Aims" 394–96 (= *Essays* 113–16); and Wick, "Alliances" 298–302. For similar reasons, a defensive alliance was concluded with Corcyra in that same year (Thuc. 1.36.2, 44.3). About the same time the Lacedaemonians concluded an alliance with the Dorian cities of Sicily (Thuc. 3.86.2).

76 For the identity of the Callias of Pl. *Alc. I* 119a with the proposer of the alliances, see ML, p. 173; cf. also Guthrie, *HGP* 2.1–2, 80–81.

Mytilene and by the plague (which, though now in abeyance, was to break out again shortly after the first twenty ships had left for Sicily).[77] Nevertheless, Athens answered its ally's call for help. That response was prompted, according to Thucydides, not only by the conventional pretext of helping their Ionian kinsmen, who were embroiled with a Dorian coalition headed by Syracuse,[78] or by the need, present already in 433/2 B.C., to prevent grain shipments from Sicily to the Peloponnesians,[79] but also by the desire to explore the possibility of gaining control over Sicily.[80] Thucydides considered this the Athenians' strongest motive even as early as 427 B.C., as is shown by his having Hermocrates later identify it as the primary Athenian aim in Sicily (4.60.1). The initial dispatch of only twenty ships under the command of Laches and Charoeades may seem to disprove such a motive; but the reinforcement of forty additional ships sent a year later under the command of Pythodorus, Sophocles, and Eurymedon indicates that the Athenians envisaged a major operation, as does also the severe treatment to which these three generals were subjected at their *euthyna* in 424 B.C. for failure to accomplish their mission.[81]

There are reasons to believe that a venture into the West enjoyed wide support in Athens at this time. The upper-class intelligentsia will have been inclined to respond favorably to Leontini's appeal because it was presented by Gorgias (Pl. *Hp.Ma.* 282b; Diod. 12.53.2–5), and the Athenians' choice of Pythodorus to replace Laches demonstrates their intentions were serious. Like Callias son

---

77 Thuc. 3.86.1–4, 87.1–3 with Westlake, "Aims" 389 (= *Essays* 105–6).

78 Ibid. 86.4: τῆς μὲν οἰκειότητος προφάσει. That οἰκειότης here refers to kinship has never been questioned, even though the noun is not used elsewhere by Thucydides as a synonym of ξυγγένεια. All Dorian cities except Camarina fought as allies of Syracuse, and all the colonies of Ionian Chalcis, including Rhegium on the Italian mainland κατὰ τὸ ξυγγενές, fought on Leontini's side; see ibid. 86.2.

79 Westlake, "Aims" 390–91 (= *Essays* 107–8). Although the Spartans had commissioned the construction of a fleet of five hundred ships and had ordered their Italian and Sicilian allies to levy a war chest at the outbreak of the Peloponnesian War (Thuc. 2.7.2), Syracuse—and perhaps some other Dorian cities as well—seems still to have traded with Athens as late as 425 B.C.; see Hermippus, fr. 63, esp. line 9 with Edmonds's comments. T. E. Wick, "Megara, Athens, and the West in the Archidamian War: A Study in Thucydides," *Hist.* 28 (1979) 1–14, esp. 6–9, tries to relate this argument somewhat too exclusively to Athens's blockade of Megara.

80 Thuc. 3.86.4: πρόπειράν τε ποιούμενοι εἰ σφίσι δυνατὰ εἴη τὰ ἐν τῇ Σικελίᾳ πράγματα ὑποχείρια γενέσθαι. Whether the control envisaged implied conquest we cannot tell, see Wick, "Megara" 7 with n. 16.

81 Id. 3.86.1, 115.2, 4–6; 4.2.2, and 65.3 with Philochorus *FGH* 328F127 and pp. 64–65 with n. 248 (Case 6) above.

of Calliades, Pythodorus had strong ties to the West; he had been a pupil and a host of Zeno of Elea some decades earlier.[82] The harassment to which Cleon subjected Laches at his *euthyna* and the severity of the penalties imposed on Pythodorus, Sophocles, and Eurymedon for having acquiesced in the settlement of Gela suggest that advocates of the war welcomed an expansionist campaign in Sicily.[83] Hermocrates' disposition of affairs at Gela only stalled Athenian aspirations in the West (Thuc. 4.58–65). Two years later we find the Athenians eager to organize a new coalition against Syracuse; they had found an opportunity in internal strife in Leontini, which had left the *dēmos* in control of two sections of the city and had caused the upper classes to take refuge with the Syracusans. It may be significant that the Athenian mission was entrusted to Phaeax, a member of the aristocratic intelligentsia, whose rhetorical prowess indicates a sophistic education. Phaeax was initially successful at Camarina and Acragas but was rebuffed at Gela, and he returned to Athens. He had accomplished little except to encourage the remaining Leontinians to keep up their resistance to Syracuse.[84]

In Thucydides' view, Egesta's appeal for help against Selinus in 416/15 B.C. merely served to reawaken and reinforce the imperialist spirit he saw in Athens as early as 426 B.C.: he prefaces both his statement of Athenian aims and his account of the embassy from Egesta with the remark that the Athenians "wanted to sail again to Sicily with a larger force than they had done under Laches and Eurymedon to conquer it if they could" (6.1.1). In basing their appeal on an alliance with Athens concluded under Laches, which will have reaffirmed a treaty of the 450s, the Egestans remind the Athenians that their inclination to expand into Sicily was already manifest in the 420s (6.2). Thucydides has no doubt what objectives the Athenians had: "The truest explanation of their aims was to rule the whole of Sicily, but at the same time they wished to project an image of coming to the aid of their kindred and of the allies they had won."[85]

---

82 Pl. *Prm*. 126c, 127a–d; *Alc*. I 119a. Whether any significance is to be attached to Pythodorus's relation with the Aristoteles who was to become a member of the Thirty (*Prm*. 127d) or to the probable identity of Sophocles with the later member of the Thirty (Xen. *Hell*. 2.3.2 with Gomme, *HCT* 2.431) remains uncertain.

83 See above, p. 212 and n. 59. Cf. Westlake, "Aims" 399–402 (= *Essays* 118–22).

84 Thuc. 5.4–5. On Phaeax see p. 233 above.

85 Id. 6.6.1: ἐφιέμενοι μὲν τῇ ἀληθεστάτῃ προφάσει τῆς πάσης ἄρξαι, βοηθεῖν δὲ ἅμα εὐπρεπῶς βουλόμενοι τοῖς ἑαυτῶν ξυγγενέσι καὶ τοῖς προσγεγενημένοις ξυμμάχοις. On text and sense, see Dover, *HCT* 4.220.

Thucydides corroborates this motive by inserting the "truest explanation" into the subsequent speeches of Nicias and Alcibiades and by attributing a like suspicion to Hermocrates.[86]

Egesta's request will have come as a godsend to Alcibiades; it offered him an opportunity for large-scale conquest. Though recognizing this ambition (6.15.2), Thucydides nevertheless minimizes Alcibiades' influence on the final decision by stressing that there was fertile ground for him to cultivate. His voice is heard only at a second meeting of the Assembly, which had four days earlier heard the report of envoys freshly returned from Egesta. At the first meeting the Assembly voted to send sixty ships to Sicily under the joint command of Alcibiades, Nicias, and Lamachus with full authority "to assist Egesta against Selinus, to cooperate in the resettlement of Leontini if that war turned out successfully, and to accomplish all else in Sicily in the best interest of Athens as they perceive it" (6.8.2). Thus in Thucydides' view the people are saddled with the responsibility for the Sicilian expedition and its failure; Alcibiades did no more than spur them on to do what they wanted to anyway,[87] corroborating the historian's express judgment in his famous comparison of Pericles with his successors.[88]

We are in no position to reject the essential features of this picture, simply because it constitutes the only testimony of a reliable and perceptive contemporary. And yet, we must recognize that it requires a skillful (but not necessarily deceitful) manipulation of historical facts. Despite Thucydides' silence on the matter, it is unthinkable that Alcibiades had not taken the floor also at the first Assembly meeting and that the tenor of his remarks then, their ξύμπασα γνώμη, was different from the speech reported at length in the second. A man of strong views, known to the public from his past

86 Nicias at 6.10.5, 20.2; Alcibiades at 6.18.3; Hermocrates at 6.33.2.

87 Ibid. 15.2: ἐνῆγε δὲ προθυμότατα τὴν στρατείαν Ἀλκιβιάδης ὁ Κλεινίου. de Romilly, *Thucydides* 203 with n. 1, aptly compares the language of Cleon's rejection of Spartan peace offers in 425 B.C. at 4.21.3: μάλιστα δὲ αὐτοὺς ἐνῆγε Κλέων ὁ Κλεαινέτου.

88 Id. 2.65.10–11, esp. ὀρεγόμενοι τοῦ πρῶτος ἕκαστος γίγνεσθαι ἐτράποντο καθ' ἡδονὰς τῷ δήμῳ καὶ τὰ πράγματα ἐνδιδόναι. ἐξ ὧν ἄλλα τε πολλά, ὡς ἐν μεγάλῃ πόλει καὶ ἀρχὴν ἐχούσῃ, ἡμαρτήθη καὶ ὁ ἐς Σικελίαν πλοῦς. Cf. J. de Romilly, "Les Problèmes de politique intérieure dans l'oeuvre de Thucydide," in *Historiographia Antiqua: Commentationes Lovanienses in Honorem W. Peremans Septuagenarii Editae* (Louvain, 1977) 77–93, esp. 83–84: "Il est donc vrai qu'au cours de la guerre le mécanisme démocratique a été modifié et que le peuple, avec ses passions et son incompétence, est devenue maître des affaires: tout l'agencement du récit laisse lire la leçon que dégage en clair le chapitre II 65."

actions and utterances, cannot have been designated as one of the generals to lead the armada—and at some point the possibility was even envisaged that he might be the sole commander[89]—if he had voiced no opinion on how to respond to Egesta's request and to the subsequent report of the Athenian envoys. A contemporary observer less astute than Thucydides might well have suggested that a rousing speech of Alcibiades' at the first Assembly meeting elicited the popular enthusiasm for the Sicilian expedition and won him his appointment as one of the *stratēgoi autokratores*,[90] so that the burden of responsibility would fall on Alcibiades and his rhetorical skills. Thucydides' choice not to interpret events in this way would accord with his recognition of the fatal weakness in popular sovereignty, which the decision to embark on the campaign against Sicily revealed for the first time: when the constitutional power to make weighty political decisions is vested in an ill-informed mob,[91] whose votes are subject to temporary enthusiasms any powerful speaker can fire, the consequences are bound to be disastrous for the state. Thus the decision to sail against Sicily becomes the turning point, the *peripeteia*, of popular sovereignty. By making that decision, the *dēmos* enabled an opposition that had been latent since at least the time of the Old Oligarch to make its political weight felt.

Whether Nicias too took the floor at the first meeting of the Assembly remains uncertain. It would be consonant with his slow, deliberate, and indecisive character not to realize at once the range and depth of the consequences Athens would incur by granting Egesta's request and thus to lose a momentum that he might have had, if he had spoken up promptly, to nip popular enthusiasm for the expedition in the bud.[92] He may have acquiesced in his election as one of the generals because he believed he could serve as a brake on Alcibiades or because he hoped the Assembly might yet reconsider.[93] But in his first speech at the second meeting of the Assembly he seems suddenly to realize that his earlier silence had made irrevoca-

89   ML, no. 78, fr. *b*2 with Dover, *HCT* 4.225.

90   This is done in Plut. *Nic.* 12.1, *Alc.* 17.2.

91   The point of inserting the account of early Sicilian history in the context in which we can find it, at 6.1.1–6.6.1, seems to be to show the extent of popular ignorance (ἄπειροι οἱ πολλοὶ ὄντες, 6.1.1).

92   Note Plutarch's remarks at *Nic.* 16.9: ἃ δὴ πάντες ᾐτιῶντο τὸν Νικίαν, ὡς ἐν τῷ διαλογίζεσθαι καὶ μέλλειν καὶ φυλάττεσθαι τὸν τῶν πράξεων ἀπολλύντα καιρόν· ἐπεὶ τάς γε πράξεις οὐδεὶς ἂν ἐμέμψατο τοῦ ἀνδρός. ὁρμήσας γὰρ ἦν ἐνεργὸς καὶ δραστήριος, ὁρμῆσαι δὲ μελλητὴς καὶ ἄτολμος. Cf. also μελλονικιᾶν at Ar. *Av.* 640 (414 B.C.) and Thuc. 5.16.1 with pp. 301–2.

93   Thuc. 6.8.4, ἀκούσιος μὲν ᾑρημένος ἄρχειν, with Dover, *HCT* 4.230.

ble what he regarded as folly.[94] His second speech, which is little more than a resigned logistic analysis of what equipment the expedition will need, he gives in the futile hope of overturning a now-irreversible decision, ending with a sigh of despair and frustration: "If anyone thinks differently, I yield my office to him" (6.23.3). He had responded similarly to Cleon's challenge in 425 B.C. (4.28.1–4) but this time no one relieved him of his burden.

The debate between Nicias and Alcibiades is less a clash of political principle than of different temperaments and generations. Nicias himself realizes that the sobriety and circumspection of his seasoned military expertise have little chance of stemming the irrational enthusiasm of the Assembly (6.9.3). Even before Alcibiades had opened his mouth, lust for adventure had made the commons deaf to Nicias' warnings: a Sicilian expedition would only swell the number of already existing enemies (6.10); even if the expedition succeeded, it would be difficult to control a large populace from a great distance, and, if it failed in any way, the Sicilians would join the Spartans, eager to recoup their lost prestige, in attacking Athens herself (6.11); and what strength had been recovered after the recent plague should not be dissipated on alien ventures (6.12). Even his censure of Alcibiades' aims and motives is of no avail. By accusing him, without mentioning his name, of having undermined the peace (6.10.2) and of being driven by a youthful lust for power to seek for his own selfish ends an appointment for which he is too young "in order to gain admiration for his horsebreeding, but also to make some profit from his command because of the expense involved in it" (6.12.2), he converts only a few of his listeners to his point of view (6.15.1) and only adds fuel to Alcibiades' passionate support of the expedition.

The paradox of Alcibiades' success with the masses is brilliantly captured by Thucydides both in his introduction to Alcibiades' speech and in the speech itself.[95] How could a young man whose aristocratic background, prodigal living, and intellectual training set him so far apart from the common man have prevailed over the prudent restraint of an old, seasoned democrat and have whipped the masses into frenzied enthusiasm for distant conquest? In Thucydides' view, his drive for personal glory and wealth, his extravagant lifestyle, and his conspicuous display of wealth not only won him

94   See especially his plea for reconsideration at 6.14.
95   For an excellent treatment of the rhetoric of this speech, see C. W. Macleod, "Rhetoric and History (Thucydides, VI, 16–18)," *Quaderni di Storia* 2 (1975) 39–65.

status and admiration but tended at the same time to corrode public confidence in him; his egocentricity was seen as containing the germ of potential tyranny (6.15.2–4). In the speech Thucydides puts in his mouth Alcibiades is unabashedly aware of his prestige and its sources and is able to manipulate them to his advantage; but he does not anticipate the deleterious effect they will have on the state as well as on himself. Alcibiades says nothing to allay the fears roused by Nicias; rather, he neutralizes them by appealing to the past, when reliance on the navy enabled the Athenians to establish an empire in the face of those who are still their enemies in Greece and of the Persians at the same time (6.17.7–8). Nicias he rebukes for a do-nothing policy (*apragmosynē*) and for creating division between young and old at a time when all should pull together for the advancement of empire (6.18.6–7). Moreover, whereas Nicias is self-effacing and from the outset disclaims any personal interest in the policy he advocates (6.9.2), Alcibiades, as if to stress Nicias's humble background, bases his own title to leadership on the distinction of his family and especially on the renown he himself brought Athens by his resplendent victories at Olympia (6.16.1–3), intimating that the state is more indebted to him than he to the state. Again, he stresses his own merit by citing his successful machinations against Sparta before Mantinea as evidence that his military and diplomatic acumen belies his youth and as credentials for assessing the current situation in Sicily, which, he believes, augurs success for the expedition (6.17.1–6). Unlike Cleon, he makes no pretense of equality with the common people; rather, he regards it as their good fortune that they have him to look up to (6.16.4–5). His use of the *nomos-physis* polarity and his analysis of Athenian imperialism show into whose hands the destiny of Athens has fallen.

Nomos and *physis* appear once together as opposites in Alcibiades' speech, and each of them appears once by itself. But surprisingly enough, and contrary to what we should expect from Alcibiades' arrogant bearing, he perversely identifies his own side of the argument with *nomos* and the opposing side with *physis*. Of his victories at Olympia he says: νόμῳ μὲν γὰρ τιμὴ τὰ τοιαῦτα, ἐκ δὲ τοῦ δρωμένου καὶ δύναμις ἅμα ὑπονοεῖται. καὶ ὅσα αὖ ἐν τῇ πόλει χορηγίαις ἢ ἄλλῳ τῳ λαμπρύνομαι, τοῖς μὲν ἀστοῖς φθονεῖται φύσει, πρὸς δὲ τοὺς ξένους καὶ αὕτη ἰσχὺς φαίνεται.[96] In other words, *nomos* is responsible for the

---

96 Thuc. 6.16.2–3: "This sort of thing is conventionally regarded as an honor, and at the same time the achievement creates an impression of power. Again, it is only natural that my fellow citizens envy me for the splendor I enjoy in the city for

honor Athens gains from his victories; the carping of *physis* tends to undermine his reputation. Are we to see here a fleeting intimation of the potential harm his conduct may bring to Athens? Again, what seemed to his opponents an "unnatural" (*para physin*) youthful madness is credited with his success in dealing with the Peloponnesians (6.17.1); and in his peroration, in language reminiscent of Cleon's tenet that "a state is stronger when it enforces inferior laws that are inviolable than when it has good laws that lack authority" (3.37.3), he exhorts the Athenians not to rescind their earlier vote, arguing that "those men live most securely whose government least deviates from the character and the *nomoi* they have, even if these are inferior" (6.18.7). There is irony in having this statement of the establishment mentality appropriated by a man whose personal conduct even Thucydides characterizes as *paranomia* (6.15.4). It is similarly ironic to have a man who has spared no effort to undermine Nicias's peace treaty with Sparta argue for the Sicilian expedition on the grounds "that we must defend our Sicilian allies, inasmuch as we have sworn to do so, without objecting that they have not defended us" (6.18.1).

Alcibiades' analysis of the dynamics of imperialism is suffused with the same kind of amoral intellectualism. After disingenuously arguing that empire is acquired by generously supplying aid to those who request it, Alcibiades varies themes that earlier in his work Thucydides had attributed to the Athenian ambassadors in Sparta (1.75–76) and to Pericles (2.62–63), namely, that an imperial power cannot stand still:

> People do not just defend themselves against the attack of a superior but strike first to prevent his attack. It is not possible for us to allocate limits to the extent to which we want empire, but, since we have reached the position in which we are, we must inevitably hatch plots against some and secure our control over others, because there is danger that we shall be ruled by others if we do not ourselves rule them. Your situation does not permit you to envisage a policy of peace as other states do, unless you will change your pursuits to their level. (6.18.2–3)

The necessity either to rule or to be ruled, combined with the maxim that the stronger will rule over the weaker, which is also embedded in the Melian Dialogue, was appealed to by the Athenians at Sparta

---

equiping choruses and providing other public services, but this too creates an impression of strength in the eyes of foreigners."

to account for their possession of empire.[97] Pericles too had seen that there was no retreat from empire—"by this time, you are holding it as a tyranny; though to have taken it seems to be unjust, it is dangerous to let it go" (2.63.2)—and although he realized that "our present naval resources are such that no king or any other nation will prevent you from sailing [wherever you want]" (2.62.2), he also knew that war was not a time to expand imperial holdings (1.144.1). Alcibiades understands the heritage of imperialism, but he takes its application to Melos a big step farther, insensitive to Pericles' advice and to the consequences of that insensitivity.

The latent conflict between the ruling democrats and the young oligarchs that the impending approach of the Athenians stirred up in Syracuse[98] manifested itself in a different guise in Athens at this time. Thucydides stresses that for the moment old and young were united in their determination to undertake the expedition (6.24.3); the ideological rift that was to come is hinted at only in Nicias's warning of Sparta's oligarchical machinations against Athens (6.11.7) and in the suspicion Alcibiades' arrogant rejection of equality aroused that he wanted to make himself a tyrant (6.16.4, cf. 6.15.4). But a remark of Nicias's indicates that the strife between old and young was already beginning to assume internal party-political dimensions. Nicias observes with alarm that Alcibiades has summoned a number of young men to his support, apparently to intimidate the Assembly, and he exhorts the older among the citizens not to let themselves be shamed by their presence into voting for war for fear of being regarded as cowards (6.13.1). Evidently, Alcibiades had organized some of his cronies as a pressure group to support his policy. Though Nicias's remark shows that they cannot have been sitting *en bloc*, a sufficiently large number will have surrounded Alcibiades, and we may infer from a regulation passed after the overthrow of the Four Hundred concerning seating arrangements in the Council[99] that

97 Id. 1.76.1–2: ἀναγκασθέντας ἂν ἢ ἄρχειν ἐγκρατῶς ἢ αὐτοὺς κινδυνεύειν ... ἀλλ᾽ αἰεὶ καθεστῶτος τὸν ἥσσω ὑπὸ τοῦ δυνατωτέρου κατείργεσθαι; cf. 5.105.2, ἡγούμεθα γὰρ τό τε θεῖον δόξῃ τὸ ἀνθρώπειόν τε σαφῶς διὰ παντὸς ὑπὸ φύσεως ἀναγκαίας, οὗ ἂν κρατῇ, ἄρχειν, and 5.95: οὐ γὰρ τοσοῦτον ἡμᾶς βλάπτει ἡ ἔχθρα ὑμῶν ὅσον ἡ φιλία μὲν ἀσθενείας, τὸ δὲ μῖσος δυνάμεως παράδειγμα τοῖς ἀρχομένοις δηλούμενον.

98 See the speeches of Hermocrates and Athenagoras, id. 6.33–34 and 36–40, esp. 38.2–39.2. Athenagoras is described as a δήμου προστάτης at 35.2; that the oligarchs are dominated by the young is suggested at 38.5.

99 Philochorus *FGH* 328F140 with Jacoby's note.

such block seating was regarded with suspicion.[100] One of these friends of Alcibiades' may well have been the person who eventually challenged Nicias to give the Assembly facts and figures about the forces required (6.25.1). Plutarch identifies him as Demostratus and credits him with the motion that gave the generals full authority to levy the required troops and undertake the expedition.[101] He belonged to the Bouzygai, one of the oldest aristocratic families of Athens, and remarks made about him in comedy suggest that, like Alcibiades, he participated in the profanations that shook the state shortly before the expedition set sail.[102]

Demostratus's name does not occur among those we know were denounced as participants in the desecration of the herms and the profanations of the Mysteries. But as we know the names of only sixty-five who were, or were intended to be, brought to trial (out of three hundred alleged to have been involved in the mutilation of the herms and out of an indeterminate number of participants in the profanation of the Mysteries),[103] the absence of his name from the surviving record is no argument against his involvement, and his support of Alcibiades as well as the fact that many of those implicated were likewise aristocrats favor the view that he was involved.

Despite some problems of detail, the sequence of events after the Sicilian expedition was ratified is clear enough for our purposes from the accounts of Thucydides, Andocides, Diodorus, and Plutarch.[104]

---

100   This does not, however, imply that those sitting together constituted an organized political party, as is argued by R. Sealey, "The Entry of Pericles into History," *Hermes* 84 (1956) 234–47, esp. 241.

101   Plut. *Nic.* 12.6, *Alc.* 18.3.

102   Eup. fr. 97 (cf. fr. 96 [*Dēmoi*, 412 B.C.]), who applies the same adjective, ἀλιτήριος, to him that Andocides (1.51; cf. Philochorus *FGH* 328F134) applies to those involved in the profanations of 415 B.C. Ar. *Lys.* 391–97 with schol. to 397 suggests that his deme may have been Cholarges, which may point to a distant relation to Pericles. See Davies, *APF* 105–6, and F. Sartori, *Una Pagina di storia ateniese in un frammento dei "Demi" eupolidei*, Università degli Studi di Padova: Pubblicazioni dell' Istituto di Storia Antica 12 (Rome, 1975) 96–98.

103   Andoc. 1.37, 51, and 58. Even if this number is to be discredited together with Diocleides' testimony (ibid. 65–66), it is still true that of the forty-two persons denounced by Diocleides, we know the names of only thirteen; see ibid. 43 and 47 with Appendix C below.

104   The most satisfactory discussion of the chronological problems is in my opinion that of O. Aurenche, *Les Groupes d'Alcibiade, de Léogoras et de Teucros* (Paris, 1974) 155–76, esp. 155–58 (based largely on Hatzfeld 158–77 and "Le Départ de l'expédition de Sicile et les Adonies de 415," *REG* 50 [1937] 293–303, and on MacDowell, *Andokides* 181–85 and 186–89). Important but less satisfactory is the discussion of Dover, *HCT* 4.271–76.

Some three or four weeks before the departure of the fleet in midsummer 415 B.C. the discovery that a large number of herms (square pillars surmounted by a bust of Hermes, commonly set up in doorways of private and public buildings) had been mutilated during the previous night[105] was taken very seriously, "for it was thought to be a bad omen for the departure and to have been undertaken as part of a conspiracy to stage a revolution and to overthrow the democracy."[106] Suspicions were intensified when, still before the departure of the fleet, the testimony of "some metics and personal servants," referring no doubt to Teucrus and Andromachus, revealed that, earlier, mutilation of sacred statues and parodies of the Mysteries had taken place in private houses and that Alcibiades was said to have been involved.[107] In addition to suspicions of a plot to overthrow the democracy, we now hear also of allegations that an oligarchy or tyranny was to be established in its place.[108]

Charges of conspiracy against the people and of attempting to establish a tyranny are known from Aristophanes' *Knights* and *Wasps* to have been bruited by Cleon in the 420s.[109] There is no reason to believe that his were anything more than the rhetorical excesses of a crude, emotional demagogue against political opponents; there is no evidence that Cleon ever seriously tried to bring formal charges on these counts against anyone. Though formal charges resulting from the mutilation of the herms and the profanation of the Mysteries were for impiety (*asebeia*) rather than for conspiracy to overthrow the democracy and/or for intending to establish a tyranny or oligarchy, the deep consternation at those events shows that this time the fears for the survival of the democracy were real and that they were felt even before the perpetrators' names were revealed.

It is difficult for us to understand why offenses of a *prima facie* religious character committed (according to Thuc. 6.28.1) as a

105 Thucydides' dating of the departure (6.30.1) is generally taken to refer to late June or early July; see MacDowell, *Andokides* 189. The mutilations, which probably involved more than the defacement mentioned by Thuc. 6.27.1 (cf. Ar. *Lys.* 1093–94 with Hatzfeld 161), took place either during a new moon (Plut. *Alc.* 20.8; so also Diod. 13.2.4) or a full moon (Diocleides' story in Andoc. 1.38). The arguments of MacDowell 187–88 for the former (= June 6/7) seem to me more convincing than those of Dover, *HCT* 4.275–76, for the latter (= May 25).

106 Thuc. 6.27.3. Cf. ibid. 28.2; Andoc. 1.36.

107 Thuc. 6.28.1; for Teucrus and Andromachus, see Andoc. 1.11–14, 15, 34–35.

108 Thuc. 6.28.2, 61.1, and Isoc. 16.6 (overthrow of democracy); Thuc. 6.60.1, 53.3 (oligarchy and/or tyranny).

109 See above, p. 224 with nn. 106–8.

drunken youthful prank should have produced profound and wide-spread political hysteria. Thucydides' own explanation does not satisfy completely: he tells us that Alcibiades' rivals for popular leadership, among whom will have been Androcles—who is later credited by Thucydides with the prime responsibility for Alcibiades' exile[110]—exploited his alleged participation in profaning the Myster-ies by combining it with the mutilation of the herms and by attributing to him the instigation of both sacrileges with a view to overthrowing the democracy. Alcibiades' own personal extravagance and arrogance, Thucydides intimates, made these charges credible (6.28.2). This is consistent with Thucydides' general interpretation of Alcibiades' role in the events of 415 B.C.: he was a victim of his own qualities. His brilliance and ambition provided the leadership whereby the common people believed their desires could be imple-mented, but his way of life undermined popular confidence in him and made him vulnerable to the attacks of political rivals, who did not shrink from citing his irreverent and drunken conduct in the privacy of Athenian homes to do irreparable damage to his public standing.

Whatever truth there may be in Thucydides' interpretation, it leaves much unexplained. Above all, why was the mutilation of the herms, in which Alcibiades was not implicated, interpreted as aimed at overthrowing the democracy, even before any perpetrator had been identified? Would its timing not suggest that it was intended to prevent the fleet from sailing? Some modern scholars have taken this to have been at least a subsidiary purpose of the mutilation[111] but we learn from Plutarch (*Alc*. 18.7–8) that a rumor at the time to that effect was no more credible than the view that it was merely an exuberant youthful prank; and Thucydides (6.27.3) calls it only a bad omen for the expedition, not an attempt to prevent the departure. The reason why this motive was shrugged off is probably that the Sicilian expedition enjoyed such broad support that no segment of Athenian society could be envisaged as opposing it, especially as opposing it in so peculiar a way.[112] Surely, Nicias and his followers

110 Thuc. 8.65.2. For Androcles' role in the events of 415 B.C., see also Plut. *Alc*. 19.1 and 3 and Andoc. 1.27; for his prominence, see Cratinus, frr. 208, 209a Edmonds, and 263; Ar. *Vesp*. 1187 with schol., Com. Adesp. fr. 48; for his rhetorical skill, see Arist. *Rh*. 2.23, 1400ᵃ 9–14.

111 E.g., Aurenche, *Groupes* 173–75.

112 C. A. Powell, "Religion and the Sicilian Expedition," *Hist*. 28 (1979) 15–31, adduces evidence (primarily from Plut. *Nic*. 13.2 and 14.7 and Paus. 8.11.12) that

were not people who would resort to violence against religious sensibilities in order to obtain what they had failed to obtain by constitutional procedures in the Assembly, and Alcibiades and his friends would hardly wish to jeopardize the political victory they had won on this occasion. Nor do we know of any other group likely to have opposed the Sicilian campaign: that such men as Callias son of Calliades, or Pythodorus, Sophocles, or Phaeax were involved in earlier attempts to establish Athenian control over Sicily suggests that the upper classes favored the enterprise,[113] and all elements of Athenian society, old and young, are said by Thucydides to have been ardent supporters both before and after the desecrations had come to light (6.24.2–4, 26.1–2, 31–32). No wonder, then, that the mutilation of the herms was not thought to have the prevention of the expedition as its purpose.

But what made people infer from the mutilations that a plot to overthrow the democracy was underway? Herms were ubiquitous in Athens, as symbols of good luck, as protectors of streets, gateways, and buildings both public and private. They were associated with the city as such rather than with its form of government;[114] the mutilation could not in itself have been regarded as an act against the democracy.[115] Nevertheless, since the outrage had been committed in a single night, and since it had been spread all over Athens,[116] there was justification for thinking that it was not just a drunken hooligans' prank but a deliberate act, a conspiratorial plan (Andoc. 1.36). The nature of the deed itself will have shown that it was the work of men who lacked conventional piety; further, it was not the sort of thing adults did. Suspicions will therefore naturally have focused on young men whose religious sensibilities had been so undermined by the teachings of the sophists as to believe "how pleasant it is to be familiar with the latest clever things and to be able to soar so high in

various prophecies encouraged the Athenians to undertake the expedition of 415 B.C. However, this cannot have been as strong a motivating factor as Powell believes, especially since the counteromens, discussed by Powell on pp. 18–19, were at least equally potent.

113   See above, pp. 313–15.

114   They were originally set up by the Peisistratid Hipparchus; see [Pl.] *Hipparch.* 228d. Three herms are known to have been dedicated to and by the *dēmos* in honor of Cimon's victory at the Strymon in 476/5 B.C.; see Aeschin. 3.183–85; Plut. *Cim.* 7.4–6. For the herms in general, see R. E. Wycherley, *The Stones of Athens* (Princeton, 1978) 38, 186–87.

115   Differently Aurenche, *Groupes* 174–75.

116   Thuc. 6.27.1; Andoc. 1.36, 62; Plut. *Alc.* 18.6.

thought as to look down on the established laws" of the Athenian democracy.

These suspicions will have been further fueled by the revelations before the fleet departed that the Mysteries had been parodied in private. Although all our evidence indicates that such parodies had often been performed in various houses long before the night the herms were damaged[117] it will have been clear at once that they were informed by the same irreverence as the mutilations. Further, their secrecy made them too appear conspiratorial, and Alcibiades' alleged involvement will have exacerbated such suspicions, because he had summoned a band of cronies to the decisive Assembly meeting. We know now with the benefit of hindsight that Alcibiades did not strive to establish himself as tyrant in Athens,[118] but would his contemporaries not have thought so once his profanations of the Mysteries had been revealed? Surely, they would not have believed that he wanted to undermine the enterprise he had so ardently advocated; but would it have been utterly unreasonable to surmise from his overbearing personal demeanor that he was aiming to restrict the government of Athens to himself and his young aristocratic boon companions? It is worth noting again that suspicions of tyrannical or oligarchical designs arose only after Alcibiades had been inculpated:[119] his implication in the parodies and the suspected involvement of his social peers in the mutilations made this at the time the only sensible explanation of the incidents. Androcles will have had no difficulty in persuading the common people that such suspicions were correct.

We shall never know the true motives of those involved in the mutilations and parodies, and the fact may well be that both acts had no political purpose and were merely the unmotivated result of youthful drunkenness and exuberance. It is not surprising that Alcibiades' implication caused concern, but it is curious that when the majority of Athenians of all ages and social classes favored a Sicilian expedition, the desecrations should have been linked to fears of a widespread conspiracy against the democracy. Under the surface of a united support of the expedition, there had evidently long been simmering a tension between the democratic establishment and the

117   The evidence is collected and well discussed by Aurenche, *Groupes* 160–65.

118   See R. Seager, "Alcibiades and the Charge of Aiming at Tyranny," *Hist.* 16 (1967) 6–18.

119   See n. 108 above.

upper classes, which could ignite what would normally have been an insignificant incident into a major crisis.

We have seen how the upper classes had become increasingly disenchanted with democratic processes and concomitantly the masses had been growing antagonistic toward upper-class behavior since the 420s. The upper classes resented the demagogues and their manipulation of the masses in Council, Assembly, and especially in the jury courts, where their wealth could be threatened after their *euthynai*; they looked with disapproval at the treatment of the allies, who were being bled to pay for an unnecessarily protracted war; and they were beginning to understand that it was risky to entrust major political decisions to unpredictable and gullible masses. Led by the demagogues, the lower classes had already in the 420s suspected conspiracies and attempts at tyranny;[120] but whereas such charges were thought extravagant at that time, they were taken seriously in 415 B.C. A few specific indications may explain why this was so.

As soon as the mutilation of the herms became known, suspicion fell on Andocides because the herm of the tribe Aigeis, which stood near his house, was one of the few left undamaged (Andoc. 1.62; Plut. *Alc*. 21.2–3). We cannot tell whether he was guilty, but he was regarded as the most deeply implicated.[121] We know that even before these events he had the reputation of being μισόδημος καὶ ὀλιγαρχικός, "a hater of the masses and oligarchical" (Plut. *Alc*. 21.2). Plutarch testifies that Andocides incited his oligarchical boon companions (*hetairoi*) against the *dēmos* in a speech he probably delivered well before 415 B.C.; in it he alleged that upon discovering the ashes of their erstwhile hero Themistocles, the fickle and ungrateful Athenians had scattered them to the winds.[122] A fragment perhaps from the same speech contains unmistakable overtones of social snobbery, possibly in a context deploring the consequences of war for Athens: "May we never again see the charcoal burners coming from the mountains into the city, nor their sheep, their cattle, their wagons, and their pusillanimous womenfolk, nor old men and

---

120   See above, pp. 219–29.

121   Thuc. 6.60.2, ὅσπερ ἐδόκει αἰτιώτατος εἶναι, with Andoc. 1.48–53; cf. Plut. *Alc*. 21.1–6. MacDowell, *Andokides* 173–76 believes that he was guilty of profaning the Mysteries but not of mutilating the herms.

122   Plut. *Them*. 32.4. The authenticity of the speech πρὸς τοὺς ἑταίρους is questioned by Dover, *HCT* 4.286 n. 1, on the grounds that "it does not seem to have been known to the author of *Vit. X Or*. ([Plu.] *Mor*. 835a)." However, this omission does not seem to me to constitute sufficient reason for regarding it as spurious.

working-class people putting on full hoplite armor. May we never again have to eat wild herbs and chervil."[123] Clearly, these are the sentiments of a member of the upper class looking back upon the crowded conditions in Athens during the Archidamian War, when he had to share the city with riffraff. If this gives us 421 B.C. as a *terminus post quem* for this speech, the generally accepted attribution to this speech of a further Andocidean fragment gives us a *terminus ante*: "Of Hyperbolus I blush to speak. His father is even now working as a branded slave in the public mint, and he himself, a foreigner and not even a Greek, manufactures lamps."[124] Invective so vitriolic cannot have been written after Hyperbolus's ostracism, in 416 B.C., and it can have been written only by one who hated Hyperbolus for social as well as for political reasons. Moreover, since this speech was apparently addressed to close personal and political associates (whether organized or not) it is not surprising that in 415 B.C. the unbroken herm near Andocides' house aroused suspicions that the violence was directed at the democracy, however unrelated the mutilations may in fact have been to political subversion.

Andocides is the only person implicated in whose case we can see prior political conduct that justified suspecting that the incident of the herms signaled an attempt against the democracy. But there must have been many like Andocides among those accused. The use of *eisangelia*, the procedure appropriate in crimes against the state, on the charge of *asebeia* against them indicates that these offenses against religion were felt to threaten the political security of the state. We have seen that the same charge and the same procedure had been used two decades before to prosecute Anaxagoras and Protagoras.[125] But whereas they were foreigners and teachers, the attacks on whose teachings were merely a screen for political vindictiveness against their democratic patrons, those incriminated in 415 B.C. were Athenian citizens and political activists. But, as we shall

---

123 Andoc. fr. 4 Blass: μὴ γὰρ ἴδοιμέν ποτε πάλιν ἐκ τῶν ὀρέων τοὺς ἀνθρακευτὰς ἥκοντας εἰς τὸ ἄστυ, καὶ πρόβατα καὶ βοῦς καὶ τὰς ἁμάξας καὶ γύναια . . . , καὶ πρεσβυτέρους ἄνδρας καὶ ἐργάτας ἐξοπλιζομένους· μηδὲ ἄγρια λάχανα καὶ σκάνδικας ἔτι φάγοιμεν. For a discussion of text and interpretation, see Maidment *Orators* 1.582–83.

124 Id. fr. 5 Blass: περὶ Ὑπερβόλου λέγειν αἰσχύνομαι, οὗ ὁ μὲν πατὴρ ἐστιγμένος ἔτι καὶ νῦν ἐν τῷ ἀργυροκοπείῳ δουλεύει τῷ δημοσίῳ, αὐτὸς δὲ ξένος ὢν καὶ βάρβαρος λυχνοποιεῖ. For the attribution to the speech πρὸς τοὺς ἑταίρους, see Maidment, *Orators* 1.582–83.

125 See above, pp. 194–98, 274, and Appendix B below.

see, they came from the same intellectual circles in which Anaxa-goras and Protagoras had moved in Athens, and many of them will have been influenced by them or by other foreign intellectuals who had come to Athens in the 420s. The charges against them were no indirect attack on the leaders of the Athenian democracy but will have been regarded as defending the democratic establishment against members of the upper class just old enough to compete for the highest offices in the state.

Of the three hundred persons implicated in the mutilation of the herms alone[126] and of the unknown number alleged to have profaned the Mysteries, we know the names of only sixty-five who were (or were to be) brought to trial for impiety under the procedure of *eisangelia*.[127] Of over half of them we know only that they were inculpated, fled, were condemned to death in absentia, and in some cases had their property confiscated and sold by the *pōlētai*. For twenty-seven our information is a bit more detailed. We are con-strained to use this small percentage to draw some tentative conclu-sions about the nature of and reasons for the suspicions about them if we do not want to resign ourselves to ignorance of the social groups incriminated at this time.

Only six of the twenty-seven are likely to have been over forty years of age. Five of these may have come under suspicion partly because they had sons[128] or nephews among the younger alleged offenders.[129] The twenty-one younger suspects were all between the ages of twenty-five and thirty-five. Since all twenty-seven came from prosperous and eminent families and since three of the older and four of the younger men were members of Socrates' circle,[130] we may assume that many of the accused counted themselves as part of the Athenian intelligentsia and that the younger men among them would have been followers or pupils of the sophists in the 420s. Indeed, six of the twenty-seven are found in Plato's *Protagoras* lis-

126 See n. 103 above.
127 The detailed argument for the following will be found in Appendix C below.
128 Acumenus was the father of Eryximachus; see Andoc. 1.18 and 35. Leogoras was Andocides' father; see ibid. 17, 20–22, 50–59. Nisaeus was the son of Taureas; see ibid. 47.
129 Axiochus was close to his nephew Alcibiades; see ibid. 16 and Lys. fr. 4 Thalheim. Callias son of Alcmeon was the uncle of Nisaeus; see Andoc. 1.47 with Davies, *APF* 29.
130 Axiochus, Acumenus, and Critias; Alcibiades, Charmides, Eryximachus, and Phaedrus.

tening to Protagoras, Hippias, and Prodicus.[131] Nine of the twenty-seven can be regarded as intellectuals;[132] if we may draw general inferences from this proportion, the number of intellectuals among the allegedly impious of 415 B.C. will have been large.

More remarkable, though not surprising, is the political orientation of the accused, insofar as that can be ascertained. We have some information on thirteen of the twenty-seven; among these, only for Andocides and Alcibiades do we know anything about political leanings before 415 B.C. Andocides' antagonism to the democracy has already been discussed; Alcibiades, if Thucydides' testimony is reliable, was willing to exploit democratic institutions to satisfy his own political aims, but he left no doubt in his speech advocating the expedition that he scorned the principle of equality, and he later declared at Sparta how little he cared for democracy.[133] The remaining eleven all displayed antipathy in varying degrees toward the established democracy after 415 B.C., ranging from Critias's rabid hatred to Charmides' aristocratic reserve.[134] No Thrasybulus and no Thrasyllus is to be found among them.

The spokesmen for the democratic establishment against them are harder to identify. We know nothing of the background of Pythonicus, Teucrus, or Diocleides. But we do have a little information about Thessalus, who lodged the later *eisangelia* against Alcibiades, as well as about four others whom Andocides describes as marginally involved in bringing actions against the offenders. The youngest son of Cimon, Thessalus was about sixty years old in 415 B.C.[135] He may like his father have desired peaceful relations with Sparta, which Alcibiades had undermined; but as an older landed aristocrat he may have championed, if not the democratic order, at least the Athenian religious majority, which supported it. On the other side of the political spectrum we find Androcles, one of the eight προστάται τοῦ δήμου on Reverdin's list.[136] According to Thucydides, he was the

---

131 See Pl. *Prt.* 315a for Charmides, 315c for Phaedrus and Eryximachus, 315e for Adeimantus, and 316a for Critias and Alcibiades.

132 I am including Andocides in this number, despite the lack of evidence for sophistic training or intellectual affiliations in his case, because his accomplished speechwriting and its publication suggest formal training.

133 Thuc. 6.16.4, 89.6.

134 For details, see below, Appendix C, pp. 542–43, 545, and 549–50.

135 Plut. *Alc.* 19.3 and 22.4, with Davies, *APF* 307.

136 See above, p. 201 with n. 10.

popular leader most responsible for Alcibiades' exile in 415 B.C. and was for that reason killed by some oligarchs in 411 B.C.[137] In 415 B.C. he was a member of the Council and claimed in its behalf the rewards for information leading to the apprehension of those guilty of profaning the Mysteries (Andoc. 1.27). Whether he ever held a higher office we do not know, but that he had political influence is obvious from his being pilloried by several comic writers for grubbing money and for his appeal to the lower classes.[138] It is easy to imagine Androcles eagerly making political hay of the scandal of 415 B.C. and condemning it as a threat to the fabric of the democracy.

Also on the side of the democratic establishment were Cleonymus and Peisander, on whose joint motion the rewards Androcles later claimed were offered (Andoc. 1.27). Cleonymus was of the same cast as Androcles. We remember him as one of Cleon's lieutenants in the early 420s, when (probably as a councilor in 426/5 B.C.) he concerned himself with such economic matters as appointing local *eklogeis* for more stringent exaction of tribute[139] and with regulations of grain imports at Methone.[140] Between the dates of the *Acharnians*, in 425 B.C., and of the *Birds*, in 414 B.C., he was a constant target of Aristophanes' barbs. Although Aristophanes never calls him a demagogue or a popular leader,[141] he is painted in the same colors as the demagogues: he is pushy and associates with Hyperbolus (*Ach*. 844); he poses pompously as a champion of the masses in advocating a strong war policy[142] but is himself a draft dodger whose only military distinction was throwing away his shield to run from battle;[143] he is a fraud (*Ach*. 88), an embezzler (*Eq*. 958), a glutton (*Eq*. 1294; *Av*. 289–91), a perjurer (*Nub*. 400).

Peisander seems to have been a staunch populist and democrat—until he turned oligarch in 411 B.C. Andocides calls him one of "the most ardent supporters of the democracy" in 415 B.C. and describes

137 Thuc. 8.65.2; cf. 6.28.2 and Plut. *Alc*. 19.1–3. See n. 110 above.

138 Ar. *Vesp*. 1187 with schol., which cites Cratinus, Aristophanes (fr. 570), Telecleides (fr. 15), and Ecphantides (fr. 4); cf. also Cratinus, frr. 208, 263, and 458.

139 ML, no. 68.5 and p. 188, with p. 205 above.

140 Ibid. 65.34.

141 But schol. Ar. *Nub*. 673 calls him τῶν πολιτευομένων εἷς, and schol. *Vesp*. 822 refers to him as a χαλεπὸς δημαγωγός.

142 Ar. *Vesp*. 592–95; *Pax* 673–78; *Av*. 1475.

143 Id. *Eq*. 1372; *Nub*. 353 (cf. also the charge of effeminacy at 673); *Vesp*. 19–20, 592, 822; *Pax* 446, 677–78, 1295; *Av*. 290, 1475–77.

him as an alarmist foremost in interpreting the sacrileges as an attempt to overthrow the democracy.[144] His affinity with demagogues is evident from the abuse comedy heaps upon him: he is ridiculed for his burly appearance;[145] his is presented as a glutton[146] and a corrupt politician.[147] Like Cleonymus, he was a warmonger— but a man of such signal cowardice that it became proverbial in later times.[148]

Androcles, Cleonymus, and Peisander will have been a bit younger than Thessalus. Androcles' earliest known public appointment was to a sacred embassy about 422 B.C.,[149] but allusions to him in the comedies of Cratinus, Telecleides, and Ecphantides suggest that he was prominent considerably earlier.[150] He cannot, therefore, have been born much later than 460 B.C. Cleonymus had to be at least thirty to serve on the Council in 426/5 B.C. Peisander was lampooned by Aristophanes in the *Babylonians* as a corrupt politician in 426 B.C., and we cannot go far wrong in thinking he was about the same age as Cleonymus. Thus the three identifiable politicians who took part in prosecuting the sacrileges will have been between fifty and forty-five in 415 B.C., that is, about the same age as the older known accused. We may therefore conclude that different attitudes toward religion brought to a head in 415 B.C. other polarizations in Athenian society: the older generation tended to be aligned with the religious and political establishment of the Athenian democracy;

144 Andoc. 1.36: (Peisander and Charicles) δοκοῦντες δ' ἐν ἐκείνῳ τῷ χρόνῳ εὐνούστατοι εἶναι τῷ δήμῳ, ἔλεγον ὡς εἴη τὰ ἔργα τὰ γεγενημένα οὐκ ὀλίγων ἀνδρῶν ἀλλ' ἐπὶ τῇ τοῦ δήμου καταλύσει. Since they are described as ζητηταί, both are likely to have been councilors at this time. For Peisander, it is explicitly stated ibid. 43. For the ζητηταί as members of the Council, see B. Keil, "Das System des kleisthenischen Staatskalenders," *Hermes* 29 (1894) 321–72, esp. 354–55 n. 1; B. D. Merritt, "The Departure of Alcibiades for Sicily," *AJA* 34 (1930) 125–52, esp. 146–48; and A. D. J. Makkink, *Andokides' eerste rede met inleiding en commentaar* (Amsterdam, 1932) 103.

145 Hermippus, fr. 9; Eup. fr. 182; Phrynichus, fr. 20.

146 Eup. *Dēmoi* fr. 1 Austin; cf. Ael. *VH* 1.27.

147 Ar. fr. 81 (*Babylonians*); *Lys.* 490.

148 Ar. *Pax* 395 with schol., *Av.* 1556 with schol.; Eup. fr. 31; cf. Xen. *Symp.* 2.14, Ael. *NA* 4.1; *Suda* s.vv. δειλότερος τοῦ παρακύπτοντος and Πεισάνδρου δειλότερος. It may here also be noted that Plato Comicus wrote a *Peisandros* (frr. 95–105), probably produced in 422 B.C. (see A. Körte, "Platon (Komiker)," *RE* 20. Band [1950] 2537–41, esp. 2539), but little historical information can be gleaned from it.

149 See Ar. *Vesp.* 1187 with schol. Although we know of no minimum age for *theōroi*, the fact that they were selected from among councilors in the time of Demosthenes (see Busolt-Swoboda 1102 with n. 1) permits the inference that they tended to be at least thirty years old.

150 See n. 138 above.

arrayed against it stood a young generation of well-born and wealthy men of intellectual and oligarchical leanings.

However keenly the young, upper-class intellectuals may have disliked the democracy and however deeply the masses may have suspected their aims, it is remarkable that no *stasis* (civil strife) followed the desecrations of 415 B.C. This suggests that a well-organized conspiracy against the democracy did not exist, and that, in different ways, Andocides' confession and Alcibiades' conduct constituted the lightning rod that kept the spark from igniting. According to Thucydides, Andocides' confession did not bring out the whole truth, but it calmed the excited spirits of the people and minimized the number of victims.[151] Alcibiades' correct behavior in offering to stand trial before the departure of the fleet prevented the turmoil from undermining the expedition at its outset. Later in the summer his flight when the *Salaminia* came to Sicily to recall him for trial seemed an admission of guilt; he thereby became a scapegoat, temporarily liberating the city from the fear of a tyrannist coup. Resentment against Alcibiades could then crystallize around Thessalus's *eisangelia* for profaning the Mysteries, and all Athenians at home will have approved of the death sentence that removed Alcibiades from the internal political scene.[152] No reader can find a trace in Aristophanes' *Birds*, performed only a year later, of the political disturbances that surrounded the dispatch of the Sicilian expedition.

151 Thuc. 6.60.4. Cf. Andoc. 1.59, 66, and 68.
152 Thuc. 6.61.4–7; Plut. *Alc*. 22.

Part III

TOWARD THE
SOVEREIGNTY OF LAW

CHAPTER SEVEN

The Problem of the *Patrios Politeia* (Ancestral Constitution)

AFTER SICILY

The disastrous end of the Sicilian expedition in the autumn of 413 B.C. showed that popular sovereignty was vulnerable.[1] To expect with Thucydides that the Athenians ought to have been angry with themselves for having voted the enterprise into existence instead of venting their ire against the politicians who had favored it and against the soothsayers and oraclemongers who had encouraged them (Thuc. 8.1.1; cf. Lys. 18.2) is to exceed political and psychological reality. Still, we can accept Thucydides' analysis that the major blame for the fiasco fell upon the institutions of the Athenian democracy. The Assembly had spurned Nicias's cautions and voted for the expedition and had even chosen him, unwilling though he was, as one of the generals to command it; and the *dēmos* after letting Alcibiades arouse its enthusiasm for the expedition turned against him and voted for his recall, thus unleashing a series of events that made it indirectly responsible for the Spartan occupation of Deceleia in the summer before the Sicilian debacle.[2] And again, when common sense demanded a withdrawal from Sicily, the *dēmos* had opted for sending reinforcements (Thuc. 7.15.1 and 7.16); these served only to increase the magnitude of the defeat.

1   W. S. Ferguson, "The Athenian Expedition to Sicily," *CAH* 5.310 with n. 1, estimates that of the forty-five or fifty thousand men who had been sent to Sicily only two generals and seven thousand men remained to enter Syracuse as prisoners in September, 413 B.C.; Busolt, *GG* 3.2.1400, believes that Athens had no more than one hundred usable ships left after the defeat.
2   Thuc. 7.19.1–2 and 27.3–5 with 6.91.6–7 and 93.2.

In view of the despair in which the defeat left the state, an attempt to overthrow the democracy at this time would not have been surprising, especially since an oligarchical revolution could presumably have counted on the support of the Spartan garrison at Deceleia. Perhaps there was no such attempt because anyone capable of leading it had fled or been exiled in the wake of the desecrations of 415 B.C. But more important will have been the astounding resilience of the democratic establishment. The state's finances had already been basically restructured by the introduction of a five-percent tax on sea-borne traffic shortly after the Spartan occupation of Deceleia; this produced more revenue than the allied tribute, which could no longer be effectively collected.[3] After the defeat in Sicily, the Athenians immediately began building a new fleet to try to retain control over the allies, who saw in the condition of Athens an opportunity to revolt. Drastic economic measures were taken to finance the new fleet, including, after the revolt of Chios, the use of the emergency reserve of one thousand talents, which had remained untouched since the outbreak of the Peloponnesian War (Thuc. 8.1.3, 8.2.1 and 4, 8.4, 8.15.1). Although the Athenians could not prevent the defection of Chios and Miletus, the effort they put up to keep those islands from joining the Peloponnesian camp surprised the Greek world and helped Athens retain firm control of Lesbos and Samos.[4]

Of greater interest for our purposes is the political resilience with which the Athenians met the emergency in 413 B.C. Thucydides' terse statement "and to appoint a magistracy of older men who should conduct the initial deliberations [προβουλεύσουσιν] on problems of current concern as occasion should arise" (8.1.3) can be supplemented by what we learn from the decree of Pythodorus as reported in Aristotle's *Constitution of Athens* (29.2): there were ten such magistrates; they bore the official title of *probouloi*; and they had to be over forty years of age. Moreover, since they are described as "already existing" in 411 B.C., their office will not have been subject to the usual limitation of one year's tenure only. Their number suggests that each tribe contributed one *proboulos*, and this is corrob-

---

3   Thuc. 7.28.4 with Dover, *HCT* 4.401–2.
4   For the revolt of Chios, see Thuc. 8.6.3–4, 14.2. For Athenian countermeasures, see 8.9.2–3; 10.2–3, 11, 24.2–3 and 5, 30. For the revolt of Miletus, see 8.17; for countermeasures 8.24.1, 25–27, 30. For the revolt and recapture of Clazomenae, see 8.14.3, 23.6. For Lesbos, see 8.22, 23.2–3 and 6; cf. also 8.32.1 and 3.

orated by a late lexicon.[5] The verb ἑλέσθαι, used by both Thucydides and Aristotle, provides no unequivocal clue to the manner of their appointment. If Diodorus's report (12.75.4) that "the Athenians gave by popular decree ten men the power to deliberate [βουλεύεσθαι] about the welfare of the city" refers to the appointment of the *probouloi* in 413 B.C. rather than to an otherwise unattested commission created immediately after the Peace of Nicias (where Diodorus places it), we may conclude that their office was established by a vote of the Assembly.[6] There is further evidence for this conclusion: the *probouloi* had authority to convoke meetings of Council and Assembly,[7] which suggests that both these organs were responsible for the creation of this board; the Council continued to exist until it was paid off and disbanded by the oligarchs in the summer of 411 B.C. (Thuc. 8.69.4; Arist. *Ath.Pol.* 32.1); and generals were elected— presumably by the Assembly—for 412/11 B.C.[8]

The concurrent existence of the Council and the ten *probouloi* raises the interrelated questions of the purpose and functions of the new board. Although the board did not make normal democratic processes obsolete, its very presence will inevitably have restricted the activities of Council and Assembly.[9] The board will have been created to stabilize the government of Athens in the present emergency in a way the conventional prytany system could not,[10] yet we

---

5   *Lex.Seguer.* 298.25: πρόβουλοι· ἄρχοντες ἐννέα, ἐξ ἑκάστης φυλῆς εἷς, οἵτινες συνῆγον τὴν βουλὴν καὶ τὸν δῆμον. The incorrect number of nine given here is canceled out by attributing one *proboulos* to each tribe; see Rhodes, *AB* 216 n. 2, and H. Schaefer, "πρόβουλος," *RE* 23. Band (1957) 1221–31, esp. 1225.

6   However, A. Andrewes and D. M. Lewis, "Note on the Peace of Nikias," *JHS* 77 (1957) 177–80, have shown that this interpretation is far from certain.

7   See n. 5 above.

8   Fornara, *ABG* 66.

9   Ar. *Thesm.* 78–79 (City Dionysia of 412/11 B.C.: see Dover, *Aristophanic Comedy* 162, 169; Andrewes, *HCT* 5.184–93) suggests that the Council and the jury courts continued to meet. That there was some restriction on the competence of the Council seems confirmed ibid. 808–9, ἀλλ' Εὐβούλης τῶν πέρυσίν τις βουλευτής ἐστιν ἀμείνων / παραδοὺς ἑτέρῳ τὴν βουλείαν, with Wilamowitz, *Aristoteles* 2.344–45. The functions assigned to the *proboulos* in Ar. *Lys.* are no reliable indicator of historical facts: his mission to get money from the Acropolis to buy oars (420–23), the Scythian archers at his disposal (433–34, 441–42, 445, 449, 455, 462), and his reception of the Spartan herald (whom he sends back to request the dispatch of ambassadors plenipotentiary from Sparta, promising that he himself will request the Council to appoint Athenian ambassadors [1009–12]) may but need not reflect actual powers of the *probouloi*.

10   On this point, see F. Ruzé, "La Fonction des probouloi dans le monde grec antique," in *Mélanges d'histoire ancienne offerts à William Seston* (Paris, 1974) 443–62, esp. 446–49.

know that it did not replace the prytanies.[11] Aristotle's statement in the *Politics* (4.15, 1299[b]36–38) that the coexistence of *probouloi* and councilors in the same state constitutes a check on the latter (since a Council is democratic and a board of *probouloi* is oligarchical) has caused some scholars to interpret the appointment of *probouloi* in 413 B.C as an oligarchical or at least an antidemocratic measure; they believe the age requirement supports this contention.[12]

But the two *probouloi* we know by name can hardly be described as oligarchs or opponents of the democracy. Hagnon, the father of Theramenes, was a general with Pericles in the Samian campaign in 440/39 B.C. and took Pericles' side in the Phidias affair two years later; a year after that he established the colony at Amphipolis. He was a general again in 431/0 and 429/8 B.C.; he was a signatory of the Peace of Nicias as well as of the Athenian alliance with Sparta in 421 B.C.;[13] and even Lysias (12.65) admits that he was "regarded as a strong supporter of the system" when he was appointed *proboulos*. The other *proboulos* whose name we know is Sophocles; that he is the tragedian can no longer be doubted.[14] He served as general at least once, in the Samian campaign of 441/0 B.C. with Pericles,[15] and two years earlier, in 443/2 B.C. he had been a *hellēnotamias*.[16] If association with Pericles is not sufficient to clear him of the suspicion of oligarchical sympathies, the story Aristotle tells of him in the *Rhetoric* (3.18, 1419[a]25–30), where we are also told that he was one of the *probouloi*, indicates that a man who regarded the oligarchy of the

---

11 Ar. *Thesm.* 654, 764, 854, 923, 929–46, 1084; cf. Busolt, *GG* 3.2.1409 n. 2.

12 E.g., Hignett, *HAC* 269; H. Schaefer, "πρόβουλος" 1225–26; A. E. Raubitschek, "Eine Bemerkung zu Aristoteles, Verfassung von Athen 29.2," *Chiron* 4 (1974) 101–2.

13 See Davies, *APF* 227–28.

14 The doubts voiced by H. Schaefer, "πρόβουλος" 1225 and by H. C. Avery, "Sophocles' Political Career," *Hist.* 22 (1973) 509–14, esp. 513–14, are less cogent than the arguments of M. H. Jameson, "Sophocles and the Four Hundred," *Hist.* 20 (1971) 541–68, esp. 541–46, and of P. Karavites, "Tradition, Skepticism, and Sophocles' Political Career," *Klio* 58 (1976) 359–65, esp. 363–65.

15 Androtion *FGH* 324F38. For his relation to Pericles at that time, see Ion of Chios *FGH* 392F6; Strab. 14.1.18; Plut. *Per.* 8.8. Whether he owed his election to his success with the *Antigone*, as the first argument to that play states, remains doubtful. A second generalship, attested by Plut. *Nic.* 15.2 for the 420s, has been shown to lack historical foundation by L. Woodbury, "Sophocles among the Generals," *Phoenix* 24 (1970) 209–24, esp. 211–17.

16 *ATL* 2, list 12.36 with B. D. Meritt, "The Name of Sophokles," *AJP* 80 (1959) 189, and Jameson, "Sophocles" 541–42. The identification of the *hellēnotamias* with the poet is doubted by Avery, "Sophocles' Career" 509–13.

Four Hundred only as a necessary evil is not likely to have been an oligarch. When appointed *probouloi*, Hagnon will have been about fifty-seven years old and Sophocles about eighty-four;[17] neither of them was a career politician, and neither had been outstanding as a statesman. It appears from their appointment "that the Athenians were looking to trusted, sober, and experienced men, but men not associated with the recent disastrous ventures."[18] They had seen too much of life to be influenced by demagogues, and their age will at least initially have been a safeguard against the machinations of antidemocratic and oligarchical forces dominated by younger men who had reached maturity in the 420s. What the appointment of the *probouloi* may reflect about the political tensions in Athens in 413 B.C. is that under the democracy popular sovereignty was strong and flexible enough to adjust its institutions to a very grave emergency.

The Athenians thus turned at this critical moment to seasoned men respected for their competent (if uninspiring) leadership in the past. The reason why they did so is suggested by the remnants of Eupolis's *Dēmoi*, which can be dated with some confidence to the City Dionysia of 412 B.C.[19] The central feature of this play was the resurrection of a number of great Athenians of the past—Miltiades, Pericles, Aristides, Myronides, and perhaps also Solon, Nicias, and Harmodius and Aristogeiton—no doubt in order to show on the stage a leadership Athens seriously missed and to remind the city of its erstwhile greatness.[20] The nature of the ailment is defined in two fragments lamenting the quality of present-day generals. In one of these Miltiades and Pericles are invoked to see to it that debauched striplings "who trail the generalship around their ankles behind them" are no longer allowed to hold office.[21] The other fragment, probably from the parodos, looks back to the past: "Believe me, though there is much to talk about, I don't know what to say, so intense is the pain I get when I look at the state as it is now. So long as

17   Davies, *APF* 228, suggests ca. 470 B.C. as the year of Hagnon's birth; for Sophocles the birthdate of 497/6 B.C., given by the *Marmor Parium* (*FGH* 239A56 and 64), is generally accepted.

18   So Jameson, "Sophocles" 545.

19   For the date, see Sartori, *Pagina* 11–15; the social and political implications of the play are discussed ibid. 31–85.

20   For an imaginative reconstruction of the plot, see J. M. Edmonds, "The Cairo and Oxyrhynchus Fragments of the Δῆμοι of Eupolis," *Mnemos.*, 3d ser., 8 (1939) 1–20, and *The Fragments of Attic Comedy* 1 (Leiden, 1957) 978–94.

21   Eup. fr. 100: καὶ μηκέτ᾽, ὦναξ Μιλτιάδη καὶ Περίκλεες, / ἐάσατ᾽ ἄρχειν μειράκια βινούμενα, / ἐν τοῖν σφυροῖν ἕλκοντα τὴν στρατηγίαν.

we old men used to run it, we did not run it in this way. To start with, we had generals for the city from the most eminent families, first in wealth and first in birth, whom we worshiped as if they were gods, and that's what they were. As a result, we lived securely; but now, whenever it turns out that we have to go to war, we elect rubbish for generals."[22] It is tempting but futile to speculate which generals were the target of these barbs.[23] But it is noteworthy how many of the generals known to have been elected for 413/12 and 412/11 B.C. came from obscure or unknown families and/or had never served as generals before.[24] Although the administration of the state was entrusted to men whose contributions to public life inspired confidence that their character was incorruptible, they had made their active contribution a generation before; no energetic leadership could be expected from them now, and the present military fortunes of Athens lay in yet-untested hands.

Like Eupolis's *Dēmoi*, the appointment of the ten *probouloi* shows that immediately after the Sicilian disaster the Athenians looked to the past to provide guidance for the present. But the appointment of

22 Id., fr. 117: καὶ μὴν ἐγὼ πολλῶν παρόντων οὐκ ἔχω τί λέξω· / οὕτω σφόδρ' ἀλγῶ τὴν πολιτείαν ὁρῶν παρ' ἡμῖν. / ἡμεῖς γὰρ οὐχ οὕτω τέως ᾠκοῦμεν οἱ γέροντες, / ἀλλ' ἦσαν ἡμῖν τῇ πόλει πρῶτον μὲν οἱ στρατηγοί / ἐκ τῶν μεγίστων οἰκιῶν, πλούτῳ γένει τε πρῶτοι, / οἷς ὡσπερεὶ θεοῖσιν ηὐχόμεσθα· καὶ γὰρ ἦσαν· / ὥστ' ἀσφαλῶς ἐπράττομεν· νυνὶ δ', ὅταν τύχωμεν, / στρατευόμεσθ' αἱρούμενοι καθάρματα στρατηγούς.

23 Connor, *New Politicians* 147, has seen a reference to Alcibiades in fr. 100, but, as Sartori, *Pagina* 83–84 has pointed out, Alcibiades was no longer a stripling at this time—nor, we might add, a general—and he was not in Athens. Surely, there will have been many other upper-class striplings in Athens whose trailing robes and political aspirations aroused apprehensions among many citizens: see Plut. *Alc.* 1.8 (quoting Archippus, fr. 45), 16.1; Ar. *Nub.* 987.

24 Of the generals active in 413/12 B.C. after the deaths of Nicias, Demosthenes, and Eurymedon, none had served as general before; but Strombichides and Aristocrates came from "propertied families," and Aristocrates had been a signatory of the Peace of Nicias and of the alliance with Sparta (see Davies, *APF* 161–62, 56–57); nothing is known about Diphilus and Hippocles, except that they served as generals in this year (Thuc. 7.34.3, 8.13). The only general known to have been reelected for 412/11 B.C. was Strombichides; all the rest seem to have been elected for their first term. Like Aristocrates, Thrasycles had signed the Peace of Nicias and the alliance with Sparta in 421 B.C.; Eucrates was the younger brother of Nicias, who had been denounced by Diocleides for participation in the mutilation of the herms in 415 B.C. but was acquitted through the testimony of Andocides (Andoc. 1.47, 68; see below, Appendix C, pp. 547–48); and Phrynichus is alleged to have come from lowly beginnings in the country to the city ([Lys.] 20.11–12), where he became prominent enough as a politician (Lys. 25.9) to have rated a mention in *Vesp.* 1302, in 422 B.C. No family or earlier prominence is attested for Onomacles, Diomedon, Leon, Scironides, Euctemon, or Charminus.

the ten *probouloi* was never more than a temporary expedient: no provisions seem to have been made either for filling vacancies, which were bound to occur within the next few years because of the age of the incumbents, or for perpetuating or replacing the board. Clearly, the intention was merely to create a stopgap in a crisis. The Athenians will meanwhile have gone on thinking about how the democratic government ought to be modified in order to find a lasting solution to the constitutional crisis into which defeat had thrown the city. Between the reforms of Solon and the defeat in Sicily, Athens had indeed developed democratic institutions, but neither Athens nor any other Greek city had developed a theory of democracy—or, for that matter, a consistent view of oligarchical government—of articulate principles of popular sovereignty, to provide any guidelines in 413 B.C.[25] Herodotus in the constitutional debate (3.80–82) had tried to enumerate in broad outline the respective advantages of democracy, oligarchy, and monarchy, but the manner and context of that discussion provided little guidance for reform. The Old Oligarch had offered trenchant criticisms of democratic society but had ended up acknowledging its effectiveness, in a time when the failures from which it was now suffering could not have been envisaged. The sophists had stimulated critical analysis of the institutions of the democracy but had provided few constructive ideas on how to alter or improve them; and the political ideas of Hippodamus of Miletus (Arist. *Pol*. 2.8, 1267^b22–1268^a14) were too eccentric and too little rooted in Athenian traditions to be serviceable for restructuring the state. Thus concerned Athenians had to find in their own political heritage a model to create a system of government that would not repeat the mistakes of the immediate past. Accordingly, about this time Athenians became concerned to bring the constitution of this state back into line with the *patrios politeia* (ancestral constitution), the *patrioi nomoi* (ancestral laws), and all the other *patria* that they believed had once guaranteed the political stability and greatness of Athens. Even opponents of the democracy had to present their programs as attempts to restore the political conditions of a rosier past. The wish to bring the past to bear upon reshaping the present did not abate until a stabler democracy, based on the principle of the sovereignty of law, emerged in the years following the overthrow of the Thirty Tyrants.

25   Cf. Jones, *AD* 41.

THE FIRST OLIGARCHICAL CHALLENGE

Preliminaries

The costs of a renewed war effort after the defeat in Sicily will have been most burdensome for the upper classes. The Spartan occupation of Deceleia exposed their lands to enemy raids depriving them of crops and cattle, and the defection to Deceleia of more than twenty thousand slaves, many of them skilled craftsmen, will have affected the industrialists among them most severely.[26] Yet their losses notwithstanding, they had to continue to undertake costly liturgies, of which the trierarchy will have been the most frequent and oppressive; and at the same time they were the main targets of special property taxes (*eisphorai*), which the ever-present emergency will have frequently necessitated.[27] Their hopes either for an early end to hostilities or for new sources of revenue are likely to have been more fervent than those of people who had less property to lose and were paid for military service. But with military operations in Ionia stalemated no end was in sight, and with popular sovereignty still basically intact, despite the appointment of the ten *probouloi*, hopes of wealthy Athenians will have been frustrated by the goals of the majority.

There is no evidence that in the two years following the Sicilian defeat the frustrations of the upper classes resulted in a clear program of political action, to say nothing of an organization to implement it; but their latent anger remained waiting to be activated. For the revolution of the Four Hundred, our only source, Thucydides, leaves no doubt that Alcibiades provided the impetus. But, just as in his prelude to the Sicilian expedition, Thucydides presents Alcibiades as exploiting a ripe situation for his own political aims without either foreseeing or being able to control the consequences of what he instigated.

The scene of his intrigues shifts from Athens to Samos, which with the arrival of Strombichides as general in command of eight ships became the Athenians' base of Ionian operations in the early summer of 412 B.C.[28] Not long after the establishment of the base,

26 Thuc. 7.27.3–5; Lys. 7.6–7, [20].33; Xen. *Vect.* 4.25, with Busolt, *GG* 3.2.1401–2.

27 See Lys. 21, esp. 1–4, and the copious evidence cited by Busolt, *GG* 3.2.1404–5 with 1405 n. 1.

28 Thuc. 8.16.1. It may be assumed on the basis of 8.30.2 the twelve ships that soon followed under the command of Thrasycles (8.17.3) and the sixteen under Diomedon (8.19.2) were also to be based in Samos.

when all but three Athenian ships were gone on missions against the enemy, the Samian *dēmos* with the support of the remaining Athenians rose in a bloody insurrection against the ruling oligarchy.[29] What role the Athenians played in this revolt we are not told, but its success will not have been unwelcome to them, and its course will have had an effect not only on those among them who witnessed it[30] but also on further Athenian contingents that kept on arriving. The Athenian fleet at Samos numbered seventy-four ships by the early winter of 412 B.C.[31] If we assume that each ship carried a normal complement of two hundred men,[32] about fifteen thousand Athenian military personnel will have been stationed in Samos at this time. Only ten of these are known to us by name, eight of them as generals.

Between November and mid-December of 412 B.C. negotiations took place between Alcibiades and certain Athenian leaders.[33] Thucydides represents these negotiations as motivated by mutual interest, but he describes Alcibiades' motives in greater detail than the others'. Having lost the confidence of the Peloponnesians, Alcibiades worked hard to strengthen his influence with Tissaphernes (8.45.1) by advising him to support neither Greek side but to let the Athenians and Peloponnesians wear each other out, thus allowing the Persian king to play one against the other (8.46.1). He gave this advice, Thucydides asserts, partially because he believed this policy was in the best Persian interest and partially "to lay careful plans for his return to his own country, realizing that, if he was not going to destroy it, the day would come when he could persuade the Atheni-

29   Ibid. 21, where the oligarchical nature of the government emerges from the terms δυνατοί, δυνατώτατοι, and γεωμόροι. For the government of Samos between 441 and 412 B.C., see Andrewes, *HCT* 5. 44–47, and T. J. Quinn, *Athens and Samos, Lesbos and Chios: 478–404 B.C.* (Manchester, 1981), 13–19.

30   This is indicated by Thucydides' statement at 8.21 that the Athenians decreed αὐτονομία for Samos and by *IG* I³ 96, for which see *HCT* 5.46

31   Thuc. 8.30.2. On the problems of this number, see Andrewes, *HCT* 5.73 with 28–29; for the thorny chronology here and in the following, the account of Andrewes, *HCT* 5.185–93, seems to me the most sensible.

32   See Taillardat, "Trière" 189 with n. 31.

33   The negotiations seem to be subsumed under the date ἐν δὲ τούτῳ καὶ ἔτι πρότερον, πρὶν ἐς τὴν Ῥόδον αὐτοὺς ἀναστῆναι, with which Thucydides opens his account of Alcibiades' machinations at 8.45.1. The *terminus post quem* for the entire story of Alcibiades' falling out with the Peloponnesians and its sequel probably goes as far back as the late summer of 412 B.C. (see Andrewes, *HCT* 5.93), and the removal of the Peloponnesian base to Rhodes, coming as it did at a point when Lichas's demands had already strained relations between the Peloponnesians and Tissaphernes (43.3–44.1), may be close to the time at which Alcibiades and the Athenian leaders established contact. The arrival of Lichas is dated at 39.1–2 about the time of the winter solstice of 412 B.C. See Andrewes, *HCT* 5.185–86.

ans to let him come back. The most effective basis of persuasion, he believed, would be their impression that Tissaphernes was at his disposal. This was precisely what happened."[34]

With an unerring eye for Athenian weaknesses, Alcibiades now approached the most influential men (ἐς τοὺς δυνατωτάτους) in the Athenian camp at Samos "to let it be known among the upper classes [ἐς τοὺς βελτίστους] that, if an oligarchy were to replace the rascally regime of the democracy, which had expelled him, he was eager to return to his country as a full citizen and to secure the friendship of Tissaphernes for them."[35] Only at this juncture does Thucydides state that "the trierarchs and the most influential [δυνατώτατοι] of the Athenians on Samos had on their own initiative already started a movement to overthrow the democracy."[36] This is our first inkling that any leading Athenians were actively promoting the overthrow of the democracy. Thucydides leaves it unclear whether they or Alcibiades took the first step in the negotiations. But when Alcibiades warns that unless the democratic regime is abandoned there is no hope of obtaining the friendship of Tissaphernes and the king, three motives are evident in the Athenians' reaction: a desire to relieve the war's economic burden, a hope of controlling the government, and a hope that Persian assistance would mean victory over the Peloponnesians.[37] The recall of Alcibiades had not yet been broached.

We can obtain further clues about these men's motivation by investigating the identity of the δυνατώτατοι with whom Alcibiades negotiated. Since only ten of the fifteen thousand Athenians on Samos are known to us by name, we have to infer what we can from this slender evidence. Of the eight generals among them, only

34 Thuc. 8.47.1: ἅμα δὲ τὴν ἑαυτοῦ κάθοδον ἐς τὴν πατρίδα ἐπιθεραπεύων, εἰδώς, εἰ μὴ διαφθερεῖ αὐτήν, ὅτι ἔσται ποτὲ αὐτῷ πείσαντι κατελθεῖν· πεῖσαι δ' ἂν ἐνόμιζε μάλιστα ἐκ τοῦ τοιούτου, εἰ Τισσαφέρνης φαίνοιτο αὐτῷ ἐπιτήδειος ὤν· ὅπερ καὶ ἐγένετο.

35 Ibid. 2: Ἀλκιβιάδου προσπέμψαντος λόγους ἐς τοὺς δυνατωτάτους αὐτῶν ἄνδρας ὥστε μνησθῆναι περὶ αὐτοῦ ἐς τοὺς βελτίστους τῶν ἀνθρώπων ὅτι ἐπ' ὀλιγαρχίᾳ βούλεται καὶ οὐ πονηρίᾳ οὐδὲ δημοκρατίᾳ τῇ αὐτὸν ἐκβαλούσῃ κατελθὼν καὶ παρασχὼν Τισσαφέρνην φίλον αὐτοῖς ξυμπολιτεύειν. On the distinction between δυνατώτατοι and βέλτιστοι see Andrewes, *HCT* 5.106.

36 Thuc. 8.47.2: τὸ δὲ πλέον καὶ ἀπὸ σφῶν αὐτῶν οἱ ἐν τῇ Σάμῳ τριήραρχοί τε τῶν Ἀθηναίων καὶ δυνατώτατοι ὥρμηντο ἐς τὸ καταλῦσαι τὴν δημοκρατίαν. Note the pluperfect, ὥρμηντο.

37 Ibid. 48.1: τῷ τε Ἀλκιβιάδῃ διαβάντες τινὲς ἐκ τῆς Σάμου ἐς λόγους ἦλθον, καὶ ὑποτείνοντος αὐτοῦ Τισσαφέρνην μὲν πρῶτον, ἔπειτα δὲ καὶ βασιλέα φίλον ποιήσειν, εἰ μὴ δημοκρατοῖντο (οὕτω γὰρ ἂν πιστεῦσαι μᾶλλον βασιλέα), πολλὰς ἐλπίδας εἶχον αὐτοί θ' ἑαυτοῖς οἱ δυνατώτατοι τῶν πολιτῶν τὰ πράγματα, οἵπερ καὶ ταλαιπωροῦνται μάλιστα, ἐς ἑαυτοὺς περιποιήσειν καὶ τῶν πολεμίων ἐπικρατήσειν.

three—Strombichides, Diomedon, and Leon—seem clear of suspicion of having participated in any movement against the democracy. For Strombichides, who belonged to a "notable and wealthy family, whose political allegiance was consistent in support of the full democracy and in opposition to Sparta,"[38] this can be inferred from his active opposition to the peace and oligarchy of 404/3 B.C. and from his execution by the Thirty.[39] Diomedon and Leon were upright and loyal democrats, as the *dēmos* indicated shortly before the oligarchical coup, by sending them to the Ionian front to replace Phrynichus and Scironides, who had been denounced by Peisander. Thucydides states that "the respect Diomedes and Leon enjoyed among the common people made them put up with the oligarchy unwillingly" and that they supported the Samian *dēmos* against the oligarchical counterrevolutionaries.[40] We can be certain that four of the remaining five generals sided with the oligarchs against the democracy; only in the case of Euctemon do we lack any relevant information.[41] Onomacles' leanings are known from Andron's motion to try him, Archeptolemus, and Antiphon for treason they committed as members of the Four Hundred[42] and from his membership among the Thirty in 404/3 B.C.[43] Scironides' oligarchical sympathies can be inferred only from his being removed from office together with Phrynichus by the Athenian *dēmos* early in 411 B.C.,[44] and Charminus's from his being called upon to prove allegiance to

38 Davies, *APF* 161.

39 Lys. 13.13 and 30.14. Thuc. 8.30.1 states that he was a general in 412/11 B.C.; cf. 8.15.1, 16.1–2, 17.1 and 3, 62.2, 63.1, 79.3 and 5.

40 Their generalship in 412/11 B.C. is attested in the passage about their appointment as replacements, Thuc. 8.54.3. On their attitude toward the oligarchy, see 8.73.4: οὗτοι γὰρ οὐχ ἑκόντες διὰ τὸ τιμᾶσθαι ὑπὸ τοῦ δήμου ἔφερον τὴν ὀλιγαρχίαν. The two always appear together in Thucydides (see also 8.23.1, 24.2, 55.1, and 73.5), and they served again together on the board of generals after Alcibiades' second exile, in 406/5 B.C. (Xen. *Hell.* 1.5.16; cf. Diod. 13.74.1). Diomedon also participated in the battle of Arginusae (Xen. *Hell.* 1.6.29) and was one of the six generals executed in its aftermath (ibid. 1.7.2, 34; Philochorus *FGH* 328F142); Diod. 13.102.1–3 assigns a patriotic speech to him as he was led to his death. Leon may well be identical with the Salaminian victim of the Thirty; see Andrewes and Lewis, "Note" 179 n. 10, and W. J. McCoy, "The Identity of Leon," *AJP* 96 (1975) 187–99.

41 All we hear of him is that he was an Athenian general in Samos in 412/11 B.C. (Thuc. 8.30.1). Busolt, *GG* 3.2.1466–67 with 1412 and n. 6, classifies him as an oligarch but without evidence.

42 [Plut.] *X orat.* 833f. For his generalship, see Thuc. 8.25.1.

43 Xen. *Hell.* 2.3.2 with Andrewes, *HCT* 5.60.

44 Generalship: Thuc. 8.25.1; recall: 54.3. The interesting possibility that he may be identical with the wealthy Cyronides of Isae. 10 has been raised by W. E. Thompson, "Thucydides 8, 25,1 and 8, 54.3," *MH* 22 (1965) 238.

the oligarch's cause by murdering Hyperbolus.[45] The most interesting of the oligarchical generals is the one about whom we are also best informed, Phrynichus.

Little is known about this complex character before he appears in the late summer of 412 B.C. as one of three generals commanding forty-eight ships and 3,500 hoplites at Samos, soon to begin operations against Miletus (Thuc. 8.25.1). We have no earlier indication of his service to the democracy, except that a reference to a fine he had to pay into the treasury ([Lys.] 20.12) may mean he had been convicted after a *euthyna* for public office. The story that he spent his youth as a poor shepherd in the country and moved into the city upon reaching manhood to become a sycophant (ibid. 11–12) need not be taken literally, as a rags-to-riches story, but it helps us compare his age with that of Polystratus and to determine that he will have been in his sixties at the time of his generalship.[46] Since it is difficult to believe that a man of no previous distinction could be elected general for the first time at so advanced an age, it is tempting to identify this general with the Phrynichus who appears a decade earlier at the center of a group of men-about-town including Antiphon, Lycon, and Lysistratus (Ar. *Vesp.* 1301–3). There is no reason to attribute a political purpose to this group,[47] but Lysistratus was one of the four denounced by Andocides (1.52, 67, and 122) as participants in the mutilation of the herms in 415 B.C., and Antiphon became one of the oligarchical leaders in 411 B.C. If Lycon, however, is the same person who in 399 B.C. joined Anytus and Meletus in prosecuting Socrates,[48] his sympathies are not likely to have been with the oligarchs. But Plato's allegation that he prosecuted Socrates "on behalf of the public speakers" (ὑπὲρ τῶν ῥητόρων), when added to Antiphon's renown as an orator, suggests that Phrynichus's group consisted of upper-class men favorably disposed toward the sophists and influenced by them, while Phrynichus's description as a sycophant ([Lys.] 20.12) suggests that they kept busy in the law courts. Intellectual prowess, which does not exclude sophistic influence, also shines through Thucydides' praise of Phrynichus (8.27.5) as οὐκ

---

45 Generalship: Thuc. 8.30.1, 41.3–4, and 42.2. Murder of Hyperbolus: ibid. 73.3. Charminus is also mentioned at Ar. *Thesm.* 804.

46 See Andrewes, *HCT* 5.59.

47 See MacDowell, *Wasps* 302–3.

48 Pl. *Ap.* 23e and 36a. According to D.L. 2.38, he was called a δημαγωγός by Hermippus.

ἀξύνετος, "not without intellectual insight", an epithet elsewhere reserved for such outstanding statesmen as Themistocles (1.138.3), Pericles (2.34.6), Brasidas (4.81.2), and Hermocrates (6.72.2).

The occasion of Phrynichus's praise is his decision, momentous both for Athens and for himself and taken in defiance of his colleagues, not to offer battle off Miletus to a superior number of Peloponnesian ships because victory would not be assured.[49] His judgment may have been sound, but it caused the Argive hoplites to go back home in anger, led to the loss of Iasus to the Peloponnesians, and let the Persian rebel Amorges fall into enemy hands. Not long thereafter, it led to Peisander's charge of treason against him and to his and Scironides' recall by the Athenian *dēmos*.[50] His insight that the military strength of Athens was too precarious to risk a showdown in Ionian waters explains why he may have been willing to listen to any possibility of enlisting Persian aid for Athens. His position and his views will almost certainly have made him one of the δυνατώτατοι who entered into negotations with Alcibiades.

We do not know whether Phrynichus was among the Athenians who crossed over to the mainland for talks with Alcibiades (Thuc. 8.48.1). We do know he was the only Athenian leader intelligent enough to oppose Alcibiades' plan of replacing the democracy with an oligarchy. He could see that Alcibiades was less interested in oligarchy and democracy than in manipulating the situation to secure his own return to Athens and that the divisiveness of revolution had to be avoided. Further, he objected, an alliance with Athens would not be in Persia's interest at that time; and an oligarchy in Athens would not be able to control the allies any better than the democracy, since the allies' interest was in their own freedom from domination and allied states would find the upper classes more oppressive rulers than the commons (8.48.4–7). But Phrynichus did not prevail: the other δυνατώτατοι had already organized themselves into a ξυνωμοσία to implement Alcibiades' proposals.

Phrynichus's conversion from this stance to ardent support for the

49 Thuc. 8.27. The Athenian fleet contained probably sixty-eight ships over against eighty on the Peloponnesian side; see Andrewes, *HCT* 5.66. That Phrynichus's judgment prevailed suggests that he was already the senior Athenian officer on Samos; he is this at 8.51.1, where ἐστρατήγει δὲ καὶ κύριος ἦν αὐτὸς πράσσων ταῦτα.

50 Ibid. 27.6, 28.2–4, 54.3. Cf. schol. *Ran*. 688 (= *Suda* s.v. παλαίσμασιν) and Andrewes, *HCT* 5.66–67. This also explains Lysias's incredible allegation twelve years later (25.9) that, like Peisander, Phrynichus established the oligarchy because he feared retribution for crimes committed against the people.

oligarchy can be explained only by his obsession with preventing the return of Alcibiades to Athens, which he now regarded as inevitable. Fear of the *dēmos*'s vengeance should Alcibiades return (8.50.1) cannot have been Phrynichus's only motive, else he would have escaped into voluntary exile when recalled to Athens at Peisander's instigation (8.54.3). It rather seems he was so genuinely apprehensive of the the political consequences Alcibiades' return would have for Athens that, in order to prevent them, he was willing to risk being suspected of treasonous machinations with the enemy, although he eventually proved his integrity as an Athenian patriot.[51] Only when the oligarchs had dissociated themselves from Alcibiades months later did he join the oligarchical leadership to make doubly sure that his enemy would not return.[52] In short, though Phrynichus's upper-class intellectual background and his old ties to Antiphon suggest that he would not have been averse to seeing an oligarchical regime replace the democracy, he may like Antiphon[53] have recognized the dangers inherent in Alcibiades' character as soon as Alcibiades had entered politics and now may have feared what his return would do to Athens.

Two of the ten identifiable Athenians on Samos when the first contacts were established with Alcibiades are not described as generals. Of Thrasycles little is known: he was an officer, perhaps a general, in the Athenian forces (Thuc. 8.15.1, 17.3, 19.2); he was a signatory of the Peace of Nicias and of the Fifty-Year Alliance (5.19.2, 24.1); and he was probably the same Thrasycles who proposed a proxeny decree for Asteas of Alea in 421/0 B.C.[54] The other person was certainly one of the δυνατώτατοι Alcibiades approached: Peisander.

Peisander's past does not provide much of a clue for his appearance as a leader of the oligarchical movement in 411 B.C. In his earliest known political post, he appears as a trusted democrat (Andoc. 1.36), a member of the Council in 415/14 B.C. appointed ζητητής (investi-

---

51 Thuc. 8.50.2–51.3; Plut. *Alc.* 25.6–13; schol. Ar. *Av.* 750; *Suda* s.v. Φρυνίχου πάλαισμα; Polyaenus 3.6.

52 Thuc. 8.68.3; Ar. *Ran.* 689; Lys. 25.9; Artist. *Pol.* 5.6, 1305ᵇ 27.

53 The ʼΑλκιβιάδου λοιδορίαι that Plut. *Alc.* 3 and Ath. 12.525b attribute to Antiphon must be dated before Alcibiades' first exile, since the latter quotes a fragment in the second person singular. Blass, *AB*² 1.106 suggests ca. 418 B.C. as a date.

54 *IG* I³ 80.7 with Andrewes and Lewis, "Note" 178, where the suggestion is made that he may have been a general.

gator) in the incident of the herms and the Mysteries.[55] One of his colleagues in that capacity was Charicles, who later became prominent among the Thirty and may have followed Peisander into the oligarchical camp as one of the Four Hundred.[56] Remarks by comic poets about Peisander from 426 B.C. on attest his prominence but tell us nothing about his political activities in the 420s; they do permit the inference that he was in his mid-forties in 411 B.C.[57] The fact that Plato Comicus wrote a play about him, as he did also about Hyperbolus and Cleophon, suggests that Peisander had the reputation of a demagogue;[58] his reputation as a warmonger and bribetaker gives him an affinity to Cleon.[59] He is not marked as a "salesman" (-πωλης) as other demagogues are, but the unique epithet ὀνοκίνδιος applied to him by Eupolis (fr. 182) and alluded to by Hermippus (fr. 9) may mean that donkey driving played an important part in his economic activities. He seems to have been a man of some wealth: he was probably Peisander son of Glaucetes of Acharnae, who was appointed to supervise the production of the cult images of Hephaestus and Athena for the temple of Hephaestus in 421/0 B.C.,[60] and we know he had landholdings enough to be confiscated after he escaped to Deceleia in 411 B.C.[61]

Wealth is our only possible clue to explain Peisander's conversion to the oligarchical cause in 412/11 B.C. Since he was not in Samos as a general at that time, the most satisfactory explanation for his presence among the δυνατώτατοι is that he must have been one of the seventy-four trierarchs who had accompanied their ships to the island.[62] The trierarchs were hit hardest by the economic distress that followed the Sicilian defeat (8.48.1; cf. 8.63.4). Though their

---

55 Andoc. 1.36 with pp. 331–32 above.

56 His membership in the Four Hundred can be inferred only from Lys. 13.74; he seems to have gone into exile after their fall (Isoc. 16.42 with Lys. 13.73), returned, and became a member of the Thirty in 404 B.C. (Xen. *Hell.* 2.3.2, *Mem.* 1.2.31; Andoc. 1.101; Lys. 12.55; Arist. *Pol.* 5.6, 1305[b] 26). See Davies, *APF* 502–3.

57 See A. G. Woodhead, "Peisander," *AJP* 75 (1954) 131–46, esp. 133, and above, Chap. 6, nn. 145–48.

58 See Woodhead, "Peisander" 132–33 with n. 6.

59 Ar. fr. 81. Cf. schol. Ar. *Lys.* 490; *Pax* 390–95.

60 *IG* I[3] 472.1–3 with Makkink, *Rede* 129.

61 Lys. 7.4. A further indication that he was a man of substance may be seen in his moving the proxeny decree for Lycon of Achaea (*IG* I[3] 174) at some point between 425 and 410 B.C.

62 Asserted without argument by G. Reincke, "Peisandros," *RE* 19. Band (1937) 142–44, esp. 142; cf. also Woodhead, "Peisander" 140 with n. 21, who rightly rejects Nepos's assertion (*Alc.* 5.3) that he was a general.

income had dwindled because of the Spartan occupation of Deceleia, there was no letup in the demands the state made of them year after year to equip and run the fleet: the allies still had to be kept in check and the war against the Peloponnesians still had to be waged in the waters off Ionia. They were probably ready to overthrow the democracy even before negotiations with Alcibiades began;[63] the prospect that with Alcibiades' intercession Tissaphernes might ease their financial burden will have proved attractive. The Sicilian expedition had shown that the judgment of the people could not be relied on to get Athens out of her present difficulties.

Peisander's emergence as the main spokesman and agent of the δυνατώτατοι suggests that he was one of the delegates who negotiated with Alcibiades on the mainland (8.48.1) and that he joined or perhaps even organized the ξυνωμοσία (conspiracy) formed as soon as the delegates returned to Samos, presumably because without concerted action Alcibiades' package deal could not be brought off.[64] He may well have considered that his past activities had won him the trust of the common people, so that he could best be depended on to persuade the masses of the need for strong measures. There is no reason to assume that "a revision of principles tested and found wanting, and a well-grounded calculation of expediency . . . combined to cause Peisander to make a statesmanlike move into the oligarchic camp":[65] his own trierarchies may well have convinced him to look to Persia for financial relief; once he had arrived at that conviction, he worked for it with the same zeal and ruthlessness with which he had gone after those he had believed were the culprits in 415 B.C. He dealt both with the soldiers on Samos and with the Assembly in Athens as squarely as was politic but withheld from both the plan of installing an oligarchy in place of the democracy. The soldiers were told that friendship with the Persian king could be obtained if Alcibiades were recalled and the democracy were overthrown; their disapproval of these conditions was soon overcome by the hope of pay the plan offered (8.48.2–3). Phrynichus's objections that Alcibiades' return and establishing an oligarchy would be counterproductive *vis-à-vis* the allies were overruled as overlooking

63   Thuc. 8.47.2 with p. 346 and n. 36 above.
64   Ibid. 48.2. We learn at 48.3 that the members of the ξυνωμοσία included τοῦ ἑταιρικοῦ τῷ πλέονι in their deliberations. These included probably personal likeminded friends not prominent enough to be members of the delegation that negotiated with Alcibiades.
65   Woodhead, "Peisander" 140.

the most serious issue, the procurement of funds to carry on the war
(8.48.4–6). It was left to Peisander to ensure by recalling Phrynichus
to Athens that his opposition would not impair the conspiracy's
chance of success (8.49, 54.3).

There is no need to regard as disingenuous the arguments with
which Peisander soon after his arrival in Athens[66] prepared the
Assembly for the things to come. The reason why they carried
conviction may well have been that Peisander was himself convinced of their validity. If he was right in believing that the survival
of Athens depended on solving the state's financial difficulties, his
arguments are unanswerable:

In view of the facts that the Peloponnesians have no fewer ships than the
Athenians for confronting them at sea, that more cities are allied with
them, and that the king and Tissaphernes are giving them money, whereas
the Athenians have none left, is there any hope of survival unless someone
can prevail upon the king to switch his support to Athens? . . . The only way
to make that happen is to install a more moderate regime and to make fewer
men eligible for office, in order to gain the confidence of the king; the issue
at this juncture is less the form of government under which Athens is to live
than how it is to survive. We shall be able to change our government again
later, if we do not like it. Alcibiades is the only person alive able to work this
out successfully, and we must bring him back. (8.53.2–3)

66   For a judicious treatment of the chronological problems of Peisander's
mission to Athens, see Andrewes, *HCT* 5.184–93, who argues cogently that he
reached Athens in early January 411 B.C., that he was present in Athens when
Aristophanes' *Lysistrata* was performed at the Lenaea (in February), but that he had
departed for Asia Minor by the time the *Thesmophoriazusae* was performed (about
April) at the Dionysia, since his conference with Tissaphernes will have taken place
before the middle of April. Andrewes believes that contrary to the impression
conveyed by Thuc. 8.53.1, Peisander had not yet addressed the Assembly by the time
of the performance of the *Lysistrata*, and "that at first all that was generally known
was that he had a plan to obtain money from the Persians" (*HCT* 5.189). This leaves
the reason for Peisander's delay somewhat of a puzzle, unless we assume that his
overtures to the clubs preceded his first address to the Assembly and that the address
was a stratagem from the very start. Since, however, his overriding concern was to
create the preconditions for obtaining Persian funds, it would be strange if he did
not address the Assembly as soon as possible after his arrival. It is also unlikely that
the Assembly immediately appointed him and ten others to negotiate with Tissaphernes and Alcibiades: Thucydides' use of the present participle διδασκόμενος
(8.54.1) preceding the aorist ἐψηφίσαντο (54.2) suggests that more than one Assembly meeting was needed to obtain the desired result. Peisander's concern with
funding the war is attested by the only reference to him in Aristophanes' *Lysistrata*
(490–91); the absence of any reference to the possibility that the democracy might
have to be sacrificed to satisfy this need might simply mean that this aspect of
Peisander's mission had not left any deep impression and that it was hoped
Alcibiades' recall could be brought about without radical constitutional changes.

The view that Peisander held these opinions not because he had become a doctrinaire oligarch but because, like the *proboulos* Sophocles, he saw no alternative[67] is not inconsistent with the ruthlessness, duplicity, and deceit with which he worked for what he believed was in the Athenians' best interest. As he had with the soldiers in Samos, he concealed at Athens the full extent of the constitutional changes Alcibiades demanded, at first using the phrase μὴ τὸν αὐτὸν τρόπον δημοκρατουμένοις (53.1) and leaving it ambiguous whether a modification or the abolition of the democratic form of government was required. Later he explained that the adjustment would merely entail moderation in public policy and a restriction of eligibility—presumably to those most involved in financing the war—for public office. Was this approach born of an honest conviction that a few cosmetic changes sufficient to bring about Alcibiades' recall would obtain the desired funds from Persia? Or was it merely a stratagem to pave a devious way for oligarchy?[68] Peisander will have been prepared for the political, legal, and religious outcry his proposal evoked. By challenging each of his opponents to produce a better solution for the financial predicament of the city, he made the *dēmos* accept the inevitable in the hope that any change to come would be reversible. His appointment by the Assembly to head a team of eleven envoys with full powers to negotiate with Tissaphernes and Alcibiades, and the removal of Phrynichus and Scironides from their generalships on his motion show that he enjoyed the confidence of the people (8.53.2–54.3).

Peisander, however, did not reciprocate this trust. Before his departure for Asia Minor, Thucydides states, he approached all ξυνωμοσίαι whose members were sworn to help one another in lawsuits and in realizing their personal political ambitions (ἐπὶ δίκαις καὶ ἀρχαῖς), urging them to work together to overthrow the democracy.[69] This is the first time we hear of such ξυνωμοσίαι; Thucydides informs us that they existed in Athens before 411 B.C., although he does not say how much earlier. The context makes clear that the term does not here have its usual meaning, "conspiracies,"

---

67   See Arist. *Rh*. 3.18, 1419ᵃ 25–30: οὐ γὰρ ἦν ἄλλα βελτίω.
68   The latter seems to be the interpretation adopted by Arist. *Pol*. 5.4, 1304ᵇ 10–15, if, as is likely, it refers to this stage of the development.
69   Thuc. 8.54.4: καὶ ὁ μὲν Πείσανδρος τάς τε ξυνωμοσίας, αἵπερ ἐτύγχανον πρότερον ἐν τῇ πόλει οὖσαι ἐπὶ δίκαις καὶ ἀρχαῖς, ἁπάσας ἐπελθὼν καὶ παρακελευσάμενος ὅπως ξυστραφέντες καὶ κοινῇ βουλευσάμενοι καταλύσουσι τὸν δῆμον.

but has been chosen to indicate groups bound together by mutual oaths, much as it is applied in external affairs to compacts that parties confirm by oaths between them.[70] Unlike conspiracies, these domestic associations were not formed *ad hoc* but were intended for permanent social and private cooperation among friends in litigation and in furthering the political careers of one another. Before this period such groups, which surely must have existed at least informally from early times, were not called ξυνωμοσίαι. That term appears for the first time in a private political sense in Thucydides' account of the scandal of 415 B.C., when a conspiracy to overthrow the democracy and establish a tyranny or oligarchy in its place was widely suspected.[71]

We have already observed that these acts were attributed to groups of like-minded young aristocrats known because of their origins and education to be unsympathetic to the democracy.[72] It is therefore safe to infer that much of the help they gave one another ἐπὶ δίκαις will have been in trials arising from *euthynai*, to which one of their number might be subjected or to which a member might wish to subject a political opponent. Organizations of such men could easily be mobilized to take action against the democracy even if their basic purpose was social and personal rather than ideological.[73] Peisander will have recognized that the ruthless ambition of many of these young men, whose intellectual and critical faculties will have been sharpened by sophistic training and influence, could be used to ensure that the momentum of his enterprise would not be lost in his absence. Not until Peisander encouraged the various ξυνωμοσίαι to cooperate with one another were they united in common political purpose.[74] Any political pressure they exerted before that time will

---

70   Id. 3.64.2, 5.83.4. For the verb ξυνομνύναι used in this sense, see id. 1.58.1, 71.5; 2.72.1; 3.63.3, 64.3; 64.3; 5.38.2 and 3, 48.2, 80.2; 6.18.1; 8.75.3. Cf. also τὸ ξυνώμοτον at 2.74.2. In general, see Andrewes, *HCT* 5.128–31.

71   Thuc. 6.27.3, 60.1, and 61.1 with pp. 322–26 above.

72   See above, pp. 325–27.

73   The only other fifth-century passage in which ξυνωμοσία is used in this sense is Ar. *Eq.* 476, where the term refers collectively to specific acts of which Cleon had recklessly accused ξυνωμόται in lines 257, 452, 628, and 862. For ξυνωμότης in the sense "conspirator," see also Ar. *Vesp.* 345, 483, 488, 507, 953. In his discussion of the conspiracy of Harmodius and Aristogeiton Thucydides does not use ξυνωμοσία, but οἱ ξυνομωκότες (6.56.3) and ξυνωμόται (6.57.2). The discussions of these terms by Calhoun, *Clubs* 4–7, and Sartori, *Eterie* 17–33, are less satisfactory than that of Aurenche, *Groupes* 32–41 with table on p. 33.

74   Note Thuc. 8.54.4: ξυστραφέντες καὶ κοινῇ βουλευσάμενοι.

have been to support members or their policies: Alcibiades, for example, could count on a group of like-minded young men to try to intimidate the Assembly into voting for his policy and against Nicias's.[75] Now they were pressed into supporting not a person or policy but a political principle.

Thucydides uses the term ἑταῖροι (friends; boon companions) of these groups when he reports that they had completed their assigned task by the time Peisander and his associates returned to Athens in the summer of 411 B.C. ready to install an oligarchical regime.[76] The word indicates how Peisander had changed these originally private and personal associations. From Homer down, through all periods of Greek literature, ἑταῖροι are characterized by a close personal relationship inaccessible to outsiders because of its closeness and therefore easily suspected of secret activities, political or otherwise.[77] It is not until Peisander's politicization of the ξυνωμοσίαι that the words ἑταῖροι and ἑταιρεία are used to describe essentially political groups. The two exceptions to this statement are only apparent. The speech Andocides is said to have addressed πρὸς τοὺς ἑταίρους, presumably earlier than 415 B.C.,[78] is clearly political and antidemocratic in character, but that does not imply that the *hetairoi* he addressed were his friends in a primarily political rather than a social sense. Decidedly political associations are, however, referred to by Thucydides (3.82.5 and 6; cf. 3.82.4) as ἑταιρία and τὸ ἑταιρικόν in his discussion of *stasis* on Corcyra. Yet this passage is generally agreed to have been composed long after the event; Thucydides may well be using a vocabulary developed after 413 B.C. to describe a situation that existed in 427 B.C.[79] About this time, too, the word τὸ ἑταιρικόν

---

75 Thuc. 6.13.1 with pp. 321–22 above.

76 Thuc. 8.65.2: καὶ καταλαμβάνουσι τὰ πλεῖστα τοῖς ἑταίροις προειργασμένα.

77 None of the eight occurrences in Hdt. (3.14.7 and 10, 51.3, 125.1; 5.95.2; 6.62.1 [*bis*] and 2) has any political overtones, and even Thuc. (6.30.2; 7.73.3, 75.4) occasionally uses the term in a purely social sense. Moreover, in Thucydides' report (8.48.4) of Phrynichus's suspicions that Alcibiades was trying to engineer his return to Athens ὑπὸ τῶν ἑταίρων παρακληθείς, it remains ambiguous whether the *hetairoi* in question are personal friends, political partisans, or both; cf. also Ar. *Lys.* 1153, Andoc. 1.54 and [4].14, Lys. 13.19. Further, the tragedians' use of ἑταιρ(ε)ία to describe the bond of friendship (Soph. *Aj.* 683; Eur. *Or.* 1072, 1079) should make us wary of assuming a primarily political meaning of Cylon's ἑταιρηίη τῶν ἡλικιωτέων at Hdt. 5.71.1. Calhoun, *Clubs* 4–9, Sartori, *Eterie* 18–30, and Aurenche, *Groupes* 15–32 with tables on pp. 16–18, all tend to see earlier traces than warranted of the political corporations attested from the late fifth century on.

78 See Plut. *Them.* 32.4, as discussed above, pp. 327–28 with nn. 122–24.

79 For the date of composition, see O. Luschnat, "Thukydides," *RE* Suppl. 12 (1971) 1201; *HCT* 2.372 (on 3.82.1), 5.408.

seems to have been coined to describe any ἑταιρεῖα constituted for political action,[80] and "action" in its most concrete sense, at that. Unlike our modern political parties, the *hetaireiai* were not united by any ideological principle, other than the views dictated by a common upper-class background. We know of no *hetaireia* organized to champion the interests of the common people.

Whether Peisander foresaw what his organization of the clubs would lead to we do not know. Thucydides' description (8.65–66) of the terror and intimidation they spread applies to the weeks immediately preceding the coup in early June of 411 B.C.; it will have taken several weeks after Peisander's departure to develop its full fury. By the time of the production of the *Thesmophoriazusae*, in April, there was, as Andrewes has shown, apprehension that the democracy was endangered, but the clubs had not yet resorted to terror.[81] Of special interest in the *Thesmophoriazusae* are the curses uttered by the female herald (331–51) and echoed in lyrics by the chorus (352–71), parodying those formally pronounced at the opening of Assembly meetings. The inclusion among the former of anyone "negotiating with Euripides and the Medes to the detriment of the Assembly of women" may be humorous, because it puts Euripides on the same level as the traditional enemy. But the fact that added to it is a curse against anyone "planning to establish a tyranny or abetting the return of the tyrant" suggests that the recall of Alcibiades as the price for Persian help is envisaged with some genuine trepidation.[82] Even more ominous fears ring through the lyric curses against "all those who deceive and transgress against the oaths sanctioned by tradition for the sake of profit and to the detriment [of the city], or who seek to move decrees and law in the reverse direction, and who tell our enemies what must not be revealed, or bring the Medes into our land for the sake of profit and to the detriment [of the city], who act impiously and unjustly toward the city."[83] Intimidation has not yet

80 Again at Thuc. 8.48.3, and most strikingly in the νόμος εἰσαγγελτικός cited by Hyperides 4 (*Eux.*) 8.
81 For this and the following, see Andrewes, *HCT* 5.190–93.
82 Ar. *Thesm*. 336–39: ἢ 'πικηρυκεύεται / Εὐριπίδῃ Μήδοις <τ'> ἐπὶ βλάβῃ τινὶ / τῇ τῶν γυναικῶν, ἢ τυραννεῖν ἐπινοεῖ / ἢ τὸν τύραννον συγκατάγειν.
83 Ibid. 356–67: ὁπόσαι δ' / ἐξαπατῶσιν παραβαίνουσί τε τοὺς / ὅρκους τοὺς νενομισμένους / κερδῶν οὕνεκ' ἐπὶ βλάβῃ, / ἢ ψηφίσματα καὶ νόμον / ζητοῦσ' ἀντιμεθιστάναι, / τἀπόρρητά τε τοῖσιν ἐ-/χθροῖς τοῖς ἡμετέροις λέγουσ', / ἢ Μήδους ἐπάγουσι γῇ / κερδῶν οὕνεκ' ἐπὶ βλάβῃ, / ἀσεβοῦσιν ἀδικοῦσίν τε τὴν πόλιν. Since the manuscript reading of lines 365–66 makes no sense, I retain, with the Oxford text, the emendations of Velsen and Reiske and accept in general the interpretation of Andrewes, *HCT* 5.190–192.

banished free speech from the stage either here or in the invocation to Athena, Protector of the City, toward the end of the play, in which the *dēmos* of women pointedly appeals to the goddess's hatred of tyrants (1143–46). Still, a threat to the democracy is clearly being found in quarters that put profit ahead of such traditional values as oaths sworn, decrees passed, and the democratic order embodied in *nomos*—quarters that do not shrink from treasonous dealings with the Persians for the sake of profit and lack religious (ἀσεβοῦσιν) and moral scruples.

The Four Hundred

There is no evidence that Peisander or those in whose name he had come from Samos had any idea what the oligarchical regime that would recall Alcibiades would look like, and it is doubtful that any specifics had been discussed with Alcibiades. There is accordingly no reason to believe that Peisander's ideas went any farther than the vague statements on greater moderation and a restriction on eligibility for office that Thucydides attributes to his address to the Assembly. If this is correct, we may think of Peisander as a skillful organizer who depended on others to inspire him with ideas for his political abilities to effect.

Ideas can be dangerous, but lack of ideas can be more dangerous still. If Peisander gave any positive guidance to the clubs of young aristocrats before he embarked on his mission to Ionia, we are not told about it. His only known instruction is negative: to work together for the overthrow of the democracy (Thuc. 8.54.4). The actions taken by the young conspirators before Peisander's return in early June reflect this lack of a positive principle. Restriction of pay for public service to the soldiers in the field and of the franchise to the five thousand citizens most capable of serving the state with their persons and their fortunes were the only ideas that reached the level of public discussion (8.65.3); no legislative action seems to have been taken on them. Apart from that, the young gentlemen did no more than terrorize and intimidate. Alcibiades' old enemy Androcles was murdered lest he be an obstacle to the recall of Alcibiades, and a number of other potential obstructionists suffered a similar fate. Council and Assembly meetings were formally held, but their agenda were controlled by the conspirators, because ignorance of their identities and their number reduced the masses to silence and to suspecting their neighbors. They had seen the unexplained fate of those who offered resistance (8.65.2, 8.66). We learn of no preparation for Peisander's return other than intimidating the populace so that he could do with it as he pleased.

And yet, the events preceding the coup as related by Aristotle (*Ath.Pol.* 29.1–3) and especially the elaborate constitutional schemes for the present and the future (ibid. 30–31) can only be the result of prolonged discussion, extending at least over the three months of Peisander's absence and probably initiated considerably before his departure on his mission. Peisander is likely to have been in touch with the participants in these discussions during his stay in Athens, but being preoccupied with negotiating with Alcibiades and obtaining Persian funds he was probably not worried about constitutional structures at this time. He was an organizer, but for creative political thought he depended on others.

The documents Aristotle incorporates in the *Constitution of Athens* (30–31) leave no doubt that the "others" were intellectually and ideologically committed to abolishing or at least modifying the principle of popular sovereignty and to putting control of the government into the hands of the upper classes. According to Aristotle (*Ath.Pol.* 29.2, 30.1, 31.1; cf. Thuc. 8.67.1) a board of thirty commissioners (συγγραφεῖς) was established upon Peisander's return to promulgate new constitutional proposals, but their recommendations will have incorporated ideas hatched by the opponents of the democracy and submitted by them to the commission. Our sources do not name those who devised the constitution of the Four Hundred, but Thucydides identifies the leading spirit among them. Peisander, he says, made the motion to create a Council of Four Hundred with absolute power, "but the person who had organized the method by which the whole affair should come to this issue and who had devoted himself to it for the longest time was Antiphon, second to none of the Athenians of his time in excellence and most forceful in conceiving ideas and in communicating his conclusions. He was reluctant to address the Assembly and to engage in any public argument, because the reputation of his formidable talent rendered him suspect in the eyes of the masses. But he was the one man most capable of helping people in a critical contest, whether in the jury courts or in the Assembly, when they sought his advice on any point."[84]

---

84 Thuc. 8.68.1: ὁ μέντοι ἅπαν τὸ πρᾶγμα ξυνθεὶς ὅτῳ τρόπῳ κατέστη ἐς τοῦτο καὶ ἐκ πλείστου ἐπιμεληθεὶς Ἀντιφῶν ἦν ἀνὴρ Ἀθηναίων τῶν καθ᾽ ἑαυτὸν ἀρετῇ τε οὐδενὸς ὕστερος καὶ κράτιστος ἐνθυμηθῆναι γενόμενος καὶ ἃ γνοίη εἰπεῖν, καὶ ἐς μὲν δῆμον οὐ παριὼν οὐδ᾽ ἐς ἄλλον ἀγῶνα ἑκούσιος οὐδένα, ἀλλ᾽ ὑπόπτως τῷ πλήθει διὰ

This is higher praise than Thucydides gives Phrynichus (8.27.5); it can be compared only with the historian's opinion of the intellect of Themistocles or Pericles.[85] Some modern scholars have been baffled here because Thucydides attributes ἀρετή (excellence) to a man who condoned, if not initiated, the terror and deceit that characterized the establishment of the Four Hundred, a man who joined the treasonous embassy to Sparta. But it becomes less surprising once we recognize that Antiphon is praised not for his virtue but for his *virtù*, that is, not as a paragon of conventional morality but as a thinker (ἐνθυμηθῆναι), as an articulate expounder of his views (ἃ γνοίη εἰπεῖν), and as an effective advocate of clients and of causes (τοὺς ἀγωνιζομένους ὠφελεῖν). His precise role is far from clear. Since no element in the constitution for the present or for the future is assigned to him, and since he is not credited with any of the motions establishing the Four Hundred's power, we have to interpret Thucydides' words as indicating that Antiphon shunned public exposure and operated powerfully behind the scenes, using Peisander and others as his agents. Moreover, the crucial phrase ὁ μέντοι ἅπαν τὸ πρᾶγμα ξυνθεὶς ὅτῳ τρόπῳ κατέστη ἐς τοῦτο, "but the person who had organized the method by which the whole affair should come to this issue," leaves ambiguous whether Antiphon merely "managed the mechanics of the business,"[86] or whether he designed the oligarchy. Thucydides' use of the intransitive aorist κατέστη in conjunction with ἐς τοῦτο, which can define as the "issue" only the form the oligarchical regime eventually took, suggests that Antiphon also determined the goals of the revolution, in other words, that he was its theoretician.[87] If that was the case, what made him oppose the democracy and promote oligarchy?

Reliable information about Antiphon is difficult to obtain.[88] There is some broad agreement that the oligarch is identical with the orator under whose name three speeches in homicide cases, three rhetorical

---

δόξαν δεινότητος διακείμενος, τοὺς μέντοι ἀγωνιζομένους καὶ ἐν δικαστηρίῳ καὶ ἐν δήμῳ πλεῖστα εἷς ἀνήρ, ὅστις ξυμβουλεύσαιτό τι, δυνάμενος ὠφελεῖν.

85   Id. 1.138.3; 2.34.6 and 65.5–6, 13; cf. Andrewes, *HCT* 5.171–72, who also includes Hermocrates, Brasidas, and Alcibiades in his comparison.

86   So Andrewes, *HCT* 5.170.

87   E. Meyer, *Geschichte des Altertums* 4.2⁴, *Der Ausgang der griechischen Geschichte* (Basel and Stuttgart, 1956) 140 and 282; L. Gernet, ed. and tr. *Antiphon: Discours* (Paris, 1923) 3.

88   The most important biography that has come down to us from antiquity ([Plut.] *X orat.* 832b–834b), which depends on Caecilius of Calacte, a contemporary of Augustus, confuses the oligarch with other contemporaries of the same name; see

exercises (the *Tetralogies*), and fragments of some twenty speeches have come down to us, among them a papyrus of the defense he delivered before his execution in 411 B.C.[89] Dover has plausibly argued that none of the speeches was delivered before 422/1 B.C. and that the *Tetralogies* were composed earlier in Antiphon's career.[90] Considered together with Thucydides' statement that Antiphon was averse to appearing in public (8.68.1), this suggests that Antiphon appeared in the courts only in the last decade of his life and was prior to that time occupied with theoretical problems of rhetoric.

This conclusion tallies well with other information. There is no reason to disbelieve the tradition that Antiphon was first taught by his father, Sophilus, who also counted Alcibiades among his pupils.[91] Further, we can accept Plato's statement (*Menex.* 236a) that Antiphon himself taught rhetoric[92] without our being compelled also to accept the tradition that he was Thucydides' teacher.[93] A verdict on his relations with Thucydides depends on what the age difference was between them. Most scholars believe Antiphon was born about 480 B.C.,[94] but this is unlikely, because a man would probably not

---

Blass, *AB*[2] 1.93–94; dependent on it are Philostr. *VS* 1.15, Phot. *Bibl.* 485b–486b (ed. R. Henry, *Photius: Bibliothèque* 8 [Paris, 1977] 41–43), and a Γένος Ἀντιφῶντος included in the manuscripts of Antiphon. It is not difficult to distinguish the oligarch from the son of Lysonides and victim of the Thirty ([Plut.] *X. orat.* 832f–833b; Xen. *Hell.* 2.3.40), or from the tragic poet executed by Dionysius I of Syracuse ([Plut.] *X orat.* 833b–c), but it is impossible confidently to determine the oligarch's relation to the sophistic author of treatises περὶ ἀληθείας and περὶ ὁμονοίας and to the sophistic interlocutor of Socrates (Xen. *Mem.* 1.6.1; he is probably identical with the soothsayer mentioned, according to D.L. 2.46, in the third book of Aristotle's *Poetics*). The most important recent studies of this problem are: E. Bignone, "Antifonte oratore e Antifonte sofista," *Rend.Ist.Lomb.* 52 (1919) 564–78 (reprinted in *Antifonte Oratore e Antifonte Sofista* [Urbino, 1974] 7–20); J. S. Morrison, "Antiphon," *PCPS* 187, n. s. 7 (1961) 49–58; S. Luria, "Antiphon der Sophist," *Eos* 53 (1963) 63–67 (reprinted in Classen, ed., *Sophistik* 537–42); Guthrie, *HGP* 3.292–94; Kerferd, *SM* 49–51.

89 For Antiphon's life, see Andrewes, *HCT* 5.170–76 and 198–201 with bibliography on p. 170.

90 Dover, "Chronology" 44–60.

91 [Plut.] *X orat.* 832b–c with Blass, *AB*[2] 1.95 with n. 2.

92 The doubts expressed by Dover, "Chronology" 59, and seconded by Andrewes, *HCT* 5.174, have been effectively answered by Morrison, "Antiphon" 49 n. 3.

93 Caecilius in [Plut.] *X orat.* 832e (with Wyttenbach's emendation of μαθητήν to καθηγητήν); Marcellin. *Vit. Thuc.* 22 (cf. *Vit.anon.* 2); Hermog. *Id.* 2 (Antiphon 87A2 DK[6], pp. 334.22–335.3). On the ancient accounts of the relation between Antiphon and Thucydides, see Morrison, "Antiphon" 53, 56.

94 Based on the doubtful statement at [Plut.] *X orat.* 832f that he was born at the time of the Persian Wars and that he was a little younger than Gorgias, and on

begin publishing his speeches about the age of sixty or become politically most active as he approached his seventies. A birthdate some ten years later, suggested by Aristophanes' associating him with the high-living men about Phrynichus (*Vesp.* 1301–2; the earliest known reference to Antiphon), seems more probable and would make a relationship (as friend or teacher) with Thucydides, his junior by ten or fifteen years, more likely.[95] Moreover, Aristophanes' reference to him falls in 422 B.C., the same year, according to Dover, as Antiphon's earliest datable speech.[96] It is therefore reasonable to suppose that this was one of his earliest public appearances and that the allusion in the *Wasps* to his constant hunger may reflect the large fees he exacted from his clients,[97] a charge hurled at him again by one of his prosecutors in 411 B.C.[98]

The reference to Antiphon in the *Wasps* enables us to say something about his social and political orientation. Phrynichus's group consisted of men from the upper classes whose common interest in rhetoric suggests their close relationship to the sophists. The presence in that group of the Lysistratus who was to participate in the mutilation of the herms some seven years later may indicate that its members shared an aversion to the established democracy.[99] This observation is reinforced in *On the Choreutes* by Antiphon's mentioning that the same (apparently) Lysistratus was an earlier target of his client's adversaries.[100] Chief among these adversaries was Philinus, whose conviction for embezzlement Antiphon had secured a year earlier, on which occasion Antiphon accused him of trying to "make all thetes into hoplites."[101] This statement alleges a radical proposal, tantamount to freeing the lowest property class altogether (ἅπαντας) from its most glaring disability. Whatever the context of the allegation, it can only have been made by a spokesman for the upper classes

---

the slanderous allegation at his trial that his grandfather had supported the tyrants (Antiphon, fr. 1 Thalheim); see Andrewes, *HCT* 5.172.

95 See above, pp. 348 and 350.

96 Antiphon, frr. 21–24 Thalheim (= κατὰ Λαισποδίου) with Dover, "Chronology" 54, 55.

97 Ar. *Vesp.* 1270, πεινῇ γὰρ ἥπερ 'Αντιφῶν, with MacDowell's note.

98 Antiphon, fr. 1a Thalheim. His fondness for money was also ridiculed by Plato Com. fr. 103 (*Peisander*), dated 422 B.C. by Körte, "Platon (Komiker)" 2537–41, esp. 2539, and before 411 B.C. by P. Geissler, *Chronologie der altattischen Komödie* (Berlin, 1925) 51.

99 See above, p. 348.

100 Antiphon 6.36, dated by Dover, "Chronology" 55 and 60, to 419/18 B.C.

101 Antiphon, 6.36 with 12, 21, 35, 38, with Dover, "Chronology" 55; and fr. 61 (XVIII κατὰ Φιλίνου): τούς τε θῆτας ἅπαντας ὁπλίτας ποιῆσαι.

against a champion of the democracy. The antidemocratic bias shown here may also be in evidence in Antiphon's charge that Philocrates, who had been suborned by Philinus and his friends to prosecute the *choreutēs*, had the habit of "shaking down and bringing frivolous suits against" magistrates at their *euthynai*.[102] Such charges are also made against the demagogues in comedy, but there is a difference between the comic stage and a courtroom. An antidemocratic attitude in these passages would be consistent with Antiphon's aversion to seeing the allies pay excessive tribute, evident in his pleading the causes of the people of Lindos (before 419/18 B.C.) and of Samothrace (between 418/17 and 414/13 B.C.).[103] The upper classes had been showing the same concern for the allied states since as early as Thucydides son of Melesias and continued to do so through the 420s.[104] Our evidence points therefore to an upper-class, antidemocratic outlook for Antiphon from at least the late 420s, and it suggests that his motive for wanting to establish an oligarchy in 411 B.C. was unlike the motive of Peisander and his associates. Antiphon acted not out of a desire to accommodate Alcibiades, against whom he had inveighed as early as 418 B.C.,[105] but out of a deeply ingrained temperamental and ideological predisposition that presumably also underlies Thucydides' assertion of his reluctance to appear before the people.

The possible identity of the oligarch and orator Antiphon with the author of the sophistic tract *On Truth*, though an important problem in its own right, is of only marginal interest to understanding the role Antiphon played in the revolution of 411 B.C. We have shown already that the oligarch was associated with men whose thinking had been shaped by the sophists. *On Truth* seems to have been written in the 420s, or at least during the orator Antiphon's lifetime; unless such a date for *On Truth* can be disproved, it must obviously be considered evidence for the identity of the orator with the author.[106] The question thus is whether the tract displays such oligarchical

---

102   Antiphon 6.43; ἑτέρους τῶν ὑπευθύνων ἔσειε καὶ ἐσυκοφάντει. Cf., e.g., Ar. *Eq.* 258–65, 840.

103   Antiphon, frr. IX and XV with Dover, "Chronology" 54, 55.

104   See above, pp. 187–88.

105   See above, p. 350 with n. 53.

106   See Guthrie, *HGP* 3.286 with n. 2, and C. Moulton, "Antiphon the Sophist *On Truth*," *TAPA* 103 (1972) 329–66, esp. 330 with n. 2. The most influential modern argument against the identity of sophist and orator-politician is that of Bignone, "Antifonte," still accepted by Guthrie, *HGP* 3.292–94. The most powerful argument for identity is that of Morrison, "Antiphon"; see also H. C. Avery, "One Antiphon or Two?" *Hermes* 110 (1982) 145–58.

leanings as we detected in the orator, but its fragments provide no conclusive answer. They are indeed the most elaborate surviving statement of the *nomos-physis* controversy and are thus consonant with the orator's sophistic training, but they show no preference either for democracy or for oligarchy.[107] Although *On Truth* neither contradicts nor confirms the identity of its author with the politician, its theoretical bent tempts one to believe that the author was Antiphon the theoretician and prime mover of the revolution of the Four Hundred.

καὶ Θηραμένης ὁ τοῦ ῞Αγνωνος ἐν τοῖς ξυγκαταλύουσι τὸν δῆμον πρῶτος ἦν, ἀνὴρ οὔτε εἰπεῖν οὔτε γνῶναι ἀδύνατος.[108] This judgment of Thucydides', echoed by Aristotle (*Ath.Pol.* 32.2), warrants our including him among those who paved the way for the coup in Athens even though he is not known to have participated in any of the activities that preceded it. Yet what we know of his background and his later outlook suggests that he may have considerably influenced the course of events in 411 B.C. from the beginning. His family had been prominent in Athens for at least one generation. His father, Hagnon, had distinguished himself as a general and as an associate of Pericles from the early 430s, had represented Athens at the signing of the Peace of Nicias and the alliance with Sparta in 421 B.C., and had been appointed as one of the ten *probouloi* in 413 B.C.[109] What we know of the social and economic situation of his grandfather Nicias depends, unfortunately, on a passage in Cratinus's *Ploutoi*, first performed about 430 B.C., that is susceptible to two very

107 In addition to the works mentioned in nn. 88 and 106 above, the following seem to me the most illuminating studies of Antiphon's thought: S. Luria, "Eine politische Schrift des Redners Antiphon aus Rhamnus," *Hermes* 61 (1926) 343–48; E. Bignone, "Le Idee morali di Antifonte sofista," in *Studi sul pensiero antico* (Naples, 1938) 66–159; G. B. Kerferd, "The Moral and Political Doctrines of Antiphon the Sophist. A Reconsideration," *PCPS* 184, n.s. 4 (1956–57) 26–32; E. A. Havelock, *The Liberal Temper in Greek Politics* (New Haven, 1957) 255–94; J. S. Morrison, "The Truth of Antiphon," *Phronesis* 8 (1963) 35–49; T. J. Saunders, "Antiphon the Sophist on Natural Laws (B 44 DK)," *Proceedings of the Aristotelian Society*, n.s. 78 (1977–78) 215–36; J. Barnes, *The Presocratic Philosophers* 2 (London, 1979) 206–14; D. J. Furley, "Antiphon's Case against Justice," in G. B. Kerferd, ed., *The Sophists and Their Legacy*, Hermes Einzelschrift 44 (Wiesbaden, 1981) 81–91; and C. H. Kahn, "The Origins of Social-Contract Theory," ibid. 92–108.

108 Thuc. 8.68.4: "Also Theramenes son of Hagnon was a principal among those who joined in overthrowing the democracy, a man who lacked competence neither in speaking nor in the formulation of policy."

109 See above, pp. 340–41 with nn. 13 and 17.

different interpretations. It may indicate either that Hagnon's family had long been wealthy landowners or that Hagnon had himself become rich dishonestly in public office.[110] Theramenes, however, was clearly born into an upper-class family that belonged to the democratic establishment as it was constituted in the days of Pericles. What prompted him to support the oligarchy in 411 B.C.?

We first hear of him in 422 B.C., in Eupolis's *Poleis*, as Hagnon's adopted son, whose real home is Ceos.[111] The point of this remark is obviously that Theramenes was a pupil of Prodicus of Ceos,[112] that is, he too was a young upper-class devotee of the sophists in the 420s. Since he will have been at least thirty when he first became a general under the oligarchy, in 411 B.C., he will have been born no later than 441 B.C. and probably no earlier than 450 B.C.;[113] this makes him a few years younger than Alcibiades. There is no evidence that he ever either supported or opposed Alcibiades' early career, or that, like other young aristocrats who had been exposed to sophistic training, he opposed the democracy or got involved in the profanation of the Mysteries in 415 B.C. On the contrary, if we are to take charges hurled at him by Critias in 404/3 B.C. at their face value, he was a beneficiary of his father's prestige, perhaps to the extent of holding public office earlier than is attested for him.[114] Any transformation he may have undergone from democrat to oligarch was less spectacular than in Peisander's case. The nickname "Buskin" (κόθορνος) seems to have been attached to him for his later tergiversations, not for an initial conversion in 411 B.C.;[115] therefore, only inferences from his later policies and attitudes can help us guess what prompted Theramenes in 411 B.C. to support the oligarchical revolution. The initiative he took in recalling Alcibiades after the fall of the Four

110 Cratinus, *Ploutoi*, in C. Austin, ed., *Comicorum Graecorum Fragmenta in Papyris Reperta* (Berlin and New York, 1973) 43, lines 70–71, as restored by D. L. Page, ed., *Greek Literary Papyri* i (London and Cambridge, Mass., 1941) 196–201, fr. 38b29–33, esp. 32–33, ἀλλὰ μὴν ἀρχαιόπλουτός γ' ἐστὶν ἐξ ἀρχ[ῆς ἔχων] / πάνθ' ὅσ' ἔστ' αὐτῷ, τὰ μὲν [γ'] ἐξ [οἰκι]ῶν, τὰ δ' [ἐξ ἀγρῶν], with Page's note c on p. 201. As Davies, *APF* 228, rightly observed, the remark at line 35 that Nicias was a stevedore has no historical value.

111 Eup. fr. 237 (= schol. Ar. *Ran.* 970, commenting on a verse in which Theramenes is called a Cean). Cf. Plut. *Nic.* 2.1.

112 Ath. 5.220b; schol. Ar. *Nub.* 361.

113 Thuc. 8.92.9 with Davies, *APF* 228.

114 Xen. *Hell.* 2.3.30 with Andrewes, *HCT* 5.177.

115 Xen. *Hell.* 2.3.31, 47; Plut. *Nic.* 2.1; scholl. Ar. *Ran.* 47 and 541, and *Nub.* 361; *Suda* s.vv. δεξιός, εὐμεταβολώτερος κοθόρνου, and κόθορνος.

Hundred[116] may mean that after 413 B.C. he was as disillusioned with the leadership of the democracy as he later became with the oligarchy and that he saw strong leadership as the only hope for the state's survival in 411 B.C., worth the price of overthrowing the democracy. Further, the pressure he exerted on the Four Hundred to publish the promised list of the Five Thousand and the support he received from the hoplites to establish the Five Thousand in power[117] suggest he sincerely believed already before the revolution "that pay should be abolished for all except those serving in the field, that no more than five thousand should be given a share in government, and that these should consist of the persons best able to serve with their fortunes and their persons" (Thuc. 8.65.3). His response to Critas indicates that such beliefs may have been a matter of principle with him: "I have always been at war with those who believe that one cannot have a good democracy until slaves and those who because of their poverty would sell the city for a drachma have a share in it, and I am, conversely, also opposed to those who do not believe that a good oligarchy can be installed until they bring the city to the point of being tyrannized by a few" (Xen. *Hell*. 2.3.48). A man animated by such convictions in 404 B.C. may well have believed after the Sicilian disaster that the salvation of Athens depended on the leadership of an Alcibiades and on the restriction of active citizenship to men of property. He may have embraced the cause of the oligarchs when Peisander presented to the Athenian Assembly the conditions for the return of Alcibiades and for Persian aid. This would explain why he broke with the oligarchs when he did, namely, when those most opposed to Alcibiades' return, Antiphon and Phrynichus, who had become the most influential revolutionaries, were showing little inclination to give the Five Thousand the promised share in their power. Unlike Antiphon, Theramenes will not have had oligarchical sympathies before the defeat in Sicily. Though many who shared his social and intellectual background will have been members of the ξυνωμοσίαι Peisander politicized, it is not likely that he was among them or participated in their terrorism.[118]

---

116   Diod. 13.38.2, 42.2; Nep. *Alc*. 5.4. However, Thuc. 8.97.3 does not mention Theramenes in this connection.

117   Thuc. 8.89.2, 92.11 with 92.5–10; Arist. *Ath.Pol*. 33.1–2; Diod. 13.38.1–2, where I prefer Krüger's emendation ὁπλιτῶν to the πολιτῶν of the manuscripts.

118   Arist. *Ath.Pol*. 34.3 explicitly dissociates Theramenes and his group from the members of the *hetaireiai* in the politics after the end of the Peloponnesian War.

The constitutional conference at Colonus reported by Thucydides (8.67.3) and by Aristotle (*Ath.Pol*. 29.5, 31.1) proposed establishing a Council of Four Hundred, in which Theramenes does not seem to have had much interest, and limiting the franchise to five thousand citizens, a proposal dear to Theramenes but one the hard-core oligarchs gave only perfunctory support. This suggests that these two programs were contributed by two different political orientations, which had crystallized amid revolutionary debates in Athens after the defeat in Sicily. There is sufficient evidence that these attitudes were based on different conceptions of the *patrios politeia*, the predominant political theme of that time.[119] A continuing dispute about its nature is clearly attested in a speech of about 411 B.C. written by the sophist Thrasymachus of Chalcedon for a young Athenian disenchanted with the internal political rivalries the war had brought. Both sides, he claims, are confused about the ancestral constitution, "although it can very easily be ascertained and constitutes the very bond that makes a community out of the citizens."[120] It is also reflected in passages of Aristophanes' *Thesmophoriazusae* that reveal a fear of danger to the democracy of imminent tyranny, of an antidemocratic trend in Athenian decrees and law.[121] There is no evidence to link either Antiphon or Theramenes to any debate over the *patrios politeia* in 411 B.C., although Aristotle (*Ath.Pol*. 34.3) associates Theramenes with this slogan in 404 B.C. Yet clearly the sides both men favored were prominent in such political discussions,

---

119   See above, pp. 342–43. A lively discussion of the *patrios politeia* was initiated by A. Fuks, *The Ancestral Constitution* (London, 1953), who argues that it represents the program of a return to the constitutions of Solon and Cleisthenes adopted by the Theramenean moderates in opposition to the designs of the oligarchs and that this program in turn evoked the opposition of the soldiers on Samos on the grounds that the true *patrioi nomoi* were those of the democracy (1–51 with 107–13). But, as we shall see, his exclusion of the oligarchs from this quest is not warranted, and, above all, the contention of Fuks that it was a "party" program developed by the moderates by the time of Cleitophon's amendment is open to grave doubts. The contention of K. R. Walters, on the other hand ("The 'Ancestral Constitution' and Fourth-Century Historiography in Athens," *AJAH* 1 [1976] 129–44), that a *patrios politeia* program cannot have been conceived before the fourth century, has been effectively refuted by P. Harding, "O Androtion, You Fool!" ibid. 3 (1978) 179–83. Other important contributions to this discussion are: E. Ruschenbusch, "Πάτριος πολιτεία," *Hist*. 7 (1958) 398–424; S. A. Cecchin, Πάτριος Πολιτεία (Turin, 1969); and M. I. Finley, *The Ancestral Constitution* (Inaug. Lect., Cambridge, 1971).

120   Thrasymachus 85B1 DK⁶: πρῶτον μὲν ἡ πάτριος πολιτεία ταραχὴν αὐτοῖς παρέχει ῥάστη γνωσθῆναι καὶ κοινωτάτη τοῖς πολίταις οὖσα πᾶσιν.

121   Ar. *Thesm*. 336–39 and 356–67 with pp. 357–58 and nn. 82 and 83 above.

which were vigorously renewed soon after Peisander's return to Ionia and were translated into official motions when Peisander came back to Athens in late May or early June.[122]

It is inconceivable that a commission of *syngrapheis*, or the proposals submitted by interested citizens to it or to the Colonus meeting, or the measures and proposals resulting from that meeting (including the constitutions for the future and for the present; *Ath.Pol.* 30, 31)[123] could have taken shape without several weeks of discussion, during which a number of political positions could harden. In particular, unless we assume intense discussions to have preceded the appointment of the commissioners, we cannot explain the short time they were given to prepare their report.[124]

Thucydides, with his penchant for *Realpolitik*, describes these discussions as a "specious ploy aimed at the masses" (εὐπρεπὲς πρὸς τοὺς πλείους), but he belies this in his account of the forces that overthrew the Four Hundred.[125] There was much thinking about the *patrios politeia*, as is seen in Aristotle's report of the Assembly

122   The problem of integrating the two main sources for the content and the chronology of the revolution of the Four Hundred, which has vexed classical scholarship since the discovery of Aristotle's *Ath.Pol.,* need not be raised here, since it has been discussed fully and satisfactorily by Andrewes, *HCT* 5.184–256, esp. 211–56, and by Rhodes, *CAAP* 362–67. Both scholars happily agree that the major discrepancies between Thucydides and Aristotle are confined to the number of συγγραφεῖς and to the existence or nonexistence of the Five Thousand during the time when the Four Hundred were in power; despite other minor differences, the two narratives complement rather than contradict one another: "Thucydides provides *A.P.*'s narrative background, and on the establishment of the intermediate régime *A.P.* tells us nothing that is not in Thucydides except the change of archon. On the establishment of the Four Hundred the points of detail on which *A.P.* supplements Thucydides or diverges from him appear to be derived from a series of documents" (Rhodes, *CAAP* 365–66). For a full discussion and bibliography of earlier attempts to reconcile the two accounts, see U. Hackl, "Die oligarchische Bewegung in Athen am Ausgang des 5. Jahrhunderts v. Chr." (diss. Munich, 1960) 23–50, who revives the fantastic and historically incredible theory of M. Lang, "The Revolution of the 400," *AJP* 69 (1948) 272–89, refuted by Hignett, *HAC* 362–64, and restated with slight changes by Lang, "Revolution of the 400: Chronology and Constitutions," *AJP* 88 (1967) 176–87, that the thirty συγγραφεῖς of *Ath.Pol.* 29 were appointed during Peisander's first return from Samos and that the ten συγγραφεῖς of Thucydides 8.67 were appointed after his second return to Athens. On this point, see D. Flach, "Der oligarchische Staatsstreich in Athen vom Jahr 411," *Chiron* 7 (1977) 9–33, esp. 12–13; Andrewes, *HCT* 5.255; Rhodes, *CAAP* 363–65.

123   That both these documents are genuine products of the revolution of 411 B.C., even though the proposals of neither were ever fully implemented, has been convincingly argued by Andrewes, *HCT* 5.242–46.

124   Thuc. 8.67.1–2 with Andrewes, *HCT* 5.187.

125   Thuc. 8.66.1 with 97.1–2 and Andrewes, *HCT* 5.163.

meeting Peisander called upon returning to Athens with his allied hoplite contingents (Thuc. 8.65.1). A certain Melobius, later one of the Thirty, spoke in favor of establishing an oligarchy in order to obtain an alliance with the Persian king.[126] It is difficult to say whether his proposal was deliberately deceitful, as Aristotle seems to imply in the *Politics*,[127] or whether there was still a possibility that Persia could be won over to the Athenian side (Thuc. 8.65.2). But since Melobius's speech seems to have been the keynote address of an assembly Peisander engineered and since Thucydides intimates that Peisander implemented Antiphon's designs, it is not eccentric to regard Antiphon as the author of what ensued (8.67.1, 68.1). Antiphon is even more likely to have influenced Pythodorus, who first formally moved overthrowing the democracy. That he should subsequently himself have become a member of the Four Hundred is only to be expected, and it is surely a strange coincidence that he was archon when the Thirty came to power (Arist. *Ath.Pol.* 35.1). More remarkable is his having prosecuted Protagoras (D.L. 9.54); if as is likely, he accused the sophist of charging too much for his training,[128] we may infer that he came from a well-to-do family and like Antiphon and Theramenes had had a sophistic education. In short, Pythodorus may well have been among the intellectuals promoting the revolution.

Pythodorus's motion, quoted verbatim by Aristotle presumably from a document (*Ath.Pol.* 29.2), called for the Assembly to elect twenty men over forty years of age to constitute (together with the ten *probouloi* of 413 B.C.) a commission of *syngrapheis*. These were to be sworn to draft proposals in the best interest of the state and to submit recommendations to ensure its safety; any interested citizen was permitted to submit proposals to the commission, so that the best of all could be recommended. Thucydides gives an abbreviated version of the same motion but does not say who proposed it. He mistakenly speaks of only ten *syngrapheis* but adds the interesting information, not found in Aristotle, that a deadline was set for submitting recommendations to the Assembly.[129] Thucydides makes

126   Arist. *Ath.Pol.* 29.1, with Xen. *Hell.* 2.3.2, Lys. 12.12, and Harp. s.v. Μηλόβιος (= Hyperides, fr. 61).

127   Arist. *Pol.* 5.4, 1304^{b}10–15, seems to fit this Assembly meeting better than the meetings described at Thuc. 8.53–54.1–2.

128   See below, Appendix B, pp. 532–33 with nn. 19–22.

129   Thuc. 8.67.1. Aristotle's number of thirty is supported by Androtion *FGH* 324F43 and Philochorus *FGH* 328F136.

no reference to Cleitophon's amendment to Pythodorus's motion, which Aristotle also quotes verbatim; it indicates that Aristotle has not given us the full text of Pythodorus's proposal. The text runs: Κλειτοφῶν δὲ τὰ μὲν ἄλλα καθάπερ Πυθόδωρος εἶπεν, προσαναζητῆσαι δὲ τοὺς αἱρεθέντας ἔγραψεν καὶ τοὺς πατρίους νόμους, οὓς Κλεισθένης ἔθηκεν ὅτε καθίστη τὴν δημοκρατίαν, ὅπως <ἂν> ἀκούσαντες καὶ τούτων βουλεύσωνται τὸ ἄριστον. The next eleven words are generally regarded as a motivation added by Aristotle: ὡς οὐ δημοτικὴν ἀλλὰ παραπλησίαν οὖσαν τὴν Κλεισθένους πολιτείαν τῇ Σόλωνος.[130] As an amendment, the text Aristotle gives is comprehensible only if the prior motion proposed investigating something known or presupposed, and that something can only have been the laws of Solon, especially those that were thought to affect the Athenian constitution.[131] This is corroborated by the comparison between the Cleisthenic and Solonian constitutions in the phrase just quoted. Aristotle had no reason to include Solon in the motivation he imputed to Cleitophon's amendment unless Solon's legislation figured prominently in Pythodorus's motion to start with. That he omitted it can be explained by a desire to quote for brevity's sake only the language that was enacted. On this reasoning, we may conclude that those for whom Pythodorus acted as the spokesman presented their proposal of instituting a Council of Four Hundred as a return to the *patrioi nomoi*, presumably as the manifestation of the *patrios politeia*, of Solon, as they saw it.[132] The historicity of a

---

130   Arist. *Ath.Pol.* 29.3: "Cleitophon supported the motion of Pythodorus but added the motion that those elected should in addition investigate also the ancestral laws that Cleisthenes enacted when he established the democracy, in order that they should give heed to them, too, in deliberating on the best course; he did so in the conviction that the constitution of Cleisthenes was not populist but very close to Solon's constitution." For Aristotle as the author of the last clause, see Andrewes, *HCT* 5.215.

131   This is proved by the use of προσαναζητῆσαι (which does not occur elsewhere in Greek literature; see Andrewes, *HCT* 5.214–15) and by the double καί preceding, respectively, τοὺς πατρίους νόμους and τούτων, which reiterate the point already made by the prefix προσ-, namely, that the search for the ancestral laws of Cleisthenes is to be added to the search for another set of ancestral laws enjoined by the main motion. See F. Sartori, *La Crisi del 411 a.C. nell' Athenaion Politeia di Aristotele*, Università di Padova: Pubblicazioni della Facoltà di Lettere e Filosofia 26) (Padua, 1951) 27, cited with approval by J. Bibauw, "L'Amendement de Clitophon," *Ant.Class.* 34 (1965) 464–83, esp. 470 with n. 36; cf. also Walters, "Ancestral Constitution" 136–37 with n. 40.

132   Thuc. 8.67.3 and Arist. *Ath.Pol.* 31.1, with M. I. Finley, *Ancestral Constitution*, esp. 7–9.

Solonian Council of Four Hundred, which is a problem to some modern scholars, was no problem to them; what mattered was that it seemed to them the true traditional form of Athenian government before it came to be perverted by the populist excesses of the late fifth century. This is why the constitution for the present, whether intended as a blueprint for action or not, could state βουλεύειν μὲν τετρακοσίους κατὰ τὰ πάτρια.[133] But we cannot know whether Pythodorus genuinely wanted a reformed constitution modeled on the greatest Athenian lawgiver's or was merely invoking the Solonian constitution as a persuasive disguise for making oligarchy more palatable to the Athenians.

A similar doubt surrounds Cleitophon's amendment. By presenting the ancestral laws of Cleisthenes as having established *dēmokratia*, he implies that the present system of government is a perversion of what its originator had intended. Aristotle's comment that Cleitophon did not regard the Cleisthenean constitution as populist (δημοτικήν) but as close to Solon's shows that, like Pythodorus, Cleitophon believed popular sovereignty had gone too far and that, again like Pythodorus, he tried to justify his changes to the current constitution as a return to past traditions. But he differed from Pythodorus in his view of which ancestral laws would be most desirable in stemming the tide of popular sovereignty. Again, it is difficult to decide whether Cleitophon sincerely wanted features of the Cleisthenean democracy restored[134] or was merely saying so to cover oligarchical designs.[135] Identifying specific later measures inspired by his proposal is more difficult to do for Cleitophon than for Pythodorus. The amendment is usually thought to reflect the views of the moderates, but this is because we know Cleitophon to have been later closely associated with Theramenes, the "moderate" *par excellence*. In Aristophanes' *Frogs* (967), Euripides claims both men as his disciples, a sure indication that, like Theramenes, Cleitophon was close to sophists. Indeed, we know from Plato's *Republic* and from the *Cleitophon* that he frequented the company of both Thrasymachus and Socrates,[136] and Aristotle (*Ath.Pol.* 34.3) names

133 Arist. *Ath.Pol.* 31.1: "There shall be a Council of four hundred members, according to ancestral usage." For the Council under Solon, see ibid. 8.4.

134 So Fuks, *"Ancestral Constitution,"* 1–32.

135 So Hignett, *HAC* 130.

136 Pl. *Resp.* 1.328b and *Clitoph.* 406a and 410c, with S. R. Slings, "A Commentary on the Platonic Clitophon" (diss. Amsterdam, 1981) 63–65. I owe this reference to the kindness of Professor D. A. F. M. Russell.

him as one of four colleagues of Theramenes who worked to reestablish the *patrios politeia* after the peace with Sparta in 404 B.C. But even if, as is likely, the two men had relations in 411 B.C., and if Cleitophon in moving his amendment spoke for Theramenes, as Melobius and Pythodorus spoke for Antiphon or Peisander, it still remains difficult to link any of the measures Theramenes favored to known features of the constitution of Cleisthenes. The consideration that the number five thousand is ten times the membership of the Cleisthenic Council of Five Hundred leads us nowhere. Perhaps the ancestral laws of Cleisthenes meant to Cleitophon simply the constitution as it existed before the development of the Athenian navy gave the thetes a greater voice in the state and before Pericles introduced pay for public service.

Initially after Peisander's return no one openly advocated oligarchy. Upper-class intellectuals agreed that popular sovereignty needed to be curbed and that a constitutional change should follow a traditional ancestral pattern, but they differed about whether the ancestral laws of Solon or of Cleisthenes were the better model. Objectively, both constitutions were equally ancestral. But in preferring one or the other their partisans were not searching for historical truth; they were trying to find support in the political traditions of Athens for their programs for the future. Pythodorus's motion clearly intended to roll popular sovereignty too far back for Cleitophon.

After proposing the commission of thirty *syngrapheis* and giving them their charge,[137] the intellectuals Pythodorus and Cleitophon temporarily disappear from the political scene, leaving center stage

137 Since the question of what the ἀναζήτησις of Solon's and the προσαναζήτησις of Cleisthenes' ancestral laws entailed, with which the *syngrapheis* were charged, is only of marginal relevance to our concerns, we shall relegate it to this footnote. As Andrewes, *HCT* 5.214–15, has pointed out, ἀναζητεῖν means "to investigate something whose existence is already known or presupposed;" the question is, therefore, in what form were Solon's and Cleisthenes' laws available for investigation in 411 B.C. R. Stroud, *The Axones and Kyrbeis of Drakon and Solon*, University of California Publications in Classical Studies 19 (Berkeley and Los Angeles, 1979), esp. 3–10 and 41–44, has shown that the Solonian *kyrbeis* and *axones* were physically available for inspection. But it is doubtful that they contained any constitutional provisions defining the structure of the state, and similar doubts may be entertained about constitutional provisions surviving in whatever written ancestral laws of Cleisthenes existed in any public depository before the establishment of a state archive between 409 and 405 B.C.: see Walters, "Ancestral Constitution" 131–32; and for the archive, A. L. Boegehold, "The Establishment of a Central Archive at Athens," *AJA* 76 (1972) 23–30. In correctly inferring from Cleitophon's amendment that Cleisthenes' laws were extant in 411 B.C., Wade-Gery, *Essays* 139–

to the practical businessman Peisander. A date a few days before 14 Thargelion (the date on which the old Council of the Five Hundred was dissolved) had been set for the *syngrapheis* to submit their report,[138] and "when the day came, they packed the Assembly into Colonus" (Thuc. 8.67.2). One would like to know who "they" were and what their purpose was in convening the Assembly outside the city, not on the Pnyx, where its meetings were normally held. It is constitutionally improbable that the *syngrapheis* convened the Assembly; Thucydides' text rather suggests οἱ περὶ τὸν Πείσανδρον as the subject of ξυνέκλησαν.[139] But one wonders on what authority they could convene an Assembly at all and convene it in such an unusual place. Probably the conspirators had so infiltrated and intimidated the Council of the Five Hundred and its prytanies that Peisander had an easy time in getting them to do his bidding, in this instance, in having a meeting held at a place sacred to the knights, the property class to which most of his supporters will have belonged.[140] Moreover, holding the meeting outside the city at

---

40, went beyond the warrant of this scanty evidence in his further inference that they existed as written *psēphismata* and could be "searched out" (προσαναζητῆσαι) in an archive. The inevitability of this inference falls with the observation of Andrewes that ἀναζητεῖν does not have the meaning "search out" before the fourth century and regularly means in its few fifth-century occurrences "investigate" (without deliberate search) something known to exist—e.g., at Thuc. 2.8.3, 8.33.4; Ar. *Lys.* 26; Hdt. 1.137.2. In other words, it is possible to assume that the ancestral *nomoi* to be considered by the *syngrapheis* were to be found in written documents, but there is no need for this assumption in order to explain their task: προσαναζητῆσαι implies no more than that the content of the relevant ancestral laws of Solon and Cleisthenes was ascertainable, and the very short interval between the appointment of the commissioners and the due date of their report makes it difficult to imagine that an elaborate archival search was expected of them. It was believed either that the relevant facts of the two constitutions were sufficiently well known to all citizens— as is indeed also intimated in Thrasymachus's assertion (above, n. 120) that the *patrios politeia* "can very easily be ascertained and constitutes the very bond that makes a community out of the citizens"—to enable them to communicate their ideas about their relevance to new constitutional proposals to the commissioners, or that any research (pretended, forged, or actual) required to ascertain them had already been done in the course of the political debates about the *patrios politeia* that had been triggered by the defeat in Sicily in 413 B.C.

138 Arist. *Ath.Pol.* 32.1 with the comments of Andrewes (*HCT* 5.235) and Rhodes *ad loc*.

139 Against P. Siewert, "Poseidon Hippios am Kolonos und die athenischen Hippeis," in *Arktouros: Hellenic Studies Presented to Bernard M. W. Knox on the Occasion of His Sixty-Fifth Birthday* (Berlin and New York, 1979) 280–89, esp. 286.

140 See Thuc. 8.66.1–2: ἐβούλευον δὲ οὐδὲν ὅτι μὴ τοῖς ξυνεστῶσι δοκοίη, ἀλλὰ καὶ οἱ λέγοντες ἐκ τούτων ἦσαν καὶ τὰ ῥηθησόμενα πρότερον αὐτοῖς προύσκεπτο. ἀντέλεγέ τε οὐδεὶς ἔτι τῶν ἄλλων, δεδιὼς καὶ ὁρῶν πολὺ τὸ ξυνεστηκός. For the association of Colonus with the knights, see Siewert, "Poseidon" 282–87.

Colonus will have discouraged the lower classes from attending, since they could not provide their own arms, and would therefore have been unlikely to venture beyond the city walls when the Spartans were occupying Deceleia. Since discouragement was the effect, it may well have been the purpose.[141]

It goes without saying that those pushing for a constitutional change will have made sure that their interests were represented on the board of *syngrapheis*. In view of the mixture of staid, respectable *probouloi* and oligarchical sympathizers among them, it is not surprising that the commissioners as a group could not agree on any substantive recommendations but merely proposed the suspension of all safeguards protecting the sovereignty of the people in order that the opponents of democracy might come forward with their proposals. No threat of *graphē paranomōn* or *eisangelia*, no summons to appear before a magistrate was to prevent any person from offering concrete proposals, however offensive they might be to democratic sensibilities. Any interference with or obstruction of such proposals would result in arrest and capital punishment (Thuc. 8.67.2; Arist. *Ath.Pol*. 29.4). Up to this point there is no disagreement between the accounts of Thucydides and Aristotle, and the divergences between their reports of the recommendations immediately following the suspension of constitutional safeguards are minimal and merely formal.[142] These resolutions will have represented the consensus of Peisander, Theramenes, Antiphon, and presumably of all those, including Pythodorus and Cleitophon, who wanted to restore the *patrios politeia* to what it was before pay for public service had been introduced; it is almost certain that these principles were affirmed, regardless of who proposed them, immediately after the suspension of constitutional safeguards.

141   Cf. Thuc. 8.71.1. Andrewes, *HCT* 5.165–67, remains skeptical.

142   Both authors agree that pay for public service was abolished, but whereas Thuc. 8.67.3 reports the abolition not only of pay but of all offices that existed under the democracy, Arist. *Ath.Pol*. 29.5 quotes the motion that limited the abolition of pay to the duration of the war, exempting the nine archons and the prytaneis and adding that all revenues were to be spent exclusively on the war effort. Further, Thucydides emphatically confines the recommendations of the *syngrapheis* to the suspension of constitutional safeguards and has all the other proposals openly advocated (λαμπρῶς ἐλέγετο) in a general discussion; Aristotle's language, on the other hand, μετὰ δὲ ταῦτα τὴν πολιτείαν διέταξαν τόνδε <τὸν> τρόπον, suggests that this was part of the proposals submitted by the *syngrapheis*; see Hignett, *HAC* 356–57, 362, and Rhodes, *CAAP* 379–80, both of whom also consider the possibility, accepted by Andrewes, *HCT* 5.217, that οἱ Ἀθηναῖοι might have to be supplied as the subject of διέταξαν. However, the use of συνέγραψαν at *Ath.Pol*. 30.1 makes it fairly certain that οἱ συγγραφεῖς is a more appropriate subject.

There are some serious divergences between Thucydides' and Aristotle's accounts of the rest of the meeting at Colonus. Thucydides (8.67.3–68.1) has Peisander propose the appointment of five *proedroi*, who are to select one hundred men, each of whom in turn is to coopt three men; the resulting four hundred are thenceforth to constitute a council with unrestricted authority (αὐτοκράτορας) to make policy and to convene the Five Thousand at their discretion. Nothing is said about the appointment of the Five Thousand, presumably because Thucydides regarded the reference to them in the discussions before the revolution (8.65.3) as sufficient and because the Four Hundred never appointed them (8.89.2, 92.11, 93.2). Aristotle, on the other hand, says nothing about the appointment of the Four Hundred at this point, but subjoins to the recommendation of the *syngrapheis* concerning the abolition of pay for public service the proposal that "all other affairs of state be turned over for the duration of the war to those Athenians who are most competent [δυνατωτάτοις] to render public service with their persons and their fortunes, no less than five thousand in number, and that they shall have full authority to make treaties with anyone they wish; ten men of over forty years of age are to be appointed from each tribe to draw up the list [καταλέξουσι] of the Five Thousand, after having sworn an oath over a perfect sacrifice" (*Ath.Pol.* 29.5). Subsequently, he reports that the Five Thousand appointed from among their own number one hundred *anagrapheis*, who drafted two constitutional documents, one for the future (30.2–6) and one for the present (31). Only in the quoted text of the latter (31.1) are the Four Hundred mentioned, but the method of their selection differs from what we have been told by Thucydides. Tribesmen are to select candidates from among those over thirty years old; from these, forty men from each tribe are to be elected. As Aristotle's text stands, it appears that the two constitutions were put to the vote by one Aristomachus (otherwise unknown) and approved by the πλῆθος (32.1); he adds that the old Council was dissolved in the archonship of Callias (412/11) on 14 Thargelion, before the expiration of its term of office (due on 14 Skirophorion), and that the Four Hundred took over on 22 Thargelion.[143]

---

143   Arist. *Ath.Pol.* 32.1. On the basis of the tables in B. D. Meritt, *The Athenian Year* (Berkeley and Los Angeles, 1961) 218, and "The Chronology of the Peloponnesian War," *Proceedings of the American Philosophical Society* 115 (1971) 114, Rhodes, *CAAP* 405–6, equates 14 Thargelion with June 9th, so that 22 Thargelion = June 17th.

Aristotle's account bristles with difficulties. Since he tells us (32.3) in agreement with Thucydides (8.92.11), that the Five Thousand were only nominally chosen but never actually appointed until after the fall of the Four Hundred, how can they have selected one hundred *anagrapheis* from among their own number? Moreover, if the proposal to appoint a Council of Four Hundred was promulgated only in the constitution drafted by the *anagrapheis* for the present (31.1), how can it have been ratified by the πλῆθος (if that term refers to the democratic Assembly; 32.1), which had by that time already been superseded by the Five Thousand (29.5)? Were the Four Hundred appointed as Thucydides says, or as prescribed in the document drafted, according to Aristotle (31.1), by the *anagrapheis*? If the two constitutions are, as is now believed, documents of about 411 B.C.,[144] what is their status, since the constitution for the future was never put into effect and the constitution for the present was not administered quite as stated? What sense can be made of Aristotle's dates (32.1), especially since they suggest that an entire week elapsed between the dissolution of the old Council and the assumption of power by the Four Hundred? Was Athens without a Council for a whole week at so critical a time?

Thucydides' and Aristotle's accounts of the events after the constitutional safeguards were suspended are not irreconcilable with one another, but they are accounts of the same proceedings given by men of different preoccupations: Thucydides concentrates on measures concretely realized in the sequel, whereas Aristotle is more interested in the formalities.[145] But what has not been observed adequately is that both Thucydides and Aristotle discuss the transactions of the meeting at Colonus as proposals and motions passed; neither of them states that any of the measures taken at Colonus was implemented on the spot.[146] Thucydides (8.68.1) presents the appointment of the Four Hundred as Peisander's γνώμη (motion), and Aristotle includes the appointment of the Five Thousand and of the *katalogeis*, who were to register them, among the recommendations of the *syngrapheis* (29.5). Neither author says when these proposals were put into effect. Only the appointment of one hundred *anagrapheis* seems to have taken immediate effect (30.1). Moreover, it is *a priori* difficult, if

---

144   Andrewes, *HCT* 5.243–46; Rhodes, *CAAP* 366, 386–87.
145   So Flach, "Staatsstreich" 13–20; Rhodes, *CAAP* 380.
146   *Contra* Andrewes, *HCT* 5.168 and 205, and Rhodes, *CAAP* 380, who allege that Thucydides has the Four Hundred appointed at the Colonus meeting.

not impossible, to imagine the measures voted at Colonus being acted on at the same meeting, considering that it will have lasted only one day and will have had many agenda. Once it is recognized that Thucydides and Aristotle attribute only resolutions and the votes taken on them to the meeting at Colonus, the differences between their accounts become minimal.

On this basis, the following sequence of events can be reconstructed. The meeting at Colonus opened with the recommendation of the *syngrapheis* as a body to suspend all constitutional safeguards (Thuc. 8.67.2; *Ath.Pol.* 29.4). When this was approved, individual *syngrapheis*[147] first moved that all revenues be expended for the war only and that all pay for public office be suspended, except for the nine archons and the prytaneis (*Ath.Pol.* 29.5; Thuc. 8.67.3); next that the franchise be limited to the five thousand citizens most competent to serve with their persons and their fortunes; and that one hundred *katalogeis* over forty years of age, ten from each tribe, be appointed to select them (*Ath.Pol.* 29.5; cf. Thuc. 8.65.3).[148] We are not told whether *katalogeis* were selected after the resolution to appoint them was passed, nor whether the tribes or the Assembly as a whole was to elect the ten *katalogeis* from each tribe.[149] It is, however, safe to assume that the appointment of the *katalogeis* cannot have been long delayed. The selection of the Five Thousand is a different matter.

These proposals will have embodied all shades of opinion among those who believed that a change in the democratic government was called for. But then the radicals took over. Peisander, who may well have been one of the thirty *syngrapheis*,[150] used his office to move in his own name that the old democratic structure of the state be

---

147 See n. 142 above.

148 Thucydides' silence on that matter has already been explained (p. 375 above) by the fact that the list of the Five Thousand was not made public until after the overthrow of the Four Hundred. [Lys.] 20.13–14 proves that the motion to limit the franchise was passed and that *katalogeis* were appointed before the Four Hundred seized power, and the occasion can only have been the Colonus meeting; cf. Andrewes, *HCT* 5.203.

149 Andrewes, *HCT* 5.205, rightly stresses that the statement at [Lys.] 20.2 (sc. that Polystratus ἡρέθη ὑπὸ τῶν φυλετῶν) must be taken with caution, especially since it is not clear whether his appointment as a *katalogeus* or as a member of the Four Hundred is at issue.

150 First suggested by E. Meyer, *Forschungen zur alten Geschichte* 2 (Halle a.S., 1899), 419, opposed by Busolt-Swoboda 1.71 with n. 2 and, most recently, by Flach, "Staatsstreich" 20 with n. 68; but see Rhodes, *CAAP* 380–81.

abolished and that full authority be vested in a Council of Four Hundred constituted in the manner detailed by Thucydides (8.67.3). The tenor of this motion betrays its ideology and permits us to interpret Thucydides (8.68.1) as pointing to Antiphon's mind behind it. The proposal for a Council of Four Hundred is clearly a call to return to the *patrios politeia* of Solon, as Pythodorus had advocated, probably as the spokesman of Antiphon's group.[151] But two elements in Peisander's motion are new. In the first place, the full authority envisaged for the Four Hundred, if borrowed from any *patrios politeia* at all, resembles the power of the pre-Cleisthenic Areopagus more than the Solonian Four Hundred. Secondly, entrusting the first step in their selection to only five well-chosen *proedroi* ensured extremist control of membership in the Four Hundred.

Thucydides reports only this enabling resolution; nothing is said about the body that was to appoint the *proedroi* or about when and how Peisander's motion was carried out. It was obviously effected sooner than the resolution to draw up a register of the Five Thousand; Thucydides' account of how the Four Hundred were appointed may be corroborated by a decree of 411 B.C. that seems to have listed five *proedroi* as presiding over the Council of Four Hundred.[152] On the natural assumptions that the appointment of the five *proedroi* was left to the meeting at Colonus and that Peisander had their nominations ready, it is likely that they were appointed immediately at Colonus. However, even if Peisander and his associates were also prepared to produce a list of the Four Hundred, it will have taken a day or two to complete their designation in the manner specified by Thucydides; hence this is not likely to have been accomplished at the Colonus meeting.[153] If, as is probable, 14 Thargelion (Aristotle's date for the dissolution of the old Council; *Ath.Pol.* 32.1) was when the appointment of the Four Hundred had been completed, the Colonus meeting will have taken place a few days before.[154]

151   Arist. *Ath.Pol.* 29.2 as interpreted above, pp. 369–71, and corroborated by the constitution for the present, which calls for the appointment of the Four Hundred κατὰ τὰ πάτρια. I do not understand why Flach, "Staatsstreich" 19, relates Peisander's motion to Cleitophon's appeal to the *patrioi nomoi* of Cleisthenes.

152   ML, no. 80.5–7 with comment on p. 249 and with Andrewes, *HCT* 5.196, 226.

153   To the best of my knowledge, this has been recognized only by J. M. Moore, *Aristotle and Xenophon on Democracy and Oligarchy* (London, 1975) 263.

154   See n. 138 above. The same conclusion is reached for different reasons by Flach, "Staatsstreich" 25.

The agenda of the Colonus meeting will have included one final item, the appointment of one hundred *anagrapheis,* of which we are informed only by Aristotle. Since Aristotle (30.1) states that they were appointed by the Five Thousand from among their own number but contradicts himself by admitting that the appointment of the Five Thousand was purely nominal (32.3; corroborated by Thuc. 8.89.2, 92.11, and 93.2), some scholars have refused to believe that the *anagrapheis* were ever appointed and that the πλῆθος ever approved their proposals when Aristomachus put them to the vote (*Ath.Pol.* 32.1).[155] But if one believes that the Colonus meeting abolished the democracy, limited the franchise, established a Council of the Four Hundred, and set in motion the machinery for appointing the Five Thousand and the Four Hundred, then one must posit also the appointment of a body to define the functions of these new institutions in governing Athens. There is no good reason to reject Aristotle's contention that *anagrapheis* were appointed for that purpose.

If they were, we can begin to explain the unsatisfactory state of the two constitutions Aristotle attributes to them (30.2–6 and 31).[156] These documents are now recognized as authentic products of the revolution of 411 B.C., even though the *anagrapheis* are—unnecessarily, I think—denied authorship; the constitutions are thought to be "derived either from a proclamation made by the Four Hundred, or

155   So, most recently, Andrewes, *HCT* 5.240–42.

156   The name *anagrapheis* (*Ath.Pol.* 30.1, 31.1, 32.1) given to this body has occasioned surprise, since in the period with which we are dealing ἀναγράφειν and ἀναγραφεύς are normally used of recording what has already been worked out by some other body, whereas the drafting of new proposals is usually described as συγγράφειν, and a commission entrusted with this task as συγγραφεῖς; see Andrewes, *HCT* 218–19, and Rhodes, *CAAP* 387. However, the *anagrapheis* may well have received their name not only to differentiate their task from that of the thirty *syngrapheis,* who had been entrusted with drafting new recommendations for presentation at the Colonus meeting, but also because their job was envisaged as the implementation of measures passed at Colonus, perhaps embodying points made in debate but not included in formal motions. What cannot be right is that they were appointed by the Five Thousand, as these had not yet been constituted. Still, since the Assembly convened at Colonus will have been attended predominantly by the members of the upper classes, who were likely to be enrolled among the Five Thousand anyway (see above, pp. 373–74 with nn. 140 and 141), it may well have been falsely remembered by Aristotle or his source as an assembly of the Five Thousand, which appointed one hundred *anagrapheis* from among its own number; see Rhodes, *CAAP* 386–87. It may also be conjectured, although there is no explicit warrant in Aristotle, that the *anagrapheis* were given a deadline by which to complete their task of preparing a draft constitution to coincide as closely as possible with the actual appointment of the Four Hundred.

less probably from drafts circulating in Athens at the time of the revolution."[157] Scholars are apparently reluctant to assign them to the *anagrapheis* because neither constitution was ever fully put into effect and because the documents are incomplete and often incoherent. However, their implementation has nothing to do with either the mandate under which they were prepared or the intent of those who prepared them: the *anagrapheis* could control only the recording of constitutional measures proposed, but presumably not yet ratified, at Colonus; the autocratic nature of the regime they were trying to define provided no guarantee that the constitutions would be adhered to. The obscurities and omissions in the documents can be explained as due to any or all of three causes: Aristotle or his source may have condensed a more explicit original; these constitutions had to be produced quickly; and much that is obscure to us may have been clear to contemporaries.

Nothing in the constitution for the present (*Ath.Pol.* 31) prevents us from accepting it as a genuine, official document drafted almost immediately after Colonus to lay down how the transition from the democracy to the oligarchy of the Four Hundred was to be effected. It is not and does not purport to be a complete instrument of government; it lays down guidelines effective for the remainder of the year (412/11, which was about to end in a few weeks),[158] and, as far as the election of generals is concerned, also for the next, ending with some basic provisions to prepare for implementing the constitution for the future (*Ath.Pol.* 30).[159] The political powers granted to the Four Hundred are absolute: the appointment of all magistrates and the formulation of the oaths they are to swear is left to them, evidently to ensure the magistrates' allegiance; they have the sole power to legislate and to demand an accounting (*euthyna*) from all officials (31.1); and they can enact any constitutional law they deem

157   Andrewes, *HCT* 5.242–51; quote from p. 251.
158   On 14 Skirophorion for the Council, according to Arist. *Ath.Pol.* 32.1, and a little over two weeks later, on 1 Hekatombaion, for all other magistrates.
159   The recent discussions of the two constitutions by Andrewes, *HCT* 5.218–33, 242–51, and by Rhodes, *CAAP* 387–404, make a detailed treatment here unnecessary. I differ from Rhodes only in that I believe more emphatically that the *anagrapheis* began the preparation of these two documents immediately after Colonus, that is, before the appointment of the Four Hundred had been implemented. The position of Rhodes on that point is not clear: his dating of the documents "between the Colonus assembly and 22 Thargelion" so as to "refer to the 'establishment' of the boule of Four Hundred as an event still in the future" (p. 402), with which I agree, seems to me irreconcilable with his dating "at beginning of the rule of the Four Hundred" (p. 387).

desirable. The provisions made for the appointment of the military leadership are especially illuminating: for the present (τὸ νῦν εἶναι) any member of the Five Thousand is to be eligible for the generalship; but once established, the new Council (that is, of the Four Hundred) is to appoint ten new generals and a secretary for the following year, with no restriction upon their powers (αὐτοκράτορας), except that they are to consult the Council as need may arise (31.2). The only new requirement for generalship for the present is that any member of the Five Thousand is eligible; nothing is said about how or by whom they are to be appointed. But since their appointment is contrasted with the new Council's appointment of the ten αὐτοκράτορας, we may presume that the Athenians were to elect them exactly as they had under the democracy and that unlike the new board of generals they would be subject to a *euthyna* when their term of office expired. In order to qualify, they had to be members of the Five Thousand, but since the Five Thousand had not yet been officially designated, I take this to mean—as in the case of the *anagrapheis*—they had to be members of the Assembly at Colonus. In practice this is likely to mean that such men as Phrynichus and Scironides were reinstated in office; that Diomedon and Leon, who had been sent to replace them, and possibly also Strombichides(?), were deposed; and that men like Onomacles and Charminus were permitted to continue in office.[160] In short, the appointment of the generals for the present can be construed as merely confirming the generals already elected under the democracy for 412/11 B.C., with only a few exceptions, who were, as usual, subject to a *euthyna* at the end of their term. However, since the new Council of the Four Hundred has the authority once established to appoint its own generals and their secretary with no restriction on their power (evidently meaning that they will not be subject to a *euthyna*), clearly this part of the document was drafted before the Four Hundred had been appointed and the generals for the present could look forward to only a brief tenure.

The δέκα αὐτοκράτορες accompanied the Four Hundred when they took over the Bouleuterion on 22 Thargelion; the provisions for their appointment were therefore obviously carried out. The stipulation that they were to hold office "for the following year" (τὸν εἰσιόντα ἐνιαυτόν) will then mean that they were to serve out what remained of 412/11 and that their appointment was to last also for the

160 See pp. 346–47 above.

coming year, 411/10 B.C.[161] Appointing civilian officials was a less urgent matter: the archon Callias was permitted to serve out his term before the Four Hundred appointed one of their own number, Mnasilochus, as archon for 411/10 B.C. (*Ath.Pol.* 32.1, 33.1). But the election of the cavalry commander and the commanders of the tribal cavalry contingents (*phylarchoi*) was left unaltered for the time being, "but in the future the Council is to make their election in accordance with the written regulations" (31.3).

Whether this future was envisaged as beginning immediately when the new Council was established, or at the new year, or even at some later point, depends on the meaning of the phrase κατὰ τὰ γεγραμμένα, "in accordance with the written regulations". Arguing that the cavalry commanders, as military officers, must have been subject to the same rules as the generals, some scholars have supposed "the written regulations" refers to the procedure for appointing generals in this same document (31.2).[162] This argument is, however, not compelling. We can assume that the knights, the property class from which the cavalry was recruited, were more sympathetic to the revolutionaries than were the generals (*stratēgoi*),[163] who would in any event be their superiors; hence an immediate change of command in the cavalry was not necessary. It is therefore preferable to relate "the written regulations" to the provision of the constitution for the future that the cavalry commanders, together with other magistrates, be elected from among and (presumably) by the members of the Council.[164]

---

161   There seems to me no need to see, with Andrewes, *HCT* 5.230-31, a contrast between τὸ νῦν εἶναι at *Ath.Pol.* 31.2 and τὸ δὲ λοιπόν at 31.3, not only because the two expressions are too far separated from one another, but also because the former refers to the generals, whereas the latter refers to the cavalry officers. Moreover, nothing compels to interpret τὸ νῦν εἶναι as referring to the remainder of 412/11 B.C., as both Andrewes, *HCT* 5.230-31, and Rhodes, *CAAP* 401, assume. On the contrary, the fact that the new αὐτοκράτορες accompanied the Four Hundred when they occupied the Bouleuterion shows that the tenure of the τὸ νῦν εἶναι had come to an end by 22 Thargelion.

162   Sartori, *Crisi* 97-98, followed by Rhodes, *CAAP* 402-3, both of whom regard the "future" as beginning with the new year 411/10 B.C., as they do in the case of the generals. However, since we have seen that the change in the election of generals is not tied to the new year, the appointment of the cavalry officers is not tied to it, either.

163   See Siewert, "Poseidon" 282-87, as cited in n. 140 above; cf. also Thuc. 8.92.6.

164   Arist. *Ath.Pol.* 30.2 with Andrewes, *HCT* 5.231, 243; cf. also Beloch, Ferrabino, Ehrenberg, and de Sanctis as cited by Sartori, *Crisi* 97 n. 42.

This in turn suggests that the constitution for the present (*Ath.Pol.* 31) formed one package with the constitution for the future (30.2–6) and that the latter preceded the former in this package, prepared by the *anagrapheis*. The final provision of the constitution for the present corroborates this assumption: after stipulating that only councilors and generals be allowed to occupy the same office more than once, it enjoins the one hundred *anagrapheis* to distribute the Four Hundred among the four sections (*lēxeis*) provided for in the constitution for the future, which is assumed to have been already proposed. Therefore, the constitution for the present must have been intended by the *anagrapheis* as a temporary expedient, preparatory to a more extensive reorganization of the government.

This permanent scheme of government need not be discussed in detail; it was never carried out. Despite some obscurities, the document as a whole is not unintelligible and contains measures streamlining the government of Athens that were, or were soon to be, translated into practice. For example, the treasury of Athena was combined with that of the Other Gods in 406/5 B.C.[165] and the *kōlakretai* were absorbed into an enlarged board of *hellēnotamiai* to receive and disburse secular funds.[166] What remains puzzling is how a Council of about 875 men (855, if we subtract the twenty *hellēnotamiai*)[167] could efficiently administer the state without being divided into executive committees, like the prytanies under the democracy, and how this departure from Athenian traditions, that is, from the *patrios politeia*, to form four rotating Councils (paralleled only by the federal constitution of Boeotia and its constituent cities in the fifth and fourth centuries)[168] is to be explained.

To answer these questions, especially the second, we ought to know more about the person or group who proposed the constitution for the future. But we cannot even make an informed guess,

---

165   W. S. Ferguson, *The Treasurers of Athena* (Cambridge, Mass., 1932) 4–7 and 104–6, and W. E. Thompson, "Notes on the Treasurers of Athena," *Hesp.* 39 (1970) 54–63, esp. 61–63, as cited by Andrewes, *HCT* 5.220, and Rhodes, *CAAP* 391.

166   For details, see ML, p. 258; Andrewes, *HCT* 5.220–21; and Rhodes, *CAAP* 391–92. There may also be a relationship between the five councilors chosen by lot to count votes and determine the agenda to be presented to the Council (30.5) and the five *proedroi* of Thuc. 8.67.3, often related to the five presiding officers of ML, no. 80.5–7; but the nature of that relation remains obscure.

167   Andrewes, *HCT* 5.225.

168   *Hell.Oxy.* 16.2–4 Bartoletti, with Thuc. 5.38.2–4.

except by general inference from the document itself. If the Boeotian model was deliberately adopted for Athens, its proponents must have been familiar with foreign ways. Upper-class Athenians who cultivated relations with foreign lands will have had such knowledge, especially intellectuals among them who had learned the rudiments of comparative government from itinerant sophists. Yet although this draft is farther removed from any *patrios politeia* than is the constitution for the present, it is closer in spirit to the old democratic institutions of Athens: neither the Council nor the generals are given unchecked power (αὐτοκράτορες), as they were under the Four Hundred (Thuc. 8.67.3; *Ath.Pol*. 31.2); the lot is to be used in appointing the first group of councilors in setting the terms of councilors for subsequent years, and in appointing the minor magistrates to be selected from outside the Council currently serving; and all terms of office are limited to one year. By implication, active citizenship is limited to the five thousand "best able to serve with their persons and their fortunes" (Thuc. 8.65.3; *Ath.Pol*. 29.5); but of these all are eligible for any office, provided that they have reached the age of thirty and, if serving as councilors, that they attend Council meetings at the appointed time on pain of a fine of one drachma a day for each absence (*Ath.Pol*. 30.6). The only features of this scheme that one might call oligarchical are the limitation of citizenship, the abolition of any pay for any office at all—a point on which this constitution goes even beyond the recommendations Aristotle attributes to the *syngrapheis* (29.5)—and the provision that nonmembers of a current Council can be coopted for consultation, evidently in place of holding a plenary session of the Five Thousand. Clearly, those who persuaded the *anagrapheis* to propose this constitution as permanent were more concerned to rid Athens of what they regarded as the democracy's shortcomings than to establish an oligarchy: all those who had the franchise could hold any office, and they were to serve without pay. The absence of a *euthyna* procedure or of any regulation concerning the administration of justice may be due either to the neglect or indifference of this document's authors or to incomplete reporting by Aristotle or his source.

If the two constitutions (*Ath.Pol*. 30.2–6, 31) are part of the same package, the chief mandate given to the *anagrapheis* at the Colonus meeting will have been to draft a new, permanent constitution, to which the constitution for the present was merely to provide the transition—perhaps analogous to Marx's idea of a dictatorship of the proletariat as a necessary prelude to the classless society. Of course, only the constitution for the present ever materialized. This may have been partially because absolute power is difficult to dislodge once it is installed and partially because dissension soon became rife among the Four Hundred. Some of them apparently were content to treat the constitution for the future as a statement of pious intention, useful for propaganda purposes; others, namely, those who later demanded the publication of the list of the Five Thousand, took it seriously and worked for it.

What is especially noteworthy about the entire enterprise is that constitutional formalities were observed throughout, at least on the surface. Even the oligarchical extremists, who did not shy from using covert intimidation and violence, acquiesced to documentary publication of their immediate intentions. A mask of legality was important to their designs, since without one they would have had stiffer opposition from the people. For that reason it is rash to dismiss as fictional Aristotle's report (*Ath.Pol.* 32.1) that the constitutional package was put to the vote by Aristomachus (otherwise unknown) and ratified by the πλῆθος.[169] Although πλῆθος usually refers to the democratic Assembly, which cannot very well have been held after the Colonus meeting, ratification of some kind must be assumed. Aristomachus may well have been a councilor who put some or all of the Colonus meeting's proposals to a vote at the first official meeting of the Four Hundred.[170]

Although the proposals of the Colonus meeting had been accepted without opposition (Thuc. 8.69.1), Peisander had to have foreign hoplites police the streets of Athens, and the Four Hundred had to use weapons and an armed gang of 120 (presumably upper-class) young men to evict the old, democratic Council from the Bouleuterion a few days later.[171] The measures voted at Colonus,

---

169   So most recently Andrewes, *HCT* 5.241, 244–46, 247–51, 255.

170   So Rhodes, *CAAP* 386–87, 404–5. Alternatively, it is not completely unreasonable, though unsupported by any ancient evidence, to conjecture that the Four Hundred convoked a mass meeting of their supporters (who, since they had not yet formally been constituted as the Five Thousand, might have ben vaguely referred to as τὸ πλῆθος) shortly before their inauguration on 22 Thargelion for the ratification of the two constitutions.

171   I interpret the ἤδη ὕστερον at Thuc. 8.69.1 as meaning "later, as soon as they had been appointed." This point is presumably identical with 14 Thargelion, the date on which Aristotle says (*Ath.Pol.* 32.1) the old Council was dissolved; this will consequently be when the designation of the Four Hundred, authorized a couple of

then, must not have enjoyed popular support, perhaps because that meeting was thought unrepresentative of the Athenian *dēmos* as a whole and because the measures had been approved under duress (8.69.2–4, 65.1).

Neither Thucydides nor Aristotle specifies any changes introduced by the Four Hundred in internal matters. Thucydides merely states (8.70.1–2) that their administration was considerably different from the democracy's and that they ran the city "forcefully" (κατὰ κράτος): they executed a few men they considered especially dangerous; others they imprisoned or exiled. Thucydides gives no further details, and though it conveys an impression of ruthlessness, his phrase κατὰ κράτος does not connote illegality. The only change in fiscal administration for which we have documentary evidence shifted from the people to the Council the authority to disburse public funds in the treasury of Athena;[172] other epigraphical evidence suggests that the democratic treasurers were left to serve out their term, as was also the archon Callias.[173] The Four Hundred's only departure in internal matters—not merely from democratic but from general Greek practice—was their refusal to recall those exiled under the democracy, for fear that Alcibiades would have to be included among them (Thuc. 8.70.1). This policy will have had the support of Phrynichus, Antiphon, and Peisander, among others, but it excluded from Athens also those who had been exiled for the profanations in 415 B.C.[174] Their widest departure from democratic policies was in external affairs: despite the conspirators' resolution a few months earlier on Samos, they made immediate peace overtures to Agis, commander of the Spartan garrison at Deceleia, on the grounds that the Spartans would be more reliable contractual partners than the

---

days earlier at Colonus, had been completed. His statement that they "entered" (εἰσῇεσαν) on 22 Thargelion probably means that they let a week elapse before their official inauguration with prayer and sacrifice—that is, before the *anagrapheis* had their constitutions ready for publication, the prytaneis had been selected, and ten new generals had been appointed; see Thuc. 8.70.1 and Arist. *Ath.Pol.* 32.1 with Rhodes, *CAAP* 402 and 406, and Andrewes, *HCT* 5.181–82, 235–36.

172 ML, no. 81.14–15, with Andrewes, *HCT* 5.195, who also remarks on the appearance of some Ionic letters in this inscription and on the dating by month and day rather than by prytany and day.

173 See Andrewes, *HCT* 5.194–95.

174 This policy may have been a subsidiary reason for Andocides' imprisonment by the Four Hundred upon his return to Athens in 411 B.C. (Andoc. 2.13–15; [Lys.] 6.27) despite the fact that, strictly speaking, the decree of Isotimides had not stipulated exile for him (Andoc. 1.71; [Lys.] 6.9, 24).

democrats (8.70.2, 63.4). This led to a rift among the Four Hundred and to their eventual downfall; but it was not the only major cause of their demise. Equally important was counterrevolutionary ideology, which was strongest among the armed forces on Samos. This era saw the first clear ideological split in Athenian politics.

The Four Hundred knew that the Athenian forces on Samos, dominated by the lower classes, which manned the navy, would not take kindly to an oligarchical government. Accordingly, they promptly dispatched ten envoys to Samos to explain that the oligarchy had been established for the good of the city and that sovereignty was vested in the Five Thousand, not merely in the Four Hundred.[175] But events on Samos had meanwhile so polarized the Athenian camp that the envoys' mission was foredoomed to fail. Like the initiative for the overthrow of the democracy, so did the initiative for its restoration originate in Samos.

The movement was galvanized by two opponents of Peisander's conspiracy, the trierarch Thrasybulus and the hoplite Thrasyllus. After the failure of Peisander's negotiations with Alcibiades, some three hundred erstwhile Samian revolutionaries (Thuc. 8.21) established their ideological credentials by helping the Athenian oligarchical general Charminus dispose of Hyperbolus and by then turning upon the Samian *dēmos*. The latter appealed for help to the Athenian generals Leon and Diomedon, who were known to be unsympathetic toward their colleagues' oligarchical plot. Diomedon and Leon in their turn enlisted the help of Thrasybulus and Thrasyllus, who proceeded to forge the Athenian army and navy into a potent democratic weapon against the oligarchical movement, first on Samos and then at Athens, on ideological grounds (8.73.1–4).

Nothing is known of either man's ancestry. In the case of Thrasyllus, we are ignorant even of his father's name and of his deme. His bare identification as a hoplite suggests his origin was humbler than that of the trierarch Thrasybulus. To judge from their later actions, they had different motives for opposing the oligarchy.

175   Thuc. 8.72. Flach, "Staatsstreich" 29 has made the attractive suggestion that this indicates completion of the constitution for the future by the time of the envoys' departure and that the constitution formed the basis of the propaganda they were to spread. Andrewes, *HCT* 5.184 and 285, believes on the basis of 8.86.3 that the envoys did not leave until after the attack of Agis, reported in Thuc. 8.71, had been repulsed. However, it is unlikely that the Four Hundred would have waited so long before communicating with Samos, and it seems more probable that the envoys received news of Agis's attack during their stay on Delos.

Thrasyllus's primary aim was to restore the democracy at all costs, even if that meant enlisting Alcibiades' aid—though once it was reestablished, he wanted no further truck with Alcibiades. Both Thrasyllus and Thrasybulus served in the fleet at the siege of Eresus and, with Alcibiades, participated in the stunning naval victories over Mindarus at Cynossema and Abydos;[176] but thereafter Thrasyllus did not return to the Hellespont from his mission to Athens. Evidently he shared the restored democracy's distrust of such men as Theramenes and Alcibiades, who after having a major part in overthrowing the democracy a year earlier were now guarding its lifeline in the Hellespont.[177] His loyalty to the restored democracy seems unquestionable: he was elected general when Alcibiades, Theramenes, and probably also Thrasybulus were passed over;[178] he was sent to Ionia rather than to the Hellespont in the early summer of 410 B.C.; and after the defeat at Notium he was appointed one of the generals, all with unimpeachable democratic credentials, who replaced the board Alcibiades had served on.[179] But a year later he was one of the six generals condemned to death for dereliction of duty at Arginusae.[180]

Thrasybulus, by contrast, was not averse to Alcibiades' rehabilitation, if Athens could prevail over Sparta in no other way, but not at the price of overthrowing the democracy (Thuc. 8.73.4). That is why he organized a democratic resistance first to the Samian and then to the Athenian oligarchs (8.73.5, 75.2–77) and did not broach the subject of Alcibiades' recall until after the oligarchs' negotiations with Alcibiades had broken down. Moreover, though he believed that Alcibiades alone had any chance of transferring Tissaphernes' support from the Peloponnesians to the Athenians, Thrasybulus did not bring him to Samos until after the assembly of soldiers had approved the recall (8.76.7, 81.1). Recognition of the possible value of Alcibiades' service to the state may well have been Thrasybulus's

176   Thuc. 8.100.4, 104.3–105.3; Xen. *Hell*. 1.1.3–7; Diod. 13.38.3, 39.4–40.6, 45.7–46.6.

177   A. Andrewes, "The Generals in the Hellespont, 410–407 B.C.," *JHS* 73 (1953) 2–9. The views of Andrewes are not affected by the chronology proposed by N. Robertson, "The Sequence of Events in the Aegean in 408 and 407 B.C.," *Hist*. 29 (1980) 282–301.

178   Andrewes, "Generals" 4 with n. 12. For Thrasyllus's generalship, see Xen. *Hell*. 1.1.34, 1.2.1. Cf. also Dion. Hal. *Lys*. 21, 25.

179   Xen. *Hell*. 1.5.16; Lys. 21.7–8; and Diod. 13.74.1 (who mistakenly names Thrasybulus in place of Thrasyllus) with Andrewes, "Generals" 4.

180   Xen. *Hell*. 1.6.30, 1.7.2, 29, 34; Philochorus *FGH* 328F142; Diod. 13.101.5.

motive for his constant cooperation with him and Theramenes in the Hellespont from the summer of 411 to the battle of Arginusae in 406 B.C.: regardless of the suspicions with which the restored democracy may have viewed his colleagues for their political past and him for his association with them, Thrasybulus may have regarded present service in the interest of the survival of Athens as more vital than the memory of past wrongs, provided that service had the willing consent of the soldiers and sailors.

Whereas Peisander six months earlier had succeeded in eliciting from the soldiery at Samos only their reluctant acquiescence in the planned overthrow (Thuc. 8.48.3), Thrasybulus and Thrasyllus will have had little trouble in winning the overwhelming support of the troops for the Samian *dēmos* once the plans of the Samian oligarchs had been exposed. When Chaereas, whose family had strong ties to the Samian democratic establishment,[181] returned to Samos with the horror stories of the oligarchical coup at Athens (8.74.3), Thrasybulus and Thrasyllus were able to exact an oath from all the Athenian troops and from the Samians of military age "to live united under a democratic form of government, to fight the war against the Peloponnesians energetically through to the end, and to be enemies of the Four Hundred and not to make any peace overtures to them."[182] The army now constituted itself into an Assembly, deposed politically suspect generals and trierarchs, and elected new ones to fill their places. Thucydides (8.76.2) reports only the election as generals of Thrasybulus and Thrasyllus and later of Alcibiades (8.82.1); he makes no mention either of Leon and Diomedon or of Chaereas, who Diodorus tells us was a commander at Cyzicus later that year.[183] The split between an oligarchical home government invested with political power and a democratic army controlling the bulk of Athenian military resources was now complete: the army claimed to be the true upholders of the *patrioi nomoi* their political

181 See above, pp. 311–12 with n. 70.
182 Thuc. 8.75.2: ἦ μὴν δημοκρατήσεσθαί τε καὶ ὁμονοήσειν καὶ τὸν πρὸς Πελοποννησίους πόλεμον προθύμως διοίσειν καὶ τοῖς τετρακοσίοις πολέμιοί τε ἔσεσθαι καὶ οὐδὲν ἐπικηρυκεύσεσθαι.
183 Diod. 13.49.6. It is *a priori* likely that he was elected on this occasion. Andrewes, *HCT* 5.268, believes that the same may be true of Eumachus, Diodorus, and Mantitheus, all of whom were active in the Hellespont later: see Xen. *Hell.* 1.1.22; Diod. 13.68.2. Of Leon and Diomedon nothing further is heard until they appear on the board of generals to replace those deposed after Alcibiades' failure at Notium in 406/5 B.C.; see above, n. 40.

opponents had enlisted to help their own cause a few weeks before (Thuc. 8.76.6; cf. Arist. *Ath.Pol.* 29.3, 31.1).

The envoys of the Four Hundred had only reached Delos when they learned of these developments and wisely decided to proceed no farther for the time being (Thuc. 8.77). When they finally reached Samos, they had to negotiate with Alcibiades, who had the situation well in hand (8.86.1). Thrasybulus despite some opposition (of which Thrasyllus may have been a part) had persuaded the assembly of soldiers to support Alcibiades' recall and immunity by arguing that he could win Tissaphernes' support for the Athenians;[184] Alcibiades, who since negotiating with Peisander had seen his influence over Tissaphernes slipping (8.56.4), had accepted Thrasybulus's invitation as an opportunity to improve his own status at Athens and his standing with Tissaphernes at the same time (8.82.3). Upon his election as general by the troops, he immediately left to negotiate with Tissaphernes and had just returned to Samos—with what result we are not told—when the envoys of the Four Hundred landed (8.82, 85.4). At this point Alcibiades' potential as a great leader appeared at its best. His charismatic influence restrained the soldiers from lynching the oligarchical emissaries and from deciding to sail at once to attack the Piraeus (8.86.2–4), and he persuaded them to concur in his response, which the envoys took back to Athens: that a government of the Five Thousand was acceptable so long as the Four Hundred be deposed and a Council of Five Hundred be restored; that any economies would be welcomed if they ensured pay for the troops; and that there should be no slackening in the resistance to the enemy, because the troops' reconciliation with the home government was designed to save the city (8.86.6–7).

The firm yet conciliatory tone of this response rallied those among the Four Hundred who had joined the revolution in the hope that restricting the franchise to the five thousand "best able to serve with their fortunes and persons" would rid the democracy of its most blatant shortcoming by vesting sovereignty in those who had a "stake in the country." They had accepted membership in the Council content that the appointment of *katalogeis* would take care of their concerns, but they will have bristled at the peace feelers stretched out to Agis soon after the seizure of power (8.70.2) and will have felt relief when the subsequent mission of Laispodias, Aristo-

---

184 Thuc. 8.81.1. On the possibility of Thrasyllus's opposition, see Andrewes, "Generals" 4 and *HCT* 5.275.

phon, and Melesias to sue for peace at Sparta was aborted.[185] The major issue for them, however, was the extremists' reluctance to expedite the work of the *katalogeis* and to publish the list of the Five Thousand. The news that the armed forces in Samos were now led by Alcibiades and would not be reconciled to the regime of the Four Hundred encouraged Theramenes and Aristocrates son of Scellias to demand the list of the Five Thousand be published as a prelude to introducing more equality into the constitution, but they still lacked the confidence to demand an end to the extreme oligarchy.[186] Despite its malice, Lysias's statement (12.66–67) that Aristocrates was the more vocal of the two and was less actuated by personal ambition

185 Thuc. 8.86.9 with 89.2, where ἄνευ τῶν πλεόνων suggests a majority of the Four Hundred. Although the three ambassadors are said to have been fairly prominent in the overthrow of the democracy at 8.86.9, little is known about them: Laispodias was general in 415/14 B.C., and we know from Thuc. 6.105.2 that he commanded raids on Epidaurus, Limera, Prasiae, and other parts of the coast of the Peloponnese. In that same year, Ar. *Av*. 1569 apparently alludes to a physical defect of his; according to the scholiast on this passage, he had a deformed shin, for which he was ridiculed also by Eupolis (fr. 102), Strattis (fr. 16) and Theopompus (fr. 39). That he was called πολεμικός by Phrynichus (fr 16) and φιλόδικος by Philyllius (fr. 9), and that Antiphon had delivered a speech against him (frr. 21–24 Thalheim) ca. 422 B.C. (see n. 96 above), is not sufficient proof that he was one of the democrats who had a change of heart in 411 B.C., as J. Beloch, *Die attische Politik seit Perikles* (Leipzig, 1884) 62–63, has it. Nothing else is known of Aristophon, who must have been older than the Aristophon of whom we first hear as an opponent of the Thirty; see Davies, *APF* 65. Melesias may well have been the now-aging son of Thucydides son of Melesias, who, according to Pl. *Lach*. 178a–179d, never achieved any distinction despite his good education (*Meno* 94c–d).

186 Thuc. 8.89.1–2. The text is corrupt toward the end of the passage, and it is difficult to decide whether οὐ τὸ† ἀπαλλαξείειν τοῦ ἄγαν ἐς ὀλίγους οἰκεῖν (*sic* M) hides the kind of meaning we have given it here, or whether, with Andrewes, *HCT* 5.297–98, the οὐ τὸ† ought to be completely disregarded, giving the sense that an end to extreme oligarchy was in fact demanded. The issue cannot be decided on the basis of the present passage alone, and we must interpret it in the light of the subsequent narrative. This seems to me to argue against an early demand for an end to radical oligarchy. Thucydides presents the actions of the rebels as a crescendo: Theramenes' first step is merely to allege that the fortification of Eëtioneia does not have its avowed purpose (8.90.3). Next—but only after the return of the ambassadors from Sparta—he expresses his conviction κινδυνεύσειν τὸ τεῖχος τοῦτο καὶ τὴν πόλιν διαφθεῖραι (91.1) and advocates that measures be taken to guard the city (91.2); only the murder of Phrynichus emboldens Theramenes and Aristocrates into taking action, especially since the Peloponnesian ships are coming uncomfortably close (92.2–3). But even then Theramenes avoids a confrontation with the Four Hundred: when threatened in Council for collusion in the arrest of Alexicles, he denies complicity and offers to obtain Alexicles' release (92.6), and once in the Piraeus he does not openly turn against Aristarchus but pretends to join his angry outbursts against the hoplites and only after that leaves it to the hoplites to decide whether the fortifications should be built or destroyed (92.9–10). This chain of development

may be correct.[187] A choregic dedication in the Pythion leaves no doubt that, like Theramenes, he came from a prominent family.[188] The fact that he was among the younger signatories of the Peace of Nicias and the alliance with Sparta in 421 B.C. (Thuc. 5.19.2, 24.1) indicates that he was a solid citizen and trusted by the democratic establishment when Theramenes was still a pupil of Prodicus.[189] There is no indication that he was an intellectual, and this may in part explain why the Athenian *dēmos* looked more kindly on him in the following years than on Theramenes. He was sufficiently in the public eye in 414 B.C. to rate a pun in Aristophanes' *Birds* (125–26), and he held his first known generalship a year later.[190] But whereas Theramenes was appointed general by the Four Hundred (Thuc. 8.92.9), Aristocrates served only as a taxiarch, commanding the hoplites of his tribe (8.92.4); for another generalship he had to await the restoration of the democracy (ML, no. 84.35). This suggests that he was no more than "a trusted soldier with no strong political feelings, drawn into the Four Hundred by the hope of Persian help in the war."[191] He served as a hoplite general with Alcibiades in 407/6 B.C., remained on the board of generals when most of his colleagues were replaced after Notium, and was a general in the battle of Arginusae a year later, suffering the same fate as five of his colleagues.[192] It is noteworthy that Theramenes, though active in the campaigns in the Hellespont, was never elected general throughout this period, and when he was elected for 405/4 B.C., in the

does not suggest that Theramenes took a strong stand against the oligarchs immediately upon the return of the envoys from Samos, and for that reason I favor the interpretation of 89.1–2 given here. Clearly, action was taken by Aristocrates before it was taken by Theramenes. For the ambivalence of Theramenes' motives, see also G. Adeleye, "Theramenes and the Overthrow of the Four Hundred," *Mus.Afr.* 2 (1973) 77–81.

187   It seems corroborated by the sequence of names in Arist. *Ath.Pol.* 33.2 and by the general statement in Thuc. 8.89.3 that φιλοτιμία played a part in the downfall of the Four Hundred.

188   Pl. *Grg.* 472a–b with *IG* I² 772, rediscovered and discussed by T. L. Shear, Jr., "The Athenian Agora: Excavations of 1971," *Hesp.* 42 (1973) 121–79, esp. 173–75, who dates it in the 420s.

189   Andrewes and Lewis, "Note" 179–80; cf. nn. 111–12 above.

190   Thuc. 8.9.2 His service as general at some unknown point is also attested by Aristophanes, fr. 63.70–71 Austin.

191   Andrewes, *HCT* 5.295, who errs, however, in assigning to Aristocrates "a prominent part in setting up the oligarchy."

192   For 407/6, see Xen. *Hell.* 1.4.21. For post-Notium, see ibid. 1.5.16; Diod. 13.74.1. For Arginusae, see Xen. *Hell.* 1.6.29, 1.7.2 and 34; Diod. 13.101.5–6; Philochorus *FGH* 328F142.

critical period after Arginusae, he did not pass his *dokimasia*.[193] Evidently the restored democracy regarded an activist intellectual as a greater risk than an unsophisticated patriot who, despite his initial support of the Four Hundred, had demonstrated in 411 B.C. that he knew right from wrong.

Fear was the main reaction of the diehards among the Four Hundred to the news from Samos. Phrynichus had personal reasons for fearing Alcibiades, and Aristarchus, a member of the upper classes and an inveterate enemy of popular sovereignty,[194] was apprehensive lest the democratic movement should undermine the already shaky loyalty of the people and even of some of the Four Hundred. Together with other extremists, such as Peisander and Antiphon, they decided to call in the enemy rather than be certainly doomed under a restored democracy if their oligarchy and control over the allies could not be maintained (Thuc. 8.91.3). An embassy of ten was sent to Sparta to sue for peace under minimal acceptable conditions; among the ambassadors were Antiphon, Phrynichus, Onomacles, who had been an oligarchical general at Samos and later became one of the Thirty,[195] and Archeptolemus (son of the town planner Hippodamus of Miletus), who had been a partisan of peace with Sparta already after Pylos.[196] At the same time, on the initiative of Aristarchus, Melanthius, and Aristoteles, the extremists among the Four Hundred intensified the fortification of Eëtioneia at the entrance to the Piraeus in order to secure the Peloponnesians' access to the harbor (8.90.1, 91.2).[197]

There is no indication that Theramenes actively opposed sending the embassy to Sparta, nor do we know how far he let the construc-

---

193 Lys. 13.10 with Andrewes, "Generals" 2–3.

194 His upper-class status is indicated by his choregia of a boys' chorus in 422/1 B.C. (*IG* II² 2318.121–22); his hostility to democracy, by Thuc. 8.90.1 and 92.6–10, where he is aided by young knights, and not least by his betrayal of Oenoë to the Boeotians after the Four Hundred had been overthrown (Thuc. 8.98 and Xen. *Hell*. 1.7.28; referred to perhaps in Ar. frr. 550–51, if the Iberians mentioned there were the τοξόται βαρβαρώτατοι of Thuc. 8.98.1). At some point before Arginusae he returned to Athens, where he was put on trial and condemned to death (Xen. *Hell*. 1.7.28; Lycurg. 1.115).

195 [Plut.] *X orat*. 833e–f with p. 347 and nn. 42–43 above.

196 [Plut.] *X orat*. 833e–f; Ar. *Eq*. 794 with schol. and 327.

197 The three are named in Theramenes' defense speech in Xen. *Hell*. 2.3.46. Nothing else is known of Melanthius. Aristoteles will have been an aging intellectual and former pupil of Zeno (Pl. *Prm*. 127d); he had been a general in 431/0 B.C. (*IG* I³ 366.6), *hellēnotamias* in 421/0 B.C. (*ATL*, list 34, with D. M. Lewis, "Double Representation in the *Strategia*," *JHS* 81 [1961] 118–23, esp. 120–21), and was to survive to become a member of the Thirty (Xen. *Hell*. 2.3.2).

tion at Eëtioneia proceed before he voiced his suspicions about its true purpose (Thuc. 8.90.3). By the time his opposition became vocal, the ambassadors had returned without satisfactory results, and the movements of the Peloponnesian navy had substantiated his suspicions (8.91.1–2, 92.3); and by the time he and Aristocrates, together with the hoplites detailed to complete it, sabotaged the work at Eëtioneia, Phrynichus had already been murdered (8.92.2– 4). The hoplites' arrest of Alexicles, a general and member of the extremist inner circle (8.92.4; cf. 98.1), was a signal to the Four Hundred that a considerable number of the people were against them and would soon join the malcontents in their own midst in demanding at least a partial restoration of popular sovereignty. Still, Theramenes was too slow or too cautious to recognize the extent of his support at once. When threatened by the Council, he offered to prove his good faith by procuring Alexicles' release, and he was sufficiently intimidated by Aristarchus and the young knights who had been sent along to keep an eye on him[198] to join Aristarchus in angrily admonishing the hoplites in the Piraeus. Not until he saw that the fortifications were of no avail did he openly agree to demolishing them (8.92.9–10).

This demolition led to the first open declaration of popular hostility to the Four Hundred. When the hoplites appealed to the gathered crowd to join their efforts to have the Five Thousand govern in place of the Four Hundred (8.92.11), the lines were drawn. The hoplites relented to the extent of releasing Alexicles, but they continued to demolish Eëtioneia. As the Four Hundred, shaken by these events, met in the Bouleuterion the following day, the hoplites held an armed assembly in the theater of Dionysus near Munychia, where they decided to march against the city. Representatives of the Four Hundred met them at the temple of the Dioscuri and succeeded in blunting their determination by promising to publish the list of the Five Thousand, by proposing a scheme whereby the Four Hundred would be elected in rotation by and from among the Five Thousand, and by appealing to their patriotism to prevent the city from falling into the hands of the enemy. A date was set for a common Assembly meeting in the theater of Dionysus, at which the details for a reconciliation were to be worked out (8.93). But events

198   Thuc. 8.92.6. That the young, presumably upper-class, knights supported the oligarchy is shown by the escort 120 of them gave to the Four Hundred when they took over the Bouleuterion at 8.69.4.

outstripped the consummation of this agreement. Just before the appointed hour the appearance of forty-two Peloponnesian ships off Salamis quelled for the moment the differences between the opposing camps: "The Athenians, on hearing the news, ran in full force to the Piraeus, realizing that the war against their enemy, no longer distant but at their very harbor, was of greater importance than the domestic war" (8.94.3). They hastily manned their ships to prevent Euboea from falling to the enemy, but they did not succeed. Their defeat off Eretria delivered all Euboea except Oreos to the Peloponnesians. In the ensuing consternation, which according to Thucydides was kept from becoming a total disaster only by the Spartan's lack of enterprise, the authority of the Four Hundred evaporated. The Assembly meeting that officially terminated their rule was held on the Pnyx, the customary meeting place of the Assembly under the democracy (8.95–96, 97.1).

RECONSTRUCTION AND THE FIRST RESTORATION

In view of the praise showered upon it, we are tantalized that no details are known about the constitutional structure of the regime that followed the overthrow of the Four Hundred. Thucydides' celebrated comment καὶ οὐχ ἥκιστα δὴ τὸν πρῶτον χρόνον ἐπί γε ἐμοῦ ᾿Αθηναῖοι φαίνονται εὖ πολιτεύσαντες· μετρία γὰρ ἥ τε ἐς τοὺς ὀλίγους καὶ τοὺς πολλοὺς ξύγκρασις ἐγένετο καὶ ἐκ πονηρῶν τῶν πραγμάτων γενομένων τοῦτο πρῶτον ἀνήνεγκε τὴν πόλιν,[199] faintly echoed by

---

199   Ibid. 97.2: "Not least remarkable is that for the first time in my lifetime the Athenians clearly enjoyed good government. It was a judicious blend geared to the interests of the few and the many, and this fact first buoyed up the city after the wretched condition into which it had fallen." As Andrewes, *HCT* 5.331, rightly remarks in the first part of this passage, "argument is needed to elucidate every phrase but ᾿Αθηναῖοι φαίνονται." Such argument need not be given here, since it has been copiously and lucidly provided by Andrewes himself (ibid. 331–339), whose results have been incorporated into the translation given here, and by G. Donini, *La Posizione di Tucidide verso il governo dei Cinquemila,* Historia Politica Philosophica: Il Pensiero Antico, Studi e Testi 2 (Turin, 1969). My major disagreements with both Andrewes (331–35) and Donini 4–7, 96–97) are that they accept without argument a close syntactical relation between οὐχ ἥκιστα and εὖ πολιτεύσαντες (which has been the conventional interpretation at least since Classen and Steup) and that I take τὸν πρῶτον χρόνον as meaning "for the first time," although there is no parallel for it, and not as "during the first phase [of this regime]." The decisive argument against the conventional interpretation of οὐχ ἥκιστα is that, when modifying another expression of any kind, Thucydides places it in close proximity to the expression modified—e.g., 1.23.3, ἡ οὐχ ἥκιστα βλάψασα . . . ἡ λοιμώδης νόσος (for other

Aristotle's δοκοῦσι δὲ καλῶς πολιτευθῆναι κατὰ τούτους τοὺς καιρούς,[200] raises the question to what extent the sovereignty of the people was restored under this "intermediate constitution," or in other words, what role the Athenian *dēmos* played in this μετρία ξύγκρασις (judicious mixture).[201] The Assembly that deposed the Four Hundred and "voted to hand over control of affairs to the Five Thousand"[202] was convened on the Pnyx; this was no doubt a symbolic gesture to herald a greater degree of democratic freedom than had existed under the Four Hundred. The initiative in convening it came presumably from Theramenes, who is credited by Diodorus (13.38.2, 42.2) with establishing the intermediate regime. For although he will have had the support of Aristocrates and of other opponents from among the Four Hundred, the political prin-

---

participial expressions, see 2.27.1, 79.6; 6.99.2; 8.86.9); 1.35.3, καὶ οὐχ ἥκιστα ἀπὸ τῶν ὑμετέρων ὑπηκόων (for other adverbial expressions, see 1.60.2, 67.2; 2.61.3, 89.9); 1.68.2, προσήκει ἡμᾶς οὐχ ἥκιστα (for other pronouns, see 4.30.1, 47.2); 1.68.3, καὶ οὐχ ἥκιστα τοῖς ἡμετέροις ξυμμάχοις (for other nouns or names, see 1.95.1 and 5, 103.4, 130.2; 4.80.1, 96.3; 6.61.5; 7.4.6, 21.3, 86.4; 8.73.5); so also in verbs at 7.44.6 and 8.65.2, though when οὐχ ἥκιστα is placed at the end of a sentence for emphasis, it is sometimes separated from the verb: e.g., 1.3.1, δηλοῖ δέ μοι καὶ τόδε τῶν παλαιῶν ἀσθένειαν οὐχ ἥκιστα (so also at 1.140.2; 6.15.3). This usage makes it highly unlikely that it is to be taken together with εὖ πολιτεύσαντες. Moreover, this is the only Thucydidean passage in which οὐχ ἥκιστα is sandwiched between καὶ . . . δή, which separates it in a sense from the rest of the sentence and signifies, according to J. D. Denniston, *The Greek Particles*[2] (Oxford, 1959) 253, "that the addition made by καί is an important one." This removes the embarrassment of having to combine ἥκιστα with πρῶτον, which gives discomfort to Donini (pp. 5–6) and Andrewes (p. 332), and enables us to consider τὸν πρῶτον χρόνον in its own right. To take it in its natural meaning, "during the first phase," makes it not only difficult to accommodate the phrase ἐπί γε ἐμοῦ, with which it is closely associated, but also imposes the well-nigh impossible task of dividing the short-lived regime of the Five Thousand into at least two phases. The only way out of this problem, it seems to me, is either to accept with reluctance the otherwise unattested meaning "for the first time," or, less plausibly, to refer χρόνον to Thucydides' own life and interpret the phrase as "this was the first period of my lifetime in which the Athenians clearly enjoyed good government." But one would perhaps expect τὸν ἐπί γε ἐμοῦ πρῶτον χρόνον.

200 Arist. *Ath.Pol.* 33.2: "They are thought to have been well governed in that period."

201 This question has again become controversial in recent years through the publication of G. E. M. de Ste. Croix, "The Constitution of the Five Thousand," *Hist.* 5 (1956) 1–23. See also R. Sealey, "The Revolution of 411 B.C.," in his *Essays* 111–32, esp. 122–31; P. J. Rhodes, "The Five Thousand in the Athenian Revolutions of 411 B.C.," *JHS* 92 (1972) 115–27 (from which I borrow the expression "intermediate constitution"); Andrewes, *HCT* 5.323–28.

202 Thuc. 8.97.1: τοῖς πεντακισχιλίοις ἐψηφίσαντο τὰ πράγματα παραδοῦναι. On this meaning, see de Ste. Croix, "Constitution" 3, and Andrewes, *HCT* 5.325.

ciples with which Xenophon credits him (*Hell*. 2.3.48) are consonant with the intermediate constitution; and his sophistic training,
which will have given him an interest in political principles, makes
him more likely than Aristocrates to have shaped the intermediate
regime.

The Assembly that voted the new regime into existence consisted
of the people as a whole rather than of only the hoplites, who were
to dominate it. Thucydides suggests as much by using the verb
παραδοῦναι (8.97.1), which denotes "the effective hand-over to
another of something which one owns or controls,"[203] and by the
phrase εἶναι δὲ αὐτῶν ὁπόσοι καὶ ὅπλα παρέχονται, "that they shall be
all those among them who provide their own arms" (ibid.), where
αὐτῶν indicates that the vote was taken by a body larger than that of
which the Five Thousand was to consist.[204] This means that the
intermediate regime was sanctioned by the sovereign people, but it
does not imply that the people as a whole retained the franchise
under the Five Thousand in the sense that their approval was
required, as under the democracy, to validate whatever proposals
would be submitted to them. This right had clearly been ceded in
the vote "to hand over control of affairs" to the Five Thousand;
and when Thucydides mentions "frequent assemblies" (πυκναὶ
ἐκκλησίαι) in the sequel, we must understand these as assemblies of
the Five Thousand. Yet whatever the formal, legal situation may
have been, if indeed the question of popular franchise did receive a
legal formulation, the smooth restoration of the democracy in
410/09 B.C. shows that popular franchise had not been permanently
surrendered but remained latent and unclaimed during the eight
months of the intermediate regime.[205] The people were ready to
cede their powers to those with the means to serve the state with
their persons and fortunes because of their fear and helplessness after
the defeat at Eretria (Thuc. 8.96), and, in the absence of strong
leadership, because of their willingness to entrust the state to men
who had proved their dislike of autocracy by opposing the Four
Hundred.

203   Andrewes, *HCT* 5.325.
204   So U. Wilcken, "Zur oligarchischen Revolution in Athen vom Jahre 411 v.
Chr.," *Sber. d. Preuss. Ak. d. Wiss. Berlin, Philos.-hist. Kl.* 1935, no. 3, 52–53, cited
with approval by de Ste. Croix, "Constitution" 9 with n. 39.
205   de Ste. Croix's contention, "Constitution," esp. 3–4 and 13, that the thetes
retained the right to attend the Assembly throughout, has been effectively answered
by Andrewes, *HCT* 5.323–24.

This brings us to the problem of who the Five Thousand were. The list that the *katalogeis* had been commissioned at Colonus to draw up had apparently never been completed, although we know that some beginnings had been made. The speech *For Polystratus* claims that as a reluctant *katalogeus* Polystratus included nine thousand men in the register instead of five thousand and that his active service on the Council lasted only eight days before he was dispatched to Eretria.[206] If that is true, we may infer that although the *katalogeis* began their assigned task soon after Colonus by drafting a long list (which was perhaps to be whittled down to five thousand at a later stage), their function was not regarded as sufficiently urgent to make their presence in Athens imperative. This would confirm Thucydides' statement (8.92.11) that the Four Hundred were reluctant to get the list published. We hear of no resumption of activity either on the part of Polystratus or of any other *katalogeus* after these eight days, and the fact that the Assembly on the Pnyx found it necessary to define the Five Thousand shows that such a list did not exist. The definition itself gives pause: if "all those...who provide their own arms" were to be included, the "control of affairs" will have been in the hands of a body in excess of five thousand; why then was this magic number used?[207] Perhaps five thousand had indeed become a magic number, one that had lost all relation to historical reality, simply signifying all those best able to serve with their fortunes and their persons. The number is first mentioned as a maximum figure in the discussions in Athens before Peisander's return from his mission to Alcibiades (Thuc. 8.65.3); a speech attributed to Lysias (20.13) attests that a proposal to give them control of affairs was accepted by vote; and Aristotle (*Ath.Pol.* 29.5) includes five thousand as a minimum figure among the recommendations of the *syngrapheis*, presumably at Colonus. (Aristotle's mistaken assertion that the *anagrapheis* were elected by and from among the Five Thousand may indicate that the Colonus meeting either considered itself or was considered in some later tradition as equivalent to that body.)[208] Thus, the number may well have stuck, regardless of how many hoplites were now given a part in the intermediate regime.

There is evidence that a new Council of Five Hundred was chosen

206   [Lys.] 20.13–14 with Andrewes, *HCT* 5.205–6.
207   For this question, see Andrewes, *HCT* 5.328–29.
208   See above, p. 379.

not by lot, as the old one had been under the democracy,[209] but presumably by direct election from among the Five Thousand. Similarly, other officials who we know were elected—generals, thesmothetai, the Eleven, and demarchs ([Plut.] *X orat.* 833e-834a)—will have been of at least hoplite status. Whether thetes were excluded also from jury service is hard to tell, but the absence of pay for jurors suggests that in fact few if any would have been able to serve, even if they had been eligible *de iure*.[210]

Despite its claim to continuity with the various proposals of the recent past to limit the franchise to five thousand men, the intermediate regime shows hardly a trace of the elaborate constitutional structure the *anagrapheis* proposed for the future (Arist. *Ath.Pol.* 30.2-6). The Council and Assembly on which it was based are clearly democratic features, as is the resumption of the practice of dating decrees by prytanies.[211] It seems that after the Colonus meeting the adoption of a Boeotian model for the Athenian constitution, if indeed it had ever been seriously advocated, was quietly dropped in favor of a model with roots in Athenian tradition. A time of crisis was no time for constitutional experiments. All in all, the break between the intermediate constitution and the rule of the Four Hundred was more marked than the transition to the democracy, which was restored some ten months later.[212] Of the generals who

209   The prescript of the decree of Demophantus, passed early under the restored democracy, in 410/09 B.C., states that it is issued by ἡ βουλὴ οἱ πεντακόσιοι λαχόντες τῷ κυάμῳ (Andoc. 1.96), differentiating it not only from the Council of Four Hundred but also from a Council of Five Hundred not chosen by lot, which will have been the Council of the intermediate regime: see Hignett, *HAC* 372; de Ste. Croix, "Constitution" 22 with n. 98; Rhodes, "The Five Thousand" 117 with n. 24. Moreover, the decree of the intermediate regime calling for the arrest and trial of Archeptolemus, Onomacles, and Antiphon was passed by the Council ([Plut.] *X orat.* 833e).

210   The arguments of de Ste. Croix, "Constitution" 11-12, that [Lys.] 20 ought to have referred to exclusion, if there had been any, and that δικαστήριον refers to jury courts under the democracy, do not carry conviction. No inference can be drawn from the corrupt passage at Thucydides 8.68.2 about the composition of the court before which Antiphon was tried, nor can any inference be based on the ὑμᾶς in Antiphon's defense speech (fr. 1a Thalheim, *Antiphontis Orationes et Fragmenta* [Leipzig, 1914] 108.15); see Andrewes, *HCT* 5.200, 327.

211   Compare the decree in [Plut.] *X orat.* 833f with ML, no. 81.15-17; cf. Andrewes, *HCT* 5.181-82.

212   For example, the archon Mnasilochus, installed by the Four Hundred, was replaced by Theopompus; see Arist. *Ath.Pol.* 33.1 and Diod.13.38.1 with Andrewes, *HCT* 5.193-95. The Council was raised again to five hundred, and the prytany system was reinstated with the modification that ἐπιστάτης and γραμματεύς could

had served under the oligarchy, only Theramenes and Thymochares were retained;[213] Eumachus, Conon, and Chaereas, who served as generals after the overthrow of the Four Hundred, seem to have been newly appointed.[214] Whether the election of Thrasybulus, Thrasyllus, and Alcibiades by the soldiers in Samos (Thuc. 8.76.2, 82.1) was ratified we do not know.

Two characteristic policies of the intermediate regime are closely associated with Theramenes: the recall of Alcibiades and other exiles and the trials of revolutionary oligarchical extremists. The recall of Alcibiades will have been moved by Theramenes[215] soon after the beginning of the new regime not only because Alcibiades' talents and potential connections were desirable but also because the recall was a further symbolic break with the Four Hundred (Thuc. 8.70.1) and at the same time an endorsement of the action the forces in Samos took under Thrasybulus's leadership (8.81.1). Why it took almost another four years for Alcibiades to return to Athens can only be guessed. He probably knew of still-latent hostility toward him in the city, and he may have wished to allay it by first proving his patriotism in the Hellespont, where his presence was needed most. The other exiles now recalled (Thuc. 8.97.3) will have been primarily those who had fled or had been exiled in the wake of the desecrations of 415 B.C.[216] How many of them returned to Athens at this time we cannot tell. Certainly Axiochus, Alcibiades' uncle, was back in Athens by 407 B.C., at the age of about sixty;[217] Timanthes had returned before the amnesty decree of Patrocleides in 405 B.C.;[218] and Adeimantus

---

belong to the same tribe, as they could not under the democracy: see Hignett, *HAC* 376; Rhodes, *CAAP* 412. In addition, the treasurers of Athena were replaced by a new board, which served for the remainder of the year: see Ferguson, *Treasurers* 100–101 with n. 1 and 145–47; Rhodes, *CAAP* 366. Likewise the increase of the number of *hellēnotamiai* to twenty, absorbing the functions previously fulfilled by the *kōlakretai*, may have been an act of the intermediate regime; see n. 166 above.

213   For Theramenes, see Thuc. 8.92.9 with Xen. *Hell.* 1.1.22; for Thymochares, see Thuc. 8.95.2 with Xen. *Hell.* 1.1.1.

214   Xen. *Hell.* 1.1.22; Diod. 13.48.6, 49.6.

215   Diod. 13.38.2 42.2; cf. Nep. *Alc.* 5.4 and n. 116 above. The recall of Alcibiades credited to Critias by Plut. *Alc.* 33.1 probably belongs in 408/7 B.C., as argued by Andrewes, "Generals" 3 n. 7. Thuc. 8.97.3 names no proposer and includes unnamed others in the recall.

216   Of the sixty-five persons we identify in Appendix C (below) as having been incriminated, thirty-one fled and another seventeen either fled or were executed, according to Dover's list, *HCT* 4.277–80.

217   Andoc. 1.16; [Pl.] *Axioch.* 368d–369a; ML, 89.48; with Appendix C and n. 20 below.

218   Andoc. 1.35; *IG* I³ 106.21–23 with Hatzfeld 184 n. 1.

was serving as general with Alcibiades in the campaign against Andros in 407/6, was reelected as one of those to replace the Arginusae generals in 406/5, and was among the generals captured by Lysander after Aegospotami: his election as general with Alcibiades suggests that he returned well before 407 B.C.[219] Others may have returned at this time, whom Andocides (1.35) mentions as present in the city at the time of his trial. In any event, a gradual return of exiles may well have been encouraged by the intermediate regime, especially of those who could be expected to benefit the state and not cause another revolution.

But along with this conciliatory gesture went a relentless prosecution of extremist oligarchs. It was a prosecution, not a persecution: we hear of no lynchings or terrorism but only of orderly legal proceedings initiated soon after the new regime had been established. The case against Antiphon, Archeptolemus, and Onomacles is the most celebrated and most instructive because the indictment and verdict have come down to us verbatim and because some intelligible pieces of Antiphon's defense, which supplement Harpocration's meager information, were discovered in 1907 on a papyrus of the second century of our era.[220] The indictment was decreed by the Council alone, without ratification by the Assembly, but this does not permit any inferences about legislative procedure under the intermediate regime, since the proceeding was an *eisangelia*;[221] we can infer merely that the normal democratic course of initiating action before the Council was observed. The prescript indicates that the indictment was not issued until the new regime had been in power for three weeks, namely, on the twenty-first day of the (presumably first) prytany. The fact that the indictment calls for the arrest (συλλαβεῖν) of Archeptolemus, Onomacles, and Antiphon and for their appearance before a jury court (δικαστήριον) indicates that these three had remained at large and unharmed for the first few weeks after the overthrow of the Four Hundred. Apparently they felt no need to go into exile; since the new government was still in

---

219   Andoc. 1.16; Xen. *Hell*. 1.4.21, 1.7.1, 2.1.30; Diod. 13.69.3; Plut. *Alc*. 36.6, with Appendix C, p. 545 and n. 53 below.

220   [Plut.] *X orat*. 833e–f and 834a–b has preserved the text of indictment and verdict from Caecilius's collection, taken from Craterus *FGH* 342F5b; the Geneva papyrus, together with the fragments preserved by Harpocration, is most accessible as Antiphon, frr. 1–6 in Thalheim's edition, pp. 108–11; all these documents can be found with English translation in Maidment, *Orators* 1.294–99 and 314–17. For the formal aspects of this trial, see below, Appendix A, case 7.

221   [Plut.] *X orat*. 833a and d; cf. Hansen, *Eisangelia* 113–15.

the process of being organized, its attitude toward the extremists among the oligarchs was not yet clear.[222] The charge against all three was treason, on the grounds "that they had gone to Lacedaemon as ambassadors to the detriment of the Athenian state and that they had sailed from the camp on an enemy ship and had made their way on foot through Deceleia" ([Plut.] *X orat*. 833e). In other words, they were tried for going on an embassy to Sparta after the news of the opposition of the army in Samos had reached Athens (Thuc. 8.90.2), not for their revolutionary activities before and at Colonus. The reason for this is clear: their accusers had themselves been active in establishing the Four Hundred and had been members of their Council but had turned against the extremists and were now leaders of the new regime. The decree of indictment was moved by Andron, one of the younger intellectuals, who had thrown in his lot with the oligarchical movement and had become a member of the Four Hundred[223] but had evidently joined the disaffected; Theramenes played a part in the prosecution, probably as one of the generals to whom the conduct of the case was entrusted;[224] and Apolexis, an obscure participant in the prosecution, may well also have been one of the Four Hundred.[225]

We are less well informed about other prosecutions against oligarchical extremists. The most vindictive of these will have been the posthumous actions against Phrynichus, which were taken even before Archeptolemus and Antiphon were condemned.[226] We learn

---

222   So Jameson, "Sophocles" 553.

223   Andron must still have been young when he sat at Hippias's feet ca. 433 B.C. (Pl. *Prt.* 315c), since his son Androtion was not born until ca. 410 B.C.; see Davies, *APF* 34. We have already met him as a close friend of Callicles in Pl. *Grg.* 487c (above, p. 246 with n. 172), and his membership in the Four Hundred is attested by Harp. and the *Suda* s.v. Ἄνδρων.

224   Lys. 12.67 and Antiphon, fr. 1b6–8 Thalheim, with Xen. *Hell.* 2.3.40 and [Plut.] *X orat.* 833e–f.

225   Harp. s.v. στασιώτης (= Antiphon, fr. 1 Thalheim) states merely that Apolexis accused Antiphon and his grandfather of factionalism (ὡς στασιώτης ἦ <καὶ> ἐγὼ καὶ ὁ πάππος ὁ ἐμός). We can infer from this merely that he was either a general or one of the ten συνήγοροι chosen by the generals from among the councilors, to whom Andron's decree ([Plut.] *X orat.* 833f) entrusts the prosecution. However, even this is uncertain, since the decree permits ἄλλους, ἄν τις βούληται to participate in the prosecution. In any event, Harp. s.v. στασιώτης cannot be cited to support the contention that Apolexis was a συνήγορος, as is done by Gilbert, *Beiträge* 334, and by W. S. Ferguson, "The Condemnation of Antiphon," *Mélanges Gustave Glotz* 1 (Paris, 1932) 349–66, esp. 360 with n. 3.

226   [Plut.] *X orat.* 834b assumes that the decrees concerning Phrynichus are already published.

from Lycurgus (1.112–15) that his assassins were released from prison; that on the motion of Critias it was voted to try him for treason and, if he were found guilty, to exhume his body and cast it outside the borders of Attica; that it was further voted (on whose motion we are not told) that, if he were convicted, anyone who had spoken in his defense would be subject to banishment; and that Aristarchus and Alexicles were put to death and were denied burial in Attica.[227] The persons Lycurgus mentions as involved in these cases are of considerable interest. Critias's earliest attested political activity is his implication on Diocleides' testimony in the mutilation of the herms, in 415 B.C.; Critias was arrested but later released.[228] He will have been sympathetic enough to the extremists of 411 B.C. to support their fortifying Eëtioneia, but there is no evidence that he was a member of the Four Hundred.[229] The hostility toward Phrynichus evinced in his decree makes it unlikely that the two had associated in 412/11 B.C., and the fact that Critias was free to move the decree at all in the hoplite assembly shows that he was not thought an oligarchical extremist. What best explains his bitter hostility is his close friendship with Alcibiades, attested as early as 433 B.C.,[230] which was also to prompt him four years later to move Alcibiades' formal recall.[231] Aristarchus, one may suppose, might have been tried in his own right for treason not only for having promoted (together with Phrynichus, Peisander, and Antiphon) peace negotiations with Sparta and the fortification of Eëtioneia (Thuc. 8.90.1; Xen. Hell. 2.3.46) but also for his diehard loyalty to the oligarchy, which made him betray Oenoë to the Boeotians when the Four Hundred had already been overthrown.[232] If there is any truth in Lycurgus's allegations, it will be that Aristarchus did not leave Athens immediately after Oenoë but stayed long enough to defend his dead associ-

227 Lycurgus's attribution of the vote to ὁ δῆμος (1.113), which is not mentioned by de Ste. Croix, "Constitution," does of course not imply that these measures belong to the restored democracy; and the bronze tablet in [Plut.] X orat. 834b argues against that.

228 Andoc. 1.47 and 66 with Appendix C, pp. 542–43 below.

229 [Dem.] 58.67 with Wade-Gery, Essays 279–80. To this extent I agree with H. C. Avery, "Critias and the Four Hundred," CP 58 (1963) 165–67, but I cannot follow him in his statement (p. 166) that "during the first oligarchy he remained a democrat." Avery's arguments have been effectively answered by G. Adeleye, "Critias: Member of the Four Hundred?" TAPA 104 (1974) 1–9, who, however, goes beyond the evidence of [Dem.] 58 in assuming membership in the Four Hundred.

230 Pl. Prt. 316a with Appendix C, p. 543 with n. 32.

231 See n. 215 above.

232 Thuc. 8.98 with n. 194 above.

ate Phrynichus. He was not, however, executed on this charge: Euryptolemus's speech in defense of the generals of Arginusae suggests that he lived long enough to be tried under the democracy shortly before 406 B.C., probably on a charge of either treason or of subverting the democracy (κατάλυσις τοῦ δήμου), with the death penalty inflicted at that time.[233] Presumably he escaped soon after Phrynichus's trial, possibly to Deceleia, and returned to Athens a few years later. Similarly with Alexicles: if he was executed, it will have been later, since we know from Thucydides (8.98.1) that like Peisander he left Athens for the enemy camp at Deceleia under the intermediate regime; he probably did so only after his defense of Phrynichus had failed.[234]

Several other extremists will have been tried under the intermediate regime: Thucydides uses the plural ἐς ἀγῶνας in his reference to Antiphon's trial and the speech *For Polystratus* refers to the acquittal of many who had served on the Council of the Four Hundred to the bitter end.[235] Some of these escaped before the verdict was announced. Peisander may well have been among them;[236] and likewise Mnasilochus, archon under the Four Hundred, who like Onomacles is not heard from again until he shows up as one of the Thirty; and Aristoteles, who had been active in fortifying Eëtioneia, is found in the service of Lysander and then returning to Athens as a member of the Thirty.[237] But not all those tried for their involvement in the Four Hundred escaped to avoid paying for their political activities: Antiphon and Archeptolemus stood trial and were convicted ([Plut.] *X orat.* 833e–f with 834a–b); and Polystratus, a less significant figure, even returned to Athens, where he was tried and fined a substantial sum.[238]

233   Xen. *Hell.* 1.7.28 with Jameson, "Sophocles" 552–53.

234   See Jameson, "Sophocles" 552–53.

235   Thuc. 8.68.2 as discussed by Jameson, "Sophocles" 554–55; [Lys.] 20.14 with Jameson, "Sophocles" 553 and n. 35, who rightly points out that some of these trials may have taken place only after the restoration of the democracy.

236   So Jameson, "Sophocles" 556–58.

237   For Mnasilochus, see Arist. *Ath.Pol.* 33.1 and Xen. *Hell.* 2.3.2; for Onomacles, see above, p. 347 with nn. 42–43; for Aristoteles, see Xen. *Hell.* 2.3.2 and 13 with n. 197 above.

238   See [Lys.] 20.1–2 for his membership in the Four Hundred, ibid. 14 for his return to Athens, and ibid. 22 for his first trial, early under the intermediate regime. His appointment as καταλογεύς is treated as insignificant (ibid. 13–14); see ibid. 17 for the office (ἀρχή) to which he was sent out: Andrewes, *HCT* 5.202–3, suggests that he was commissioned to set up an oligarchy in Eretria and that his trial arose from his *euthyna*. The insignificance of his office is also intimated by the fact that the

Of greater importance are the positive steps taken under the intermediate regime to reform the constitution. The fact that these steps were taken shows that the Five Thousand thought of themselves from the beginning not as a permanent institution but as an intermediate regime, dissatisfied both with the oligarchy of the immediate past and with the democracy that had preceded it. Although the measures taken may have been inspired by Theramenes, Thucydides' assertion that they took place "later" (ὕστερον, 8.97.2) suggests that Theramenes played no direct part in them; his departure on military missions first to Euboea, Paros, and Pydna and then to join Thrasybulus and Alcibiades in the north will not have been delayed for many months (Diod. 13.47.6–8, 49.1; Xen. *Hell*. 1.1.12). Our only text on these constitutional reforms—Thucydides' terse statement that subsequent to the initial meeting on the Pnyx "frequent other Assembly meetings were held later on, in which it was voted to appoint *nomothetai* [lawgivers] and approve other constitutional measures,"[239]—is incommensurate with the importance of what it describes. For there are reasons to believe that the appointment of *nomothetai* ushered in a period of constitutional reform that had no precedent in Athenian history and was to last to the end of the fifth century.

There can be no doubt that these *nomothetai* were directly derived from the ten *probouloi* appointed in 413 B.C., from the thirty *syngrapheis* among whom these were included in 411 B.C., and from the *anagrapheis* appointed at Colonus.[240] Like all these earlier commissions, the *nomothetai* were elected by the Assembly, though of course the Assembly now excluded the thetes, as it had in fact also excluded them at Colonus when the *anagrapheis* were chosen.[241] As in the case of the *syngrapheis*, the proposals of the *nomothetai* were to be ratified by the Assembly; this consideration had not entered into the appointment of the *probouloi*, who were to formulate policies to meet the

---

prosecution tried to associate him with his demesman Phrynichus (ibid. 11), an attempt that would have been unnecessary in the case of a major figure; for the penalty imposed then, see ibid. 14 and 18. That he was tried again under the restored democracy—the occasion of [Lys.] 20—emerges from ibid. 17.

239 Thuc. 8.97.2: ἐγίγνοντο δὲ καὶ ἄλλαι ὕστερον πυκναὶ ἐκκλησίαι, ἀφ' ὧν καὶ νομοθέτας καὶ τἆλλα ἐψηφίσαντο ἐς τὴν πολιτείαν.

240 See above, pp. 338–41, 369–72, and 379–85.

241 For the *probouloi*, see Diod. 12.75.4 and p. 339 above, with the cautions expressed by Andrewes and Lewis, "Note"; for the *syngrapheis*, see Arist. *Ath.Pol.* 29.2: τὸν δῆμον ἑλέσθαι.

emergency situation after the defeat in Sicily rather than propose changes in the constitution (Thuc. 8.1.3, 67.1). But this measure was meant in contrast to the *anagrapheis*, whose constitutional proposals were ratified, if at all, only by the Council of the Four Hundred.[242] In view of this, ratification by the Assembly, albeit an Assembly of hoplites, marked a return to democratic procedure.

Of the earlier commissions, both the *syngrapheis* and *anagrapheis* had been mandated to submit constitutional proposals. The *syngrapheis* were enjoined by the motions of Pythodorus and Cleitophon to consider the *patrioi nomoi* of Solon and Cleisthenes, respectively; the *anagrapheis* presented two constitutions.[243] But both these commissions had to work against a deadline, which is likely to have been tight: the *syngrapheis* were to present their report ἐς ἡμέραν ῥητήν, "on an appointed day" (which turned out to be the day of the Colonus meeting), and the *anagrapheis* will have had only a little over a week to draft their proposals.[244] For the *nomothetai* we are given neither a deadline nor the length of the term for which they were appointed. Their appointment, therefore, suggests that they were to revise the constitution anew. Since the intermediate regime did not model itself on the constitution drafted by the *anagrapheis* for the long-term future, we may infer that the Boeotian pattern was rejected and that new proposals more in conformity with the *patrios politeia* were to be worked out, and not under pressure but thoughtfully, over a reasonable length of time. Further, the frequency of Assembly meetings makes it clear that new proposals were to be discussed and voted upon seriatim.

The commission's title, *nomothetai*, and precise tasks remain problematic. Since the office is not otherwise attested in Athens before 403/2 B.C. (Andoc. 1.83–84), we either have to admit that we know nothing about the *nomothetai* Thucydides (8.97.2) attributes to the intermediate regime[245] or have to assume that he is not giving us the official title of a commission but describes its activities in generic terms.[246] Although the word *nomothetēs* might in the fifth century

---

242 See above, p. 385 with n. 170.
243 Arist. *Ath.Pol.* 29.2–3, 30, and 31, with pp. 369–72 and 378–85 above.
244 Thuc. 8.67.1 with p. 369 and n. 129 above; and pp. 384–85 above.
245 This path of extreme caution was chosen by Stroud, *Drakon's Law* 22–24. The [νομο]θέτα[ι] and their task of establishing a new [δικαστέριον] in the new text of the Thudippus decree (425/4 B.C.) of *IG* I³ 71.16 are too uncertain to merit consideration here, since both title and function depend on restorations.
246 So Kahrstedt, "Untersuchungen" 9, citing Xen. *Mem.* 1.2.31 as a parallel; Hignett, *HAC* 300. For others, see Stroud, *Drakon's Law* 22 n. 13.

refer to one occupied with either *nomoi* or *psēphismata*,[247] it is clear from Thucydides' language that this commission was more concerned with fundamental legislative enactments (*nomoi*) than with drafting ephemeral measures (*psēphismata*) to meet a given situation. We know that commissions of *syngrapheis* and *anagrapheis* were active in constitutional matters before the intermediate regime was installed[248] and again after the democracy was restored in 410/09 B.C.;[249] hence it is natural to assume that Thucydides uses *nomothetai* as a collective term to cover both these commissions. Accordingly, we can interpret his statement as meaning that the *ad hoc* work the commissions he calls *nomothetai* undertook before and under the Four Hundred was transformed by the intermediate regime into a long-term enterprise that lasted until the end of the Peloponnesian War and ended only after the Thirty were overthrown.

There are some indications that the *syngrapheis* and *anagrapheis* active between 410/09 and 405/4 B.C. were originally appointed late in the intermediate regime. Nicomachus's first term was to last only four months (Lys. 30.2), which suggests that he was appointed by the intermediate regime only for the remainder of the archon year, whereupon his office was renewed or reaffirmed by the restored

247 On the lack of a clear distinction in the fifth century, see most recently M. H. Hansen, "*Nomos* and *Psephisma* in Fourth-Century Athens," *GRBS* 19 (1978) 315–30, esp. 316–17.

248 For the *syngrapheis*, see Thuc. 8.67.1, καθ' ὅτι ἄριστα ἡ πόλις οἰκήσεται, and the decree of Pythodorus at Arist. *Ath.Pol.* 29.2: ὀμόσαντες ἦ μὴν συγγράψειν ἃ ἂν ἡγῶνται βέλτιστα εἶναι τῇ πόλει, συγγράψουσι περὶ τῆς σωτηρίας. For the *anagrapheis*, see *Ath.Pol.* 30.1, 31.1, 32.1 as discussed above, p. 379.

249 See Andoc. 1.96 for the *syngrapheus* Demophantus in 410/09 B.C.; *IG* I³ 99.8 for the [γνόμ]ε τὸν συγγραφέον in that same year concerning the repayment of funds borrowed from Athena; Lys. 30.17 and 21 for the συγγραφαί from which Nicomachus was to draft his sacrificial calendar; and *IG* I² 844.4, [κατὰ τ]ὰς χσυγγραφά[ς], from the pre-Euclidean side of the sacrificial calendar. Stroud, *Drakon's Law* 27–28, does not regard this evidence as strong enough to justify belief in *syngrapheis* between 410/09 and 405/4 B.C.; but see A. R. W. Harrison, "Law-Making at Athens at the End of the Fifth Century B.C.," *JHS* 75 (1955) 26–35, esp. 33–34. Concerning the *anagrapheis*, we know from Lys. 30.2 that Nicomachus was originally appointed for a four-month term as τῶν νόμων ἀναγραφεύς but that he held this office for six years. If the terminal point of his appointment—and presumably of that of his colleagues (Lys. 30.28), too—was the fall of Athens to Lysander late in 405/4 B.C., inclusive counting will give us 410/09 B.C. as the beginning of his term, but exclusive counting would push it up to 411/10 B.C. Therefore, at least one *anagrapheus* may have been active as early as the intermediate regime and certainly was active under the restored democracy, when activity of *anagrapheis* is attested also by the republication of Draco's law on homicide, *IG* I³ 104 (= ML, no. 86) with the exemplary discussions of Stroud, *Drakon's Law*, and M. Gagarin, *Drakon and Early Athenian Homicide Law* (New Haven and London, 1981).

democracy. This would, incidentally, suggest that the intermediate regime did not begin the job of formulating new constitutional measures until it had been in power for some six months, by which time its uncertain future may have become obvious; provisions for a more permanent constitution accordingly had to be worked out.[250] The appointment of *anagrapheis* by the intermediate regime receives some additional support from Aristotle's erroneous attribution (*Ath.Pol*. 30.1) of the two constitutions of 411 B.C. to a commission of one hundred *anagrapheis* chosen by the Five Thousand from among their own number. We have seen earlier that there are reasons for believing in the reality of these *anagrapheis* while at the same time disbelieving Aristotle's account of the manner of their appointment.[251] Could his error be in confusing the *anagrapheis* at Colonus with a new commission appointed later that year by the Five Thousand? Though this may be plausible, a doubt still remains whether the number one hundred is to be associated with the former or the latter commission; there is no basis for even a conjecture on this point.

To find traces of *syngrapheis* under the intermediate regime is even more difficult, and speculation more hazardous. There is an enigmatic statement in Harpocration that Apolexis, one of Antiphon's accusers, was one of fifty *syngrapheis*.[252] When he was so appointed we are not told, and our ignorance has caused some scholars to suppose he was one of the *syngrapheis* who ushered in the Four Hundred; they emend the numeral to read either "ten," to bring the statement in line with Thucydides (8.67.1), or "thirty," to conform to the number in Pythodorus's motion in Aristotle (*Ath.Pol*. 29.2).[253] However, it makes equally good sense to follow Gilbert in retaining the numeral and to see in Harpocration's statement the survival of a tradition crediting the intermediate regime, in which we know Apolexis was involved, with the appointment of a board of fifty

---

250 On this point, see de Ste. Croix, "Constitution" 13 with n. 62, who suggests that Theramenes' departure may have been precipitated by his realization that the regime was not likely to last much longer.

251 See above, pp. 379–80.

252 Harp. s.v. Ἀπόληξις· εἷς τῶν ν′ συγγραφέων, ὃν Πλάτων κωμῳδεῖ ἐν Σοφισταῖς.

253 The former was accepted by Dindorf, following Cobet, in his edition of Harpocration; cf. also Meineke, *FCG* 2.664, and Kock, *CAF* 1.638. The latter was accepted by Kirchner, *PA* 1352.

syngrapheis.[254] Equally tenuous is a consideration based on the appointment of the *syngrapheus* Demophantus. We know that he submitted his legislation against subverting the democracy and establishing tyranny to Council and Assembly in the first prytany of the restored democracy, in 410/09 B.C.[255] If Demophantus had been appointed on the first day after the Council of the Five Hundred was restored, and if he presented his proposal on the last day of its first prytany, he will have had ample time, more than a month, to prepare his legislation under the restored democracy.[256] Although it is unlikely that he would have presented legislation against subverting the democracy while those who had abetted the establishment of the Four Hundred and had then turned against them were still in positions of power, it is not inconceivable that he could act as promptly as he did because he (and others with him) had been appointed *syngrapheus* toward the end of the intermediate regime in order to pave the way for a new regime, which turned out to be the restored democracy. If this was indeed the case, commissions of (fifty?) *syngrapheis* and (one hundred?) *anagrapheis* may have been appointed during the last four months of the intermediate regime to formulate a permanent system of government conforming to the ancestral constitution. This assumption would partially explain why the transition from the intermediate regime to the restored democracy was so smooth that it left no trace in the literary tradition.

The realization that popular sovereignty needed to be modified in order to give the city a viable government had led by the beginning of 410 B.C. to the conviction that written laws were required to bring order into the states. As far back as 423 B.C., Euripides had Theseus define written laws as the bulwark of the democracy (*Supp.* 429–37, esp. 433–434). But it took the oligarchical revolution of 411 B.C. to begin fixing constitutional matters in writing—not, to be sure, in order to strengthen the democracy but in order to find in the *patrioi nomoi* of Solon and Cleisthenes a justification for reforming the state according to their lights. The appointment of *syngrapheis* to submit constitutional measures to the Colonus meeting and the two consti-

---

254 Gilbert, *Beiträge* 342–43, who, however, identifies this board with that of 410/09 B.C., on which Demophantus served, and infers that Apolexis belonged to "the democratic party."

255 Andoc. 1.96, οἷς Κλειγένης πρῶτος ἐγραμμάτευεν, confirmed by *IG* I³ 375.1.

256 For the chronology, see Meritt, *AFD* 106–7.

tutions drafted by the *anagrapheis* appointed at Colonus were the first deliberate attempts in Athenian history to regulate constitutional matters by written legislation. These were responses to a real need: the intermediate regime felt constrained to appoint *nomothetai* for similar purposes, and *syngrapheis* and *anagrapheis* continued their work, with some interruptions, from 410/09 until 403/2 B.C.

What had created this need is not hard to guess. Most recently there had been the prerogatives that the Four Hundred had usurped and their indifference to the legislation that they had themselves commissioned at Colonus. But the need went deeper than that. We know from Lysias (10.16–20) and from Aristotle (*Ath.Pol*. 35.2) that by the end of the fifth century many of Solon's words and phrases— and consequently provisions of his *kyrbeis* and *axones*—had become so obsolete as to be unintelligible. In addition, many new statutes had been added to Solon's legislation in the form of *psēphismata* (decrees) passed by Council and Assembly ever since the reforms of Cleisthenes to meet new social and political situations as they arose. Among these may well have been measures giving the Areopagus the "added powers in which consisted its guardianship of the constitution," of which Ephialtes deprived it (Arist. *Ath.Pol*. 25.2). *Psēphismata* will also have established the various agencies needed to administer the empire, *hellēnotamiai*, *eisagōgeis*, *episkopoi*, and a host of other officials concerned with collection and disposal of the tribute and with control over the allies. Not only must it have been hard for the Athenians to be sure of what was the latest valid regulation on a given issue, but also many *psēphismata*, certainly those of Ephialtes, must have encroached upon stipulations of the Solonian code. Moreover, the published laws were scattered all over Athens—on the Acropolis, in the agora, on the Areopagus, and so forth—and in different forms: *kyrbeis*, *axones*, marble, and bronze. There must have been archives at least as early as the heyday of empire,[257] but they are not likely to have been systematic enough to keep track of every change, and we know of no attempt before the last decade of the fifth century to coordinate the various bits of legislation into a coherent whole. Obviously as long as the state functioned efficiently and successfully there was no need to remedy a confused legal situation or to question the foundations on which the

257   This is indicated, for example, by ML, no. 58A11–12, of 434/3 B.C.

Athenian democracy had been erected. But such a time was now past. The Four Hundred had provided the idea of revising the laws, but their overthrow gave the impetus to harnessing this idea into the service of good government under the *patrios politeia*.[258] Written guidelines were needed to give the law precedence over the uncontrolled sovereignty of the people.

258   On the problems discussed in the preceding paragraph, see also Stroud, *Drakon's Law* 24.

CHAPTER EIGHT

The Breakdown of Popular Sovereignty

THE series of three victories at Cynossema, Abydos, and especially at Cyzicus, about March or April of 410 B.C. under the command of Theramenes, Thrasybulus, and Alcibiades buoyed Athenian spirits and will have contributed considerably to the restoration of the democracy soon thereafter.[1] The interception of a message of despair at Mindarus's death sent by his lieutenant Hippocrates to Sparta and the news that new revenue was coming in from Cyzicus, Perinthus, and Selymbria and that a toll station had been established near Chalcedon to collect a tax from all ships sailing into and out of the Bosporus (Xen. *Hell*. 1.1.19–23; Diod. 13.64.2) deprived the intermediate regime of any economic reason for its continued existence and gave confidence to those who wanted to see the democratic principle of pay for public service restored. While the movement for political reform was kept alive, the sting had been taken out of its economic motive: there seemed no longer any need to limit the franchise to those best able to serve the state with their persons and fortunes. The advocates of this position receded into the background, leaving the stage to Cleophon, who now stepped forward for the first time, still under the intermediate regime, to oppose the Spartan offer of peace brought to Athens by Alcibiades' friend

---

1 For Cynossema, see Thuc. 8.104–6; for Abydos, Xen. *Hell*. 1.1.4–7; for Cyzicus, ibid. 1.1.11–23, Diod. 13.49.2–51. For the impact on Athens, see Diod. 13.52.1.

Endius.[2] An optimistic faith in better times to come reappeared for the first time since the disasters of Sicily and Euboea.

More thoughtful minds were less sanguine. Sophocles' *Philoctetes*, produced in the archonship of Glaucippus (410/09 B.C.), reflects the somber resignation of a man disenchanted with politics after serving as *proboulos* in the events leading up to the oligarchical revolution and as a prosecutor of Peisander after the downfall of the Four Hundred.[3] The scene of the play's action, the desolate island of Lemnos, is far removed from any focus of social life; the *raison d'état* finds an articulate representative in Odysseus, master of guile, intrigue, and deceit, willing to stop at nothing, uninhibited by moral qualms in pursuing the interests of the state. Hope for the future is embodied in young Neoptolemus, son of a noble sire, whose nature (*physis*) does not run counter to the values of society (*nomos*) like the *physis* of Antiphon's treatise *On Truth* and no doubt also the *physis* that made many young men join Peisander in overthrowing the democracy. Neoptolemus's *physis* is informed by innate nobility (τὸ γενναῖον) and shaped by an education that unlike sophistic education trains the character rather than the mind; it accepts the goals of society but will not let itself be corrupted into pursuing these goals by the immoral means demanded in politics. In the terms of the *Philoctetes*, a god would have to intervene to harness such a *physis* into the service of the community.[4] Despite obvious and fundamental differences, there is a similarity in outlook between the *Philoctetes* and Euripides' *Phoenissae*, which is the product of this same period.[5] Political power in the *Phoenissae* is equated with a tyranny that is the product of sheer personal ambition, such as Thucydides had predicated of Pericles' successors, especially of the Four Hundred.[6] Eteocles, drunk with absolute power, rides roughshod over the legitimate

2 Diod. 13.52.2–53.2; Philochorus *FGH* 328F139 dates the offer and rejection ἐπὶ ἄρχοντος Θεοπόμπου.

3 For Sophocles as *proboulos*, see pp. 340–41 above and esp. Arist. *Rh.* 3.18, 1419ᵃ 25–30; for his possible prosecution of Peisander, see Jameson, "Sophocles," esp. 555–59.

4 M. H. Jameson, "Politics and the *Philoctetes*," *CP* 51 (1956) 217–27, makes the attractive suggestion that Neoptolemus embodies the hopes Sophocles had for the younger Pericles. See also the sensitive analysis of Nussbaum, "Consequences" 25–53.

5 See D. J. Conacher, *Euripidean Drama* (Toronto, 1967) 228 with n. 2.

6 Thuc. 2.65.10–12 and 8.89.3 with J. de Romilly, "Les *Phéniciennes* d'Euripide ou l'actualité dans la tragédie grecque," *Rev. Phil.*, 3d ser., 39 (1965) 28–47.

claims of his brother; he drives Polyneices to lead a foreign army against his native land, a traitor, bringing war instead of peace, and only the patriotic self-sacrifice of young Menoeceus can restore some semblance of equilibrium to Thebes. In the *Phoenissae* we are as far from the spirit that animated the Athenian public after Cyzicus as we are in the *Philoctetes*.

THE REVISION OF THE LAWS

The hatred of tyranny expressed in the *Phoenissae* was translated into political action. The earliest known measure by which the restored democracy continued the legislative reform of the intermediate regime was against tyranny and subversion of the democracy.[7] Demophantus's decree contains two parts: the first imposes severe penalties on anyone who attempts to overthrow the Athenian democracy or holds office after its overthrow; the second consists of an oath to be sworn by all Athenians to remain faithful to the provisions of the first part, adding further injunctions against establishing or abetting tyranny, and absolving from their oaths all those who had sworn enmity to the democracy at Athens, in the army, or elsewhere.[8] We shall confine ourselves to three observations. First, the purpose of enacting such a law at this point was evidently to provide a broader legal basis for taking action against men like Antiphon, Archeptolemus, and Onomacles, who had worked to overthrow the democracy in 411 B.C. but could be charged only under the law against treason,[9] because a law against subverting the democracy (κατάλυσις τοῦ δήμου) did not yet exist. When this loophole was closed, legal action could be taken against conspirators for the crime they had perpetrated. Second, the language of Demophantus's decree leaves no doubt that in defining the new crime he consciously took earlier legislation as his model. In particular, the phrase ἐάν τις τυραννεῖν ἐπαναστῇ ἢ τὸν τύραννον συγκαταστήσῃ echoes a law to which appeal was made a hundred years earlier after the expulsion of the Peisistratids, ἐάν τινες τυραννεῖν ἐπανιστῶνται [ἐπὶ τυραννίδι], ἢ συγκαθιστῇ τὴν τυραννίδα,[10] and the oath may echo

7   Andoc. 1.96–98; see above, p. 409 with n. 255.
8   For the structure of this law, see Ostwald, "Athenian Legislation" 110–14.
9   [Plut.] *X orat.* 833f; κατὰ τὸν νόμον ὅς κεῖται περὶ τῶν προδόντων.
10   Compare Andoc. 1.97 with Arist. *Ath.Pol.* 16.10, with Ostwald, "Athenian Legislation" 111–12. For a different view on the origin of this law, see Gagarin, "Thesmothetai" 71–77.

the bouleutic oath instituted in the archonship of Hermocreon (501/0 B.C.).[11] This suggests that a concern with *patrioi nomoi* was still alive in 410/09 B.C.; Andocides (1.95) confirms as much when he introduces Demophantus's decree with the words κατά γε τὸν Σόλωνος νόμον. Surely Andocides' contemporaries will not have been offended by this blatant falsehood, because they regarded the legislation that followed as perpetuating the *patrios politeia* Solon had founded. Moreover, the belief that the democracy was the *patrios politeia* may well have led to its restoration, possibly as a result of deliberations begun when the intermediate regime was still officially in power.

This brings us to a third observation on Demophantus's decree. As already remarked, Demophantus introduced his law not *motu proprio* but in his capacity as *syngrapheus*, that is, as a person who had received the mandate to draft this legislation from an official body and was now submitting the result of his labors for the approval of Council and Assembly. We are not told by Andocides who gave Demophantus his mandate. But if the decree of Pythodorus is any guide, which created the thirty *syngrapheis* who were to present their report at Colonus, Demophantus will have been appointed by a vote of the Assembly. If it was the Assembly of the restored democracy, he will have been appointed not much more than a month before he presented his legislation to the sovereign people; but, as we saw, Thucydides' mention of *nomothetai* under the intermediate regime does not exclude the possibility that his initial appointment predates the restored democracy by a few months.

We have noted that the task of revising the laws was from at least 410/09 B.C. on in the hands of commissions of *syngrapheis* and *anagrapheis*.[12] To differentiate between their functions we have no more evidence than their names and the scanty record of their activities. The term *syngrapheus* is derived from the verb συγγράφειν, which describes the action of "composing in writing" a book, a speech, a contract, a report, and so on.[13] We should, therefore, expect a *syngrapheus* to collect facts and materials from various quarters and then weld them into a coherent whole in his written report, and

---

11 Ostwald, "Athenian Legislation" 112 with n. 45.

12 See above, pp. 407–9.

13 For a book, see, e.g., Thuc. 1.1.1, 6.7.4; Xen. *Eq.* 1.1; Pl. *Grg.* 518b, *Minos* 316d; for a speech, Isoc. 1.3; Pl. *Phdr.* 258a, *Euthyd.* 272a; for a contract or treaty (usually middle), Thuc. 5.41.3; Xen. *Eq.* 2.2; Isoc. 4.177, 12.158.

what little we know of the activities of *syngrapheis* confirms this. The *syngrapheis* of 411 B.C. were to consult others, receive testimony from those willing to give it, and investigate the *patrioi nomoi* of Solon and Cleisthenes before drawing up their new legislative recommendations (Arist. *Ath.Pol.* 29.2–3); Demophantus drew on earlier legislation against tyranny to formulate a new law against overthrowing the democracy; and earlier in the fifth century *syngrapheis* had been commissioned to draw up regulations for Miletus in 450/49 B.C. and for the offering of first fruits at Eleusis in 416/15 B.C.[14] The only analogous activity of *syngrapheis* in the period with which we are here concerned is the appointment of the Thirty by popular decree in 404/3 B.C. with the original mandate to "draft the ancestral laws [*patrioi nomoi*] by which they are to govern."[15] What other activity is ascribed to them concerns religious matters, such as drafting proposals for the repayment of sacred monies to Athena and another sacred regulation, the exact nature of which remains obscure.[16] However, Lysias (30.17, 21) gives us the valuable information that the *anagrapheus* Nicomachus was to draft his calendar of sacrifices on the basis of συγγραφαί, which suggests not only that the *syngrapheis* of this period were too busy themselves with religious affairs but also that their position may in some sense have been superior to that of the *anagrapheis*.

We are a little better informed about the *anagrapheis*, whose title is derived from the verb ἀναγράφειν, "to write up for display in public," which is frequently found in connection with the publication of laws, decrees, treaties, and the like.[17] In the present context, this would suggest that *anagrapheis* were entrusted with the final preparation of texts of laws already validated and with their publication; that suggestion is borne out by what we know of their activities during this period. Nicomachus was initially appointed in 410 B.C. as an ἀναγραφεὺς τῶν νόμων with the mandate to publish the laws of Solon.[18] If this mandate had been confined to a republication of the Solonian laws still in use,[19] the task could probably have been

---

14   Andoc. 1.96–98; *IG* I³ 21.3; ML, no. 73.3–4, 47, 48, 59–60.

15   Xen. *Hell.* 2.3.2: ἔδοξε τῷ δήμῳ τριάκοντα ἄνδρας ἑλέσθαι, οἳ τοὺς πατρίους νόμους συγγράψουσι, καθ᾽ οὓς πολιτεύσουσι. Cf. ibid. 11. For this meaning, see below, Chap. 9, n. 70.

16   *IG* I³ 99.8, and 135.3.

17   See, e.g., Thuc. 5.47.11; Andoc. 1.82; Dem. 24.23; Lyc. 1.117; Arist. *Pol.* 6.8, 1321[b] 34, etc.

18   Lys. 30.2 with p. 407 and n. 249 above.

19   So Clinton, "Nature."

completed within the four months originally allowed. But Nicomachus's term (and presumably also the terms of his associates) was extended to six years; apparently it was soon found necessary to integrate into Solon's code more recent legislation, such as the decree of Demophantus, which purported to be Solonian but was in fact new legislation based upon *patrioi nomoi*. We are better informed about how the *anagrapheis* functioned in 409/8 B.C. in republishing Draco's law on homicide: the ἀναγραφεῖς τῶν νόμων received the text from the archon basileus, assisted by the secretary of the Council, and were to have it engraved on a stone stele and set up in front of the Royal Stoa; the *pōlētai* were to let out the contracts for procuring the marble, for inscribing the text, and for erecting the stele; and the *hellēnotamiai* were to disburse the payments.[20] Notably in this case the authoritative text for publication was in the hands of the archon basileus, presumably in a depository or archive of laws whose enforcement fell into his province.[21] From the prescript of the law (line 3) we may infer that the *anagrapheis* were responsible to Council and Assembly, and Lysias (30.2) indicates that they received a daily stipend for their work. The funds needed for publishing what they had prepared seem to have been voted seriatim by Council and Assembly.[22] Moreover, *anagrapheis* seem to have been excused from submitting to an annual *euthyna* and were audited only when their job was finished (Lys. 30.2–5).

It is difficult to reconcile the activities of *anagrapheis* after 410/09 B.C. with those of the one hundred *anagrapheis* who drafted the constitution of 411 B.C. except on the assumptions already stated: namely, that the *anagrapheis* of 411 B.C. were so called in order to differentiate them from the *syngrapheis*, whose mandate expired with the report they presented at Colonus, and that their task was to summarize the proposals made on that occasion.[23] These assumptions are too daring to inspire great confidence; they rather suggest that in some areas of responsibility there was no clear boundary to distinguish *anagrapheis* from *syngrapheis*. But some support for the distinction we postulate can be found in Lysias's accusations (30.2–3, 11–14) against Nicomachus: that he took it upon himself to enter or erase laws, that he produced contradictory laws in the courts, and that he produced on the very day of the trial the law under which

20   ML, no. 86 (= Stroud, *Drakon's Law* 5–6) 5–9.
21   See Stroud, *Drakon's Law* 28–29.
22   ML, no. 86.8–9; on the whole, see Stroud, *Drakon's Law* 25.
23   See above, pp. 379–80.

Cleophon was condemned to death. However extravagant these charges may be, they do indicate that the *anagrapheis* had—or were believed to have—considerable discretion in validating laws.[24]

Demophantus's law against overthrowing the democracy was one of the very first measures, if not the first, enacted after the restoration; clearly, then, the Athenians believed that safeguarding the old democratic institutions against further subversion was their most important immediate task. The law's tone is fierce: it declares any person attempting to overthrow the democracy or holding office after such overthrow a public enemy, who may be killed with impunity and whose property is to be confiscated. Yet it is not retroactive—that is, it is not vindictive.[25] Though the conversion of those who had overthrown the Four Hundred and had installed the intermediate regime was apparently accepted, the democracy's relations with some of them, including Theramenes, remained strained.[26] Demophantus's law was a clear warning against oligarchical recidivism.

A further antisubversive measure was the new seating arrangement adopted for the Council in 410/09 B.C. (Philochorus *FGH* 328F140). Seats were to be assigned to the councilors by lot, and an oath was exacted from each councilor to abide by the new arrangement. This regulation was no doubt intended to prevent concerted action by a block of councilors—perhaps members of a *hetaireia*—to disrupt or take over any proceedings. We are reminded of Nicias's remark on Alcibiades' supporters strategically placed in the Assembly to influence the vote on the Sicilian expedition and of Plutarch's

---

24   We do not know how many *syngrapheis* and *anagrapheis* there were between 410 and 404/3 B.C. For the *syngrapheis*, thirty are attested for 411 and 404/3 B.C. (Arist. *Ath.Pol.* 29.2; Xen. *Hell.* 2.3.2); for the intermediate regime, we have suggested above (pp. 408–9 with n. 252) that Harpocration's number, fifty, can possibly be accepted. This poses the problem why Demophantus acted alone, whereas all other known proposals emanated from the *syngrapheis* as a group. Similarly with the *anagrapheis*: is the number one hundred, which Aristotle's confused account at *Ath.Pol.* 30.1 and 32.1 assigns to the *anagrapheis* of 411 B.C., in fact applicable to those of 410 B.C? Stroud, *Drakon's Law* 25 with n. 24, extrapolates twenty from schol. Aeschin. 1.39 and Poll. 8.112, who speak of twenty τοὺς ζητήσοντας καὶ ἀναγράψοντας τοὺς διεφθαρμένους τῶν νόμων after the fall of the Thirty. But in view of the magnitude of their task the larger number is not inconceivable. Can we infer from Lys. 30.2–3 and 11–14 that *anagrapheis* acted on their own on some occasions, just as the *syngrapheus* Demophantus did?

25   Andoc. 1.96: πολέμιος ἔστω Ἀθηναίων καὶ νηποινεὶ τεθνάτω, καὶ τὰ χρήματα αὐτοῦ δημόσια ἔστω, καὶ τῆς θεοῦ τὸ ἐπιδέκατον.

26   See Andrewes, "Generals."

assertion that Thucydides son of Melesias grouped together the upper class to prevent its mingling with the common people.[27] It is therefore likely that the ξυνωμοσίαι Peisander recruited for the coup of 411 B.C. had also used seating patterns as one means of intimidating the people in Council and Assembly (Thuc. 8.54.4, 66.1–2) and that the new measure was aimed at discouraging such tactics in the future.

Since Philochorus speaks of an oath imposed on the councilors, this regulation may have been part of a comprehensive law concerning the powers of the Council. We have contemporary inscriptional evidence of just such a law, dubbed by Wade-Gery "The Charter of the Democracy, 410 B.C.," which we discussed at some length above. Linguistic evidence led us to believe that it incorporates measures first enacted early in the fifth century to curb the powers of the Council, presumably the Council of the Areopagus.[28] In 410/09 B.C. the sovereign people reaffirmed their power—this time *vis-à-vis* the Council of the Five Hundred—to inflict heavy fines (*IG* I³105.32), to declare war and conclude peace (line 35), to impose the death penalty (36), and to have the final say in a number of other matters. That affirmation, and above all the new oath to be taken by the councilors (27–28), gains special point after the events of 411 B.C. If the new law incorporated and applied to the restored Council of the Five Hundred an earlier legislative restriction of Areopagite authority, then it will have been part of the enterprise early under the restored democracy to reformulate and give written expression to the *patrios politeia*. Nothing is preserved in its text to indicate who drafted the law, but since old regulations are applied to a new situation, it may be the work of one or more *syngrapheis*. The *anagrapheis* may also have had a hand in this legislation; Nicomachus was working on legislation concerning the Council about the time of Cleophon's trial (Lys. 30.10–14), perhaps arranging for the publication of a text prepared by *syngrapheis*.

Whether the work of *syngrapheis* on the repayment of funds to Athena in 410/09 B.C. (*IG* I³99.8) was connected with their work on the constitution we do not know. But constitutional issues are involved in the merger of the treasurers of Athena with the treasurers of the Other Gods, which Aristotle (*Ath.Pol.* 30.2) includes in the

---

27　Thuc. 6.13.1 with pp. 321–22 above; Plut. *Per.* 11.1–2 with pp. 185–86 above.
28　*IG* I³ 105, as discussed above, pp. 32–40.

constitution drafted for the future by the *anagrapheis* of 411 B.C. and which seems to have been implemented in 406/5 B.C.[29]

This exhausts our knowledge of Athenian legislation prior to 404 B.C. that can reasonably be attributed to the movement to revise the laws. We shall now discuss how other internal developments between 410 and 404/3 B.C. led to further revisions after the fall of the Thirty.

POPULAR SOVEREIGNTY ON TRIAL

Democracy and Alcibiades

The smooth transition from the intermediate regime to democracy, reflected in the continued revison of the laws, is also in evidence in politics. Theopompus, who had been elected archon under the intermediate regime, was left to serve out his term undisturbed,[30] and the treasurers of 411/10 B.C. seem to have handed over their office to their successors as if nothing had happened politically.[31] Yet the efforts now being made to reestablish the sovereignty of the people with a more self-consciously democratic edge contained some disturbing signs.

Apart from any legislation to guard the democracy against subversion, vindictive measures against those who had been associated with the Four Hundred widened in scope. The intermediate regime had secured a posthumous verdict to cast Phrynichus's body outside the boundaries of Attica and had released his assassins from prison;[32] in 409 B.C. the restored democracy went even farther, conferring high honors on his killers.[33] Erasinides, who made the motion on behalf of the Council (ML, no. 85.5, 15), is almost certainly the same Erasinides who was appointed to the democratic board of generals

29   See above, p. 383 with n. 165.

30   Meritt, *AFD* 106–10.

31   ML, no. 84, with commentary on p. 258. On this handover, see also Andrewes, *HCT* 5. 196.

32   See above, pp. 402–3.

33   There is some question about the identity of Phrynichus's slayers; see Andrewes, *HCT* 5.309–11. Thuc. 8.92.2 states that Phrynichus was killed by a *peripolos* (and thus presumably an Athenian) assisted by an Argive; this is at variance with literary and epigraphical evidence, which points to the two metics Thrasybulus of Calydon and Apollodorus of Megara. These men are not only named by Lys. 13.70–72 and Lycurg. 1.112 but also appear in a decree (ML, no. 85, with pp. 262–63) from late in the archonship of Glaucippus, in which honors are conferred on

that replaced those blamed with Alcibiades for the defeat at Notium in 406 B.C. (Xen. *Hell.* 1.5.16; Diod. 13.74.1), who was later condemned to death for failing to pick up the shipwrecked sailors after the victory at Arginusae.[34] Diocles, who moved the first amendment to Erasinides' motion, is possibly identical with the archon of the following year, 409/8 B.C.[35] Moreover, we learn from the pseudo-Lysianic speech *For Polystratus* that Polystratus, who had already been tried under the Five Thousand, was tried a second time soon after the democracy was restored, again on a charge related to his membership in the Four Hundred; conviction would have so increased the fine to which he had already been condemned under the intermediate regime that his entire family would have been disfranchised.[36] Further, Lysias informs us that Epigenes, Demophanes, and Cleisthenes used the courts against men who had sympathized with the Four Hundred; he accuses this trio of enriching themselves by having people condemned to death without trial, by having the property of others confiscated, and by engineering the exile and disfranchisement of yet others.[37] These are familiar charges against sycophants, but they do not entirely misrepresent the period. They attest the fervor with which the democracy tried to eliminate opposition by using the chief organ of popular sovereignty, the jury courts. The citizenship of more people beside Polystratus will have

Phrynichus's assassins. The stele, which contains a motion and two amendments, shows that honors of some kind had been voted for Thrasybulus earlier that year (17–18) and presumably also for Apollodorus. But though the motion adds a golden crown to the honors for Thrasybulus (6–14), and though the first amendment grants him citizenship and other benefits (15–25), the second amendment orders the Council to conduct an investigation into charges that bribery was involved in securing honors for Apollodorus, presumably on the same occasion on which Thrasybulus was originally honored (38–47). From Lys. 7.4 we learn that the people gave Apollodorus a plot of land from the property confiscated from Peisander and that he sold it shortly before the Thirty came to power. Plut. *Alc.* 25.14 names the *peripolos* Hermon as the assassin by confusion with the Hermon of Thuc. 8.92.5.

34 Xen. *Hell.* 1.6.29, 1.7.2 and 34, *Mem.* 1.1.18; Philochorus *FGH* 328F142; Ar. *Ran.* 1196 with schol.

35 ML, no. 85.14, with Lys. 21.2; Diod. 13.54.1; Philochorus *FGH* 328F139.

36 [Lys.] 20.17, 33–36 with Andrewes, *HCT* 5.203.

37 Lys. 25.25–26. We are ill informed about the identity of these three. Nothing is known about Demophanes; Epigenes is conceivably identical with a sick and poor man of that name who, according to Lys. fr. 35 Thalheim, was compelled to undertake the liturgy of a trierarch; and Cleisthenes may be the person frequently ridiculed as a pathic by Aristophanes and other comedians; see *Ach.* 118, *Eq.* 1374, *Nub.* 355, *Vesp.* 1187, *Av.* 831, *Lys.* 621, 1092, *Thesm.* 235, 574–654, 929, *Ran.* 48, 57, 426; Crat. fr. 195; Pherecrates, fr. 135.

stood in jeopardy because of their inability to pay the heavy fines imposed on them. We learn from Andocides (1.75) that soldiers who had stayed in Athens during the regime of the Four Hundred suffered partial loss of civil rights (*atimia*), being barred from addressing the Assembly or serving on the Council. This disability may have been inflicted by legislation or, more probably, by jury verdicts in individual cases; we are not told.

By the time of the Lenaea of 405 B.C. the divisiveness of such vengeance was so obvious that Aristophanes included an appeal to forgive the disfranchised in the parabasis of the *Frogs* (686–92). But it took the defeat at Aegospotami later that summer to get action. In order to bring unity to the city in its desperate straits, Patrocleides moved a blanket amnesty expunging all records of loss of civil rights, "except for all names publicly inscribed of those who did not stay in Athens or who, having been tried by either the Areopagus or the *ephetai* or at the prytaneion or the Delphinion under the presidency of the *basileis*, either are in some kind of exile for homicide or were condemned to death either as murderers or as tyrants."[38] The last clause, from "or who" on, is of special interest, because its language is almost identical to a Solonian amnesty law quoted by Plutarch (*Sol.* 19.4). When we add the observation that the beginning of the decree refers to amnesty decrees from the time of the Persian Wars (Andoc. 1.77), we see that it was drafted in a manner similar to how the *syngrapheis* proceeded during this period; we may wish to conclude that Patrocleides (of whom we know little else) will have been a *syngrapheus*.[39] The first group excluded from the amnesty in our quotation will certainly have included Peisander, Aristarchus, Alexicles, Onomacles, and others who had escaped from Athens soon after the overthrow of the Four Hundred and perhaps also some who had fled after the desecrations of 415 B.C.[40]

The spirit pervading these measures was manifest already under the intermediate regime in Cleophon, who became the most vocal popular leader under the restored democracy. His rising influence may have precipitated Theramenes' early departure from Athens and

38   Andoc. 1.78 as translated by MacDowell, p. 113.

39   Patrocleides may be identical with the person who moved one of the decrees honoring the people of Aphytis ca. 426 B.C. see *IG* I³ 63.10 and perhaps also with the Patrocleides of Ar. *Av.* 790 with schol.

40   Of this group Aristarchus had already returned to Athens and had been tried and executed; see Chap. 7, n. 194 above. That the decree did not constitute a blanket recall of exiles is explicitly stated by Andoc. 1.80.

may have contributed to shaping the distant attitude that the city adopted toward the generals in the Hellespont over the next two or three years. Cleophon came from an industrial family wealthy and prominent enough to have given him hoplite status and thus the franchise under the intermediate regime.[41] He was not a political unknown in 410 B.C. Six ostraka bearing his name and found in the excavations in the Athenian agora attest his prominence already before the Sicilian expedition;[42] Andocides' disgust that Cleophon occupied his house during his exile (1.146) points to his importance soon after 415 B.C.; and his mention in Aristophanes' *Thesmophoria-zusae* (805) indicates that he was already recognized as a popular leader shortly before the coup in 411 B.C. However, we have no concrete information about his political outlook or activities before he successfully spearheaded the opposition to peace with Sparta after the battle of Cyzicus.[43] What prompted his opposition can only be guessed. Personal animosity toward Alcibiades may have predisposed him against the offer brought to Athens by Endius, a former ephor and close family friend of Alcibiades;[44] but the allegation, preserved by both Philochorus and Diodorus, that Cleophon's demagoguery led to rejecting the peace against the better judgment of the upper class[45] permits us to draw two conclusions. First, he will have persuaded the people that the Spartan offer was a sign of weakness and that perseverance would result in more favorable terms in the future. Second, he will have chosen the Assembly (which under the intermediate regime will still have been made up of hoplites) as the authority he should persuade formally to reject peace with Sparta against the recommendation of the Council, thus initiating a return to the principle of popular sovereignty.

We do not know to what extent Cleophon may have been responsible for the restoration of democracy in 410 B.C. or for the

---

41 See above, p. 202 with n. 14. On the slurs about his being a foreign slave and about his obscure origins, see above, p. 215 with n. 71.

42 Thomsen, *Origin* 81 with n. 186.

43 Diod. 13.52.2–53.2; Philochorus 328F139, as cited in n. 2 above. Cleophon's name has been restored as the mover of an amendment to a decree honoring Evagoras, king of Salamis on Cyprus, *IG* I³ 113.32–33. In view of the uncertainty of the date and precise contents of the decree, I cannot attach to it the significance seen in it by Renaud, "Cléophon" 462–65.

44 Diod. 13.52.2 with Thuc. 8.6.3.

45 Diod. 13.53.1 reports that as a result of Endius's speech οἱ μὲν ἐπιεικέστατοι τῶν Ἀθηναίων ἔρρεπον ταῖς γνώμαις πρὸς τὴν εἰρήνην.

democratic measures that were enacted in the next four years.[46] His name is closely associated with the expansion and thus perhaps also the reintroduction of public pay. A hallmark of the democracy ever since Pericles' introduction of jurors' pay, the practice had been suspended even before the Four Hundred took power, and an attempt to reinstate it incurred a curse under the intermediate regime.[47] We are singularly ill-informed about the nature of the *diōbelia* (payment of two obols), which Cleophon is said to have introduced (Arist. *Ath.Pol.* 28.3). Aeschines and Aristotle treat this as an irresponsible squandering of public funds that corrupted the common people and brought democracy into disrepute.[48] But this seems far from the truth, an unwarranted equation of Cleophon's *diōbelia* with the dole Pericles is said to have introduced to enable poorer citizens to attend theatrical performances (*theōrikon*) or with the pay Agyrrhius and Heracleides introduced for attending Assembly meetings in the fourth century.[49] Unlike these the *diōbelia* seems to have been a daily payment.[50] More likely it was an allowance to feed the poorest citizens, whom the Spartan occupation of Deceleia kept from their lands or the exigencies of the war prevented from practicing their trade;[51] or else it resumed at a uniform rate of two obols per day all payments for public service (including jury duty, tenure of magistracies, etc.), which had been suspended in 411 B.C.[52] We know that it was introduced in 410/09 B.C. and that payments began in the third prytany of that year; payments are attested also for 407/6 B.C.; and in 406/5 B.C. it was administered by the popular leader Archedemus.[53] Archedemus's interest in the *diōbelia* underscores its democratic character. He was a butt of comic poets for his

46   The otherwise excellent article of Renaud, "Cléophon," suffers from attributing all democratic measures between 410 and 404 B.C. indiscriminately to the initiative and influence of Cleophon.

47   Thuc. 8.67.3, 97.1; Arist. *Ath.Pol.* 29.5, 33.1.

48   Arist. *Ath.Pol.* 28.3, where it is intimated that the death penalty was inflicted on Cleophon for having introduced it: εἴωθεν γὰρ κἂν ἐξαπατηθῇ τὸ πλῆθος ὕστερον μισεῖν τούς τι προαγαγόντας ποιεῖν αὐτοὺς τῶν μὴ καλῶς ἐχόντων. Cf. also *Pol.* 2.7, 1267[b] 1–5, where the *diōbelia* is treated as a first step in arousing greed; Aeschin. 2.76.

49   Plut. *Per.* 9.1–3; Arist. *Ath.Pol.* 41.3 with Busolt-Swoboda 921.

50   *Etym.Magn.* s.v. διωβελία = *Anecd.Bekk.* 1.237.15, with the reading καθ' ἡμέραν.

51   So Wilamowitz, *Aristoteles* 2.212–16.

52   K. von Fritz and E. Kapp, trs., *Aristotle's Constitution of Athens and Related Texts* (New York, 1950) 172–73.

53   *IG* I³ 375 (= ML, no. 84) 10, 12, 14, 22, 23; *IG* I³ 377.25, 30, 32, 33, 36, 37, 39, 41, 43, 44, 46, 48, 50, 52; Xen. *Hell.* 1.7.2.

bleary eyes, and was charged, like most popular leaders, with foreign birth and embezzlement of public monies;[54] he was also the first person to initiate proceedings against Erasinides as one of the generals of Arginusae (Xen. *Hell*. 1.7.2). But unlike other demagogues he was praised as an effective speaker and politician; and Socrates, who is not usually well disposed toward popular leaders, even recommends him to Crito as an honest watchdog against the sycophants who attacked him in the courts.[55] How long the *diōbelia* lasted and when Callicrates proposed to raise it to three obols (*Ath.Pol.* 28.3) are unknown, but it is not likely to have survived the end of the Peloponnesian War.

Two further measures in this period democratically soaked the rich to defray public expenditures. Although Cleophon's name is not associated with either, they are likely to have had his support.[56] A property tax on capital (*eisphora*), first imposed by Cleon, was twice levied in the period 410/09 to 405/4 B.C.[57] Since it will have hit the upper classes much harder than the common people, the support popular leaders probably gave it is likely to be partly responsible for the hostility with which Cleophon, like Cleon, is depicted in our sources. The second measure continued the Periclean building program on the Acropolis. Construction of the Erechtheum had begun soon after the Peace of Nicias but was interrupted by the Sicilian expedition and the hard times thereafter; it was resumed in 409 and completed in 405 B.C.[58] Building accounts (some fragmentary) covering this entire period preserve considerable detail about this enterprise. The most interesting information we can glean from them is that only twenty-four percent of the known work force consisted of citizens, all but one in supervisory roles or as skilled craftsmen, whereas metics made up thirty-nine and slaves nineteen percent.[59] If we compare these figures with those from Eleusis in the fourth century, in which metics outnumber citizens by only two percent and the number of slaves is negligible,[60] we realize how few Athe-

---

54   Ar. *Ran*. 420–25, 588; Eup. frr. 9, 71; Lys. 14.25.

55   Xen. *Mem*. 2.9.4–8; Aeschin. 3.139.

56   They are, however, attributed to Cleophon by Renaud, "Cléophon" 466–68.

57   Lys. 21.3; cf. above, pp. 204–5 with n. 23.

58   Wycherley, *Stones* 146–53.

59   *IG* I³ 474–79. For the economic and social aspects of these accounts, see R. H. Randall, Jr., "The Erechtheum Workmen," *AJA* 57 (1953) 199–210, esp. 201–3.

60   Randall, "Erechtheum Workmen" 203 n. 22. The status of the remaining eighteen percent is unknown.

nian citizens could be spared from the war effort. Why then was the construction resumed at this time? There is one possible explanation. Successes after the victory at Cyzicus by the summer of 407 B.C. had restored Athenian control over the Hellespont and had caused Thasos to revolt against the oligarchy Dieitrephes had imposed in 411 B.C. and to return to the Athenian side.[61] Perhaps these events had raised hopes in Athens that the democracy would be able to reassemble the empire from the ruin the oligarchs had precipitated. Should not the first fruits of the renewed empire be devoted to the completion of a symbol of the old? The question whether the fortunes of war made such expenditure wise does not seem to have been raised.

The paradox of the situation was that the man most responsible for the resurgence of imperial hopes was still without honor in his own country. Alcibiades had inspired the Spartan occupation of Deceleia; he had encouraged the δυνατώτατοι in the Athenian command on Samos to overthrow the democracy in the professed hope of Persian support but in the real hope of securing his own recall to Athens; but once the revolt had been set in motion, he had discovered his own impotence to make good his promises and had imposed conditions that alienated the revolutionaries. Once again a prime mover in Athenian fortunes, he was now the main architect of a successful strategy in the Hellespont. He was in this position because Thrasybulus had seen that the resistance to the Four Hundred needed a strong leader more urgently than one with unblemished democratic credentials. The soldiers on Samos had concurred with Thrasybulus: they elected Alcibiades their general, let him restrain their impulse to sail against the Piraeus, and approved his acceptance of the government of the Five Thousand.

In Athens, Theramenes, too, in moving Alcibiades' recall soon after the intermediate regime was established, seems to have been prompted by the recognition that strong leadership was imperative. Alcibiades' not returning immediately will have been due largely to the urgent military tasks that required his presence in the north. But he must also have been aware that the old enmities remained. Thrasyllus's negative attitude to his recall to Samos and to his subsequent return to Athens via Abydos late in 411 B.C. will have put him on notice that though the Athenians might agree in principle to

---

61   For these successes, see Xen. *Hell*. 1.1.20–3.22; for Thasos, see ibid. 1.1.32, Dem. 20.59 with Thucydides 8.64.2–5.

forgive and forget in order to secure his military leadership in the field, they would be reluctant to live with him in fact. Moreover, Thessalus's *eisangelia* for impiety was still hanging over him, and he was still under a curse the Eleusinian priesthood had uttered against him. Furthermore, with the democracy restored, other leaders, such as Cleophon, stauncher champions of popular sovereignty, constituted the immediate political reality, and they were not likely to let the Athenians forget what fate a Hyperbolus or an Androcles had met for opposing Alcibiades.

Though there will have been a latent animosity toward Alcibiades, the Assembly approved Theramenes' motion for his recall and ratified his election as general by the troops on Samos and likewise the election of Thrasybulus and Thrasyllus. But the atmosphere became uncongenial enough for Theramenes to leave the city on military missions not long after he had moved Alcibiades' recall. As far as we know, no voices were raised against Alcibiades by Cleophon or anyone else after democracy was restored. But as Andrewes has observed, many facts or probabilities for the years 410–407 B.C. betray the existence of serious tensions between the city and its armed forces in the Hellespont.[62] Neither Alcibiades nor Thrasybulus nor Theramenes was reelected general for 410/09 or 409/8 B.C.; only Thrasyllus was reelected. He had returned to Athens after Abydos and remained there between December 411 B.C. and the summer of 409 B.C., leaving the other three to act as generals without having been formally elected at home.[63] Not until Thrasyllus was defeated at Ephesus did he join his forces to those of the Hellespontine generals, giving them the reinforcements they needed to capture Byzantium and Chalcedon in 408 B.C., and not until these important victories had been won with the assistance of a democratic general did opinion in Athens shift sufficiently to allow Alcibiades' return.

It was symptomatic of this shift that Alcibiades and Thrasybulus were elected generals at Athens for 407/6 B.C. but (strangely enough) Thrasyllus was not. Conon, who had not been a general in 408/7 B.C., was chosen in his place. Xenophon's language underlines the significance of this change of mood: οἱ Ἀθηναῖοι στρατηγοὺς εἵλοντο Ἀλκιβιάδην μὲν φεύγοντα καὶ Θρασύβουλον ἀπόντα,

---

62 Andrewes, "Generals."
63 On this point, see Andrewes, "Generals" 2 with n. 4.

Κόνωνα δὲ τρίτον ἐκ τῶν οἴκοθεν.[64] Since despite his recall on Theramenes' motion Alcibiades is called an exile, quite likely this was the moment (that is, soon after the recovery of Byzantium and Chalcedon but before his election as general) when Critias made another formal motion for his recall, which will have included a promise of amnesty and an invitation to return to Athens.[65] There is no reason to believe that Critias had any but personal motives for doing so, the same kind of motives as had made him the author of vindictive measures against Phrynichus two years earlier. Certainly no evidence suggests that he was politically prominent at this time or connects him with any particular policy. Still, his motion will have done its part to create the new atmosphere that not only gave Alcibiades and his fellow generals in the Hellespont their long-overdue recognition but also prepared the enthusiastic welcome when he sailed into the Piraeus in May 407 "on the day on which the city celebrated the Plynteria."[66] Thrasyllus's failure to win reelection when Alcibiades and Thrasybulus were elected generals may indicate the depth of the emotions stirred by Alcibiades' impending return: perhaps the Athenians thought Alcibiades would be offended to have a colleague who had been closely identified over the past few years with such men as Cleophon, democratic leaders whose opposition to Alcibiades only the mood now prevailing had stilled.[67] The election of Conon, presumably in his place, will have been militarily sound and offensive to no one. A member of an old Athenian family, as a soldier he had loyally served the Athenian democracy; his genius and good fortune kept him out of political trouble throughout a life devoted to the service of his country. He cannot have been much more than thirty years old when during his first term as general he commanded Naupactus in 414/13 B.C.; he had been general again under the intermediate regime, when he took a contingent of six hundred Messenians from Naupactus to suppress an oligarchical revolution in Corcyra that was going to hand the island over the Spartans.[68] Apparently he was not reelected by the restored democ-

64   Xen. *Hell*. 1.4.10: "The Athenians elected as their generals Alcibiades, who was an exile, Thrasybulus, who was abroad, and as a third, Conon, from among those at home."
65   Plut. *Alc*. 33.1, with Andrewes, "Generals" 3 and n. 7.
66   Xen. *Hell*. 1.4.12; Plut. *Alc*. 34.1-2.
67   Note the hostile reception Alcibiades' troops gave to Thrasyllus's troops on their arrival in Lampsacus, Xen. *Hell*. 1.2.15 and 17.
68   Thuc. 7.31.4-5; Diod. 13.48.6-8; cf. Davies, *APF* 506-9.

racy, but we know too little about his past to guess why. Since he does not seem to have been involved in any of the political troubles of 411 B.C., he will have been acceptable to all sides in 408/7 B.C.

Some features of Alcibiades' entrance into Athens deserve notice. He is not merely given center stage in the three accounts we have;[69] none of his colleagues even shares the stage with him. We are told nothing of Thrasyllus's reception when he returned with his victorious army shortly before Alcibiades; Thrasybulus stayed in Thrace and recovered Thasos; and nothing is known of Theramenes' whereabouts at this time.[70] Moreover, Alcibiades seems to have been in no hurry to reach Athens after he had heard of his recall and his election, probably while at Samos: before he sailed triumphantly into the Piraeus, he first went to Paros, and thence to Gytheum to gather information about Spartan shipbuilding operations and to await reports about the political climate in Athens. Even then he did not dare disembark until he saw in the welcoming crowd his cousin Euryptolemus, back safe from the peace mission to Persia on which Alcibiades had dispatched him after the recovery of Chalcedon.[71] He needed the encouragement of a friendly face to be reassured that the hostility he knew was still latent in the city would not turn his landing into a disaster.[72] His apprehensions were not justified for the moment, but they were for the long run. The accolades he received, his effective speech in defense against the charges of impiety that had been pending against him, his acclamation as ἀπάντων ἡγεμὼν αὐτοκράτωρ (supreme commander with absolute authority), and his bravado in leading the procession from Athens to Eleusis overland for the first time since the Spartan occupation of Deceleia in order that by ostentatiously celebrating the Mysteries he might erase the memory of the curse and of the exile their profanation had brought him[73]—all this became meaningless when a few months later, in 406 B.C., Lysander defeated the Athenians at Notium.

69   Xen. *Hell*. 1.4.11–23; Diod. 13.68.2–69.3; Plut. *Alc*. 32.1–34.7.

70   Xen. *Hell*. 1.4.9–10. Both Diod. 13.68.3 and Plut. *Alc*. 32.3 state that other generals returned with Alcibiades, but none is named. In view of that, the statement of Nep. *Alc*. 6.3, that Theramenes and Thrasybulus accompanied him, is open to doubt.

71   Xen. *Hell*. 1.4.11–12 and 19 with 1.3.12–13; cf. also Plut. *Alc*. 32.2. On Euryptolemus and his relation to Alcibiades, see Davies, *APF* 377–78.

72   See especially Xen. *Hell*. 1.4.17, and the remarks by both Xen. ibid. 12 and Plut. *Alc*. 34.2 that his arrival fell on an unlucky day.

73   Xen. *Hell*. 1.4.20; Diod. 13.68.2–69.3; Plut. *Alc*. 32.1–34.7; Plut. *Alc*. 34.7 even asserts that the lower classes would have liked to make him tyrant.

The defeat was due to Alcibiades' helmsman Antiochus, who had attacked the Peloponnesian fleet in defiance of Alcibiades' orders,[74] but Alcibiades was nevertheless blamed both at home and by the army. He and most of his fellow generals were deposed; since a new board of ten loyal democrats was constituted to replace them, their allegiance to the democracy was evidently still regarded with suspicion.[75] Thrasybulus's close association with Alcibiades throughout the campaign in the Hellespont makes his dismissal at this time no surprise. But both the appointment and dismissal of the only other general known to have been deposed with Alcibiades is remarkable: Adeimantus son of Leucolophides had last been heard from in 415 B.C., when he escaped from Athens, denounced by Agariste for profaning the Mysteries, and his rather substantial property was confiscated and sold at auction.[76] We noted that he may well have returned to Athens with the exiles recalled by the intermediate regime;[77] but in view of how soon thereafter he was appointed general, he was probably elected for 407/6 B.C. because of his

---

74   Xen. *Hell*. 1.5.11–15; *Hell.Oxy*. IV Bartoletti; Diod. 13.71; Plut. *Alc*. 35.6–8, with A. Andrewes, "Notion and Kyzikos: The Sources Compared," *JHS* 102 (1982) 15–25, esp. 15–19.

75   Xen. *Hell*. 1.5.16–17; Diod. 13.73.3–74.2, who, however, wrongly attributes the turning of the tide to Alcibiades' treatment of Cyme (similarly Nep. *Alc*. 7.2). Moreover, Diodorus's list at 13.74.1 has Lysias in place of the Leon in Xenophon's list and Thrasybulus in place of Thrasyllus. In both cases preference is to be given to Xenophon. As far as we can determine, only Conon and Aristocrates were kept of the old board; Conon was an apolitical but loyal democratic soldier (see above, pp. 428–29 with n. 68), and Aristocrates, Theramenes' associate in overthrowing the Four Hundred, unlike Theramenes had been appointed general by the restored democracy (see above, pp. 392–93 with n. 192). Of those newly appointed, Diomedon and Leon had last been generals in 412/11 B.C., when they had been sent by the democracy to replace Phrynichus and Scironides and had helped the Samian *dēmos* against the oligarchical designs of their rulers (see above, pp. 346–47 with n. 40 and 387); Pericles, son of Pericles and Aspasia (see Davies, *APF* 458), had held his first known public office as *hellēnotamias* in 410/09 B.C. (see ML, no. 84.8, 11, 13, 18); Erasinides had made the motion to honor Phrynichus's assassins (see above, pp. 420–21). Archestratus's antecedents are unknown, except that he seems to have been a friend of Pericles' sons (Ath. 5.220d with Wilamowitz, *Aristoteles* 1.68–69 n. 40); he was to lose his life at Mytilene in 406 B.C. (Lys. 21.8). Nothing is known of Protomachus and Aristogenes, except that both were generals at Arginusae who did not return to Athens after the battle, fearful of the popular fury (Xen. *Hell*. 1.6.30, 1.7.2; Diod. 13.101.5). The most significant replacement was Thrasyllus, who, as already remarked, had not originally been elected general, presumably lest this offend Alcibiades; the significance of his appointment is underlined by the fact that Lys. 21.7 calls the whole group τοὺς μετὰ Θρασύλλου δέκα.

76   Andoc. 1.16; Aurenche, *Groupes* 130–31 with Appendix C, p. 545 below.

77   See above, pp. 400–401 with n. 219.

connection with Alcibiades, and therefore also fell from favor with him.

So transient a reconciliation with Alcibiades and his fellow generals shows their successes had not been sufficient to make deep-seated suspicions and hostilities fade away. There may have been substance to the accusation Diodorus records (13.73.6) that Alcibiades colluded with the Spartans and with the Persian satrap Pharnabazus. Again, according to Plutarch, the army sent Thrasybulus son of Thrason to accuse Alcibiades before the Assembly of relinquishing his command to incompetent fellow rakes while he himself was off building a private fort and carousing in the Thracian Chersonese.[78] If a late report can be trusted, Cleophon not only took judicial proceedings against Alcibiades about this time[79] but also secured either a verdict or a popular decree against Critias, the sponsor of Alcibiades' recall, which drove him into exile in Thessaly; he did not return until the war was over and Athens was under Lysander's control.[80] Alcibiades was never to see Athens again. Whether he was formally deposed from office and recalled we do not know. But he knew better than to submit himself to a *euthyna* at home, realizing that its results would be a foregone conclusion. He withdrew to his fortified estates in the Thracian Chersonese,[81] and when he came in the late summer of 405 B.C. to advise the Athenian generals near Aegospotami to shift their base of operations to Sestos, his advice was not wanted: "We, not you, are the generals now."[82] His political career was at an end.

The Dénouement: Arginusae and Its Aftermath

"Alarmed by the extent of his excesses in his personal life and by the mentality that pervaded his every action in every situation, the masses became his firm enemies, convinced that he was aspiring to tyranny. Although in public life his organization of the war effort had been most effective, all were offended by his private conduct; and so they entrusted the conduct of affairs to others, and it did not

---

78   Plut. *Alc.* 36.1–3. For similar charges couched in more general terms, see Xen. *Hell.* 1.5.16–17.

79   Himerius 36.18 and Phot. *Bibl.* 377a, as cited above, Chap. 5, n. 53.

80   Ar. *Rh.* 1.15, 1375ᵇ 31–35; Xen. *Mem.* 1.2.24, *Hell.* 2.3.15 (where the expression φυγὼν ὑπὸ τοῦ δήμου is to be noted) and 36.

81   Lys. 14.38; Xen. *Hell.* 1.5.17; Diod. 13.74.2.

82   Xen. *Hell.* 2.1.25–26: αὐτοὶ γὰρ νῦν στρατηγεῖν, οὐκ ἐκεῖνον. See also Diod. 13.105.3–4; Plut. *Alc.* 36.6–37.1; Nep. *Alc.* 8.2–5.

take long before they ruined the city."[83] The blame with which Thucydides saddles the masses for ruining Athens is justified insofar as in their fickleness they could so rapidly shift from enthusiastically welcoming Alcibiades to exiling him a second time. But it is not justified in view of Alcibiades' past conduct, private as well as public; the masses had good reason not to trust him blindly. The tragic aspect of the situation is that Alcibiades fell because of a failure for which he was not to blame, brought about by a subordinate officer's disregard of his explicit orders. Popular feeling toward him was too ambivalent to retain confidence in him after so serious a defeat. Under the circumstances, there was no alternative to turning the conduct of affairs over to others, and though these others could never be Alcibiades' peers in stature and ability, they inspired greater trust.

Conon, an experienced soldier and one of the two men known to have retained his generalship after Notium,[84] was a worthy enough successor to Alcibiades as commander of the Athenian fleet at Samos. He did not take long to restore morale to the dispirited troops by refraining from a major campaign and regrouping the fleet into an efficient fighting force. He then conducted raids on enemy strongholds on and off the coast of Asia Minor to provide pay and practice.[85] Internal troubles in the Spartan camp facilitated his task (Xen. *Hell*. 1.6.1–12; Plut. *Lys*. 6). But by the middle of June, the tide had turned. The Spartans, under the command of Callicratidas, had made inroads on the Athenian bases on Lesbos: Methymna was taken by storm; 30 of Conon's 70 ships were captured; and Conon was cooped up with the other 40 in the harbor of Mytilene (Xen. *Hell*. 1.6.12–18; Diod. 13.76.5–78.3). His fellow general Erasinides escaped to bring the discouraging news to Athens.[86]

We do not know who designed the astounding military and financial measures that were voted to relieve Conon in an Athens

83   Thuc. 6.15.4: φοβηθέντες γὰρ αὐτοῦ οἱ πολλοὶ τὸ μέγεθος τῆς τε κατὰ τὸ ἑαυτοῦ σῶμα παρανομίας ἐς τὴν δίαιταν καὶ τῆς διανοίας ὧν καθ' ἓν ἕκαστον ἐν ὅτῳ γίγνοιτο ἔπρασσεν, ὡς τυραννίδος ἐπιθυμοῦντι πολέμιοι καθέστασαν, καὶ δημοσίᾳ κράτιστα διαθέντι τὰ τοῦ πολέμου ἰδίᾳ ἕκαστοι τοῖς ἐπιτηδεύμασιν αὐτοῦ ἀχθεσθέντες, καὶ ἄλλοις ἐπιτρέψαντες, οὐ διὰ μακροῦ ἔσφηλαν τὴν πόλιν.
84   See n. 75 above.
85   Xen. *Hell*. 1.5.18 and 20; Diod. 13.74.1–2, 76.1, 77.1.
86   Xen. *Hell*. 1.6.19–22. That Erasinides was on board the trireme that escaped can be inferred from his presence with Conon in Mytilene, ibid. 16, and from his subsequent presence at Arginusae, ibid. 29.

already drained of human and material resources. Within the remarkably short period of thirty days (apparently spanning the final days of the archonship of Antigenes [407/6 B.C.] and the first days of the archonship of Callias [406/5 B.C.], that is, in midsummer 406 B.C.) 110 ships were mobilized to be sent to Asia Minor. Metics and slaves of military age were enticed by promises of citizenship to man them alongside free Athenians.[87] A fragment of Hellanicus suggests that even Plataean citizenship, perhaps in the Plataean settlement Athens established at Scione, was given to slaves as early as the archonship of Antigenes, presumably in its final month.[88] Aristophanes' *Frogs* attests that these slaves had won their freedom by early 405 B.C.[89] Moreover, since available funds were not sufficient to defray the tremendous expense of rearming, the Athenians voted to convert into coin seven golden statues of Nike and presumably other gold and silver offerings on the Acropolis.[90]

So extensive and energetic an effort obviously required the support of the entire people, and the result justified their faith. Under the command of the eight available generals, all of whom had been

---

87   Xen. *Hell.* 1.6.24; Diod. 13.97.1, with D. Whitehead, *The Ideology of the Athenian Metic*, *PCPS* Supplement 4 (Cambridge, 1977) 153–54.

88   Hellanicus 323a F25 with Jacoby's commentary, *FGH* 3b Suppl. 1.54–55. For the Plataeans at Scione, see Thuc. 5.32.1 I regard it as probable that the much-restored decree honoring Archelaus of Macedon (ML, no. 91) also belongs in this context. It provides for the speedy delivery of ships, whose construction in Macedonia had already been commissioned, in order to man them in Athens for dispatch to Ionia (lines 9–20), and it threatens severe penalties for obstructing its stipulations (11–14, 20–22). That the decree belongs in the archonship of Antigenes was first recognized by Meritt, who also restored the name of Pericles (lines 5–6) as one of the generals involved in the disbursement of funds for the construction of these ships, *AFD* 107–15. However, Meritt seems to be off the mark when in a later article, "Archelaos and the Decelean War," in *Classical Studies Presented to E. Capps* (Princeton, 1936) 246–52, he restores Alcibiades' name (line 4) as the mover of the decree: so far as we know, Pericles first became general only after Alcibiades' board had been deposed after Notium (see n. 75 above), and that would place the decree late rather than early in Antigenes' archonship. In short, the preparations culminating in the battle of Arginusae provide a better context for the decree.

89   Ar. *Ran.* 33, 190–91, 693–94 with scholl. on 33 and 694.

90   The literary evidence consists of Ar. *Ran.* 720 with schol., which cites Hellanicus *FGH* 323a F26 and Philochorus *FGH* 328F141. It is supported by the epigraphical evidence of *IG* I² 255a (= *IG* I³ 316) as interpreted by W. E. Thompson, "The Date of the Athenian Gold Coinage," *AJP* 86 (1965) 159–74, and J. Tréheux, *Études sur les inventaires attiques*, Annales de l'Est, publiées par la Faculté des Lettres et Sciences Humaines de l'Université de Nancy 29, Études d'Archéologie Classique 3 (Paris, 1965) 5–38. For the numismatic evidence, see C. M. Kraay, *Archaic and Classical Greek Coins* (Berkeley and Los Angeles, 1976) 68–69.

elected after Notium,[91] the fleet set out for Samos early in the archonship of Callias, that is, about the end of July or early August.[92] After adding more than 40 allied ships there, it set sail for Lesbos to relieve Conon.[93] Callicratidas, leaving 50 triremes with Eteonicus to blockade Mytilene, sailed with 120 ships to meet the Athenian 150. At the Arginusae Islands, off the southeastern tip of Lesbos, the Athenians crushed the Peloponnesian fleet in what Diodorus calls "the greatest sea battle ever fought by Greeks against Greeks."[94] Callicratidas lost his life; 9 of the 10 Laconian ships and more than 60 of their allies' were sunk, more than half their fleet; the Athenians lost only 25 ships, 12 of them still afloat (Xen. *Hell*. 1.6.34).

But the problem of rescuing these ships and their survivors turned a smashing military victory into a humiliating political defeat for the principle of popular sovereignty and stigmatized all major organs of the Athenian democracy, Council, Assembly, and the judicial system. Forty-seven ships under Theramenes and Thrasybulus, who though experienced generals had participated in the battle as trierarchs, had been detailed after the victory to pick up the shipwrecked sailors while the eight generals took the rest of the fleet to relieve Mytilene. Both plans, however, were frustrated by a storm, and the Athenians returned to their base in Samos (Xen. *Hell*. 1.6.35–38; Diod. 13.100.1–6). The generals informed Council and Assembly in Athens by letter that a storm had made it impossible to rescue the shipwrecked (Xen. *Hell*. 1.7.4).

The eight generals were consequently deposed from office, "tried," and executed. Our understanding of these events is hampered because Xenophon's account of what preceded the "trial" omits or contradicts several details of the more coherent account in Diodorus, particularly an entirely different estimate of Theramenes' role.[95] Still, certain procedural points are clear. The generals will still have been in Samos when they were informed of their recall

91   They are identical with those enumerated in Xen. *Hell*. 1.5.16, except that Conon was at Mytilene and Archestratus, who had been killed at Mytilene (Lys. 21.8), was apparently replaced by Lysias, whose name appears in place of Leon's on Diodorus's list (13.74.1); on this, see Beloch, *Politik* 312–13. Unless we are to accept Diodorus's list, we have to assume that he was still with Conon at Mytilene; see Xen. *Hell*. 1.6.16.

92   Xen. *Hell*. 1.6.25; for the date, see Arist. *Ath. Pol*. 34.1 and Ath. 5.218a.

93   Xen. *Hell*. 1.6.25.

94   Xen. *Hell*. 1.6.26–33; Diod. 13.97.2–99.6 (quotation at 98.5; cf. 102.4).

95   On this point, see especially A. Andrewes, "The Arginousai Trial," *Phoenix* 28 (1974) 112–22, to which the following is much indebted.

(*apocheirotonia*), which entailed their immediate return to Athens to submit to *euthynai*, and of the appointment of Adeimantus and Philocles to take their place with Conon in the operations in Asia Minor (Xen. *Hell*. 1.7.1; Diod. 13.101.5). Protomachus and Aristogenes showed how apprehensive the generals were about what would await them at home; they disobeyed the recall order and escaped before reaching Athens (Xen. *Hell*. 1.7.2; Diod. loc. cit.).

Andrewes has shown sound reasons for their apprehensions.[96] Theramenes and Thrasybulus, who had been closely associated with Alcibiades' operations in the Hellespont between 410 and 407 B.C., had returned to Athens before the rest (Diod. 13.101.2); and Adeimantus, who had been appointed as one of their replacements, seems to have been on close personal terms with Alcibiades and may have owed his election as general for 407/6 B.C. to him.[97] But since the generals at Arginusae owed their appointment to the removal after Notium of the board that had served with Alcibiades, they could reasonably suspect their recall and replacement had been engineered by political opponents who sought revenge for Alcibiades' exile. Whether there was substance to their suspicions or not[98] they could not know; but they now sent a second letter, addressed to the people (*dēmos*), to exculpate themselves by noting that it was to Theramenes and Thrasybulus that the task of recovering the dead after Arginusae had been assigned.[99]

96 Ibid. 116. A less convincing interpretation is given by Roberts, *Accountability* 64–69, esp. 66.

97 See above, pp. 430–31.

98 The appointment of Philocles as a replacement general along with Adeimantus tends to indicate that the fear of political resentment was groundless. The fact that he was executed by Lysander as the author of the decree, passed before Aegospotami, to cut off the right thumb (or right hand) of all prisoners taken and as having caused the cruel murder of Corinthian and Andrian captives (Xen. *Hell*. 2.1.31–32; Plut. *Lys*. 9.7; Diod. 13.106.7; Paus. 9.32.9), as well as his alleged disregard of Alcibiades' advice at Aegospotami for fear that association with him would bring him harm at Athens (Nep. *Alc*. 8.4), suggests that he shared Cleophon's policy of war to the finish and of opposition to Alcibiades. Moreover, the role of the democrat Archedemus in the treatment of the generals (Xen. *Hell*. 1.7.2) also suggests that opposition to them cannot have been due merely to the fact that they had replaced Alcibiades' board. Finally, the intervention of Alcibiades' cousin Euryptolemus on behalf of the generals shows that the issue was not "party-political." For an opposite view, see G. Németh, "Der Arginusen-Prozess," *Klio* 66 (1984) 51–57.

99 It is curious that Xenophon's emphasis is throughout on the rescue of the survivors of the shipwrecks, whereas Diod. 13.101.1 (cf. Pl. *Menex*. 243c) speaks only of the recovery of the dead.

For an understanding of the political atmosphere surrounding the "trial" of the generals, we depend entirely on Xenophon (*Hell*. 1.7). His detailed account conveys the impression that regardless of its antecedents, it was far from clear anyone would be tried when the generals were recalled. The first step in the direction of any judicial proceedings was Archedemus's action against Erasinides, which seems to have been unrelated to the battle of Arginusae. In imposing an administrative fine (*epibolē*) on Erasinides for having in his possession public funds from the Hellespont, Archedemus apparently acted as administrator of the *diōbelia*; only when Erasinides contested the fine in a jury court did Archedemus accuse him also of misconduct as general,[100] presumably at or as a preliminary action to his *euthyna*.[101] The court decided to put Erasinides under arrest pending a trial (*Hell*. 1.7.2). Xenophon does not say on which of these charges Erasinides was arrested; but since in the fourth century a general's *apocheirotonia* was normally followed by trial in a jury court,[102] we may assume that the charge of misconduct was the reason and that the arrest was precautionary to prevent him from following the example of Protomachus and Aristogenes.

Xenophon relates the case of Erasinides to the measures taken against the generals as a group only in one small but perhaps not insignificant point. He explains that the arrest of "also" (καὶ) the other generals was ordered as a result of a hearing before the Council in which the generals gave a report on the sea battle and on the severity of the storm (*Hell*. 1.7.3). Xenophon leaves the reason for this procedure unexplained. Normally, the *euthynai* of generals were the task of the thesmothetai and the jury courts;[103] since on occasions other than the *euthyna* generals may have been asked during their tenure to defend official acts before the Assembly,[104] we may suppose the purpose of the Council's hearing was to determine whether

100 Xen. *Hell*. 1.7.2, where in view of the δὲ καί following κατηγόρει, I punctuate Ἐρασινίδῃ ἐπιβολὴν ἐπιβαλὼν κατηγόρει ἐν δικαστηρίῳ· φάσκων ἐξ Ἑλλησπόντου αὐτὸν ἔχοντα χρήματα ὄντα τοῦ δήμου, κατηγόρει δὲ καὶ περὶ τῆς στρατηγίας.

101 The basis for this accusation may well have been Erasinides' advice (Xen. *Hell*. 1.7.29) to sail against Mytilene without first picking up the survivors; cf. Andrewes, "Arginousai Trial" 113 with n. 4.

102 Arist. *Ath.Pol*. 61.2, with Hansen, *Eisangelia* 41–45, and MacDowell, *LCA* 187.

103 See above, p. 63 with n. 242.

104 So, for example, Pericles' explanation ἐν τῷ τῆς στρατηγίας ἀπολογισμῷ that he had expended ten talents "for a necessary purpose" (εἰς τὸ δέον) was given to the δῆμος (Plut. *Per*. 23.1).

offenses actionable by *eisangelia* had been committed, either by the generals[105] or (as alleged by the generals in their second letter) by Theramenes and Thrasybulus.[106] This seems to be corroborated by the fact that the motion of Timocrates ordered the generals arrested and produced before the *dēmos* (*Hell*. 1.7.3), which, as we have seen some reason to believe,[107] had jurisdiction over generals in *eisangelia* proceedings for offenses alleged to have been perpetrated in their official capacity. Notably, however, Timocrates' motion merely required the generals be handed over (παραδοθῆναι) to the people; it did not recommend a trial before the Assembly.

Xenophon proceeds to describe a subsequent Assembly meeting without specifying the purpose for which it had been summoned (*Hell*. 1.7.9). Was it convoked to pass judgment on the generals who were produced before it, that is, did it meet on this occasion as a law court? Or had it been called, as in the case of Agoratus (Lys. 13.32), simply to hear for itself denunciations already made before the Council, as was mandatory in the case of generals and taxiarchs? Timocrates' motion had doubtless come as a *probouleuma* before the Assembly, and it required the generals to be produced before the *dēmos*. From Xenophon's report on how it ended, we can be sure of one thing the meeting was not: because the advanced hour made a vote on substantive issues impossible, the Assembly voted to adjourn, but not before requesting a *probouleuma* of the Council ὅτῳ τρόπῳ οἱ ἄνδρες κρίνοιντο, "in what manner the men should be judged" (*Hell*. 1.7.7). This means that, whatever the purpose of this Assembly meeting may have been, it was not to pass judgment on the generals. It is important to establish this point in order to ascertain what illegalities were perpetrated against the generals.

Theramenes' speech further indicates that the meeting was not a trial. Referring to the letter that the generals originally sent to Council and Assembly, he proposed that they should be subjected to an accounting of why they had failed to rescue the shipwrecked (*Hell*. 1.7.4). Xenophon here presents as an attack by Theramenes what sounds substantially more like a defense against the generals' allegation in their second letter, this time addressed to the *dēmos*, that he and Thrasybulus bore the responsibility for not having picked up the dead after the battle; and the substance of his remarks sounds

105 Cf. Rhodes, *AB* 148.
106 Diod. 13.101.2 with Andrewes, "Arginousai Trial" 116–17.
107 See above, pp. 65–66 with n. 252.

more like a reasonable defense than like the accusation that Xenophon imputes to him.[108] The term Theramenes uses, λόγον ὑποσχεῖν, is almost certainly a demand for the overall *euthyna* of the generals, since the finances of their administration are not being questioned.[109] Furthermore, Theramenes does not assume, as a prosecutor would, that the generals are guilty, nor does he advocate their punishment, but he proposes a procedure to ascertain whether the generals were responsible for the failure of the rescue operations or the storm was.

The sequel therefore has to be interpreted differently from how it usually is. Xenophon reports that next each general made a brief statement in his own defense; he explains the brevity by the parenthetical remark οὐ γὰρ προυτέθη σφίσι λόγος κατὰ τὸν νόμον, which is conventionally translated "for they were not granted the hearing prescribed by the law" (*Hell*. 1.7.5)[110] and interpreted as meaning the accused were denied the legal right freely to defend themselves.[111] But an alternative translation seems also possible: "For in conformity with the law no opportunity was given them to make a speech [or perhaps: "give an accounting"]," implying that a full-length defense speech (or a full accounting) could not by law be given at an ordinary meeting of the Assembly. I see no linguistic or stylistic objection to this interpretation,[112] and it finds support in the observations that the generals were able to present witnesses to corroborate even their short statements concerning the storm (1.7.6), that they were able to convince the people to the extent that several private individuals publicly offered bail for them (1.7.6–7), and that the speech of Euryptolemus nowhere suggests that the generals ought to have been given an opportunity to defend themselves on this occasion. In short, it seems that the purpose of this Assembly meeting was to

108 Andrewes, "Arginousai Trial," esp. 113. Cf. also G. Adeleye, "The Arginusai Affair and Theramenes' Rejection at the *Dokimasia* of 405/4 B.C.," *Mus.Afr.* 6 (1977–78) 94–99.

109 For the interchangeable use of λόγος and εὔθυνα as expressions for the official audit, see Hignett, *HAC* 203 with n. 9.

110 So. C. L. Brownson, tr., *Xenophon: Hellenica, Books I–V* (Cambridge, Mass., and London, 1918) 69; cf. J. Hatzfeld, ed. and tr., *Xénophon: Helléniques* 1⁴ (Paris, 1960) 60: "Car on ne leur avait pas donné d'avance le temps de parole prévu par la loi."

111 See, e.g., von Wedel, "Prozesse" 160; Harrison, *LA* 2.58; MacDowell, *LCA* 189.

112 It might even be argued on the analogy of *Hell*. 1.1.27, ὡς ἀδίκως φεύγοιεν ἅπαντες παρὰ τὸν νόμον, that the conventional interpretation could have been less equivocally expressed by Xenophon by οὐ γὰρ προυτέθη . . . παρὰ τὸν νόμον.

determine what procedures, if any, should be initiated against the deposed generals and that when it got too late to bring the matter to a decisive vote the meeting was adjourned with a simultaneous request to the Council for a *probouleuma* ὅτῳ τρόπῳ οἱ ἄνδρες κρίνοιντο (1.7.7). This was not a request for a trial but for guidance concerning the procedure to be used in the generals' case, to which the Council was free to respond by ordering a trial but might equally well order that the *euthyna* take its normal course and that its outcome determine whether judicial action was necessary. Nothing illegal had happened so far.

The *probouleuma* came a few days later in a motion presented to the Assembly by its author, Callixenus: "Since they have heard both the accusations brought against the generals and the generals' defense in the previous meeting of the Assembly, all Athenians shall now cast their votes by tribes."[113] It went on to define how the votes for the guilt or innocence of the generals were to be cast and to specify as punishments the death penalty, confiscation of property, and the payment of a tithe to Athena (*Hell.* 1.7.9–11). The motion was supported with an emotional appeal by a man who claimed to be a survivor of the shipwreck and inculpated the generals in the name of those who had perished (1.7.11).

Xenophon does not specify the grounds on which Euryptolemus immediately served a summons on Callixenus for drafting an illegal proposal (παράνομα φάσκοντες συγγεγραφέναι, *Hell.* 1.7.12), which is generally and, I believe, correctly interpreted as initiating a *graphē paranomōn*.[114] But the context alone makes it clear that the illegality consisted in treating as a judicial procedure what had been merely a deliberative meeting of the Assembly, which had indeed heard but had not given a judicial hearing to either party. Callixenus's offense was not against a particular law but against "die Rechtsordnung als Ganzes," which required that a verdict be preceded by trial in the manner prescribed by law.[115] Euryptolemus's specific legal points are designed to illustrate the central παράνομον of Callixenus's proposal, namely, that a verdict should be rendered though no trial had taken place (1.7.25).

113 Xen. *Hell.* 1.7.9: Ἐπειδὴ τῶν τε κατηγορούντων κατὰ τῶν στρατηγῶν καὶ ἐκείνων ἀπολογουμένων ἐν τῇ προτέρᾳ ἐκκλησίᾳ ἀκηκόασι, διαψηφίσασθαι Ἀθηναίους ἅπαντας κατὰ φυλάς.

114 Bonner-Smith 1.266; Wolff, *"Normenkontrolle"* 49–50; von Wedel, "Prozesse" 161–62; Hansen, *PAUP* 28–29; MacDowell, *LCA* 188–89.

115 Wolff, *"Normenkontrolle"* 49–50 with quote on p. 50.

Euryptolemus demanded that in accordance with due process the generals be given at least one day to make their defense collectively as well as individually (*Hell*. 1.7.19) and that no verdict against all be given on one ballot cast for them all (1.7.26).[116] To support his contention he cited two laws, either of which, he believed, could serve as a proper basis for a trial. The first of these was the decree of Cannonus, enacted at an unknown date and outlining the procedure in crimes against the Athenian people. According to its provisions, each accused is to make his defense[117] separately before the people,[118] and upon conviction he is to be executed, his property confiscated, and a tithe given to Athena (1.7.20). Though the punishment Callixenus proposed conformed to Cannonus's decree (1.7.10), the procedure did not. The second possible procedure Euryptolemus envisaged was to apply to the generals the law concerning treason and temple robbery,[119] which called for trial before a jury court, and upon conviction required the death penalty, refusal of burial in Attic soil, and confiscation of property (1.7.22).

Nowhere in his speech does Euryptolemus call for the generals to give an accounting of themselves, as Theramenes had demanded (*Hell*. 1.7.4). Evidently a general's *euthyna* in the fifth century was normally conducted, as in the fourth, before a *dikastērion* and with the thesmothetai presiding,[120] and it may be that this procedure had already been used in the case of Erasinides.[121] Its use against him alone of the eight would be due to the fact that he alone was accused

116 That condemnation of all eight defendants by one ballot, as would have been the effect of Callixenus's motion, was contrary to law is also stated by Pl. *Ap*. 32b and Xen. *Mem*. 1.1.18.

117 This seems to be the meaning of the rare word ἀποδικεῖν.

118 My interpretation is based on the conviction that A. von Bamberg ("Über einige auf das attische Gerichtswesen bezügliche Aristophanesstellen," *Hermes* 13 [1878] 505–14, esp. 509–14) was right in emending the manuscript reading δεδεμένον at Xen. *Hell*. 1.7.20 to διαλελημμένον on the basis of Ar. *Eccl*. 1090. On the manuscript reading, the accused would be produced "in fetters," i.e., under arrest, before the people, and since this is precisely what happened on the motion of Timocrates (Xen. *Hell*. 1.7.3–4), and since the penalty proposed by Callixenus (ibid. 10) fully complies with Cannonus's decree, there would be no point to Euryptolemus's objection. My interpretation is further supported by Euryptolemus's final motion at 1.7.34 κατὰ τὸ Καννωνοῦ ψήφισμα κρίνεσθαι τοὺς ἄνδρας δίχα ἕκαστον.

119 For this strange bracketing of two offenses, of only one of which the generals could have been considered guilty (except insofar as their failure to bury the dead might have been regarded as constituting ἱεροσυλία, for which there is no evidence), see Lipsius, *ARRV* 442–43, and Hansen, *Apagoge* 45 n. 33.

120 See above, n. 103.

121 See above, p. 436.

of embezzling public funds (1.7.2). Since the charges against the generals as a group were more serious, the purpose of their original report to the Council (1.7.3) may have been to decide whether *eisangelia* proceedings should be instituted against them in the Assembly or whether they should merely be subjected to an ordinary *euthyna* before a jury court. Since the proposal of Timocrates did not specify a trial but merely referred the question to the Assembly (1.7.3), we may assume that the Council asked the Assembly simply whether *eisangelia* proceedings should be initiated against the generals and that when the hour became too late for a vote, the Assembly referred it back to the Council for a *probouleuma*. Euryptolemus's proposals (1.7.20–23) suggest that this *probouleuma* was meant to be a recommendation either for a trial for crimes against the state (ἐάν τις τὸν τῶν 'Αθηναίων δῆμον ἀδικῇ, 1.7.20) conducted by the *eisangelia* procedure appropriate for generals before the Assembly or for a *euthyna* before a *dikastērion*, in which charges of treason or temple robbery might be brought forward. In fact, neither course of action was proposed by the Council. Whipped into a frenzy by Callixenus, it illegally proposed a verdict when there had been no trial (1.7.25).

The illegality of Callixenus's proposal was compounded by the violence with which the Assembly reacted to Euryptolemus's charge against him. The approval of some citizens notwithstanding, terror tactics compelled Euryptolemus to withdraw his summons. The majority (τὸ πλῆθος) shouted "that it is shocking not to let the people do whatever they wish,"[122] and a certain Lyciscus threatened to move that Euryptolemus and his supporters be condemned by the same vote as the generals (*Hell*. 1.7.12–13). Despite their initial sympathy for Euryptolemus, all prytaneis save Socrates also succumbed to the terror and supported the motion of Callixenus (1.7.14–15). Much to the credit of the Athenian people, despite all pressures it voted after Euryptolemus's speech in favor of his motion to try the generals separately before the Assembly in conformity with the decree of Cannonus. Only when an objection was raised by one Menecles did they change their minds and vote, to their own later regret, to condemn all eight generals with one vote and without a trial. The six present in Athens were promptly executed.[123]

---

122 Xen. *Hell*. 1.7.12: δεινὸν εἶναι εἰ μή τις ἐάσει δῆμον πράττειν ὃ ἂν βούληται.

123 It is difficult to understand the precise nature of the ὑπωμοσία raised by Menecles; the only thing of which we can be certain is that it made a new διαχειροτονία necessary. In principle, a ὑπωμοσία is a declaration on oath in Council

Two political matters in the "trial" of the Arginusae generals remain to be discussed: Theramenes' role in the proceedings and the probable motives of Euryptolemus. Theramenes' speech at the first Assembly meeting was not the attack Xenophon (*Hell.* 1.7.4) supposes but a defense.[124] Can we believe Xenophon's further allegations (1.7.8) that Theramenes used the celebration of the Apaturia, which intervened between the two Assembly meetings, to incite the populace to vent against the generals their grief for lost relatives and that he suborned Callixenus to obtain the illegal *probouleuma* from the Council and present it to the Assembly? Diodorus (13.101.6–7) contradicts the first of these allegations; he presents the mourning relatives' protestations as spontaneous and Theramenes and associates as merely supporting them. Andrewes inclines to accept this version, largely on the grounds that an attempt to inflame mourners who had been sympathetic to the generals at the first Assembly meeting might have backfired against Theramenes.[125] The strength of this argument depends, however, on our estimate of the political and rhetorical prowess of Theramenes; the possibility remains that Theramenes and his friends somehow managed to turn the real grief of the recently bereaved into antagonism against the generals.

---

or Assembly that a γραφὴ παρανόμων would be brought against the measure under discussion if it should be passed. Its intent was, therefore, to cause the motion to be withdrawn or, if it had already been passed, to prevent its implementation until its legality had been established in court; see Lipsius, *ARRV* 393–94. In the present case, Hatzfeld, *Xénophon: Helléniques*, in a note *ad loc.* believes that Menecles' threat made Euryptolemus withdraw his motion, so that the Assembly could proceed at once to voting on the motion of the Council, the only motion left on the floor. But it seems unlikely that Euryptolemus would have been scared off so easily, especially since he had himself threatened to prosecute Callixenus παρανόμων (Xen. *Hell.* 1.7.12); and it is also difficult to understand in what respect Menecles could have viewed Euryptolemus's motion as a παράνομον. Perhaps Lipsius's suggestion, *ARRV* 393–94 with n. 73, is right, i.e., Menecles declared on oath that the statement of the prytaneis on the outcome of the διαχειροτονία was false and he demanded a recount.

124   See above, pp. 437–38 with n. 108.

125   Andrewes, "Arginousai Trial" 118, whose other arguments in favor of Diodorus's version are that the assignment of the rescue of the shipwrecked sailors to Theramenes and Thrasybulus may be a later invention, thought up by the generals only after they realized they were in danger, and that in fact the tired crews refused this duty (Diod. 13.100.2); that Theramenes acted only after being accused by the generals; and that Diodorus does not suggest that Callixenus acted as Theramenes' agent. The second of these arguments can be integrated into Xenophon's elliptical account; the first is not only "unnecessary speculation," as Andrewes himself admits, but also makes the generals rather than Theramenes guilty of falsely charging their opponents, for which there is no textual warrant whatever. Furthermore, Diodorus's indifference to Callixenus (13.103.2) would not lead us to expect to hear anything about his relation to Theramenes.

The allegation that Callixenus was suborned is supported by a passage in the pseudo-Platonic *Axiochus* (368d–e), where Theramenes and Callixenus are jointly saddled with the responsibility for the generals' death without trial. But this evidence is weak; it probably depends on Xenophon's account. Further, Xenophon's presentation of Theramenes in his defense against the charges of Critias is more favorable. There he justifies his attack on the generals because they had earlier accused him, and he claims the credit for having convinced the city that in fact the storm had made the rescue impossible.[126] This defense may have been self-serving, however, and in any event Theramenes is unlikely to have mentioned any intrigues with Callixenus in this context. Thus we cannot assess the truth of Xenophon's allegation (*Hell.* 1.7.8) that Theramenes and his friends persuaded Callixenus to get his fellow councilors to approve presenting his motion as a *probouleuma* to the Assembly. Unquestionably, popular sentiment turned against both men in the immediate sequel. In the case of Callixenus, we learn from Xenophon that soon after the generals' execution "the Athenians regretted their action and voted that those who had deceived the people, among them Callixenus, should be subjected to *probolai* and that they should provide sureties until the time of their trial."[127] Most likely this revulsion arose in the spring of 405 B.C., when amid their feverish preparations for Aegospotami the Athenians will have felt the shortage of competent generals most keenly. The reaction was intense: though elected general for 405/4 B.C., Theramenes was barred from taking office at his *dokimasia* (Lys. 13.10). Callixenus, too, became its victim, but this is not strong enough evidence to argue that he and Theramenes conspired at the time of the generals' "trial."

Of greater political interest in the study of popular sovereignty is the role Xenophon assigns to Euryptolemus in the proceeding against the generals. We have no way of telling whether he was in fact the fair-minded and law-abiding patriot Xenophon makes him out to be, but that does not diminish his significance. We mentioned him earlier as Alcibiades' cousin, who had been dispatched on a mission to Persia and whose friendly face in the welcoming crowd

126 Xen. *Hell.* 2.3.35 with Andrewes, "Arginousai Trial" 114–15.
127 Xen. *Hell.* 1.7.35. The *probolē* consisted in a vote by the Assembly mandating a prosecution for having deceived the people; see Lipsius, *ARRV* 211–19, esp. 213–15. Xenophon further informs us that Callixenus escaped (to Deceleia, according to Diod. 13.103.2) in the *stasis* that followed the defeat at Aegospotami and returned to Athens "when the men of the Piraeus returned to the city [sc. ca. October 403 B.C.]; hated by all, he died of starvation."

encouraged Alcibiades to disembark when he returned to Athens.[128] There is nothing political in the narrow sense about this, and his only personal interests in the case of the generals were his kinship to Pericles, his friendship with Diomedon, and his professed patriotism (Xen. *Hell.* 1.7.16, 21). Moreover, personal interest did not make him unfair. With tongue in cheek he stressed the irony that his friends, at whose insistence the initial report of the generals to Council and Assembly had withheld the information that Theramenes and Thrasybulus had been detailed to pick up the shipwrecked sailors, should now "in return for the humanity they showed at the time have their lives endangered through the intrigues of these men and certain others" (1.7.18). He makes no vindictive suggestion that Theramenes and Thrasybulus ought to be punished instead; his emphasis is on due process for the accused generals, not on blame for anyone else. He carefully refrains from prejudging the issue and insists only that the law should take its course in establishing whether or not the generals are culpable.

The situation Euryptolemus faced was unique. For the first time in Athenian history the principle of popular sovereignty was asserted to its logical conclusion. Never before had there been a situation in which τὸ...πλῆθος ἐβόα δεινὸν εἶναι εἰ μή τις ἐάσει τὸν δῆμον πράττειν ὃ ἂν βούληται, "the masses shouted that it was monstrous for anyone not to let the people do whatever they wanted" (1.7.12). What they wanted was to spill blood. This situation was the reverse of its closest analogue, the Mytilene debate: there Cleon had based his plea for ruthless severity on the argument from *nomos*, that a decision once made should not be rescinded; Diodotus had argued for more humane treatment on the grounds that *nomos* cannot inhibit the natural inclination of men to do wrong and that expediency is the only valid criterion for political action. But in the case of the generals of Arginusae the right of the sovereign people not to be bound by their own *nomoi* is affirmed as justifying cruel and unjust action, whereas Euryptolemus invokes the *nomoi* to plead for humane proceedings under the law. After the clamor of the mob had compelled him to withdraw his charge against Callixenus under the *graphē paranomōn*, Euryptolemus still had the courage to face the hostile crowd, arguing that each of the generals should be fairly and separately tried under either the decree of Cannonus or the law

128   See above, p. 429 with n. 71.

against treason and temple robbery. However shocked we may be by the clash of the principle of popular sovereignty with the principle of due process of law, the practice of the Athenian democracy, which made Euryptolemus's motion prevail at least temporarily in this charged atmosphere and which led to revulsion against the executions, shows that the foundations already existed for establishing a principle of the sovereignty of law a few years later. Still, further ordeals awaited Athens before that point was reached.

The Debacle: Aegospotami and Peace

To the detriment of Athens, political considerations were most important when the city faced the problem of replacing the executed generals with capable successors to confront Lysander, whom the Spartans had appointed to succeed Callicratidas as commander of their fleet.[129] A late source reports a renewed Spartan peace offer after Arginusae, and Aristotle attributes its rejection to Cleophon's drunken, impassioned appeal in armor before the Assembly to refuse any peace that would not compel the Lacedaemonians to relinquish all conquered territories (schol. Ar. *Ran*. 1532; Arist. *Ath.Pol*. 34.1). This report is usually discredited, because neither Xenophon nor Diodorus mentions it and because the terms it offered are identical to those Cleophon rejected after Cyzicus.[130] Still, while Cleophon's drunkenness and extravagant attire may be discarded as literary embellishments fostered by social prejudice, Sparta's defeat at Arginusae makes the offer likely, and Cleophon's rejection tallies well with the known Athenian determination to fight to the finish.[131]

The atmosphere in Athens is well illustrated by some passages, especially in the parabasis, of Aristophanes' *Frogs*, which was produced at the Lenaea (January–February) of 405 B.C. The chorus pleads for equality among the citizens: the disfranchised should be given back their rights (687–705); well-born, level-headed, and just

129 Since Spartan law prohibited tenure of the office of ναύαρχος more than once, Aracus was formally appointed as Callicratidas's successor, and Lysander was made his second-in-command (ἐπιστολεύς) with the understanding that he would wield the real power: see Xen. *Hell*. 2.1.7; Diod. 13.100.8; Plut. *Lys*. 7.

130 See Sandys's note on *Ath.Pol*. 34.1.

131 The notice, preserved only in schol. Ar. *Ran*. 679, that Cleophon was elected general for 405/4 B.C. is of doubtful validity and should probably be rejected; see D. Lewis, "Double Representation" 123; for the opposite view, see M. H. Jameson, "Seniority in the *Stratêgia*," *TAPA* 86 (1955) 63–87, esp. 86–87 with n. 55.

gentlemen, brought up in the palaestra and with dancing and culture, should not be rejected in favor of inferior folk, but the "good men" (χρηστοί) should manage the affairs of the state (727–37). Cleophon is maligned as a foreigner and a warmonger (679–85, 1532), and his early demise, and Adeimantus's as well, is hoped for (1504–14); Theramenes is throughout presented as an opportunist whose sophistic training helps him get out of every difficulty (538–41, 967–70). Of special interest are some remarks on Alcibiades, whose name is first brought up by Dionysus in connection with his quest for someone to save the city. To Euripides' inquiry what the city thinks of him, Dionysus responds: "She longs for him yet hates him and wants to have him."[132] Both Euripides and Aeschylus mirror this ambivalence. Euripides admires his intellectual qualities but not his use of them: "I hate a citizen whose nature is slow to benefit his country but quick to inflict great harm upon it; he is resourceful when it comes to himself, but when it comes to the city he is helpless" (1427–29). Aeschylus is more inclined, but equally unenthusiastic, to accept his services: "One should not bring up a lion's whelp in the city, [to say nothing of a lion,] but if one raises him, one must humor his ways" (1430–33). None of this is sufficient to allow a clear impression of what went on in Athens in the early months of 405 B.C. But it is remarkable that practically nothing is said about the conduct of the war. What political interest there is consists in a yearning for leadership to bring unity and a sense of community to the city, which would involve a greater part for the upper classes and a reduced role for the lower classes in affairs of state. In condemning both Cleophon and Adeimantus for impeding the attainment of this goal, Aristophanes is even-handed in his criticism. Although Theramenes seems to be free from any opprobrium for his conduct against the generals of Arginusae, he is called too clever to be relied on for public-spirited counsel. The most desirable solution would be the return of Alcibiades, but there can be no confidence in a man who would as soon ruin the city as save it if it should not cater to his whims.

Strengthening the fleet at Samos against the naval power Lysander had enlarged with Persian help proved less a problem than providing competent commanders for it. Philocles and perhaps also Adeimantus had been sent out to assist Conon in his raids on the coast of

---

132 Ar. *Ran.* 1425: ποθεῖ μέν, ἐχθαίρει δέ, βούλεται δ᾽ ἔχειν.

Asia Minor in the months immediately after the battle of Argin-usae.[133] But as it became increasingly evident that a major confronta-tion with Lysander had to be prepared for, and as more ships were accordingly built—the Athenians had 180 at Aegospotami[134]—more generals were needed to command them. Under what circumstances Menander, Tydeus, and Cephisodotus were elected as generals "in addition to those already appointed" (Xen. *Hell* 2.1.16) is uncertain. Xenophon's προσείλοντο leaves open the possibility that they were appointed by special election but does not preclude the more proba-ble interpretation that they were regularly elected when Conon, Philocles, and Adeimantus were reelected for 405/4 B.C. If the latter was the case, it is significant that this will have been the same election for which Theramenes was prevented at his *dokimasia* from assuming office, allegedly because his loyalty to the democracy was in doubt (Lys. 13.10).

Loyalty to the democracy was indeed a more important criterion for election to the generalship in 405/4 B.C. than imaginative military and political leadership. Xenophon reports (*Hell*. 2.1.31–32) that shortly before the battle of Aegospotami, Adeimantus spoke against a decree proposed, according to Plutarch (*Lys*. 9.7), by Philocles that in case of victory the right hands of all prisoners should be cut off. The enactment of this decree shows that at this time those who, like Cleophon, would fight a ruthless and desperate war had the upper hand in Athens, and the presence of two generals at the voting permits the inference that the generals for 405/4 B.C. had been elected shortly before. Moreover, the presence of Adeimantus makes it plausible that he had come to propose Alcibia-des' repatriation and election as general. He failed because Alcibiades was greatly distrusted, as Aristophanes' *Frogs* attests. That distrust may have been one of the reasons why Theramenes—who had, after all, moved his recall in 410 B.C. and had been associated with him in the Hellespont—was rejected at his *dokimasia*. In fact, Adeimantus's proposal may have been counterproductive: the choice fell on Alcibi-ades' enemies, whose devotion to the democracy and the prosecution

133 Xen. *Hell*. 2.1.16; Diod. 13.100.6. Diod. 13.104.2 suggests that Philocles was sent to share his command, but that is dated just before the departure of the fleet to the Hellespont. On the garbled chronology of Diodorus here, see Busolt, *GG* 3.2.1609–10 n. 2. There is no evidence about the dispatch of Adeimantus, except that his election to succeed the generals of Arginusae is mentioned in the same breath as Philocles' at Xen. *Hell*. 1.7.1.

134 Xen. *Hell*. 2.1.20; Diod. 13.105.1; Plut. *Lys*. 9.6.

of the war were above suspicion. Nothing is known of Cephisodotus's past, but Menander and Tydeus were experienced war horses.
Both had fought in Sicily under Nicias; Menander had served as a
hoplite commander under Alcibiades at Abydos in 410 B.C.; and
Tydeus was probably the son of Lamachus.[135] Neither of them had
the distinction of an Alcibiades or even a Theramenes, but they were
politically trustworthy and, it seems, no better generals of unquestioned loyalty were available; and as the event showed, they were
opposed to Alcibiades.[136] Politics outweighed considerations of
effective military leadership and precipitated defeat: the Athenian
generals proved no match for Lysander.

The defeat exacerbated and widened already-existing political
tensions. Except for the *Paralus*, eight ships under the command of
Conon, and some isolated others, the entire fleet fell into Lysander's
hands; all captured Athenians were put to death, some three or four
thousand, foremost among them Philocles for the cruel treatment he
had meted out to some Corinthian and Andrian captives. Only
Adeimantus's life was spared, because he had opposed the decree that
the right hands of all enemy prisoners should be cut off.[137] Conon's
luck and skill removed him once again from the political consequences of the defeat by allowing him to escape to Cyprus with his
ships. The *Paralus* brought the devastating news to Athens (Xen.
Hell. 2.1.29).

The need to create unity (*homonoia*) at Athens, to make resistance
to capitulation the common purpose of all citizens, stifled partisanship for a while. The only trace of partisan excess immediately after
Aegospotami occurs in the suspicions, fueled by Lysander's clemency
toward Adeimantus, that treachery and bribery among Alcibiades'
friends and not the incompetence of the Athenian generals had
brought on the disaster.[138] Otherwise, the Athenians tried to cope

135   For Menander's elevation to the rank of general in Sicily, see Thuc. 7.16.1
(cf. also 43.2); Plut. *Nic*. 20.2 and 6. For his role in the battle of the harbor at
Syracuse, see Thuc. 7.69.4; Diod. 13.13.2. For Abydos, see Xen. *Hell*. 1.2.16. For
Tydeus as commander at Catane in 413 B.C., see [Lys.] 20.26; for his relation to
Lamachus, see Kirchner, *PA* 13885.
136   Xen. *Hell*. 2.1.26; Plut. *Alc*. 37.1, *Lys*. 10.7. On this point, see B. S. Strauss,
"Aegospotami Reexamined," *AJP* 104 (1983) 24–35, esp. 29–31.
137   Xen. *Hell*. 2.1.28–32; Diod. 13.106.6–7; Plut. *Lys*. 11.8–10, 13.1–2; Paus.
9.32.9. On the number of Athenian ships saved, see C. Ehrhardt, "Xenophon and
Diodorus on Aegospotami," *Phoenix* 24 (1970) 225–28.
138   Xen. *Hell*. 2.1.32; Lys. 14.38; Dem. 19.191; Paus. 4.17.3, 10.9.11. Lys. 14.38
also implicates Alcibiades; and Paus. 10.9.11, Tydeus.

rationally with their situation. Lysander followed up his victory by dismantling what was left of the empire, concentrating first on the reduction of such cities as Byzantium and Chalcedon, whose possession meant control over grain imports from the Black Sea. All Athenian citizens in these places were ordered to depart for Athens and nowhere else, in order to swell the number of residents so large that famine would starve the city into submission. As a complementary measure Lysander prohibited the export of grain to Athens on pain of death.[139] This influx will have brought back to Athens a number of those the democracy had exiled in the upheavals of 415 and 411/10 B.C., who could not be counted among its supporters. Possibly the decree of Patrocleides, enacted while the city was under siege after the defeat, included these in its amnesty for all citizens living in Athens under full or partial *atimia* for political reasons,[140] presumably in order to strengthen the determination to resist by creating an atmosphere of unity.

This same determination is reflected also in Athenian attempts to put relations with the remaining allies on a new footing. In recognition of the Samian democrats' resistance to Lysander's efforts to win the island over to the Peloponnesian cause (Xen. *Hell*. 2.2.6), the Athenians extended citizenship to the islanders in a decree passed somewhat before Patrocleides' amnesty. This has now been shown to be more than a sentimental gesture to reward steadfast loyalty in adversity.[141] The decree was the result of Samian, not of Athenian, initiative; it was preceded by negotiations about the relations between Athens and Samos for the remainder of the war and beyond,[142] the purpose of which was to make the Samians free and equal partners of the Athenians and not subject allies. The grant of

139 Xen. *Hell*. 2.2.1–2 speaks only of safe passage to Athens; Plut. *Lys*. 13.3–4 has the more probable version that he ordered their return on pain of death. For the prohibition of grain export, see Isoc. 18.61.

140 Andoc. 1.73–80 with p. 422 above. For the point at which it was passed, see Xen. *Hell*. 2.2.11.

141 ML, no. 94, as discussed by W. Gawantka, *Isopolitie: Ein Beitrag zur Geschichte der zwischenstaatlichen Beziehungen in der griechischen Antike*, Vestigia 22 (Munich, 1975) 178–97, to which much of the following is indebted. For a recent text, see M. J. Osborne, *Naturalization in Athens* 1, Verhandelingen van de koninklijke Academie voor Wetenschapen, Letteren en Schone Kunsten van België, Kl. Lett. 43, no. 98 (Brussels, 1981) D4 and 5, with commentary in vol. 2 (Brussels, 1982) 25–26.

142 See especially ML, no. 94, 11–12, 14, 20, and 33, as discussed by Gawantka, *Isopolitie* 191–92.

citizenship to all Samians is potential, not actual, that is only Samians settling in Athens are entitled to it.[143] Its purpose can only have been to give potential Samian exiles a home rather than a refuge in Athens. For the rest, the independence of the Samians is guaranteed: they retain complete control over the form of government under which they will live (ML, no. 94.13); they will enjoy autonomy in legislation and the administration of justice (ibid. 15–16); and all judicial disputes arising between the two states will be settled in conformity with existing treaties (ibid. 16–18). The bonds between two independent democracies are affirmed and strengthened in the face of a victorious power that has already succeeded in replacing democracies with oligarchies elsewhere; imperial rule over a subject ally is a thing of the past.

External pressures added to the determination to resist. After reducing all Athenian dependencies except Samos, Lysander began a complete blockade of the Piraeus with 150 ships. As part of the Spartan plan, both kings, Pausanias and Agis, converged on Athens by land and encamped in the Academy.[144] But Athens did not capitulate. The city's will to resist may have been stiffened by a decision Sparta and its allies reached at this time to obliterate the city.[145] The Spartans now decided to let starvation take its course: Pausanias withdrew his forces, leaving the land siege to Agis from Deceleia, and Lysander, leaving enough ships to ensure that no grain would reach Athens, took the rest of his fleet to finish his job in Ionia (Diod. 13.107.3).

By mid-November the famine had become severe enough to prompt the Athenians to sound out Agis on the possibility of a peace that would leave them their walls and the Piraeus and make them allies of Sparta.[146] Agis rightly claimed that he had no authority to

143　For the problems connected with the amendment (32–37), see Gawantka, *Isopolitie* 195–96 with n. 67. It is probable that Eumachus and others who came to Athens at this time were immediately enrolled as Athenian citizens; see J. Cargill, "IG II² 1 and the Athenian Kleruchy on Samos," *GRBS* 24 (1983) 321–32, esp. 322–23 with n. 6.

144　Xen. *Hell*. 2.2.9; Plut. *Lys*. 14.1–5 (who wrongly dates the blockade after the fall of Samos); Diod. 13.107.2. Busolt's objection (*GG* 3.2.1627 n. 2) to both Spartan kings encamping at the Academy, that Spartan law prohibited both kings from leading out an army at the same time (Hdt. 5.75.2; Xen. *Hell*. 5.3.10), is not valid, since it would have been violated even if Agis had stayed at Deceleia.

145　Paus. 3.8.6 with C. D. Hamilton, *Sparta's Bitter Victories* (Ithaca, N.Y., and London, 1979) 50–52.

146　Xen. *Hell*. 2.2.11, where παντελῶς is no doubt an exaggeration. For the date, see Krentz, *TA* 32 with n. 8. I wish to record here my gratitude to Dr. Peter Krentz

negotiate and referred them to Sparta. The Athenians duly approved an embassy, but when it arrived on the Laconian border at Sellasia, the ephors turned it back, urging the Athenians to think up more reasonable terms if they really wanted peace. The Spartans made the counterproposal that ten stades of each of the Long Walls should be torn down, but that Lemnos, Imbros, and Scyros could remain under Athenian control, with their democratic institutions undisturbed.[147] These conditions, if they could be kept, were considerably more reassuring than the annihilation Agis and Lysander desired. The lifeline across the sea would be left intact, but by land Sparta would be in complete control. But what assurance was there whether the ephors or Lysander and Agis would prevail in the end?

The reaction the ambassadors provoked by their report upon returning to Athens marked the first major breach in the unity (*homonoia*) painstakingly cultivated after Aegospotami. When the councilor Archestratus, who is otherwise unknown, recommended accepting the ephors' terms, he was thrown in prison; and a decree was passed, presumably on the motion of Cleophon, prohibiting even the discussion of peace on these terms.[148] Probably at the same Assembly meeting (Lys. 13.8–9) Theramenes promised to get Athens out of this impasse if he were entrusted with a mission, on the exact course of which we have conflicting evidence. According to Xenophon, he proposed that he be dispatched to Lysander to sound him out on Spartan intentions, in particular, whether razing the walls was to be a prelude to enslavement or merely a demonstration of good faith—in short, to find out to what extent Lysander supported the ephors' terms. His proposal was accepted; he prolonged his stay with Lysander for three months in the expectation that famine would meanwhile reduce the Athenians to accepting any peace conditions; he then returned to Athens and reported that Lysander lacked authority to answer his questions and had referred him to Sparta. Thereupon he was elected ambassador plenipotentiary (πρεσβευτὴς αὐτοκράτωρ) and was sent with nine others to Sparta to

---

for having made a copy of his dissertation available to me before it was published under the title *The Thirty at Athens* (Ithaca, N.Y., 1982).

147 Xen. *Hell*. 2.2.12–15, where only the razing of the Long Walls is mentioned, as it is in Lys. 13.8. However, the terms mentioned by Aeschin. 2.76 seem to fit no other occasion; see Krentz, *TA* 33 n. 11.

148 Xen. *Hell*. 2.2.15 with Lys. 13.8. If the information in Aeschin. 2.76 is accurate, this is probably the occasion on which Cleophon threatened to cut the throat of anyone who would even mention peace. Needless to say, if true, this can only have been part of a speech, not of a motion.

negotiate a peace (Xen. *Hell*. 2.2.16–17). The most salient differences between this account and the two of Lysias are that Theramenes was dispatched not to Lysander but to Sparta and that he was immediately appointed ambassador plenipotentiary; in other words, Lysias has one Assembly meeting and one mission where Xenophon has two of each, and he places the protracted stay, here too aimed at starving Athens into submission, in Sparta (Lys. 13.9–11). Scholars in the main believe that Lysias has telescoped the two meetings and two missions into one and that Xenophon is to be trusted in this regard.[149] However, once this is recognized, the problem remains whether Theramenes was appointed ambassador plenipotentiary at the first or, as Xenophon has it, the second Assembly meeting. On the answer to this question depends our judgment of Xenophon's report that Theramenes merely wanted to sound out Lysander. Since appointment as ambassador plenipotentiary would necessarily carry with it, as Lysias's language suggests,[150] the power to negotiate any terms of peace, there was no reason for an appointment of this nature if negotiations were not the purpose of Theramenes' mission. The discovery of the Michigan papyrus (Inv. 5982) containing a fragmentary account of the first Assembly meeting supports Lysias insofar as it reports Theramenes' appointment by the Assembly as πρεσβευτὴν [αὐ]τοκράτορα τὴν εἰρήνην [πο]ιησόμενον (lines 35–37), but it also supports Xenophon in stating that his mission was to Lysander, adding that Samos was his destination (lines 39–41).[151] Scholars generally agree that the author wrote in the fourth century B.C. and that five lines of the papyrus (5–9) are so close to the wording of Lysias (12.69) that they must depend on it. There is less agreement on

149 E. Schwartz, "Quellenuntersuchungen zur griechischen Geschichte," *RhM*, n.s., 44 (1889) 104–26, esp. 108–12; J. A. R. Munro, "Theramenes against Lysander," *CQ* 32 (1938) 18–26, esp. 21. The one dissenting note is that of R. Sealey, "Pap. Mich. Inv. 5982: Theramenes," *ZPE* 16 (1975) 279–88, esp. 286–287, who proposes the historically improbable compromise that Theramenes went to Sparta by way of Samos to negotiate with Lysander.

150 Lys. 13.9: περὶ τῆς εἰρήνης πρεσβευτὴν αὐτοκράτορα.

151 The *editio princeps* is that of R. Merkelbach and H. C. Youtie, "Ein Michigan-Papyrus über Theramenes," *ZPE* 2 (1968) 161–69. The most important discussions are: A. Henrichs, "Zur Interpretation des Michigan-Papyrus über Theramenes," *ZPE* 3 (1968) 101–8; A. Andrewes, "Lysias and the Theramenes Papyrus," *ZPE* 6 (1970) 35–38; C. San Clemente, "Teramene e un nuovo papiro di Karanis (Papiro Michigan, inv. 5982)," *Rend.Ist.Lomb.* 104 (1970) 202–18; and Sealey, "Pap. Mich. Inv. 5982." Lines 31–33 have been ingeniously restored by W. Luppe, "Die Lücke in der Theramenes-Rede des Michigan-Papyrus inv. 5982," *ZPE* 32 (1978) 14–16.

the question whether the author was a minor historian or a political pamphleteer, which is not germane to our inquiry.

We have two basic questions. What made the Athenians entrust Theramenes with such an important mission when only a few months earlier they had denied him at his *dokimasia* the generalship to which he had been elected? And what prompted them to do so at an Assembly meeting at which they passed Cleophon's motion to prohibit discussing peace on the ephors' terms? Since Xenophon gives no reasons whatever for Theramenes' appointment, we have to turn to Lysias's hostile account to glean from it what historical probability we can. Lysias makes Theramenes propose himself as "ambassador plenipotentiary concerning the peace," assuring the Assembly "that he would manage to prevent razing the walls and any other humiliation of the city and that he thought that he could also get some other good for the city from the Lacedaemonians."[152] Here, it seems to me, we get the beginnings of a plausible answer to our second question. Theramenes' promises complement rather than contravene Cleophon's motion; they add a positive, statesmanlike note to the decreed prohibition to discuss the ephors' terms. Like Cleophon, Theramenes rejects these terms, but rather than leave matters at that, he proposes to negotiate for better terms and thinks he is the man to conduct these negotiations, provided the Athenians give him a free hand. Moreover, so far Lysias's account does not contradict Xenophon's: it does make sense that such delicate negotiations should have begun somewhat informally, by sounding out a prominent Spartan official with no power of his own to conclude a peace treaty, before they were undertaken in earnest with the authorities in Sparta. The line between sounding out and negotiating is bound to be thin and vague, and Xenophon's language permits the interpretation that Theramenes proposed to discuss his own ideas about a possible treaty with him in an informal way. Moreover, the Athenians approved this mission in the knowledge that Theramenes' options would be limited by the provisions of Cleophon's decree.

But is it credible that Theramenes was appointed πρεσβευτὴς αὐτοκράτωρ for this purpose? Modern scholars believe not, because such powers had never before been given to an individual and famine

---

152 Lys. 13.9: ἐὰν αὐτὸν ἕλησθε περὶ τῆς εἰρήνης πρεσβευτὴν αὐτοκράτορα, ποιήσει ὥστε μήτε τῶν τειχῶν διελεῖν μήτε ἄλλο τὴν πόλιν ἐλαττῶσαι μηδέν· οἴοιτο δὲ καὶ ἄλλο τι ἀγαθὸν παρὰ Λακεδαιμονίων τῇ πόλει εὑρήσεσθαι.

had not yet made the Athenians desperate enough for peace.[153] Both of these arguments are strong, but neither is decisive. After Cleophon's decree had been passed, the Assembly would have been confronted with a stalemate; if no plans had been forthcoming, this would have resulted only in the indefinite continuation of the famine and the status quo. The famine increased in severity within the next three months, but that does not mean its effects were not already felt when Theramenes was sent to Lysander; nor does it prove Theramenes' delays aimed to compel Athens to accept the even less favorable conditions that according to Xenophon (*Hell.* 2.2.16) and Lysias (13.11; cf. 12.70) he really had in mind. Such motives are less likely to be historically true than to have been invented in a desire to malign the man who set the official seal on the defeat of Athens. So far as we know, Theramenes was the only man to offer any hope for better peace conditions and for putting an end to the famine. Should not the Assembly have given him a chance? To be sure, the price he put on his appointment was high, but it was the only price he could put on it, as the success of his mission depended upon his freedom to maneuver. Since the critical situation justified unusual measures, it is not inconceivable that the Athenians gave him what he asked for, relying on Cleophon's decree to tie his hands and on the knowledge that in the end any treaty would have to be validated by the vote of the sovereign people.[154]

These considerations are not yet adequate to provide an answer to our first question: would powers of this sort have been given to a man whose past career had been too ambivalent to deserve the full trust of at least the sector of the Athenian people that on this occasion had demanded the arrest of Archestratus and had supported Cleophon's motion? A partial answer can be found in some details surrounding his appointment given in the second passage from Lysias and in the Michigan papyrus. Even though Lysias's is the passage on which the Michigan papyrus doubtless depends,[155] the possibility remains that it is historically accurate. Lysias attests that Theramenes' prestige was high at this time and implies that therefore he was believed when he asserted he "had found an important

153   Henrichs, "Zur Interpretation" 105, accepted by Andrewes, "Lysias" 35. Cf. also D. J. Mosley, *Envoys and Diplomacy in Ancient Greece*, Historia Einzelschrift 22 (Wiesbaden, 1973) 30, 32, 35.

154   Cf. Xen. *Hell.* 2.2.17–22.

155   Demonstrated by Henrichs, "Zur Interpretation" 106.

and invaluable device" (πρᾶγμα ηὑρηκέναι μέγα καὶ πολλοῦ ἄξιον) to save the city and procure peace without giving hostages, tearing down walls, or surrendering ships. What this device was he would not tell, and Lysias (12.68–69) continues: "When many people spoke in opposition to Theramenes, though you knew that the rest of mankind keep secrets to mislead the enemy, whereas he was not willing to communicate to his own fellow citizens what he was going to tell the enemy, nonetheless you entrusted your country, your children, your wives, and yourselves to him." The thoughts Lysias here attributes to the Athenians become in the Michigan papyrus (lines 5–10) arguments used in the Assembly against Theramenes, against which he skillfully defends himself by pointing out that when the enemy has the upper hand, it is dangerous to discuss peace conditions thoughtlessly, since no enemy would agree to conditions less severe than those the vanquished propose; by keeping his plans secret, he says, the final decision about peace conditions will be reserved to the Athenians and not to others.[156] The speech convinced the *dēmos*, and Theramenes was elected ambassador plenipotentiary to negotiate for peace and departed for Samos and Lysander (lines 33–43).

This version makes the accounts of Xenophon and Lysias (13.9) even more convincing: Theramenes reinforces his promise to get better terms for peace by claiming to possess a secret weapon he cannot reveal to the Athenian public lest the disclosure be detrimental to Athenian interests. What made the Athenians believe him? The Michigan papyrus implies that his rhetorical acumen carried conviction. This may certainly have been one crucial factor in his success. We know that he was trained by Prodicus; and his role in establishing and then overthrowing the Four Hundred, in setting up the intermediate regime, prosecuting Antiphon, recalling Alcibiades, and, above all, condemning the Arginusae generals will have been largely due to his skill as a public speaker. Although this last had not redounded to his glory and may have been a cause for his rejection as general at his *dokimasia*, Lysias assures us that his election as πρεσβευτὴς αὐτοκράτωρ was partially due to his prestige.[157] Apparently his stature had increased again by the end of the year since the elections in the spring. One reason for that may have been

156 Pap. Mich. Inv. 5982.14–30.
157 Lys. 12.68: τιμώμενος δὲ καὶ τῶν μεγίστων ἀξιούμενος.

the return of exiles and reinstatement of disfranchised citizens after Aegospotami; and another, the dearth of strong political leaders. There simply was no one else of sufficient stature whom the Athenians could trust, and this may help to explain why they acceded to Theramenes' proposal.

Was Theramenes' "important and invaluable device" mere bluff, as Xenophon and Lysias imply, or was there substance to his promise? A recent suggestion has much to commend it, though it is merely conjectural: anticipating the death of Darius, Theramenes intended to use his perception of its probable consequences for the Greeks in private discussions with the most intelligent Spartan leader; he hoped thereby to get Athens conditions for peace more favorable than either obliteration or such terms as the ephors proposed.[158] This would explain why his stay with Lysander was protracted for three months and why negotiations broke off when it became clear that Darius would live longer than had been anticipated. Since the secret of Theramenes' device was well kept, Xenophon and Lysias had to infer Theramenes' motives from the effects his long stay inevitably had on Athens: because the famine had so weakened the Athenians during these three months that they would accept any conditions, our sources impute this effect as Theramenes' plan. On his return to Athens, Theramenes could explain his long absence only by saying that Lysander had "detained" him (Xen. *Hell*. 2.2.17); to admit that he had failed by miscalculating the death of Darius would have undermined popular confidence in him and would have led to disastrous consequences for himself.

The Athenians still trusted him when he returned in late February or early March 404 B.C. He was appointed ambassador plenipotentiary to lead a delegation of ten to Sparta to negotiate for peace (Xen. *Hell*. 2.2.17). But there is evidence that this trust was not universal and had been established by strong-arm methods. Unrest about the desirability of a peace procured by Theramenes will have erupted while he was with Lysander, and Callixenus, Theramenes' ally in the affair of the Arginusae generals, is likely to have escaped from detention at this time, when the opponents of peace had gained the upper hand.[159] But their dominance was short-lived. Cleophon's attacks on the Council, presumably for its favorable disposition toward peace, soon led to his arrest by two prominent councilors.

158   Krentz, *TA* 37–39.
159   Xen. *Hell*. 1.7.35 with n. 127 above.

One of them, Chremon, was soon to become a member of the Thirty; the other, Satyrus, "the most aggressive and shameless member of the Eleven," was later to arrest Theramenes at Critias's behest.[160] Cleophon was brought to trial on the trumped-up charge that he had been delinquent in his military duties,[161] and he was condemned to death under a procedure whose legality is doubtful because members of the Council were included among his jurors.[162] With Cleophon out of the way, the opposition to peace was weakened, and Theramenes' supporters, who will not have been well disposed toward the democracy, were riding high. There will have been little opposition to his dispatch to Sparta when he returned from Samos.

The peace conference at Sparta was attended by the member states of the Peloponnesian League as well as by representatives of Lysander, one of whom was the Athenian Aristoteles. One of Zeno's now-aging pupils, he was a former general and *hellēnotamias* who had joined the Four Hundred, had been active in the fortification of Eëtioneia, and had fled into exile after the overthrow of the Four Hundred, to emerge again at this time.[163] Lysander's purpose in sending him was, according to Xenophon, to dispel any doubts the ephors might cast upon his loyalty; he wanted it known that it was he who had impressed upon Theramenes that the authority to make peace and war belonged only to them. This shows that relations between Lysander and the ephors were not the best. But Aristoteles' presence as Lysander's representative will also have been a visible indication that Lysander no longer favored the obliteration of Athens, which was still being pressed by the Corinthian and Theban delegates (Xen. *Hell*. 2.2.19). Another purpose may have been to have Aristoteles persuade the Peloponnesians that if they would compel the Athenians to take back any exiles who had not yet returned (who would probably have been the most diehard opponents of popular sovereignty), Sparta could count on their cooperation once they reached home. A softening in Lysander's position may have resulted

---

160   Lys. 30.10–12 with Xen. *Hell*. 2.3.2 and 54.

161   Lys. 13.12. The formal charge was presumably ἀστρατείας; see Lipsius, *ARRV* 453 n. 5.

162   Lys. 30.11–13; 13.12. The procedure was probably similar to that stipulated in Andron's decree for the trial of Antiphon, Archeptolemus, and Onomacles on the charge of treason in 411/10 B.C., according to which up to ten councilors were to be members of the jury; see [Plut.] *X orat*. 833e–f.

163   Xen. *Hell*. 2.2.17–18. For Aristoteles, see above, pp. 393 with n. 197 and 404 with n. 237.

from his negotiations with Theramenes and may be reflected in the sentiments the Spartans expressed to counter the arguments of their allies: they refused "to enslave a Greek city that had rendered great service in the greatest dangers ever to befall Greece," an obvious reminder of the Persian Wars at a time when Theramenes may have warned Lysander of the fickleness of Persian support.[164] Yet the pressure of their allies and the fact that Athens was now on her knees made the Peloponnesians impose conditions more severe than the ephors had laid down earlier: the Long Walls and the fortifications of the Piraeus were to be torn down entirely; all ships except for a number to be determined by the Spartan commander on the spot were to be surrendered; all exiles were to be received back into Athens; the Athenians were to withdraw from all occupied cities; they were to have the same friends and enemies as the Lacedaemonians and to follow them wherever they might lead by land and sea; and they were to be governed under their ancestral constitution (*patrios politeia*).[165] Theramenes and his fellow ambassadors will have had little choice but to acquiesce in these conditions, which despite anything Xenophon or Lysias tells us cannot have been to their liking. Subsequent events suggest that the *patrios politeia* clause was wrung from the Peloponnesians and inserted into the treaty at Theramenes' insistence, presumably to preserve the autonomy of Athens in internal affairs and save it from decarchy, which Lysander was busy imposing on conquered Asian cities.

When Theramenes brought back these terms, there was relief in Athens that an end to death and famine was in sight. Still, the removal of Cleophon from the political scene had not stifled resistance. Some military men, including former generals and taxiarchs,

---

164   Xen. *Hell*. 2.2.20; cf. 6.5.35 and 46, Andoc. 1.142 and 3.21. Even more rhetorical is Justin 5.8.4: *negarunt se Spartani ex duobus Graeciae oculis alterum eruturos*. Lysander's influence on a more generous treatment of Athens is also attested by Polyaenus 1.45.5, where he is made to argue for the preservation of Athens as a buffer against Thebes.

165   This list appears in full in Xen. *Hell*. 2.2.20 and with minor variations in Diod. 13.107.4, Lys. 13.14, Andoc. 3.11–12 and 39, and Plut. *Lys*. 14.8. Controversial is only the *patrios politeia* clause, which is attested by Arist. *Ath.Pol*. 34.3 and Diod. 14.3.2; it is perhaps vaguely corroborated by Justin 5.8.5, who makes the acceptance of the Thirty part of the peace treaty. Against it speaks only the silence of Xenophon, Andocides, and Plutarch; see Hignett, *HAC* 285 with n. 2, and Fuks, *Ancestral Constitution* 52–61. That it formed, nevertheless, part of the treaty has been convincingly argued by W. J. McCoy, "Aristotle's *Athenaion Politeia* and the Establishment of the Thirty Tyrants," *YClS* 24 (1975) 131–45, esp. 136–39 with 136 n. 22.

protested against the terms Theramenes accepted.[166] Among them were the staunch democrat Strombichides, who had served with Leon and Diomedon in Samos in 412/11 B.C. and may have been deposed with them when the Four Hundred seized power;[167] Dionysodorus, whose murder by the Thirty became the occasion of Lysias's speech *Against Agoratus* (13); probably also an otherwise unknown Calliades;[168] and Nicias's younger brother Eucrates, who had been incriminated by Diocleides as a desecrator of the herms in 415 B.C., had been freed by Andocides' testimony, had served as general in Thrace in 412/11 B.C., and had again been appointed general after Aegospotami.[169] Although since he was well connected with those upper-class circles who were plotting to establish an oligarchy he could according to Lysias have become a member of the Thirty if he had wished, he preferred to live up to his convictions and opposed the peace (Lys. 18.4–5).

The opposition was quickly silenced. The Council seized one of the protesters, Agoratus, and compelled him to reveal the names of those generals and taxiarchs who were opposed to the peace and to lay information against them (note the irony) for "plotting against the democracy."[170] Those denounced were arrested and imprisoned pending trial. But meanwhile the Assembly had accepted the Spartan terms for peace; before they could be tried, the treaty had been implemented, and the Thirty were in control of the city.[171]

---

166   Lys. 13.13 and 16; cf. Xen. *Hell*. 2.2.22: ἀντειπόντων δέ τινων αὐτῷ.

167   See above, p. 347 and nn. 38–39, and p. 381.

168   Lys. 30.14. He may be identical with the Calliades who takes the place of Erasinides in Diodorus's list of generals at Arginusae (13.101.5).

169   See Appendix C, pp. 545–46.

170   Lys. 13.17–33; for the charge, see ibid, 48: μηνύσας αὐτοὺς [τῇ πόλει] ἐπιβουλεύειν τῷ πλήθει τῷ ὑμετέρῳ. Cf. 51 and 84.

171   Lys. 13.17 makes it clear that the denunciations took place before the Assembly ratified the peace; however, Agoratus's testimony before the Assembly meeting in the theater at Munychia (ibid. 32) will have been given after the ratification but before Lysander sailed into the Piraeus for the surrender (34). A chronological problem is posed by Xenophon's assertion that the peace proposals were presented on the day after Theramenes' return from Sparta and apparently immediately ratified by the Assembly (*Hell*. 2.2.22), which would leave very little time for Agoratus's denunciations. For that reason, some modern scholars, most recently G. A. Lehmann, "Die revolutionäre Machtergreifung der 'Dreissig' und die staatliche Teilung Attikas (404–401/0 v. Chr.)," *Antike und Universalgeschichte. Festschrift H. E. Stier* (Münster, 1972) 201–33, esp. 210–12, and Rhodes, *CAAP* 428, date the denunciations after the surrender of Athens. However, I am convinced by the arguments of Krentz, *TA* 43 with n. 35, that Lysias's account can be accepted.

CHAPTER NINE

The Second Oligarchical Challenge and Its Failure

POLITICS AFTER THE PEACE

When Lysander sailed into the Piraeus to accept the surrender of Athens on 16 Mounichion 404 B.C., that is, about late March,[1] and the dismantling of the walls was begun to the accompaniment of flutes and all but twelve ships were handed over to him,[2] the Council that had condemned Cleophon was still in office. Its determination to get peace was strengthened by the exiles who returned with—or soon after—Lysander. Primarily members of the upper classes, they had sought or had been driven into exile after the fall of the Four Hundred and had, therefore, no kind feelings for democracy (Arist. *Ath.Pol.* 34.3).

Among them was certainly Aristoteles, a former pupil of Zeno's now between sixty and sixty-five years old, who had been largely responsible for building the fort at Eëtioneia under the Four Hundred and had attended the peace conference at Sparta as Lysander's representative.[3] There will also have been two younger intellectuals who had been prominent in establishing the Four Hundred: Pythodorus (once a pupil of Protagoras's), who had moved the appointment of the thirty *syngrapheis* in 411 B.C. and had himself become a member of the Four Hundred,[4] and Melobius, who had vanished

---

1 Plut. *Lys.* 15.1. For the Julian equivalent, see the discussion in *HCT* 4.11–12 and Krentz, *TA* 32 n. 8.

2 Xen. *Hell.* 2.2.20, 23; Lys. 13.34 and 46, 18.5; Plut. *Lys.* 15.1.

3 See above, pp. 393 with n. 197, 404 with n. 237, and 457 with n. 163.

4 See above, p. 369 with n. 128, and below, Appendix B, pp. 532–33 with nn. 19–22. Since nothing is heard of Pythodorus between 411 B.C. and his appointment

from the scene after he delivered the keynote address advocating the replacement of democracy by the Four Hundred in 411 B.C. and reemerged as one of the Thirty in 404/3 B.C.[5] Mnasilochus, archon under the Four Hundred and not heard of again until he became one of the Thirty, is also likely to have returned from exile at this time.[6] Onomacles, one of the antidemocratic generals on Samos in 412/11 B.C., who had been charged with treason along with Antiphon and Archeptolemus for negotiating peace with Sparta but had escaped before his trial, also surfaces again as a member of the Thirty.[7] One of the more remarkable returnees after the peace was Charicles, whom we mentioned as the brother-in-law of Teisias, general at Melos.[8] His early history does not suggest the importance he was to assume under the Thirty, second only to that of Critias. Like Peisander, whose fellow councilor and investigator (*zētētēs*) he had been in the turmoil of 415 B.C., he is described as a staunch democrat at that time (Andoc. 1.36). A year later he was a general, leading a squadron of thirty ships against the Peloponnese together with Demosthenes (Thuc. 7.20, 26; Diod. 13.9.2). When and under what circumstances he joined the oligarchical movement of 411 B.C. we do not know; all we do know is that he spent some years—and these can only have been the years from 411/10 to 404/3 B.C.— quietly in exile and on his return "maltreated the city."[9] If we can infer back from his prominence among the Thirty, he may have been exiled for membership in or close association with the Four Hundred; he and Critias are described as the Thirty's extremist leaders by sources as disparate in their outlook as Andocides (1.101), Lysias (12.55), Xenophon (*Hell.* 2.3.2; *Mem.* 1.2.31), and Aristotle (*Pol.* 5.6, 1305^{b}26).

---

to the archonship by the Thirty (Xen. *Hell.* 2.3.1), it is likely that he spent the intervening time in exile. Arist. *Ath.Pol.* 35.1 suggests that the Thirty were established when Pythodorus was already archon; but since he also states that the Thirty established πεντακοσίους βουλευτὰς καὶ τὰς ἄλλας ἀρχὰς ἐκ προκρίτων τῶν χιλίων (cf. Xen. *Hell.* 2.3.11), it is likely that Xenophon's report of his appointment by the Thirty is correct.

5   Arist. *Ath.Pol.* 29.1 and Harp. s.v. Μηλόβιος with p. 369 with n. 126 above; Xen. *Hell.* 2.3.2; Lys. 12.12–20.

6   See above, pp. 399 with n. 212 and 404 with n. 237; Xen. *Hell.* 2.3.2.

7   See above, pp. 347 with nn. 42–43, 393 with n. 195, 401–2; Xen. *Hell.* 2.3.2.

8   See above, p. 311 with n. 68.

9   Isoc. 16.42, καὶ φεύγων μὲν ἡσυχίαν εἶχε, κατελθὼν δὲ κακῶς ἐποίει τὴν πόλιν, with MacDowell, *Andokides* 87.

Two of the known returnees in 404/3 B.C. had not been in exile for membership in the Four Hundred. It is generally believed that the Sophocles among the Thirty is identical with the general in Sicily in 426/5 and 425/4 B.C. who was recalled together with his colleagues Pythodorus and Eurymedon for having acquiesced in the settlement of Gela and was punished with exile at his *euthyna*.[10] Since we hear nothing of him thereafter until he appears as one of the Thirty (Xen. *Hell.* 2.3.2), the resentment against the democracy that had banished him may have kept him abroad until 404/3 B.C.[11] The other returnee was Critias, whom Cleophon had consigned to exile after Alcibiades' fall from favor in Thessaly.[12]

In the sense that Critias is the only member of the Thirty whose writings have survived even in fragments, we have more information about him than about any of his colleagues. And yet he remains enigmatic. What is known of his life before 404/3 B.C. is personal rather than political in nature.[13] It is no surprise that a member of one of the oldest Athenian families, a man related by marriage to other old Athenian families, should have been implicated, however unjustly, in the desecration of the herms. Critias's family connections will have drawn him inevitably into those upper-class circles whose younger members constituted the core of the *hetaireiai* and *synōmosiai* generally suspected of that impiety. Since he was born about 460 B.C., he will have been older than most of the others accused in 415 B.C., yet his sophistic training will have given him more in common with them than with their elders. If Plato's dramatic dates can be trusted, his first appearance in intellectual circles precedes his first public notice by some fifteen years. In 433 B.C. he entered Callias's house in company with Alcibiades and just behind Socrates to listen to Protagoras; a year later he sat next to Socrates (who had just returned from Potidaea) and introduced his young cousin Charmides to him (*Prt.* 316a; *Chrm.* 153c, 155a–b). A few years after that he is said to have been enthralled by Gorgias (Philostr. *VS* 1.9). A

---

10   See above, Chap. 1, n. 248 (Case 6) and p. 314 with n. 81.
11   See Gilbert, *Beiträge* 291.
12   See above, p. 431 with n. 80.
13   Since references to various facts now to be discussed are given above, pp. 402–3 with nn. 226–31, 428 with n. 65, and 431 with n. 80, and below, Appendix C, pp. 542–43 with nn. 29–30, the following will be only sparingly annotated. For an entirely different and more conjectural interpretation of the evidence on Critias's life, see G. Adeleye, "Critias: From 'Moderation' to 'Radicalism'," *Mus.Afr.* 6 (1977–78) 64–73.

little before this time he will have begun his close association with Socrates, which he maintained for nearly the rest of his life. It is attested not only by Plato's making him one of Socrates' interlocutors in the *Charmides*, *Timaeus*, and *Critias* (as also in the pseudo-Platonic *Eryxias*) but especially by Xenophon's effort to clear Socrates of any guilt by association with Critias and Alcibiades.[14] If we can trust dates that Xenophon's apologetics may have inspired, this association will have flourished in the late 430s and through the 420s; we are told that it petered out when Critias and Alcibiades opted for political careers (Xen. *Mem*. 1.2.15–16, 39).

The wide range of literary, rhetorical, and philosophical writings attested for Critias—from occasional poems to tragedies and from prose and verse studies of societies (*politeiai*) to introductions to public speeches (Δημηγορικὰ προοίμια)—will have spanned his entire adult life.[15] Though the fragments show little originality, they reveal the extensive learning and interests of an enlightened belletristic gentleman. But it is difficult to extract systematic thought from them, especially since we now know that the longest and most valuable fragment, the speech from the *Sisyphus*, is better assigned to Euripides.[16] Already in antiquity he was called "an amateur among philosophers and a philosopher among amateurs."[17] Like Antiphon and Charmides,[18] he kept aloof from political activity and the law courts well into his middle age; nothing is heard of him in contemporary literature, not even in Aristophanes, before 415 B.C. Perhaps his intellect and temperament made the people view him too, like them, with suspicion and in turn alienated him from Athenian society.

Critias kept distant from politics during the oligarchy of the Four Hundred. Although there is some evidence that he sympathized with the diehards who built Eëtioneia to let the Spartans into the Piraeus, the fact that he did not go into exile after the overthrow of the Four Hundred suggests he was not active among them.[19] However, we may have in this sympathy the first inkling of a desire to

---

14   Xen. *Mem*. 1.2.12–16, 24–39; cf. Aeschin. 1.173, who asserts that Socrates was killed for having been Critias's teacher.

15   These are collected in DK⁶ 88 and discussed by D. Stephans, "Critias: Life and Literary Remains" (Ph. D. diss., University of Cincinnati, 1939) chaps. 2–5.

16   See above, p. 281 with n. 315.

17   Schol. Pl. *Ti*. 20a: ἰδιώτης μὲν ἐν φιλοσόφοις, φιλόσοφος δ' ἐν ἰδιώταις.

18   See Thuc. 8.68.1; Xen. *Mem*. 3.7.

19   See above, p. 403 with n. 229.

translate into political reality the admiration of things Spartan that he will have shared with many of the upper-class young of his time.[20] In any event the fragments of his two works on the constitution of the Lacedaemonians (88B6–9, 32–37 DK[6]), one in verse and one in prose, make it abundantly clear that his admiration was evoked first and foremost by Spartan social customs in drinking, moral maxims, clothing, and the like; no discussion of their political institutions or organization has been preserved, and the tone of what survives makes it unlikely that there was any. This suggests that his attachment to Sparta was personal and sentimental rather than political and practical, an impression his public conduct confirms.

His earliest known public act, his vengeful motion to exhume the bones of Phrynichus (with whom one would have thought Critias should have sympathized for trying to negotiate peace with Sparta) can be explained as an act of irrational passion to take revenge on the man for opposing his friend Alcibiades' recall in 412/11 B.C.[21] Similarly, his motion to recall Alcibiades, made probably two years after Theramenes' to the same effect had been approved but not carried out, seems to have aimed to rehabilitate his friend rather than to benefit the state, since we know of no interest in politics on Critias's part at this time.[22] That Alcibiades' fall from favor after Notium should have led to Critias's exile occasions no surprise either, and Cleophon may have moved it either because of Critias's attachment to Alcibiades or because of his love for Sparta.[23] But a question remains: why did Critias not join Alcibiades in Thrace but rather go to Thessaly? An answer could contain an important clue to Critias's development into a politician, but there is no answer. One may argue that his departure for Thessaly speaks against attachment to Alcibiades as a motive for the recall or speculate that the two grew estranged after meeting again in Athens. But the truth remains that we simply do not know. Even more difficult to interpret are Critias's alleged activities in Thessaly. Our only specific source is the statement in Theramenes' hostile speech that "with Prometheus he fomented democracy and armed the *penestai* against their masters,"[24] an

20 See above, pp. 235–36 with nn. 140–41, and Ehrenberg, *People*[2] 102.
21 See above, p. 403.
22 See above, p. 428 with n. 65. A personal motive is suggested by the epigram in Plut. *Alc*. 33.1.
23 See above, p. 431 with n. 80.
24 Xen. *Hell*. 2.3.36: ἀλλ᾽ ἐν Θετταλίᾳ μετὰ Προμηθέως δημοκρατίαν κατεσκεύαζε καὶ τοὺς πενέστας ὥπλιζεν ἐπὶ τοὺς δεσπότας. Wade-Gery, *Essays* 280–81, associates

unlikely activity for so ardent an enemy of democracy and admirer of Sparta. Wade-Gery ingeniously attempts to solve the paradox by assigning to Critias the speech *On the Constitution*, traditionally attributed to Herodes, and by arguing that Critias at this time favored a hoplite democracy along the lines of the intermediate constitution at Athens in 411/10 B.C.[25] This is difficult to accept; we have no hint anywhere that Critias ever favored the intermediate regime or that any political principles he may have had were strong enough to turn him into a missionary for any cause while in exile. It would be much easier to accept the late testimony of Philostratus (*VS* 1.16), unsupported though it is by any other source, that he made oligarchies in Thessaly more oppressive by maligning the Athenians and democracy in general in his conversations with those in power. There is, however, one indication that the sojourn in Thessaly was traumatic for Critias: Xenophon's tendentious and simple-minded claim that it took him away from Socrates and brought him into contact with "men more conversant with lawless conduct than with righteousness" (*Mem*. 1.2.24) may well hide a general contemporary conviction that his exile politicized him. Lysias's assertion that the initial program of the Thirty was "to purge the city of unjust men and to turn the rest of the citizens to goodness and justice"[26] is the more credible in coming from a hostile source and has in addition the support of Plato (*Ep*. 7.324d) and Aristotle (*Ath.Pol*. 35.2–3). If, as we can safely assume, Critias was prominent in formulating their goal, we can regard this as evidence of a strong puritanical streak in him. That may well have outraged any sense of social justice in his emotional nature when he saw the condition of the *penestai* in Thessaly; it may have prompted him to use his rhetorical talents in the service of the movement Prometheus headed against local potentates. Once discovered on alien soil, these talents could later be employed to bring about what he envisaged as a moral regeneration of Athens when he returned from exile.

---

this with an agrarian revolt against the Aleuadae at Larisa, attested in Arist. *Pol*. 3.2, 1275[b]25–30; C. Mossé, *La Tyrannie dans la Grèce antique* (Paris, 1969) 122 n. 3, thinks of an insurrection against Lycophron of Pherae. Cf. also the suggestion of Stephans, "Critias" 38 that "Prometheus" may be a nickname of Jason or Lycophron of Pherae.

25 Wade-Gery, *Essays* 271–92, esp. 280–82.

26 Lys. 12.5: φάσκοντες χρῆναι τῶν ἀδίκων καθαρὰν ποιῆσαι τὴν πόλιν καὶ τοὺς λοιποὺς πολίτας ἐπ᾽ ἀρετὴν καὶ δικαιοσύνην τραπέσθαι.

Regarding these eight men as representative of those who returned from exile after the peace in 404/3 B.C., we can draw the following general conclusions. Most of the repatriates were members of the upper classes who had one reason or another to be hostile to the democracy. None except Critias had been implicated in the desecrations of 415 B.C., but six had shown their antipathy to democracy by joining the Four Hundred in 411 B.C.[27] Some, like Sophocles, may have resented being unjustly condemned at their *euthynai*. Most had held public office in the past. The oldest among them, Aristoteles and Critias, will have been between fifty-five and sixty; the rest can be assumed from their earliest known tenure of office to have been in their forties, so that their most impressionable, formative years will have fallen in the 420s. For four of them—Aristoteles, Critias, Pythodorus, and Melobius—there are good reasons to believe that they were trained or at least influenced by the sophists.

On their return to Athens the exiles found like-minded men among those who had never been banished or had returned earlier. The Thirty could count on at least one thousand supporters, some of whom they appointed to a Council of Five Hundred and to the various magistracies (Arist. *Ath.Pol.* 35.1). We know many of their names; none of them (except Theramenes, a special case) had been as prominent in the past as the known returnees. The majority are mere names to us. Still, some interesting facts emerge about the few who can be identified with any confidence. If the Dracontides who made the motion to appoint the Thirty and became subsequently one of them[28] is the same man who is mentioned in Aristophanes' *Wasps* and in the *Sophists* of Plato Comicus as involved in many lawsuits (with the verdict usually going against him; Ar. *Vesp.* 157 with schol.), he may well have been a pupil of a sophist. Charmides, who became one of the Ten in the Piraeus and lost his life in the fighting there, was Critias's cousin and like him associated with Socrates and Protagoras. Whether or not he is the Charmides who was denounced by Agariste in 415 B.C. for holding one of the profanations of the Mysteries at his house, he will have moved in the same circles

---

27 This fairly large percentage lends some support to Lysias's statement at 13.74 that the Thirty and their Council had all been members of the Four Hundred who fled after their overthrow. Needless to say, the statement cannot be taken literally, since the five hundred councilors and the Thirty add up to 530.

28 Arist. *Ath.Pol.* 34.3; Lys. 12.73. Cf. Xen. *Hell.* 2.3.2 and Harp. s.v. Δρακοντίδης.

as his cousin and guardian and shared his political sympathies.[29] The
Teisias who was to become a councilor under the Thirty is presumably identical with Alcibiades' friend who married Charicles' sister
and had been a general in the Melian campaign in 416 B.C.[30] Erasistratus's upper-class origins and possible sophistic training are suggested by his association with Critias in the pseudo-Platonic *Eryxias*
and by his probably being the nephew of Phaeax, the ambassador to
Leontini in 422 B.C. who was said to have been involved in the
intrigues surrounding the ostracism of Hyperbolus.[31] The tragic
poet Theognis should probably also be counted among the intellectuals. He will have been somewhat older than the four we have
mentioned so far, since he was prominent enough in 425 B.C. to have
been a butt to Aristophanes for his frigid compositions.[32] Nothing is
known of his politics, but his preoccupation with measures against
the metics under the Thirty may reflect a xenophobic desire to keep
Athens for the Athenians.[33]

Among those who cannot be counted as intellectuals we know
most about Eratosthenes. All our information derives from his
personal and political enemy Lysias, but the facts he mentions belie
much of the abuse he piles upon him. He was a trierarch in
412/11 B.C., probably one of those who were stationed on Samos; he
favored Peisander's designs to abolish the democracy in order to
obtain Persian aid through Alcibiades, and when negotiations with
Alcibiades had broken down he joined those who were willing to go
through with the planned revolution anyway.[34] There is no evidence
to suggest that he ever became a member of the Four Hundred:[35]
Lysias says no more than that he tried to establish oligarchy in the
army at the time of the Four Hundred and that he left his ship and
fled from the Hellespont back to Athens together with Iatrocles
(otherwise unknown) and others (Lys. 12.42). This probably happened after the fleet had rejected the oligarchy at home and had
elected Thrasybulus and Thrasyllus as its generals, and the defection
may have taken place after the indecisive battle off Byzantium
(Thuc. 8.80.4). What he did thereafter until he became one of the

29 See below, Appendix C, p. 545 with nn. 56–59.
30 See above, pp. 310–11.
31 Xen. *Hell*. 2.3.2 with [Pl.] *Erx*. 392a and p. 233 above.
32 Ar. *Ach*. 11 with schol. and 140; *Thesm*. 170.
33 Xen. *Hell*. 2.3.2; Lys. 12.6, 13–15.
34 See above, pp. 351–53; Thuc. 8.63.3–4.
35 Against Davies, *APF* 184.

five ephors who organized the overthrow of the democracy in 404/3 B.C. is unknown. Although he became one of the Thirty, he had close ties to Theramenes; he was not deposed (as all but one of his colleagues were) after the fighting in the Piraeus, and he stayed in Athens after the amnesty: all these are indications that he was no extremist. Lysias's impassioned prosecution of him for his brother's murder seems to have ended in acquittal.[36] The antidemocratic tendencies of Satyrus and Chremon—the latter became a member of the Thirty, and the former was to be Critias's henchman as one of the Eleven—are shown by their obtaining as councilors the trial and conviction of Cleophon after Aegospotami.[37] Nothing of political significance is known about the prehistory of Eucleides, who had held some religious office in 420/19 B.C. before serving as general at Eretria in 410/09 and as secretary of the Council in 408/7 B.C.;[38] nor of Chaereleos, who may have been a guardian of the temple of Poseidon Hippios in 413/12 and 412/11 B.C.;[39] nor either of Theogenes, who may be identical with an ambassador to Persia in 408 B.C.[40] The remaining members of the Thirty and their administration are only names.[41]

The six months between the conclusion of the peace in March and the appointment of the Thirty in September 404 B.C.[42] were a period of intense political activity. There are some faint indications that the usual elections for magistrates for 404/3 B.C. had not taken place in the precarious circumstances surrounding Theramenes' peace negotiations and that the Areopagus had been entrusted with or taken over the conduct of affairs.[43] Not until Pythodorus's election as

---

36 Lys. 12.43, 48, 53–54; Xen. *Hell*. 2.3.2. See Blass, *AB*[2] 1. 542–43.

37 See above, pp. 456–57 with nn. 160–62.

38 *IG* I[3] 473.8; ML, no. 84.17; *IG* I[3] 110.3–4.

39 *IG* I[3] 405.2, 16, 26.

40 Xen. *Hell*. 1.3.13; but this is highly uncertain, since Kirchner, *PA*, lists over forty men of this name. Similarly, the identification of Diocles is made impossible by the fact that *PA* lists eighty-nine.

41 Much of the preceding discussion is indebted to D. Whitehead, "The Tribes of the Thirty Tyrants," *JHS* 100 (1980) 208–13, and to Krentz, *TA* 52–56.

42 For recent arguments for this date, see Krentz, *TA* 147–52.

43 See G. Colin, *Xénophon historien d'après le livre II des Helléniques (hiver 406/5 à 401/0)* (Paris, 1933) 36. The only indication that the Areopagus had taken over is the enigmatic phrase πραττούσης μὲν τῆς ἐν Ἀρείῳ πάγῳ βουλῆς σωτήρια, Lys. 12.69; though Lysias associates this with his confused narrative of Theramenes' appointment as πρεσβευτὴς αὐτοκράτωρ, it may conceivably refer to the time before Pythodorus's election as archon. The tasks assigned to the Areopagus by Teisamenus's decree a year later (Andoc. 1.84) provide a parallel to this hypothesis.

archon, when the Thirty were already installed in power, did the administration of the city have some semblance of regularity.[44]

We saw reason to believe that at Theramenes' urging a clause had been inserted into the peace treaty to stipulate that the Athenians were to be governed under their *patrios politeia*. The purpose of this clause will have been to protect Athens against the kind of internal interference in which Lysander was indulging in the Greek cities in the East and was, as Fuks has rightly stressed, "the normal guarantee on the part of Sparta not to interfere in Athens' domestic affairs, it was not an instruction to adopt any definite constitution."[45] Aristotle informs us (*Ath.Pol.* 34.3) that three groups worked for the implementation of this clause, each in the light of its own political preference. The populists (*dēmotikoi*) wanted to preserve the established democracy. The upper classes fell into two groups: one of these, consisting of the returned exiles and those organized in *hetaireiai*, desired oligarchy; the other, consisting of the most reputable citizens who were not members of *hetaireiai*, sought to establish the "ancestral constitution." Theramenes is said to have been the leader of this last group, and Archinus, Anytus, and Cleitophon are named among its members. Diodorus also singles out Theramenes in a slightly different way, not naming any other factional leader (14.3.3); he speaks, however, of only two factions, one oligarchical and the other favoring "the constitution of their fathers, which they declared to be by common consent democracy." Theramenes emerges as the spokesman for the latter only in Diodorus's report on the constitutional assembly (14.3.6), about which more will be said presently.

The reliability of this account has been questioned by some modern scholars because no other source mentions either the *patrios politeia* clause of the peace treaty or Theramenes' subsequent championing of the *patrios politeia*. Ephorus (whose account of these events Diodorus followed) and Aristotle, it is argued, drew their information from a source, often identified as Androtion, who was intent on whitewashing Theramenes' involvement and tried to dissociate him from the oligarchy. Toward this end the source dated Theramenes' break with the oligarchs before the establishment of

---

44 See above, n. 4. The possibility that Xen. *Hell.* 2.3.1, ἐν ὀλιγαρχίᾳ ᾑρέθη, may be part of an interpolation does not prevent it from being historically accurate.

45 See above, pp. 457–58 with n. 164; cf. Fuks, *Ancestral Constitution* 61.

the Thirty instead of several months after their installation, when (it is claimed) it actually occurred.[46] However, bias is not proven to be devoid of historical fact by the discovery of its cause. The source or sources Aristotle and Ephorus may have used for a more sympathetic picture of Theramenes than others drew of him need not have invented facts but may merely have been selective in presenting them or in emphasizing actions that showed him in a favorable light while suppressing anything unfavorable. The source may like Aristotle have failed to mention Theramenes' membership in the Thirty, or it may have whitewashed unpleasant facts, as Ephorus does when he explains Theramenes' election among the Thirty as the people's attempt to check the excesses (πλεονεξία, Diod. 14.4.1) of his colleagues. The allegation of bias is not sufficient grounds on which to reject Theramenes' championing of the *patrios politeia*.

On the contrary, since other sources corroborate Aristotle's account of factionalism after the conclusion of peace, there is no reason to reject his contention that Theramenes and his associates wanted a return to what they conceived to be the *patrios politeia* in order to fill a vacuum temporarily filled by the Areopagus. Theramenes will have had little patience with the generals and taxiarchs who were dissatisfied with the terms of the peace.[47] Similarly, he will not have had much sympathy for those of the returned exiles, many of them officeholders, who had become disenchanted with the democracy and in many cases admired everything Spartan. Since he had joined no conspiracy (*synōmosia*) in 411 B.C., he will not have looked with favor on the oligarchs, who (as we know from Lysias 12.43–44) were preparing for political action through their social clubs, the *hetaireiai*, as they had in 411 B.C. How early these formulated their ideas about the kind of oligarchy they wanted to establish we do not know, and it is only an informed guess that the Laconophile intellectual Critias was prominent in developing them. The choice of Sparta as the model will have been clear to those who knew that a conspiracy was headed by five "ephors," on which board the returnees as well as the domestic opponents of the democracy were represented—we know that Critias and Eratosthenes were among them—and that these in turn had designated phylarchs to

46   The most prominent exponent of this view is Fuks, *Ancestral Constitution* 52–79, esp. 59–63. The extreme consequences of this position were drawn by Walters, "Ancestral Constitution" 137.

47   See above, pp. 458–59.

influence the tribes when measures were to be voted or magistrates were to be appointed (Lys. 12.43–44). Though these political action committees must have been secret, it is far from inconceivable that their professed aims were what Diodorus says they were, namely, "to revive the ancient system whereby very few assumed the leadership of the community as a whole."[48]

Theramenes may have been indecisive and a reluctant follower of Aristocrates in his opposition to the Four Hundred,[49] but he could not afford to waffle about implementing the peace he had negotiated. He had never favored a democracy in which pay for office was the main incentive for public service and in which sovereignty was vested in all, regardless of their ability "to serve with their fortunes and their persons."[50] When he had been unable to make his convictions stick in 410 B.C., he had left Athens to join Alcibiades and Thrasybulus in the Hellespontine war, and his relation to the democracy at home remained as frigid as theirs. To the best of our knowledge, he did not return to Athens until after Arginusae; he then attacked the generals (to save his own skin), which won him immediate success but also alienated enough people to overturn at his *dokimasia* his election as general for 405/4 B.C. But this reverse was only temporary. Thanks to his sophistic oratorical training and to his uncanny ability to land on his feet, Theramenes had become the chief negotiator plenipotentiary of the peace with Sparta. His efforts evoked the opposition of some members of the democratic establishment and the suspicions of others, yet his prestige was still great enough to make people heed him.[51] Since under the circumstances he had no choice but to defend the peace, especially if he was responsible for the *patrios politeia* clause, there seems no good reason to reject the contention of Aristotle and Diodorus that the reestablishment of the *patrios politeia* became his political slogan—even if Aristotle's wording gives the impression that only the Therameneans worked to restore the ancestral constitution. We are not told precisely what the substantive content was, although it is

48 Diod. 14.3.3: τὴν παλαιὰν κατάστασιν δεῖν ἀνανεοῦσθαι, καθ' ἣν παντελῶς ὀλίγοι τῶν ὅλων προειστήκεισαν.
49 See above, pp. 390–94.
50 See above, pp. 365–66.
51 For the opposition, see above, pp. 458–59; the suspicions are amply attested in Lys. 12.62–67, 13.9–14; and his prestige, in Lys. 12.64: νῦν δὲ ὁρῶ τάς τε ἀπολογίας εἰς ἐκεῖνον ἀναφερομένας, τούς τ' ἐκείνῳ συνόντας τιμᾶσθαι πειρωμένους, ὥσπερ πολλῶν ἀγαθῶν αἰτίου ἀλλ' οὐ μεγάλων κακῶν γεγενημένου.

reasonable to infer from Theramenes' political program in 410 B.C. and from his actions and defense speech in 404/3 B.C. that it included the abolition of pay for office and the restriction of the franchise to those able to serve with their fortunes and persons, that is, to the hoplites and upper classes. But his association at this time with Archinus, Anytus, Cleitophon, and Phormisius, none of whom became a member of the Thirty, makes it abundantly clear that Theramenes had no part in the machinations of the returned exiles and their *hetairoi* (Arist. *Ath. Pol.* 34.3).

The careers of these four associates of Theramenes indicate that all were members of the upper classes who shared in various degrees and for different reasons an aversion to the popular sovereignty practiced under the democracy but who stopped short of wanting to abolish democracy in favor of oligarchy. Cleitophon's motives are likely to have been those of a principled intellectual. He had been a friend of Socrates and Thrasymachus, and Euripides claims him and Theramenes as disciples in Aristophanes' *Frogs* (967). We saw that his amendment to Pythodorus's motion in 411 B.C., requiring "the *patrioi nomoi* that Cleisthenes had enacted when he established the democracy" to be taken into consideration in drafting proposals for constitutional reforms, was intended to ease Pythodorus's planned restrictions on popular sovereignty, and we suggested that he may have acted as a spokesman for Theramenes on that occasion.[52]

Anytus's support for the Therameneans at this time will have been motivated more by practical considerations than by principles. We learn from Plato's *Meno* that he was the wealthy son of an unassuming, respectable self-made man and that he loathed the sophists and all they stood for, being convinced that they corrupted the young, although he had never associated with them; it can be inferred from what little is said about him in the *Apology* that this was why he became one of Socrates' chief accusers.[53] Antagonism to the sophists may be one reason he did not join—and presumably was not even tempted to join—the oligarchs in 404 B.C. However, his prominence after the fall of the Thirty makes it difficult to see why he did not join the democratic faction in 404 B.C.[54] Possibly his wealth and his connections with the upper classes made him frown on the idea of

52   See above, pp. 371–72.
53   Pl. *Meno* 90a–b, 91c–92c; *Ap.* 18b, 23e. Cf. also Diod. 14.37.7; Isoc. 11 hypoth.; D. L. 2.38.
54   Isoc. 18.23; Pl. *Meno* 90b; cf. Xen. *Ap.* 29.

pay for public service, especially at a time when public funds were needed for rebuilding the Athenian economy.[55] Some facts of his generalship earlier in the decade may help explain his attitude in 404 B.C. D. M. Lewis has presented cogent reasons for dating his mission to Pylos with thirty ships not in 409/8 B.C., as Diodorus (13.64.6) has it, but a year earlier.[56] This means that Anytus was elected general under the intermediate regime, suggesting a relation to Theramenes six years before it is attested. Further, we learn that his failure to reach his destination because of storms off Cape Malea resulted in a trial for treason, at which he ensured acquittal by bribing the jury.[57] Regardless of whether it is true that he was the first ever to bribe a jury in Athens and regardless of any difficulty in understanding how he may have gone about it with so many jurors involved, the allegation not only attests his wealth but also suggests that he may have believed it impossible to obtain justice in a democratic jury court in any other way. In other words, the story may reflect his disenchantment with the judicial process of the Athenian democracy, and this in turn may explain why his idea of the *patrios politeia* was closer to Theramenes' than the democratic establishment's. In any event, unlike Theramenes, he did not become one of the Thirty and was in fact among their exiled opponents with Thrasybulus at Phyle. There, according to Lysias, he displayed a remarkable sense of fairness in preventing the murder of Agoratus.[58] His appearance as a witness in Andocides' behalf in 400 B.C. (Andoc. 1.150) and as a spokesman for the artisans and democratic politicians in the prosecution of Socrates a year later (Pl. *Ap.* 23e) seem to indicate his lack of partisanship after the restoration of the democracy.

Less is known about Phormisius and Archinus. Aristophanes treats Phormisius as one who hankered after the good old times before the democracy went out of hand;[59] after the fall of the Thirty and his return from exile, his motion to restrict citizenship also reflects such an attitude to landowners (Dion. Hal. *Lys.* 32). This motion may indicate opposition to Thrasybulus, who had proposed that citizen-

55   For his wealth and social connections, including the allegation that he had been Alcibiades' lover, see Davies, *APF* 40–41.

56   D. M. Lewis, *Sparta and Persia* (Leiden, 1977) 126 n. 112; cf. also MacDowell, *Andokides* 166.

57   Diod. 13.64.6; Arist. *Ath.Pol.* 27.5; Plut. *Cor.* 14.6; schol. Aeschin. 1.87; Harp. s.v. δεκάζων.

58   Xen. *Hell.* 2.3.42, 44; Lys. 13.78, 82.

59   Ar. *Ran.* 965 with Didymus's scholion; cf. also *Eccl.* 97.

ship be granted to all who had returned from the Piraeus, a measure that would have enfranchised a thousand foreigners; it is noteworthy in this respect that Phormisius is not mentioned among the exiles who had joined Thrasybulus at Phyle. Archinus, however, who is known to have been a leader both at Phyle and in the return of the exiles and who is praised for his moderating influence in the reconciliation after the return,[60] also opposed Thrasybulus's motion by lodging a *graphē paranomōn* against it.[61] But otherwise, less is known of him than his reputation in the fourth century as a leader of those exiled by the Thirty would cause us to expect.[62]

Thrasybulus is conspicuously absent from the list of Theramenes' followers. Ever since he had saved the Athenian fleet at Samos from falling into the hands of the Four Hundred by entrusting it to Alcibiades, he had fought alongside Alcibiades and Theramenes around the Hellespont and Thrace between 410 and 408/7 B.C. without the support of the home government. Though elected general with Alcibiades and Conon for 407/6 B.C., like Theramenes he had not joined Alcibiades' triumphant return to Athens, and after Notium he had suffered the same fate as the other generals on Alcibiades' board. His name is also linked to Theramenes' at Arginusae, where as trierarchs they were jointly assigned the task of picking up the survivors. After that he vanishes from view: Theramenes alone is involved in the defense against the generals' charges and in launching the attack that led to their execution.[63] We next encounter him in Thebes, in exile from the Thirty and busy organizing the resistance (Xen. *Hell*. 2.4.2, cf. 2.3.42, 44; Diod. 14.32.1). Both in exile and prominently in restoring the democracy his name is associated with that of Anytus (Xen. *Hell*. 2.3.42, 44; Isoc. 18.23). Why is his name not found among the Therameneans? Our ignorance of his whereabouts after the execution of the generals allows the possibility that he was abroad at the time the peace was concluded and that he went to Thebes after the installation of the Thirty without first returning to Athens. If so, he will have been

60 Dem. 24.135; Aeschin. 2.176, 3.187. Cf. also Arist. *Ath.Pol.* 40.1–2. For his oratorical skill, see Pl. *Menex*. 234b, Deinarchus 1.76.

61 Arist. *Ath.Pol.* 40.2; Aeschin. 3.195; and [Plut.] *X orat.* 835f, where we learn that Lysias was among those to be enfranchised.

62 The significance of his only known political action before 404 B.C. escapes us: Ar. *Ran.* 367 with scholl., which also cite Plat. Com. fr. 133 and Sannyrion, fr. 9, mention a measure curtailing payments to comic poets.

63 See above, pp. 387–89, 427–29, and 434–37.

absent during the six months when the political discussions took place. However, since he was officially exiled by the Thirty (Xen. *Hell*. 2.4.14), it is equally likely that he went into exile from Athens. If that was the case, there will have been a parting of the ways between him and Theramenes at some point, most probably caused by Thrasybulus's disapproval of Theramenes' action against the generals of Arginusae. His exile and subsequent resistance to the oligarchy can best be explained by the assumption that he had become an outspoken champion of the democracy as the *patrios politeia* during the six months after the peace. It is noteworthy, however, that despite any differences between them Theramenes' respect for Thrasybulus remained undiminished (Xen. *Hell*. 2.3.42, 44).

THE THIRTY

The "Good" Period

Since relations between Theramenes and Critias were still cordial after the establishment of the Thirty, it is safe to assume a measure of cooperation between them also during the six months following the peace (Xen. *Hell*. 2.3.15). After all, they were united in opposition to the unlimited popular sovereignty that characterized the democracy, differing only on how much it was to be restricted, and Theramenes may have been fully aware of the extent to which the *hetaireiai* were planning to remodel Athens. Both will have favored the prompt implementation of the peace treaty, Theramenes because he had negotiated it, and Critias because it brought Athens closer to Sparta; and both will consequently have been dismayed by how long the democrats took in dismantling the walls. Moreover, Pythodorus's presence in the oligarchical camp and the Theramenean alignment of Cleitophon, who had proposed in 411 B.C. that thirty *syngrapheis* be commissioned to reform the constitution and restore the *patrioi nomoi*, makes it a reasonable assumption that Theramenes and Critias favored—at least officially—settling the constitutional question by appointing a new commission of *syngrapheis*. This idea will have appeared sensible to the general public, especially since *anagrapheis* had been active establishing a new code of laws at least as recently as the trial of Cleophon (Lys. 30.11–14).

A new commission of thirty *syngrapheis* was indeed elected, but in an unexpected manner and under extraordinary circumstances, in an assembly convoked in September to settle the issue of the constitution. Our main sources, Lysias and Diodorus, agree that a constitutional assembly was held, that it was addressed by Lysander and Theramenes, that Lysander called attention to the failure of Athens to abide by the treaty in not having demolished the walls on schedule, that the *dēmos* opposed abolishing the democracy but was beaten down by Lysander, and that the Thirty were elected on the motion of Dracontides.[64] But our sources disagree about the context in which these proceedings took place. Lysias, intent on maximizing Theramenes' responsibility for the Thirty, states that he had summoned Lysander and his fleet from Samos to be present for the meeting, that he proposed to entrust the city to thirty men in conformity with "the constitution Dracontides had delineated," and that Lysander lent him his support. But Diodorus says that the oligarchs summoned Lysander in the expectation that he would support them; he has Lysander not only convoke the Assembly but also propose the election of thirty men "to take over the leadership of the state and manage all the affairs of the city." Further, when Theramenes protested that this interference in the internal affairs of Athens contravened the *patrios politeia* clause of the treaty, according to Diodorus, Lysander quashed his objections by responding that Athens had already broken the treaty and by threatening to kill Theramenes if he did not stop opposing the Lacedaemonians. Under the circumstances Theramenes had no choice but to go along with Lysander's proposal.

In the absence of any other evidence or of any objective criteria to weigh these two biased accounts against one another, most scholars accept Lysias without argument.[65] However, it has been shown that the two accounts can be reconciled if we assume that Theramenes spoke twice in the Assembly, once to oppose the oligarchy Lysander was imposing contrary to the terms of the peace (Diodorus) and again, after realizing that resistance to Lysander was futile, to support the motion of Dracontides (Lysias).[66] If, then, Theramenes'

64 Lys. 12.71–76; Diod. 14.3.2–7. Cf. Arist. *Ath.Pol*. 34.3, cited also by schol. Ar. *Vesp*. 157.

65 Most recently, Rhodes, *CAAP* 434, states that "all that we know of Theramenes suggests that Lysias' account of his part in the setting up of the Thirty is correct," forgetting that most of what we know of Theramenes is controversial. For a list of other scholars accepting Lysias, see P. Salmon, "L'Établissement des Trente à Athènes," *Ant.Class*. 38 (1969) 497–500, esp. 498 nn. 4–8.

66 Salmon, "Établissement," accepted by McCoy, "Aristotle's *Athenaion Politeia*" 142–44, and Krentz, *TA* 49 n. 21. The advantage of this hypothesis is that it would enable us to fault Lysias only for reversing the order in which Theramenes and Lysander spoke.

support for the Thirty came only after a realistic reappraisal of the situation, it is less likely that he had summoned Lysander than that Lysander had been called in by the oligarchical conspirators to support their cause. This seems also confirmed by Aristotle.[67] Moreover, it seems that his change of mind alienated Theramenes' supporters, which would explain why none of those known to us became a member of the Thirty.

Both Lysias and Diodorus convey the impression that Dracontides' motion instituted a new form of government.[68] Lysias adds to this the information that ten of the Thirty were nominated by Theramenes, ten by the "ephors," and ten "from among those present," meaning presumably from among those opponents of democracy who had not left the meeting when they saw which way the wind was blowing (Lys. 12.75–76). That Theramenes was permitted to designate one-third of them may well have been a concession on Lysander's part when he realized that Theramenes was now willing to support him. Another concession to Theramenes may be contained in the motion that is the only item Xenophon reports of this assembly: ἔδοξε τῷ δήμῳ τριάκοντα ἄνδρας ἑλέσθαι, οἳ τοὺς πατρίους νόμους συγγράψουσι, καθ' οὓς πολιτεύσουσι.[69] Although this is too terse to reflect the original decree as a whole, which will have been more explicit about the powers conferred on the Thirty, it leaves no doubt that part of their mandate was to draft written laws (συγγράψουσι) on which to base their government.[70] The fact that these were to be "ancestral laws" would indicate that the principles of their government were to be rooted in Athenian traditions and that they were to continue the legislative work Pythodorus's motion

67 Arist. *Ath.Pol.* 34.3: Λυσάνδρου δὲ προσθεμένου τοῖς ὀλιγαρχικοῖς.

68 Lys. 12.73: ἀναστὰς δὲ Θηραμένης ἐκέλευσεν ὑμᾶς τριάκοντα ἀνδράσιν ἐπιτρέψαι τὴν πόλιν καὶ τῇ πολιτείᾳ χρῆσθαι ἣν Δρακοντίδης ἀπέφαινεν. Diod. 14.3.5: τριάκοντα ἄνδρας τοὺς ἀφηγησομένους τῆς πολιτείας καὶ πάντα διοικήσοντας τὰ κατὰ τὴν πόλιν.

69 Xen. *Hell.* 2.3.2: "The people decided to elect thirty men who would draft the ancestral laws by which they were to govern." The question of historical accuracy is not affected by the possibility that this passage has been interpolated.

70 I believe that Krentz, *TA* 50, is right in his suggestion that οἱ τριάκοντα is the subject of πολιτεύσουσι. This is confirmed by the fact that the active sense of πολιτεύειν is in Xenophon invariably "to establish a political order," "to run the state"; see *Hell.* 1.4.13, 5.19; 3.1.21; 5.2.12 (συμπολιτεύειν); *An.* 3.2.26; cf. also the passive at *Mem.* 4.4.16. He uses the middle πολιτεύεσθαι in the sense "to live under a social or political order"; see *Hell.* 2.3.11, 4.22, 4.43 (*bis*); 5.3.25; *Mem.* 2.6.26; 4.3.12; *Cyr.* 1.1.1; and *Ages* 1.37. The middle participle οἱ πολιτευόμενοι seems to refer in Xenophon invariably to the leaders of a political system in which these view themselves as participants; see *Mem.* 1.2.47; 2.1.14; 4.4.13.

had initiated in 411 B.C., which had continued ever since the over-throw of the Four Hundred. As the initial enterprise had the support of Theramenes' associate Cleitophon, and since Aristotle presents Theramenes as the main champion of the *patrios politeia* clause of the treaty, we may infer that Lysander permitted this mandate to be inserted into Dracontides' motion in deference to Theramenes. Moreover, when taken in conjunction with that of Lysias and Diodorus, Xenophon's testimony suggests that the original model for the Thirty was the board of *syngrapheis* Pythodorus's motion commissioned in 411 B.C. but that unlike them the Thirty were also entrusted with the actual government of the city, at least on a provisional basis until a new constitution should have been introduced.[71]

According to Xenophon, then, the Thirty were not originally established as the ruling body of an oligarchy, since an oligarchy of thirty men was alien to Athenian traditions; and indeed neither Lysias nor Diodorus speaks of oligarchy in connection with their appointment. But this means also that the oligarchical rule on which they embarked some time after their installation was not illegal, since the *dēmos* had conferred upon them the power to govern as well as to formulate the constitution, and that it became illegitimate only because they ignored the mandate to base their rule upon the *patrioi nomoi*. How soon after their accession the oligarchy began is not known, but in general our sources agree that it was preceded by a period of government of which at least the respectable members of the upper classes approved.[72] To this period must be assigned their appointment of a Council of Five Hundred and of the other magistrates and the revisions of the laws that they are said to have undertaken. According to Aristotle, all officials were recruited from among a preselected group of one thousand; on what criteria this group was constituted is not known.[73] Signs of what was to come will not have been hidden for long. According to Lysias, most of the councilors, whose task it was to ratify the measures of the Thirty (Arist. *Ath.Pol.* 37.1) were carried over from the previous year, that is from the Council that illegally condemned Cleophon to death and

---

71 Hignett, *HAC* 383.

72 Diod. 14.4.2: καὶ μέχρι τούτου τοῖς ἐπιεικεστάτοις τῶν πολιτῶν εὐαρέστει τὰ γινόμενα. Cf. Xen. *Hell.* 2.3.12; Arist. *Ath.Pol.* 35.2–3. Cf. also Lys. 12.5; Pl. *Epistle* 7 324d.

73 Arist. *Ath.Pol.* 35.1–2 with Rhodes, *CAAP* 438 and Krentz, *TA* 57 n. 1.

arrested the generals and taxiarchs who opposed the terms of the peace.[74] Other magistrates were chosen from among the friends of the Thirty.[75] Unprecedented among the appointments were the designation of ten archons for the Piraeus, the economic nerve center of Athens, controlling access to and from the sea, and home of many metics;[76] and, on a lower level, the employment of three hundred "whip-bearing servants" (μαστιγοφόροι ὑπηρέται) to do their bidding.[77]

Even though no positive constitutional measures were forthcoming from the Thirty,[78] their one negative constitutional action, lifting the restrictions that Ephialtes and Archestratus had imposed on the political competence of the Areopagus (Arist. *Ath.Pol.* 35.2), will have been a point on which the followers of Critias and of Theramenes could readily agree, since they regarded them as a perversion of the *patrios politeia* of Solon and Cleisthenes.[79] (Similarly, the Thirty had democratic legislation erased from a wall

74   Lys. 13.20 with pp. 456–57 and 458–59 above. The three names known to us are not sufficient to corroborate or deny his statement: Epichares (Andoc. 1.95) does not seem to be identical with the member of the Ten, who succeeded the Thirty (Lys. 12.55; see MacDowell, *Andokides* 133); nothing else is known of him. Euandros was unsuccessfully attacked by Lysias at his *dokimasia* for the archonship for 382/1 B.C. but was admittedly a good citizen under the democracy (Lys. 26.10; cf. 3–5). Teisias (Isoc. 16.43) was the brother-in-law of Charicles and had been one of the generals against Melos in 416 B.C.; see p. 311 with n. 68 and p. 467. However, we have already noted that the councilors Chremon and Satyrus became members of the Thirty and the Eleven, respectively; see above, p. 457 with n. 160.

75   Xen. *Hell.* 2.3.11; Diod. 14.4.2. Of the archons, only Pythodorus, the eponymous archon, is otherwise known; see above, n. 4. Nothing else is known of Patrocles, who served as archon basileus under the Ten, who succeeded the Thirty (Isoc. 18.5), and is therefore likely to have served also under the Thirty in this capacity.

76   Arist. *Ath.Pol.* 35.1; Pl. *Epistle* 7 324c; Plut. *Lys.* 15.6. One of these was Critias's cousin Charmides; see above, pp. 466–67 with n. 29, and Xen. *Hell.* 2.4.19. Another was Molpis, otherwise unknown; see Androtion *FGH* 324F11.

77   Arist. *Ath.Pol.* 35.1. These are presumably identical with the dagger-bearing young men who took Theramenes to his death; see Xen. *Hell.* 2.3.23, 54–55; Diod. 14.5.1.

78   Xen. *Hell.* 2.3.11; Arist. *Ath.Pol.* 35.1; Diod. 14.4.2.

79   Arist. *Ath.Pol.* 35.2. The identity of Archestratus remains enigmatic. If he was an associate of Ephialtes in 462/1 B.C., nothing earlier is known of him. Wilamowitz, *Aristoteles* 1.68 n. 40, may have been right in identifying him with the Archestratus who offered an amendment to the Chalcis decree in 446/5 B.C. (ML, no. 52.70), with the son of Lycomedes who was a general against Potidaea in 433/2 B.C. (Thuc. 1.57.6), and with a treasurer of Athena in 429/8 B.C. (*IG* I³ 297.1).

adjacent to the Royal Stoa; this is archaeologically attested.)[80] If Aristotle (*Ath.Pol.* 35.2) is right in asserting that in removing ambiguities from the Solon's legislation "they eliminated the discretionary authority of the jurors, in that they claimed to be correcting the constitution and freeing it from dispute," the opponents of popular sovereignty will have approved of their action. However, the improvements Aristotle cites apply to the Solonian inheritance laws and seem more like the work of the *anagrapheis* who published Draco's laws on homicide in 410 B.C. than constitutional legislation.

The only other "good," pre-oligarchical activity attested for the Thirty is judicial; it was primarily directed at eliminating sycophants[81] and shows the transition from the "good" period to the oligarchy. Since the primary targets of sycophants had been members of the upper classes who had to pass *euthynai* upon the expiration of their terms of office,[82] it is only natural that the Thirty as members of the upper classes and in many cases past victims of sycophants would give proceedings against them a high priority. Since there were no jury courts, they were tried before the Council, which was packed with supporters of the Thirty; what charges were brought against them we are not told, but the only penalty inflicted was death. However enthusiastically the respectable class of citizens may have applauded the removal of this nuisance, it was attained by high-handed methods of questionable legality.[83]

The trial of the generals and taxiarchs who had been arrested for opposition to the terms of the peace about March 404 B.C. presumably also took place early in the Thirty's administration. They too were condemned to death by the Council, even though the decree under which they had been arrested stipulated a trial by a jury of two thousand. Among them were Strombichides, Dionysodorus, Calliades, Eucrates, and possibly Aristophanes (otherwise unknown), who had stood surety for Agoratus.[84]

---

80   A. Fingarette, "A New Look at the Wall of Nikomakhos," *Hesp.* 40 (1971) 330–35. This interpretation makes more sense than Clinton's suggestion, "Nature" 32, that the erasure was made by the restored democracy in 403.

81   Curiously enough, Arist. *Ath.Pol.* 35.2, in giving the motive for the reform of the Solonian inheritance laws as ὅπως μὴ ᾖ τοῖς συκοφάνταις ἔφοδος, seems to define legacy hunting as a kind of συκοφαντία. This is unusual, since sycophants are known to have been active only in public suits, whereas problems of inheritance were commonly private δίκαι.

82   See above, pp. 202 and 209–12 for demagogues as sycophants.

83   Xen. *Hell.* 2.3.12; Diod. 14.4.2; Arist. *Ath.Pol.* 35.3. Approval is indicated even by Lys. 25.19.

84   Lys. 13.34–38, 58–60; cf. above, pp. 458–59.

Oligarchy and Repression

The problem of sources. Our understanding of the motives underlying the Thirty's shift to oligarchy depends on the chronology of three events about which our sources show serious discrepancies:[85] the garrisoning of Athens by seven hundred Lacedaemonian troops under the harmost Callibius at the Thirty's request; the execution of Theramenes; and the seizure and fortification of Phyle by the exiles under the leadership of Thrasybulus. If we accept Xenophon's version, with which Diodorus and Justin concur, the Spartan garrison was called in at the beginning of the oligarchical period, and in due course Theramenes was executed and Phyle was occupied;[86] Theramenes' opposition to the Thirty, then, was principled and born of resentment of their violent, arbitrary methods, and the futility of his protests will have inspired the exiles to take action. If we accept Aristotle's order of events (*Ath.Pol.* 37), Phyle was occupied before Theramenes was killed and the Spartan garrison was installed; and the growing strength of the exiles motivated both Theramenes' opposition and the request for Spartan troops.

Modern orthodoxy favors Xenophon's chronology, largely because he was a contemporary of the events and may even have taken part in them.[87] But some curious omissions and differences in treatment give pause; these emerge from a comparison with other sources, especially in his account of the events after the Thirty were deposed. He does not tell us that the Ten, who replaced them, were given full powers to bring an end to hostilities between the city and the Piraeus (Arist. *Ath.Pol.* 38.1; Diod. 14.33.5); instead he confines his narrative to the horrors they perpetrated and makes them participate only in the appeal for Spartan help that the remnant of the Thirty initiated, isolated in Eleusis (*Hell.* 2.4.24–28). Moreover, in Xenophon's account Pausanias, motivated by rivalry with Lysander, is entirely responsible for the reconciliation; whereas Aristotle gives

---

85 The most extensive discussion of the sources and the discrepancies among them is Hignett's, *HAC* 384–89, expanded and clearly tabulated by Rhodes, *CAAP* 416–19.

86 Xen. *Hell.* 2.3.13–4.2; Diod. 14.4.3–5.4, 32.1; Justin 5.8.11, 9.1–6.

87 Most elaborately argued by Hignett, *HAC* 384–89; cf. also Rhodes, *CAAP* 420–22, and the works cited by Krentz, *TA* 133 nn. 2 and 3. For Xenophon's participation, see Schwartz, "Quellenuntersuchungen" 164–65, and more recently, J. K. Anderson, *Xenophon* (London and New York, 1974) 55–60, and W. E. Higgins, *Xenophon the Athenian* (Albany, N.Y., 1977) 22–24 with n. 18.

the credit to a second set of ten, led by Rhinon and Phayllus and appointed after the overthrow of the first.[88] To dismiss the second board of ten as tendentious fiction, largely on the grounds that it is contrived to give the Athenians the credit for settling their own differences,[89] does not satisfactorily resolve the discrepancies between the two sources: Xenophon can be accused of the opposite bias of stressing the humanity and compassion of Pausanias. Since there is no good reason for Aristotle to have invented this board to stress the merits of Rhinon and Phayllus, and since the existence of this board does not contradict facts otherwise known, there is no strong reason to reject his testimony.[90] By contrast, there are some strange omissions from Xenophon's account. We depend on Diodorus (14.6.1–3) and Justin (5.9.4–5) for the information that the Spartans demanded all Greek states deliver all Athenian refugees to the Thirty on pain of a fine of five talents and that Argos and Thebes refused. Xenophon either did not know this or suppressed it in a desire to make the Spartans look less vindictive.[91] He says nothing about the offer to Thrasybulus that he might replace Theramenes as a member of the Thirty (Diod.14.32.5–6; Justin 5.9.13–14); if this was in fact made, it was a shrewd maneuver to take the sting out of the opposition by coopting its leader. Nor does he mention the Thirty's futile attempt

88   Xen. *Hell.* 2.4.35–39 (cf. Diod. 14.33.6; Justin 5.10.7–8); Arist. *Ath.Pol.* 38.3–4.

89   The most detailed argument against the second board is that of P. Cloché, *La Restauration démocratique à Athènes en 403 avant J.-C.* (Paris, 1915) 170–83. See also A. Fuks, "Notes on the Rule of the Ten at Athens in 403 B.C.," *Mnemos.*, 4th ser., 6 (1953) 198–207 with bibliography on p. 198 n. 2; Rhodes, *CAAP* 420, 459–60.

90   Isoc. 18.6 and 8 merely confirms Rhinon's presence on a board of Ten in 403 B.C. Cloché's argument (*Restauration* 112–14) that this must have been the first board rests on confused chronological data in Isoc. 18.17 and 49, which cannot be decisive. Other omissions by Xenophon are of lesser moment. The statement in Arist. *Ath.Pol.* 36.2 that the Thirty delayed and kept altering the list of the Three Thousand before Theramenes' death is rejected by Hignett, *HAC* 388, on the grounds that the delay would have played into Theramenes' hands. But surely this is not a sufficient reason for rejection, and, if true, the statement affects no major issue. Further, it is of little consequence that Arist. *Ath.Pol.* 37.1 mentions two laws on the basis of which Theramenes was condemned, whereas Xen. *Hell.* 2.3.51 refers only to one: the law disfranchising those who had dismantled Eëtoneia and opposed the Four Hundred cannot possibly have been enacted before the crucial Council meeting and may well have been the enabling motion that made Theramenes' removal from the list of the Three Thousand mandatory and thus provided the legal basis for inflicting the death penalty.

91   Similarly, Xenophon may have been ignorant of, or wished to suppress, the support given to the exiles by the Theban Ismenias and by Lysias; see Justin 5.9.8–9.

to intercept the exiles on their way to the Piraeus from Acharnae (Diod. 14.32.6–33.1) or, again, that the people of Salamis shared the fate of the Eleusinians at the Thirty's hands (Diod. 14.32.4; Lys. 12.52). Though none of these omissions affects either a major issue or his chronology, it is strange that all these incidents should be missing from so full an account.

The real difficulty in accepting Xenophon's sequence of events is that one has to accept his characters' motivations with it, and these are too naive and simplistic to explain why and by what steps the Thirty veered from a reasonable policy that had the approval of respectable upper-class citizens to embark on a program of repressive oligarchy. Nothing but a lust for power motivates their appeal for a Spartan garrison;[92] Critias's thirst for blood is explained by the fact that the democracy had sent him into exile (*Hell.* 2.3.15); the wholesale slaughter of citizens and metics is prompted by power madness, greed, and the need to pay the Spartan garrison (2.3.21, 4.1); Theramenes is removed as an obstacle to the unrestrained exercise of power (2.3.23); and Pausanias's conciliatory attitude is motivated only by his jealousy of Lysander's success (2.4.29). There may be truth in all these allegations; but they tend to explain events as a struggle between "goodies" and "baddies," Critias and his gang being interested only in power and money, opposed by Theramenes as the champion of good government by superior citizens (καλοὶ κἀγαθοί) and by Thrasybulus as the embodiment of the principle χαλεπὰ τὰ καλά (noble things are difficult), with Pausanias being pitted against Lysander's rough-and-ready strong-arm methods. Surely, this is too simple an explanation of responses to a very complex political development, even if it does have an inner logic and is the work of a contemporary. But being a contemporary does not guarantee political acumen, and since modern scholars are agreed that this part of the *Hellenica* is not contemporary but was composed several decades after the events,[93] Xenophon's experiences cannot guarantee the accuracy of his memory.

Aristotle (or his sources) also show bias—in favor of the Therameneans and of the restored democracy—and his compressed

92   Xen. *Hell.* 2.3.13: ὅπως ἂν ἐξείη αὐτοῖς τῇ πόλει χρῆσθαι ὅπως βούλοιντο.
93   M. MacLaren, "On the Composition of Xenophon's *Hellenica*," *AJP* 55 (1934) 121–39, 249–62, esp. 122; H. R. Breitenbach, "Xenophon," *RE* 2. Reihe, 9. Band (1967) 1569–1910, esp. 1679–80; Higgins, *Xenophon* 101.

narrative contains a number of obscurities.[94] But his sequence of events yields nevertheless a more credible historical picture.[95] Aristotle's bias is made more palpable by his omissions (such as his failure to mention Critias's name or Theramenes' membership in the Thirty) than by his rearranging the sequence of events. Dating the Thirty's failure to prevent Thrasybulus from seizing Phyle before Theramenes' execution and the summoning of the Spartan garrison after it, Aristotle provides a better framework to explain the development of the oligarchy. Contrary to Xenophon's belief, Theramenes' objections to the Thirty's excesses seem not merely an internal squabble within the ruling clique but a reasonable response to the external threat posed by the exiles' success, and the appeal to Sparta seems sensible as prompted by the Thirty's inability to cope with the increasing number of opponents who were willing to resort to arms after Theramenes' death.[96] Even though neither Xenophon's chronology nor Aristotle's is susceptible of proof, Aristotle's seems to correspond more intelligibly to historical reality.

Theory and practice.   All our sources agree that the Thirty's excesses followed the elimination of sycophants and other undesirables and began with the killing of wealthy and respectable citizens.[97] What made the Thirty turn against those who had initially approved of their actions? Their high-handed illegality in prosecuting the sycophants, generals, and taxiarchs who were regarded as enemies of the new order[98] may have made some respectable citizens victims of the fervor with which the city was being purged, and this may explain the development of an opposition and the official or voluntary exile of men like Thrasybulus and Anytus. But they do not account for the scale of the slaughter to which, according to all

94   For details, see Hignett, *HAC* 387–89, and Rhodes, *CAAP* 420–21. The most glaring flaws are his failure to mention that Theramenes became a member of the Thirty and his omission of Critias's name from his account altogether. The most important of Hignett's objections have been effectively answered by Krentz, *TA* 144–45.

95   G. Busolt, "Aristoteles oder Xenophon?" *Hermes* 33 (1898) 71–86; O. Armbruster, "Über die Herrschaft der Dreissig zu Athen 404/3 v. Chr." (diss. Freiburg, 1913) 14–22; Colin, *Xénophon* 41–43; Krentz, *TA* 131–47.

96   Aristotle's conjunction of the request for help with the denunciation of Theramenes (*Ath.Pol.* 37.2: τοῦ τε Θηραμένους κατηγόρουν καὶ βοηθεῖν αὐτοῖς ἠξίουν) does not imply that Theramenes was still alive but is rather intended to justify the appeal for help.

97   Xen. *Hell.* 2.3.13–14; Arist. *Ath.Pol.* 35.4; Diod. 14.4.3–4; Justin 5.8.11–12.

98   See above, p. 480.

our sources, Theramenes first objected.[99] This intensification of terror can be explained only by the assumption that Athenian society and government were to be restructured on the basis of some master plan, to realize which the Thirty willingly turned to violence. If Theramenes knew of this plan, he will have acquiesced at the beginning, when he did not realize what would follow, but once he saw how narrowly and brutally it was enforced he began to oppose it.[100] As early as 1932 scholars suggested that this plan entailed remaking Athenian society on the Spartan model, but the details have only recently been extrapolated from the acts of the Thirty by two independent studies.[101] Obviously, not every feature of the Spartan system was suitable for transplantation to Attica. There was nothing in the Athenian social structure on which to graft a dual kingship, and nothing that could be transformed into a helot class. The absence of kings, in turn, made it unnecessary to find an equivalent for ephors to supervise them. But, as these studies have persuasively demonstrated, not only did the Thirty come to think of themselves as a *gerousia*, a body of thirty aristocrats in whom supreme authority was vested, but they also tried to create an upper-class elite of *homoioi*, who were to enjoy full citizen rights, excluding all others by reducing them to a status analogous to that of the *perioikoi*.

We cannot pinpoint when this plan became the Thirty's deliberate policy. As we have noticed, the appointment of five "ephors" by the *hetaireiai* after the peace indicates that the extremists envisaged a Spartan model for Athens well before the Thirty were installed and that Theramenes may well have gone along with the idea of restricting full citizenship.[102] Since our sources agree that Theramenes first began to object when men were put to death for no reason other than their prominence,[103] he clearly resented including such persons

99   Xen. *Hell.* 2.3.15; Arist. *Ath.Pol.* 36.1; Diod. 14.4.5.
100   Xen. *Hell.* 2.3.15–17; Arist. *Ath.Pol.* 36.1–2; Diod. 14.4.5.
101   Krentz, *TA* 64–67—who cites A. P. Dorjahn, "The Athenian Senate and the Oligarchy of 404/3 B.C.," *PhQ* 11 (1932) 57–64, esp. 64, and F. Ollier, *Le Mirage spartiate* (Paris, 1933) 167, as providing earlier hints—establishes political and institutional borrowing from Sparta by the Thirty; D. Whitehead, "Sparta and the Thirty Tyrants," *Ancient Society* 13/14 (1982–83) 106–30, emphasizes the social affinities that linked members of the Thirty to Sparta and prompted them to view themselves as a *gerousia*. The following is heavily indebted to both these works.
102   See above, pp. 470–71 and 475.
103   Xen. *Hell.* 2.3.15 simply speaks of prominence; Arist. *Ath.Pol.* 35.4 speaks of prominence in terms of property, wealth, and status; Diod. 14.4.4 speaks of

among the undesirables; further, since fear that Theramenes might become the focal point of opposition is given as a motive for the subsequent publication of the list of the Three Thousand, we can infer that Theramenes had insisted from the beginning on the publication of a list of eligible citizens but that the extremists had procrastinated, uncertain whom to include and whom to omit (Arist. *Ath.Pol.* 36.2), and had meanwhile killed a number of those Theramenes had wished to include. The circumstances under which the list was published, however, will have alienated Theramenes still further. For presumably simultaneously with its publication, the Thirty decreed that none of the Three Thousand could be put to death without a verdict of the Council but that the Thirty had the right to put to death anyone not on the list.[104] This made it at least implicitly clear that a class analogous to the Spartan *homoioi* was to be created as an entity separable from the rest (in analogy with the *perioikoi*), with the Thirty as the *gerousia* wielding the power over the life and death of the latter.[105] The number three thousand was not necessarily chosen with reference to the Spartan *homoioi*;[106] but it is

---

wealth. It is probable that the three men lamented in Theramenes' speech as unjust victims of the Thirty were among these (*Hell.* 2.3.39–40): Niceratus was the son of Nicias and had been a trierarch at Samos in 409 B.C.; see ML, no. 84.36. According to Xenophon, he was killed "as a wealthy man who, like his father, had never shown any populist sympathies"; cf. also Diod. 14.5.5, who dates his death after Theramenes' execution. Cf. also Lys. 18.6 and 19.47, and Plut. *Mor.* 998b as discussed by Davies, *APF* 405–6. Leon the Salaminian is probably identical with the colleague of Diomedon in the generalships at Samos in 412/11 B.C. and again after Notium; see above, pp. 346–47 with n. 40, 387, and Chap. 8, n. 75. His dislike of the oligarchy of the Four Hundred will have made him suspect to the Thirty, but his integrity is assured by the fact that Socrates, alone of the five sent for that purpose to Salamis by the Thirty, refused to arrest him; see Pl. *Ap.* 32c–d, *Epistle* 7 324e–325a; Xen. *Mem.* 4.4.3; cf. also Andoc. 1.94. Antiphon's wealth and patriotism are attested only by Xenophon's statement (*Hell.* 2.3.40) that he equipped two triremes for the war; see Davies, *APF* 327–28 for the information about him that can be disentangled from [Plut.] *X orat.* 832f–833b.

104 Xen. *Hell.* 2.3.18; Arist. *Ath.Pol.* 36.1. Justin 5.8.10 speaks of *tria milia satellitum* but may have in mind the three hundred ὑπηρέται μαστιγοφόροι. I have cited the longer version of the law as given in Xen. *Hell.* 2.3.51 in preference to the version preserved in Arist. *Ath.Pol.* 37.1. Since neither author mentions the occasion on which this law was enacted, it is reasonable to assume that it accompanied the list of the Three Thousand. Krentz, *TA* 76, dates both laws mentioned by Aristotle (*Ath.Pol.* 37.1) to the time after Thrasybulus's seizure of Phyle.

105 According to Isoc. 12.181, the ephors had this right in Sparta, but since the constitution of the Thirty had nothing analogous to them it will have embodied the principle of the superiority of the *homoioi* in the "*gerousia*" of the Thirty.

106 So Krentz, *TA* 64–65. But Krentz is no doubt right in including the knights among them.

noteworthy that this number is much smaller than the five thousand who were regarded as constituting the hoplite class in 411 and 410 B.C. No wonder Theramenes was moved to protest once again that so small a group had no monopoly on excellence (Arist. *Ath.Pol.* 36.2; Xen. *Hell.* 2.3.19).

The measures against the metics were probably taken after the publication of the list but before the expulsion of those excluded from it. The motive given for their murder is gain;[107] but if, as is likely, emulation of the Spartan practice of expelling foreigners (*xenēlasia*) was part of the reason, Theramenes may well have gone along with it until the Thirty required each of their members to prove his mettle by killing one metic—no doubt in imitation of the *rite de passage* to which the members of the Spartan *krypteia* were subjected.[108]

The seizure of Phyle by Thrasybulus and his band of seventy Athenian exiles early in the winter (about January or February) of 403 B.C. is dated by Aristotle (*Ath.Pol.* 37.1) after the publication of the list of the Three Thousand,[109] suggesting that the attempted laconization of Athens spurred Thraybulus into action. The defeat the exiles dealt them made the Thirty fear the rise of an internal opposition spearheaded by Theramenes. Theramenes was accordingly arrested and tried before the Council; intimidated by the presence of young men carrying concealed daggers, the councilors first gave the proceedings an air of legality by passing a law that removed from the list of citizens any participant in the dismantling of Eëtioneia in 411 B.C. and any opponent of the Four Hundred (Arist. *Ath.Pol.* 37.1).[110] They then condemned Theramenes to death on this basis (Xen. *Hell.* 2.3.23, 50–56; Diod. 14.4.5–6). It thus became clear that Athens would not be laconized without violence.

---

107 Xen. *Hell.* 2.3.21 (who gives need for money to pay the Spartan garrison as an additional incentive); Diod. 14.5.6 (who associates their murders with those of respectable Athenians).

108 Xen. *Hell.* 2.3.22, 41 with Whitehead, "Sparta." Lys. 12.6–7 attests the personal participation of the Thirty in the action against the metics but makes only ten (including two paupers) their target; Diod. 14.5.6 gives the number of victims as sixty. It is possible that the law prohibiting the teaching of rhetoric (λόγων τέχνην μὴ διδάσκειν) attested by Xen. *Mem.* 1.2.31 also belongs in this context, since many sophists were foreigners.

109 Xen. *Hell.* 2.4.2, though dating this event after the death of Theramenes, confirms that the Three Thousand were included among the force that the Thirty led into the field against them.

110 *Pace* Hignett, *HAC* 389, I believe that Kenyon was right in assigning this law to the Council meeting at which Theramenes was condemned.

The disarming, expulsion, and expropriation of all those not listed among the Three Thousand will have followed soon, including the enactment of a law that barred them from reentering the city.[111] The excluded[112] were settled in the Piraeus, whence some proceeded to Thebes and Megara.[113] The Thirty apparently intended to deprive them of their lands and to restrict them to shipping, commerce, and industry, occupations that, like the Spartans, the Thirty will have regarded as beneath the dignity of a citizen.[114] Isocrates (7.67) puts the number of those compelled to move to the Piraeus at over five thousand; Diodorus (14.5.7) has more than half the Athenians take refuge there. Flight abroad meant no safety: most Greek cities seem to have been intimidated by the Spartan demand (probably made at the Thirty's request) to deliver Athenian refugees back into the Thirty's hands on pain of a fine of five talents;[115] the refusal of Thebes and Argos was long remembered with admiration.[116]

Aristotle dates the summoning of Spartan aid that resulted in Callibius's occupation of the Acropolis with his seven hundred troops after the death of Theramenes and the disarming of the excluded (*Ath.Pol.* 37.2). Xenophon, however, dates this early in the oligarchical period.[117] The discrepancy cannot be explained by investigating Aristotle's possible sources,[118] since judgment about them is too uncertain to be free of subjectivity; there is at present no incontrovertible evidence by which a subjective judgment can be avoided. If we believe that the combined pressures of external and internal opposition after the death of Theramenes provide a more

---

111   Arist. *Ath.Pol.* 37.2 says nothing about the expulsion; Xen. *Hell.* 2.3.20 and 4.1 make the disarming precede, and the expulsion follow, the execution of Theramenes. For the expulsion, see also Lys. 25.22.

112   I prefer this term, coined by Cloché, *Restauration* 2 *et passim* and appropriated by Krentz, to "unprivileged," which is used by Hignett and Rhodes.

113   Diod. 14.32.4 and Justin 5.9.12 speak of compulsory settlement in the Piraeus; Xen. *Hell.* 2.4.1 conveys the impression that the settlement in the Piraeus was voluntary and alone mentions the further migrations.

114   I know of no evidence to support Krentz's contention (*TA* 66) that the expulsion represents an attempt to orient the Athenians toward the land.

115   Diod. 14.6.1; Justin 5.9.4. Cf. Lys. 12.95, 97; Deinarchus 1.25; Plut. *Lys.* 27.5.

116   Diod. 14.6.2–3; Justin 5.9.4–5; Deinarchus 1.25; Plut. *Lys.* 27.6–7.

117   Xen. *Hell.* 2.3.13–14. Diod. 14.4.3–4 with 32.6 and Justin 5.8.11 with 9.14, in an apparent attempt to reconcile their sources with one another, have the Spartans summoned both at the beginning of the oligarchical period and after Theramenes' death. On the preferability of Aristotle's date, see Armbruster, "Herrschaft" 17.

118   This is the path taken by Busolt, "Aristoteles?" and Krentz, *TA* 131–47.

convincing motive for calling in the Spartans than Xenophon's statement that the Thirty did so "in order that they could manage the city any way they wished" (*Hell*. 2.3.13), our position may be more plausible but not less vulnerable than preferring Xenophon. For those who accept Xenophon's chronology will have to explain the inactivity of the Spartan garrison until after the death of Theramenes.[119]

The measures against the metics and the expulsion of the excluded will have swelled the ranks of the opposition to the Thirty. But it remained latent and disorganized until Thrasybulus felt that the force he had gathered at Phyle was strong enough to make an attempt on the Piraeus. It had taken him a long time to increase the number of his followers from the seventy with whom he had captured Phyle in the winter to the seven hundred with whom he could strike out by the end of April (Xen. *Hell*. 2.4.5). Of that force only a hundred seem to have been Athenians; the rest were evenly divided between foreigners and mercenaries.[120] Xenophon associates the defeat that this force inflicted on the Thirty and their cavalry with the Thirty's seizure of Eleusis and the brutal treatment they meted out to the inhabitants (*Hell*. 2.4.5–10); Lysias (12.52; 13.44) and Diodorus (14.32.4) report that Salamis and its people suffered the same fate. The Thirty were in the grip of panic: potential foci of unrest could not be allowed to develop into strategic points from which their opponents might attack them.[121] At the same time, if we can trust Diodorus's chronology, a desperate attempt was made to weaken the opposition by offering Thrasybulus the place left vacant by Theramenes' execution.[122] The appeal allegedly made to Sparta

---

119   Xen. *Hell*. 2.3.14 has Callibius's garrison participate in the arrest of respectable citizens, has some Laconian troops join two Athenian cavalry squadrons in patrolling the countryside after the initial setback of the Thirty at Phyle (2.4.4), and also partly motivates the killing of metics by the need to pay the Spartan garrison (2.3.21). After that, Λακωνικοὶ φρουροί appear only as packing the Odeum when the Eleusinians were condemned to death (2.4.10). Diod. 14.32.4 may be thinking of the Spartan garrison when he states that the Thirty depended ξενικοῖς ὅπλοις to control the city after the expulsion of the excluded.

120   Krentz, *TA* 83–84.

121   Note that at Xen. *Hell*. 2.4.20, Cleocritus, the herald of the initiates, addresses the army of the exiles.

122   Diod. 14.32.5–6; Justin 5.9.13–14. Krentz, *TA* 64 with n. 35, makes the attractive suggestion that the place was eventually filled by Satyrus, the notorious leader of the Eleven, who had served as Critias's henchman in arresting Theramenes: see Xen. *Hell*. 2.3.54–56; cf. Lys. 30.12.

after Thrasybulus's refusal (Diod. 14.32.6; Justin 5.9.14) may in fact refer to the Thirty's first use of Spartan troops.

Although Xenophon has the Thirty and their Spartan allies take no action against Thrasybulus and his troops, by this time increased to one thousand, until he had reached the Piraeus (*Hell*. 2.4.10–11), it is unthinkable that they did not expect him to try to bring the excluded in the Piraeus under his banner and that they will not have tried to intercept him. Since the occupation of Eleusis will have made it difficult for the men of Phyle to reach the Piraeus by a route west of Mount Aegaleos, probability favors Diodorus's account (14.32.6–33.1) that a battle took place at Acharnae in which the Thirty were aided by the Spartans, presumably the same battle that Xenophon mistakenly dates soon after the capture of Phyle (*Hell*. 2.4.4–7). The rout the Thirty suffered did not discourage them from striking again five days later, this time in full force and again with Spartan support, after the rebels had seized Munychia (2.4.13). The defeat of the Thirty in the Piraeus, including the death of two of their members, Critias and Hippomachus, and of Charmides, one of the ten commanders of the Piraeus, marked the beginning of the end of their rule.[123]

DISSOLUTION AND RECONSTITUTION

The five months between the overthrow of the Thirty in May and the restoration of democracy in October 403 B.C. present few chronological problems. With the Piraeus firmly in the hands of the rebels, the remnant of the Thirty led their adherents back to Athens. Thenceforth all our sources describe the two parties as "city people" (οἱ ἐν ἄστει) and "Piraeus people" (οἱ ἐν Πειραιεῖ), respectively, which shows that the arbitrary way the Thirty had tried to laconize Athenian society had split the state geographically as well as ideologically. The problem was on what terms a government could be created that would effect a reconciliation. This was impossible so long as the seat of government remained in the control of the oligarchs, who could count on Spartan assistance to enforce their will. The dissension that arose among the oligarchs immediately after the battle in the Piraeus cleared the way for the reconciliation a few months later.

123   Xen. *Hell*. 2.4.10–22; Diod. 14.33.2–4; Justin 5.9.14–10.3; Arist. *Ath.Pol*. 38.1.

A meeting of the Three Thousand—their only one ever, so far as we know—was convened by the remnant of the Thirty the day after their withdrawal into the city.[124] A board of ten men, one from each tribe, was elected to replace the Thirty and was given full power to bring hostilities to an end.[125] Its membership included, according to Lysias (12.55), "Pheidon [a member of the Thirty], Hippocles, Epichares of Lamptrae, and others thought to be most opposed to Charicles, Critias, and their gang [*hetaireia*]"; most scholars add Rhinon to this list.[126] Of these men we know Pheidon as a member of the Thirty (Xen. *Hell*. 2.3.2); Epichares was a councilor under the Thirty and was one of the accusers of Andocides in 400 B.C.;[127] and Rhinon is listed as having held public office (*paredros* of the *hellēnotamiai?*) in 417/16 B.C. (ML, no. 77.26–27). However opposed Lysias makes them out to have been to the Thirty, there is no evidence that they attempted a reconciliation; on the contrary, they continued the divisive policies of the Thirty even after these had retired to Eleusis.[128]

The knights seem to have been especially prominent under their rule. They had, to be sure, already been important to the Thirty in the operations against Thrasybulus after the seizure of Phyle (Xen. *Hell*. 2.4.2, 4, 6–7) and in the action against Eleusis (2.4.8–10); but the Ten are said to have made the hipparchs partners of their rule (2.4.24); and since the cavalry, together with the Spartan garrison, are singled out as participants in the fighting against the Piraeus people (Xen. *Hell*. 2.4.24, 26–27, 31–32; Arist. *Ath.Pol*. 38.2), they

124   That the Thirty convened this meeting is nowhere stated, but it can be inferred from the fact that they were deposed and the Ten elected by a formal vote of the Three Thousand: see Xen. *Hell*. 2.4.23; Arist. *Ath.Pol*. 38.1; Diod. 14.33.5; Justin 5.10.4–5; cf. Lys. 12.54–55.

125   Xen. *Hell*. 2.4.23; Arist. *Ath.Pol*. 38.1; Diod. 14.33.5; cf. Justin 5.10.4. Their appointment as αὐτοκράτορες to end hostilities appears only in Aristotle and Diodorus.

126   Rhinon is added on the strength of Isoc. 18.6 and 8. However, there is still controversy whether he was a member of the first or second board of Ten or of both; see n. 90 above.

127   Andoc. 1.95. But, as MacDowell rightly remarks *ad loc*., Andocides would have mentioned his membership in the Ten if he had held one.

128   Xen. *Hell*. 2.4.24; Justin 5.10.4–5. There is no evidence for the contentions of Fuks, "Notes," that they either enlarged the citizen body (pp. 202–5) or initiated negotiations with the Piraeus people (pp. 205–7). On the contrary, they put to death an eminent citizen, Demaretus (of whom nothing else is known; Arist. *Ath.Pol*. 38.2), and were responsible for the slaughter of the peasants of Aexone by the cavalry commander Lysimachus (Xen. *Hell*. 2.4.26).

probably constituted under the Ten the hard core of the oligarchy, ready to prevent a resurgence of popular sovereignty by force of arms.[129] This is confirmed by what we know of the attitude toward the knights in the early years of the restored democracy: in response to a request by Thibron in 400 B.C., the Athenians gladly contributed three hundred cavalry recruited from among those who had served under the Thirty, "believing that the people stood only to gain from their absence and possible death" (Xen. *Hell*. 3.1.4); and even in the 390s and late 380s to charge at a *dokimasia* that a person had served in the cavalry under the Thirty could be sufficient to bar him from membership in the Council (Lys. 16.3–8; 26.10).

The Ten's repressive measures swelled the numbers of the Piraeus people still further, and the promise of *isoteleia* (taxation equal to that of an Athenian citizen) made as many as nine hundred foreigners join their ranks.[130] Though equipped only with makeshift armor, they controlled the countryside, repelled attacks by the city cavalry, and were getting ready to move siege engines to the walls of the city (Xen. *Hell*. 2.4.25–27). Unable to cope, the Ten sent to Sparta for aid; the embassy included Pheidon as well as representatives of the Thirty from Eleusis.[131] By representing the rebels as Boeotian agents (Lys. 12.58) and by accusing the *dēmos* of "revolt against the Lacedae-monians" (Xen. *Hell*. 2.4.28), they humiliated themselves as mere representatives of Sparta and showed that the oligarchs in the city had overtly turned into Spartan puppets.

The Spartan response was surprisingly half-hearted. Lysander and his brother Libys were dispatched to besiege the Piraeus by land and sea, respectively, but they were given no Spartan troops. Instead, a loan of one hundred talents was made available to the Athenian oligarchs, with which to hire one thousand Peloponnesian merce-naries to serve under Lysander and to man the forty ships.[132] The disappointment this response evoked among the oligarchs in the city

129 The fact that the Piraeus people had some seventy cavalrymen fighting on their side (Xen. *Hell*. 2.4.25) does not affect this argument, since the vast majority will have fought on the oligarchical side.

130 Xen. *Hell*. 2.4.25 with P. Krentz, "Foreigners against the Thirty: *IG* 2² 10 Again," *Phoenix* 34 (1980) 298–306.

131 That the embassy was sent by the Ten is stated by Arist. *Ath.Pol*. 38.1 and by Diod. 14.33.5. Xen. *Hell*. 2.4.28 attributes the initiative to the Thirty at Eleusis and has them accompanied by τῶν ἐν τῷ καταλόγῳ ἐξ ἄστεως (sc. some of the Three Thousand). Pheidon's name is mentioned by Lys. 12.58–59.

132 Xen. *Hell*. 2.4.28–29; Lys. 12.59–60; Diod. 14.33.5; Plut. *Lys*. 21.4.

plausibly accounts for the replacement of the oligarchical Ten by a new board of ten men "of the highest integrity" (Arist. *Ath.Pol.* 38.3).[133] Aristotle has preserved the names of two of them: little of significance is known about Phayllus;[134] Rhinon may have been carried over from the earlier board of Ten, but whatever public recognition he received followed the reconciliation, to which he is said to have made an important contribution.[135] How large a role this second board of ten played in the reconciliation is unknown; probably they would have achieved little without Pausanias's support.

The motivation and timing of Pausanias's entrance into Attica are by no means clear.[136] It is hard to believe he intended to effect a reconciliation when he set out on his expedition. Though Xenophon (*Hell*. 2.4.31–32) suggests that Pausanias attacked the Piraeus because he wanted to hide his true sympathies for the Piraeus people (31: ὅπως μὴ δῆλος εἴη εὐμενὴς αὐτοῖς ὤν), the intensity of the attack belies this allegation. Rivalries between a king and a brilliant general were nothing new in Sparta, as the example of Pleistoanax (Pausanias's father) and Brasidas shows.[137] Pausanias and possibly also Agis, lacking a firm policy of their own, may have viewed Lysander's activism with alarm, especially since it was beginning to make

133   Krentz, *TA* 96–97 with n. 28, and M. B. Walbank, "The Confiscation and Sale by the Poletai in 402/1 B.C. of the Property of the Thirty Tyrants," *Hesp.* 51 (1982) 74–98, esp. 93–94 n. 47. Since Aristotle dates their election to a point at which the Piraeus people were winning the war but before Pausanias arrived and states that its purpose was to initiate peace negotiations, the time immediately following the return of the ambassadors from Sparta but before the arrival of Lysander's troops appears to be the most suitable occasion.

134   He is mentioned as having transferred some objects to Poseidon Hippios in 406/5 B.C.; see *IG* I³ 405.25. His son Aristion was a victor at the Thargelia in 359/8 B.C. (*Arch.Delt.* 25 [1970] 146.5) and a trierarch in the 330s (*IG* II² 1624.71–72; see Davies, *APF* 53–54, and Rhodes, *CAAP* 460.

135   See above, p. 491 with n. 126. He was elected general for 403/2 B.C. (*Ath. Pol.* 38.4) and probably treasurer of Athena in 402/1 B.C. (*IG* II² 1370 + 1371.10 with *Addenda*, p. 797). He was enough of a public figure to have Archippus name a comedy (frr. 40–42) and the Socratic Aeschines a dialogue (D.L. 2.61; Poll. 7.103) after him; cf. Davies, *APF* 67.

136   Xen. *Hell*. 2.4.29 gives jealousy of Lysander as a motive; Diod. 14.33.6 adds concern for Sparta's prestige; Justin 5.10.7 motivates his attempt to reconcile the city and Piraeus people by compassion; Plut. *Lys*. 21.4–6 makes jealousy of Lysander the motive of both kings, support of the tyrants the pretext, and reconciliation the means by which Lysander was to be undermined; Lys. 12.60 has no reconciliation planned, but only the destruction of the state. For a full discussion see Cloché, *Restauration* 200–213.

137   Cloché, *Restauration* 204 n. 3, citing Thuc. 5.16.

Athens the general's own province. They must have influenced the decision to deny Lysander the use of the Spartan army, and his successful siege of the Piraeus may have spurred them to enlist the help of three of the five ephors to let Pausanias take the regular Spartan army into the field lest Lysander claim victory for himself. The refusal of the Boeotians and Corinthians to join him will have been a warning that his own actions and Lysander's were giving Sparta a bad image in the Greek world (Xen. *Hell*. 2.4.30), and the resistance the Piraeus people put up will have convinced Pausanias that no purpose would be served by using the Spartan army to prop up an unpopular regime in Athens. Reconciliation of the two factions with himself as mediator will have appeared to him as the only viable policy. The change of mind was to cost him the support of his fellow king, Agis, who had him impeached when he returned to Sparta (Paus. 3.5.2). If Aristotle (*Ath.Pol*. 38.3) is right in asserting that a new board of ten had already been elected by the city people to negotiate a settlement with the Piraeus, Pausanias's task will have consisted in first securing the consent of the Piraeus people and then assuring them that the negotiations with the board of ten would have the support of the city. The Piraeus people quickly accepted, and Pausanias persuaded a majority of the city people that a reconciliation of the two factions was a precondition for friendly relations with Sparta, as relations with only one Athenian faction would have been pointless. The assent of the two ephors who accompanied the king sealed the agreement, and thereby Lysander and his policy stood isolated (Xen. *Hell*. 2.4.35–36).

The Piraeus people were easier to move than the city people. A delegation from the Piraeus was soon on its way to Sparta with proposals for a peace based on reconciliation under Spartan auspices and a treaty of friendship with Sparta that would withdraw all Lacedaemonian forces from Attic soil. The delegation was joined by two private citizens from the city, Cephisophon and Meletus (2.4. 36–37), who were eager to demonstrate a sense of urgency about coming to terms with the Piraeus people before the city would make up its mind to send official emissaries. They evidently realized that the days of the oligarchy were numbered and wanted to throw their lot in with the democrats, whose return to power they saw as imminent. The foresight was duly rewarded: Cephisophon became secretary of the Council as soon as the democracy was restored. During his tenure of office the decree passed in 405 B.C. was inscribed, granting the Samians Athenian citizenship in gratitude for their loyalty to the democracy, with two new decrees added, one moved by Cephisophon himself, confirming and expanding the privileges then granted.[138] Moreover, it may have been under his chairmanship (*epistatēs*) of the Council that Archinus's decree honoring the heroes of Phyle was passed.[139] Why he had not joined the exiles earlier we cannot guess. As for Meletus, he is difficult to identify, because so many isolated details are known about men with his name from the end of the fifth century; the burden of sorting the pieces into coherent pictures has been left almost entirely to modern scholars. MacDowell reconstructed four individuals from the eight pieces of information we possess and stated that the most famous Meletus, the accuser of Socrates, is unrelated to the other three.[140] Scholarly opinion has since come more and more to identify Socrates' accuser also as the accuser of Andocides.[141] Once this is accepted, the accuser of Socrates becomes the very man who participated in the arrest of Leon the Salaminian at the bidding of the Thirty when Socrates refused to do so,[142] and it becomes reasonable to assume that he was also the Meletus who left the city in order to join the Piraeus delegation to Sparta when he saw that the oligarchy would not be able to maintain itself.[143] In short, Meletus's part in the prosecution of Andocides and Socrates, both of whom were tainted by association with oligarchs, may be seen as an attempt to distance himself from the Thirty, and his joining the Piraeus delegation to Sparta may well have been his first step in that direction.[144]

The departure of the Piraeus delegation to Sparta, accompanied by two private citizens from Athens, put pressure on the city people to

138 *IG* II² 1.1–2; cf. 56, 42, 51, with P. Cloché, "Les Décrets athéniens de 403/2 en faveur des Samiens," *REG* 40 (1927) 197–207. Cf. above, pp. 449–50.

139 So A. E. Raubitschek, "The Heroes of Phyle," *Hesp.* 10 (1941) 284–95, esp. 287–95, no. 78.78, with Davies, *APF* 148.

140 MacDowell, *Andokides* 208–10.

141 Dover, *Lysias* 80 n. 30; H. Blumenthal, "Meletus the Accuser of Andocides and Meletus the Accuser of Socrates; One Man or Two?" *Philol.* 117 (1973) 169–78; J. J. Keaney, "Plato, *Apology* 32c8–d3," *CQ*, n.s., 30 (1980) 296–98. The main stumbling block to an identification of the two, Socrates' statement at Pl. *Euthyphr.* 2b that Meletus was νέος καὶ ἀγνώς, has been effectively removed by the explanation of Blumenthal, "Meletus" 176–78.

142 Andoc. 1.94 with above, n. 103.

143 So Blumenthal, "Meletus" 175. For the possibility that he is also identical with the Meletus implicated in both the desecration of the herms and the profanation of the Mysteries in 415 B.C., see Appendix C, p. 543.

144 Cf. Blumenthal, "Meletus" 174–75.

send official ambassadors of its own to join in the negotiations. According to Xenophon (*Hell*. 2.4.37), they proposed surrendering to the Spartans, who were to impose whatever conditions they might choose about them and their walls, and demanded that as a precondition for friendship with Sparta the other side surrender the Piraeus and Munychia. Reconciliation was not on their minds. The Spartans wisely refrained from making a decision at home and appointed a commission of fifteen to go to Athens to assist Pausanias in effecting a reconciliation on the spot.[145] What they helped negotiate began a new chapter in Athenian history.

145 Xen. *Hell*. 2.4.38. Aristotle, *Ath.Pol*. 38.4, gives the commission a membership of only ten.

CHAPTER TEN

Toward a New Order: Democracy under the Law

THE RESTORATION OF ORDER

The nexus of events that ended the war between Athens and the Lacedaemonians and at the same time terminated the hostilities between the oligarchical remnant in the city and its opponents in the Piraeus constitutes one of the most inspiring episodes in Athenian history, if not even in human history. The reconciliation between the two factions worked and proved durable, thanks largely to the self-restraint of the Athenian *dēmos*. But its most remarkable feature is that it was achieved through written laws and agreements, voluntarily accepted by a majority of both parties, that inhibited what rancor was still at large among the victims of the oligarchy and prevented it from disrupting the precarious unity of the state. A new social and political order was created that retained the characteristic institutions of the Athenian democracy while subordinating the principle of popular sovereignty to the principle of the sovereignty of law.

The negotiations between the city and the Piraeus, conducted under the auspices of Pausanias and the Spartan mediators (*diallaktai*), resulted in what Aristotle calls τὴν εἰρήνην καὶ τὰς διαλύσεις, "peace and reconciliation" (*Ath.Pol.* 38.4).[1] Regardless of whether one or two instruments were drafted, it is clear that an internal settlement was a precondition for the peace treaty, since the Spartans

---

1 That both terms were used is also indicated by Xen. *Hell.* 2.4.38: οἱ δὲ διήλλαξαν ἐφ' ᾧτε εἰρήνην μὲν ἔχειν πρὸς ἀλλήλους. Whether these were one instrument or two (as Cloché, *Restauration* 242–44, believes) cannot be decided on the basis of the surviving evidence.

will have required a definition of the partner with whom they were going to conclude peace. Accordingly, both peace and reconciliation will have been based on the terms preserved by Xenophon (*Hell*. 2.4.38): cessation of hostilities between the two Athenian factions and the return of what was their own to the members of each, excluding only the Thirty, the Eleven, and the ten governors of the Piraeus; the peace treaty will also have required the withdrawal of all Lacedaemonian troops from Attic soil and an assurance that the Spartans would no longer interfere in internal Athenian affairs. This is shown by the fact that the reconciliation agreement, which is much better attested, does not mention Sparta at all, leaving its implementation entirely in Athenian hands.[2] The detailed text, preserved with only minor omissions by Aristotle, leaves no doubt that it was a written document; this is confirmed by the fact that Isocrates had it read into his speech *Against Callimachus*.[3]

The most remarkable feature of the document is that five of its six clauses (Arist. *Ath.Pol.* 39.1–5) are devoted to establishing Eleusis as a semi-independent enclave for city people who did not wish to stay in Athens under a new regime and to regulating the relationship of this new political unit to Athens. The new settlers in Eleusis were guaranteed autonomy in their internal administration, except that the sanctuary of Demeter was to be accessible to both parties, especially at the celebration of the Mysteries, and remain under the traditional administration of the Kerykes and Eumolpids; for all other purposes each side was barred from access to the other. Eleusis was to contribute to the defense fund on the same terms as the Athenians; no Eleusinian houses could be expropriated for occupancy by the new settlers. Citizens were given ten days after the reconciliation was ratified in which to register for joining the settlement and twenty days in which to emigrate to Eleusis; settlers at Eleusis were barred from holding office at Athens unless they returned and registered as city residents. Finally a provision that any who had with their own hands committed murder or inflicted wounds with intent to kill should be tried for homicide in the

---

2   The agreement is variously referred to as διαλύσεις (cessation of hostilities), διαλλαγαί (reconciliation), συνθῆκαι (compact), or their verbal forms. For the relevant passages, see Rhodes, *CAAP* 463.

3   Arist. *Ath.Pol.* 39.1–6. Rhodes, *CAAP* 463, notes only two omissions and two obscurities. Cf. Isoc. 18.19. For its contents, see the fundamental discussion of Cloché, *Restauration* 251–77; for a good recent discussion, see Krentz, *TA* 102–8.

ancestral way, which applied both to the new settlers and the Athenians, led over to the amnesty clause. Obviously, protecting the supporters of the oligarchy, whom we can assume to have been the hard core of the Three Thousand, was the major concern of the reconciliation agreement. The possibility of a complete symbiosis of the two parties, if considered at all, was not regarded as feasible.

Of greater immediate moment was the amnesty clause, which concluded the agreement (Arist. *Ath.Pol.* 39.6). It barred vindictive action of any kind (μὴ μνησικακεῖν) by or against any person of either party, excepting only actions against the Thirty, the Ten (no doubt the successors of the Thirty were meant), the Eleven, and the ten governors of the Piraeus under the Thirty;[4] but even these were to be included in the amnesty if they would submit to and successfully pass *euthynai* for acts committed under the oligarchy. Moreover, fairness in these *euthynai* was assured by the provision that only "those who had taxable property" should conduct audits affecting city people: no thetes would sit in judgment over them and former members of the Three Thousand would be well represented.[5] The last major provision of the agreement stipulated that each party was to be responsible for whatever debts it had incurred during the civil war.

Pausanias and his forces withdrew as soon as the reconciliation agreement was ratified, and on 12 Boedromion, that is, in late September or early October 403 B.C., the Piraeus people began their return to the city with a formal procession in arms up the Acropolis

4 The fact that Xen. *Hell*. 2.4.38 omits the Ten, and Andoc. 1.90 both the Ten and the Piraeus ten, does not affect the credibility of Aristotle's list. I believe that the second board of ten (see above, p. 493) were not excepted and that Rhinon's *euthyna* is no proof to the contrary; see below, n. 5.

5 Arist. *Ath.Pol.* 39.6, ἐν τοῖς τὰ τιμήματα παρεχομένοις, with Cloché, *Restauration* 268–72. It may be well to point out that this kind of *euthyna* applied only to those excluded from the amnesty. It does not mean that other officials of the oligarchy did not have to undergo a *euthyna*, though this will have been of the normal type, in which any citizen regardless of social status could air his complaints. In other words, non-excluded officials had the same option as the excluded, to emigrate to Eleusis without *euthyna* or to stay in Athens if they were cleared of wrongdoing at their *euthynai*; moreover, I believe the unemended next sentence, εἶθ᾽ οὕτως ἐξοικεῖν τοὺς ἐθέλοντας (for the problems with which, see Rhodes, *CAAP* 471), to include under ἐθέλοντας also the non-excluded who as a result of their *euthynai* preferred emigration to a continued stay in Athens. Rhinon, as a member of the second board of ten, may well have been one of those who submitted to and were cleared by ordinary *euthynai*.

to offer sacrifice to Athena.[6] The first problem to be faced was to fill the vacuum left by the collapse of the oligarchy. We learn from Andocides that an interim government was elected consisting of "twenty men to take care of the city until a law code be enacted, pending which the laws of Solon and the statutes of Draco should be in force," that a Council was chosen by lot, and that lawgivers (*nomothetai*) were elected.[7] How the Twenty were recruited we are not told, but the contribution of ten each from city and Piraeus would be in tune with the spirit of the reconciliation, with each side choosing one man from each tribe (as had been done in the selection of the Ten, successors to the Thirty; cf. Xen. *Hell*. 2.4.23), so that both parties and all tribes were equally represented. In other words, the tone for a return to democratic institutions was set in that the appointment of a Council and a continuation of the revision of the laws received the highest priority in the restoration of social and political order. With the arrangements for the election of the magistrates (Xen. *Hell*. 2.4.43) and the restoration of the jury courts to their functions, the task of the Twenty will have been completed, except that they will still have administered to all Athenians, to the Council, and to all jurors the oaths binding them to observe the terms of the amnesty (Andoc. 1.90–91).[8]

THE PROBLEMS OF THE AMNESTY

The amnesty's success already impressed its contemporaries, though different authors distribute the credit differently according to their own political persuasions. Opponents of popular sovereignty tend to attribute it to the patriotism of the Athenians as a whole,[9] whereas its friends praise the forbearance and decency of the Piraeus

6   Xen. *Hell*. 2.4.39. Cf. Lys. 13.80–81, where ἔθεντο τὰ ὅπλα πρὶν εἰσιέναι εἰς τὸ ἄστυ must mean "rested arms [in an easy position but ready for action]"; see LSJ s.v. τίθημι AII.10.a. The date (wrongly assigned to the return from Phyle) is given by Plut. *Mor*. 349f (*De glor. Ath*. 7).

7   Andoc. 1.81–82: δόξαντα δὲ ὑμῖν ταῦτα, εἵλεσθε ἄνδρας εἴκοσι· τούτους δὲ ἐπιμελεῖσθαι τῆς πόλεως, ἕως ἂν οἱ [Stahl; MS ἄλλοι] νόμοι τεθεῖεν· τέως δὲ χρῆσθαι τοῖς Σόλωνος νόμοις καὶ τοῖς Δράκοντος θεσμοῖς. ἐπειδὴ δὲ βουλὴν ἀπεκληρώσατε νομοθέτας τε εἵλεσθε.... Cf. Poll. 8.112 and schol. Aeschin. 1.39.

8   The clause πλὴν τῶν φυγόντων in the bouleutic oath may well refer to those exiles who had not returned to Athens even after the amnesty had been extended to the oligarchs at Eleusis in 401/0 B.C. and may therefore have been added only after that date. However, this does not affect the date of the rest of the bouleutic oath as cited by Andocides; see Cloché, *Restauration* 274–76.

9   Andoc. 1.140; Isoc. 18.46; Pl. *Menex*. 243e.

people.[10] Even the one apparent breach of the provision that peaceful means be used to settle differences attests its success: at some point after the reconciliation the oligarchs, sequestered in Eleusis, began to hire mercenaries with the obvious intent of regaining power in Athens by violent means, and treachery and violence were used to bring this insurrection to an end;[11] but the Athenians were united (πανδημεί) in opposing the oligarchs, and we hear of no attempt on the part of the Lacedaemonians to interfere, however sympathetic they may have been to the insurgents. Moreover, when these hostilities came to an end, in the archonship of Xenaenetus (401/0 B.C.), there was no vindictiveness: friends and relatives of the oligarchs were enlisted to appease them, and the terms of the treaty were extended now also to Eleusis (Xen. *Hell.* 2.4.43; Arist. *Ath.Pol.* 40.4).

But there were other, more immediate problems. Since the purpose of the amnesty was to proscribe vindictive actions (μὴ μνησικακεῖν), it was a foregone conclusion that the city people, who had perpetrated or abetted the crimes of the oligarchy, stood to gain more from the amnesty than the Piraeus people, who had been their victims. The economic rehabilitation of the Piraeus people was the most important issue. The city people were made to return to their former owners any real property acquired as a result of expropriation by the Thirty, but expropriated movable property had to be repurchased by those who had returned from the Piraeus from those to whom it had been sold.[12] Thus, though the city people will have lost their investments in real estate, the Piraeus people lost the value of what they had lost by expropriation. Moreover, no property was confiscated or sold at auction except of those who had been excluded from the amnesty, and even these could avoid confiscation by submitting to a *euthyna*;[13] what movable property was confiscated was not diverted to private use but was sold to pay for processional implements.[14] Most of the Piraeus people reclaimed the property they had lost (Isoc. 16.46), but their leaders, Thrasybulus and Anytus,

10   Lys. 25.2, 28; Isoc. 7.68; Dem. 20.11–12.
11   Xen. *Hell.* 2.4.43 simply says ὑστέρῳ χρόνῳ; Justin 5.10.8 speaks of an attack, which he dates "some days later" (*interiectis diebus*); cf. Isoc. 7.67.
12   Lys. fr. I. 34–47 Gernet-Bizos (= *POxy.* 1606). According to Harp. s.v. σύνδικοι, a commission by that name was established to supervise the disposal of properties confiscated under the oligarchy. If these σύνδικοι are, as is likely, identical with those mentioned in Lys. 16.7, 17.10, 18.26, and 19.32, they will have functioned for several years under the restored democracy; see Lipsius, *ARRV* 115–17.
13   Walbank, "Confiscation," esp. 94–96.
14   Philochorus *FGH* 328F181. According to *Anecd.Bekk.* 1.304, συλλογεῖς were elected to list the properties thus confiscated.

had the magnanimity not to reclaim theirs (Isoc. 18.23). A similar spirit informed the settlement of public debts. Although the reconciliation agreement had stipulated that each faction be responsible for settling the war debts it had incurred, the repayment of the oligarchs' debt to Sparta was in fact shouldered by the people as a whole.[15] Aristotle aptly contrasts this with the situation in other states after a democratic victory, where the democrats not only refuse to make contributions of their own but redistribute the land at the expense of the vanquished.[16]

In social and political matters it was more difficult to effect the terms of the amnesty. The return of the Piraeus people created tensions graphically mirrored in the address that Xenophon says Thrasybulus delivered to the assembled people after the procession to the Acropolis:

My advice to you, men of the city, is to know yourselves. The best way of doing this is for you to figure out what grounds you have for arrogance that would make you attempt to rule over us. Are you more righteous? No: although the common people are poorer than you are, they have never wronged you for the sake of money; whereas you, though richer than all the rest, have perpetrated many disgraceful acts for your own profit. But since righteousness is not a standard that applies to you, consider whether you have any reason for arrogance on the score of courage. What better criterion is there for that than the manner in which we waged war against one another? Well, would you maintain that you are superior in intelligence when with a wall, weapons, money, and Peloponnesian allies you were trapped by men who had none of these things? All right, then, do you believe that the support of the Lacedaemonians gives you grounds for arrogance? How can it? They have handed you over to the common people here, hurt as these are by the wrongs done to them, collared like vicious dogs, and now they are gone. Nevertheless, I do not expect that you, gentlemen, will violate any of the oaths you have sworn, but rather that in addition to your other good qualities you will demonstrate that you abide by your oaths and fear the gods. (*Hell*. 2.4.40–42)

Regardless of whether this speech is historical or not—and even if, as Xenophon goes on to report in indirect speech, Thrasybulus reassured the city people that there was no cause for alarm so long as the "ancient laws" (presumably those in force under the democracy) should be observed—those who had stayed in the city during the

15   Arist. *Ath.Pol*. 40.3; Isoc. 7.67–69; Dem. 20.11–12.
16   Arist. *Ath.Pol*. 40.3 with Rhodes, *CAAP* 479.

civil war, especially those who had been on the list of the Three Thousand or had supported the oligarchy, were filled with fear for the security of their persons, their families, and their property, apprehensive lest the reconciliation agreement would not be adequate to protect them. Legally, to be sure, they were more than adequately protected. They were liable to prosecution for crimes under the oligarchy only for murder by their own hands (Arist. *Ath.Pol.* 39.5); they could not be prosecuted for having instigated, suborned, or abetted the killing of a person. Although verdicts passed under the oligarchy were declared null and void (Andoc. 1.87), former oligarchs could serve on juries and participate in Assembly meetings (Lys. 26.2) and could run for office; and though membership in the cavalry under the oligarchy could be prejudicial to them at their *dokimasiai* (Lys. 26.10; cf. 16.3–8), many are alleged to have been elected councilors, generals, and cavalry commanders nonetheless (Lys. 16.8). We even know of one official under the Thirty who survived a challenge to his election as archon some two decades later.[17] And of course all city people who like Rhinon had submitted to a *euthyna* immediately upon the restoration of democracy or who like Meletus and Cephisophon had dissociated themselves from the oligarchy in good time were automatically exempted from all disabilities.[18]

Nevertheless, the reconciliation agreement could not prevent frictions from arising on the related issues of citizenship and of rewarding those who had actively participated in the overthrow of the oligarchy. A promise of *isoteleia* had been given to foreigners fighting alongside the Piraeus people (Xen. *Hell.* 2.4.25);[19] in fulfillment of that promise "in the period of anarchy preceding the archonship of Eucleides," that is, in the first flush of victory, when archons had not yet been elected, Thrasybulus moved that citizenship be granted to all those who had returned from the Piraeus.[20]

17 Lys. 26 (*On the Scrutiny of Evander*) with Cloché, *Restauration* 398–404. Cf. also Lys. 25, in which a candidate for an unidentified magistracy defends himself, presumably at his *dokimasia*, against allegations associating him with the Thirty.

18 See above, pp. 493 and 494–95. Cf. also Lys. 26.17–20.

19 I find it difficult to accept the view of D. Whitehead "'Ισοτέλεια, a Metaphor in Xenophon," *Eirene* 16 (1978) 19–22, esp. 21, that *isoteleia* does not have a technical meaning in this passage.

20 Since Thrasybulus's motion to grant citizenship to Lysias, attested by [Plut.] *X orat.* 835f–836a, was no doubt identical with his motion, preserved by Arist. *Ath.Pol.* 40.2, to grant citizenship to all returnees from the Piraeus, it is reasonable

However well intentioned, the proposal will have alarmed the city people: the influx of an unknown number of slaves and of a thousand foreigners would have tipped the electoral balance in their disfavor, and the successful passage of the motion by the Assembly gave their fear substance.[21] In the interest of allaying these apprehensions and of not jeopardizing the reconciliation, Archinus had the decree annulled through a *graphē paranomōn*,[22] not on grounds of its content but on the legal technicality that Thrasybulus's motion had not come to the Assembly as a *probouleuma* of the Council.[23] With a similar aim, Archinus intervened again when he saw indecision about whether or not to join the exodus to Eleusis bedevil those who had fought on the side of the Thirty. By arbitrarily lowering the deadline for registration for emigration to Eleusis, he compelled many of them to stay in the city willy-nilly; he hoped that enforcing the reconciliation agreement would restore their self-confidence (Arist. *Ath.Pol.* 40.1).

The defeat of Thrasybulus's decree in the courts may have encouraged Phormisius to offer about this time a restrictive citizenship regulation designed to allay the fears of the wealthy.[24] It proposed the recall of the oligarchs from Eleusis and the restriction of citizenship to landowners; the measure had the approval of the Lacedaemonians, we are told, and would have disfranchised five thousand

---

to assume the date given by [Plut.] for Aristotle also. For it is unlikely that Archinus brought two *graphai paranomōn* against Thrasybulus for similar proposals; see Osborne, *Naturalization* 2.30 n. 77.

21   For the passage of the proposal by the Assembly, see [Plut.] *X orat.* 835f; the number of foreigners is estimated by Krentz, "Foreigners," esp. 305–6, at ca. 1,200, and by Osborne, *Naturalization*, 2.35–42, at between 920 and 960.

22   See pp. 473–74 with n. 61 above. Whether Thrasybulus (Aeschin. 3.195) or his ψήφισμα (Arist. *Ath.Pol.* 40.2; [Plut.] *X orat.* 835f–836a) were the target of Archinus's *graphē paranomōn* is immaterial to the present issue; for a *graphē paranomōn* against a decree already validated by the Assembly, see Hansen, *PAUP* 49 with n. 3, who cites among others the case against Theozotides' decree, which belongs to this period. [Plut.]'s remark on Lysias, ἀπελαθεὶς τῆς πολιτείας (836a), shows, however, that Lysias enjoyed citizenship for a brief span. It is tempting to assume that he was still a citizen when he prosecuted Eratosthenes.

23   [Plut.] *X orat.* 835f–836a; *POxy* 1800, fr. 6 + 7. If indeed the motion was passed as early as [Plut.] says it was, there was no Council yet to have approved it; see Planudes' comment on Hermog. Στάσεις, as quoted by Sandys, *Aristotle's Constitution*[2] 154: οὐ γὰρ ἦν πω καταστᾶσα ἡ βουλή. Cf. Rhodes, *CAAP* 474–75.

24   Dion. Hal. *Lys.* 32, which must be dated before the end of hostilities with Eleusis in 401/0 B.C., because the exiles whose recall is advocated can only have been the oligarchs at Eleusis, since the exiles from the Piraeus are said already to have returned.

Athenian citizens.[25] Phormisius's purpose can be inferred from what we have already found out about his personality: his old-fashioned outlook and his sympathy for Theramenes in the period between the peace with Sparta and the installation of the Thirty[26] suggest that he was an unregenerate adherent of the principle current in 411 B.C.— that citizenship be confined to "those best able to serve the state with their persons and their fortunes" (Thuc. 8.65.3; Arist. *Ath.Pol.* 29.5), whom he believed to be those who owned land. Thus, he will have opposed popular sovereignty, which considered as citizens all Athenians regardless of the source of their income, but not a narrowly based democracy such as the intermediate regime of 411/10 B.C. If his proposal had excluded no more than five thousand Athenians from citizenship rights, it would still have had a broader base than the intermediate regime, which at least in theory restricted citizenship to this number of people. No doubt the city people will have been pleased that this scheme, which would have swelled their numbers by eliminating the oligarchical enclave at Eleusis and would have given them a preponderance of the electorate, was put forward by one of the returnees from the Piraeus. The Piraeus people will have been less happy, for the bill would have excluded from citizenship those of them who derived their livelihood from industry and sea-borne commerce and those whose support had enabled them to prevail over the oligarchs. Accordingly, Phormisius's bill was defeated.[27]

Though unsuccessful, the proposals of Thrasybulus and Phormisius show that the problem of admitting foreigners to citizenship became acute after the oligarchy was overthrown. Uneasiness about this problem is reflected also in a number of measures designed to honor those who had joined the resistance. General agreement could be secured to reward all those who had fallen in the struggle against the oligarchy, including foreigners, with a public funeral and to grant them in perpetuity the same posthumous honors as citizens (Lys. 2.66). Also acceptable to both sides was a decree Archinus proposed (perhaps to counter suspicions that his opposition to Thrasybulus's bill showed he was more concerned to assuage the city people's fears than to give the Piraeus people their due) that all

25   Ibid.
26   See pp. 473–74 above.
27   The purpose of Lys. 34, preserved in Dion. Hal. *Lys.* 33, was to secure the defeat of Phormisius's bill.

citizens who could prove they participated in the defense of Phyle should be rewarded with a gift of money for sacrifices and dedicatory offerings and with a crown of wild olive and that their names should be inscribed on a public monument.[28] Since this decree honored only citizens, and of them only the few who had joined the anti-oligarchical movement early, it was a safe decree; it cannot have offended the now-important former supporters of the oligarchy left in the city, who by this time realized that the Thirty's excesses had deserved opposition. The masses who had returned from the Piraeus were as yet unrewarded.

The same delicate balance in matters of citizenship is noticeable shortly after the restoration in two decrees Theozotides proposed, which also ignored the noncitizens' contribution in overthrowing the oligarchy.[29] The purpose of the earlier of these, which reduced the pay of cavalrymen from one drachma to four obols a day and increased that of the *hippotoxotai* (mercenary mounted archers) from two to eight obols a day,[30] is hard to envisage. Quadrupling the pay of one branch of the armed services while cutting that of another by only one-third cannot have been dictated by reason either of economy or military effectiveness. Perhaps it can be explained as calculated to insult the aristocratic knights, who had been a mainstay of the oligarchy, by raising the importance of mercenary troops,[31] thus attaching a greater value to the services of paid foreigners than of citizen supporters of the oligarchy.

Questions of citizenship were more deeply involved in Theozotides' second decree, passed not long after the first. Its purpose was to extend the same public support that had in the past been reserved for war orphans to the sons of "all those Athenians who met a violent

28   Aeschin. 3.187–90. Fragments of the inscription have been published and restored by Raubitschek, "Heroes," where Archinus's name, intelligible in line 55, is restored as the mover of the decree in line 78 on the strength of Aeschines. Cephisophon (line 78) was the *epistates* of the Council on this occasion; see Chap. 9, n. 139 above.

29   Of Theozotides' antecedents we know only that he was prominent enough to have been mentioned by Cratinus (fr. 337) in the 420s. His sons Nicrostratus and Theodotus were among Socrates' followers, but Theodotus was already dead by the time of Socrates' trial; see Pl. *Ap*. 33e. Theozotides himself was apparently born shortly before 450 B.C.; see Davies, *APF* 222–23.

30   Lys. fr. VI.3.II Gernet-Bizos.

31   See R. S. Stroud, "Theozotides and the Athenian Orphans," *Hesp.* 40 (1971) 280–301, esp. 298–99.

death fighting for the democracy during the oligarchy,"[32] but it explicitly excluded νόθοι and ποιητοί (bastards and adopted sons) from its benefits.[33] This meant exclusion not only of the sons of non-Athenians who had participated in the struggle against the oligarchy but also of the sons of the slaves, metics, and foreigners enfranchised after Arginusae, of the Samians who were granted citizenship after Aegospotami, and of the Euboeans to whom the privilege of inter-marriage (*epigamia*) with Athenians was given sometime before 405 B.C. It meant in effect a reversion to the discriminatory legislation enacted by Pericles in 451/0 B.C.[34] The decree became law, as its publication on a marble stele shows. It is difficult for us to square its restrictive character with the anti-oligarchical spirit of the earlier decree except by assuming that it intended to implement the recon-ciliation agreement even-handedly, counterbalancing discrimination against the knights with discrimination against non-Athenians in order to consolidate unity among Athenians.

There is further evidence, however, of successful attempts imme-diately after the restoration to revive the stringent provisions of Pericles' citizenship law. On the motion of Aristophon a law was passed in the archonship of Eucleides that declared illegitimate anyone not born of an Athenian mother.[35] If the late and scrappy evidence for this law can be taken at face value, it would imply that the sons of enfranchised foreigners would be citizens only if their mothers were free native Athenian women and that the sons of men who had married foreign women while in exile were excluded.[36] Because this measure reversed the value of citizenship awards made in recognition of services rendered to the state when they were most needed, it was soon superseded by the decree of Nicomenes, which reintroduced the Periclean requirement that both parents had to be Athenian citizens, but it stipulated that this criterion be applicable

---

32 Ibid. 281–82, lines 4–6: ὁπόσοι Ἀθηναίω[ν] ἀ[πέθαν]ον [β]ιαί/ωι θανάτωι ἐν τῆι ὀλιγ[αρχίαι β]ο[ηθ]ὅντ/ες τῆι δημοκρατίαι.

33 Lys. fr. VI. 1 and 2 Gernet-Bizos, with Stroud, "Theozotides" 297–98 with bibliography in n. 47.

34 See above, pp. 433 with nn. 87–89 and 449–50; Lys. 34.3 with Stroud, "Theozotides" 299 with nn. 58–62.

35 Carystius, fr. 11 (*FHG* 4.358 = Ath. 13.577b): Ἀριστοφῶν δ' ὁ ῥήτωρ, ὁ τὸν νόμον εἰσενεγκὼν ἐπ' Εὐκλείδου ἄρχοντος, ὃς ἂν μὴ ἐξ ἀστῆς γένηται νόθον εἶναι.

36 See A. Schaefer, *Demosthenes und seine Zeit*[2] 1 (Leipzig, 1885) 138–40.

only to those coming of age after the archonship of Eucleides.[37] This legislation remained in force until the demise of the Athenian democracy after Chaeronea.[38]

If the decree of Nicomenes was an attempt to normalize citizenship after the anomalies of the last phase of the Peloponnesian War by returning to the *patrios politeia*, it did nothing to resolve the problem of rewarding noncitizens with anything more substantial than a public funeral. Though our literary evidence would lead us to believe that indeed nothing more was done, epigraphical evidence in the form of a decree passed in the archonship of Xenaenetus (401/0 B.C.), after the end of the war with Eleusis, shows that two years after his enfranchisement decree had been declared unconstitutional Thrasybulus himself, in all probability, finally succeeded in fulfilling the promise he had given at Munychia.[39] Though the fragmentary and composite nature of the inscription makes certainty unattainable, it is now possible to be confident that at least three groups of non-Athenians were rewarded: "those who returned from Phyle or [gave assistance] to those who did"; "those who participated in the battle of Munychia"; and "those who remained loyal to the *dēmos* in the Piraeus when the reconciliation took place."[40] Only the first of these groups seems to have received full citizenship. Consequently they were now exempted from the restrictions imposed two years earlier, that is, they were no longer excluded from the benefits that Theozotides' second decree had conferred upon the sons of those who had lost their lives in the struggle against the oligarchy. The privileges granted to the other two groups seem to have been less

37 Schol. Aeschin. 1.39, citing the Peripatetic Eumelus: Νικομένη τινὰ ψήφισμα θέσθαι μηδένα τῶν μετ' Εὐκλείδην ἄρχοντα μετέχειν τῆς πόλεως, ἂν μὴ ἄμφω τοὺς γονέας ἀστοὺς ἐπιδείξηται, τοὺς δὲ πρὸ Εὐκλείδου ἀνεξετάστους ἀφεῖσθαι. On the importance, see Patterson, *Pericles' Law* 145–47.

38 See Dem. [43].51, 57.30; Isae. 6.47, 8.19 and 43; cf. Harrison, *LA* 1.25–29, for this and later developments.

39 *IG* II² 10 with additions, most recently edited by Osborne, *Naturalization* 1.D6 with commentary ibid. 2.26–43 and bibliography 26 n. 66, on whose text the following discussion will be based. An earlier recent text is that of Krentz, "Foreigners" 304.

40 Osborne, *Naturalization* 1.D6, Face A (a), lines (a) 4, ὅσοι συνκατῆλθον ἀπὸ Φυλῆς ἢ τοῖς κατελ[θõσι συνελάβοντο ἐς τὴν κάθοδον τὴν εἰς Πειραιᾶ]; (b) 7, συνεμάχησαν δὲ τὴμ μάχην τὴμ Μονιχίασιν; (c) 8, [ὅσοι δὲ παρέμενον τῶι ἐμ Πειραιεῖ δήμωι ὅ]τε αἱ διαλλαγαὶ ἐγένοντο, where the restoration is guaranteed by the subheading of the Aegina fragment; see *SEG* 12.84.79–80 (= Face B, lines 56–57). What followed line 4 can only be conjectured; different solutions are accepted by Osborne and Krentz.

extensive. It is reasonable to assume that both received the *isoteleia* that had been promised them at Munychia (Xen. *Hell*. 2.4.25) and perhaps also the right to marry Athenian citizens (ἐγγύησις, line 9); all else is conjecture. The first group, which had joined Thrasybulus early, will have consisted largely of hoplites and is the smallest of the three; the second and third groups, which had flocked to Thrasybulus only after he had entrenched himself in the Piraeus, will have been considerably more numerous.[41] In short, by the time the Eleusinian oligarchs had been reintegrated into the body politic, the atmosphere in Athens had changed sufficiently to enable Thrasybulus to try again, this time with more discrimination and with success, to fulfill his promise to those who had fought on his side. The harmony that had been restored made the Athenians ready to integrate into the order also the foreigners who had helped establish it.

RECONCILIATION AND LAW PAST, PRESENT, AND FUTURE

The elegiac couplets Archinus's motion had inscribed on the stele honoring the heroes of Phyle praise them for having taken the initiative "in putting an end to those who ruled the city with unjust *thesmoi*."[42] Describing the ordinances of the Thirty as *thesmoi* brands them as "imposed" regardless of the will of the people, and it is not too fanciful to infer that the new order purports to be a revival of the Cleisthenic constitution, at least in the sense that it is to be governed by *nomoi*, norms accepted as valid and binding by those who live under them.[43] Indeed, it is no exaggeration to say that the reconciliation agreement, including the amnesty, represents a triumph of *nomos* not only over arbitrary government but even over the kind of popular sovereignty that found its extreme expression in the clamor

---

41 Osborne, *Naturalization* 2.32–43, estimates the first group (a) to have numbered 70–90, the second group (b) ca. 290, and the third group (c) 560–80. D. Whitehead, "A Thousand New Athenians," *LCM* 9 (1984) 8–10, believes that all three groups were awarded full citizenship.

42 Raubitschek, "Heroes" 289, lines 63–76, as restored on the basis of Aeschin. 3.190: τούσδ' ἀρετῆς ἕνεκα στεφάνοις ἐγέαιρε παλαίχθων / δῆμος 'Αθηναίων, οἵ ποτε τοὺς ἀδίκοις / θεσμοῖς ἄρξαντας πόλιος πρῶτοι καταπαύειν / ἦρξαν, κίνδυνον σώμασιν ἀράμενοι.

43 See Ostwald, *Nomos* 55–56 and 158–60.

of the masses at the Arginusae "trial" that "it would be a terrible thing not to let the *dēmos* do whatever it pleases."[44]

Although we are not told who formulated the reconciliation agreement, there can be little doubt that Thrasybulus and Archinus had a hand in it and that it formed the written legal instrument on which everything that followed was based. Its implementation was regarded as paramount and in Archinus's view even justified two illegal acts to ensure its effectiveness. The first of these was his arbitrary curtailment of the registration period for emigration to Eleusis (Arist. *Ath.Pol.* 40.1); since Archinus lacked the power to decree this in his own name, it must have involved collusion with some authoritative body, such as the Council. The second consisted in his arrest of a returnee from the Piraeus who had violated the amnesty, haling him before the councilors and persuading them, despite their lack of authority to inflict the death penalty on an Athenian citizen, to execute him without a trial as a warning to others. This act had the desired effect: according to Aristotle, no further vindictive actions were taken after the man's execution.[45]

But apart from these measures, both of which clearly belong to the unsettled times immediately following the reconciliation agreement, Archinus used only the letter and spirit of the law (*nomoi*) to enforce the amnesty in the face of considerable pressure to have it repealed (Isoc. 18.26). He met the threat of Thrasybulus's decree by using due process in the courts to have it invalidated on the basis of a legal technicality.[46] More important, after the end of the war with Eleusis, when the return of former oligarchical diehards was likely to revive old hostilities, he instituted the procedure of *paragraphē*, which made it possible for a person who believed that a case against him violated the amnesty first to demand a decision whether the case was admissible at all. Whoever lost the *paragraphē* case had to pay one-sixth of the amount at issue as a penalty.[47] Its effectiveness in inhibiting vindictive prosecutions is no doubt one of the reasons for the praise given to Archinus in the decades immediately following the restoration; but there was equally good reason to include the

44 Xen. *Hell.* 1.7.12: δεινὸν εἶναι εἰ μή τις ἐάσει τὸν δῆμον πράττειν ὃ ἂν βούληται.
45 Arist. *Ath.Pol.* 40.2 with Rhodes, *CAAP* 477–78.
46 Arist. *Ath.Pol.* 40.2 with pp. 503–4 above.
47 Isoc. 18.1–3, which opens the first case ever heard under this procedure; cf. also schol. Aeschin. 1.163. The magisterial study of the procedure is H. J. Wolff, *Die attische Paragraphe* (Weimar, 1966); for other studies and the date of its introduction, see Rhodes, *CAAP* 473.

Athenian *dēmos* as a whole in this praise:[48] because even potentially explosive situations had been handled with restraint and because due process had been rigidly observed, no new outbreaks of violence occurred. Even the *euthyna* of a former member of the Thirty proceeded "in accordance with the law" (Lys. 12.82); and Thrasybulus acquiesced in the defeat of his decree, though it had been duly passed by the Assembly: he did not use violence to get his way but bided his time until it was possible for him to reward his foreign supporters legally. A determination to let legal procedures prevail is also seen in the orderly defeat of Phormisius's bill, which must have offended many, and in the way Nicomenes' decree rectified the rigid application of Pericles' citizenship law that Aristophon's law had advocated.

The Athenians insisted that the new order be based on written law. The revisions that had been launched in 411 B.C. with the appointment of thirty *syngrapheis* were now once again resumed and at last completed.[49] How seriously this task was taken is shown by the appointment of *nomothetai* immediately after the reconciliation agreement, even before the election of new magistrates.[50] For our knowledge of who they were and what functions were assigned to them we depend largely on the decree of Teisamenus as quoted by Andocides (1.83–84), supplemented by some background provided by Andocides and by Lysias's speech *Against Nicomachus* (30).

Thucydides uses the term *nomothetai* in a nontechnical sense to describe the *syngrapheis* and *anagrapheis* appointed under the intermediate regime and active thereafter until 405/4 B.C.[51] From Lysias we learn that one of the ἀναγραφεῖς τῶν νόμων, Nicomachus, who had served throughout this period, passed his *euthyna* for this service under the restored democracy and was thereupon appointed to a similar office, which he held for the four years from 403/2 to 400/399 B.C.[52] Among his colleagues in this second term Lysias names Teisamenus son of Mechanion, of whom he speaks abusively as associated with Nicomachus; he contrasts the legislation of great men of the past—Solon, Themistocles, and Pericles—with that of these two *hypogrammateis* (Lys. 30.27–28). We must take this not as

---

48 Arist. *Ath.Pol.* 40.2–3; Dem. 24.135; Aeschin. 2.176.
49 See above, pp. 369–72, 404–9, and 414–20.
50 See above, p. 500 with n. 7, and especially schol. Aeschin. 1.39.
51 Thuc. 8.97.2 with pp. 404–9 above.
52 Lys. 30.2–4; see above, pp. 407–8.

their official title, since the rest of the speech leaves no doubt that at least Nicomachus continued to be an ἀναγραφεὺς τῶν νόμων (Lys. 30.2, 4, 19, *et passim*), but rather as an attempt to disparage them as mere underlings.[53] We have seen earlier that the work of the *anagrapheis* and *syngrapheis* during Nicomachus's first term consisted in an attempt to coordinate scattered legislation into a coherent whole and to prepare and publish authoritative texts of the *patrioi nomoi*, especially those of Solon; but it also seems to have included drafting new legislation, such as that concerned with administering sacred funds.[54] All we know about Nicomachus's second term is that work was done then on a new sacrificial calendar, substantial portions of which have been preserved on stone.[55] Since it is only marginally relevant to the new political order, we need not consider it here and may turn instead to the activity of the *nomothetai* attested by the decree of Teisamenus and by Andocides.

Nicomachus was probably appointed to his second term as *anagrapheus* about the same time as the *nomothetai* were appointed, though the functions of the latter were clearly different. Teisamenus's decree cannot be exactly dated, but clearly both sets of *nomothetai* to which it refers had already been established by the time Teisamenus proposed it in the Assembly.[56] However, it is also clear that these two boards had not been appointed at the same time. The earlier of them, described as "the five hundred *nomothetai* elected by the demesmen," the decree of Teisamenus directs to join the five hundred members of the Council in subjecting to scrutiny (*dokimasia*) the laws proposed by a second group of *nomothetai*, about whom more will be said presently. We are not told what functions this first commission had before Teisamenus's decree, but it is a natural inference from Ando-

53   The term is taken literally by Gernet-Bizos, *Lysias* 2.158, and by MacDowell, *Andokides* 122.

54   See above, pp. 415–20. Their work on the administration of sacred funds, described on pp. 419–20 above, invalidates much of the argument of Clinton, "Nature" 28–30.

55   They are best known through three distinguished publications of Sterling Dow: "The Law Codes of Athens," *Proceedings of the Massachusetts Historical Society* 71, Proceedings 1953–1957 (1959) 3–36; "The Athenian Calendar of Sacrifices: The Chronology of Nikomakhos' Second Term," *Hist.* 9 (1960) 270–93; and "The Walls Inscribed with Nikomakhos' Law Code," *Hesp.* 30 (1961) 58–73.

56   Andoc. 1.83 and 84, respectively, use the perfect ᾑρημένοι of one set and the aorist εἵλοντο of the other. On the decree of Teisamenus, see the discussion in MacDowell, *Andokides* 194–99, where the most important scholarly discussions up until 1961 are listed on p. 194. To them add Clinton, "Nature," and R. Sealey, "On the Athenian Concept of Law," *CJ* 77 (1982) 289–302, esp. 293–96.

cides' narrative (1.82) that they were to examine "the laws of Solon and Draco" with a view to definitive publication. We cannot go far wrong in believing that included among them were all those laws published or cleared for publication by the *anagrapheis* and *syngrapheis* active between 410 and 404 B.C., especially since some of their work had been erased by the Thirty.[57] The composition of this board shows that the laws in question were to be scrutinized in the most democratic manner conceivable, that is, not by an Assembly, which might be more or less poorly attended, but by a group of five hundred citizens, like the Council representing all the demes but unlike the Council chosen not by the lot but by election.[58]

In the course of their labors, Andocides (1.82) informs us, these *nomothetai* "discovered that there were many laws of Solon and Draco under which many citizens were liable to punishment for earlier incidents"—in short, that the laws investigated contravened the spirit of the amnesty. Reluctant to undertake on their own the changes needed to make the new code conform to the amnesty, they requested the Council to appoint a second set of *nomothetai* to consider the problem. The Council complied by appointing (perhaps from among its own members) a smaller group of *nomothetai*, which may have numbered ten or, more probably, fifty.[59] Their appointment was ratified by the Assembly; a scrutiny of all laws was ordered and as well the subsequent publication in the Royal Stoa of all that were acceptable.[60] Selection and ratification will have been completed immediately before Teisamenus moved his decree. The

57 See above, p. 479 with n. 80.

58 Note the language at Andoc. 1.82 ἐπειδὴ δὲ βουλήν τε ἀπεκληρώσατε νομοθέτας τε εἵλεσθε.

59 These numbers are based on emendations of the corrupt οἵδε by Sluiter and Reiske, respectively, to read οἱ δέκα or οἱ ΛΕ (δεκάκις πέντε); see MacDowell, *Andokides* 122, and Hignett, *HAC* 300–301. That they numbered fifty has the rather weak support (but support, nevertheless) of the possibility that the *nomothetai* of the intermediate regime may have consisted of fifty *syngrapheis*; see Harp. s.v. Ἀπόληξις, as discussed above, pp. 408–9 with nn. 252 and 254. For the method of their selection, see Andoc. 1.83. Andocides' assertion that all laws were to be scrutinized has been doubted by Clinton, "Nature" 30–33, largely on the basis of the space available on the wall in the Royal Stoa. His argument is weakened by the probability that that publication was to be provisional and in ink, pending a permanent publication on stone; see n. 82 below.

60 Andoc. 1.82: δοκιμάσαντες πάντας τοὺς νόμους, εἶτ᾽ ἀναγράψαι ἐν τῇ στοᾷ τούτους τῶν νόμων οἳ ἂν δοκιμασθῶσι. We can infer the στοά in question is the Royal Stoa because the *kyrbeis* of Solon were displayed there (Arist. *Ath.Pol.* 7.1) and because the prescript of the republished Draconian homicide law specifies it be set up in front of the Royal Stoa (ML, no. 86.7–8).

attractive suggestion has been made that Teisamenus was himself a councilor elected to serve on the new board of *nomothetai*;[61] if this is true, he may have moved his decree from the floor of the Assembly as a councilor without the customary *probouleuma* of the Council, which would explain why the Council does not appear in the prescript of his decree.

Teisamenus, then, intended not to commission new *nomothetai* but to assign a task to ones just appointed and to integrate that with the revision of the laws as a whole, in which the first *nomothetai* had played an important part. The nature of these two assignments is best seen through a detailed examination of the decree in the context in which Andocides sets it. Drafting a new code of laws had already been envisaged immediately after the reconciliation, when the Twenty were appointed, and the *nomoi* of Solon and the *thesmoi* of Draco were to remain in force until it should be completed.[62] Although Andocides creates the impression that this resolution preceded the appointment of the Council and of the first *nomothetai*, his narrative cannot be pressed to contradict the historically more sensible assumption that this stopgap use of the Solonian and Draconian legislation was formally voted at the same time as the new *anagrapheis* and the first *nomothetai* were appointed. In any event, the use of the laws of Solon and Draco is here clearly intended as a temporary expedient, pending approval of a revised code.

The *anagrapheis* and the five hundred deme-elected *nomothetai* will have set about their work at once. How long it took them to discover the conflicts between the laws of Solon and Draco as revised in the period from 410 to 404 B.C. and the amnesty clause we can only guess. It will certainly have been several weeks or even months before they appealed to the Council for help and before the second *nomothetai* were appointed. In other words, Teisamenus will have moved his decree in late November or early December 403 B.C.

The decree opens with the simple statement that the new order is to conform to the *patrios politeia*: "The government of Athens is to follow its ancestral pattern [κατὰ τὰ πάτρια], the laws [*nomoi*] of Solon and his measures and weights shall be used, as also the ordinances [*thesmoi*] of Draco, which we used in former times."[63]

---

61   A. R. W. Harrison, "Law-Making" 33.

62   Andoc. 1.81 with p. 500 and n. 7 above.

63   Ibid. 83: πολιτεύεσθαι ᾿Αθηναίους κατὰ τὰ πάτρια, νόμοις δὲ χρῆσθαι τοῖς Σόλωνος καὶ μέτροις καὶ σταθμοῖς, χρῆσθαι δὲ καὶ τοῖς Δράκοντος θεσμοῖς οἷσπερ ἐχρώμεθα ἐν τῷ πρόσθεν χρόνῳ. MacDowell, *Andokides* 122, refers the last clause only

Here the laws of Solon and Draco are not prescribed as a stopgap, as they were immediately after the reconciliation, but as the basis of the final code. The addition of the phrase "which we used in former times" indicates that the reference is not to the ancient documents as such but to the old legislation as revised, amended, and rescinded in the period from 410 to 404 B.C.—as it stood before the Thirty came to power, and as it had been scrutinized by the five hundred deme-elected *nomothetai* until they had found that some of its provisions conflicted with the amnesty, or perhaps more correctly, until its inadequacies were discovered in the light of the experiences of 404/3 B.C.[64] Probably the Solonian weights and measures were included in this fundamental statement in order to reassure all Athenians that no economic changes were envisaged.

Teisamenus turns next to defining the job for which the second *nomothetai* has been appointed: they are "to publish any additional measures in writing on tablets and display them near the statues of the Eponymous Heroes so that interested persons may inspect them. These are to be handed over to the magistrates within the current month."[65] The measures to be published and presumably also to be drafted are clearly additional to the code as it had been revised by the time the Thirty came to power. Interestingly enough, only additions are envisaged, not changes, deletions, or revisions.[66] These additions are likely to have included clauses such as that Andocides cited (1.87), affirming the validity of verdicts and arbitrations under the democracy and of laws enacted after the archonship of Eucleides and thus declaring the judicial acts of the oligarchy null and void, and Nicomenes' modifications of Aristophon's citizenship law, introducing a distinction between those who had reached maturity before and after the archonship of Eucleides. The one-month deadline suggests that the task was not enormous. Moreover, by the end of that month, as the decree goes on to specify, the finished product was to be in the hands of the magistrates within whose competence each given measure fell. This means that by then the new laws had to be

---

to Draco's laws, but, as I hope to show in the sequel, it is better applied to the laws of both Solon and Draco.

64 See A. R. W. Harrison, "Law-Making" 33.

65 Andoc. 1.83: ὁπόσων δ' ἂν προσδέῃ, †οἵδε† ᾑρημένοι νομοθέται ὑπὸ τῆς βουλῆς ἀναγραφέντας ἐν σανίσιν ἐκτιθέντων πρὸς τοὺς ἐπωνύμους σκοπεῖν τῷ βουλομένῳ, καὶ παραδιδόντων ταῖς ἀρχαῖς ἐν τῷδε τῷ μηνί.

66 This is emphasized by MacDowell, *Andokides* 195.

not only drafted but displayed on temporary tablets and approved by a process also established by Teisamenus's decree.

Thus, the second *nomothetai* seem to have fulfilled a function similar to that of the *syngrapheis* in 411 and in the period from 410 to 404 and to that of the Thirty in their original conception, namely, in order to draft legislation and submit it to Council and Assembly for validation.[67] But there is a crucial difference in procedures. The requirement that the proposed revisions are to be published in a temporary form is not attested for any earlier Athenian legislation. Although this cannot be used as an *argumentum e silentio* that the practice did not exist, it is significant that this procedure was now specified in a written decree. It means that every citizen was to have a chance to peruse at his leisure before their final enactment the laws under which he was to live and to voice any objection before a commission of one thousand, consisting of the Council and the first *nomothetai* (sc. the five hundred elected by the demesmen), now designated to scrutinize under oath each revised law as it was approved.[68] The Assembly was to have no voice in the final validation of the law code beyond passing the enabling resolution for this procedure in the present decree. As in the appointment of the first *nomothetai*, the task of validating the new code was to be left not to the chance of a possibly sparsely attended Assembly meeting but to a body representing every deme of Attica and constituted partially by lot and partially by election. Moreover, this body added to the Council, from among whom the second *nomothetai* had been drawn, the first set of *nomothetai*, who had discovered the inadequacies in the laws it had scrutinized. Imposing an oath on this new body meant it was to function as a unit in seeing without fear or favor that the additions drafted conformed to the amnesty. This procedure guaranteed that all laws were subjected to scrutiny before the final code was validated; the first *nomothetai* scrutinized the laws approved between 410 and 404 B.C. and additions to them in conjunction with

---

67   See above, pp. 369, 405, 408–9, 415–20, and 475–78. A. R. W. Harrison, "Law-Making" 33, suggests that they were called *nomothetai* because "the action of the *syngrapheis* in 411 had given that title a bad odour."

68   Andoc. 1.84: τοὺς δὲ παραδιδομένους νόμους δοκιμασάτω πρότερον ἡ βουλὴ καὶ οἱ νομοθέται οἱ πεντακόσιοι, οὓς οἱ δημόται εἵλοντο, ἐπειδὰν ὀμωμόκασιν. That this step was to precede the handing over of each validated law to the magistrate entrusted with its enforcement is indicated by πρότερον; the use of the present tenses παραδιδόντων and παραδιδομένους shows that the additional measures were to be approved by the enlarged Council seriatim and not *en bloc*.

the Council (Andoc. 1.82). Nothing was to be done without due deliberation; no part of the new code could be proposed from the floor of the Assembly.

If the Assembly played no part in validating the final code, that did not mean the code was not democratically approved. In laying the groundwork for the final procedure without a *probouleuma* of the Council, the Assembly had made sure that even the smallest community in Attica, not merely those happening to attend a given meeting of the Assembly, would be represented in validating the old laws and doubly represented in approving additions to them. Moreover, it encouraged "any interested private citizen to present himself before the Council to offer what good advice he could concerning the laws."[69] A similar invitation had been issued to all citizens in 411 B.C., when Pythodorus's decree had established the thirty *syngrapheis* (Arist. *Ath.Pol.* 29.3). There is no evidence that either at that time or in 403/2 B.C. anyone took advantage of the offer. But surely whatever advice may have been forthcoming in 403/2 B.C. will have been the better informed for being based on texts that had been provisionally displayed at the statues of the Eponymous Heroes in the agora. It is not clear whether comments were invited only on the additions or on the code as a whole, but the latter seems the likelier alternative: only the Council is named as the forum before which the interested parties are to present their suggestions. Probably therefore the formal and final approval of the new code was also left to the Council.

The final provision of the decree of Teisamenus is baffling: "Once the laws have been enacted, the Council of the Areopagus shall take care of the laws and see that the magistrates employ the laws enacted."[70] We noticed some evidence for a possible resurgence of the power of the Areopagus about this time: in the six months between the peace with Sparta and the accession of the Thirty, it may have taken over the control of the city *faute de mieux*, and the Thirty's repeal of the restrictions that the legislation of Ephialtes and Archestratus had placed upon the Areopagus also points in the direction of increased prestige.[71] Not only is it difficult to believe that the

69   Ibid.: ἐξεῖναι δὲ καὶ ἰδιώτῃ τῷ βουλομένῳ εἰσιόντι εἰς τὴν βουλὴν συμβουλεύειν ὅ τι ἂν ἀγαθὸν ἔχῃ περὶ τῶν νόμων.

70   Ibid.: ἐπειδὰν δὲ τεθῶσιν οἱ νόμοι, ἐπιμελείσθω ἡ βουλὴ ἡ ἐξ Ἀρείου πάγου τῶν νόμων, ὅπως ἂν αἱ ἀρχαὶ τοῖς κειμένοις νόμοις χρῶνται.

71   See above, pp. 468–69 with n. 43 and 479 with n. 79.

restored democracy should have retained this part of the Thirty's legislation, but there is no evidence that the Areopagus possessed between 403/2 B.C. and the mid-fourth century such functions as Teisamenus's decree provides for it.[72] The fundamental question is what precisely is envisaged by the "care of the laws" and by the supervision of the magistrates to make sure they enforce the new code. Similar powers are ascribed to the Areopagus by Aristotle for the pre-Draconian constitution, for the constitution under Draco, and for the Solonian constitution; and the powers of which Ephialtes is said to have deprived it are those that constituted its "guardianship of the constitution" (τῆς πολιτείας φυλακή) and its "caretaking" (ἐπιμέλεια).[73] Although none of these passages is as specific as we should like, we saw earlier that expressions such as φύλαξ ἦν τῶν νόμων καὶ διετήρει τὰς ἀρχάς, ὅπως κατὰ τοὺς νόμους ἄρχωσι,[74] which is verbally very close to Teisamenus's clause, and the definition of the νομοφυλακία of the Areopagus under and after Solon as consisting in overseeing the constitution, including the task defined as καὶ τοὺς ἁμαρτάνοντας ηὔθυνεν κυρία οὖσα καὶ ζημιοῦν καὶ κολάζειν,[75] suggest that power to conduct *euthynai* was vested since pre-Solonian times in the Areopagus and that it retained this function until Ephialtes' reforms took it away.[76] There is no evidence that the Council and the *euthynoi* and *logistai*, who were recruited from among its members, were now deprived of these powers or that they were restored to the Areopagus. Possibly, as MacDowell suggests, "it was thought that the existing constitutional safeguards were not enough to ensure that there would be no fresh revolution like those of 411 and 404."[77] But in that case the Areopagus will not have retained these powers for long. Alternatively, Teisamenus may have enjoined the Areopagus to be more watchful that the magistrates employ only the new laws and to be more rigorous in initiating actions (but not to conduct the hearings) at the annual *euthynai* of magistrates than the ordinary citizen (ὁ βουλόμενος), who in the fourth century never lost the

72 For a good discussion of the problems of interpreting this clause, see MacDowell, *Andokides* 124–25. Cf. also Ostwald, "Athenian Legislation" 126.

73 Arist. *Ath.Pol.* 3.6, 4.4, 8.4, 25.2, 26.1

74 Ibid. 4.4, "was guardian of the laws and supervised the magistrates so that they would follow the laws in their administration."

75 Ibid. 8.4: "It called to an official accounting those who had done wrong, having the authority to inflict fines and penalties."

76 See above, pp. 12–13 with n. 33 and pp. 40–42.

77 MacDowell, *Andokides* 125.

right he had in the fifth to lodge complaints against magistrates at their *euthynai* or to initiate *eisangeliai* against them for "not using the laws."[78]

Teisamenus's decree ends by specifying where the new code is to be published: τοὺς δὲ κυρουμένους τῶν νόμων ἀναγράφειν εἰς τὸν τοῖχον, ἵνα περ πρότερον ἀνεγράφησαν, σκοπεῖν τῷ βουλομένῳ.[79] This rather routine statement is of interest for two reasons. In the first place, the τοῖχος is located by Andocides in "the stoa," which is to be identified as the Royal Stoa; according to Aristotle this had been the repository of Solon's legislation (*Ath. Pol.* 7.1). This means that the conviction was visibly expressed that the new code stood in the tradition of the *patrios politeia* and was to perpetuate it. The second point of interest is that the American excavations of 1970 and 1973 in the Athenian agora have given us a very good idea of the physical setting for the revised code, though some details remain obscure.[80] The existence of an excellent summary of these finds, including a history of the Royal Stoa as a repository for the Athenian law code, enables us to confine our remarks to features germane to Teisamenus's decree.[81] What was to become the Royal Stoa was not erected until the second quarter of the fifth century, initially as a new home for the Solonian *axones* when they were brought down from the Acropolis in connection with Ephialtes' reforms. Homer A. Thompson has made the attractive suggestion that the "wall" on which the new code was to be inscribed was the rear wall of this stoa; it was probably made of brick and covered with plaster, unlike the end walls, which were of fine stone masonry. The revised code may have been inscribed on this wall in ink in the first instance, to be available to the public as speedily as possible pending a more lasting publication on marble stelai.[82]

78 Aeschin. 3.23 with pp. 13–14 and n. 37 above; Arist. *Ath.Pol.* 48.4 with pp. 55–56 and n. 214 above; and 45.2 with pp. 53–55 and n. 208 above.

79 Andoc. 1.84: "As the laws are being validated they shall inscribe them on the wall where they have formerly been inscribed for the inspection by any interested person."

80 See the excavation reports of T. L. Shear, Jr., "The Athenian Agora: Excavations of 1970," *Hesp.* 40 (1971) 241–79, esp. 243–60 with plates 45–50, and "The Athenian Agora: Excavations of 1973–1974," ibid. 44 (1975) 365–70 with plate 82.

81 Rhodes, *CAAP* 134–35 and 441–42. I am deeply grateful to Professor Homer A. Thompson for help in drafting the following.

82 See Rhodes, *CAAP* 134–35, citing *IG* I² 94 (= *IG* I³ 84) 22–25 as evidence for temporary publications in ink. We do not know where the marble stelai containing the definitive version of the new code were to be placed. The fact that

We do not know whether the code that the two sets of *nomothetai* scrutinized and the Council ratified was ready to be handed over to the magistrates within the month Teisamenus's decree had stipulated for its completion. We do know, however, that it took another four years before the calendar of sacrifices was published on which the *anagrapheus* Nicomachus had been working,[83] and it may well have been at this point, in 400/399 B.C., that the job of inscribing the code on stone was begun. Part of the revised code, enacted in 403/2 B.C., or soon thereafter, contained two new procedures for amending old or enacting new laws (*nomoi*); these resemble the procedure outlined in Teisamenus's decree only in that they deprive the Assembly of the validating power it had possessed in the fifth century and transfer it to boards of *nomothetai*.[84]

For an outline of one of the new procedures we depend on Demosthenes (20.89–99). Any interested citizen who wished to propose a new law had to do so in writing. We are not told to what body he had to submit it, but if later practice is any guide, it will have been before the thesmothetai.[85] The proposal had to include a statement of which law of the existing code was to be replaced and in what respects the new law diverged from any old legislation; at the same time, measures to repeal conflicting legislation had to be initiated.[86] The new proposal had to be publicly displayed in front of the statues of the Eponymous Heroes before it was discussed at

---

the republication of Draco's law on homicide in 409/8 B.C. was placed outside the building of the official charged with its administration (sc. the Royal Stoa) suggests that they were set up in the vicinity of the buildings that housed the various magistrates charged with their enforcement. Possible corroboration of this may be found in the discovery of a base incorporated into the north annex of the Royal Stoa, which carried multiple stelai, presumably containing the known marble fragments of Nicomachus's calendar of sacrifices; see Shear, "Excavations 1970" 251 with plate 49a and 255.

83   Lys. 30.4, where the τριάκοντα ἡμερῶν presumably refers to Teisamenus's decree.

84   See D. M. MacDowell, "Law-Making at Athens in the Fourth Century B.C.," *JHS* 95 (1975) 62–74, esp. 63–65, "The Old Legislation Law," and 66–69, "The Review Law," which, as MacDowell conjectures, were valid between 403/2 and ca. 370 B.C.; cf. MacDowell, *LCA* 48–49. For an earlier account of fourth-century procedure, see Hignett, *HAC* 299–300. Cf. also Sealey, "On the Athenian Concept" 289–302.

85   For the "inspection law" to which they were central, see Aeschin. 3.38–39 with MacDowell, "Law-Making" 71–72.

86   It is not clear whether the repeal procedure took the form of a γραφή to be decided by a jury court or of a vote by the Assembly; see MacDowell, "Law-Making" 64.

several (possibly three) Assembly meetings. But the Assembly's approval was not an enactment: the decision whether the proposed law was to replace the older legislation was left to a board of *nomothetai* chosen, presumably by the Assembly, from among those who had sworn the jurors' oath in the current year.[87] We can only guess why the *nomothetai* were chosen from this group: the jurors' oath contained the clause περὶ ὧν ἂν νόμοι μὴ ὦσι, γνώμῃ τῇ δικαιοτάτῃ κρινεῖν (in matters not covered by laws I shall pass judgment on the basis of my perception of what is most just); this and other provisions of the jurors' oath will have been seen as a safeguard for preserving the integrity of the law code as a whole.[88] The display of the new proposal in front of the Eponymous Heroes and the importance of *nomothetai* are clearly taken over from Teisamenus's decree.

This procedure was reinforced by another, called ἐπιχειροτονία νόμων (review law) by Demosthenes, which despite some similarities seems distinct from the rules laid down for enacting new legislation. This law, which Demosthenes cites verbatim (24.20–23), provides for an annual review of all laws in a prescribed order—laws pertaining to the Council, to all magistrates, to the nine archons, and to other officials—and stipulates that the question whether the laws in each category are satisfactory or not be raised in an Assembly meeting to be held on the eleventh day of the first prytany of each year. If the laws in each group are found satisfactory, the matter rests there; if objections are raised to any law or laws in any of the groups, the prytaneis and *proedroi* under threat of severe penalties are to set aside the last of the three Assembly meetings of their prytany to elect an unspecified number of *nomothetai*, again from among those who have sworn the jurors' oath. The number of *nomothetai* will have varied from case to case but will have been fairly large: on the occasion of which Demosthenes speaks it was fixed at 1,001. Since they are to be recruited from the same body as the *nomothetai* we discussed in the preceding paragraph, we may assume that here too the final decision whether the old law or the new prevails is in their hands. Similarly to the first procedure the new law must be displayed in front of the Eponymous Heroes every day between the first

---

87 Dem. 20.92–94 and 99, as discussed by MacDowell, "Law-Making" 63–65. This procedure was later modified by the "inspection law," for which see n. 85 above.

88 For a version of the jurors' oath, see Dem. 24.149–51; for the clause quoted, id. 20.118, 23.96, 39.40, 57.63.

meeting of the Assembly and the third. Moreover, at the first Assembly meeting, that is, when review of the laws is on the agenda, the Assembly selects five of its members to speak in defense of the laws proposed for repeal at the sessions of the *nomothetai* (Dem. 24.23). When, where, and for what length of time these sessions are to be held we are not told.

Nothing is known about how these two procedures may have been related; we have rehearsed them in some detail because they are likely to have become part of the revised code in or soon after 403/2 B.C. and because they perpetuate Teisamenus's provision to take the final validation of laws (*nomoi*) out of the hands of the Assembly and entrust it to a special board of *nomothetai* appointed for each occasion from among those who have sworn to uphold the existing laws. The procedures are democratic, since they mandate repeated discussion in the Assembly before a new law can be validated, but they represent a restriction on popular sovereignty because the validation does not come from the Assembly but from a broadly based group of *nomothetai*. Further, the detailed delineation of the procedures and the heavy penalties imposed on the relevant magistrates for noncompliance, especially in the case of the review law, show that law was to be supreme in the new democracy and that the *dēmos* could no longer regard whatever it pleased as valid and binding.[89]

The Athenians who had effected the reconciliation were aware that the revised code constituted a landmark in their history, as is shown by two further pieces of legislation the code included. A law moved soon after 403/2 B.C. by a certain Diocles declares three kinds of *nomoi* valid: those enacted under the democracy before the archonship of Eucleides, which no doubt refers to the *patrioi nomoi* validated by *syngrapheis* and *anagrapheis* in the period from 410 to 404 B.C. and confirmed by the first *nomothetai* in Teisamenus's decree; the laws written and published in the archonship of Eucleides, that is, the laws added by the second *nomothetai* and the Council; and all laws duly enacted or hereafter to be enacted after the

---

89 The significant difference between validation of laws by Council and Assembly alone (which constitutes an integral part of popular sovereignty) and validation by the procedure of *nomothesia* (which asserts the primacy of the sovereignty of law) is neglected by Sealey, "On the Athenian Concept," esp. 301–2.

archonship of Eucleides.[90] Athens could not have cleansed itself more unequivocally from the results of the oligarchy or established the restored new democracy on a firmer legal basis.

The second law, which set the seal on the process of revision, is remarkable for how it defines the new boundaries between popular sovereignty and the sovereignty of the law: ἀγράφῳ δὲ νόμῳ τὰς ἀρχὰς μὴ χρῆσθαι μηδὲ περὶ ἑνός. ψήφισμα δὲ μηδὲν μήτε βουλῆς μήτε δήμου νόμου κυριώτερον εἶναι. μηδὲ ἐπ' ἀνδρὶ νόμον ἐξεῖναι θεῖναι, ἐὰν μὴ τὸν αὐτὸν ἐπὶ πᾶσιν 'Αθηναίοις, ἐὰν μὴ ἑξακισχιλίοις δόξῃ κρύβδην ψηφιζομένοις—"The magistrates shall under no circumstances whatever employ a law that is not part of the written code. No decree of either Council or Assembly shall have higher authority than a law. The enactment of a law directed at an individual shall not be permitted, unless the same law be applicable to all Athenians and unless it has been passed by the secret ballot of six thousand voters."[91] The fifth-century democracy, in which the popular will had been sovereign, had differentiated between *nomos* and *psēphisma* not in substance but only in form. Both were equally authoritative, but whereas *nomos* stressed the general acceptance of a given measure as valid and binding, the emphasis in *psēphisma* was that its authentication had taken the form of approval by Council and Assembly.[92] Things were henceforth to be different. The written law, praised by Theseus in Euripides' *Supplices* (433–37) two decades earlier as the guarantor of equal justice for rich and for poor, was now officially accepted as having precedence over anything decreed by Council and Assembly to meet a particular situation, and any such decree was declared null and void unless it conformed to the code of written laws.[93] There is evidence that this distinction was observed for most of the fourth century, except for the critical period between

90   Dem. 24.42: Διοκλῆς εἶπεν· τοὺς νόμους τοὺς πρὸ Εὐκλείδου τεθέντας ἐν δημοκρατίᾳ καὶ ὅσοι ἐπ' Εὐκλείδου ἐτέθησαν καὶ εἰσὶν ἀναγεγραμμένοι, κυρίους εἶναι. τοὺς δὲ μετ' Εὐκλείδην τεθέντας καὶ τὸ λοιπὸν τιθεμένους κυρίους εἶναι ἀπὸ τῆς ἡμέρας ἧς ἕκαστος ἐτέθη, πλὴν εἴ τῳ προσγέγραπται χρόνος ὄντινα δεῖ ἄρχειν. For the date, see Hignett, *HAC* 302.

91   Andoc. 1.87; cf. also 85 and Dem. 24.30. For the last clause, cf. also id. 23.86 and 218, 24.59, and [46].12. On Clinton's belief that Andocides omitted the crucial clause "if there is a written law concerning the same matter" from his citation, see above, Chap. 3, n. 79.

92   See Ostwald, *Nomos* 2 with n. 2, and most recently, Hansen, "*Nomos*" 316.

93   For a striking example recently discovered, see R. S. Stroud, "An Athenian Law on Silver Coinage," *Hesp.* 43 (1974) 157–88, esp. 157–59, lines 55–56.

340 and 338 B.C.[94] At the same time equal protection under the law was guaranteed to every citizen by the prohibition that no law could be directed against an individual unless its provisions were applicable to all Athenians. Only the Cleisthenic law on ostracism was exempted from that provision; though this had never been used again after the intrigues against Hyperbolus in 416 B.C., it was still on the books as an empty shell.[95] Athens was still a democracy in the mold of the *patrios politeia* as it had existed since the days of Ephialtes. But Council and Assembly receded into the background in matters of internal policy, and the jury courts held center stage. Prosecutions of crimes against the state could still be initiated by any citizen, however humble, and every citizen still had the right to air his dissatisfaction with the administration of the state at the *dokimasiai* and *euthynai* to which all officials had to submit. But in matters of legislation the Assembly relinquished its final say to *nomothetai*. Thus the democracy achieved stability, consistency, and continuity when the higher sovereignty of *nomos* limited the sovereignty of the people.

94 Hansen, *"Nomos"* and "Did the Athenian *Ecclesia* Legislate after 403/2 B.C.?" *GRBS* 20 (1979) 27–53; Rhodes, *CAAP* 329.

95 MacDowell, *Andokides* 127–28, suggests that "a vote of 6,000 was regarded as virtually equivalent to a vote of the whole Athenian people, presumably because more than this number could not be expected to attend a meeting of the assembly." However, since a total of six thousand votes had also to be cast in an ostracism, the context makes the specific occasion more likely; cf. Hignett, *HAC* 165–66. For ὀστρακοφορία in the fourth century, see Arist. *Ath.Pol.* 43.5.

APPENDIX A:
EISANGELIA CASES
IN THE FIFTH CENTURY

AN *eisangelia* procedure is mentioned in connection with the following fifth-century cases:

1. Anaxagoras's indictment was based on a ψήφισμα proposed by Diopeithes, probably about 437/6 B.C., permitting εἰσαγγέλλεσθαι τοὺς τὰ θεῖα μὴ νομίζοντας ἢ λόγους περὶ τῶν μεταρσίων διδάσκοντας (Plut. *Per*. 32.2–3).[1] We are not told what juridical steps were taken in consequence of this decree, and our information on Anaxagoras's fate is conflicting. According to Plutarch (*Per*. 32.5), Pericles helped him escape from Athens; from Diogenes Laertius (2.12, 14) we learn that according to Satyrus he was prosecuted by Thucydides (doubtless the son of Melesias is meant) and was condemned to death *in absentia*; that Sotion asserted that Cleon was his accuser, Pericles his defender, and the penalty exile and a fine of five talents; and that, according to Hieronymus, Pericles produced him before a jury court in such a sickly and emaciated condition that he was acquitted.[2]

2. Lampon's amendment to the decree regulating the offering of first fruits at

---

1 The arguments against authenticity advanced by Dover, "Freedom" 39–40, fail to carry conviction; they are mainly based on the silence of other ancient sources and on the *a priori* assumption that the decree may have been fabricated on the basis of "fulminations attributed to Diopeithes in a comedy." Hansen, *Eisangelia*, ignores this case completely.

2 On the trial, see von Wedel, "Prozesse" 139–40. That a trial took place at all is doubted by Dover, "Freedom" 31–32, whom the conflicting evidence leads to suggest that "we have to deal . . . with ancient ideas about what must have happened, ideas generated by a historical attitude which is itself rooted in the condemnation of Socrates." However, the authenticity of the trial and its date have now been convincingly established by Mansfeld, "Chronology," part 1, 39–69, and part 2, 17–95, esp. 80–84.

Eleusis of about 422 B.C. prohibits erecting altars on the Pelargikon without the approval of Council and Assembly or cutting and removing stones or earth from the Pelargikon, stipulating the archon basileus must lodge an *eisangelia* against the offender before the Council and a penalty of five hundred drachmas must be imposed upon conviction (ML, no. 73.55–59). Since no provision for appeal is mentioned, we may assume that the verdict of the Council was final.

3. Antiphon's speech *On the Choreutes* (6.35; cf. 12, 36) mentions an *eisangelia* for embezzlement that the speaker had lodged in 420/19 B.C. before the Council against three individuals and the undersecretary of the thesmothetai, but the only additional information we get is that the trial was to be conducted before a jury court (ibid. 37–38).

4. Of the three *eisangeliai* of which we hear in connection with the profanation of the Mysteries in 415 B.C., Pythonicus's revelation of Alcibiades' involvement, made just before the fleet sailed, is the only one of which we know in the fifth century that was first given in the *ekklēsia*.[3] Whether Pythonicus's information constituted a formal *eisangelia* is debatable: the Assembly meeting at which it was offered was extraordinary and had been hurriedly convoked as soon as the profanation of the Mysteries had become known, in order to settle the matter before the expedition should sail.[4] But procedurally it is important to note that his charges were immediately investigated by the prytaneis (Andoc. 1.12), that after more information had come out a commission of inquiry (ζητηταί) was established (ibid. 14, 40, 65), and that the Council was given full powers to deal with the situation (αὐτοκράτωρ, 15). This meant at least that it could give immunity from prosecution (ἄδειι) to new informers. Some of those denounced fled (25, 34, 52); others were arrested by the Council (36) and put to death (34, 52, 59), whether by the verdict of the Council in this unusual situation or of a *dikastērion* we are not told.

5. Diocleides laid before the Council the *eisangelia* implicating the largest number of people at this time, forty-two, concerning the mutilation of the herms (Andoc. 1.37, 43). The Council then decided to arrest those he denounced (ibid. 45) and agreed to their pleas not to examine them by torture but to release them on bail pending a trial (43–44). Of those who did not escape, Andocides won freedom for himself and his relatives (56, 59) by informing against four (53). His testimony before the Council convicted Diocleides of lying; the latter was handed over to a *dikastērion* and condemned to death (65–66).

6. Thessalus son of Cimon lodged the most celebrated *eisangelia* of this period against Alcibiades apparently a short time after the departure of the fleet. Its main interest for us lies in the fact that its text has been preserved verbatim by Plutarch (*Alc*. 22.4; cf. 19.3), although we depend on Isocrates (16.6) for the information that it was lodged before the Council. Plutarch's document defines the charge as ἀδικεῖν περὶ τὼ θεώ and lists in detail the acts allegedly committed, but Plutarch himself (*Alc*. 20.5) and Isocrates as well speak of revolutionary designs attributed to Alcibiades. From Thucydides we learn that Alcibiades was condemned to death *in*

---

3   Andoc. 1.14 and 27, referring to 11.
4   See MacDowell, *Andokides* 68.

absentia, and his wording and Isocrates' suggest that Alcibiades was tried in the Assembly.[5]

7. Antiphon's trial after the overthrow of the Four Hundred in 411/10 B.C. was initiated as an *eisangelia* ([Plut.] X *orat*. 833a, d), and a decree is preserved, copied by the author from Caecilius's collection, that proves it was laid before the Council and referred to a *dikastērion* for trial by their decree (ibid. 833e–f). We learn more details about the procedure of *eisangelia* in the fifth century from this document than from any other. The generals produced information before the Council alleging specified treasonous acts of Archeptolemus, Onomacles, and Antiphon. The Council then ordered the accused to be arrested and placed in the custody of the generals and of up to ten members of the Council whom they would select to prevent the prisoners' escape and ensure their appearance before a jury court. The thesmothetai were instructed to issue summonses to the accused the next day to appear in court at a specified time, when the generals, their chosen associates, and any citizen who so desired would act as prosecutors. The decree further stipulates that the accused are to be tried for treason and that upon conviction the penalty appropriate to traitors be inflicted upon them.

The text of the verdict is also preserved (ibid. 834a–b). Onomacles probably escaped before the trial, but Archeptolemus and Antiphon were to be handed over to the Eleven for execution; their property was to be confiscated, their houses razed, their bodies denied burial on Attic soil, and their citizen rights and those of their descendants forfeited.

8. The final cases explicitly attested as *eisangeliai* were based on Agoratus's denunciations of Theramenes' enemies shortly before the Thirty were installed in power (Lys. 13.50). Procedurally, the noteworthy points are that the crime alleged was conspiracy (ibid. 21), that the denunciations were made before the Council (30–31), that pressure was exerted to repeat the charges before the Assembly—a proceeding deemed necessary in the case of *stratēgoi* and *taxiarchoi* (32)—and that the Assembly voted to have the accused arrested and the case tried in a *dikastērion* of two thousand jurors (34–35). The stipulations of this decree were not implemented, with the result that the trial was conducted by the Council, but this was only because the Thirty had meanwhile come to power: riding roughshod over proper legal procedure, they condemned all the accused to death and declared Agoratus a public benefactor (35–38).

---

5   Thuc. 6.61.7 has οἱ ᾿Αθηναῖοι pronounce the verdict ἐρήμη δίκη (cf. Plut. *Alc*. 22.5) and attributes at 6.60.4 to ὁ δῆμος the death penalty imposed upon those who had fled after being denounced as participants in the sacrilegious acts. Isoc. 16.7 suggests that the βουλή suborned τοὺς ῥήτορας to bring the matter to trial, leaving some doubt whether "the orators" spoke before the δικαστήριον or the ἐκκλησία. von Wedel, "Prozesse" 145 seems to think that the case was tried before the Assembly; Hansen, *Eisangelia* 76–77 (Case 12), at one point accepts the statement of Diod. 13.5.4 that the trial took place before a δικαστήριον (n. 12) and at another cites ibid. 69.2 and Plut. *Alc*. 22.5 to show that the sentence took the form of a ψήφισμα of the Assembly (n. 2).

APPENDIX B:
THE EARLIEST TRIALS FOR
IMPIETY (*ASEBEIA*) AT ATHENS

THERE seem to me to be strong reasons for believing that the decree of Diopeithes constituted the earliest attempt in Athens to make *asebeia* a punishable offense and that the legal concept was invented to check what was regarded as an offense against society—or rather, an offender against society—that (or who) could not be dealt with in any other way. Since Greek religion stressed ritual and sacrifice but was indifferent to belief—Xenophanes (frr. 10, 11, 12–14, 19–22 Diehl) was not regarded as a heretic for espousing unconventional ideas about the gods, and Pindar (*Ol.* 1.52) was not thought irreverent for his disgust at the story that the gods had feasted on the flesh of Pelops—we should expect ἀσέβεια to denote any violation of cultic rules, violations that must in one form or another have been perpetrated ever since cults and the rules they prescribed were established. It is no surprise that no evidence of this use of ἀσέβεια or of its punishment, if any, has survived: the offense is likely to have been detected by an officiating religious functionary, and what penalties he is likely to have caused to be inflicted will have been along the lines of acts of atonement or, at worst, exclusion from the cult. Accordingly, such matters are not likely to have come to public attention and are therefore not likely to be recorded in our sources, at least not before the fifth century. The earliest public religious infractions of which we hear in Athens are the conduct of the archon Megacles at the time of the Cylonian revolt and Aeschylus's divulgence of secrets to be revealed only to initiates of the Eleusinian Mysteries.

Our sources leave us ill informed about the precise nature of the offense and the procedure followed in these cases. Only Aristotle and Plutarch ascribe the offense against the Cylonians to Megacles;[1] our earliest and most reliable sources, Herodotus and Thucydides, ascribe it (directly and by innuendo, respectively) to the

---

1   Arist. *Ath.Pol.* fr. 8 Oppermann; Plut. *Sol.* 12.1.

Alcmaeonids collectively.[2] All our sources unequivocally assert that it consisted in butchering suppliants in contravention of a promise to spare them and put them on trial,[3] and the same sources attest the curse (ἄγος) that consequently fell upon the Alcmaeonids and their descendants. However, no such technical term as ἀσέβεια is given to identify the nature of their offense,[4] nor are we told what organs pronounced the curse. From Thucydides we learn the bare fact that the accursed were exiled; and the mutilated opening of Aristotle's *Constitution of Athens*, made more intelligible by Plutarch, suggests that at some later date a special tribunal of three hundred nobles confirmed the curse on them. The perpetrators' bones were exhumed and thrown beyond the borders, and their descendants were condemned to permanent exile.[5] Of importance for our purposes is only the unequivocal conclusion that in this exceptional situation no traditional judicial procedure was followed to deal with a religious offense; and the fact that the expulsion of the accursed could be demanded in 508/7 and again in 432/1 B.C. (Thuc. 1.126.12–127.1) shows that no verdict could be permanently enforced.

The details about Aeschylus's alleged offense are veiled in even greater darkness. Our earliest testimony is Aristotle's bare statement in the *Nicomachean Ethics*, adduced as an example of an act involuntary because committed in ignorance, that Aeschylus pleaded "that he did not know he was divulging a secret when he divulged matters pertaining to the Mysteries."[6] We are not told under what circumstances the offense was committed or the plea was made, and the plea of ignorance does not appear in the version found in Aristotle's pupil Heracleides Ponticus. From him we learn that the offense was committed in one of Aeschylus's plays, that Aeschylus fled to the altar of Dionysus for protection when he realized what he had done, that he was prevailed upon by members of the Areopagus to stand trial, and that he was acquitted by a δικαστήριον—whether this was the Areopagus or a jury court remains unclear—exonerated by his own valor and that of his brother Cynegeirus in the battle of Marathon.[7] Heracleides' story was further elaborated in

---

2   Hdt. 5.71.2 names the πρυτάνιες τῶν ναυκράρων as having given them an assurance that they would not be killed and the Alcmaeonids as accused of having slain them; Thuc. 1.126.8–11 names the nine archons as charged with their custody, attributes the assurance and the murder to those charged with guarding them, and mentions that these and their descendants were called ἐναγεῖς καὶ ἀλιτήριοι τῆς θεοῦ as a result. For a recent discussion of the Cylonian affair, see E. Lévy, "Notes sur la chronologie athénienne au VIᵉ siècle. I. Cylon," *Hist.* 27 (1978) 513–21 with bibliography in n. 1, who proposes a date of 597/6 or 596/5 B.C.

3   In addition to the passages cited in nn. 1–2 above, see schol. Ar. *Eq.* 445.

4   The closest identification is schol. Ar. *Eq.* 445: ὅτι ἐκ τῶν ἀρχαίων νόμων παρέβησαν τοὺς ἱκέτας φονεύσαντες.

5   Thuc. 1.126.12 with Arist. *Ath.Pol.* fr. 8 Oppermann; *Ath.Pol.* 1 with Plut. *Sol.* 12.3–4. Thuc. 1.126.12 assigns the exhumation and a renewal of the exile to the struggle between Cleomenes and Cleisthenes in 508/7 B.C.; see Gomme, *HCT* 1 *ad loc.*

6   Arist. *EN* 3.1, 1111ᵃ6–10: ἢ οὐκ εἰδέναι ὅτι ἀπόρρητα ἦν, ὥσπερ Αἰσχύλος τὰ μυστικά.

7   Heraclid. Pont. fr. 170 Wehrli; cf. H. G. Gottschalk, *Heraclides of Pontus* (Oxford, 1980) 128–39, esp. 135–36.

the second century of our era. Clement of Alexandria (*Strom*. 2.14, 60.3), citing it for much the same purposes as Aristotle had done, has Aeschylus acquitted by the Areopagus on the plea that he was not an initiate of the Mysteries. Aelian (*VH* 5.19) dramatizes the story incredibly: Aeschylus, he claims, was tried—before which tribunal he does not say—for impiety (ἀσέβεια) committed in one of his plays. When the Athenians were on the verge of stoning him to death, his younger brother Ameinias, who had lost his hand in the battle of Salamis, procured his acquittal by pulling the stump of his arm from under his robe and showing it to the judges. Attempts have been made to lend credibility to the story of Aeschylus's trial for impiety by fusing elements from these divergent accounts.[8] Since, however, Clement's statement looks very much like an elaborated misunderstanding of Aristotle's account, and since Aelian's story is a grossly dramatized and distorted version of Heracleides', the latter's lone voice is no sufficient basis to assert that impiety had been the formal charge against Aeschylus; and the lone voice of Clement is not sufficient to lend credibility to a trial before the Areopagus, especially since we know of no role of the Areopagus in cases of impiety before the late fourth century.[9] The farthest we can go is to accept Heracleides' statement: some sort of trial did take place on the charge that Aeschylus had revealed in one of his plays matters whose knowledge was to remain confined to initiates of the Mysteries, and he was acquitted. But we remain ignorant of the formal charge against him, of what tribunal tried him, and of the grounds of his acquittal, since Heracleides' testimony on these points conflicts with the more trustworthy account of Aristotle.[10]

If, then, neither the offense against the Cylonians nor the offense of Aeschylus can be regarded as ἀσέβεια in a formal legal sense, the trial of Anaxagoras is the earliest case of impiety of which we know. Some scholars believe that the novelty of Diopeithes' decree consists in extending earlier legislation against impious acts to the control of impious thought.[11] It may be doubted that such thinking constituted in itself a crime without the teaching Diopeithes added to it,[12] and it is legitimate to wonder whether there existed any legislation against impiety before Diopeithes. There is, to the best of my knowledge, only one indication in all Greek literature that suggests any may have existed.

In a passage we had occasion to cite earlier,[13] a Eumolpid prosecutor of Andocides asserts, καίτοι Περικλέα ποτέ φασι παραινέσαι ὑμῖν περὶ τῶν ἀσεβούντων μὴ μόνον χρῆσθαι τοῖς γεγραμμένοις νόμοις περὶ αὐτῶν, ἀλλὰ καὶ τοῖς ἀγράφοις, καθ' οὓς Εὐμολ-πίδαι ἐξηγοῦνται.[14] If the substance of this statement is correct, it seems written

---

8   E.g., MacDowell, *LCA* 198–99.

9   Lipsius, *ARRV* 367 with n. 38.

10   Ibid. 361 with n. 12. Cf. also F. W. Schneidewin, "Die didaskalie der Sieben gegen Theben," *Philol.* 3 (1848) 348–71, esp. 366–68.

11   Derenne, *Procès* 23; J. Rudhardt, "La Définition du délit d'impiété d'après la législation attique," *MH* 17 (1960) 87–105, esp. 92 and 102–3; MacDowell, *LCA* 200.

12   This is already suggested by Rudhardt, "Définition" 92, 102–3.

13   See above, p. 166 with n. 82.

14   [Lys.] 6.10: "And yet they say that Pericles once recommended to you that in the case of impious people, one should use not only the written laws that deal with them, but also the unwritten ones, on the basis of which the Eumolpids expound."

legislation against impiety existed in the time of Pericles and that on an unknown occasion Pericles recommended unwritten laws administered by the Eumolpid priesthood should also be brought to bear upon the offender. If we knew of the existence of such earlier written legislation from other sources, we could leave matters at that and try to discover what else we might about the "unwritten laws" mentioned here. But since there is no independently attested earlier legislation against impiety, and since we know of no circumstances before the late 430s or early 420s in which the state might have felt sufficiently threatened to enact legislation against impiety, a different interpretation of the historical facts underlying this passage can be envisaged.

Such an interpretation will have to start from the perception that the Eumolpid prosecutor's purpose was to make the Eleusinian functionary Callias's exegesis of a *patrios nomos* prevail over the written statute Cephalus appealed to in the matter of the supplicatory offering Andocides allegedly deposited.[15] For that reason, he invokes Pericles' authority as having affirmed on an unspecified occasion the equal validity of unwritten and written legislation and as having directed his remarks in particular to the unwritten laws that would apply to Andocides, that is, the regulations the Eumolpid priesthood enforced. The issue of a conflict between written and unwritten laws, which was essential to this point of the case against Andocides, need not have been an issue for Pericles at all. A historical core of the statement remains intelligible if Pericles merely recommended in a particular case of alleged impiety that the accused should not be prosecuted under written laws, by which the state tries and punishes offenders, but that the charge should be handled by the religious authorities responsible for the administration of the cult against which the impious act had been perpetrated, using as a basis the (unwritten or unpublished) rules governing their cult. Moreover, there is no need to assume that Pericles' statement addressed itself specifically to the unwritten laws "on the basis of which the Eumolpids expound": though this part of the prosecutor's version is germane to the case of Andocides, the story remains historically intelligible also if Pericles spoke of unwritten laws administered by a different group of priests. In short, Pericles in one case may well have advocated recourse to cultic regulations enforceable by priests rather than to written laws.

If this reconstruction is plausible, it is not a necessary inference from the pseudo-Lysianic *Against Andocides* (6.10) that written legislation against impiety existed when Pericles made the statement attributed to him. He may well have recommended that if the alleged offender had indeed committed an act of impiety, those in charge of the violated cult should deal with him and that there was no reason to employ or even introduce written legislation. We are given no context for Pericles' statement at all, but it would fit perfectly as an argument against Diopeithes when the latter proposed his decree against Anaxagoras. It would have been a powerful and clever argument in behalf of his friend, especially if Anaxagoras had never been suspected of impious behavior toward a religious cult. And, as we noted, there is no indication in any of our sources that Anaxagoras had given any cause for suspicion of impiety of this sort. In suggesting that charges of impiety be left to religious functionaries, Pericles may have wished to forestall or oppose in debate the kind of

---

15 Andoc. 1.115–16, as discussed above, pp. 166–67.

legislation Diopeithes was about to get enacted; but Pericles' attempt failed. If this hypothesis is correct, it suggests that Diopeithes' decree may in fact have been the earliest attempt to introduce written legislation against impiety.

A small measure of support for this hypothesis can be found in the fact that Diopeithes proposed an *eisangelia* procedure against the alleged offender. There can no longer be any doubt that the range of crimes to be dealt with by *eisangelia* was still wide and flexible in the fifth century and perhaps included any "crimes against the state for which no written legislation exists" (ἄγραφα δημόσια ἀδικήματα):[16] for Diopeithes' purposes it would be the logical procedure to adopt against Anaxagoras, whose conduct had not (so far as we know) made him culpable of violating an established law against impiety.

Even without the reconstruction it is clear that Diopeithes' decree, if not the earliest legislation of this kind, constitutes a landmark attesting the threat that intellectuals were believed to pose to the religious sensibilities of many Athenians during the Periclean era. Whether Anaxagoras, against whom it was directed, was ever tried under it remains uncertain;[17] if he was, the accusers named by different traditions, Cleon and Thucydides, son of Melesias, are of such disparate political orientations and the punishment of death or exile plus heavy fine of such severity, that it is safe to say that the case was remembered as serious indeed. We do not know whether Aspasia's trial, alleged to have taken place about the same time (Plut. *Per.* 32.1), was also initiated by an *eisangelia*. Plutarch calls it a δίκη, but this does not argue that it was not an *eisangelia*, since a δίκη might be private (ἰδία) or public (δημοσία); Plutarch is indifferent, anyway, to the finer points of Athenian legal procedure. The charge against Aspasia would certainly have fallen within the wide range of cases actionable by *eisangelia* in the fifth century. In fact, it is hard to think of a procedure other than *eisangelia* by which religious opponents could have more effectively attacked Pericles through two closely associated foreigners who were not guilty of any crime defined in Athenian law. The tradition about both trials shows that this era was remembered in late antiquity as one of polarization between popular religious sentiments and the values of the enlightenment.

The tradition about a trial of Protagoras points in the same direction. It is most explicitly attested by Diogenes Laertius as having been based on Protagoras's professed agnosticism about the existence of the gods;[18] his accuser is said to have been the same Pythodorus who became one of the Four Hundred. Protagoras was expelled from Athens, and his books were burned in the agora; he died on a voyage to Sicily.[19] A variant recorded by Sextus Empiricus has him condemned to death but escaping before the execution.[20] We have no information what the specific charges against him were or what tribunal condemned him. Some scholars have dated the

---

16   See above, p. 53 with n. 202.

17   On this point, see Jacoby, *Diagoras* 41 n. 159.

18   Protogoras 80B4 DK[6]: περὶ μὲν θεῶν οὐκ ἔχω εἰδέναι, οὔθ' ὡς εἰσὶν οὔθ' ὡς οὐκ εἰσὶν οὔθ' ὁποῖοί τινες ἰδέαν· πολλὰ γὰρ τὰ κωλύοντα εἰδέναι ἥ τ' ἀδηλότης καὶ βραχὺς ὢν ὁ βίος τοῦ ἀνθρώπου.

19   D.L. 9.52, 54, 55; similarly with insignificant variants Cic. *Nat.D.* 1.23.63, schol. Pl. *Resp.* 600c; cf. Plut. *Nic.* 23.4, Philostr. *VS* 1.10.

20   Sext. Emp. *Math.* 9.55–56; cf. Joseph. *Ap.* 2.266.

trial in 416/15 B.C. because Pythodorus is said to have been his accuser.[21] However, since the context in which Diogenes gives Pythodorus's name is not Protagoras's trial and exile but the suit Euathlus initiated against him, it is more likely that, like Euathlus, Pythodorus was one of Protagoras's pupils who brought suit against the master for having charged an excessive fee.[22] In any event, the evidence we have is not strong enough to support the view of some scholars that Protagoras was tried in an *eisangelia* proceeding based on the decree of Diopeithes,[23] but it is too strong to reject the notion of a trial for impiety altogether,[24] especially since Eupolis's *Flatterers* in 421 B.C. calls him (in a phrase reminiscent of Diopeithes' decree) ἀλιτήριος περὶ τῶν μετεώρων, which suggests Protagoras's presence in Athens about this time.[25] This unflattering remark is in itself insufficient for an inference that Protagoras was tried and convicted at this time, but it would support other evidence to that effect, if we had any; yet the date is too early if indeed Pythodorus was his accuser. Still, whatever the truth about Protagoras's charge of impiety may be, the fragment of Eupolis, together with the tradition about a trial and conviction, corroborates our conclusion that between intellectuals and the religious majority there existed an entrenched polarization in Athens in the 420s.[26]

The events surrounding the mutilation of herms and the profanation of the Mysteries in 415 B.C. provide the most striking evidence that Athens had been polarized along religious lines. Although these desecrations evoked a fear of conspiracies to supplant the democracy with an oligarchical or even tyrannical government,[27] it is indicative of the close relation between religious and democratic sentiment that none of the charges and trials arising from these incidents was for subversion of the democracy (κατάλυσις τοῦ δήμου), but all were for impiety.[28] These two religious offenses were interpreted as crimes against the state, which demonstrates that the democratic establishment felt threatened by them, and their enormity is shown by the dimensions of the witch hunt they provoked.

Andocides, our most important source for these events, tells us regrettably little

---

21 So Derenne, *Procès* 51–54, accepting the argument of T. Gomperz, *Greek Thinkers* 1, tr. L. Magnus (London, 1920) 440 with note on p. 587.

22 D.L. 9.54, 56; Quint. 3.1.10; Gell. *NA* 5.10. Cf. pp. 231–32 with n. 127 above.

23 So Rudhardt, "Définition" 91, and MacDowell, *LCA* 201.

24 So J. Burnet, *Greek Philosophy*, vol. 1, *Thales to Plato* (London, 1914) 111–12 with 112 n. 1; K. von Fritz, "Protagoras," *RE* 23. Band (1957) 910–11; and Dover, "Freedom" 34–37.

25 Eupolis, fr. 146a and b, "the sinner concerning celestial phenomena."

26 For the sake of completeness, it should be mentioned here that a scholiast to Pl. *Resp.* 600c (= *Suda* s.v. Πρόδικος) states that Prodicus of Ceos was condemned by the Athenians for corrupting the young. Lack of additional and more detailed evidence makes an evaluation of this statement impossible. The same is true of an alleged prosecution of Euripides for ἀσέβεια, for which Satyrus, *Vita Euripidis* (*POxy.* 1176) fr. 39, col. x, 15–21, is our only source; cf. Dover, "Freedom" 29, 42.

27 Thuc. 6.27.3–28.2, 53.3, 60.1, 61.1–3; Andoc. 1.36. See above, pp. 323–26.

28 Thuc. 6.53.1: περὶ τῶν μυστηρίων ὡς ἀσεβούντων; Andoc. 1.10, 29, 30, 31, 32, 58, 71; Poll. 10.97 with *SEG* 13 (1956) 18.1; cf. also Xen. *Hell.* 1.4.20, concerning Alcibiades. Isocrates' assertion (16.6) that subversion was included among the charges against Alcibiades is worthless historically; see Ostwald, "Athenian Legislation" 111 n. 37.

about the judicial procedures employed against the alleged offenders. But in the two sets of cases in which we get a hint, it is clear that *eisangelia* was applied, the procedure for crimes against the state and the same procedure Diopeithes advocated against Anaxagoras: we learn that Pythonicus's charges against Alcibiades for participation in the profanation of the Mysteries took the form of an *eisangelia* before the Assembly[29] and that Diocleides' accusations against the alleged desecrators of the herms before the Council constituted a formal *eisangelia*.[30] Similarly, Thessalus's indictment of Alcibiades shortly after the expedition had set sail was an *eisangelia* before the Council for his participation in the profanation of the Mysteries,[31] and there is reason to believe that all the other denunciations Andocides reports for either of these crimes may have been part of *eisangelia* proceedings, even though he does not so describe them, contenting himself with calling them μηνύσεις and ἀπογραφαί before the Council and informing us that their victims either fled or were arrested and condemned to death or exile.[32]

What interests us here is that though the offenses were entirely different kinds of impiety from that with which Anaxagoras was charged, the same procedure, *eisangelia*, was used against the suspected offenders. Whatever the legal basis of the charges against those denounced in 415 B.C. may have been, it was not disbelief in the divinity of celestial bodies or teaching about celestial phenomena. In fact, we do not know whether the law under which they were prosecuted clearly defined the offense they had allegedly committed. Plutarch (*Alc.* 22.4) has preserved for us the text of the *eisangelia* Thessalus brought against Alcibiades after the fleet had set sail; but like the decree of Diopeithes it is little more than a bill of specifics, accusing Alcibiades of "having committed an offense against the Two Goddesses by parodying the Mysteries and performing them before his close friends in his own house, clad in the ceremonial attire in which the hierophant shows the sacred objects, and calling himself 'hierophant,' and addressing Poulytion as '*dāidouchos*,' Theodorus of Phegaia as 'herald,' and his other close friends as 'initiates' and '*epoptai*' in contravention of the rules and regulations of the Eumolpids, Kerykes, and the priests of

---

29   Andoc. 1.14, referring to 11. MacDowell's view in his note on 14 (p. 73), that εἰσήγγειλεν does not have its technical meaning here, is disproved by the use of the same verb of Pythonicus's charge at 27.

30   Andoc. 1.37.

31   Plut. *Alc.* 22.4, with Isoc. 16.6; see above, Appendix A, case 6.

32   μήνυσις and ἀπογραφή are mentioned for the denunciations of Andromachus (Andoc. 1.12–13), Teucrus (15, 34–35), and Lydus (17); for Agariste any details beyond μήνυσις are omitted (16); and Diocleides is credited with εἰσαγγελία and ἀπογραφή (37 with 43). Despite the fact that fifteen of the names of the denounced mentioned by Andocides are also found on the Attic Stelai, which record the sale of the property of the convicted, it is likely that ἀπογραφή refers here merely to a list of the accused submitted in conjunction with the denunciation against them (see Lipsius, *ARRV* 301–2 with n. 11), not to a list of property that the accused, if convicted, will forfeit to the state (see Lipsius, 300–304; MacDowell, *LCA* 58, 62, 166, 256). For the Attic Stelai, see W. K. Pritchett, "The Attic Stelai," part 1, *Hesp.* 22 (1953) 225–99, and part 2, II, ibid. 25 (1956) 178–317, and "Five New Fragments of the Attic Stelai," ibid. 30 (1961) 23–29. The fifteen names are listed in MacDowell, *Andokides* 71–72, and in Aurenche, *Groupes* 191–92.

Eleusis."[33] Rudhardt sees an explicit legal sanction in the last clause: he believes that the relevant priestly authorities kept and interpreted unwritten laws that defined the nature of ritual infractions and could form the basis for prosecution on a charge of impiety in the courts of the state.[34] This is likely; but it means merely that by the late fifth century priestly authorities had no jurisdiction of their own and had to take legal action through the tribunals of the state. It does not mean, as Rudhardt seems to believe, that the public law against impiety contained even in the fifth century rigorous definitions of what constituted an impious act.[35] On the contrary, Diopeithes' decree and the wording of Thessalus's indictment of Alcibiades suggest that no stipulations of a law were invoked to support the charges but rather that it was left to the bill of particulars brought against the alleged perpetrator of an impious act to define the offense. This explains also why Thessalus, like Diopeithes, proceeded by *eisangelia*. For not only could this procedure be applied in the fifth century as a catchall in any "crimes against the state for which no written legislation exists,"[36] but it was brought before the Council, the same body by which new legislation had to be initiated in the fifth century. The lack of any general definition of impiety in the body of written laws is also suggested by the following consideration: though we can reasonably expect the *eisangeliai* against others accused of profaning the Mysteries in 415 B.C. to have been couched in language similar to Thessalus's indictment of Alcibiades, it is unthinkable that the same language would have been used also to indict those charged at that time with the mutilation of the herms. It seems, accordingly, that fifth-century law did not define *asebeia* but permitted any act offensive to the religious sensibilities of the people to become actionable before a court of law through the presentation of an *eisangelia* in the form of a bill of particulars before the Council.

The judicial proceedings of 415 B.C. were (so far as the extant evidence permits us to judge) the last *eisangelia* procedures used in cases of impiety. The next action for impiety of which we hear was instituted by Andocides within ten days of resuming residence in Athens in 403 B.C. against a certain Archippus for having multilated his family's herm.[37] The charge is called a δίκη ἀσεβείας, which was lodged not before

---

33   Plut. *Alc.* 22.4: ἀδικεῖν περὶ τὼ θεώ, ἀπομιμούμενον τὰ μυστήρια καὶ δεικνύοντα τοῖς αὐτοῦ ἑταίροις ἐν τῇ οἰκίᾳ τῇ ἑαυτοῦ, ἔχοντα στολὴν οἵανπερ ὁ ἱεροφάντης ἔχων δεικνύει τὰ ἱερά, καὶ ὀνομάζοντα αὐτὸν μὲν ἱεροφάντην, Πουλυτίωνα δὲ δᾳδοῦχον, κήρυκα δὲ Θεόδωρον Φηγαιᾶ, τοὺς δ' ἄλλους ἑταίρους μύστας προσαγορεύοντα καὶ ἐπόπτας παρὰ τὰ νόμιμα καὶ τὰ καθεστηκότα ὑπό τ' Εὐμολπιδῶν καὶ Κηρύκων καὶ τῶν ἱερέων τῶν ἐξ Ἐλευσῖνος.

34   Rudhardt, "Définition" 97–98.

35   This is the thesis of Rudhardt's article as a whole. He sees two such definitions in the decree of Diopeithes (pp. 89–92: disbelief in the gods and the teaching of celestial phenomena) and takes as a third definition the introduction of foreign cults, attested by Joseph. *Ap.* 2.267 (pp. 92–93); to these he adds ritual infractions of rules stated on sacred calendars and preserved in such inscriptions as the Hecatompedon decree as well as "unwritten laws" in the keeping of priestly families.

36   See n. 16 above.

37   [Lys.] 6.11–12. For the date of Andocides' return to Athens, see MacDowell, *Andokides* 204.

the Council but before the archon basileus; the offense was therefore to be prosecuted through a procedure other than *eisangelia*, presumably a δημοσία δίκη (usually called simply γραφή), which was preceded by a formal citation of the accused (πρόσκλησις) and was initiated by a formal presentation of the complaint before the competent magistrate (λῆξις).[38] Since this procedure, which we encounter again in the trial of Socrates,[39] is regularly employed in cases of impiety in the fourth century, it is likely that the change in procedure was effected through the revised law code 403/2 B.C.[40] Whether the new code contained a more stringent definition of *asebeia* remains doubtful. In any event, Andocides' case against Archippus may have been one of the earliest to be handled by a γραφή.[41] It is ironic that it should have been used by a former oligarch, perhaps in an attempt to rehabilitate his standing in the restored democracy.

---

38   See Lipsius, *ARRV* 815–18 with 815 n. 40 and 817 n. 47.

39   See Pl. *Euthyphr.* 2a–c; Xen. *Mem.* 1.1.1; D.L. 2.38, 40.

40   Hypereides 4.6; Arist. *Ath.Pol.* 57.2; [Dem.] 35.48; Poll. 8.90 with Derenne, *Procès* 236–39, and MacDowell, *LCA* 199–200. MacDowell believes that cases of ἀσέβεια could be handled by γραφή already in the fifth century. But there is no evidence for that, and there is no reason to believe that such trials were a frequent occurrence.

41   The case against Andocides himself in 400 B.C. was apparently not on a charge of impiety but an ἔνδειξις for exercising rights to which he was not entitled; see MacDowell, *Andokides* 13–14.

APPENDIX C:
THE SOCIAL AND INTELLECTUAL
BACKGROUND OF THE ἀσεβοῦντες
OF 415 B.C.

WE learn from Andocides that some three hundred people were implicated in the mutilation of the herms in 415 B.C.;[1] neither he nor our other sources, Thucydides and Plutarch, say how many were alleged to have been involved in the profanation of the Mysteries. In a painstaking examination of all persons known to have been incriminated in either or both of these offenses, Aurenche has compiled a list of seventy names,[2] at best a fraction of those under suspicion at that time.

Yet even though this is only a fraction, not all of those Aurenche includes can have been incriminated. Ingenious and suggestive as Aurenche's work is as an examination of the factors that went into forming social and political groups in Athens in the late fifth century, his list can be used only with great caution. Surely, the mere fact that Callias son of Hipponicus was Alcibiades' brother-in-law does not make him a participant in the profanation of the Mysteries,[3] especially since as dàidouchos and a high Eleusinian functionary he could hardly have condoned the desecration.[4] Nor can Euryptolemus be implicated by the mere fact that he was Alcibiades' cousin and is later attested as his close associate.[5] In the absence of any

---

1 This figure is first attributed to Diocleides at Andoc. 1.37, but Andocides makes it his own ibid. 51 and 58.

2 Aurenche, *Groupes*, esp. 191–228. A shorter list of sixty-five identifiable plus a few unidentifiable names can be found in Dover, *HCT* 4.277–80, not mentioned by Aurenche.

3 As Aurenche, *Groupes* 46 n. 5 with 104, will have it.

4 Xen. *Hell*. 6.3.3; Arist. *Rh*. 3.2, 1405ᵃ19–20.

5 Aurenche, *Groupes* 60 with 104.

evidence, it is injudicious to make Nicias a participant in the profanation of the Mysteries merely because he had conspired with Alcibiades on an earlier occasion to obtain the ostracism of Hyperbolus or because he was rich and two of his brothers were involved:[6] Thucydides would hardly have had him affirm his own piety or have praised him for ordering his life by high moral standards if he had been implicated in any way in the profanations of 415 B.C.[7] Moreover, Agariste's denunciation does not automatically make her a participant in the profanations, to say nothing of her husband, Alcmeonides.[8]

In the remaining sixty-four cases of Aurenche's list, some degree of involvement in one or both of the sacrileges is indeed likely, even if we cannot be sure in every case whether implication resulted in an *eisangelia* for impiety against the person involved. On the basis of Andocides' *On the Mysteries*, we can feel confident that at least forty-nine persons were—or were to be—tried for impiety: eleven denounced for profaning the Mysteries by Alcibiades' slave Andromachus in support of Pythonicus's *eisangelia* (Andoc. 1.12–14);[9] twelve denounced by Teucrus for profaning the Mysteries (ibid. 15)[10] and eighteen for mutilation of the herms, including Meletus, also denounced by Andromachus for profanation of the Mysteries (ibid. 35); four denounced by Agariste for participation in the Mysteries, including Alcibiades, already denounced by Teucrus (ibid. 16);[11] four denounced for the same offense by the slave Lydus, including his master, Pherecles, also denounced by Teucrus for mutilating the herms (ibid. 17–18); and four against whom Andocides informed for mutilation of the herms, including Panaetius, already denounced by Teucrus for profaning the Mysteries (ibid. 52, 67). To these forty-nine, we can add the two βουλευταί and the eleven members of Andocides' family who were among the forty-two Diocleides denounced for mutilation of the herms by way of *eisangelia* (ibid. 37, 43–44, 47)—even though apparently none were tried because Diocleides' testimony was later found false and he was executed for it (ibid. 65–66). We can be reasonably certain also of the conviction of Alcibiades Phegousios, who fled from Athens together with Amiantus of Aegina after Diocleides had testified that they had suborned him (ibid.), because his name appeared on the lists of those whose property was auctioned off by the *pōlētai*.[12] Callias son of Telocles should be included among those Diocleides denounced; for although Andocides (1.47) does not list him as incriminated by Diocleides, his brother Euphemus, who was implicated no more deeply than Callias in the attempt to bribe Diocleides, is listed among the accused (Andoc. 1.40–42 with 47). Finally, although the evidence is late and slender for Timaeus, Plutarch names him as a person with whom Andocides developed a close

6   Aurenche, *Groupes* 47 n. 1, 77–78, 151–52.

7   Thuc. 7.77.2, καίτοι πολλὰ μὲν ἐς θεοὺς νόμιμα δεδιῄτημαι, πολλὰ δὲ ἐς ἀνθρώπους δίκαια καὶ ἀνεπίφθονα, and 86.5: διὰ τὴν πᾶσαν ἐς ἀρετὴν νενομισμένην ἐπιτήδευσιν, with Dover, *HCT* 4.463.

8   As in Aurenche, *Groupes* 46 with nn. 2 and 4, 103–4.

9   Included among the eleven is Poulytion, at whose house the profanations were said to have taken place.

10   Including Teucrus himself.

11   Including Charmides, at whose house the profanation was alleged to have taken place.

12   Stelai 1.viii.3–4 in *IG* I^3 428.

relationship in prison and says he persuaded Andocides to give the information that Andocides says Charmides persuaded him to give;[13] this deserves some attention, even if we cannot do much with it.

The list of those thought with some probability to have been incriminated for impiety in 415 B.C. will then look as follows:[14]

A. Denounced by Andromachus for Mysteries (Andoc. 1.12–14)
    1. Alcibiades (see also C)
    2. Archebiades
    3. Archippus
    4. Aristomenes
    5. Diogenes
    6. Meletus (see also E)
    7. Nicides
    8. Oeonias
    9. Panaetius (see also F)
    10. Polystratus
    11. Poulytion

B. Denounced by Teucrus for Mysteries (Andoc. 1.15)
    12. Antiphon
    13. Cephisodorus
    14. Diognetus
    15. Gniphonides
    16. Hephaestodorus
    17. Isonomus
    18. Pantacles
    19. Phaedrus
    20. Philocrates
    21. Smindyrides
    22. Teisarchus
    23. Teucrus

C. Denounced by Agariste for Mysteries (Andoc. 1.16)
    24. Adeimantus
        Alcibiades (= A1)
    25. Axiochus
    26. Charmides (son of Glaucon?)

D. Denounced by Lydus for Mysteries (Andoc. 1.17–18)
    27. Acumenus
    28. Autocrator
    29. Leogoras (see also G)
    30. Pherecles (see also E)

---

13 Plut. *Alc.* 21.4; cf. Andoc. 1.48 with MacDowell, *Andokides* 177–80, esp. 179–80.

14 This list is identical with that of Dover, *HCT* 4.277–80, but differently organized. Unlike Dover, I do not believe in two Panaetii.

E. Denounced by Teucrus for herms (Andoc. 1.35)
   31. Alcisthenes
   32. Antidorus
   33. Archidamus
   34. Charippus
   35. Eryximachus
   36. Euctemon
   37. Euphiletus
   38. Eurydamas
   39. Eurymachus
   40. Glaucippus
       Meletus (= A6)
   41. Menestratus
       Pherecles (= D30)
   42. Platon
   43. Polyeuctus
   44. Telenicus
   45. Theodorus
   46. Timanthes

F. Denounced by Andocides for herms (Andoc. 1.52, 67)
   47. Chaeredemus
   48. Diacritus
   49. Lysistratus
       Panaetius (= A9)

G. Denounced by Diocleides for herms (Andoc. 1.43–47)
   50. Andocides
   51. Apsephion
   52. Callias son of Alcmeon
   53. Callias son of Telocles
   54. Charmides son of Aristoteles
   55. Critias
   56. Eucrates
   57. Euphemus
       Leogoras (= D29)
   58. Mantitheus
   59. Nisaeus
   60. Phrynichus
   61. Taureas

H. Others
   62. Alcibiades Phegousios
   63. Amiantus
   64. Timaeus

Of these sixty-four names, fifteen are also preserved on the Attic Stelai registering the sale of property of those convicted of impiety in 415 B.C.[15] Together with what

---

15   The classic publication is that of W. K. Pritchett, "Attic Stelai," part 1, most accessible in *SEG* 13 (1956) nos. 12–22, with corrections and additions cited in

literary evidence there is apart from Andocides, these give us information on twenty-seven of those inculpated, that is, on less than half. For the rest, we have no more than Andocides' meager information, in most cases merely by whom they were denounced, for which of the two offenses, and what verdict was passed upon them. Moreover, the identification of many individuals remains uncertain: was the Antiphon denounced by Teucrus (12) the orator and/or sophist, or some other Antiphon? Is the Charmides presumably denounced by Agariste (26) the same Charmides (54) against whom Diocleides informed? Is the inference correct that the Meletus on Andromachus's list (6) is identical with the one Teucrus denounced? Several similar problems could be cited to demonstrate that the conclusions drawn from the twenty-seven names we believe we are able to identify can be no more certain than their identification. But however precarious such conclusions may be, we must try to draw them or abandon all hope of gaining any insight into the events of 415 B.C. Moreover, we must take the still more precarious step of assuming that this fraction of a fraction is a representative sample of all those inculpated at that time.

Dover has used the list to demonstrate that "the identifiable participants in the profanations are connected, directly or through intermediaries, with Alkibiades";[16] Aurenche's work leaves no doubt that most of the accused of 415 B.C. came from aristocratic families or from families of sufficient wealth to be considered upper-class.[17] None of those incriminated was so far as we can ascertain a member of the lower classes.[18] Since our concern here is to establish that these offenders were chiefly men between the ages of twenty-five and thirty-five, that a large number among them were part of the Athenian intelligentsia, which had been sitting at the feet of the sophists, and that many among them are known to have been later averse or even hostile to the principles of the Athenian democracy, we shall have to subject our list to a renewed scrutiny from these points of view.

Of the twenty-seven identifiable persons, only six seem to belong to an older generation: Axiochus (25) Acumenus (27), Leogoras (29), Callias son of Alcmeon (52), Critias (55), and Taureas (61). *Axiochus* (25) was an uncle of Alcibiades, in whose debaucheries at Abydus he is unreliably said to have shared.[19] He will have been over fifty in 415 B.C., and the records of the *pōlētai* prove he was a wealthy real-estate owner.[20] The ties linking him and his son Cleinias to Socrates are attested in Platonic writings and show a close relationship to the intellectual circles of Athens,[21]

Appendix B, n. 32. All these are now in *IG* I³ 421–30. For the list of these fifteen, see MacDowell, *Andokides* 71–72.

16 Dover, *HCT* 4.276–88; quote from 283.

17 Aurenche, *Groupes* 51–81, 123–53.

18 Note, for example, that even someone like Apsephion, of whom or of whose connections we know no more than what Andocides relates at 1.43–44, must have been wealthy enough to own a horse on which to escape to the enemy.

19 Lys. fr. 4 Thalheim, from Ath. 12.534f–535a and 13.574d–e.

20 Davies, *APF* 16–17; Aurenche, *Groupes* 128–30. Davies believes him to have been over seventy years old in 406 B.C. But his escapades with Alcibiades suggest that he was considerably younger than his brother Cleinias, perhaps by as much as ten years; see Hatzfeld 29 with n. 2.

21 Pl. *Euthyd.* 271a–b, 275a; [Pl.] *Axioch.* 364b–c *et passim*.

and his political outlook may be reflected in caricature in what he is represented as saying in a dialogue, probably of the first century B.C.: "For the people, my dear Socrates, are an ungrateful, fickle, brutal, maliciously slanderous, and uneducated thing, as if slapped together from the scum of a mob and of blabberers of violence. To cultivate its friendship is to increase one's own misery."[22] Another passage in the same dialogue intimates that Axiochus had at least the courage of his convictions; he is said to have joined Euryptolemus in defending the generals of Arginusae in 406 B.C. ([Pl.] *Axiochus* 368e–369a).

Axiochus's presence among the accused for profaning the Mysteries may be explained by his attachment to his nephew Alcibiades (1); for *Acumenus* (27) and *Leogoras* (29) a probable reason is the involvement of their sons, Eryximachus (35) and Andocides (50), respectively. Acumenus's paternity is our only indication of his age; nothing else is known about him, except that like his son he was a physician and a friend of Socrates.[23] On Leogoras we are better informed. He was born about 470 B.C. into one of the oldest aristocratic families of Athens,[24] so he will have been about fifty-five by the time he was denounced by Lydus for profaning the Mysteries and by Diocleides for mutilating the herms (Andoc. 1.17, 47). Though we are told that he was active in public affairs, his only known engagement was as an Athenian ambassador to Macedonia in 426 B.C., where his family had connections with the royal house.[25] Comedies of the 420s allude to his luxurious and spendthrift life.[26]

The only indications of the age of *Callias son of Alcmeon* (52) are that he was a brother of Taureas (61), that both were cousins of Leogoras, and that Taureas had a son, Niseaus (59), old enough to be incriminated along with his father. This permits the guess that the two brothers will have been born between 465 and 460 B.C., that is, they were about forty-five or fifty in 415 B.C.[27] Nothing else is known about Callias. Taureas is generally taken to be the choregus, on whose altercation with Alcibiades we remarked earlier.[28]

Critias (55), the cousin of Leogoras, is almost certainly the son of Callaeschrus who gained notoriety as leader of the Thirty in 404 B.C. Since he is believed to have been born about 460 B.C. or not much thereafter,[29] he will have been between forty and forty-five in 415 B.C. and can be regarded either as the youngest among the older identifiable offenders or as the oldest of the younger. He came from an old aristocratic family that traced its descent back to Dropides, variously called Solon's

---

22 [Pl.] *Axioch*. 369a–b: δῆμος γάρ, ὦ φίλε Σώκρατες, ἀχάριστον, ἀψίκορον, ὠμόν, βάσκανον, ἀπαίδευτον, ὡς ἂν συνηρανισμένον ἐκ συγκλύδων ὄχλου καὶ βιαίων φλυάρων. ὁ δὲ τούτῳ προσεταιριζόμενος ἀθλιώτερος μακρῷ. For the date, see J. Souilhé, ed. and tr., *Platon: Oeuvres complètes* 13.3 (Paris, 1962) 132–36.

23 Pl. *Phdr*. 227a, 268a; Xen. *Mem*. 3.13.2.

24 Andoc. 1.147; Davies, *APF* 30.

25 Schol. Ar. *Nub*. 109; ML, no. 65.51; Andoc. 2.11 with B. D. Meritt, H. T. Wade-Gery, and M. F. McGregor, *The Athenian Tribute Lists* 3 (Cambridge, Mass., 1950) 136 with n. 15.

26 Ar. *Nub*. 109 with schol.; *Vesp*. 1269; Eup. fr. 44; Plato Com. fr. 106.

27 Davies, *APF* 29.

28 [Andoc.] 4.20–21 and Dem. 21.147 with pp. 120–21 above. Davies, *APF* 29, dates this conflict between 430 and 415 B.C.

29 Davies, *APF* 326–27. Guthrie, *HGP* 3.301, dates his birth ca. 453 B.C.

brother, friend, or successor as archon.[30] His political activities have been sufficiently discussed above.[31] It remains a question whether we are justified in retrojecting the evidence of his later political leanings back onto his alleged participation in the mutilation of the herms, especially since Diocleides' testimony against him did not prevail over Andocides' testimony, which obtained his release (Andoc. 1.47, 68). And yet the similar political orientation of many of those incriminated with him suggests that he was merely the most extreme oligarch among the Athenian upper classes in 415 B.C.

Of the twenty-one younger alleged offenders, the best known is *Alcibiades* (1), who is often associated with Critias.[32] He was born in 451/0 or 450/49 B.C. into the aristocratic family of the Salaminioi on his father's side and as an Alcmaeonid on his mother's; he will have been about thirty-five when accused of profaning the Mysteries.[33] His close relationship to Socrates since before the Potidaea campaign of 432/1 B.C., amply attested by Plato and Xenophon, establishes his intellectual credentials;[34] his wealth is shown by his ostentatious displays, especially in the five years between 421 and 416 B.C.;[35] and his shifting political allegiances, never favorable to democracy as such, are too well known to require detailed documentation here.

That *Archebiades* (2) belonged to the younger group can be inferred from a statement in Lysias (14.27) that he became a lover of Alcibiades' son upon Alcibiades' death. Nothing else is known of him.

The identification of *Meletus* (6) is bedeviled by the fact that eight Athenians of that name are known from the end of the fifth century.[36] Probability favors the identity of the person Andromachus denounced for profanation of the Mysteries with the Meletus denounced by Teucrus for mutilating the herms (Andoc. 1.12, 13, 35, 63). If he is also identical with the Meletus who after the fall of the Thirty joined the delegation from the Piraeus as a private individual from the city to negotiate peace with Sparta,[37] we may infer that he was about thirty-five in 415 B.C., that his sympathies were sufficiently oligarchical for him to have remained in the city undisturbed by the Thirty, that he had survived their regime, and that he was now eager for reconciliation and a policy of no recriminations in Athens.

Poulytion's (11) house, where the profanations in which Alcibiades was implicated took place (Andoc. 1.12, 14),[38] was proverbial for its splendor already in antiquity[39] and attests its owner's wealth and high connections. Little else is known about him;

---

30 Brother in D. L. 3.1; relative in Pl. *Chrm*. 155a, 157e; friend, id. *Ti*. 20e–21a; successor in Philostr. *VS* 1.16.

31 See above, pp. 462–65.

32 Xen. *Mem*. 1.2.12–18, 24–28; Pl. *Prt*. 316a; cf. also Plut. *Alc*. 33.1.

33 Davies, *APF* 10–12, 18.

34 E.g., Pl. *Symp*. 213e–214a, esp. 219e–221b; *Prt*. 309a; *Alc. I* 135d; Xen. *Mem*. 1.2.12, 24; cf. also Plut. *Alc*. 4.1–4, 6.1, 7.3–6.

35 For details, see Davies, *APF* 20–21.

36 See MacDowell, *Andokides* 208–10; cf. above, pp. 494–95.

37 Xen. *Hell*. 2.4.36. The identification is admitted as possible by MacDowell, *Andokides* 209–10, and accepted by Aurenche, *Groupes* 63 with n. 7.

38 That he was a metic is suggested by Diod. 13.2.4.

39 Pherecrates, fr. 58; [Pl.] *Erx*. 394b–c, 400b; Paus. 1.2.5.

his membership in a *hetaireia* allegedly organized by Alcibiades may indicate that he and Alcibiades were the same age.[40]

The *Diognetus* (14) whom Teucrus denounced for profaning the Mysteries is believed to have been a brother of Nicias and thus also of the Eucrates (56) whom Diocleides denounced for mutilating the herms.[41] Their family's wealth is well attested.[42] A Diognetus likely to be the one Teucrus denounced is mentioned in Eupolis's *Dēmoi* in 415 B.C. as τῶν πανούργων . . . τῶν νεωτέρων / πολλῷ κράτιστος,[43] which suggests he was considerably younger than Nicias, who was Socrates' senior,[44] but also younger than Eucrates, who, as we shall see below, was probably born shortly before 451/0 B.C. and was a general in Thrace when Eupolis's *Dēmoi* was first performed.[45] We shall therefore not be far wrong in estimating that Diognetus was between thirty and thirty-five at the time of his denunciation. His political stance is indicated by a hint that he may have been one of the Four Hundred in 411 B.C.[46] and by the fact that Lysias has no stronger defense for him than that his exile—presumably in 415 B.C.—was due to sycophants, that he did not join the enemy, and that he held no office under the Thirty.[47] He certainly was not sympathetic to the democratic establishment.

If Aurenche is right in identifying a councilor of 336/5 B.C. as a grandson of the *Isonomus* (17) denounced by Teucrus for profaning the Mysteries,[48] Isonomus will have been in his twenties in 415 B.C.

We are better informed about *Phaedrus* (19), whom the Attic Stelai identify as the well-to-do son of Pythocles, that is, the friend of Socrates after whom Plato's *Phaedrus* is named.[49] If he was born about 450 B.C., he will have been thirty-five when he was denounced.[50] He is marked as a member of the intellegentsia not only by his friendship with Socrates but also by his admiration for Lysias's rhetorical prowess, by his appearance with Eryximachus (35) intently listening to Hippias in the *Protagoras*, and by his speech in the *Symposium*.[51] Of his political orientation nothing is known.

---

40 Isoc. 16.6. We learn from Thessalus's *eisangelia* of Alcibiades also that he played *dāidouchos* to Alcibiades' hierophant (Plut. *Alc.* 22.4).

41 Andoc. 1.15; cf. 47. In view of what else is known about him, this is the more likely Diognetus than the ζητητής mentioned ibid. 14.

42 See Davies, *APF* 403–7.

43 Eup. fr. 122B, C.b 15–18 Edmonds, "The strongest by far of the younger rascals," where he is also called a ἱερόσυλος, possibly with reference to his involvement in the sacrilege against the Mysteries. Edmonds suggests in a note that he is described as "younger" because "he is old enough to know better" and that he was between fifty and sixty years old in 411 B.C. However, the fact that Lys. 18.10 exonerates him from having held office under the Thirty indicates that he was considerably younger.

44 Pl. *La.* 186c with Davies, *APF* 404.

45 See Ar. *Lys.* 103 with schol., and below, pp. 547–48 with n. 77.

46 Lys. 18.9 with Gernet-Bizos, *Lysias* 2.32 n. 1.

47 Lys. 18. 9–10; cf. 19.

48 Bouleutai list in *Hesp.* 30 (1961) 30–57, esp. 31, line 59, with Aurenche, *Groupes* 78–80, who erroneously dates the list in 337/6 B.C.

49 MacDowell, *Andokides* 74; Aurenche, *Groupes* 111–12, 150–51.

50 Davies, *APF* 201.

51 Pl. *Phdr.* 244a, 227a–228a; *Prt.* 315c; *Symp.* 176d, 178a–180b.

Adeimantus (24) is described in the *Protagoras* (315e) as a μειράκιον sitting at Prodicus's feet and will accordingly have been a little over thirty when he was denounced by Agariste. The Attic Stelai attest his considerable wealth.[52] Though he was exiled in 415 B.C., we find him as a general and colleague with Alcibiades in the expedition against Andros in 407/6 B.C., reelected as general to replace those deposed after the battle of Arginusae a year later, and, again, as one of the generals Lysander captured after Aegospotami, in 405/4 B.C.[53] These posts may show the Athenians' confidence in his military ability, but they indicate political reliability no more than they do in the case of Alcibiades. There are derogatory remarks about him in Aristophanes' *Frogs* (406 B.C.), and a scholiast on the passage informs us that Adeimantus's notoriety had been remarked as early as 422 B.C., in Eupolis's *Poleis*.[54] He was the only Athenian spared by Lysander, and this was taken as evidence that he was bribed to betray the fleet at Aegospotami.[55] Like Alcibiades, Adeimantus seems to have been a capable general whose devotion to the state was doubted.

Possibly the *Charmides* (26) whom Agariste denounced for lending his house, near the Olympieion, for the profanation of the Mysteries was the son of Glaucon, and not the one Diocleides denounced, who was the son of Aristoteles (54) and cousin of Andocides.[56] If that is the case, he was the friend of Socrates, after whom his nephew Plato named the dialogue, where we learn that he belonged to the same old aristocratic family as his cousin Critias, that he was much admired for his beauty, and that he was still a youngster in 432 B.C. (Pl. *Chrm.* 154a–b, 155a). This suggests he was born about 450 B.C., which would make Charmides the same age as Alcibiades.[57] His intellectual interests are indicated by his association not only with Socrates[58] but also with Protagoras, in whose train he appears in the house of Callias (Pl. *Prt.* 315a). His aversion to public speaking may well have been due to his personal shyness, but it may equally well reflect a dislike of democratic process:[59] he served as one of the ten archons of the Piraeus under the Thirty and was killed in the streetfighting in the Piraeus after the Thirty's overthrow, in 403 B.C. (Xen. *Hell.* 2.4.19).

Eryximachus (35) son of Acumenus (27, q.v.) probably was between twenty-five and thirty-five when Teucrus denounced him for mutilation of the herms.[60] Of his political views we know nothing; like his father he was a physician and a friend of Phaedrus (19, q.v.; cf. Pl. *Phdr.* 268a–b; *Symp.* 185d, 186a; *Prt.* 315c).

The close relationship between Andocides and *Euphiletus* (37) may indicate that they were roughly the same age and shared political views we will presently discuss (Andoc. 1.51, 61; cf. 61–64). *Menestratus* (41) may have held similar views; he saved

---

52   Aurenche, *Groupes* 130–31.

53   Xen. *Hell.* 1.4.21; Diod. 13.69.3; Xen. *Hell.* 1.7.1, 2.1.30; Plut. *Alc.* 36.6; see pp. 446–48 above.

54   Ar. *Ran.* 1513 with schol. (= Eup. fr. 210).

55   Xen. *Hell.* 2.1.32; Lys. 14.38; Paus. 4.17.3, 10.9.11. Cf. also Dem. 19.191, where Conon is said to have accused him.

56   Andoc. 1.16 with Aurenche, *Groupes* 70–71. MacDowell, *Andokides* 76, regards this identification as "possible."

57   Davies, *APF* 330–31.

58   Pl. *Symp.* 222b; *Theages* 128d; Xen. *Symp.* 1.3, 3.1–2; *Mem.* 3.6.1.

59   Xen. *Mem.* 3.7.1–9; cf. D.L. 2.29.

60   Andoc. 1.35 with Davies, *APF* 462–63.

his skin under the Thirty by informing against others and was therefore executed under the restored democracy (Lys. 13.55–57).

Lysistratus (49), whom Andocides denounced for mutilating the herms seems like Euphiletus (37) to have been one of Andocides' associates and was presumably of roughly the same age.[61] Nothing is known about his economic status, but since he is a frequent butt of Aristophanes for hanging around the agora with a lean and hungry look[62] and for his practical jokes and verbal witticisms at others' expense,[63] he may well have been one of the clever well-to-do young men who could be seen among the followers of the sophists. There is no evidence relating Lysistratus to any sophist, but his social milieu and its political leanings are shown in his affiliation in 422 B.C., together with other budding politicians, with the same Phrynichus who was to become a leader of the oligarchical movement a decade later.[64]

This brings us to *Andocides* (50) himself. He came from an old and distinguished family, as we mentioned in connection with his father, Leogras (29).[65] Since he was over forty years old at his trial in 400 B.C., he will have been about twenty-five in 415 B.C.[66] Only the fact that he prided himself enough on his oratory to have his speeches published suggests his affiliation with the intellectual circles of Athens. An insight into his political thinking can be gleaned from the fragments of some of his writings. We learn from Plutarch's *Themistocles* that his speech πρὸς τοὺς ἑταίρους was aimed at "inflaming the oligarchs against the people";[67] if as is generally believed his virulent attack on Hyperbolus's parentage and occupation formed part of that speech,[68] his oligarchical sympathies and his strong aversion to the demagogues and to the people supporting them will have been on record well before 415 B.C. The depth of this feeling is revealed in yet another passage attributed to this speech: "May we never again see the charcoal burners coming from the mountains into the city, nor their sheep, their cattle, their wagons, and their pusillanimous womenfolk, nor old men and working-class people putting on full hoplite armor.

---

61 Andoc. 1.52 and 67 with 122, and MacDowell, *Andokides* 151.

62 Ar. *Ach*. 854–59; *Eq*. 1267.

63 Id. *Vesp*. 787–90, 1301–3, 1308–10; fr. 198 (*Daitaleis*).

64 Id. *Vesp*. 1301–3 with Macdowell's notes *ad loc*. and on 787. It must, however, remain doubtful whether this Phrynichus is identical with the ὀρχησάμενος denounced by Diocleides for mutilation of the herms at Andoc. 1.47. MacDowell doubts the identity in his note on Andocides 1.47 but identifies him with the Phrynichus of *Vesp*. 1302, whereas in his note on the latter passage he identifies Phrynichus as the oligarch. Lysistratus's involvement in politics may also be reflected in a statement in Antiphon 6.36 that he was accused of homicide by Philinus—possibly a brother of Cleophon; see A. E. Raubitschek, "Philinos," *Hesp*. 23 (1954) 68–71—in order to prevent him from taking action against him.

65 Andoc. 1.147 with n. 24 above.

66 [Lys.] 6.46, corroborated by his own attributing to νεότητί τε καὶ ἀνοίᾳ his participation in the sacrileges of 415 B.C. at Andoc. 2.7.

67 Plut. *Them*. 32.4 (= Andoc. fr. 3 Blass): ἐπὶ τὸν δῆμον παροξύνων τοὺς ὀλιγαρχικούς. Cf. id. *Alc*. 21.2 for Andocides' reputation as μισόδημος καὶ ὀλιγαρχικός.

68 Andoc. fr. 5 Blass: περὶ Ὑπερβόλου λέγειν αἰσχύνομαι, οὗ ὁ μὲν πατὴρ ἐστιγμένος ἔτι καὶ νῦν ἐν τῷ ἀργυροκοπείῳ δουλεύει τῷ δημοσίῳ, αὐτὸς δὲ ξένος ὢν καὶ βάρβαρος λυχνοποιεῖ.

May we never again have to eat wild herbs and chervil."[69] This is not an attack on the horrors of war but on its social consequences, by an aristocrat who had nothing but contempt for the common people. However, it seems that he modified his views after the events of 415 B.C. The immunity he received for turning state's evidence[70] did not save him from voluntary exile,[71] and the help he gave to the Athenians in Samos in 411 B.C. won him the enmity of Peisander and the Four Hundred (Andoc. 2.11, 13–15; [Lys.] 6.27). He was tried and imprisoned, and was freed only after their fall ([Lys.] 6.27; [Plut.] X orat. 834f). Apparently the restored democracy did not want him either, for he went into exile again, and his professions of loyalty to the democracy were not sufficient to gain him his return a few years later, probably about 407 B.C. (Andoc. 2.16, 27). He seems to have remained in exile under the Thirty ([Plut.] X orat. 834f) and not to have returned to Athens until the amnesty of 404/3 B.C. The action for impiety that he brought within ten days of his return against a certain Archippus ([Lys.] 6.11–12) will have been part of an effort to clear his name, which he succeeded in doing: within the next three years he held the office of gymnasiarch, led two sacred embassies, and was a treasurer of the Sacred Monies and a councilor (Andoc. 1.132; [Lys.] 6.33); and he successfully defended himself against a charge of unlawfully participating in the celebration of the Mysteries. He had obviously made his peace with the democracy.

Callias son of Telocles (53) was married to Andocides' only sister (Andoc. 1.50) and is therefore likely to have been approximately the same age as his brother-in-law. No more is known about him, except that he was a gymnasiarch at some point in the late fifth century.[72] Since Euphemus (57) is identified as Callias's brother (and not vice versa) and since he is deferential to his brother and to his brother's in-laws, he was probably somewhat younger than Callias (ibid. 40–42).[73]

We have it on Andocides' authority that his cousin Charmides son of Aristoteles (54) was the same age as himself (ibid. 48). Since the cousins were brought up together at Leogoras's house, Charmides may have been orphaned at an early age; in that case his father will not have been the general and hellēnotamias of the 420s who later became one of the Thirty Tyrants.[74]

Eucrates (56) was a brother of Nicias and Diognetus (14) and can therefore be assumed to have been wealthy. Like Diognetus he seems to have been considerably younger than Nicias; his children were not yet of age in 404 B.C. (Lys. 18.10), so his marriage to the (presumably elder) sister of Callias (53) and Euphemus (57)[75] is not likely to have taken place earlier than the 420s, when Nicias had already won distinction as a general. He seems to have been older than Diognetus: in 412/11 B.C.,

---

69   Id. fr. 4 Blass: μὴ γὰρ ἴδοιμέν ποτε πάλιν ἐκ τῶν ὀρέων τοὺς ἀνθρακευτὰς ἥκοντας εἰς τὸ ἄστυ, καὶ πρόβατα καὶ βοῦς καὶ τὰς ἁμάξας καὶ γύναια . . . , καὶ πρεσβυτέρους ἄνδρας καὶ ἐργάτας ἐξοπλιζομένους· μηδὲ ἄγρια λάχανα καὶ σκάνδικας ἔτι φάγοιμεν. Cf. MacDowell, Andokides 191.

70   Andoc. 2.23; Thuc. 6.60.3–4; Plut. Alc. 21.5–6.

71   As a result of the decree of Isotimides; see Andoc. 1.71, 2.24 and 27.

72   IG II² 3018 with Davies, APF 253.

73   Note also that at 47 Eucrates is identified as Callias's in-law (rather than Euphemus's).

74   Andoc. 1.48 with Davies, APF 30; differently MacDowell, Andokides 97.

75   Andoc. 1.47 with Davies, APF 253 and 404.

when Eupolis called Diognetus "one of the younger rascals," Eucrates was already a general in Thrace.[76] On the basis of a scholion to Aristophanes (*Lys.* 103), which says Εὐκράτης κωμῳδεῖται ὡς...ξένος, Davies has advanced the interesting hypothesis that Eucrates and Diognetus may be children of a second marriage of Niceratus, contracted with a foreign woman, to whom Eucrates was born before 451/0 B.C., when Pericles' citizenship law was enacted.[77] If this can be accepted, Eucrates will have been a few years older than Alcibiades, that is, about thirty-six or thirty-seven in 415 B.C. There seems to have been some ambivalence in his political attitude, our only knowledge of which comes in Lysias's attempt to paint it in colors pleasing enough to a democratic law court not to deprive his sons of their inheritance. His election as general after Aegospotami suggests that he was believed to be acceptable to the Spartans, and this seems corroborated by the fact that he was invited to join the oligarchy of the Thirty (Lys. 18.4–5). Having sufficient character to decline the offer, he was put to death by the Thirty.[78]

If *Mantitheus* (58) is identical with the companion of Alcibiades in the Ionian war,[79] he may have been approximately the same age. He was at least thirty in 415 B.C., since he was a councilor when Diocleides denounced him (Andoc. 1.43–44). *Nisaeus's* (59) youth can be inferred only from the fact that his father, Taureas (61), was inculpated with him.[80] Since Taureas was a cousin of Leogoras, not many years will have separated Nisaeus from Andocides.

The identification of *Phrynichus* (60) is beset with difficulties. We can be certain only that he was a cousin of Andocides (ibid. 47). The manuscripts identify him as ὀρχησάμενος, which would indicate that he had once been a dancer. The invention of new dance figures is attributed in Plutarch to Phrynichus the tragic poet (Plut. *Mor.* 732f, *Quaest. conv.* 8.9); but since he lived early in the fifth century, he is not likely to have been implicated in the affairs of 415 B.C. An interest in dancing is attested for the oligarch-to-be Phrynichus, in whose following we noted Lysistratus (49),[81] and the possibility cannot be excluded that he is indeed the ex-dancer and cousin of Andocides. Still, the identification merely as an ex-dancer remains strange and has induced scholars either to explain it as an intrusive gloss or to resort to the desperate expedient of making Phrynichus's father bear the otherwise unattested name Orchesamenus.[82] It makes more sense to accept Aurenche's suggestion that Phrynichus was the comic poet, a fragment from one of whose plays pokes fun at Diocleides for alleging deliberate mutilations of fallen herms and also mentions Teucrus's attempt to get a reward for his denunciations.[83] Not only may he well have celebrated his own acquittal and the discredit of Diocleides in this way (Andoc. 1.65–68), but as MacDowell has shown, several comic writers seem to have been

---

76 See n. 44 above for Diognetus; for Eucrates, see Ar. *Lys.* 103 with schol. and *Suda* s.v. ἄπεστιν.

77 Davies, *APF* 404.

78 Lys. 18.5; *Suda* s.v. ἄπεστιν.

79 Xen. *Hell.* 1.1.10, 1.3.13; Diod. 13.68.2.

80 Andoc. 1.47, 68 with p. 542 above.

81 Ar. *Vesp.* 1490, 1524; cf. 1301–3 with nn. 61–64 above.

82 MacDowell, *Andokides* 97, believes it is a gloss; A. Wilhelm, "Vermuthungen," *Philol.* 60 (1901) 481–90, esp. 485, reads Ὀρχησαμενοῦ.

83 Phrynichus, fr. 58, with Aurenche, *Groupes* 75–76.

incriminated in 415 B.C.[84] However, this leaves the appellations ὀρχησάμενος unexplained, Aurenche's ingenious attempt notwithstanding, and it would make Phrynichus a good decade older than his cousin Andocides, since his first production is attested for the eighty-sixth Olympiad, that is, for the years 431 to 428 B.C.[85]

Finally, we know a little about *Alcibiades Phegousios* (62), who together with *Amiantus* (63) of Aegina had suborned Diocleides to give false testimony and had escaped from Athens when he was found out (Andoc. 1.65–66). Of his personal implication we know only from the Attic Stelai, which list him as owning property at Oropus.[86] He is probably identical with the cousin and fellow exile of Alcibiades (1) who was captured by Thrasyllus from a Syracusan ship off Methymna in 409/8 B.C.[87] This makes it legitimate to infer that he was approximately the same age as Alcibiades and that he had reason to fear a return to democratic Athens.

It is now time to take stock of what we have learned. Of the sixty-four persons inculpated on one or the other of the sacrileges in 415 B.C., twenty-seven members of the upper classes can be identified with greater or less confidence. Only six of these are likely to have been over forty years of age at the time: Critias (55) was probably the youngest of these, followed in ascending order by Callias son of Alcmeon (52), Taureas (61), Acumenus (27), Leogoras (29), and Axiochus (25); the remaining twenty-one seem to have been between the ages of twenty-five and thirty-five, that is, they will have gone through their formative and most impressionable years in the late 430s and the 420s, when many young men of the upper classes associated with sophists. Their number suggests that they constituted the core of the suspects in 415 B.C.

Our information on the intellectual affiliations of the accused depends exclusively on Plato and regards only eight of the twenty-seven. Three members of the older group (Axiochus [25], Acumenus [27], and Critias [55]) and four of the younger (Alcibiades [1], Phaedrus [19], Charmides [26], and Eryximachus [35]) are known to have been associated with Socrates; of these Critias (55), Alcibiades (1), and Charmides (26) are also shown in the company of Protagoras, and Phaedrus (19) and Eryximachus (35) in the company of Hippias. In addition, Adeimantus (24) is shown listening to Prodicus. If we assume that Andocides' (50) oratorical skill was the result of sophistic training, we have a list of nine attested members of the intelligentsia. Although this constitutes only one-third of the twenty-seven, our general ignorance of who the sophists' followers were makes this an impressive number; it suggests that the number of intellectuals among the three hundred said to have been incriminated in 415 B.C. will have been considerable.

We get a hint of the political orientation of thirteen of the twenty-seven, that is, of about half. The remarkable fact here is that all evince antipathy toward the Athenian democracy. The opportunism of Alcibiades (1) made him at best indifferent to such constitutional niceties as democracy and oligarchy; but Adeimantus's

---

84 MacDowell, *Andokides* 211, where Phrynichus is, however, not named.
85 *Suda* s.v. Φρύνιχος.
86 *SEG* 13 (1956) 19.3–7.
87 Xen. *Hell*. 1.2.13, where the text says that he was stoned to death (κατ-έλευσεν). Since the context makes this intrinsically improbable, Wade-Gery's emendation κατελε<ήσας ἀπέλ>υσεν, "took pity and freed him," deserves serious consideration; see Andrewes, "Generals" 4 n. 11.

opportunism (24) incurred him the suspicion of treason. Andocides (50) too can be regarded as an opportunist after his voluntary exile in 415 B.C., but he seems to have been violently antidemocratic and oligarchical in his outlook before then. Oligarchical and pro-Spartan sympathies are most pronounced in Critias (55) and Meletus (6), but Euphiletus (37) and Menestratus (41) will not have been free of them. Antidemocratic sentiments can be detected in Axiochus (25), Charmides (26), Lysistratus (49), Eucrates (56), and Alcibiades Phegousios (62); and Diognetus (14) may have been a member of the Four Hundred in 411 B.C. All this suggests that there were substantive reasons for the democratic establishment to suspect an oligarchical coup behind the profanation of the Mysteries and the desecration of the herms in 415 B.C., of which the younger aristocrats who had been tinged with sophistic teaching were the main promoters.

BIBLIOGRAPHY

Adeleye, G. "The Arginusai Affair and Theramenes' Rejection at the *Dokimasia* of 405/4 B.C." *Mus.Afr.* 6 (1977–78) 94–99.

———. "Critias: From "Moderation" to "Radicalism." *Mus.Afr.* 6 (1977–78) 64–73.

———. "Critias: Member of the Four Hundred?" *TAPA* 104 (1974) 1–9.

———. "The Purpose of the *Dokimasia*," *GRBS* 24 (1983) 295–306.

———. "Theramenes and the Overthrow of the Four Hundred." *Mus.Afr.* 2 (1973) 77–81.

Amit, M. "The Melian Dialogue and History." *Athenaeum*, n.s., 46 (1968) 216–35.

Ampolo, C. "Politica istituzionale e politica edilizia di Pisistrato." *Parola del Passato* 28 (1973) 271–74.

Anderson, J. K. Review of *Nomos and the Beginnings of the Athenian Democracy*, by M. Ostwald. *CJ* 66 (1971) 369–71.

———. *Xenophon*. London and New York, 1974.

Andrewes, A. "The Arginousai Trial." *Phoenix* 28 (1974) 112–22.

———. "The Generals in the Hellespont, 410–407 B.C." *JHS* 73 (1953) 2–9.

———. *The Greeks*. London, 1967.

———. "The Growth of the Athenian State." *CAH*, 2d ed., vol. 3, part 3 (1982) 360–91.

———. "Lysias and the Theramenes Papyrus." *ZPE* 6 (1970) 35–38.

———. "The Melian Dialogue and Perikles' Last Speech." *PCPS* 186, 6 (1960) 1–10.

———. "The Mytilene Debate: Thucydides 3.36–49." *Phoenix* 16 (1962) 64–82.

———. "Notion and Kyzikos: The Sources Compared." *JHS* 102 (1982) 15–25.

———. "The Opposition to Perikles." *JHS* 98 (1978) 1–8.

Andrewes, A., and D. M. Lewis. "Note on the Peace of Nikias." *JHS* 77 (1957) 177–80.

Armbruster, O. "Über die Herrschaft der Dreissig zu Athen 404/3 v. Chr." Diss. Freiburg, 1913.

Arrighetti, G., ed. *Satiro: Vita di Euripide*. Studi Classici e Orientali 13. Pisa, 1964.

551

Ast, F. *Lexicon Platonicum*. 2d ed. 3 vols. Leipzig, 1908.

Aurenche, O. *Les Groupes d'Alcibiade, de Léogoras et de Teucros*. Paris, 1974.

Austin, C., ed. *Comicorum Graecorum Fragmenta in Papyris Reperta*. Berlin and New York, 1973.

Avery, H. C. "Critias and the Four Hundred." *CP* 58 (1963) 165–67.

———. "One Antiphon or Two? *Hermes* 110 (1982) 145–58.

———. "Sophocles' Political Career." *Hist*. 22 (1973) 509–14.

Badian, E. "Archons and *Strategoi*." *Antichthon* 5 (1971) 1–34.

Baldwin, B. "Notes on Cleophon." *Acta Classica* 17 (1974) 35–47.

———. "Notes on Hyperbolus." *Acta Classica* 14 (1971) 151–56.

von Bamberg, A. "Über einige auf das attische Gerichtswesen bezügliche Aristophanesstellen." *Hermes* 13 (1878) 505–14.

Barnes, J. *The Presocratic Philosophers*. 2 vols. London, 1979.

Barrett, J. F. "The Downfall of Themistocles." *GRBS* 18 (1977) 291–305.

Barrett, W. S., ed. *Euripides: Hippolytos*. Oxford, 1964.

Bartoletti, V., ed. *Hellenica Oxyrhynchia*. Leipzig, 1959.

Bayer, E., and J. Heideking. *Die Chronologie des perikleischen Zeitalters*. Erträge der Forschung 36. Darmstadt, 1975.

Beazley, J. D. *Attic Red-Figure Vase-Painters*, vol. 2. 2d ed. Oxford, 1963.

Bekker, I. *Anecdota Graeca*. 3 vols. Berlin, 1814–21.

Beloch, J. *Die attische Politik seit Perikles*. Leipzig, 1884.

Bengtson, H., ed. *Die Staatsverträge des Altertums*, vol. 2. 2d. ed. Munich and Berlin, 1975.

Benveniste, E. *Noms d'agent et noms d'action en indo-européen*. Paris, 1948.

Berneker, E., ed. *Zur griechischen Rechtsgeschichte*. Wege der Forschung 45. Darmstadt, 1968.

Bibauw, J. "L'Amendement de Clitophon." *Ant.Class*. 34 (1965) 464–83.

Bicknell, P. J. *Studies in Athenian Politics and Genealogy*. Historia Einzelschrift 19. Wiesbaden, 1972.

Bignone, E. "Antifonte oratore e Antifonte sofista." *Rend.Ist.Lomb*. 52 (1919) 564–78. [Reprinted in *Antifonte oratore e Antifonte sofista*, pp. 7–20.]

———. *Antifonte oratore e Antifonte sofista*. Ed. B. Gentili and G. Morelli. Urbino, 1974.

———. "Le Idee morali di Antifonte sofista." *In Studi sul pensiero antico*, pp. 66–159. Naples, 1938.

Blass, F. *Die attische Beredsamkeit*. 2d ed. 4 vols. Leipzig, 1887–98.

———. ed. *Andocidis et Antiphontis Orationes*. Leipzig, 1881.

Bloedow, E. F. *Alcibiades Reexamined*. Historia Einzelschrift 21. Wiesbaden, 1973.

Bluck, R. S. *Plato's Meno*. Cambridge, 1961.

Blumenthal, H. "Meletus the Accuser of Andocides and Meletus the Accuser of Socrates: One Man or Two?" *Philol*. 117 (1973) 169–78.

Boegehold, A. L. "The Establishment of a Central Archive at Athens." *AJA* 76 (1972) 23–30.

Bona, G. "ὑψίπολις e ἄπολις nel primo stasimo dell'Antigone." *Riv.Filol*. 3d ser., 99 (1971) 129–48.

Bonner, R. J., and G. Smith. *The Administration of Justice from Homer to Aristotle*. 2 vols. Chicago, 1930–38.

von Bothmer, D. "New Vases by the Amasis Painter." *Antike Kunst* 3 (1960) 71–80.

Bowersock, G. W., ed. and tr. *Pseudo-Xenophon: Constitution of the Athenians.* In *Xenophon: Scripta Minora*, ed. and tr. E. C. Marchant. Cambridge, Mass., and London, 1968.

Bradeen, D. W. "The Fifth-Century Archon List." *Hesp.* 32 (1963) 187–208.

———. "The Popularity of the Athenian Empire." *Hist.* 9 (1960) 257–69.

———. "The Trittyes in Cleisthenes' Reforms." *TAPA* 86 (1955) 22–30.

Bradeen, D. W., and M. F. McGregor. *Studies in Fifth-Century Attic Epigraphy.* Norman, Okla., 1973.

Breitenbach, H. R. "Xenophon." *RE* 2. Reihe, 9. Band (1967) 1567–1928.

Brownson, C. L., tr. *Xenophon: Hellenica, Books I–V.* Cambridge, Mass., and London, 1918.

Bruce, I. A. F. "The Corcyrean Civil War of 427 B.C." *Phoenix* 25 (1971) 108–17.

Brunt, P. A. "Thucydides and Alcibiades." *REG* 65 (1952) 59–96.

Buchner, E. "Die Aristophanes-Scholien und die Frage der Tributpflicht von Melos." *Chiron* 4 (1974) 91–99.

Bultmann, R. "Polis und Hades in Sophocles' *Antigone.*" In *Essays Philosophical and Theological*, pp. 22–35. London, 1955. [Originally published in 1936.]

Burian, P. "Pelasgus and Politics in Aeschylus' Danaid Trilogy." *WS*, n.s., 8 (1974) 5–14.

Burkert, W. *Griechische Religion der archaischen und klassischen Epoche.* Stuttgart, 1977.

Burn, A. R. *Persia and the Greeks.* London, 1962.

Burnet, J. *Greek Philosophy.* Vol. 1, *Thales to Plato.* London, 1914.

Busolt, G. "Aristoteles oder Xenophon?" *Hermes* 33 (1898) 71–86.

———. *Griechische Geschichte bis zur Schlacht bei Chaeronea.* 3 vols. in 4. Gotha, 1893–1904.

Busolt, G., and H. Swoboda. *Griechische Staatskunde.* 2 vols. Munich, 1920–26.

Cadoux, T. J. "The Athenian Archons from Kreon to Hypsichides." *JHS* 68 (1948) 70–123.

Calder, W. M. III. "Sophokles' Political Tragedy, *Antigone.*" *GRBS* 9 (1968) 389–407.

Calhoun, G. M. *Athenian Clubs in Politics and Litigation.* Bulletin of the University of Texas 262, Humanistic Series 14. Austin, Tex. 1913.

Camon, F. "Le Cariche pubbliche di Iperbolo." *Giornale Italiano di Filologia* 16 (1963) 46–59.

———. "La Demagogia di Iperbolo." *Giornale Italiano di Filologia* 15 (1962) 364–74.

Cargill, J. "*IG* II² 1 and the Athenian Kleruchy on Samos." *GRBS* 24 (1983) 321–32.

Cawkwell, G. L. "Agesilaus and Sparta." *CQ*, n.s., 26 (1976) 62–84.

———. "The Fall of Themistocles." In B. F. Harris, ed., *Auckland Classical Essays Presented to E. M. Blailock*, pp. 39–58. Auckland and Oxford, 1970.

Cecchin, S. A. Πάτριος Πολιτεία. Turin, 1969.

Chambers, M. "Notes on the Text of the *Ath. Pol.*" *TAPA* 96 (1965) 31–39.

Chantraine, P. *La Formation des noms en grec ancien.* Paris, 1933.

Classen, C. J. "The Study of Language amongst Socrates' Contemporaries." In C. J. Classen, ed., *Sophistik*, pp. 215–47. [q. v.]

———, ed. *Sophistik.* Wege der Forschung 187. Darmstadt, 1976.

Classen, J., and J. Steup, eds. *Thukydides*. 8 vols. Vols. 1,2: 5th ed.; vols. 3–8: 3d ed. Berlin, 1963.

van Cleef, F. L. *Index Antiphonteus*. Cornell Studies in Classical Philology 5. Ithaca, N.Y., 1895.

Clinton, K. "The Nature of the Late Fifth-Century Revision of the Athenian Law Code." In *Studies in Attic Epigraphy, History, and Topography Presented to Eugene Vanderpool*, Hesperia Supplement 19, pp. 27–37. Princeton, N.J., 1982.

Cloché, P. "Le Conseil athénien des Cinq Cents et la peine de mort." *REG* 33 (1920) 1–50.

———. "Les Décrets athéniens de 403/2 en faveur des Samiens." *REG* 40 (1927) 197–207.

———. *La Restauration démocratique à Athènes en 403 avant J.-C.* Paris, 1915.

Cogan, M. "Mytilene, Plataea, and Corcyra: Ideology and Policy in Thucydides, Book Three." *Phoenix* 35 (1981) 1–21.

Cole, J. R. "Cimon's Dismissal, Ephialtes' Revolution and the Peloponnesian Wars." *GRBS* 15 (1974) 369–85.

Colin, G. *Xénophon historien d'après le livre II des Helléniques (hiver 406/5 à 401/0)*. Paris, 1933.

Colonna, A., ed. *Himerii Declamationes et Orationes*. Rome, 1951.

Commentaria in Aristotelem Graeca. 23 vols. in 29. Berlin, 1882–1909.

Conacher, D. J. *Euripidean Drama*. Toronto, 1967.

Connor, W. R. *The New Politicians of Fifth-Century Athens*. Princeton, 1971.

———. "Two Notes on Diopeithes the Seer." *CP* 58 (1963) 115–18.

Corbato, C. *Sofisti e politica ad Atene durante la Guerra del Peloponneso*. Università degli Studi di Trieste, Istituto di Filologia Classica 4. Trieste, 1958.

Cornford, F. M. *Plato's Theory of Knowledge*. London, 1935.

Crawley, L. W. A. "Γραφὴ συκοφαντίας." In B. F. Harris, ed., *Auckland Classical Essays Presented to E. M. Blailock*, pp. 77–94. Auckland and Oxford, 1970.

Dalfen, J. "Gesetz ist nicht Gesetz und fromm ist nicht fromm. Die Sprache der Personen in der sophokleischen Antigone." *WS*, n.s., 11 (1977) 5–26.

Dalmeyda, G., ed. and tr. *Andocide: Discours*. Paris, 1960.

Daube, B. *Zu den Rechtsproblemen in Aischylos' Agamemnon*. Zurich and Leipzig, 1938.

Davies, J. K. "Athenian Citizenship: The Descent Group and the Alternatives." *CJ* 73 (1977–78) 105–21.

———. *Athenian Propertied Families 600–300 B.C.* Oxford, 1971.

———. Review of *The New Politicians of Fifth-Century Athens*, by W. R. Connor. *Gnomon* 47 (1975) 374–78.

———. Review of *Nomos and the Beginnings of the Athenian Democracy*, by M. Ostwald. *CR* 87, n.s., 23 (1973) 224–27.

Davison, J. A. "Protagoras, Democritus, and Anaxagoras." *CQ*, n.s., 3 (1953) 33–45.

Deane, P. *Thucydides' Dates: 465–431 B.C.* Don Mills, Ont., 1972.

Degani, E. "Arifrade l'anassagoreo." *Maia* 12 (1960) 190–217.

De Laix, R. A. *Probouleusis at Athens: A Study of Political Decision-Making*. University of California Publications in History 83. Berkeley and Los Angeles, 1973.

Demiańczuk, I., ed. *Supplementum Comicum: Comoediae Graecae Fragmenta post editiones Kockianam et Kaibelianam reperta vel indicata*. Cracow, 1912.

Denniston, J. D. *The Greek Particles*. 2d ed. Oxford, 1959.

————, ed. *Euripides: Electra*. Oxford, 1939.

Derenne, E. *Les Procès d'impiété intentés aux philosophes à Athènes au Vme et au IVme siècles avant J.-C.* Bibliothèque de la Faculté de Philosophie et Lettres de l'Université de Liège 45. Liège and Paris, 1930.

Deubner, L. *Attische Feste*. Berlin, 1932. Reprint. Darmstadt, 1969.

Diamantopoulos, A. "The Danaid Tetralogy of Aeschylus." *JHS* 77 (1957) 220–29.

Diehl, E., ed. *Anthologia Lyrica Graeca*. 3d ed. 3 fasc. Leipzig, 1949–52.

Diels, H., ed. *Doxographi Graeci*. Berlin, 1879.

Diels, H., and W. Kranz, eds. *Die Fragmente der Vorsokratiker*. 6th ed. 3 vols. Berlin, 1951–52.

Dihle, A. "Das Satyrspiel 'Sisyphos,'" *Hermes* 105 (1977) 28–42.

Dindorf, W., ed. *Aristeidis Opera*, vol. 2. Leipzig, 1829.

Dodds, E. R., ed. *Euripides: Bacchae*. 2d ed. Oxford, 1960.

————, ed. *Plato: Gorgias*. Oxford, 1959.

Donini, G. *La Posizione di Tucidide verso il governo dei Cinquemila*. Historia Politica Philosophica: Il Pensiero Attico, Studi e Testi 2. Turin, 1969.

Donnay, G. "La Date du procès de Phidias." *Ant. Class.* 37 (1968) 19–36.

Dorjahn, A. P. "The Athenian Senate and the Oligarchy of 404/3 B.C." *PhQ* 11 (1932) 57–64.

Dover, K. J. *Aristophanic Comedy*. London, 1972.

————. "The Chronology of Antiphon's Speeches." *CQ* 44 (1950) 44–60.

————. "The Freedom of the Intellectual in Greek Society." *Talanta* 7 (1975) 24–54.

————. *Greek Popular Morality in the Time of Plato and Aristotle*. Oxford, 1974.

————. *Lysias and the Corpus Lysiacum*. Berkeley and Los Angeles, 1968.

————, ed. *Aristophanes: Clouds*. Oxford, 1968.

Dow, S. "The Athenian Calendar of Sacrifices: The Chronology of Nikomakhos' Second Term." *Hist.* 9 (1960) 270–93.

————. "The Law Codes of Athens." *Proceedings of the Massachusetts Historical Society* 71, Proceedings 1953–1957 (1959) 3–36.

————. "Studies in the Athenian Tribute Lists. I." *CP* 37 (1942) 371–84.

————. "The Walls Inscribed with Nikomakhos' Law Code." *Hesp.* 30 (1961) 58–73.

Dunbar, H. *A Complete Concordance to the Comedies and Fragments of Aristophanes*. Oxford, 1883.

Eberhardt, W. "Der Melierdialog und die Inschriften ATL A9 und IG I² 97 +." *Hist.* 8 (1959) 284–314.

Eberlein, E. "Über die verschiedenen Deutungen des tragischen Konflikts in der 'Antigone' des Sophokles." *Gymnasium* 68 (1961) 16–34.

Edmonds, J. M. "The Cairo and Oxyrhynchus Fragments of the Δῆμοι of Eupolis." *Mnemos.*, 3d ser., 8 (1939) 1–20.

————, ed. and tr. *The Fragments of Attic Comedy*. 3 vols. in 4. Leiden, 1957–61.

Edmunds, L., and R. Martin. "Thucydides 2.65.8: ἐλευθέρως." *HSCP* 81 (1977) 187–93.

Ehrenberg, V. *The Greek State*. 2d ed. London, 1969.

————. "Origins of Democracy." *Hist.* 1 (1950) 515–48.

————. *The People of Aristophanes*. 2d ed. Oxford, 1951.

———. "Polypragmosyne: A Study in Greek Politics." *JHS* 67 (1947) 46–67.

———. *Sophocles and Pericles*. Oxford, 1954.

Ehrhardt, C. "Hair in Ancient Greece." *Classical News and Views* 15 (1971) 14–19.

———. "Xenophon and Diodorus on Aegospotami." *Phoenix* 24 (1970) 225–28.

Eliot, C. W. J. *Coastal Demes of Attika. A Study of the Policy of Kleisthenes*. Phoenix Supplement 5. Toronto, 1962.

Erbse, H., ed. *Scholia Graeca in Homeri Iliadem*. 6 vols. Berlin, 1969–83.

Erdmann, W. *Die Ehe im alten Griechenland*. Münchener Beiträge zur Papyrusforschung und antiken Rechtsgeschichte 20. Munich, 1934.

Fahr, W. ΘΕΟΥΣ ΝΟΜΙΖΕΙΝ: *Zum Problem der Anfänge des Atheismus bei den Griechen*. Spudasmata 26. Hildesheim and New York, 1969.

Feaver, D. D. "Historical Development in the Priesthoods of Athens." *YClS* 15 (1957) 123–58.

Ferguson, W. S. "The Athenian Expedition to Sicily." *CAH* 5 (1935) 282–311.

———. "The Condemnation of Antiphon." In *Mélanges Gustave Glotz*, vol. 1, pp. 349–66. Paris, 1932.

———. *The Treasurers of Athena*. Cambridge, Mass., 1932.

Fiehn, K. "Taureas." *RE* 2. Reihe, 4. Band (1932) 2536–37.

Fingarette, A. "A New Look at the Wall of Nikomakhos." *Hesp.* 40 (1971) 330–35.

Finley, J. H., Jr. "Euripides and Thucydides." *HSCP* 49 (1938) 23–68.

Finley, M. I. *The Ancestral Constitution*. Inaugural Lecture, Cambridge, 1971.

———. "Athenian Demagogues." *Past and Present* 21 (1962) 3–24.

Flach, D. "Der oligarchische Staatsstreich in Athen vom Jahr 411." *Chiron* 7 (1977) 9–33.

Forman, L. L. *Index Andocideus Lycurgeus Dinarcheus*. Oxford, 1897.

Fornara, C. W. *The Athenian Board of Generals from 501 to 404*. Historia Einzelschrift 16. Wiesbaden, 1971.

———. "Cleon's Attack against the Cavalry." *CQ*, n.s., 23 (1973) 24.

———. "The *Diapsephismos* of *Ath. Pol.* 13.5." *CP* 65 (1970) 243–46.

Forrest, W. G. "Aristophanes' *Acharnians*." *Phoenix* 17 (1963) 1–12.

———. "An Athenian Generation Gap." *YClS* 24 (1975) 37–52.

———. "Themistokles and Argos." *CQ*, n.s., 10 (1960) 221–41.

Foucart, P. *Les Mystères d'Éleusis*. Paris, 1914.

Frei, P. " Ἰσονομία. Politik im Spiegel griechischer Wortbildungslehre." *MH* 38 (1981) 205–19.

Frisch, H. *The Constitution of the Athenians*. Copenhagen, 1942.

von Fritz, K. "Protagoras." *RE* 23. Band (1957) 908–21.

von Fritz, K., and E. Kapp, trs. *Aristotle's Constitution of Athens and Related Texts*. New York, 1950.

Frost, F. J. "Pericles and Dracontides." *JHS* 84 (1964) 69–72.

———. "Pericles, Thucydides, Son of Melesias, and Athenian Politics before the War." *Hist.* 13 (1964) 385–99.

Fuks, A. *The Ancestral Constitution*. London, 1953.

———. "Notes on the Rule of the Ten at Athens in 403 B.C.." *Mnemos.*, 4th ser., 6 (1953) 198–207.

Furley, D. J. "Antiphon's Case against Justice." In G. B. Kerferd, ed., *The Sophists and Their Legacy*, pp. 81–91. [q.v.]

Gagarin, M. "*Dikē* in Archaic Greek Thought." *CP* 69 (1974) 186–97.

———. "*Dikē* in the *Works and Days*." *CP* 68 (1973) 81–94.

———. *Drakon and Early Athenian Homicide Law*. New Haven and London, 1981.

———. "The Thesmothetai and the Earliest Athenian Tyranny Law." *TAPA* 111 (1981) 71–77.

Garvie, A. F. *Aeschylus' Supplices: Play and Trilogy*. Cambridge, 1969.

Gawantka, W. *Isopolitie: Ein Beitrag zur Geschichte der zwischenstaatlichen Beziehungen in der griechischen Antike*. Vestigia 22. Munich, 1975.

von Geisau, J. "Praxiergidai." *RE* 22. Band (1954) 1761.

Geissler, P. *Chronologie der altattischen Komödie*. Berlin, 1925.

Gerner, E. "Παρανόμων γραφή." *RE* 18. Band (1949) 1281–93.

Gernet, L. "Notes sur Andocide." *Rev. Phil.*, 3d ser., 5 (1931) 308–26.

———, ed. and tr. *Antiphon: Discours*. Paris, 1923.

Gernet, L., and M. Bizos, eds. and trs. *Lysias: Discours*. Vol. 1. 4th ed. Paris, 1959.

Ghinatti, F. *I Gruppi politici ateniesi fino alle guerre persiane*. Università degli Studi di Padova: Pubblicazioni dell'Istituto di Storia Antica 8. Rome, 1970.

Gilbert, G. *Beiträge zur innern Geschichte Athens im Zeitalter des peloponnesischen Krieges*. Leipzig, 1877.

Gillis, D. "Murder on Melos." *Rend.Ist.Lomb.* 112 (1978) 185–211.

Gluskina, L. M. "The Athenian Metics in the Struggle for the Re-Establishment of Democracy at the End of the Fifth Century B.C." *VDI* (1958) 70–89. [In Russian.]

Gomme, A. W. "Aristophanes and Politics." *CR* 52 (1938) 97–109. [Reprinted in *More Essays in Greek History and Literature*, pp. 70–91; and in H.-J. Newiger, ed., *Aristophanes und die alte Komödie*, Wege der Forschung 265 (Darmstadt, 1975), pp. 75–98.]

———. *More Essays in Greek History and Literature*. Oxford, 1962.

———. "Thucydides and Kleon." In *More Essays in Greek History and Literature*, pp. 112–21.

Gomme, A. W., A. Andrewes, and K. J. Dover. *A Historical Commentary on Thucydides*. 5 vols. Oxford, 1948–81.

Gomperz, H. *Sophistik und Rhetorik*. Leipzig and Berlin, 1912.

Gomperz, T. *Greek Thinkers*, vol. 1. Tr. L. Magnus. London, 1920.

Gottschalk, H. G. *Heraclides of Pontus*. Oxford, 1980.

Gould, J. "Hiketeia." *JHS* 93 (1973) 74–103.

Grant, J. A. "A Note on the Tone of Greek Diplomacy." *CQ*, n.s, 15 (1965) 261–66.

Grensemann, H., ed. and tr. *Die hippokratische Schrift "Über die heilige Krankheit."* Berlin, 1968.

Griffith, G. T. "Isegoria in the Assembly at Athens." In *Ancient Society and Institutions: Studies Presented to V. Ehrenberg*, pp. 115–38. Oxford, 1966.

Griffith, M. *The Authenticity of the "Prometheus Bound."* Cambridge, 1977.

Gronewald, M. "Ein neues Protagoras-Fragment." *ZPE* 2 (1968) 1–2.

Gülke, C. *Mythos und Zeitgeschichte bei Aischylos*. Beiträge zur klassischen Philologie, ed. R. Merkelbach, Heft 31. Meisenheim am Glan, 1969.

Gundert, H. "Grösse und Gefährdung des Menschen. Ein sophokleisches Chorlied und seine Stellung im Drama (Sophokles, Antigone 332–375)." *Antike und Abendland* 22 (1976) 21–39.

Guthrie, W. K. C. *A History of Greek Philosophy*. 6 vols. Cambridge, 1962–81.

Hackl, U. "Die oligarchische Bewegung in Athen am Ausgang des 5. Jahrhunderts v. Chr." Diss. Munich, 1960.

Hamilton, C. D. *Sparta's Bitter Victories*. Ithaca, N.Y., and London, 1979.

Hammond, N. G. L. "Strategia and Hegemonia in Fifth-Century Athens." *CQ*, n.s., 19 (1969) 111–44.

Hansen, M. H. *Apagoge, Endeixis and Ephegesis against Kakourgoi, Atimoi and Pheugontes: A Study in the Administration of Justice in the Fourth Century B.C.* Odense, 1976.

———. "The Athenian *Heliaia* from Solon to Aristotle." *C&M* 33 (1981–82) 9–47.

———. "*Demos*, *Ecclesia* and *Dicasterion* in Classical Athens." *GRBS* 19 (1978) 127–46.

———. "Did the Athenian *Ecclesia* Legislate after 403/2 B.C.?" *GRBS* 20 (1979) 27–53.

———. "Eisangelia in Athens: A Reply." *JHS* 100 (1980) 83–95.

———. *Eisangelia: The Sovereignty of the People's Court in Athens in the Fourth Century B.C. and the Impeachment of the Generals and Politicians*. Odense, 1975.

———. "*Nomos* and *Psephisma* in Fourth-Century Athens." *GRBS* 19 (1978) 315–30.

———. "The Number of Athenian Hoplites in 431 B.C." *SO* 56 (1981) 19–32.

———. "Seven Hundred *Archai* in Classical Athens." *GRBS* 21 (1980) 151–73.

———. *The Sovereignty of the People's Court in Athens in the Fourth Century B.C. and the Public Action against Unconstitutional Proposals*. Odense, 1974.

Harding, P. "O Androtion, You Fool!" *AJAH* 3 (1978) 179–83.

Harrison, A. R. W. "Law-Making at Athens at the End of the Fifth Century B.C." *JHS* 75 (1955) 26–35.

———. *The Law of Athens*. 2 vols. Oxford, 1968–71.

Harrison, E. B. "Hesperides and Heroes: A Note on the Three-Figure Reliefs." *Hesp*. 33 (1964) 76–82.

Harrison, E. L. "Was Gorgias a Sophist?" *Phoenix* 18 (1964) 183–92.

Hart, H. L. A. *The Concept of Law*. 3d ed. Oxford, 1972.

Harvey, F. D. "The Conspiracy of Agasias and Aischines (Plutarch, Aristeides 13)." *Klio* 66 (1984) 58–73.

Hatzfeld, J. *Alcibiade*. Paris, 1951.

———. "Le Départ de l'expédition de Sicile et les Adonies de 415." *REG* 50 (1937) 293–303.

———, ed. and tr. *Xénophon: Helléniques*, vol. 1. 4th ed. Paris, 1960.

Haussoulier, B. *La Vie municipale en Attique*. Paris, 1883.

Havelock, E. A. *The Liberal Temper in Greek Politics*. New Haven, 1957.

Heckenbach, J. "Hochzeit." *RE* 8. Band (1913) 2129–33.

Heiberg, I. L., et al., eds. *Hippocrates: Opera*. Leipzig, 1927.

Heinimann, F. *Nomos und Physis*. Schweizerische Beiträge zur Altertumswissenschaft 1. Basel, 1945.

Henrichs, A. "The Atheism of Prodicus." *Cronache Ercolanesi* 6 (1976) 15–21.

———. "Two Doxographical Notes: Democritus and Prodicus on Religion." *HSCP* 79 (1975) 93–123.

———. "Zur Interpretation des Michigan-Papyrus über Theramenes." *ZPE* 3 (1968) 101–8.

Henry, A. S. "The Dating of Fifth-Century Attic Inscriptions." *CSCA* 11 (1979) 75–108.

Henry, R., ed. and tr. *Photius: Bibliothèque*. Vols. 6, 8. Paris, 1971, 1977.

Hereward, D. "New Fragments of *IG* II² 10." *BSA* 47 (1952) 102–17.

Herington, C. J. *The Author of the "Prometheus Bound."* Austin, Tex., and London, 1970.

Hermann, K. F., and H. Blümner. *Lehrbuch der griechischen Privatalterthümer*. 3d ed. Freiburg and Tübingen, 1882.

Herrmann, J. "Nomos bei Herodot und Thukydides." In *Gedächtnisschrift Hans Peters*, pp. 116–24. Berlin, 1967.

Hester, D. A. "Sophocles the Unphilosophical. A Study in the *Antigone*." *Mnemos.*, 4th ser., 24 (1971) 11–59.

Higgins, W. E. *Xenophon the Athenian*. Albany, N.Y., 1977.

Hignett, C. *A History of the Athenian Constitution to the End of the Fifth Century B.C.* Oxford, 1952.

————. *Xerxes' Invasion of Greece*. Oxford, 1963.

Hill, G. F. *Sources for Greek History between the Persian and Peloponnesian Wars*. Ed. R. Meiggs and A. Andrewes. Oxford, 1951.

Hohl, E. "Zeit und Zweck der pseudoxenophontischen *Athenaion Politeia*." *CP* 45 (1950) 26–35.

Holmes, D. H. *Index Lysiacus*. Bonn, 1895.

Hommel, H. *Heliaia*. Philologus Supplement 19, Heft 2. Leipzig, 1927.

Hopper, R. J. *The Basis of the Athenian Democracy*. Inaugural Lecture, Sheffield, 1957.

Hudson-Williams, H. L. "Conventional Forms of Debate and the Melian Dialogue." *AJP* 71 (1950) 156–69.

Ireland, S. "The Problem of Motivation in the *Supplices* of Aeschylus." *RhM* 117 (1974) 14–29.

Jacoby, F. *Atthis: The Local Chronicles of Ancient Athens*. Oxford, 1949.

————. *Diagoras ὁ Ἄθεος*. Abh. d. Deutschen Ak. d. Wiss. Berlin, Kl. f. Sprachen, Literatur und Kunst 3. Berlin, 1959.

————. "Γενέσια: A Forgotten Festival of the Dead." *CQ* 38 (1944) 65–75.

————, ed. *Die Fragmente der griechischen Historiker*. 3 Teile in 14 vols. Berlin and Leiden, 1923–58.

Jameson, M. H. "Politics and the *Philoctetes*." *CP* 51 (1956) 217–27.

————. "Seniority in the *Stratêgia*." *TAPA* 86 (1955) 63–87.

————. "Sophocles and the Four Hundred." *Hist.* 20 (1971) 541–68.

Jeffery, L. H. *The Local Scripts of Archaic Greece*. Oxford, 1961.

Jocelyn, H. D. "A Greek Indecency and Its Students: Λαικάζειν." *PCPS* 206, n.s. 26 (1980) 12–66.

Jones, A. H. M. *Athenian Democracy*. Oxford, 1957.

Jordan, B. *The Athenian Navy in the Classical Period*. University of California Publications in Classical Studies 13. Berkeley and Los Angeles, 1975.

Just, M. "Die ἀποδοκιμασία der athenischen βουλή und ihre Anfechtung." *Hist.* 19 (1970) 132–40.

Kahn, C. H. *Anaximander and the Origins of Greek Cosmology*. New York, 1960.

————. "The Origins of Social-Contract Theory." In G. B. Kerferd, ed., *The Sophists and Their Legacy*, pp. 92–108. [q. v.]

Kahrstedt, U. "Untersuchungen zu athenischen Behörden." *Klio* 31 (1938) 1–32.

Kaibel, G., ed. *Sophokles Elektra*. Leipzig, 1896.

Kapp, E. Review of ΔΟΞΙΣ ΕΠΙΡΥΣΜΙΗ. *Studien zu Demokrits Ethik und Erkenntnislehre*, by H. Langerbeck. *Gnomon* 12 (1936) 65–77.

Karavites, P. "Tradition, Skepticism, and Sophocles' Political Career." *Klio* 58 (1976) 359–65.

Keaney, J. J. "Plato, *Apology* 32c8–d3." *CQ*, n.s., 30 (1980) 296–98.

Keil, B. "Das System des kleisthenischen Staatskalenders." *Hermes* 29 (1894) 321–72.

Kerferd, G. B. "The First Greek Sophists." *CR* 64 (1950) 8–10.

———. "The Moral and Political Doctrines of Antiphon the Sophist. A Reconsideration." *PCPS* 184, n.s. 4 (1956–57) 26–32.

———. "Plato's Treatment of Callicles in the 'Gorgias'." *PCPS* 200, n.s. 20 (1974) 48–52.

———. *The Sophistic Movement*. Cambridge, 1981.

———, ed. *The Sophists and Their Legacy*. Hermes Einzelschrift 44. Wiesbaden, 1981.

Kienast, D. "Die innenpolitische Entwicklung Athens im 6. Jh. und die Reformen von 508." *HZ* 200 (1965) 265–83.

Kinzl, K. H. "Δημοκρατία. Studie zur Frühgeschichte des Begriffes." Parts 1, 2. *Gymnasium* 85 (1978) 117–27, 312–26.

Kirchner, J. *Prosopographia Attica*. 2 vols. Berlin, 1901–3.

Kirk, G. S., tr. *Euripides: Bacchae*. Englewood Cliffs, N.J., 1983.

Kirk, G. S., J. E. Raven, and M. Schofield. *The Presocratic Philosophers*. 2d. ed. Cambridge, 1983.

Kleingünther, A. Πρῶτος Εὑρέτης. Philologus Supplement 26, Heft 1. Leipzig, 1933.

Kluwe, E. "Bemerkungen zu den Diskussionen über die drei 'Parteien' in Attika zur Zeit der Machtergreifung des Peisistratos." *Klio* 54 (1972) 101–24.

Knight, D. W. *Some Studies in Athenian Politics in the Fifth Century B.C.* Historia Einzelschrift 13. Wiesbaden, 1970.

Knox, B. M. W. *The Heroic Temper: Studies in Sophoclean Tragedy*. Berkeley and Los Angeles, 1964.

———. Review of *Sophokles: Antigone*, by G. Müller, *Gnomon* 40 (1968) 747–60.

Körte, A. "Platon (Komiker)." *RE* 20. Band (1950) 2537–41.

Kraay, C. M. *Archaic and Classical Greek Coins*. Berkeley and Los Angeles, 1976.

Krentz, P. "Foreigners against the Thirty: *IG* 2² 10 Again." *Phoenix* 34 (1980) 298–306.

———. *The Thirty at Athens*. Ithaca, N.Y., 1982.

Kroll, J. H. *Athenian Bronze Allotment Plates*. Cambridge, Mass., 1972.

Kron, U. *Die zehn attischen Phylenheroen*. Mitteilungen des Deutschen Archäologischen Instituts, Athenische Abteilung, Beiheft 5. Berlin, 1976.

Kühner, R., and B. Gerth, *Ausführliche Grammatik der griechischen Sprache*. 2 vols. in 4. Hannover and Leipzig, 1890–1904.

Landfester, M. "Beobachtungen zu den *Wespen* des Aristophanes." *Mnemos.*, 4th ser., 29 (1976) 26–32.

Lang, M. "The Revolution of the 400." *AJP* 69 (1948) 272–89.

———. "Revolution of the 400: Chronology and Constitutions." *AJP* 88 (1967) 176–87.

Larsen, J. A. O. "Liberalism in Greek Politics." *Phil.Rev.* 68 (1959) 103–9.

————. *Representative Government in Greek and Roman History*. Berkeley and Los Angeles, 1955.

Lee, E. N., A. P. D. Mourelatos, and R. M. Rorty, eds. *Exegesis and Argument: Studies in Greek Philosophy Presented to Gregory Vlastos*. Assen, 1973.

Lefkowitz, M. R. "The Euripides *Vita*." *GRBS* 20 (1979) 187–210.

Lehmann, G. A. "Die revolutionäre Machtergreifung der 'Dreissig' und die staatliche Teilung Attikas (404–401/0 v. Chr.)." In *Antike und Universalgeschichte. Festschrift H. E. Stier*, pp. 201–33. Münster, 1972.

Lenardon, R. J. "The Chronology of Themistocles' Ostracism and Exile." *Hist.* 8 (1959) 23–48.

————. *The Saga of Themistocles*. London, 1978.

Lesky, A. *A History of Greek Literature*. Tr. J. Willis and C. de Heer. New York, 1966.

Lévy, E. *Athènes devant la défaite de 404*. Bibliothèque des Écoles Françaises d'Athènes et de Rome 225. Paris, 1976.

————. "Notes sur la chronologie athénienne au VIe siècle. I. Cylon." *Hist.* 27 (1978) 513–21.

Lewis, D. M. "Cleisthenes and Attica." *Hist.* 12 (1963) 22–40.

————. "Double Representation in the *Strategia*." *JHS* 81 (1961) 118–23.

————. "The Kerameikos Ostraka." *ZPE* 14 (1974) 1–4.

————. "A Note on *IG* i^2 114." *JHS* 87 (1967) 132.

————. "Notes on Attic Inscriptions." *BSA* 49 (1954) 17–50.

————. Review of *Die Trittyen Attikas und die Heeresreform des Kleisthenes*, by P. Siewert. *Gnomon* 55 (1983) 431–36.

————. *Sparta and Persia*. Leiden, 1977.

————. "The Treaties with Leontini and Rhegion." *ZPE* 22 (1976) 223–25.

Lewis, J. D. "Isegoria at Athens: When Did It Begin?" *Hist.* 20 (1971) 129–40.

Lipsius, J. H. *Das attische Recht und Rechtsverfahren*. Leipzig, 1905–15.

Lobel, E., and D. Page, eds. *Poetarum Lesbiorum Fragmenta*. Oxford, 1955.

Lofberg, J. O. *Sycophancy in Athens*. Menasha, Wis., 1917.

Losada, L. A. *The Fifth Column in the Peloponnesian War*. Mnemosyne Supplement 21. Leiden, 1972.

Luppe, W. "Die Lücke in der Theramenes-Rede des Michigan-Papyrus inv. 5982." *ZPE* 32 (1978) 14–16.

Luria, S. "Antiphon der Sophist." *Eos* 53 (1963) 63–67 [Reprinted in C. J. Classen, ed., *Sophistik*, pp. 537–42. (q.v.)]

————. "Eine politische Schrift des Redners Antiphon aus Rhamnus." *Hermes* 61 (1926) 343–48.

Luschnat, O. "Thukydides." *RE* Supplement 12 (1971) 1085–1354.

McCoy, W. J. "Aristotle's *Athenaion Politeia* and the Establishment of the Thirty Tyrants." *YClS* 24 (1975), 131–45.

————. "The Identity of Leon." *AJP* 96 (1975) 187–99.

MacDowell, D. M. *Athenian Homicide Law in the Age of the Orators*. Manchester, 1963.

————. *The Law in Classical Athens*. London, 1978.

————. "Law-Making at Athens in the Fourth Century B.C." *JHS* 95 (1975), 62–74.

————, ed. *Andokides: On the Mysteries*. Oxford, 1962.

————, ed. *Aristophanes: Wasps*. Oxford, 1974.

McDowell, J., tr. *Plato: Theaetetus*. Oxford, 1973.

McGregor, M. F. "The Genius of Alcibiades." *Phoenix* 19 (1965) 27–46.

MacLaren, M. "On the Composition of Xenophon's *Hellenica*." Parts 1, 2. *AJP* 55 (1934) 121–39, 249–62.

Macleod, C. W. "Form and Meaning in the Melian Dialogue." *Hist.* 23 (1974) 385–400.

———. "Rhetoric and History (Thucydides, VI, 16–18)." *Quaderni di Storia* 2 (1975) 39–65.

Màddoli, G. "Responsabilità e sanzione nei 'decreta de Hecatompedo.'" *MH* 24 (1967) 1–11.

Madsen, D. W., and M. F. McGregor, "Thucydides and Egesta." *Phoenix* 33 (1979) 233–38.

Maidment, K. J., ed. and tr. *Minor Attic Orators*, vol. 1. London and Cambridge, Mass., 1941.

Makkink, A. D. J. *Andokides' eerste rede met inleiding en commentaar*. Amsterdam, 1932.

Mansfeld, J. "The Chronology of Anaxagoras' Athenian Period and the Date of His Trial." Parts 1, 2. *Mnemos.*, 4th ser., 22 (1979) 39–69; 23 (1980) 17–95.

Martin, J. "Von Kleisthenes zu Ephialtes." *Chiron* 4 (1974) 5–42.

Mathieu, G., and E. Brémond, eds. and trs. *Isocrate*, vol. 1. 2d ed. Paris, 1956.

Mattingly, H. B. "Athens and Eleusis: Some New Ideas." In ΦΟΡΟΣ : *Tribute to B. D. Meritt*, pp. 90–103. Locust Valley, N.Y., 1974.

———. "Athens and the Western Greeks: c. 500–413 B.C." In *Atti del I Convegno del Centro Internazionale di Studi Numismatici*, AIIN Supplement 12–14, p.201–21. Rome, 1969.

———. "The Financial Decrees of Kallias." *Proceedings of the African Classical Associations* 7 (1964) 35–55.

———. "The Growth of Athenian Imperialism." *Hist.* 12 (1963) 257–73.

Meier, C. "Clisthène et le problème politique de la polis grecque." *RIDA*, 3d ser., 20 (1973) 115–59.

Meiggs, R. *The Athenian Empire*. Oxford, 1972.

———. "The Dating of Fifth-Century Attic Inscriptions." *JHS* 86 (1966) 86–98.

———. "A Note on the Population of Attica." *CR*, n.s., 14 (1964) 2–3.

Meiggs, R., and D. [M]. Lewis, *A Selection of Greek Historical Inscriptions to the End of the Fifth Century B.C.* Oxford, 1969.

Mele, A. "La Lotta politica nell'Atene arcaica." *Riv.Filol.* 3d ser., 101 (1973) 385–95.

Meritt, B. D. "Archelaos and the Decelean War." In *Classical Studies Presented to E. Capps*, pp. 246–52. Princeton, 1936.

———. *Athenian Financial Documents*. Ann Arbor, Mich., 1932.

———. *The Athenian Year*. Berkeley and Los Angeles, 1961.

———. "The Chronology of the Peloponnesian War." *Proceedings of the American Philosophical Society* 115 (1971) 97–124.

———. "The Departure of Alcibiades for Sicily." *AJA* 34 (1930) 125–52.

———. *Documents on Athenian Tribute*. Cambridge, Mass., 1937.

———. "The Early Athenian Tribute Lists." *CP* 38 (1943) 223–39.

———. "Greek Inscriptions (14–27)." *Hesp.* 8 (1939) 59–65.

———. "The Name of Sophokles." *AJP* 80 (1959) 189.

Meritt, B. D., and H. T. Wade-Gery. "The Dating of Documents to the Mid-Fifth Century." Parts 1,2. *JHS* 82 (1962) 67–74; 83 (1963) 100–117.

Meritt, B. D., H. T. Wade Gery, and M. F. McGregor. *The Athenian Tribute Lists.* 3 vols. Cambridge, Mass., 1939–50.

Meritt, B. D., and A. B. West. *The Athenian Assessment of 425 B.C.* Ann Arbor, Mich., 1934.

Merkelbach, R., and H. C. Youtie. "Ein Michigan-Papyrus über Theramenes." *ZPE* 2 (1968) 161–69.

Meyer, E. *Forschungen zur alten Geschichte.* 2 vols. Halle a.S., 1892–99.

———. *Geschichte des Altertums.* Bd. 4, Abt. 2, *Der Ausgang der griechischen Geschichte.* 4th ed. Basel and Stuttgart, 1956.

Meyer, H. D. "Thukydides Melesiou und die oligarchische Opposition gegen Perikles." *Hist.* 16 (1967) 141–54.

Mikalson, J. D. "Religion in the Attic Demes." *AJP* 98 (1977) 424–35.

Moore, J. M. *Aristotle and Xenophon on Democracy and Oligarchy.* London, 1975.

Morrison, J. S. "Antiphon." *PCPS* 187, n.s.7 (1961) 49–58.

———. "The Place of Protagoras in Athenian Public Life (460–415 B.C.)." *CQ* 35 (1941) 1–16.

———. "The *Truth* of Antiphon." *Phronesis* 8 (1963) 35–49.

Mosley, D. J. *Envoys and Diplomacy in Ancient Greece.* Historia Einzelschrift 22. Wiesbaden, 1973.

Mossé, C. "Classes sociales et régionalisme à Athènes au début du VIe siècle." *Ant. Class.* 33 (1964) 401–13.

———. *La Tyrannie dans la Grèce antique.* Paris, 1969.

Moulton, C. "Antiphon the Sophist *On Truth.*" *TAPA* 103 (1972) 329–66.

Müller, G. *Sophokles: Antigone.* Heidelberg, 1967.

Munro, J. A. R. "Theramenes against Lysander." *CQ* 32 (1938) 18–26.

Münsterberg, R. "Zum Rennstallprozess des Alkibiades (Isokrates περὶ τοῦ ζεύγους)." In *Festschrift Theodor Gomperz*, pp. 298–99. Vienna, 1902.

Nauck, A., ed. *Tragicorum Graecorum Fragmenta.* 2d ed. Leipzig, 1889.

Németh, G. "Der Arginusen-Prozess." *Klio* 66 (1984) 51–57.

Nilsson, M. P. *Geschichte der griechischen Religion.* Vol. 1, 3d ed. Munich, 1967; Vol. 2, 2d ed. Munich, 1961.

Nussbaum, M. C. "Consequences and Character in Sophocles' *Philoctetes.*" *Philosophy and Literature* 1 (1976–77) 25–53.

Oliver, J. H. *The Athenian Expounders of the Sacred and Ancestral Law.* Baltimore, 1950.

Ollier, F. *Le Mirage spartiate.* Paris, 1933.

O'Neil, J. L. "The Exile of Themistokles and Democracy in the Peloponnese." *CQ*, n.s., 31 (1981) 335–46.

Osborne, M. J. *Naturalization in Athens.* 4 vols. Verhandelingen van de Koninglijke Academie voor Wetenschapen, Letteren en Schone Kunsten van België, Kl. Lett. 43–45, nos. 98, 101, and 109. Brussels, 1981–83.

Ostwald, M. "The Athenian Legislation against Tyranny and Subversion." *TAPA* 86 (1955) 103–28.

———. *Autonomia: Its Genesis and Early History.* Chico, Calif., 1982.

————. *Nomos and the Beginnings of the Athenian Democracy*. Oxford, 1969.

————. "The Reform of the Athenian State by Cleisthenes." In *CAH*, vol. 4, 2d ed. [Forthcoming.]

————. "Was There a Concept ἄγραφος νόμος in Classical Greece?" In E. N. Lee, A. P. D. Mourelatos, and R. M. Rorty, eds., *Exegesis and Argument: Studies in Greek Philosophy Presented to Gregory Vlastos*, pp. 70–104. [q.v.]

Page, D. [L.] *Sappho and Alcaeus*. Oxford, 1955.

————, ed. and tr. *Greek Literary Papyri*, vol. 1. London and Cambridge, Mass., 1941.

————, ed. *Poetae Melici Graeci*. Oxford, 1962.

————, ed. and tr. *Select Papyri*, vol. 3. London and Cambridge, Mass., 1950.

Parke, H. W. *Festivals of the Athenians*. London, 1977.

Paton, J. M., ed. *The Erechtheum*. Cambridge, Mass., 1927.

Patterson, C. *Pericles' Citizenship Law of 451–50 B.C.* New York, 1981.

Pearson, A. C., ed. *Euripides: Phoenissae*. Cambridge, 1909.

Peremans, W. "La Juridiction pénale de la Boulè à Athènes au début du Ve siècle avant J.-C." *LEC* 10 (1941) 329–37.

Pernice, E. *Griechisches und römisches Privatleben*. Vol. 2, part 1 of *Einleitung in die Altertumswissenschaft*, ed. A. Gercke and E. Norden, 4th ed. Leipzig and Berlin, 1932.

Piérart, M. "Les εὔθυνοι athéniens." *Ant.Class.* 40 (1971) 526–73.

Pleket, H. W. Review of *Nomos and the Beginnings of the Athenian Democracy*, by M. Ostwald. *Mnemos.* 4th ser., 25 (1972) 454–57.

Podlecki, A. J. *The Life of Themistocles*. Montreal and London, 1975.

————. *The Political Background of Aeschylean Tragedy*. Ann Arbor, Mich., 1966.

Powell, C. A. "Religion and the Sicilian Expedition." *Hist.* 28 (1979) 15–31.

Pritchett, W. K. *Ancient Greek Military Practices, Part 1*. University of California Publications in Classical Studies 7. Berkeley and Los Angeles, 1971.

————. "The Attic Stelai." Parts 1, 2. *Hesp.* 22 (1953) 225–99; 25 (1956) 178–317.

————. "Five New Fragments of the Attic Stelai." *Hesp.* 30 (1961) 23–29.

————. *The Greek State at War, Part 2*. Berkeley and Los Angeles, 1974.

Quinn, T. J. *Athens and Samos, Lesbos and Chios: 478–404 B.C.* Manchester, 1981.

Randall, R. H., Jr. "The Erechtheum Workmen." *AJA* 57 (1953) 199–210.

Raubitschek, A. E. "Eine Bemerkung zu Aristoteles, Verfassung von Athen 29.2." *Chiron* 4 (1974) 101–2.

————. *Dedications from the Athenian Acropolis*. Cambridge, Mass., 1949.

————. "The Heroes of Phyle." *Hesp.* 10 (1941) 284–95.

————. "Philinos." *Hesp.* 23 (1954) 68–71.

————. "Theopompos on Hyperbolos." *Phoenix* 9 (1955) 122–26.

————. "War Melos tributpflichtig?" *Hist.* 12 (1963) 78–83.

Reincke, G. "Peisandros." *RE* 19. Band (1937) 142–44.

Renaud, R. "Cléophon et la guerre du Péloponnèse." *LEC* 38 (1970) 458–77.

Reverdin, O. "Remarques sur la vie politique d'Athènes au Vᵉ siècle." *MH* 2 (1945) 201–12.

Rhodes, P. J. *The Athenian Boule*. Oxford, 1972.

————. *A Commentary on the Aristotelian Athenaion Politeia*. Oxford, 1981.

————. "Εἰσαγγελία in Athens." *JHS* 99 (1979) 103–14.

———. "The Five Thousand in the Athenian Revolutions of 411 B.C." *JHS* 92 (1972) 115–27.

———. "Thucydides on Pausanias and Themistocles." *Hist.* 19 (1970) 387–400.

Roberts, J. T. *Accountability in Athenian Government*. Madison, Wis., 1982.

Robertson, N. "The Sequence of Events in the Aegean in 408 and 407 B.C." *Hist.* 29 (1980) 282–301.

Robinson, J. M. "On Gorgias." In E. N. Lee, A. P. D. Mourelatos, and R. M. Rorty, eds., *Exegesis and Argument: Studies in Greek Philosophy Presented to Gregory Vlastos*, pp. 49–60. [q.v.]

Rocchi, G. D. "Aristocrazia genetica ed organizzazione politica arcaica." *Parola del Passato* 28 (1973) 92–116.

Roesch, P. *Thespies et la confédération béotienne*. Paris, 1965.

de Romilly, J. *La Loi dans la pensée grecque*. Paris, 1971.

———. "Les *Phéniciennes* d'Euripide ou l'actualité dans la tragédie grecque." *Rev.Phil.*, 3d ser., 39 (1965) 28–47.

———. "Les problèmes de politique intérieure dans l'oeuvre de Thucydide." In *Historiographia Antiqua: Commentationes Lovanienses in Honorem W. Peremans Septuagenarii Editae*, pp. 77–93. Louvain, 1977.

———. *Thucydides and Athenian Imperialism*. 2d ed. Tr. P. Thody. Oxford, 1963.

Ronnet, G. *Sophocle, poète tragique*. Paris, 1969.

Rosenmeyer, T. G. "Notes on Aristophanes' *Birds*." *AJP* 93 (1972) 223–38.

Roux, J. *Euripide: Les Bacchantes*. 2 vols. Bibliothèque de la Faculté des Lettres de Lyon 21. Paris, 1970–72.

Rudhardt, J. "La Définition du délit d'impiété d'après la législation attique." *MH* 17 (1960) 87–105.

Ruschenbusch, E. "Δικαστήριον πάντων κύριον." *Hist.* 6 (1957) 257–74.

———. "Πάτριος πολιτεία." *Hist.* 7 (1958) 398–424.

———. *Untersuchungen zur Geschichte des athenischen Strafrechts*. Graezistische Abhandlungen 4. Cologne and Graz, 1968.

Ruzé, F. "La Fonction des probouloi dans le monde grec antique." In *Mélanges d'histoire ancienne offerts à William Seston*, pp. 443–62. Paris, 1974.

de Ste. Croix, G. E. M. "The Constitution of the Five Thousand." *Hist.* 5 (1956) 1–23.

———. "Notes on Jurisdiction in the Athenian Empire." Parts 1, 2. *CQ*, n.s., 11 (1961) 94–112, 268–80.

———. *The Origins of the Peloponnesian War*. London, 1972.

Salmon, P. "L'Établissement des Trente à Athènes." *Ant.Class.* 38 (1969) 497–500.

San Clemente, C. "Teramene e un nuovo papiro di Karanis (Papiro Michigan, inv. 5982)." *Rend.Ist.Lomb.* 104 (1970) 202–18.

Sandys, J. E., ed. *Aristotle's Constitution of Athens*. 2d ed. London, 1912.

Sartori, F. *La Crisi del 411 a. C. nell'Athenaion Politeia di Aristotele*. Università di Padova: Pubblicazioni della Facoltà di Lettere e Filosofia 26. Padua, 1951.

———. *Le Eterie nella vita politica ateniese del VI e V secolo a.C.* Rome, 1957.

———. *Una Pagina di storia ateniese in un frammento dei "Demi" eupolidei*. Università degli Studi di Padova: Pubblicazioni dell'Istituto di Storia Antica 12. Rome, 1975.

Saunders, T. J. "Antiphon the Sophist on Natural Laws (B 44 DK)." *Proceedings of the Aristotelian Society*, n.s., 78 (1977–78) 215–36.

Schaefer, A. *Demosthenes und seine Zeit*. 2d ed. 3 vols. Leipzig, 1885–87.

Schaefer, H. "πρόβουλος." *RE* 23. Band (1957) 1221–31.

Schmid, W., and O. Stählin, *Geschichte der griechischen Literatur*. 5 vols. Munich, 1929–48.

Schneidewin, F. W. "Die didaskalie der Sieben gegen Theben." *Philol.* 3 (1848) 348–71.

Schuller, W. *Die Herrschaft der Athener im ersten attischen Seebund*. Berlin and New York, 1974.

Schulthess, O. "Λογισταί." *RE* 13. Band (1926) 1012–19.

Schwartz, E. "Quellenuntersuchungen zur griechischen Geschichte." *RhM*, n.s., 44 (1889) 104–26.

Schwyzer, E. *Dialectorum Graecarum Exempla Epigraphica Potiora*. Leipzig, 1923.

———. *Griechische Grammatik*. 2d ed. 3 vols. Munich, 1953–71.

Scodel, R. *The Trojan Trilogy of Euripides*. Hypomnemata 60. Göttingen, 1980.

Seager, R. "After the Peace of Nicias. Diplomacy and Policy, 421–416 B.C." *CQ*, n.s., 26 (1976) 249–69.

———. "Alcibiades and the Charge of Aiming at Tyranny." *Hist.* 16 (1967) 6–18.

Sealey, R. "The Entry of Pericles into History." *Hermes* 84 (1956) 234–47.

———. *Essays in Greek Politics*. New York, 1967.

———. "On the Athenian Concept of Law." *CJ* 77 (1982) 289–302.

———. "The Origins of *Demokratia*." *CSCA* 6 (1973) 253–95.

———. "Pap. Mich. Inv. 5982: Theramenes." *ZPE* 16 (1975) 279–88.

———. "Regionalism in Archaic Athens." *Hist.* 9 (1960) 155–80.

———. "The Revolution of 411 B.C." In *Essays in Greek Politics*, pp. 111–32.

Sencie, J., and W. Peremans. "La Juridiction pénale de la Boulè à Athènes au début du Ve siècle avant J.-C." *LEC* 10 (1941) 193–201.

Shear, T. L., Jr. "The Athenian Agora: Excavations of 1970." *Hesp.* 40 (1971) 241–79.

———. "The Athenian Agora: Excavations of 1971." *Hesp.* 42 (1973) 121–79.

———. "The Athenian Agora: Excavations of 1973–1974." *Hesp.* 44 (1975) 365–70.

Sheppard, J. G., and L. Evans. *Notes on Thucydides*. 2d ed. London, 1870.

Siewert, P. "Poseidon Hippios am Kolonos und die athenischen Hippeis." In *Arktouros: Hellenic Studies Presented to Bernard M. W. Knox on the Occasion of His Sixty-Fifth Birthday*, pp. 280–89. Berlin and New York, 1979.

———. *Die Trittyen Attikas und die Heeresreform des Kleisthenes*. Vestigia 33. Munich, 1982.

Simon, E. *Festivals of Attica: An Archaeological Commentary*. Madison, Wis. 1983.

Slings, S. R. "A Commentary on the Platonic Clitophon." Diss. Amsterdam, 1981.

Smart, J. D. "Athens and Egesta." *JHS* 92 (1972) 128–44.

Smith, C. F., tr. *Thucydides*. 4 vols. Cambridge, Mass., and London, 1919–23.

Snell, B., ed. *Pindari Carmina cum Fragmentis*, vol. 2. 3d ed. Leipzig, 1964.

———, ed. *Tragicorum Graecorum Fragmenta*, vol. 1. Göttingen, 1971.

Sokolowski, F., ed. *Lois sacrées des cités grecques*. École Française d'Athènes. Travaux et Mémoires 18. Paris, 1969.

Solmsen, F. *Hesiod and Aeschylus*. Ithaca, N. Y., 1949.

————. *Intellectual Experiments of the Greek Enlightenment*. Princeton, 1975.

Souilhé, J., ed. and tr. *Platon: Oeuvres complètes*, vol. 13, part 3. Paris, 1962.

Stählin, O., and L. Früchtel, eds. *Clemens Alexandrinus*, vol. 2. Berlin, 1960.

Stephans, D. "Critias: Life and Literary Remains." Ph.D. diss., University of Cincinnati, 1939.

Stevens, T. P. "Euripides and the Athenians." *JHS* 76 (1956) 87–94.

Stockton, D. "The Death of Ephialtes." *CQ*, n.s., 32 (1982) 227–28.

Stoessl, F. *Die Hiketiden des Aischylos als geistesgeschichtliches und theatergeschichtliches Phänomen*, Sber. d. Österr. Ak. d. Wiss., Philos.-hist. Kl. 356. Vienna, 1979.

Strauss, B. S. "Aegospotami Reexamined." *AJP* 104 (1983) 24–35.

Stroud, R. S. "An Athenian Law on Silver Coinage." *Hesp.* 43 (1974) 157–88.

————. *The Axones and Kyrbeis of Drakon and Solon*. University of California Publications in Classical Studies 19. Berkeley and Los Angeles, 1979.

————. *Drakon's Law on Homicide*. University of California Publications in Classical Studies 3. Berkeley and Los Angeles, 1968.

————. "Theozotides and the Athenian Orphans." *Hesp.* 40 (1971) 280–301.

Sutton, D. "Critias and Atheism." *CQ*, n.s., 31 (1981) 33–38.

Swoboda, H. "Hyperbolos." *RE* 9. Band (1914) 254–58.

————. "Über den Process des Perikles." *Hermes* 28 (1893) 536–98.

Taillardat, J. "La Trière athénienne et la guerre sur mer aux Ve et IVe siècles." In J. P. Vernant, ed., *Problèmes de la guerre en Grèce ancienne*, pp. 183–205. [q.v.]

Thalheim, T., ed. *Antiphontis Orationes et Fragmenta*. Leipzig, 1914.

————, ed. *Lysiae Orationes*. Leipzig, 1901.

Thompson, H. A., and R. E. Wycherley. *The Athenian Agora*. Vol. 14, *The Agora of Athens*. Princeton, 1972.

Thompson, W. E. "The Date of the Athenian Gold Coinage." *AJP* 86 (1965) 159–74.

————. "Notes on the Treasurers of Athena." *Hesp.* 39 (1970) 54–63.

————. "Thucydides 8, 25. 1 and 8, 54. 3." *MH* 22 (1965) 238.

Thomsen, R. *Eisphora: A Study of Direct Taxation in Ancient Athens*. Copenhagen, 1964.

————. *The Origin of Ostracism*. Copenhagen, 1972.

Tod, M. N. *A Selection of Greek Historical Inscriptions*. 2 vols. Oxford, 1946–48.

Toepffer, J. *Attische Genealogie*. Berlin, 1889.

Traill, J. S. *The Political Organization of Attica*. Hesperia Supplement 14. Princeton, 1975.

Tréheux, J. *Études sur les inventaires attiques*. Annales de l'Est, publiées par la Faculté des Lettres et Sciences Humaines de l'Université de Nancy 29, Études d'Archéologie Classique 3. Paris, 1965.

Treu, M. "Athen und Karthago und die thukydideische Darstellung." *Hist.* 3 (1954–55) 58–59.

————. "Athen und Melos und der Melierdialog des Thukydides." *Hist.* 2 (1953–54) 253–73.

————. "Ps. Xenophon: D. Πολιτεία Ἀθηναίων." *RE* 2. Reihe, 9. Band (1967) 1928–82.

Ullmann, W. *A History of Political Thought: The Middle Ages*. Baltimore, 1965.

Vanderpool, E. "Kleophon." *Hesp.* 21 (1952) 114–15.

———. *Ostracism at Athens*. Lectures in Memory of Louise Taft Semple, 2nd ser., no. 6. Cincinnati, 1970.

Verdelis, N., M. H. Jameson, and I. Papachristodoulou. " Ἀρχαϊκαί ἐπιγραφαί ἐκ Τίρυνθος." *AE*, 1975, 150–205.

Vernant, J.-P., ed. *Problèmes de la guerre en Grèce ancienne*. Paris and The Hague, 1968.

Vidal-Naquet, P. "La Tradition de l'hoplite athénien." In J.-P. Vernant, ed. *Problèmes de la guerre en Grèce ancienne*, pp. 161–81. [q.v.]

Voros, F. K. "The Ethical Fragments of Democritus: The Problem of Authenticity." Ἑλληνικά 26 (1973) 193–206.

Wachsmuth, C., and O. Hense, eds. *Johannis Stobaei Anthologium*. 5 vols. Berlin, 1884–1923.

Wade-Gery, H.T. *Essays in Greek History*. Oxford, 1958.

———. "Studies in Attic Inscriptions of the Fifth Century B.C." *BSA* 33 (1932–33) 101–35.

Walbank, M. B. "The Confiscation and Sale by the Poletai in 402/1 B.C. of the Property of the Thirty Tyrants." *Hesp.* 51 (1982) 74–98.

Wallace, R. W. "Ephialtes and the Areopagus." *GRBS* 15 (1974) 259–69.

Walsh, J. "The Dramatic Dates of Plato's *Protagoras* and the Lesson of *Arete*." *CQ*, n.s., 34 (1984) 101–6.

Walters, K. R. "The 'Ancestral Constitution' and Fourth-Century Historiography in Athens." *AJAH* 1 (1976) 129–44.

von Wedel, W. "Die politischen Prozesse im Athen des fünften Jahrhunderts." *Bolletino del'Istituto di Diritto Romano*, 3d ser., 13 (1971) 107–88.

West, M. L., ed. *Hesiod: Theogony*. Oxford, 1971.

———, ed. *Iambi et Elegi Graeci ante Alexandrum Cantati*. Oxford, 1971.

Westlake, H. D. "Athenian Aims in Sicily, 427–424 B.C." *Hist.* 9 (1960) 385–402. [Reprinted in *Essays on the Greek Historians and Greek History*, pp. 101–22.]

———. *Essays on the Greek Historians and Greek History*. Manchester, 1969.

———. *Individuals in Thucydides*. Cambridge, 1968.

———. "Thucydides and the Uneasy Peace. A Study in Political Incompetence." *CQ*, n.s., 21 (1971) 315–25.

Whitehead, D. *The Ideology of the Athenian Metic*. PCPS Supplement 4. Cambridge, 1977.

———. " Ἰσοτέλεια, a Metaphor in Xenophon." *Eirene* 16 (1978) 19–22.

———. "Sparta and the Thirty Tyrants." *Ancient Society* 13/14 (1982–83) 106–30.

———. "A Thousand New Athenians." *LCM* 9 (1984) 8–10.

———. "The Tribes of the Thirty Tyrants." *JHS* 100 (1980) 208–13.

Wick, T. E. "Athens' Alliances with Rhegion and Leontinoi." *Hist.* 25 (1976) 288–304.

———. "The Date of the Athenian-Egestan Alliance." *CP* 76 (1981) 118–21.

———. "Megara, Athens, and the West in the Archidamian War: A Study in Thucydides." *Hist.* 28 (1979) 1–14.

———. "A Note on the Date of the Athenian-Egestan Alliance." *JHS* 95 (1975) 186–90.

von Wilamowitz-Moellendorff, U. *Aischylos Interpretationen*. Berlin 1914.

———. *Aristoteles und Athen*. 2 vols. Berlin 1893. Reprint. Berlin, 1966.

————. *Aus Kydathen*. Vol. 1 of *Philologische Untersuchungen*. Berlin, 1880.

————, ed. *Aristophanes: Lysistrate*. Berlin, 1927.

Wilcken, U. "Zur oligarchischen Revolution in Athen vom Jahre 411 v. Chr." *Sber. d. Preuss. Ak. d. Wiss. Berlin, Philos.-hist. Kl*. 1935, no.3, 34—61.

Wilhelm, A. "Vermuthungen." *Philol*. 60 (1901) 481–90.

Will, E. "Bulletin historique: Histoire grecque." *Rev. Hist*. 238 (1967) 377–452.

————. "Bulletins historiques: Histoire grecque." *Rev.Hist*. 233 (1965) 393–432.

————. "Deux livres sur les guerres médiques et leur temps." *Rev. Phil*., 3d ser., 38 (1964) 70–88.

————. *Le Monde grec et l'orient*, vol. 1. Paris, 1972.

————. "Un Nouvel Essai d'interprétation de l'*Athènaiôn Politeia* pseudo-Xénophontique." *REG* 91 (1978) 77–95.

————. Review of *Nomos and the Beginnings of the Athenian Democracy*, by M. Ostwald. *Rev. Phil*., 3d ser., 45 (1971) 102–13.

Willemsen, F. "Die Ausgrabungen im Kerameikos." *Arch.Delt*. 23, part 2, no.1 (1968) 24–32.

————. "Ostraka." *Mitteilungen des Deutschen Archäologischen Instituts. Athenische Mitteilungen* 80 (1965) 100–126.

Williams, G. M. E. "The Kerameikos Ostraka." *ZPE* 31 (1978) 103–13.

Wolff, H. J. *Die attische Paragraphe*. Weimar, 1966.

————. *"Normenkontrolle" und Gesetzesbegriff in der attischen Demokratie*. Sber. d. Heidelberg. Ak. d. Wiss., Philos.-hist. Kl. 1970, 2. Abh. Heidelberg, 1970.

Woodbury, L. "The Date and Atheism of Diagoras of Melos." *Phoenix* 19 (1965) 178–211.

————. "Socrates and Archelaus." *Phoenix* 25 (1971) 299–309.

————. "Sophocles among the Generals." *Phoenix* 24 (1970) 209–24.

Woodhead, A. G. "I.G., I², 95, and the Ostracism of Hyperbolus." *Hesp*. 18 (1949) 78–83.

————. " Ἰσηγορία and the Council of 500." *Hist*. 16 (1967) 129–40.

————. "Peisander." *AJP* 75 (1954) 131–46.

Wycherley, R. E. *The Athenian Agora*. Vol. 3, *Literary and Epigraphical Testimonia*. Princeton, 1957.

————. *The Stones of Athens*. Princeton, 1978.

Ziehen, L. "Πλυντήρια." *RE* 21. Band (1951) 1060–65.

Zoepffel, R. "Aristoteles und die Demagogen." *Chiron* 4 (1974) 69–90.

INDEX LOCORUM

A. LITERARY TEXTS

571

GENERAL INDEX

to *hēliaia* becomes referral to *thesmothetai* and jury courts, 39, 71; from Council to Assembly in *eisangeliai* resulting from *euthynai* of generals, 60

Ephesus, 427

Ephetai, 422

Ephetic courts, verdicts of, not subject to appeal, 34

Ephialtes: livelihood of, 214; attack of, on Areopagus, 36, 41–42, 180; reforms of, xx, 34–36, 48–50, 70–73, 175–76, 179; gives powers of Areopagus to Council and *dēmos*, 70–73, 78, 518; in crimes against the state to Council, 37; deprives Areopagus of control of *euthynai*, 42, 518; institutes *euthynoi*, 61; makes *euthyna* mandatory and regular, 42, 61, 64, 71, 72, 74, 75, 78; modifies *euthynai* of generals, 64; changes in *dokimasia* introduced by, 43, 43n158, 46; restrictions on Areopagus of, rescinded by Thirty, 479, 517; meets violent death, 175–76, 180; takes final step in formation of Athenian democracy, 48, 78, 149; establishes popular sovereignty, 47, 49–50, 78, 80, 179; and Cimon, 41, 179; and Pericles, 42; and Themistocles, 30, 36

Ephors: at Sparta, oppose Peace of Nicias, 297; rebuff Athenian peace proposals (405/4), 451; and Pausanias (403), 494

Ephors (in Athens) appointed by oligarchical conspirators after Aegospotami, 128, 470, 477, 485

Ephorus, as source for Diodorus, 469–70

Epibatai (ἐπιβάται), 230

Epibolē (ἐπιβολή) administrative fine, imposed by Archedemus on Erasinides (406/5), 436

Epichares of Lamptrae, councilor under Thirty, member of Ten, accuser of Andocides, 491

Epicheirotonia (ἐπιχειροτονία) generals subject to, 63

Epicheirotonia nomōn (ἐπιχειροτονία νόμων). *See* Review law

Epicureanism, 271

Epidaurus, 64n248, 119, 191, 212

Epigamia (ἐπιγαμία) = right of intermarriage with Athenians, given to Euboea (before 405), 507

Epigenes, prosecutes oligarchs, 421

Episkopoi (ἐπίσκοποι), 410

Epistatai (ἐπιστάται), pay of, 183

Epistatai (ἐπιστάται), board of, at Eleusis, created by Assembly, 140

Epistatēs (ἐπιστάτης), Pericles as, of work on Parthenon, 193

Eponymous Archon: religious functions of, 138; prosecution before, can be initiated by *ho boulomenos*, 81

Eponymous Heroes, 56, 58, 515, 517, 520–22

Epoptai (ἐπόπται), 534

Erasinides: councilor, motion to honor Phrynichus's assassins (410/09), 420; general after Notium (406), 420; executed as one of Arginusae generals (406), 420; fellow general of Conon at Mytilene, reports to Athens, 432; and Archedemus, 425, 436, 440–41

Erasistratus: nephew of Phaeax, possibly among Thirty, 233, 467; and Critias, 467

Eratosthenes: trierarch on Samos (412/11), 467; as oligarchical ephor (404/3), 128, 467–68, 470; member of Thirty, 468; stays in Athens after amnesty (403/2), 468; and Lysias, 467–68; and Theramenes, 468

Erechtheum: construction of (409–405), 425; construction of, accounts of, 425–26

Eresus, Thrasyllus and Thrasybulus at siege of (411/10), 388

Eretria, 398; battle of, gives Euboea to Peloponnesians (411), 395, 397

Eryximachus: denounced for herms (415), 540, 542, 544, 545, 549; and Hippias, 549; and Phaedrus, 545

Establishment mentality, 83, 231, 249, 250–55, 273, 298

Eteobutads, as priests of Athena Polias, 193. *See also* Dracontides; Lycurgus

Eteocles: in Sophocles, 151, 152, 154; in Euripides, 104, 413–14

Eteonicus, Spartan naval commander, Mytilene (406/5), 434

Ethiopia, 271

Euathlus: sues Protagoras for excessive fee, 231–32, 533; as *synēgoros* at *euthyna* of Thucydides son of Melesias, 221, 231, 237, 292

Euboea, 395, 405, 413

Euboeans, granted *epigamia* (before 405), 507

Eubulia (εὐβουλία) = "sound judgment" as educational aim of Protagoras, 239, 240

Eucleides: general at Eretria (410/09), secretary of Council (408/7), member of the Thirty, 468; archonship of 403/2, as landmark in Athenian legislation, 503, 507–8, 515, 522–23

Eucles, 162

Eucrates, 128, 201n11; denounced but acquitted through testimony of Andocides (415), general in Thrace (412/11) and after Aegospotami, 342n24, 459, 540,